D1068134

This book examines Prussia's response to Napoleon and Napoleonic expansionism in the years before the crushing defeats of Auerstedt and Jena, a period of German history as untypical as it was dramatic.

Between the years 1797 and 1806 Prussia shocked Europe not by her assertiveness but by her acquiescence, not by her contempt for international norms but by her trust in such norms long after they had been abandoned by her neighbours. Throughout this period the main fear of Prussian statesmen was French power, rather than revolution from below. This threat spawned a foreign-policy debate characterised by geopolitical thinking: the belief that Prussian policy was conditioned by her unique geographic situation at the heart of Europe. Similar thinking underlay a parallel debate on the organisation of the executive: Prussian politicians felt that a swifter and more balanced process of decision-making was needed.

The book breaks new ground both methodologically and empirically. By combining high-political and geopolitical analysis, it is able to present a more comprehensive and nuanced picture than earlier interpretations. The book also draws on a very wide range of sources – official and unofficial – many previously unused.

The impact of Napoleon

The impact of Napoleon

Prussian high politics, foreign policy and the crisis of the executive, 1797–1806

Brendan Simms

Peterhouse, Cambridge

CAMBRIDGE
UNIVERSITY PRESS

Published by the Press Syndicate of the University of Cambridge
The Pitt Building, Trumpington Street, Cambridge CB2 1RP
40 West 20th Street, New York, NY 10011-4211, USA
10 Stamford Road, Oakleigh, Melbourne 3166, Australia

First published 1997

Printed in Great Britain at the University Press, Cambridge

A catalogue record for this book is available from the British Library

Library of Congress cataloguing in publication data
Simms, Brendan.
The impact of Napoleon: Prussian high politics, foreign policy
and the crisis of the executive, 1797–1806 / Brendan Simms.
     p.   cm.
Includes bibliographical references.
ISBN 0 521 45360 7
1. Prussia (Germany) – History – Frederick William III, 1797–1840.
2. Napoleon I, Emperor of the French, 1769–1821. 3. Prussia
(Germany) – Foreign relations – 1786–1806. I. Title.
DD420.S56 1996   943'.073 – dc20   96–6483   CIP

ISBN 0 521 45360 7 hardback

WD

Contents

Contents   ix

Maps

Acknowledgments

In the course of writing this book, I incurred many personal and intellectual debts, not all of them obvious from the footnotes. The advice and assistance of my wife Anita was invaluable. Without the counsel and encouragement of Tim Blanning, the original research could not have been undertaken. Hamish Scott and Derek Beales made most helpful suggestions of how my work could be expanded and improved. Philip Dwyer read the first draft and offered very useful comments. Thomas Stamm-Kuhlmann kindly read the first draft and was courteous about his reservations. The organisers of the Cambridge German Studies Group – in particular Chris Clark and Niall Ferguson – helped me to clarify my thoughts. Rafael Gross is responsible for introducing me to Carl Schmitt. Colin Armstrong was kind enough to proof-read the original draft and make useful suggestions. I also benefited from the comments of the Cambridge Modern European History Seminar, the Oxford European History Seminar, the European History Seminar at the Institute for Historical Research and the Sussex History Seminar. I am especially grateful to the Institute for European History in Mainz, then under Karl Otmar von Aretin, which not only helped to fund my research, but also allowed me to address its famous *Kaffeerunde*. I thank all those who made my stay there such a pleasant and fruitful one, in particular Martin Vogt, Claus Scharf, Ralph Melville, Frau Dascalescu, Frau Ries, Herr Koch, and, of course, my fellow *Stipendiaten*, Peter Borschberg, Eckhard Buddruss, Bruce Gordon, Michael Hundt, Jürgen Jüngling and Michael Seid. Christoph Dipper (Darmstadt), Dieter Langewiesche (Tübingen) and Winfried Baumgart (University of Mainz) provided further opportunities to address an indulgent, but critical, German audience. Earlier drafts were read and commented upon by Peter Nitschke, Dirk Schumann, Christoph Nonn, Eva Kell, Christoph Cornelissen and Heinz Kathe. Thanks are due to the archivists of the Geheimes Staatsarchiv, latterly Merseburg now Berlin-Dahlem, especially Herr Tempel, Frau 'Olé' and Frau Dr Gundermann. I am grateful to the Master and Fellows of Peterhouse for many discussions on the possibilities and limits of politics under absolutism. Needless to say, the responsibility for this book is mine alone.

I also thank the various institutions which financed my research as a graduate student, a Research Fellow and Official Fellow: the British Council, the British Academy, the Prince Consort and Thirlwall Fund, Christ Church, Oxford, and Peterhouse, Cambridge.

Finally, I thank my parents, Anngret and David Simms, for all their love and encouragement. I dedicate this book to them.

Abbreviations

ADB	*Allgemeine Deutsche Biographie*
BL	British Library
CEH	*Central European History*
FBPG	*Forschungen zur brandenburgisch-preussischen Geschichte*
FO	Foreign Office
GG	*Geschichte und Gesellschaft*
GStA	Geheimes Staatsarchiv Preussischer Kulturbesitz, Berlin-Dahlem.
GWU	*Geschichte in Wissenschaft und Unterricht*
HJ	*Historical Journal*
HZ	*Historische Zeitschrift*
IHR	*International History Review*
NDB	*Neue Deutsche Biographie*
NJBLG	*Niedersächsisches Jahrbuch für Landesgeschichte*
PJ	*Preussische Jahrbücher*
P&P	*Past and Present*
PROL	Public Record Office London
RHD	*Revue d'Histoire Diplomatique*
StaH	Niedersächsisches Hauptstaatsarchiv Hannover
TRHS	Transactions of the Royal Historical Society
VSWG	*Vierteljahrshefte für Sozial- und Wirtschaftsgeschichte*
ZfG	*Zeitschrift für Geschichtswissenschaft*
ZfHF	*Zeitschrift für Historische Forschung*

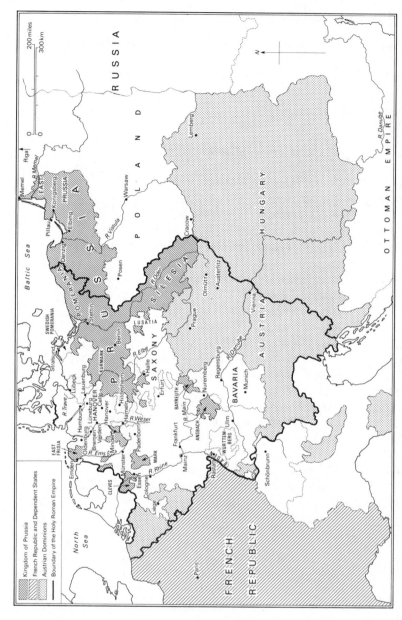

1 Geography and politics: Prussia and her neighbours in 1792. Note the Polish buffer in the east.

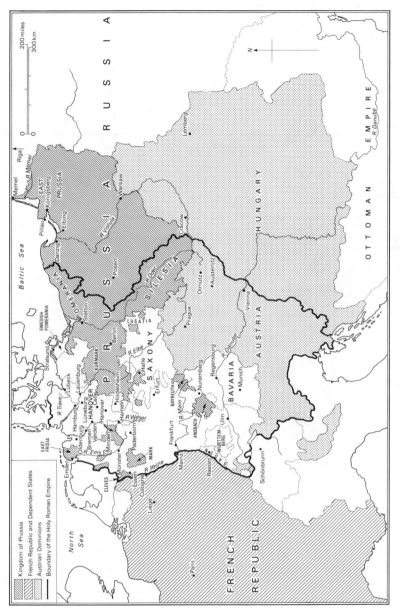

2 Geography and politics: Prussia and her neighbours in 1795. Note the disappearance of the Polish buffer and the encroachment of France.

Kingdom of Prussia
French Republic and Dependent States
Austrian Dominions
Boundary of the Holy Roman Empire

RUSSIA

Baltic Sea

North Sea

Memel
Riga
R.Memel
Pillau
EAST
Königsberg
PRUSSIA
Elbing
Danzig
Posen
SWEDISH POMERANIA
Stralsund
Stettin
Berlin
LUSATIA
R.Oder
SILESIA
Lübeck
Hamburg
Lauenburg
KURMARK
R.Elbe
Halle
SAXONY
Bremen
Lüneburg
Celle
Hildesheim
Erfurt
Oldenburg
Verden
Hanover
PRUSSIA
HANOVER
R.Weser
Minden
Hameln
EAST FRISIA
Emden
R.Ems
Paderborn
BAYREUTH
Münster
MARK
Frankfurt
Nuremberg
Regensburg
ANSBACH
R.Main
Essen
Cleves
CLEVES
Cologne
R.Rhine
Liège
Mainz
WÜRTTEM-BERG
Ulm
Munich
BAVARIA
Rastatt
Schönbrunn

POMERANIA
Cracow
Lemberg
Warsaw
Olmütz
Austerlitz
Prague
Vienna
AUSTRIA
HUNGARY
R.Danube

FRENCH REPUBLIC
Paris

OTTOMAN EMPIRE
R.Danube

200 miles
300 km

N

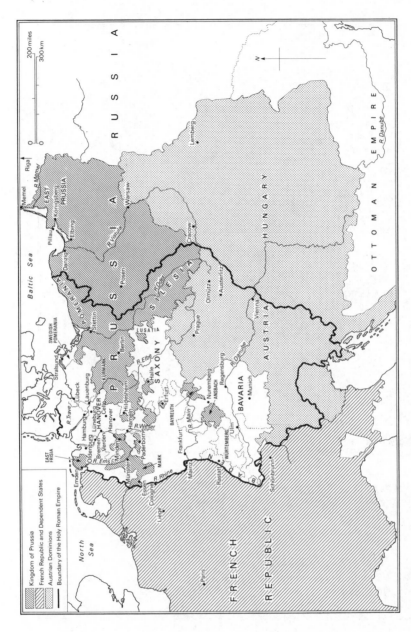

3 Geography and politics: Prussia and her neighbours in 1803.

1 Introduction

'The first decade of Frederick William III's reign', Heinrich von Treitschke writes, 'is the most traduced and least-known epoch of Prussian history'.[1] Indeed, H. M. Scott describes the whole fifty-year period from 1763 to 1806 as 'one of the most neglected half-centuries in Hohenzollern history'.[2] The relative obscurity of the period from 1797 to 1806 can be explained by the fact it is apparently untypical of what we are accustomed to think of as typically Prussian. The early reign of Frederick William III lacks the clear contours of the Great Elector's state-building; the stern militarism of Frederick William I; the unprecedented expansion of Frederick the Great; and the later achievements of the Prussian reform period after 1806. Unlike many other periods, the years from 1797 to 1806 saw Prussia shock Europe not by her assertiveness, but by her quiescence, not by her contempt for international norms, but by her trusting belief in such norms long after they had been abandoned by her neighbours; and when Prussia was punished in 1806, it was not for her aggression, but for her diffidence. Yet – as this book attempts to show – Prussian statesmen before Jena did not regard themselves as untypical. They were no less beholden to the doctrine of the primacy of foreign policy, and the demands of geopolitics, than their predecessors or successors. The decisive difference lay not so much in the unspoken assumptions underlying Prussian deliberations, but in the resulting responses: timidity, indecision, opportunism, miscalculation, high-political intrigue, royal preference and sheer necessity sustained the neutrality policy until the bitter reckoning at Jena and Auerstedt. The years 1797 to 1806 thus constitute a unique alternative narrative of Prussian history in which the price of passivity

---

[1] Heinrich von Treitschke, *Deutsche Geschichte im neunzehnten Jahrhundert* (Leipzig, 1879), I, p. 145: 'Das erste Jahrzehnt Friedrich Wilhelms III, ist die bestverleumdeste und unbekannteste Epoche der preussischen Geschichte.'
[2] H. M. Scott, 'Introduction: Prussia from Rossbach to Jena', *German History*, 12 (1994), 280 [Special Issue: Prussia from Rossbach to Jena. Guest editor H.M. Scott, 279–85].

and vacillation in a predatory environment was spelt out with unambiguous clarity.

Method: the primacy of foreign policy; geopolitics; high politics; the antechamber of power

The chief theoretical inspiration behind this book is the primacy of foreign policy. First articulated by Ranke and refined by Dilthey,[3] the primacy of foreign policy soon rose to a position of near hegemony, not merely in late-nineteenth century German historiography but in public life as well. 'Foreign affairs', Bismarck announced in 1866, 'are a purpose in themselves. I rate them higher than all other matters.'[4] Some fifty years later Hermann Oncken could declare without serious risk of contradiction that the primacy of foreign policy was not merely a 'dynamic basic law' of German political life, but 'a biological statement of fact'.[5]

---

[3] Leopold von Ranke, 'Das politische Gespräch', in Leopold von Ranke, *Das politische Gespräch und andere Schriftchen zur Wissenschaftslehre* (Halle/Saale, 1925), pp. 10–36; Leopold von Ranke, 'Die grossen Mächte', in Leopold von Ranke, *Völker und Staaten in der neueren Geschichte*, edited by Leonhard von Muralt (Zurich, 1945), pp. 44–88; Wilhelm Dilthey, 'Friedrich der Grosse und die deutsche Aufklärung', in Wilhelm Dilthey, *Studien zur Geschichte des deutschen Geistes*. Collected Works, vol. III (Göttingen, 1959), pp. 176–205. Hermann von Caemmerer, 'Ranke's große Mächte und die Geschichtsschreibung des 18. Jahrhunderts', in *Studien und Versuche zur neueren Geschichte, Max Lenz gewidmet* (Berlin, 1910), p. 309. There is a good introduction in Bernd Faulenbach, *Ideologie des deutschen Weges. Die deutsche Geschichte in der Historiographie zwischen Kaiserreich und Nationalsozialismus* (Munich, 1980), pp. 181–8; Ernst-Otto Czempiel, 'Der Primat der Auswärtigen Politik. Kritische Würdigung einer Staatsmaxime', *Politische Vierteljahrsschrift*, 4 (1963), 266–87; and Rudolf L. Bindschedler, 'Zum Primat der Außenpolitik', in Urs Altermatt and Judit Garamvölgyi (eds.), *Innen- und Aussenpolitik. Primat oder Interdependenz? Festschrift zum 60. Geburtstag von Walter Hofer* (Berne and Stuttgart, 1980), pp. 27–36. Also relevant are Heinrich August Winkler, 'Gesellschaftsform und Aussenpolitik: eine Theorie Lorenz von Steins in zeitgeschichtlicher Perspektive', *HZ* 214, 2 (1972), 335–62; Henry A. Kissinger, 'Domestic structure and foreign policy', *Daedalus*, 95 (1966), 503–29; Ernst-Otto Czempiel, 'Strukturen absolutistischer Außenpolitik', *ZfHF*, 7 (1980), 445–51. Newer discussions and applications of the theory are: F. A. J. Szabo, 'Prince Kaunitz and the balance of power', *IHR*, 1, 3 (1979), 401–8; D. E. D. Beales and T.C.W. Blanning, 'Prince Kaunitz and the primacy of domestic policy', *IHR*, 2 (1980), 618–24; F. A. J. Szabo, 'Prince Kaunitz and the primacy of domestic policy: a response', *IHR*, 2 (1980), 625–35; Horst Möller, 'Primat der Aussenpolitik: Preussen und die französische Revolution', in Jürgen Voss (ed.), *Deutschland und die französische Revolution* (Munich, 1983), pp. 65–81.

[4] Cited in Klaus Hildebrand, 'Geschichte oder "Gesellschaftsgeschichte"? Die Notwendigkeit einer politischen Geschichtsschreibung von den internationalen Beziehungen', *HZ*, 223 (1976), 346.

[5] Hermann Oncken, 'Über die Zusammenhänge zwischen äußerer und innerer Politik', *Vorträge der Gehe Stiftung zu Dresden* (Dresden/Leipzig, 1918), p. 16: 'dynamisches Grundgesetz . . . eine biologische Feststellung'.

Soon after, Wilhelm Mommsen was merely reflecting the consensus view when he said that it was the duty of the historian to 'hammer the notion of the "the primacy of foreign policy" into every German brain'.[6] In short, the concept of the primacy of foreign policy has both historiographical and political implications. In the political sense – as in Wilhelmine or Weimar Germany – it signifies a *prescriptive* demand for the strict subordination of all other matters to the external security of the state; this aspect need not concern us here. Used historiographically, on the other hand, the concept can be purely *descriptive*; it records but does not necessarily endorse the decisive role played by foreign policy – and its resulting internal consequences – in the historical development of the Prusso-German state.

Like all interpretative frameworks, the primacy of foreign policy involves a set of basic assumptions about the historical process. First of all, it postulates that international relations are conducted quite independently of ideological and societal considerations.[7] 'There is no trend of opinion, however dominant', Ranke writes, 'which can break the force of political interests.'[8] Hence the primacy of foreign policy not merely allowed the state to override domestic opposition, it also sanctioned agreements with ideological adversaries abroad. Secondly, the emphasis on foreign policy is justified by the 'irrevocability' of decisions in that sphere.[9] Whereas erroneous domestic policies could be reversed, there was no appeal from the harsh arbitrament of partition, annexation and war. Consequently, the historian must focus on the

---

[6] Cited in Faulenbach, *Ideologie des deutschen Weges*, p. 25. On the ascendancy and reception of Ranke see also Hans-Heinz Krill, *Die Rankerenaissance. Max Lenz und Erich Marcks. Ein Beitrag zum historisch-politischen Denken in Deutschland 1880–1935* (Berlin, 1962).

[7] Andreas Hillgruber, 'Methodologie und Theorie der Geschichte der internationalen Beziehungen', *GWU*, 27 (1976), 196: 'internationale Politik als eine in sich geschlossene Sphäre originärer Machtpolitik verstanden, die eigenen "Gesetzen" unterliegt'.

[8] Leopold von Ranke, 'A dialogue on politics', in Theodor von Laue (ed.), *Leopold von Ranke. The formative years* (Princeton, N.J., 1950), p. 172. German original: 'Es gibt keine so entschieden herrschende Tendenz der Meinung, daß die Interessen vor ihr zurücktraten', in Ranke, 'Das politische Gespräch', p. 28; Winkler, 'Gesellschaftsform und Außenpolitik'. See also the preamble to Uta Krüger-Löwenstein, *Rußland, Frankreich und das Reich, 1801–1803. Zur Vorgeschichte der 3. Koalition* (Wiesbaden, 1972): 'Anders als heute . . . trafen die Politiker jener Zeit ihre Entscheidungen weitgehend unabhängig von wirtschafts- und gesellschaftspolitischen Erfordernissen'; H. Gollwitzer, 'Ideologische Blockbildung als Bestandteil internationaler Politik im 19. Jahrhundert', *HZ*, 201 (1965), 306–33; Hans Rothfels, *Gesellschaftsform und auswärtige Außenpolitik* (Laupheim, 1951), p. 11.

[9] Ibid., p. 22.

'moment of decision' in international relations.[10] It is this emphasis on drama, not *longue durée*, which distinguishes the primacy of foreign policy from the more gradual explanatory models of Marxists, modernisation theorists and others. Thirdly and relatedly, the primacy of foreign policy insists that the outcome of a given historical situation is always 'open', never pre-determined;[11] hence the focus on the moment of decision and the free will of the protagonists. 'Political history', as Jacques Julliard has written, 'measures the contribution of voluntary actions in the unfolding of history.'[12] However, fourthly and paradoxically, the primacy of foreign policy also stresses the constraints on human volition and the dictates of 'necessity': an external threat may be so acute as to nullify free will and admit of only one course of action. This tension between freedom and necessity has repeatedly been referred to by both critics and champions of the primacy of foreign policy, but it has never been satisfactorily resolved.[13]

If the primacy of foreign policy was mainly deployed to describe Prussia-Germany's historical role within the international state system, it also served to explain her constitutional development. 'The degree of independence', Ranke wrote, 'determines a state's position in the world, and requires that the state mobilize all its inner resources for the goal of self-preservation. This is its supreme law.'[14] 'The internal history of a state', Dilthey maintained, 'is entirely determined by its external experience.'[15] Politically, this argument was used to counter demands for political reforms in late nineteenth-century Germany. Bismarck spoke for many when he insisted that one first had to make a house safe from the (external) elements before addressing specific questions of interior

---

[10] Andreas Hillgruber, 'Politische Geschichte in moderner Sicht', in Andreas Hillgruber, *Die Zerstörung Europas. Beiträge zur Weltkriegsepoche 1914 bis 1945* (Frankfurt/Main and Berlin, 1988), p. 14; Hillgruber, 'Methodologie und Theorie der internationalen Beziehungen', pp. 193, 198: 'Moment der freien Entscheidung'.

[11] See Winfried Baumgart, *The peace of Paris. Studies in war, diplomacy and peace-making*, translated by Ann Pottinger Saab (Santa Barbara, 1981), p. xviii; Hillgruber, 'Politische Geschichte in moderner Sicht', p. 22: 'Offenheit der jeweiligen Zukunft'.

[12] Jacques Julliard, 'Political history in the 1980s. Reflections on its present and future', *Journal of Interdisciplinary History*, 12, 1 (1981), 29.

[13] On the tension between necessity and free will see: Hillgruber, 'Politische Geschichte in moderner Sicht', p. 20, on 'Zwänge'; Hildebrand, 'Geschichte oder "Gesellschaftsgeschichte"?', p. 329; Winfried Baumgart, *Der Friede von Paris 1856* (Munich and Vienna, 1972), p. 14: 'Das methodische Grundprinzip, von dem wir uns leiten lassen, ist, die tatsächlich geschehene Geschichte nicht als einzig mögliche zu verstehen, sondern der Geschichte in ihren inneren Spannung zwischen Freiheit und Notwendigkeit, in ihrer Entscheidungscharakter nachzuspüren'.

[14] 'Politisches Gespräch': see the translation in von Laue (ed.), *Leopold von Ranke*, p. 169.

[15] Dilthey, 'Friedrich der Grosse und die deutsche Aufklärung', p. 181: 'Die innere Geschichte ist ganz bedingt von der äußeren.'

decoration.[16] Historiographically, it encouraged the tendency to see the internal development of Germany as a function of her foreign-political position. 'Perhaps the most powerful motive for the great domestic reforms of the era of enlightened absolutism', Dilthey wrote, 'was the need to mobilize resources for the external struggle through the most intensive cultivation of all spiritual and material strengths of the state.' The degree of possible internal freedom, J. R. Seeley maintained, was inversely proportional to the external pressure on its borders.[17]

This link between foreign policy and internal structure was put on a sound empirical footing by Otto Hintze.[18] Hintze's theories were a direct challenge to Marx, and all those who saw the historical process in purely endogenous terms; he argued that the constitutional development of a state was also powerfully influenced by its relations with other states. 'As a result of constant rivalry and competition between themselves', Hintze wrote, 'individual states find themselves forced into a continuous intensivisation and rationalisation of its administrative apparatus.'[19] In particular, Hintze focussed on the search for efficient institutions – military, administrative and executive – to facilitate the formulation and execution of foreign policy. Of course, while internal cohesion might be a necessary response to external pressure, it was far from automatic; but the fate of the German Reich and Poland between 1772 and 1806 showed that the result could be political extinction.[20]

Until the outbreak of the First World War, the primacy of foreign policy was generally interpreted to the disadvantage of broader popular

---

[16] Cited in Faulenbach, *Ideologie des deutschen Weges*, p. 132.

[17] Dilthey, 'Friedrich der Grosse und die deutsche Aufklärung', p. 179: 'Mittel für den Kampf nach außen zu gewinnen durch die intensivste Förderung aller materiellen und geistigen Kräfte des Staates, das ist vielleicht das mächtigste Motiv für die großen inneren Reformen im Zeitalter des aufgeklärten Absolutismus.'

[18] Otto Hintze, 'Staatsverfassung und Heeresverfassung', in Otto Hintze, *Staat und Verfassung. Gesammelte Abhandlungen zur allgemeinen Verfassungsgeschichte*, edited and introduced by Gerhard Oestreich (Göttingen, 1962), esp. pp. 55, 78; 'Die Entstehung der modernen Staatsministerien', ibid., esp. p. 276; 'Staatenbildung und Verfassungsentwicklung, Eine historisch-politische Studie', ibid., esp. pp. 34–5; 'Machtpolitik und Regierungsverfassung', ibid., esp. pp. 425–6. In a similar vein see also the rather abstract reflections of Georg Simmel, *Soziologie. Untersuchungen über die Formen der Vergesellschaftung* (Leipzig, 1908), pp. 310–11. For a more recent work on Hintzian lines see Johannes Kunisch, *Staatsverfassung und Mächtepolitik. Zur Genese von Staatenkonflikten im Zeitalter des Absolutismus* (Berlin, 1979), p. 11; Czempiel, 'Strukturen absolutistischer Außenpolitik'.

[19] Hintze, 'Weltgeschichtliche Bedingungen der Repräsentativverfassung', p. 147: 'Durch beständige Rivalität und Konkurrenz untereinander, sehen sich dabei die einzelnen Staaten gezwungen zu einer fortschreitenden Intensivierung und Rationalisierung ihres Betriebes.'

[20] Hintze, 'Machtpolitik und Regierungsverfassung', pp. 433–4.

political participation. 'The main determining factor for our monarchic-constitutional system of government', Hintze argued, 'lies in the fact that we are surrounded by the greatest military powers on the continent and that an enormous military-political external threat faces our long and unprotected borders. Strict internal cohesion is necessary in order to withstand this pressure; and this strict cohesion demands a primarily dominatory, that is to say monarchical spirit in our governmental and administrative system.'[21] During the later years of the Weimar Republic, the controversial German lawyer Carl Schmitt took this theme a step further in his attack on the parliamentary system. Instead of 'government by discussion', Schmitt demanded a 'decisionist' executive; when the preservation of the state was at stake, he argued, *any* decision was better than none.[22] But the link between foreign-political strength and authoritarian rule was not an immutable one. During the Prussian Reform period (1807–1815/19), for example, the demand for agrarian, economic, social and constitutional changes was justified by the need to free Germany of Napoleon and restore Prussia to her rightful place in the European pentarchy of powers. During the First World War and after, Max Weber, Otto Hintze and others came to realise that the foreign-political salvation of the *Reich* could only be achieved through greater popular political participation. 'Only he who sees internal politics from the perspective of its inevitable arrangement according to the needs of foreign policy', Weber argued, 'is a politician. Those who do not like the "democratic" consequences which come from this should do without the great power policy which they require.'[23] After 1918, Hintze claimed

---

[21] Ibid., p. 439: 'Der wesentlichste Bestimmungsgrund unseres monarchisch-konstitutionellen Regierungssystems liegt in der Tatsache, daß wir von den größten Militärmächten des Kontinents umgeben sind und daß ein enormer militärisch-politischer Druck von außen auf unseren langen, von Natur ungeschützten Grenzen lastet. Es bedarf einer straffen Zusammenfassung im Innern, um diesem Druck Widerstand zu leisten; und diese straffe Zusammenfassung bedingt einen vorwiegend herrschaftlichen, d.h. monarchischen Geist in unserem Regierungs- und Verwaltungssystem.'

[22] Carl Schmitt, *Politische Theologie. Vier Kapitel zur Lehre von der Souveränität* (Munich and Leipzig, 1922), pp. 9, 32; Carl Schmitt, *Die geistesgeschichtliche Lage des heutigen Parlamentarismus* (Berlin, 1926), pp. 12–13. On Schmitt see also Hermann Lübbe, 'Dezisionismus- eine kompromittierte politische Theorie', *Praxis Philosophie. Praktische Philosophie. Geschichtstheorie* (Stuttgart, 1978), pp. 61–77. For a useful definition of *dezisionismus* see Christian Graf von Krockow, *Die Entscheidung. Eine Untersuchung über Ernst Jünger, Carl Schmitt, Martin Heidegger* (Frankfurt/Main, 1990), p. 2.

[23] Max Weber, 'Innere Lage und Außenpolitik', in Max Weber, *Zur Politik im Weltkrieg. Schriften und Reden 1914–1918*, edited by Wolfgang J. Mommsen (Tübingen, 1988), pp. 191–201: 'Nur der ist ein *nationaler* Politiker, der die innere Politik unter dem Gesichtspunkt der unvermeidlichen Anpassung an die außenpolitischen Aufgaben ansieht. Wem die daraus folgenden "demokratischen" Konsequenzen nicht passen, *der verzichte* auf eine Großmachtpolitik, die sie unvermeidlich macht' (p. 192).

that Seeley's dictum about the relationship between external pressures and internal freedom now had to be reversed.[24] In short, as Karl Rotthaus pointed out, there was no 'correct' form of government *per se*; what mattered was whether a given system served the foreign-political purposes of the state or not.[25]

Despite serious challenges from Karl Lamprecht and Eckart Kehr, the primacy of foreign policy remained the dominant theoretical model until the 1960s; thereafter, it came under increasing attack from a younger generation of German historians. Their objectives were both political and methodological. Politically, these critics took exception to the apologetic baggage of the primacy of foreign policy, which potentially excused not merely Germany's aberrant behaviour on the international stage, but also her illiberal constitutional arrangements.[26] The primacy of foreign policy, in Ziebura's view, was thus an 'anti-democratic ideology'.[27] Methodologically, the objection was to the neglect of social and economic forces; the emphasis on the 'moment of decision' – it was argued – obscured the deeper, long-term forces at work in the historical process.[28] These differences were comprehensively aired in the Fischer controversy about German responsibility for the First World War, which was in turn part of a much wider debate about the relationship between foreign policy, society and elite manipulation throughout the Wilhelmine period. Indeed, far from conceding a primacy of foreign policy, the new generation of historians argued for a 'primacy of domestic policy' – *Primat der Innenpolitik* – according to which Germany's external relations were instrumentalised to perpetuate the status quo at home. No clear victor emerged from this debate. On the one hand, the new social history of politics rapidly established itself as something of a 'new orthodoxy' until itself attacked from the left towards the close of the 1970s. On the

---

[24] Otto Hintze, 'Liberalismus, Demokratie und auswärtige Politik', in Otto Hintze, *Soziologie und Geschichte. Gesammelte Abhandlungen zur Soziologie, Politik und Theorie der Geschichte*, edited and introduced by Gerhard Oestreich (Göttingen, 1964), p. 202. In the same vein see also Hermann Oncken, 'Über die Zusammenhänge zwischen äußerer und innere Politik', pp. 22, 36.

[25] Karl Rotthaus, 'Staatsform und auswärtige Politik. Eine Rankestudie', *PJ*, 179 (1920), 19.

[26] Ziebura, 'Die Rolle der Sozialwissenschaften in der westdeutschen Historiographie der internationalen Beziehungen', *GG*, 16 (1990), 93.

[27] Ibid., 87.

[28] Hans-Ulrich Wehler, 'Moderne Politikgeschichte oder "Große Politik der Kabinette"', *GG*, 1 (1975), 351 and *passim*; Wehler, 'Was bedeutet Leopold von Ranke heute?', in Hans-Ulrich Wehler, *Aus der Geschichte lernen? Essays* (Munich, 1988), pp. 98–100; Ulrich Muhlack, 'Leopold von Ranke', in *Deutsche Geschichtswissenschaft um 1900* (Stuttgart and Wiesbaden, 1988), pp. 11–36, defends Ranke against the charge of neglecting socio-economic factors.

other hand, the pendulum has now begun to swing back towards a more self-consciously *political* interpretation of key events in German history. This shift has been most marked for the Wilhelmine period,[29] but it is also evident for Revolutionary and Napoleonic Germany. 'If ever there was a country whose history was moulded by international relations', Tim Blanning writes, 'it was surely Prussia.'[30] Indeed, the more reductionist doctrines of the *Primat der Innenpolitik* have long since been retracted by some of its most passionate advocates.[31] But what is beyond all doubt is that societal historians have so far advanced no serious interpretative framework of their own to explain foreign policy; they have admitted as much themselves.[32]

---

[29] A typical example of this is the recent collection edited by Gregor Schöllgen (ed.), *Flucht in den Krieg? Die Aussenpolitik des kaiserlichen Deutschland* (Darmstadt, 1991).

[30] Tim Blanning, 'The death and transfiguration of Prussia', *HJ*, 29, 2 (1986), 459. For a recent interpretation of the Revolutionary and Napoleonic period in Germany on Rankean lines see the work of T.C.W. Blanning, 'The French Revolution and the modernisation of Germany', *CEH*, 22 (1989), 116; T. C. W. Blanning, *The origins of the French Revolutionary wars* (London, 1986); Thomas Nipperdey, *Deutsche Geschichte 1800–1866. Bürgerwelt und starker Staat* (Munich, 1983), p. 11: 'seldom have all aspects of life been determined to such an extent by power politics and external pressure'. In the Blanning school see also Peter Wilson, *War, state and society in Württemberg, 1677–1793* (Cambridge, 1995). A recent stimulating and unjustly neglected restatement of the *Primat der Aussenpolitik* is Ulrike Müller-Weil, *Absolutismus und Außenpolitik in Preußen. Ein Beitrag zur Strukturgeschichte des des preußischen Absolutismus*, Frankfurter Historische Abhandlungen 34 (Stuttgart, 1992), *passim*, especially pp. 21, 231–2. This study is indebted to and amplifies Gottfried Niedhart, 'Aufgeklärter Absolutismus oder Rationalisierung der Herrschaft', *ZfHF*, 6 (1979), 199–211.

[31] E.g. Hans-Ulrich Wehler, 'Geschichtswissenschaft heute', in Jürgen Habermas (ed.), *Stichworte zur 'Geistigen Situation der Zeit'*. Vol. II: *Politik und Kultur* (Frankfurt/Main, 1979), pp. 709–53: 'Inzwischen hat der "Primat der Innenpolitik" als harter Keil auf einem groben Klotz seine Schuldigkeit getan. Eine Dogmatisierung muß selbstverständlich vermieden werden' [p. 736]. See translation in: Hans-Ulrich Wehler, 'Historiography in Germany today', in Jürgen Habermas (ed.), *Observations on the 'spiritual situation of the age'. Contemporary German perspectives* (Cambridge, Mass. 1984), pp. 221–59: 'Meanwhile the primacy of domestic policy has doggedly done its job. Naturally, a dogmatizing of issues must be avoided' [p. 239].

[32] Ziebura, 'Die Rolle der Sozialwissenschaften', p. 90; Hillgruber, 'Die Diskussion über den "Primat der Aussenpolitik" und die Geschichte der internationalen Beziehungen in der westdeutschen Geschichtswissenschaft seit 1945', in Hillgruber, *Die Zerstörung Europas*, pp. 39–40: 'Bilanzierend kann man feststellen, daß die Vertreter der "Gesellschaftsgeschichte" zwar theoretisch für Interdependenz von Innen- und Außenpolitik plädieren, diese aber nicht praktizieren, sondern die internationalen Beziehungen in ihren Forschungen strikt ausklammern.' For a recent attempt at a *zeitgemäße Politikgeschichte* see Paul Nolte, *Staatsbildung als Gesellschaftsreform. Politische Reformen in Preußen und den süddeutschen Staaten, 1800–1820* (Frankfurt, 1990), p. 15. An interesting attempt to marry Hintzian themes and the primacy of foreign policy to the *Zeitgeist* was undertaken by Winfried Schulze in *Landesdefension und Staatsbildung. Studien zum Kriegswesen des innerösterreichischen Territorialstaates (1564–1619)* (Vienna, Cologne and Graz, 1973), especially pp. 16–18 and 24, and in *Reich und Türkengefahr im späten 16. Jahrhundert. Studien zu den politischen und gesellschaftlichen Auswirkungen*

The second theoretical inspiration for this book is the fraught and problematic concept of 'geopolitics'. Of course, the idea of a close relationship between geography, politics and history has a very long tradition. 'La politique des états', Napoleon famously remarked, 'est dans leur géographie'; history, Herder writes, 'is geography which has been set in motion'.[33] But the (pseudo-) science of 'geopolitics' – as championed by Ratzel, Haushofer, Kjellen, Mackinder and others – only emerged around the turn of the century. In its crudest form, 'geopolitics' was a geographically determinist variant of the primacy of foreign policy in which the interest, fears and policies of the state were merely a function of its location on the map. 'Man and not nature initiates', Sir Halford Mackinder wrote, 'but nature in large measure controls.'[34] On this reading, the geographic centrality of Germany in general and Prussia in particular – the German *Mittellage* in Europe – explained not only her aggressive foreign policy, but also her unique constitutional development. The widespread fear of encirclement (*Einkreisung*), the idea of preventive war, and the maintenance of authoritarian politics at home, so the argument ran, simply reflected the laws of geopolitics. 'The German *Mittellage*', Hermann Oncken wrote, was the 'fundamental fact of our national existence'.[35] Even such a liberal figure as Franz Schnabel spoke of the 'particular geographic burden (*Belastung*) of Germany'.[36]

This sense of Germany's unique geopolitical exposure was buttressed by the comparison with Britain. Historians such as Otto Hintze, Hermann Oncken and Gerhard Ritter distinguished between 'insular' and 'continental' state forms; Carl Schmitt spoke of '*Land*' and '*Meer*'.[37]

---

einer äußeren Bedrohung (Munich, 1978), especially pp. 12–14. An example of neo-Hintzeanism with foreign policy left out is Wolfgang Neugebauer, *Politischer Wandel im Osten. Ost- und Westpreußen von den alten Ständen zum Konstitutionalismus*, Quellen und Studien zur Geschichte des östlichen Europa 36 (Stuttgart, 1992), especially p. 489.

[33] Napoleon cited in Yves Lacoste, *Geographie und politisches Handeln. Perspektiven einer neuen Geopolitik* (Berlin, 1990), p. 17; Herder cited in Wolf D. Gruner, *Die deutsche Frage. Ein Problem der europäischen Geschichte seit 1800* (Munich, 1985), p. 38: 'Geschichte ist in Bewegung gesetzte Geographie.'

[34] Halford Mackinder, 'The geographical pivot of history', *The Geographical Journal*, 23, 4 (1904), 422.

[35] Oncken, 'Über den Zusammenhänge zwischen äußerer und innerer Politik', p. 36: 'Grundtatsache unserer nationalen Existenz.'

[36] Quoted in Gruner, *Deutsche Frage*, p. 38 (1985).

[37] Hintze, 'Machtpolitik und Regierungsverfassung', pp. 424–56, esp. 427–8; see also Hintze, 'Staatenbildung und Verfassungsentwicklung', p. 49; O. Hintze, 'Das monarchisches Prinzip und die konstitutionelle Verfassung', in Oestreich (ed.), *Staat und Verfassung*, p. 365. Hermann Oncken, 'Über die Zusammenhänge zwischen äusserer und innerer Politik', esp. pp. 17–19; Gerhard Ritter, *Die Dämonie der Macht: Betrachtungen über Geschichte und Wesen des Machtproblems im politischen Denken der*

Whereas the 'insular' location of Great Britain permitted the development of a representative political culture, the 'continental' situation of Prussia-Germany compelled her to achieve the internal cohesion necessary to survive in the predatory international system. Similarly, whereas Britain could concentrate on a remunerative maritime foreign policy, Prussia-Germany was entirely focussed on the mainland of Europe. While Britain could afford to uphold the European balance of power at a safe distance, Prussia-Germany enjoyed no such latitude. Indeed, it is not difficult to sense the suspicion, hostility, but also envy in Fritz Wagner's description of British policy during the French Wars of 1792 to 1815. 'Until the fall of Napoleon', he wrote, 'British capital was active in inciting one state after another, and even the peasants of remote mountain valleys, to launch a war of liberation . . . while Britain enriched herself at the expense of European colonial property overseas.'[38] British observers, of course, saw things differently. According to Spencer Wilkinson, the 'historical function of Great Britain' was to 'hold the balance between the divided forces which work on the continental area'.[39] Indeed, to quote Alfred Thayer Mahan's graphic image, Britain's role during the Napoleonic period was that of a 'fruitful mother of subsidies, upon whose bountiful breasts hung the impoverished and struggling nations of the continent'.[40] On this reading, Prussian behaviour throughout the period resembled that of a rebarbative infant, resentfully suckling on a patient and maternal Britain.

The obvious apologetic implications of geopolitical arguments often obscured their intrinsic explanatory power. For this reason, criticism of geopolitics has tended to be part of a much broader assault on traditional political history in general, and the primacy of foreign policy in particular. Historians such as as Hans-Ulrich Wehler, Gilbert Ziebura, H.-D. Schultz and Jürgen Kocka objected both to the idea of geographic determinism itself and to its exculpatory potential. The *Mittellage*, Schultz argued, was merely an intellectual stratagem designed to 'turn

Neuzeit (Munich, 1948), *passim*. Carl Schmitt, *Der Nomos der Erde im Völkerrecht des Jus Publicum Europaneum* (Berlin, 1988), p. 19 and *passim*; *Der Leviathan in der Staatslehre des Thomas Hobbes* (Hamburg, 1938), esp. pp. 120–1; Carl Schmitt, *Land und Meer. Eine weltgeschichtliche Betrachtung* (Cologne, 1981).

[38] Fritz Wagner, *England und das Europäische Gleichgewicht 1500–1914* (Munich, 1947), p. 42. In a similar vein see Ulrich Scheuner, *Das europäische Gleichgewicht und die britische Seeherrschaft* (Hamburg, 1943), pp. 5–11, 76; Adolf Rein, 'Über die Bedeutung der überseeischen Ausdehnung für das europäische Staaten-System. Ein Beitrag zur Bildungsgeschichte des Welt-Staatensystems', *HZ*, 137 (1928), esp. pp. 67–73.

[39] Spencer Wilkinson's response to Mackinder's article, 'The geographical pivot of history', p. 438.

[40] Alfred Thayer Mahan, *The influence of sea power upon the French Revolution and Empire, 1793–1812* (London, 1893), II, p. 381.

perpetrators into victims'.[41] After all, as Kocka pointed out, both Poland and Switzerland were located in the heart of Europe but had developed very differently from Germany; this reference to Poland turned out to be something of an 'own goal'. Moreover, as Gilbert Ziebura argued, geopolitical 'constraints' could hardly be reconciled with the simultaneous insistence on the free will of states and statesmen characteristic of traditional political history.[42] These were telling criticisms, but they had already been anticipated. As far back as 1921, Karl Hoffmann had understood that foreign policy 'rests on a continuous tension between space and the human will'.[43] Some fifty years later Klaus Hildebrand – a traditional but non-determinist political historian – stressed that a rigidly geopolitical view risked underestimating the role of human agency in the historical process.[44]

In any case, far from being buried by the tide of historiographical progress, the idea of geopolitics has undergone a remarkable renaissance in recent years. At the theoretical level, this has been most evident in France, where Yves Lacoste has set up a course in 'geopolitics'.[45] In Germany, the revival of geopolitical models has been led by Immanuel Geiss and Gregor Schöllgen.[46] But even more traditional empirical historians such as Wolf Gruner now routinely refer to the importance of

---

[41] H.-D. Schultz, 'Deutschlands "natürliche Grenzen"', in Alexander Demandt (ed.), *Deutschlands Grenzen in der Geschichte* (Munich, 1990), p. 74; Hans-Ulrich Wehler, *Entsorgung der deutschen Vergangenheit? Ein polemischer Essay zum 'Historikerstreit'* (Munich, 1988), pp. 174–89: 'Die Dogmen der Geopolitik als Denkverbot'; Jürgen Habermas, 'Eine Art Schadensabwicklung. Die apologetischen Tendenzen in der deutschen Zeitgeschichtsschreibung', in *Historikerstreit. Die Dokumentation der Kontroverse um die Einzigartigkeit der nationalsozialistischen Judenvernichtung* (Munich and Zurich, 1987), p. 75: 'geopolitischen Tamtam von "der alten europäischen Mittellage der Deutschen"'; Jürgen Kocka, 'Hitler sollte nicht durch Stalin und Pol Pot verdrängt werden', in *Historikerstreit*, p. 141. For a recent attack on the renaissance of geopolitics see Rudolf Walther, 'Man braucht mehr Platz', *Die Zeit*, 21.7.1995, p. 28.

[42] Ziebura, 'Die Rolle der Sozialwissenschaften', p. 87.

[43] Karl Hoffmann, 'Innen- und Außenpolitik', *Deutsche Rundschau* 189 (1921), 287: 'beruht auf einer unaufhörlichen Spannung zwischen dem Raum und dem menschlichen Willen'.

[44] Klaus Hildebrand, 'Staatskunst oder Systemzwang? Die "Deutsche Frage" als Problem der Weltpolitik', *HZ*, 228 (1979), esp. p. 644.

[45] See Anne Corbett on French enthusiasm for geopolitics, *Times Higher Educational Supplement*, 11.3.1994. Lacoste publishes a triennial journal: *Hérodote. Revue de géographie et de géopolitique*.

[46] Immanuel Geiss, 'Geographie und Mitte als historische Kategorien. Anmerkungen zur einem Aspekt des "Historikerstreits"', *ZfG*, 10 (1991), 979–94; Gregor Schöllgen, *Die Macht in der Mitte Europas. Stationen deutscher Außenpolitik von Friedrich dem Großen bis zur Gegenwart* (Munich, 1992); Heinz Brill, *Geopolitik heute. Deutschlands Chance?* (Frankfurt and Berlin, 1994).

Germany's central location.[47] As Dag Krienen has argued, the *Mittellage* may not be Germany's 'fate', but her history cannot satisfactorily be explained without it.[48] Hence the aim of historians like Geiss is to 'rescue geography as an historical category' and use it 'as a heuristic instrument for the pragmatic interpretation of history'.[49] But this new 'geopolitics' is far removed from the the dogmatic schemas of Kjellen, Haushofer, Mackinder and the old school; unlike Ratzel, it makes no claims to formulate 'laws' of political geography.[50] Instead, the new 'geopolitics' is in the 'possibilist' tradition of Vidal de la Blache: conscious of, but not enthralled by geography. As Yves Lacoste stresses, neither geography nor the geographer determines policy; this is the preserve of the supreme warlord.[51] Geography may counsel, but it cannot command: the primacy of politics remains decisive at all times.

The third main theoretical inspiration for this book is the concept of 'high politics'. Much of 'high politics' is obvious and commonsensical. 'What', Vaclav Havel was asked, 'have you found surprising in the world of the powerful?' 'I realize again and again', Havel answered, 'how terribly important the personal characteristics of politicians are, their relationships and mutual animosities.'[52] This view of politics and political history has been developed into a coherent method by Maurice Cowling, John Vincent, Alistair Cooke and others. High politics focusses on individual politicians; unlike the traditional 'great men' school of history, however, it is concerned with the collectivity not the individual. But in contrast to that other famous student of the political collectivity, Lewis Namier, 'high politics' tends to be less interested in the broader 'political nation' and more focussed on the 'monastic', 'rotarian' and 'closed' world of Westminster.[53] In this environment political substance

---

[47] Wolf D. Gruner, *Deutschland mitten in Europa. Aspekte und Perspektiven der deutschen Frage in Geschichte und Gegenwart* (Hamburg, 1992); Gruner, *Die Deutsche Frage*, section 2.3: 'Die Geographie', pp. 38–40; Müller-Weil, *Absolutismus und Außenpolitik*, pp. 32–3, 41–4, 37, 53 and *passim* for references to geopolitical factors.

[48] See Dag Krienen's review of Alexander Demandt, *Deutschlands Grenzen in der Geschichte* (Munich, 1990) in *Der Staat*, 30, 2 (1991), p. 304.

[49] Geiss, 'Geographie und Mitte als historische Kategorien', pp. 982–3.

[50] Cited in Lacoste, *Perspektiven einer neuen Geopolitik*, p. 24.   [51] Ibid., p. 57.

[52] Interview with Vaclav Havel, *New York Review of Books*, 15.8.1991, p. 6.

[53] Paradigmatic: Lewis Namier, *The structure of politics at the accession of George III* (2nd edn, London, 1961); John Brooke, 'Namier and Namierism', *History and Theory*, 3 (1964), 335; Alistair Cooke and John Vincent, *The governing passion. Cabinet government and party politics in Britain, 1885–1886* (Brighton, 1974): 'closed world', pp. 21–2; Maurice Cowling, *The impact of Labour. The beginning of modern British politics* (Cambridge, 1971), p. 10: 'monastic or rotarian world'; p. 414 : 'malice'. For a critique see: Richard Brent, 'Butterfield's Tories: "High politics" and the writing of modern British political history', *HJ*, 30, 4 (1987), 943–54; J. P. Parry, 'The state of Victorian political history', *HJ*, 26 (1983), 469–84; J. P. Parry, 'High and low politics in modern Britain', *HJ*, 29, 5 (1986), 753–70; Peter Clarke, 'Political history in the

mattered very little, whereas 'party', 'malice' and 'the cut and thrust of personal competition' mattered a great deal.[54] 'Ambition and manoeuvre', to borrow Richard Brent's phrase, not issues and debates characterise political life.[55] 'An important factor in any political decision or any political career', Maurice Cowling writes, 'was a capacity for polarizing differences, while working within a framework of common assumptions'; this tendency towards 'synthetic conflict' meant that actions and events were 'unintelligible' outside the context of 'party'.[56] Issues were thus often reduced to mere rhetorical devices, to be taken up and dropped at will in the pursuit of power and favour. Indeed, the keenest political enmity is generally to be found amongst men of similar views, who are divided only by irreconcilable personal ambition.

High politics tends to be corrosive of long-term explanations for political change and sceptical of individual motivations; it is also deeply relativist, almost nihilist. 'It is wrong', Maurice Cowling wrote, 'to think of the division between Gladstone and Disraeli as a division of basic and fundamental principle.'[57] Some years later, Cowling extended this insight to the study of party politics in the 1920s. 'Anxiety to be Prime Minister blunted the effect of constant purpose', which helps to explain why Lord Derby 'held a variety of opinions and gave prominence to each according to their relevance to the tactical situation'. On this reading, the arrival of Labour was significant primarily because it 'enabled the second rank of Conservative ministers to overthrow their leaders'.[58] But perhaps the most controversial application of high politics was Cowling's study of the impact of Hitler on the Conservative party before 1940. 'In the early thirties', Cowling concluded, 'foreign policy was the form that party conflict took. Politicians conducted it in the light of party considerations.'[59]

But if historians of high politics are strident in their assault on liberal and other teleological pieties, they are modest, not to say pessimistic about the value of their own results. The primary concern of high politics has always been the construction of a coherent narrative centred

1980s', *Journal of Interdisciplinary History*, 12, 1 (1981), 45–7. For more recent alternative views of nineteenth-century British politics see: David Mayfield and Susan Thorne, 'Social history and its discontents: Gareth Stedman Jones and the politics of language', *Social History*, 17 (1992), 165–88; Jon Lawrence and Miles Taylor, 'The poverty of protest: Gareth Stedman Jones and the politics of language – a reply', *Social History*, 18 (1993), 1–16.

54 Cooke and Vincent, *The governing passion*, p. 948: 'cut and thrust of personal competition'.
55 Brent, 'Butterfield's Tories', p. 944.
56 Maurice Cowling, *1867. Disraeli, Gladstone and revolution. The passing of the second Reform Bill* (Cambridge, 1967), pp. 1–5.   57 Ibid., p. 308.
58 Cowling, *The impact of Labour*, pp. 417–18, 429.
59 Maurice Cowling, *The impact of Hitler. British politics and British policy, 1933–1940* (Cambridge, 1975), p. 5.

around those issues and rivalries which most exercised politicians at the time; Michael Bentley described this as the 'centre-of-attention method'.[60] In assembling such narratives, historians of high politics have shown an intense – almost fetishistic – interest in archival records. Only a detailed study of the links between individual politicians, they believed, could hope to reveal their real intentions. Yet at the same time, these historians are acutely conscious of the limitations of their evidence. 'The historian cannot know completely', Maurice Cowling writes, 'and intentions can seldom be established certainly.'[61] Indeed, Cowling admits that often 'evidence of intention is so fragmentary that the author has little confidence that the narrative structure could not be reversed'.[62] The 'nihilism' of the politician thus finds its echo in the scepticism of the historian.

Perhaps surprisingly, there is no equivalent school of high politics in German historiography. To the societal school, of course, the study of personalities is anathema. When John Röhl's account of 'personal rule' under Wilhelm II harnessed high-political themes to a Fischerite critique of Imperial Germany, his approach was widely dismissed as 'personal-istic'.[63] Indeed, 'high politics' has suffered from the strong German historiographical tradition which favours the study of the collective over the individual. There is the long-established preoccupation with the study of elites going back to Robert Michels; the much more complex exercise in political sociology recently attempted by Wolfgang Reinhard; and the 'polycratic' interpretation of the Third Reich which highlights the 'war of all against all' between the various organs of party and state.[64]

---

[60] See Michael Bentley, *Politics without democracy. Great Britain, 1815–1914. Perception and preoccupation in British government* (Oxford, 1984), pp. 13–14.

[61] Cowling, *1867*, pp. 7, 289. In the same vein see Cooke and Vincent, *The governing passion*, pp. xii–xiii. On the limits to historical knowledge see Patrick Joyce, 'History and post-modernism', *P&P*, 83 (1991), 201; Lawrence and Taylor, 'The poverty of protest', p. 190: 'Joyce's claim amounts to the "anti-system challenging the very possibility of objective knowledge" warned of by the History Workshop editorial in 1980.'

[62] Cowling, *1867*, p. 339.

[63] E.g. see Geoff Eley, 'The view from the throne: the personal rule of Kaiser Wilhelm II', *HJ*, 20 (1985), 469–85. Eley (p. 485) attacks Röhl's view of personal rule as a 'chimera'. For Röhl's defence see John Röhl, 'Introduction', in John Röhl and Nicolaus Sombart (eds.), *Kaiser Wilhelm II. New interpretations* (Cambridge, 1982), p. 9 and *passim*. See also John Röhl (ed.), *Der Ort Kaiser Wilhelms II in der deutschen Geschichte* (Munich, 1991), and John Röhl, *Kaiser, Hof und Staat. Wilhelm II und die deutsche Politik* (Munich, 1987). It is too early to judge the German response to David Barclay, *Frederick William IV and the Prussian monarchy, 1840–1861* (Oxford, 1995), which devotes considerable attention to high-political dimensions.

[64] Wolfgang Reinhard, *Freunde und Kreaturen. "Verflechtung" als Konzept zur Erforschung historischer Führungsgruppen. Römische Oligarchie um 1600* (Munich, 1979); Robert Michels, *Zur Soziologie des Parteiwesens in der modernen Demokratie. Untersuchungen über*

On the other hand, significant sections of German historiography have always remained open to the importance of personalities. The biographical tradition is still vibrant and steadily (re-)gaining respectability. Similarly, the great classic accounts of Prussian-German foreign policy generally – albeit fitfully and often unwillingly – concede the importance of personal rivalries; of this, more later. Finally, there are a number of sophisticated interpretations of the early modern court which emphasise the tendency of factional alignments to transcend divisions of rank and gender.[65] But none of this amounts to a systematic high-political approach; even the 'polycratic' model tends to see conflicts in terms of institutions and not personalities. On the whole, therefore, German historians have been interested in great men and great issues. They have only peripherally concerned themselves with personal rivalry as a subject of enquiry in its own right.

The great exception is Carl Schmitt, whose thoughts on the 'antechamber of power' provide the fourth and final theoretical inspiration for this book. Although very much on the margins of high politics throughout the Third Reich, Schmitt was well placed to observe the crucial role played by personal advisors, secretaries and others who monopolised Hitler's immediate surroundings.[66] If Schmitt had previously emphasised the importance of political enmity between nations, or among groups within nations – the *Freund–Feind* thesis[67] – he was now sensitised to the importance of *personal* antipathy and ambition. In his *Gespräch über die Macht*, Schmitt attempts both a complement and a partial refutation of Ranke's *Politisches Gespräch*; he implicitly rebukes the great master for neglecting the antechamber of power. 'Even the most

---

die oligarchischen Tendenzen des Gruppenlebens, edited by Werner Conze (Stuttgart, 1970); Martin Broszat, *Der Staat Hitlers. Grundlegung und Entwicklung seiner inneren Verfassung* (Munich, 1969); a good cross-section of Mommsen's work is available in Hans Mommsen, *Der Nationalsozialismus und die deutsche Gesellschaft. Ausgewählte Aufsätze* (Hamburg, 1991).

65 Norbert Elias, *Die höfische Gesellschaft. Untersuchungen zur Soziologie des Königstums und der höfischen Gesellschaft* (Neuwied, 1969), pp. 181–2: 'Menschen verschiedener Gruppen und Rangstufen verbinden sich miteinander. Bestimmte Herzöge, Minister, und Prinzen verbinden sich, zum Teil unterstützt durch ihre Frauen, gegen andere.' In the same vein see Reinhard's analysis of the Conseil d'Etat under Louis XIV, 'Verflechtung' als, p. 43. See also Jürgen von Krüdener, *Die Rolle des Hofes im Absolutismus* (Stuttgart, 1973): 'Tatsächlich ist am absolutistischen Hofe die Abstammung als Quelle sozialer Ehre und als Ordnungsfaktor des Ranges im Prinzip aufgehoben und durch ein anderes ersetzt worden: die Nähe zum Thron.'

66 For an imaginative analysis of Schmitt's views on the antechamber of power see Nicolaus Sombart, *Die deutschen Männer und ihre Feinde. Carl Schmitt – ein deutsches Schicksal zwischen Männerbund und Matriarchatsmythos* (Munich and Vienna, 1991), pp. 182–202.

67 Carl Schmitt, *Der Begriff des Politischen* (Hamburg, 1933; 1st edn 1927), p. 7.

absolute prince relies on reports and information and is dependent on his advisors', Schmitt writes. 'Whoever briefs or informs the potentate', he continues, 'is already participating in power, irrespective of whether he is a responsible countersigning minister.' The inevitable corollary of this was the formation of an 'antechamber of power' in which several rival advisors competed for the ear of the potentate.[68] The key to this struggle, Schmitt argues, was access and favour;[69] the one was, of course, impossible without the other. If the existence of such an antechamber was deplorable, Schmitt concludes, it was also inevitable. 'Not even the wisest institution, not even the most ingenious organisation can entirely eliminate the antechamber [of power]; no tantrum against the *Camarilla* or *Antichambre* can completely remove it; the antechamber itself cannot be circumvented.'[70]

It is one of the contentions of this book that all of these approaches can be synthesised into a single method. This method follows the primacy of foreign policy in its recognition that external relations was the central preoccupation in Prussian politics throughout the Revolutionary and Napoleonic period. Because this method is deployed to interpret a pre-industrial polity, the continuing debate between Wehler, Hillgruber, Hildebrand and others on the respective merits of political and societal history is not directly relevant; accepting the primacy of foreign policy in one historical period does not necessarily involve accepting it for all times and in all contexts.[71] It also accepts that the demands of foreign policy were often reflected in domestic structure, especially in the organisation of the executive. On this reading, foreign policy does not determine every aspect of internal development; instead, the primacy of foreign policy functions as what Otto Hintze has called a 'general regulatory principle'.[72] Foreign policy only overrides domestic considerations where

---

[68] Carl Schmitt, *Gespräch über die Macht und den Zugang zum Machthaber* (Pfullingen, 1954), pp. 14–15.

[69] Carl Schmitt, 'Der Zugang zum Machthaber. Ein zentrales verfassungrechtliches Problem', in Carl Schmitt, *Verfassungsrechtliche Aufsätze aus den Jahren 1924–1954* (Berlin, 1958), p. 430; Schmitt, *Gespräch über die Macht*; Röhl also places considerable emphasis on the importance of access – *Immediatrecht* – under Wilhelm II: see Eley, 'The view from the throne', 475.

[70] Schmitt, *Gespräch über die Macht*, p. 16.

[71] This point has been made by Alexander Novotny, 'Über den Primat der äußeren Politik. Bemerkungen zu einem Gedankengang Leopold von Rankes', in *Österreich und Europa. Festgabe für Hugo Hantsch zum 70. Geburtstag* (Graz, Vienna, Cologne, 1965), p. 319, and Heinrich Heffter, 'Vom Primat der Aussenpolitik', *HZ*, 171 (1951), 3. Both argue that the primacy of foreign policy may have been applicable to the nineteenth century, but had lost its validity by the mid-twentieth century.

[72] Hintze, 'Staatenbildung und Verfassungsentwicklung', p. 51.

these imperil the interests of the state, but it then does so absolutely. In short, the primacy of foreign policy is employed in a descriptive, not a normative sense.

While this book also borrows heavily from geopolitics, it eschews the rigid determinism of the older school. Geography *by itself* proves nothing; and a strict geopolitical determinism depoliticises history by removing the element of choice and conflict. At the same time, however, this study gives greater weight to compelling geopolitical forces than the 'possibilist' tradition of French geopolitics inspired by Vidal de la Blache. 'Des nécessités', Fevbre wrote, 'nulle part. Des possibilités, partout.'[73] But while this may have been true for France, it is less persuasive for Prussia. There were no iron laws of geopolitics engraved on stone tablets, but Prussian and German statesmen ignored the implications of geography at their peril. Nor is this emphasis on geographic considerations the result of an artificial and retrospective interpretative framework. Rather, it reflects the implicit and explicit presence of such arguments in the deliberations of statesmen at the time. In short, this book sees Prussian politics as not determined, but certainly conditioned by geography.

Simultaneously, however, the methodology of this book accepts the central premise of high politics. It recognises that all politicians are preoccupied with their own advancement in the antechamber of power. The objective issues of policy are thus also part of a much broader picture of ambition and manoeuvre. This is most obvious in an absolutist polity, such as *ancien régime* Prussia; the common objection – often levelled at Röhl and Cowling – that high politics fails to consider socio-economic interest groups, parliamentary structures and other forces is hardly relevant to an era in which such representative institutions barely existed. Another strength of high politics is that it restores free will to the protagonists. If the objective demands of policy tended to promote consensus, the quest for personal advancement tended to produce synthetic conflict. At the same time, external forces and external crisis could be manipulated for individual gain in the antechamber of power. The relationship between freedom and necessity was thus not so much competitive as symbiotic.

In short, the methodology of this book combines the narrative and the thematic. While the thematic approach highlights underlying forces, the narrative will tend to stress the contextual and the contingent. This method is not without its dangers. The construction of such a narrative is potentially an arbitrary exercise of judgment – of selection and

---

[73] Quoted in Peter Burke, *The French historical revolution. The 'Annales' school, 1929–89* (Oxford, 1990), pp. 14–15.

omission – quite apart from the possibility of crucial missing evidence. A certain scepticism about the results of the present study therefore seems appropriate. Furthermore, a rigorously high-political method of analysis risks being cynical, destructive and even nihilistic. This is perhaps unavoidable. Yet if the short-term effect of high politics and the 'antechamber of power' is 'to take the content'[74] out of Prussian politics, then it is to be hoped that geopolitics and the primacy of foreign policy will put the content back in. In short, the method employed here is a fusion of high politics, geopolitics and the primacy of foreign policy. It shows that the historian of the pre-industrial age has more to learn from Ranke and Otto Hintze than from Marx, and as much to learn from Carl Schmitt or Maurice Cowling as from Max Weber.

The political history of Prussia before Jena: the state of research

Traditionally, Prussian policy before 1806 has been seen as a morality play. In this cautionary tale the vacillating king Frederick William III plays the role of ineffectual dupe; his traitorous favourites in the Kabinett, Haugwitz, Lombard and Beyme, are cast as the villains. Thus Treitschke speaks of the 'clueless weakness (ratlose Schwäche)' of a Prussia which had lost not only its prestige but also its sense of German mission; Johann Gustav Droysen condemned the 'cowardly and greedy policy of Haugwitz and Lombard'; and Rudolf Usinger railed against the 'shameful Haugwitz and the equally worthless foreigners Lombard and Lucchesini'.[75] In this picture of unrelieved gloom, only Hardenberg, Stein and a few others stand out as isolated warning voices against French encroachments, but they are powerless in the face of royal indecision and the duplicity of their rivals; the defeats at Auerstedt and Jena are thus an inevitable nemesis. After 1806, however, virtue triumphs

---

[74] Namier was accused of 'taking the mind out of history': Brooke, 'Namier and Namierism', 339.

[75] Treitschke, *Deutsche Geschichte im neunzehnten Jahrhundert*, I, p. 137; Johann Gustav Droysen, *Das Leben des Feldmarschalls Grafen York von Wartenburg* (Leipzig, 1850/1913), pp. 103–4: 'feige und habgierige Politik der Haugwitz und Lombard'; Rudolf Usinger, 'Napoleon und der nordische Bund', *PJ*, 14 (1864) 2: 'schmach-bedeckten Haugwitz und der nichts besseren Ausländer Lombard und Lucchesini'. See also p. 12: 'Labyrinth von Schwankungen . . . Halbheit folgte auf Halbheit.' In a similar vein see *inter alia* Heinrich von Sybel, *Geschichte der Revolutionszeit von 1789 bis 1800* (Stuttgart, 1898), VIII, pp. 203–4. The judgments surveyed by Karl Disch, 'Der Kabinetsrat Beyme und die auswärtige Politik Preußens in den Jahren 1805/6', *FBPG*, 41 (1928), 333, show just how tenacious the belief in Beyme's malign influence was among historians and contemporaries.

as the erstwhile dissidents take control and put Prussia on the road to reform, national awakening and liberation. These historians generally did not ask to what extent a figure like Hardenberg was implicated in the situation he inherited in 1807 and how far his relations with Haugwitz and other rivals affected the position he had previously adopted.[76] For them, the decade immediately preceding Jena simply served to throw the subsequent 'heroic' age of Prussian history into sharper relief.

For a variety of reasons this 'classic' interpretation of Prussian policy continues to find an echo among diverse historiographical traditions. Many foreign historians have been concerned to contrast the prescience and consistency of British policy or of individual allied statesmen – such as Czartoryski – with Prussian cowardice before 1806. Their strictures are correspondingly harsh: Alfred Thayer Mahan spoke of Prussia's 'hesitating, selfish and timid policy' and her 'time-serving opportunism'; Piers Mackesy speaks of the 'contemptible neutrality of Prussia' and her 'timid and greedy betrayals'; and Waclav Zawadzki refers to the 'devious policies of the court of Berlin'.[77] Similar charges were levelled by Karl Otmar von Aretin, foremost champion of the old Holy Roman Empire and no defender of traditional Borussian pieties. Prussia, he wrote, had played the role of 'Judas' to a martyred *Reich*.[78] Even Marxist historians such as Ernst Engelberg have castigated the 'weak, antinational policy of Frederick William III'.[79] Finally, some attenuated strains of the 'classic' interpretation can also be found in Paul Schroeder's recent erudite and nuanced, but often moralistic *Transformation of European politics*. Impatient with Prussia for failing to cast off the bad habits of the eighteenth century in the interests of a durable international order, Schroeder condemns her for 'choosing to be a lion only after trying long

---

[76] The exception here would be Treitschke, *Deutsche Geschichte im neunzehnten Jahrhundert*, I, p. 209, who had no illusions about Hardenberg's early positive attitude towards France.

[77] Mahan, *Influence of seapower*, II, pp. 31, 40; Piers Mackesy, *The war in the Mediterranean, 1803–1810* (London, 1957), pp. 97, 160; W. H. Zawadzki, *A man of honour. Adam Czartoryski as a statesman of Russia and Poland, 1795–1831* (Oxford, 1993), p. 125. For a sound counter to the relentless Anglo-centricity of Mackesy's work see Paul Schroeder, 'Old wine in new bottles: recent contributions to British foreign policy and European international politics, 1789–1848', *Journal of British Studies*, 26 (1987), 19–20 and *passim*.

[78] Karl Otmar von Aretin, *Heiliges römisches Reich 1776–1806. Reichsverfassung und Staatssouveränität* (Wiesbaden, 1967), I, p. 347.

[79] Ernst Engelberg, 'Preußische Militärs und das antinapoleonisch-bürgerliche Reformwerk', in Gustav Seeber and Karl-Heinz Noack (eds.), *Preußen in der deutschen Geschichte nach 1789* (Berlin/GDR, 1983), p. 51: 'schwächliche, anti-nationale Politik Friedrich Wilhelms III'.

and hard to remain a jackal', while individuals such as Lombard are dismissed as 'greedy and gullible'.[80]

The dominant Borusso-nationalist interpretation of Sybel, Treitschke and Droysen coexisted with a less heroic but more empirical school of Prussian history led by Paul Bailleu, Karl Griewank and others. They shared many of the assumptions of the heroic school, especially the centrality of foreign policy. But at the same time, these historians stressed the severe constraints upon the Prussian leadership before Jena.[81] The events of 1806 were interpreted as a political, not a moral failure. 'The collapse of the Prussian state in 1806', Szymanski claimed, 'was not the result of internal factors, but rather the direct consequence of the controversial neutrality policy';[82] Heinrich Doerries saw Jena as 'the culmination of a development which was largely the result of a series of mistakes in foreign policy';[83] and Colmar von der Goltz, eager to exculpate the nobility, states simply that 'the unfortunate [neutrality] policy was the foremost cause of the catastrophe'.[84] This school argued that it was neither depravity which determined policy up to October 1806, nor a reign of virtue that began thereafter. In particular, they exploded the myth that Hardenberg had somehow been a consistent resister *avant la lettre*.[85] Above all, scholars such as Noack, Oncken and

---

[80] Paul Schroeder, *The transformation of European politics, 1763–1848* (Oxford, 1944), pp. 303, 285.

[81] For the rehabilitation of Prussian policy: Friedrich Noack, *Hardenberg und das geheime Kabinett Friedrich Wilhelms III vom Potsdamer Vertrag bis zur Schlacht von Jena* (Giessen, 1881), pp. 46–7, 89 and *passim*; Adolf Wohlwill, 'Frankreich und Norddeutschland von 1795–1800', *HZ*, 51 (1883), 400–1; Guy Stanton Ford, *Hanover and Prussia: a study in neutrality, 1795–1803* (New York, 1903), p. 9.

[82] Hans Szymanski, *Brandenburg-Preussen zur See, 1605–1815. Ein Beitrag zur Frühgeschichte der deutschen Marine* (Leipzig, n.d.), p. 144: 'Der Zusammenbruch des Staates Preußen im Jahre 1806 war kein innerlich begründetes Ereigniß, vielmehr zweifellos eine unmittelbare Folge der so umstrittenen Neutralitätspolitik.'

[83] Heinrich Doerries, 'Friedrich von Gentz "Journal de ce qui m'est arrivé de plus marquant . . . au quartier-general de S.M. le roi de Pruse" als Quelle preussischer Geschichte der Jahre 1805–1806' (DPhil dissertation, University of Greifswald, 1906), p. 1: 'der Abschluß einer Entwicklung, die in der Hauptsache durch eine Reihe von Fehlern in der auswärtigen Politik verschuldet war'.

[84] Colmar von der Goltz, *Von Roßbach bis Jena und Auerstädt: ein Beitrag zur Geschichte des preußischen Heeres* (Berlin, 1906), p. 495: 'Unter den Ursachen der Katastrophe steht obenan die unglückliche Politik.'

[85] See the two detailed and well-crafted demolitions by Max Duncker: 'Die Denkwürdigkeiten des Staatskanzlers Fürsten von Hardenberg', *PJ*, 39 (1877), 606–43; 'Graf Haugwitz und Freiherr von Hardenberg. Aktenstücke zu den Denkwürdigkeiten des Fürsten von Hardenberg, Bd 5', *PJ*, 42 (1878), 571–625; Paul Bailleu, 'Vor hundert Jahren. Der Berliner Hof im Herbst und Winter 1805', *Deutsche Rundschau*, 125 (1905), 206–7, says that the neutrality policy was a consensus between Hardenberg and his rivals; Griewank, 'Hardenberg und die preussische Politik, 1804 bis 1806', *FBPG*, 47 (1935), 227–308.

Hüffer tried to be fair to the Kabinett.[86] Lombard, Beyme and Haugwitz were rehabilitated; all accusations of treason were rejected. Indeed, according to Otto Hintze, the Prussian collapse should be blamed on the structure of the Kabinett itself rather than the individuals within it. 'It is well known', he wrote, 'that this mistaken form of government is largely to blame for the catastrophe of 1806.'[87] Conversely, Hintze also showed that many of the reforms inaugurated after 1807 had been prepared in the preceding decade.[88]

In the 1960s, the 'paradigm shift' in German historiography replaced the traditional focus on foreign policy and individual inadequacy with that of a rigorous study of structural weaknesses in state and society: the unreformed agrarian system; the 'anachronistic' division of society into estates, rather than classes; the persistence of guilds and other pre-modern restrictive practices; and widespread fiscal chaos, to name but a few. Only the shattering defeat at Jena permitted the necessary programme of intensive socio-economic modernisation which took place after 1807, even if the lack of any simultaneous political reform meant that Prussia experienced a flawed 'partial modernisation'.[89] The years 1797 to 1806 were thus a stagnatory period in which the Prussian state vainly tried to shore up the status quo. According to this reading there is

[86] Paradigmatic: Hermann Hüffer, *Die Kabinetsregierung in Preussen und Johann Wilhelm Lombard – Ein Beitrag zur Geschichte des preussischen Staates vornehmlich in den Jahren 1797 bis 1810* (Leipzig, 1891). See also Wilhelm Oncken's preface to Noack, *Hardenberg und das geheime Kabinett*, pp. vi, ix–x, on the Kabinett; Wilhelm Oncken, *Österreich und Preußen im Befreiungskriege. Urkundliche Aufschlüsse über die politische Geschichte des Jahres 1813* (Berlin, 1879), I, pp. 139–45; Selma Stern, *Karl Wilhelm Ferdinand Herzog zu Braunschweig und Lüneburg* (Hildesheim and Leipzig, 1921), pp. 294–5.

[87] Hintze, 'Die Entstehung der Ministerien', p. 31: 'Es ist bekannt, daß diese verkehrte Regierungsweise großenteils die Schuld an der Katastrophe von 1806 trägt.'

[88] Otto Hintze, 'Preußische Reformbestrebungen vor 1806', in Oestreich (ed.), *Regierung und Verwaltung*, pp. 504–29. In a similar vein see now the reassessments by Dennis E. Showalter, 'Hubertusberg [sic] to Auerstädt: the Prussian army in decline', *German History*, 12 (1994), 309–33 and Edgar Melton, 'The decline of Prussian *Gutsherrschaft* and the rise of the Junker as rural patron, 1750–1806', ibid., 334–5.

[89] Paradigmatic: Hans-Ulrich Wehler, *Deutsche Gesellschaftsgeschichte*. Vol. I: *Vom Feudalismus des Alten Reiches bis zur Defensiven Modernisierung der Reformära 1700–1815* (Munich, 1987). For the theoretical antecedents of this view see Hans-Ulrich Wehler's introduction to his edited collection of Kehr's articles, *Der Primat der Innenpolitik. Gesammelte Aufsätze zur preußisch-deutschen Sozialgeschichte im 19. und 20. Jahrhundert* (Berlin, 1965), p. 3; Hans Rosenberg, *Bureaucracy, aristocracy, and autocracy. The Prussian experience 1660–1815* (Cambridge, Mass., 1958); Eckart Kehr, 'Zur Genesis der preußischen Bürokratie und des Rechtsstaats', in Wehler (ed.), *Der Primat der Innenpolitik*, pp. 31–55. Hanna Schissler, *Preußische Agrargesellschaft im Wandel. Wirtschaftliche, gesellschaftliche und politische Transformationsprozesse von 1763 bis 1847* (Göttingen, 1978); Barbara Vogel, *Allgemeine Gewerbefreiheit. Die Reformpolitik des preußischen Staatskanzlers Hardenberg (1810–20)* (Göttingen, 1983).

really nothing to explain about the débâcle of 1806. The Prussian state simply collapsed under the weight of its own contradictions, those structural societal deficiencies which rendered it incapable of mastering the threat of revolutionary and Napoleonic France.[90] Underlying this 'critical' interpretation was a strident socio-economic reductionism. 'The participants believe they are acting,' Eckart Kehr wrote of the Wilhelmine naval race, 'but they are doing nothing through their intrigues but bringing about what was ordained by the alignment of social forces.'[91] Similarly, Hanna Schissler saw individual politicians as merely 'the exponents of larger social groups or the spectrum of possibilities'.[92] This was the kind of thinking that led Marcel Adler-Bresse to interpret Haugwitz's support for the Second Coalition against France as 'une solidarité de classe avec les "nobiliaires" des autres états monarchiques';[93] as we shall see, nothing could be further from the truth.

The 'critical' interpretation of Napoleonic Prussia was part of a broader campaign to rehabilitate the 'Third Germany'. Viewed from the perspective of modernisation theory, states such as Bavaria, Baden and Württemberg – once dismissed as miserable collaborationist principalities by the Borusso-nationalist school[94] – emerged as the harbingers of progress. The intensive programme of bureaucratic, social and legal reform carried out in western and southern Germany under French tutelage was favourably contrasted not only with the stubborn immobilism of pre-Reform Prussia, but with the compromises and half-measures of the post-1807 period. In short, the paradigm change in German historiography not only shifted the focus from politics and foreign policy to socio-economic structures; it also led to a greater interest in the smaller German states – welcome in itself – at Prussia's

---

[90] A particularly strong statement of the case for structural and administrative 'overload' is William W. Hagen, 'The partitions of Poland and the crisis of the Old Regime in Prussia 1772–1806', CEH, 9 (1976), 115–28, which argues that Prussia expired from indigestion induced by annexing more of Poland than she could cope with.

[91] Quoted in James J. Sheehan, 'The primacy of domestic politics: Eckart Kehr's essays on modern German history', CEH, 1, 2 (1968), 173.

[92] Schissler, Preußische Agrargesellschaft im Wandel, p. 14: 'Exponenten größerer sozialer Einheiten oder des Handlungsspektrums.'

[93] Marcelle Adler-Bresse, Sièyes et le monde allemand (Lille–Paris, 1977), I, p. 204: 'Sans doute, le "nobiliaire" s'est reveillé en lui, il a ressenti en lui, une solidarité de classe avec les "nobiliaires" des autres états monarchiques.' For similar socio-economic reductionism – for a later period – concerning the motivations of politicians see Marion W. Gray, Prussia in transition: society and politics under the Stein reform ministry of 1808 (Philadelphia, 1986), pp. 43, 51 and passim.

[94] For a particularly crude example of this view see Wilhelm Koppen, Deutsche gegen Deutschland. Geschichte des Rheinbundes (Hamburg, 1936).

expense. This shift was reinforced by developments in other areas of the historical profession. First of all, there was the growth of *Reichsgeschichte*, the sympathetic study of the old Holy Roman Empire pioneered by Karl Otmar von Aretin. Secondly and relatedly, the triumph of German federalism after 1945 encouraged historians to build on the vibrant tradition of regional history; this approach united both south German conservative Prussophobes and left-liberals in search of Germany's 'democratic potential'.[95] Moreover, there were also practical archival reasons to abandon the study of Prussian politics and foreign policy. Most of the relevant records were now located in the remote – but by no means inaccessible – German Democratic Republic (GDR). The net result was that for many years after 1945, the high-political history of Prussia became virtually the preserve of biographers such as Peter Thielen and Hans Hausherr;[96] the steady trickle of specialist studies on intellectual, military, administrative and other matters hardly touched on high politics and foreign policy.[97]

In the last five years, however, the political history of Napoleonic Prussia has experienced a renaissance.[98] First of all, the work of Thomas Stamm-Kuhlmann has restored King Frederick William III to his

---

[95] For a long time Heinrich von Srbik was a lonely battler against Prusso-centricity. Paradigmatic: Heinrich Ritter von Srbik, *Deutsche Einheit. Idee und Wirklichkeit vom heiligen Reich bis Königsgrätz*, 4 vols. (Munich, 1935–42); Heinrich Ritter von Srbik, 'Das österreichische Kaisertum und das Ende des Heiligen Römischen Reiches, 1804–1806', *Archiv für Politik und Geschichte*, 2 and 3 (1927), 131–71, 301–35; Enno Kraehe, *Metternich's German policy*. Vol. I: *The contest with Napoleon, 1799–1814* (Princeton, 1963), p. viii, opposes Prussian-centred historiography; James J. Sheehan, *German history, 1770–1866* (Oxford, 1989) self-consciously avoids Prusso-centricity.

[96] Peter Gerrit Thielen, *Karl August von Hardenberg, 1750–1822. Eine Biographie* (Cologne and Berlin, 1967); Hans Hausherr, *Hardenberg. Eine politische Biographie*. Vol. I: *1750–1800*, edited by Karl Erich Born (2nd edn Cologne and Graz, 1965); Hans Hausherr, *Hardenberg. Eine politische Biographie*. Vol. III: *Die Stunde Hardenbergs* (2nd edn Cologne and Graz, 1965).

[97] Robert M. Berdahl, *The politics of the Prussian nobility 1770–1848* (Princeton, 1989); Klaus Epstein, *The genesis of Prussian conservatism* (Princeton, N.J., 1966); Hermann Büschleb, *Westfalen und die preußischen Truppen, 1795–1802. Ein Kapitel Militärpolitik und Landesgeschichte* (Osnabrück, 1987).

[98] Since I began this research in 1989 the following have appeared: Otto Büsch and Monika Neugebauer-Wölk (eds.), *Preußen und die revolutionäre Herausforderung seit 1789* (Berlin, 1991), which has comparatively little on 'pure' political history; Dominique Bourel, 'Zwischen Abwehr und Neutralität. Preußen und die Französische Revolution 1789 bis 1795/ 1795 bis 1803/6', in Büsch and Neugebauer-Wölk (eds.), *Preußen und die revolutionäre Herausforderung*, pp. 43–57, which is quite detailed for the period before 1800 but has less than two pages on 1801–6; it is mainly concerned with the story up to 1795 and uses no MSS sources after 1800. See also Brendan Simms, 'The road to Jena; Prussian high politics, 1804–1806', *German History*, 12 (1994), 374–94.

rightful centrality in Prussian politics.[99] In so doing, he gave the lie to Friedrich Schulze's confident prediction that 'Frederick William will hardly be put back at the "centre of things".'[100] Instead, Stamm-Kuhlmann took up Ranke's dictum on the importance of the monarch in absolutist polities. 'However highly one rates the general circumstances and their inner necessity', Ranke wrote, 'the monarchic element, that is the character and inclination of the prince remains decisive in a monarchic state.'[101] As Stamm-Kuhlmann shows, Frederick William was not merely the focal point of Prussian politics, he was also its ultimate arbiter; no major political decision was taken without his approval. 'He wanted to be king', Treitschke wrote, 'and he was. Nobody ever controlled him.'[102] But what Treitschke merely claimed, Stamm-Kuhlmann has proved beyond all doubt: far from being manipulated by evil advisors, Frederick William was very much his own political master. Secondly, Philip Dwyer has defended the much-criticised neutrality policy as a 'perfectly legitimate exercise in *Realpolitik*';[103] in particular, he argues that the Prussian occupation of Hanover in 1801 was more rational and less frantic than hitherto believed.[104] Both Dwyer and Stamm-Kuhlmann reject any suggestion that Hardenberg was any less

---

[99] Thomas Stamm-Kuhlmann, *König in Preussens großer Zeit. Friedrich Wilhelm III, der Melancholiker auf dem Thron* (Berlin, 1992), pp. 9, 11 and *passim*. For the centrality of Frederick William see also Simms, 'The road to Jena', and Dwyer, 'The politics of Prussian neutrality, 1795–1806', *German History*, 12 (1994), 351–74.

[100] Friedrich Schulze, 'Die Beurteilung Friedrich Wilhelms III in der Geschichtsschreibung des 19. Jahrhunderts', in *Studium Lipiense. Ehrengabe für Karl Lamprecht* (Berlin, 1909), p. 342: 'In den "Mittelpunkt der Dinge" wird sich Friedrich Wilhelm wohl niemals wieder stellen lassen.'

[101] Leopold von Ranke (ed.), *Denkwürdigkeiten des Staatskanzlers Fürsten von Hardenberg*, I, p. 396: 'Wie hoch man auch die allgemeinen Verhältnisse und ihre innere Nothwendigkeit anschlagen mag so hat doch in dem monarchischen Staat eben das monarchische Element, d.h. die Natur und Sinnesweise des Fürsten einen Alles bestimmenden Einfluß.' See also the recent comments by Wolfgang Neugebauer, 'Zur neueren Deutung der preußischen Verwaltung im 17. und 18. Jahrhundert in vergleichender Sicht', in Otto Büsch and Wolfgang Neugebauer (eds.), *Moderne preußische Geschichte, 1648–1947. Eine Anthologie* (Berlin and New York, 1981), II, p. 558, that the 'Faktor Herrscherperson aus der Analyse den Verfassungsstrukturen im "ancien régime" und ihrer Fortbildung nicht eliminiert werden kann, auch wenn die Forschung mit Nachdruck die Frage nach "Sachzwängen" und Kollektiv-phänomenen zu stellen hat.'

[102] Treitschke, *Deutsche Geschichte im neunzehnten Jahrhundert*, I, p. 142: 'Er wollte König sein und er war es. Niemand hat ihn je beherrscht.'

[103] Dwyer, 'The politics of Prussian neutrality', 358.

[104] Philip G. Dwyer, 'Prussia and the second armed neutrality, 1799–1801' (PhD dissertation, University of Western Australia at Perth, 1992). See also Philip G. Dwyer, 'Prussia and the Armed neutrality: the invasion of Hanover in 1801', *IHR*, 15 (1993), 661–87.

implicated in the policy errors before 1806, which places them firmly in the tradition of Bailleu and Duncker.[105]

No historian is an island entirely to himself. Much of this book could not have been written without the work of scholars such as Leopold von Ranke, Paul Bailleu, Otto Hintze, Rudolf Krauel, Karl Griewank and many others. There is no need to reinvent the wheel: what this book has to say about the primacy of foreign policy, the link between external pressures and internal structures, and the degree to which Hardenberg was implicated in the neutrality policy before 1806 may not be fashionable, but it is hardly revolutionary.[106] The book accepts Stamm-Kuhlmann's arguments about the centrality of Frederick William, and it echoes – with reservations – the more sympathetic view of the neutrality policy advanced by Philip Dwyer. Finally, this book recognises the immense contribution of historians such as Eckart Kehr, Hans Rosenberg and other 'critical' historians to the general history of the old Prussia; and it certainly does not dispute that the cumulative 'modernisation deficits' of the Prussian state, most notably its unreformed agrarian system, were a contributory factor in the catastrophes of Auerstedt and Jena.

But if this study is heavily indebted to the existing literature on pre-Reform Prussia, it also hopes to transcend it. First of all, this book challenges the socio-economic reductionism of the 'critical' school; the study of Prussian policy during the Hanoverian crisis – to name only the most striking instance – shows that necessity of state could override the clamour of powerful interest groups in the economy and the bureaucracy. Indeed, the socio-political strength of the aristocracy must be strictly distinguished from their high-political irrelevance. Secondly, this book addresses a gap in the literature. The work of Stamm-Kuhlmann is – unsurprisingly – largely biographical in focus. Reasonably enough, he draws on those sources directly concerned with the king, in preference to – though certainly not to the exclusion of – those records relating to broader issues of foreign policy.[107] Philip Dwyer's research, on the other hand, is largely concentrated on Prussian foreign policy: the

---

[105] Stamm-Kuhlmann, *Friedrich Wilhelm III*, pp. 197, 211 and *passim*; Dwyer, 'The politics of Prussian neutrality', p. 367 and *passim*.

[106] E.g. see: Griewank, 'Hardenberg und die preussische Politik'; Paul Bailleu, 'Haugwitz und Hardenberg', *Deutsche Rundschau*, 20 (1879), 268–98; Ludwig Dehio, 'Eine Reform Denkschrift Beymes aus dem Sommer 1806', *FBPG*, 18 (1926), 321–38.

[107] This is reflected in Stamm-Kuhlmann's use of sources, which includes the Nachlässe of Frederick William and Hardenberg but not many diplomatic sources, or even those parts of Nachlaß relating to foreign policy. For foreign policy Stamm-Kuhlmann relies largely on printed sources.

documents he uses sustain a detailed diplomatic narrative, but they are much less useful for high politics; Dwyer is also handicapped by the fact that Hardenberg's *Denkwürdigkeiten* do not start until 1803/4. Hausherr's biography does not deal with the years 1798 to 1806, in many ways the most controversial and least edifying period of Hardenberg's career. The detailed studies by Griewank, Ulmann, Disch and others cover only part of the period. Conversely, the short surveys by Bourel and Dwyer are – in the nature of things – too brief to provide more than a general outline. Finally, the volume of the *Handbuch der preußischen Geschichte* relating to the political history of Prussia before 1806 has not yet appeared.[108] In short, this book is a first attempt to provide a detailed and integrated study of Prussian policy and politics during the first decade of Frederick William III's reign.

Yet this study intends not merely to supplement and synthesise the existing literature, but also to enhance our understanding of the period through theoretical inspirations derived from high politics and geo-politics. Of course, historians have often noted the adversarial under-current in Prussian politics before 1806. 'Hardenberg', Ranke wrote, 'believed that he could perceive personal jealousy against his activities and success in the conduct of the *Kabinett*.'[109] Griewank, Hausherr, Hintze, Kieseritzky, Meyer, Kohnke, Olden, Schroeder and many others, have all noted – albeit only in passing – the role of personal ambition and antipathy in pre-reform Prussia.[110] But they were curiously reluctant to recognise these sentiments as a formidable political force in their own right. Indeed, Ranke explicitly refused to address such 'unedifying' personal animosities between Prussian statesmen, while Karl Griewank referred to 'openly manifested personal motives and irritations', only 'in order to assess them correctly and silently ignore

---

[108] Otto Büsch (ed.), *Handbuch der preußischen Geschichte.* Vol. II: *Das 19. Jahrhundert und große Themen der Geschichte Preussens* (Berlin and New York, 1992).

[109] Ranke (ed.), *Denkwürdigkeiten Hardenbergs*, I, p. 365: 'Hardenberg glaubte in dem Verfahren des Kabinetts persönliche Eifersucht gegen seine Thätigkeit und seinen Erfolg wahrzunehmen.'

[110] Hintze, 'Das preußische Staatministerium im 19. Jahrhundert', in Otto Hintze, *Regierung und Verwaltung. Gesammelte Abhandlungen zur Staats-, Rechts-, und Sozialgeschichte*, ed. and introduced by Gerhard Oestreich (Göttingen, 1967), p. 536; Ernst Kieseritzky, 'Die Sendung von Haugwitz nach Wien' (PhD dissertation, University of Göttingen, 1895), p. 14; Hans Hausherr, 'Stein und Hardenberg', *HZ*, 190 (1960); Hans Peter Olden, 'Napoleon und Talleyrand. Die französische Politik während des Feldzugs von 1805 in Deutschland', (PhD dissertation, University of Tübingen, 1928), pp. 72–3; Meta Kohnke, 'Das preußische Kabinettsministerium. Ein Beitrag zur Geschichte des Staatsapparates im Spätfeudalismus', *Jahrbuch für die Geschichte des Feudalismus*, 2 (1978), 345; Christian Meyer, *Preußen und Frankreich, 1795–1800* (Munich, 1903), p. 78; Schroeder, *The transformation of European politics*, p. 304.

them'.[111] It is true that Stamm-Kuhlmann and Dwyer both emphasise the importance of high-political manoeuvres. 'The influence of the individual factions at court and in government', Kuhlmann points out, 'was dependent upon who, when and under which circumstances somebody enjoyed the confidence of the king'.[112] But none of this amounts to a systematic analysis of Prussian high politics, which would reveal the complex adversarial agenda underlying every ostensibly objective policy debate.

Similarly, historians have noted – but not systematically analysed – the role of geopolitical considerations in Prussian policy before 1806.[113] Gregor Schöllgen's synoptic overview of the German *Mittellage* does not cover the Napoleonic period, while the various contributions by Wolf Gruner do not deal with the pre-1815 period in any detail.[114] By examining the role of geopolitical thinking in pre-reform Prussia, this book will both enhance our understanding of Prussian policy before Jena and help close a gap in the history of the German *Mittellage*. Inevitably, the focus on high politics, geopolitics and foreign policy means that many aspects of Prussian history before 1806 are either neglected or excluded altogether. The book largely ignores socio-economic problems except where they relate to foreign policy. There is no mention of cultural history: the Jewish salons, court rituals, popular piety and related phenomena. Intellectual developments, and even the emergence of a

111 Ranke (ed.), *Denkwürdigkeiten Hardenbergs*, I, p. 365: 'Hardenberg glaubte in dem Verfahren des Kabinetts persönliche Eifersucht gegen seine Thätigkeit und seinen Erfolg wahrzunehmen. Wir wollen das weder bestätigen, noch ableugnen'; Griewank, 'Hardenberg und die preussische Politik', p. 308: 'offen hervortetenden persönlichen Motiven und Gereiztheiten hat der historische Betrachter nur zu erkennen, um sie richtig einzuschätzen und dann ruhig zu übergehen'; '*unerfreulich*': Ranke, 'Die Memoiren des Grafen Haugwitz', p. 295.
112 Stamm-Kuhlmann, *Friedrich Wilhelm III*, p. 12: 'Das Gewicht der einzelnen Strömungen in Hof und Regierung war schließlich davon abhängig, wer wann und unter welchen Bedingungen das Ohr des Königs hatte' (see also p. 169); Dwyer, 'The politics of Prussian neutrality', p. 365. A high-political approach for the period *after* was also adopted by R. C. Raack, *The fall of Stein*, Harvard Historical Monographs 58 (Cambridge, Mass., 1965), p. viii: 'I have taken as my special province for detailed investigation the personal intrigues and infighting among the small circle of men near the court just before Stein's resignation. The evidence I have found seems to show the need to explore the relation between what historians view as the large historical movements – in this case the reform effort – and the constant harassments embodied in social and institutional life and the game of politics itself.'
113 Stamm-Kuhlmann, *Friedrich Wilhelm III*, pp. 163, 181, 206 on *Mittellage*; Ford, *Hanover and Prussia*, pp. 22–3; Dwyer, 'The politics of Prussian neutrality', p. 366; Disch, 'Der Kabinettsrat Beyme und die auswärtige Politik', 42 (1929), p. 100, hints at but does not develop the role of geopolitics in Beyme's thinking.
114 Schöllgen, *Die Macht in der Mitte Europas*; Gruner, *Deutschland mitten in Europa*; Gruner, *Die Deutsche Frage*.

'public sphere' are not our concern. This is a book about political action, not political thought, a book about those who held high political office, not those who occupied the high moral ground.

Sources

This book draws upon a wide range of manuscript sources. These include the relevant official diplomatic correspondence, the private papers of Prussian statesmen, diplomats and King Frederick William III, the general Prussian memoranda on foreign affairs, the representations of various economic interest groups and the records of the relevant branches of the Prussian administration.[115] The intensive use made of the correspondence with the embassy in London throughout part II reflects the bilateral focus of my original research. Unfortunately, one of the key figures – Count Haugwitz – seems to have left no private papers.[116] Other documents are known to be lost, including official correspondence relating to August-October 1806, burned by Haugwitz to prevent it from falling into French hands,[117] and much of the Hohenzollern *Hausarchiv* in Charlottenburg which was destroyed by Anglo-American terror-bombing during the Second World War.

In addition, this book is fortunate in being able to draw upon a vast array of printed source material. Three of these collections were particularly informative: Paul Bailleu's edition of the Prussian diplomatic documents which proved invaluable for an understanding of the general international context;[118] the *Denkwürdigkeiten* (memoirs) of Hardenberg, edited by Leopold von Ranke, which contain crucial information on

[115] The records of the British embassy at Berlin, containing the reports from, and instructions for, the ambassador, Francis Jackson, PRO FO 64/66–71; the records of the Prussian embassy at London, containing the reports from, and instructions for, the ambassador, Baron Jacobi-Kloest, GStA Rep.XI.73 *England* 178B–181D [GStA Rep.XI.73.178–] and Rep.XI.81 *London* 228–44 [GStA Rep.XI.81.228–]; the records of general conferences on foreign affairs in Prussia and those relating to relations with France, GStA Rep.XI.89 *Frankreich* 394–411 [GStA Rep.XI.89.394–]. General deliberations relating to Russia and the reports of Baron von der Goltz, Prussian ambassador at St Petersburg, GStA Rep.XI.175 *Russland* 154–157 [GStA Rep.XI.175.154–]; the papers of Frederick William III, king of Prussia relating to foreign affairs and high politics, GStA Rep.92.*Friedr. Wilh. d. Dritte*.B.VI.18–22; the papers of Count Hardenberg, the Prussian foreign minister, relating to foreign policy and high politics, GStA Rep.92 *Hardenberg* E8–9; and GStA Rep. 92 *Schöll* 18–21.
[116] I thank Hamish Scott and Philip Dwyer for their help in tracking down such papers. See also Anna Coupkova, 'Über das Familenarchiv Haugwitz in Namiest', *Adler. Zeitschrift für Genealogie und Heraldik*, 17, 3 (1993), 81–7.
[117] Bailleu (ed.), *Briefwechsel Alexanders*, p. 117.
[118] Paul Bailleu (ed.), *Preussen und Frankreich bis 1795–1807. Diplomatische Corresponden-zen*, 2 vols. (Leipzig, 1881–7).

Prussian policy and high politics before Jena;[119] and Georg Winter's collection on the governmental reform debate of 1806/7, which reproduces nearly all the relevant documents.[120] Without Winter's work, chapter 5 could not have been written; without Bailleu's and Ranke's labours the rest of the book would have taken much longer to write. The *Briefe und Amtliche Schriften* of Stein are far less informative for high politics and foreign affairs, excepting the documentation on the British–Prussian war of 1806, which Richard Krauel has already evaluated.[121] Useful collections of documents were also assembled by Melle Klinkenborg (on Finckenstein), Albert Naudé (on Schulenburg) and Gustav Roloff (on the reorganisation of the Prussian executive, 1800–2).[122] Finally, there are the letters and memoirs of more peripheral figures. The *Vertraute Briefe* of Friedrich von Cölln provide a penetrating critique of pre-Reform Prussia. Colonel von Massenbach's *Memoiren über meine Verhältnisse zum preußischen Staat* are disappointing;[123] on the other hand, his *Memoiren zur Geschichte des preußischen Staates* are very informative indeed.[124] The memoirs of Friedrich August von der Marwitz have generally been regarded as a contribution to the development of German conservative thought, but they also give an insight into high politics; Marwitz was, after all, a disappointed politician himself.[125]

The selected correspondence of British statesmen such as Charles James Fox, William Lord Grenville and Robert Stewart, Viscount Castlereagh contain much valuable material on policies and attitudes

---

119 Ranke (ed.), *Denkwürdigkeiten.*
120 Georg Winter (ed.), *Die Reorganisation des preussischen Staates unter Stein und Harden-berg* (Berlin, 1931), part I/vol. I.
121 There are two overlapping editions: Erich Botzenhart (ed.), *Stein. Briefwechsel, Denkschriften und Aufzeichnungen im Auftrag der Reichsregierung, der Preussischen Staatsregierung und des Deutschen und Preussischen Städtetages* (Berlin, 1931), vols. I and II; Walther Hubatsch and Manfred Botzenhart (eds.), *Stein. Briefe und amtliche Schriften*, 10 vols. (Stuttgart, 1957–74).
122 Melle Klinkenborg, 'Materialen zur Geschichte des Geheimen Staatsministers Karl Wilhelm Finck von Finckenstein', *FBPG*, 28 (1915), 563–74; Albert Naudé, 'Die Denkwürdigkeiten des Ministers Grafen von Schulenburg', *FBPG*, 15 (1902), 385–419; Gustav Roloff (ed.), 'Die Neuorganisation im Ministerium des Auswärtigen im Jahre 1802. Briefe von Haugwitz und Lombard', *FBPG*, 5 (1892), 265–73; 7 (1894), 97–111.
123 Christian von Massenbach, *Memoiren zur Geschichte des preußischen Staates unter den Regierungen Friedrich Wilhelm II. und Friedrich Wilhelm III.* (Amsterdam, 1809). Also disappointing is Maurice Weil (ed.), *D'Ulm à Jena. Correspondance inédite du Chevalier de Gentz avec Francis James Jackson, ministre de la Grande Bretagne à Berlin (1804–6)* (Paris, 1921).
124 Christian von Massenbach, *Memoiren zur Geschichte des preußischen Staates unter den Regierungen Friedrich Wilhelm II und Friedrich Wilhelm III* (Amsterdam, 1809), especially vol. III.
125 Friedrich Meusel (ed.), *Friedrich August von der Marwitz. Ein märkischer Edelmann im Zeitalter der Befreiungskriege.* Vol. I: *Lebensbeschreibung* (Berlin, 1908), especially p. 169.

towards Prussia.[126] Also extremely useful are the diaries and letters of George Jackson, brother of Francis Jackson, the British ambassador at Berlin.[127] J. H. Rose's *Select Dispatches* provides a selection of British diplomatic documents for the period 1804 to 1805, especially those concerning Lord Harrowby's mission to Berlin.[128] Finally, extensive use was made of the remarkably comprehensive Soviet collection of documents on Russian foreign policy in the nineteenth century.[129]

My research complements rather than duplicates existing source collections. For example, the majority of the documents relating to the secret policy with Russia – outlined in chapter 7 – were neither printed in the appendix to the *Denkwürdigkeiten*, nor referred to by Hardenberg in his text. Similarly, historians have tended to ignore the records relating to Hardenberg's move to the foreign office in 1804, preferring to rely on Ranke's rather sketchy exegesis. Moreover, to the best of my knowledge, the archival material quoted is not accessible elsewhere in printed form. Whenever a printed source has been available, it has been cited in preference to the manuscript source, even in those cases where the manuscript source was consulted first.

But if the documentation used is copious, it is far from unproblematic. First of all, these records may just be the tip of the iceberg; there could well be a vast subterranean rock of evidence sufficient to sink the arguments advanced in this book. Secondly, there is an in-built inverse relationship between action, reflection and composition. The more historical figures act the less they tend to reflect; the more they confer in person, the less they write. For example, we are well informed about Queen Louise's political stance in the summer of 1806, because her letters to Frederick William from Pyrmont have been preserved. Normally, however, she would have spoken directly with her husband; such conversations are much more difficult, not to say impossible, to reconstruct. Similarly, some of the most familiar documents of the Napoleonic period – the memoranda of Friedrich Gentz, Stein's Nassau memorandum and Hardenberg's Riga memorandum – were written during periods of forced inactivity; the manoeuvres of a politician caught

[126] Lord John Russell (ed.), *Memorials and Correspondence of Charles James Fox*, 4 vols. (London, 1853–7); Dropmore, *The MSS of J. B. Fortescue Esq. preserved at Dropmore (1892–1927)*, vols. VII–VIII; Charles Vane (ed.), *Robert Stewart, Viscount Castlereagh. Memoirs and Correspondence*, 12 vols. (London, 1850–3).

[127] Lady Jackson (ed.), *The diaries and letters of Sir G. J. Jackson from the Peace of Amiens to the Battle of Talavera*, 2 vols. (London, 1872).

[128] J. H. Rose (ed.), *Select Dispatches from the British Foreign Office archives relating to the formation of the Third Coalition against France, 1804–1805* (London, 1904).

[129] *Vneshnaya Politika Rossii XIX ee Nachala XX Veka*, edited by Ministerstuo inostranmykh, vols. V and VI (Moscow, 1961).

up in the cut and thrust of high office generally leave no such traces. Thirdly, while the main contours of foreign policy and the executive reform debate are richly documented, evidence for the crucial high-political context often has to be assembled from much more disparate and patchy sources. Fourthly, it is a historiographical truism that a document can be intended to obfuscate as much as enlighten. The British ambassador to Prussia, for example, urged his brother and deputy to 'shade [his] picture according to the sentiments of your employer';[130] to a greater or lesser degree, all the actors in this book were guilty of such manipulation. Fifthly and finally, the ample memoir literature of the period is fraught with the usual problems of that *genre*: apologetics, bias, selective memory and sheer sleight of hand.[131] However, these difficulties can be reduced – though not entirely overcome – through a critical handling of even the most compromised sources. In the last century, for example, Max Lehmann and Max Duncker subjected Hardenberg's *Denkwürdigkeiten* to a searching critique which revealed them to be both biased and accurate: biased in that Hardenberg's intent was obviously polemical and apologetic; accurate in that he often freely produces documents that dispute his own case.[132] Besides, the (incomplete) *Denkwürdigkeiten* were never published during Hardenberg's lifetime, so that they constitute the raw material for an apologia rather than the finished product itself.

This book is divided into three parts. The first part – which blends narrative and analysis – sets out both the structure of Prussian politics and the assumptions underlying Prussian foreign policy during the first seven years of Frederick William III's reign. This is followed by the main narrative of the years 1804 to 1806, which shows the corrosive effect of

---

130 Jackson, *Diaries*, II, p. 125.
131 See the cautionary remarks of Klinkenborg, 'Materialen zur Geschichte des Geheimen Staatsministers von Finckenstein', p. 564. Naudé, 'Denkwürdigkeiten des Ministers Grafen Schulenburg', p. 387, believes that Schulenburg's recollection is basically accurate.
132 Max Lehmann, 'Hardenberg's Memoiren', *HZ*, 39 (1878), 83, 88; Duncker, 'Die Denkwürdigkeiten Hardenbergs', p. 633. See also Hans Hausherr, 'Die Lücke in den Denkwürdigkeiten des Staatskanzlers Fürsten Hardenberg', in *Archivar und Historiker. Studien zur Archiv- und Geschichtswissenschaft zum 65. Geburtstag von Heinrich Otto Meissner* (Berlin, 1956), pp. 497–510. The documents in *Nachlaß Schöll* were selected by one of Hardenberg's assistants for another *apologia*, concentrating only on his foreign policy (Hausherr, *Hardenberg*, I, pp. 10–16). Hardenberg's 'diary' must also be used with caution: circumstantial evidence and layout suggest it to have been more of an *aide mémoire* for the compilation of the *Denkwürdigkeiten* dating from 1807–8 than a contemporary record of the years 1797–1806. This notwithstanding, it is a useful and often candid source.

events on these structures. The third and final part analyses the impact of Napoleon on Prussian high politics, foreign policy and the executive apparatus of state in the period leading up to Jena. These dates are carefully chosen: 1797 marked both the accession of Frederick William III and the Napoleonic coup of Fructidor; 1804 brought both a significant increase in French pressure on Northern Germany and the rise of Hardenberg; and 1806 saw the collapse of the old Prussia at Auerstedt and Jena. This approach has its dangers. By blending narrative and analysis for the period before 1804 (part I: 'The structures'), and emphasising the force of events thereafter (part II: 'The events'; part III: 'The responses'), the book risks exaggerating the dramatic at the expense of the thematic in the years immediately preceding Jena. Conversely, the analysis in part III – especially chapter 8 – cannot escape repeating, or at least recalling, some of the main narrative. Finally, there is the danger of slipping back into the political narratives of yesteryear. If G. M. Young said that the greater part of what passed for diplomatic history was merely what 'one clerk said to another',[133] then much of this book may seem to be just what one Prussian politician said to another. The author is aware of these and other pitfalls; whether he has avoided them is for the reader to judge.

---

[133] Quoted in Alexander de Conde, 'Essay and reflection: on the nature of international history', *IHR*, 10 (1988), 283.

Part I

The structures

2 The structure of Prussian politics during the early reign of Frederick William III

From discussion to decision: the development of the decision-making process in Prussia and its underlying assumptions

> The head of state must imbue the machinery with an independent spirit; his words should resonate through every string of the instrument like an electric shock.[1]

Almost from its very conception in the early modern period, the Prussian political system was characterised by an emphasis on decision. In institutional terms this found expression in the creation of the Geheimer Rat (Privy Council) in 1604, which was a direct response to severe foreign-political pressure upon the state.[2] It signalled a move away from simple, untrammelled princely self-government to a more formal decision-making process which coupled the sovereign's will to an advisory body. The Geheimer Rat was thus the first example of the constant Prussian search to harness the information, advice and expertise of many to the decisiveness of one man. For the ultimate power of decision rested always with the prince who, though he did not always attend the meetings of the Rat, had complete power to determine its agenda and had the last say in all matters.[3] Towards the end of the century the Great Elector summed up the reasoning behind the Rat in the following advice to his successor:

Do not decide anything important, or that which requires secrecy, in the presence of advisors. Rather, you should retire to reflect on the matter and let the

---

[1] G. F. W. von Cölln, *Vertraute Briefe über die innern Verhältnisse am preussischen Hofe seit dem Tode Friedrichs II* 6 vols. (Amsterdam and Cologne, 1807–9), I, p. 128: 'Der Staatschef muß nur durch Befehle, die nicht motiviert sind auf die Staatsmaschine wirken; wie ein elektrischer Schlag müssen seine Worte jede Saite des Instruments durchbeben.'

[2] Gerhard Oestreich, *Der brandenburgisch-preußische Geheime Rat vom Regierungsantritt des großen Kurfürsten bis zu der Neuordnung im Jahre 1651. Eine Behördengeschichtliche Studie*, edited by F. Hartung, vol. I, 1937, p. 4.

[3] Ibid., p. 5.

one or the other privy councillor or secretary come to you and weigh all opinions again. Then make your decision, so that you are like bees who draw the best nectar out of a flower.[4]

Thus, so the theory went, far from surrendering any power, or allowing the Rat to share in it, the prince shared in the knowledge of his councillors, like the bee drawing nectar out of a flower, but reserved the ultimate decision to himself. The result was a highly cohesive and dynamic polity in which all resources were subordinated to the will of one man. In the startling and unhappy formulation of Gerhard Oestreich, this made Prussia a seventeenth-century *Führerstaat*.[5]

The reign of Frederick William I saw the creation of two key institutions which were to dominate the governmental structure of Prussia until the reform period. In 1723, the Generaldirektorium (General Directory) united – for the time being at least – all the important administrative bodies into one consultative council; this brought some kind of rationality into the internal government of the state, however unsatisfactory the arrangement proved in the long term. Much more important for the purposes of this study, though, was the establishment of the Kabinettsministerium – or foreign ministry – in 1728.[6] With this measure, Frederick William put the conduct of Prussian foreign policy, previously the fiefdom of his closest advisor, Heinrich Rüdiger von Ilgen, on a more formal basis. At the same time, the move marked Ilgen's personal apotheosis after years of ruthless infighting. Not long after, when Ilgen's death seemed near, an anxious Frederick William asked him to submit his views on the best possible conduct of foreign affairs. Ironically, Ilgen suggested a collegial system of two or more equally placed, collectively responsible foreign ministers; this was the very same arrangement which he himself had spent all of his working life trying to circumvent. His justification was that no other single man, apart from himself, was capable of running Prussian foreign policy. Ilgen's action

---

[4] Quoted in Hintze, 'Die Entstehung der Modernen Staatsministerien', p. 297: 'Concludiret in Gegenwart der Räten in wichtigen Dingen und da Verschwiegenheit vonnöten, nichts, sondern nehmet solches zu bedenken anheim, lasset nochmals einen oder den andern Geheimen Rat und einen Secretarium zu Euch kommen, überleget nochmals alle Vota, so da geführet worden sein und resolviret darauf; und wird wie der Bienen, die den besten Saft aus den Blumen saugen.'
[5] Oestreich, *Der brandenburgisch-preußische Geheime Rat*, p. 1.
[6] See Peter Baumgart, 'Zur Gründungsgeschichte des Auswärtigen Amtes in Preussen, 1713–1728', *Jahrbuch für die Geschichte Mittel- und Ostdeutschlands*, 7 (1958), 229–48; Reinhold Koser, 'Die Gründung des Auswärtigen Amtes durch König Friedrich Wilhelm I im Jahre 1728', *FBPG*, 2 (1889), 161–97; Kohnke, 'Das preußische Kabinettsministerium', pp. 319–22; Müller-Weil, *Absolutismus und Außenpolitik*, pp. 170–2.

was important in two respects. First, it showed how little Prussian politicians were able to think of institutional change in isolation from narrower political issues, especially their own personal advancement. As we shall soon see, this remained unchanged until the collapse of the old Prussia. Ilgen's interest in the structure of the foreign office ended with the prospect of his own death. Indeed, there is a certain indifference, or at least intellectual laziness, about the way in which he reverted to the traditional collegial principle at the end of his career, having hitherto been a passionate advocate of a monocratic foreign ministry, headed by himself. Secondly, it saddled Prussia with that selfsame collegial system of foreign policy making for the best part of the next hundred years. In theory – to quote Max Weber – the collegial principle was an attempt 'to fashion a sort of synthesis of specialized experts into a collective unit';[7] in practice, this could only work wherever there was a sufficiently strong monarchic will to check the inevitable rivalries between ministers.

Decision-making in Prussia was complicated by the loose overall structure of the Prussian polity. Contrary to what one might imagine, Prussia had never experienced rigorous centralisation and remained a patchwork quilt of territories with widely diverging local legal, political and fiscal traditions. In foreign policy, Prussia spoke – or aimed to speak – with one voice, but no such cohesion existed in her domestic administration. As Ludwig Tümpel has pointed out, Prussia was certainly no unitary state.[8] It remains a remarkable fact that while diplomatic documents at the close of the eighteenth century referred to *La Prusse*, the internal documents of the Prussian state invariably spoke of 'His Majesty's states and provinces (*Seiner Maj. Staaten und Provinzen*)'. Indeed, to quote the words variously attributed to Stein and Schulenburg, pre-reform Prussia was a 'federal state'.[9] In fact, apart from the person of the monarch himself, the only administrative focal point for the *whole* kingdom was the Council of State, or Staatsrat. It was only in the Staatsrat that all the various branches of government – the Generaldirektorium, the Kabinettsministerium and subsequently the Silesian department – were combined into one great advisory body for the benefit of the monarch. It was only there that a considered foreign policy, taking full account of the internal capabilities and interests of the

---

[7] H. H. Gerth and C. Wright Mills (eds.), *From Max Weber. Essays in sociology* (New York, 1970), pp. 236–7.

[8] Ludwig Tümpel, *Die Entstehung des brandenburgisch-preusischen Einheitsstaates im Zeitalter des Absolutismus 1609–1806*, Untersuchungen zur deutschen Staats- und Rechtsgeschichte 124 (Breslau, 1915), p. 240.

[9] Ibid., p. 241; C.B.A. Behrens, *Society, government and the Enlightenment. The experiences of eighteenth-century France and Prussia* (London, 1985), p. 29.

monarchy, could be agreed. It was, after all, the Staatsrat which was theoretically invested with monarchic authority in the event of the king being called away on an emergency.[10] The fact that the Staatsrat never developed into such a pivotal decision-making structure was due less to its own shortcomings than to the determination of Prussian monarchs to maintain their authority through the creation of parallel advisory structures.

During the reign of Frederick the Great, the formal arrangements regarding foreign policy were a largely academic affair. Unlike his father, Frederick pursued an often expansionist and always activist foreign policy centred on his own person. 'He bore the responsibility for everything, he evaluated everything, he decided everything', in the words of one historian of Prussian institutions.[11] As Wilhelm Dilthey put it in a classic essay, Frederick's 'ideal monarchy rests entirely upon the person of the prince'.[12] Indeed Frederick's political testaments highlight his preoccupation with decision and his strident insistence on personal rule. 'Un prince qui sait bien les affaires', he wrote in 1752, 'qui les combine et qui calcule juste, va seul plus loin que tous les conseils. Il agit avec vigueur, avec activité, avec secret, ce que ne peut jamais arriver, quand sept ou huit personnes doivent se réunir, pour adhérer au même sentiment.'[13] The king must serve as *point de ralliement* for the whole system and make the decisions *en dernier ressort de toutes les affaires*.[14] Unlike his two successors, Frederick II was entirely open about the exercise of monarchic power, but his thinking probably reflects general Hohenzollern preoccupations. Frederick rejected the 'customary' system of government in which the king presided over a ministerial council.[15] First of all, he doubted whether such a large body could produce any sensible resolutions. Secondly, he feared that rival ministers would distort the affairs of state through intrigue and ambition. Thirdly, he believed that extensive and acrimonious oral debate tended to obscure rather than enlighten. Fourthly, such widespread consultations

---

[10] Carl Wilhelm Cosmar and C. A. L. Klaproth, *Der königl. Preußische Churfürstl. Brandenburgische Wirklich Geheime Staatsrath* (Berlin, 1805), p. 222.

[11] Rudolf Schmidt-Bückeburg, *Das Militärkabinett der preußischen Könige und deutschen Kaiser. Seine geschichtliche Entwicklung und staatsrechtliche Stellung, 1787–1918* (Berlin, 1933), p. 4.

[12] Dilthey, 'Friedrich der Grosse und die deutsche Aufklärung', p. 184.

[13] Quoted in Alexander von Hase, 'Der Absolutismus an den Grenzen seiner selbst', *Archiv für Kulturgeschichte*, 73, 2 (1991), 356; Hintze, 'Die Entstehung der modernen Staatsministerien', p. 299; Friedrich von Oppeln-Bronikowski (ed.), *Friedrich der Große. Das politische Testament von 1752* (Stuttgart, 1974), p. 53 and *passim*.

[14] Quoted in von Hase, 'Der Absolutismus an den Grenzen seiner selbst', p. 357.

[15] Oppeln-Bronikowski (ed.), *Friedrich der Große*, pp. 54–5.

endangered the essential confidentiality of matters of state. But there was another objection to a council of ministers, which Frederick II articulated equally frankly. This was the fear of ministerial encroachment on royal power. 'Jealous of their own reputation and power', Frederick wrote, 'the ministers want to leave the monarch with only the external appearance (of power) . . . They themselves wish to rule, but their master is supposed to be content with the empty prerogative of issuing their orders in his name.'[16]

There was no danger of this happening under Frederick the Great. Instead, ministers and departmental chiefs were relegated to the margins of political action. In part this should be seen as a direct by-product of Frederick's ruthless subordination of domestic matters to foreign political considerations. The various heads of department who made up the General Directory, for example, normally only saw the king once a year;[17] moreover, they were explicitly denied any right of initiative.[18] Admittedly, the foreign ministers saw him much more frequently, as befitted their higher standing in the Prussian polity.[19] Indeed, H. O. Meissner has stressed that even Frederick the Great did not achieve complete absolutism and draws attention to the extent to which he was dependent on ministerial research and preparation.[20] However, since Frederick effectively acted as his own foreign minister, their overall role was also limited. Hamish Scott recently characterised ministerial tasks as being little more than 'secretarial'.[21] This is precisely the phrase which springs to mind when one reads Thomas Steavens's description of Frederick's unfortunate foreign minister Count Podewils, who was directed 'to write such letters, draw up such memorials, signe [sic] such decrees as are directed by the King his master'.[22]

To make matters worse, the ministers were increasingly forced to share this lowly function with the technically far more junior cabinet secretaries and councillors. These men, who were almost invariably of humble birth, enjoyed more frequent contact with the monarch than the noble

16 Ibid., p. 139.
17 Hintze, 'Die Entstehung der modernen Staatsministerien', p. 299.
18 Walter Dorn, 'The Prussian bureaucracy in the eighteenth century', *Political Science Quarterly*, 46 (1931), 414.
19 Hans-Otto Meissner, 'Die monarchische Regierungsform in Brandenburg-Preussen', in *Festschrift für Fritz Hartung* (Berlin, 1958), p. 232.
20 Ibid., p. 233.
21 Hamish Scott, 'Aping the great powers: Frederick the Great and the defence of Prussia's international position, 1763–1786', *German History*, 12 (1994), 291: 'Ministers . . . were more like secretaries than advisers.'
22 Von Hase, 'Der Absolutismus an den Grenzen seiner selbst', p. 358. See also Müller-Weil, *Absolutismus und Außenpolitik*, pp. 205–9.

ministers. Collectively they were known as the Kabinett – not to be confused with the Kabinettsministerium – and came to be the butt of mounting criticism both of the pamphlet press and disgruntled senior bureaucrats as the century drew to a close. Very little is known about the precise origins of the Kabinett.[23] It appears to have been another of Frederick William I's innovations. But what may originally have just arisen out of a need to communicate quickly with the individual branches of the administration[24] soon had the effect of by-passing the responsible ministries. An advocate of rapid decisions, Frederick William used the secretaries to send his orders in writing to avoid long policy discussions with the ministers.[25] There can be no doubt that under his son Frederick II the effective influence of the Kabinett in politics was minimal, but the seeds of later developments were already clearly identifiable. In a revealing passage in his political testament of 1752 Frederick wrote that 'I keep my own counsel; I have only one secretary of whose trustworthiness I am convinced.'[26] Towards the end of his reign the number of cabinet secretaries multiplied so that eventually they came to be, in the words of the most distinguished historian of the Kabinett, a 'reproduction of the whole structure of the state',[27] with councillors and secretaries for each major branch of the administration. One of the young men recruited by Frederick for such administrative purposes was Johann Wilhelm Lombard, the man whose position under Frederick William III was to be so exalted that he later characterised his own role as effectively that of a minister.[28]

Despite various institutional transformations, the general principles upon which Prussian decision-making was based remained unchanged from the early seventeenth century onwards. The aim was to find the right blend of information, deliberation and execution, especially in the formulation of foreign policy. In its concern to find this blend, the Prussian political system increasingly resembled a machine. As such it corresponded to the graphic prescription of the Prussian civil servant and

---

[23] Max Lehmann, 'Der Ursprung des preussischen Kabinets', *HZ*, 63 (1889), 266.

[24] Hermann Hüffer, 'Die Beamten des älteren preussischen Kabinets von 1713–1808', *FBPG*, 5 (1892), 158.

[25] Lehmann, 'Der Ursprung des Kabinets', 271.

[26] Oppeln-Bronikowski (ed.), *Friedrich der Große*, p. 55.

[27] Hüffer, 'Die Beamten des Kabinets', p. 181.

[28] Johann Wilhelm Lombard, *Materiaux pour servir à l'histoire des années 1805, 1806 et 1807, dédié aux Prussiens par un ancien compatriote* (Frankfurt and Leipzig, 1808), p. 51: 'les secrétaires ou conseillers de cabinet étoient dans le fait des ministres auxquels il ne manquoit que le titre'.

political theorist, Johann Heinrich Gottlieb von Justi, that: 'A properly constituted state must be exactly analogous to a machine, in which all the wheels and gears are precisely adjusted to one another; and the ruler must be the master mechanic, the mainspring or the soul – if one may use the expression – which sets everything in motion.'[29] This is exactly what Frederick the Great meant when he said that 'a system can only emerge out of one mind, which must be the mind of the ruler'.[30] Of course, it is true that the conception of the state as a machine was widespread among German states in the eighteenth century;[31] however, it was only in Prussia that the process of decision-making and the decision itself were positively sacralised. This comes across most strikingly in the introduction to Klaproth and Cosmar's two-hundred-year anniversary history of the Prussian Staatsrat which appeared in 1806. The purpose of a commemoratory medal which showed the Elector Joachim Friedrich standing before an altar-like table, they explained, was in order to show 'that important decisions which secure the future welfare of the state are something sacred'.[32] It would be difficult to find a better example of Carl Schmitt's notion of the decision as 'secularised miracle'.[33] We shall see presently how this 'cult' of the decision remained part of political practice and rhetoric right up to the defeats of Auerstedt and Jena.

Discussion instead of decision: structural weaknesses in the political system of post-Frederician Prussia

Nobody can escape observing that the various branches of the state, who should be cooperating with each other, in order to further the common good as best they can, actually undermine each other. Nobody can escape observing that often one head of department publicly or

---

[29] I have blended the translations from Geraint Parry, 'Enlightened government and its critics in eighteenth-century Germany', *HJ*, 6 (1963), 182; Sheehan, *German history*, p. 34; and T. C. W. Blanning, *Reform and revolution in Mainz, 1743–1803* (Cambridge, 1974), p. 19.

[30] Oppeln-Bronikowski (ed.), *Friedrich der Große*, p. 53; in almost exactly the same words, p. 104.

[31] Barbara Stollberg-Rillinger, *Der Staat als Maschine. Zur politischen Metaphorik des absoluten Fürstenstaates* (Berlin, 1986), especially p. 125: 'absolute Monarchie als die vollkommendste Maschine'; Harm Klueting, *Die Lehre von der Macht der Staaten. Das außenpolitische Machtproblem in der 'politischen Wissenschaft' und in der praktischen Politik im achtzehnten Jahrhundert* (Berlin, 1986).

[32] Cosmar and Klaproth, *Staatsrat*, p. xxii: 'wichtige auf alle Zukunft reichende Handlungen zum besten des Vaterlandes etwas Heiliges sind'.

[33] Schmitt, *Politische Theologie*, p. 37.

secretly obstructs another in order to delay the progress of his rival so that *he* himself can steal a march and thus portray his own actions in a more favourable light.[34]

Thanks to the extraordinary force of Frederick the Great's personality, the structural weaknesses of the Prussian political system remained largely dormant throughout his reign. Yet already before 1786, the leading members of the Kabinett were regarded as unsavoury *éminences grises* operating out of the shadows, chiefly for their own benefit and often to the detriment of the state and ruler. Pride of place in the demonology of ministerial and pamphleteering critics of the system went to August Friedrich Eichel, the man who accompanied Frederick on all occasions. He was certainly privy to secrets which the ministers were not, for Frederick admitted as much in his testament; moreover, what Eichel chose to keep from the king often simply never reached him.[35] Indeed, some years after the death of the great Frederick, an anonymous memorialist warned the new king that even his vigilant predecessor had been unable to prevent widespread manipulation of petitions by the cabinet councillors, who could 'encourage or suppress at their whim'.[36] Admittedly, these criticisms of Eichel and the lesser councillors centred on nepotism and corruption rather than the making or distortion of 'high' matters of state. While such abuses did go a long way towards undermining the confidence of the subjects in their monarch and the system of appeal, their eradication could in no way be regarded as essential to the political survival of the state. What was important for the future was not so much the concrete influence of the individual cabinet secretaries – which was still negligible at this stage – but the high-political structures which Frederick left behind. By marginalising his responsible ministers, he potentially deprived himself of their expertise; by allowing the development of a personal Kabinett, he was seen to nourish a serpent at the heart of the Prussian monarchy whose toxin was

---

[34] Massenbach, *Memoiren zur Geschichte des preußischen Staates*, III, pp. 268-9: 'Niemanden kann die Bemerkung entgehen, daß öfters die verschiedenen Staatsfächer, die einander mit wechselseitiger Unterstützung entgegenkommen sollten, um das gemeinsame Beste mit vereinigten Kräften zu befördern, vielmehr gegen einander arbeiten. Niemanden kann die Bemerkung entgehen, daß oft ein Departements-Chef dem andern, heimlich oder öffentlich, in den Weg tritt, um den Gang seines Nebenbuhlers aufzuhalten, damit er selbst den Vorsprung gewinne und dadurch seine eigenen Schritte, unbekümmert um andere, glänzender mache.'

[35] Hüffer, *Die Kabinetsregierung in Preussen*, p. 501; Hüffer, 'Die Beamten des Kabinets', 162-3.

[36] Quoted in Hüffer, *Die Kabinetsregierung in Preussen*, p. 507: 'nach belieben protegiren oder zurückweisen konnten'. On the role of Eichel see Dorn, 'The Prussian bureaucracy in the eighteenth century', 419–20.

to paralyse decision-making under his much less able successors. In short, Frederick the Great bequeathed a system in which ministerial competence was already a hollowed-out shell and in which the cabinet secretaries were long ensconced in the *entourage* of the king.

After 1786, the change in monarch made itself immediately felt. The erratic and contradictory character of Frederick William II was reflected in the turbulent and colourful machinations of the court; in the meanderings of Prussian foreign policy; and in the the complete sub-version of traditional principles of decision-making through favouritism and sloth.[37] But if the alleged vices of his father's reign were largely condemned in personal terms, the critique of his son and successor Frederick William III was structural; that this masked a strong element of personal animosity will become apparent in due course. The Kabinett, once merely the butt of frustrated petitioners, now metamorphosed into the focus of ministerial discontent. Paradoxically, it was Frederick William's decision to reduce the number of cabinet councillors to three and ultimately two, thereby increasing the individual importance of the remainder, which hastened the development of the Kabinett into a serious political force. If under Frederick the Great the councillors had proliferated to become parallel, but powerless, ministers, they were cut back under Frederick Wiliam III but went on to flourish nonetheless.[38]

Leaving aside the supposed moral deficiencies of its members, two main criticisms were levelled at the Kabinett. The first charge was that the Kabinett, far from expediting monarchic decision, actually consider-ably delayed it. Rather than simply executing the royal will, the cabinet secretaries were increasingly invited to partcipate in the deliberation of policy; this inevitably slowed things down. To make matters worse, the Kabinett tended not merely to reflect, but actually to magnify the hesitation of the monarch; whenever Frederick William found himself pressed by ministerial councils, he could always look to his Kabinett for

---

[37] W. M. von Bissing, *Friedrich Wilhelm II. König von Preussen* (Berlin, 1967); Reinhold Koser, 'Die preußische Politik von 1786 bis 1806', *Deutsche Monatsschrift*, 6 (1907), 453–80, 612–37, is critical but fair.

[38] This is a classic illustration of Eberhard Naujoks' argument, *pace* Rosenberg, that the personality of the ruler influences the structure of the state. See: Eberhard Naujoks, 'Die Persönlichkeit Friedrichs des Großen und die Struktur des preußischen Staates', *Historische Mitteilungen*, 2, 1 (1989), p. 18; Hans Rosenberg, 'Die Überwindung der monarchischen Autokratie (Preußen)', in K. O. von Aretin (ed.), *Der Aufgeklärte Absolutismus* (Cologne, 1967), p. 182. Similarly Karl Griewank, 'Hardenberg und die preussische Politik', p. 235, argues that the development of the Prussian governmental system was very much a function of the '*persönliche Veranlagung*' of Frederick William III. In the same vein see Hermann Hüffer, *A. L. Mencken, der Großvater des Fürsten Bismarck, und die Kabinetsregierung in Preußen. Vortrag zum Antritt des Rektorates der Rheinischen Friedrich Wilhelms Universität am 18. Oktober 1890* (Bonn, 1890), p. 19.

support. The second charge concerned the complete lack of accountability of the Kabinett. Whereas the ministers were responsible for their actions, the cabinet councillors could hide behind the authority of the king. 'The worst thing about it was', wrote one contemporary Prussian critic, 'that the cabinet councillors appeared subordinate to the ministers, but in reality they stood in the background and issued the ministers with instructions under the aegis of royal authority without, however, being responsible for them.'[39] Finally, the ministers of the Kabinettsministerium and the bureaucrats of the Generaldirektorium were incensed by the degree of control exercised by the Kabinett over access to the king. All correspondence – both diplomatic and administrative – passed through the hands of the relevant cabinet secretary; all military business reached the king via his adjutants. Moreover, the senior bureaucratic ministers of the Generaldirektorium did not enjoy *Immediatrecht*, that is the right of access to the king. They continued to meet Frederick William about once a year on ceremonial occasions. Only the foreign ministers of the Kabinettsministerium possessed *Immediatrecht*, but even they were hard pressed to compete with the near monopoly of the royal ear enjoyed by the Kabinett.

Another grave structural problem which Frederick the Great bequeathed to his successors was the continuing tension in the General Directory between the *Realsystem* and the *Territorialsystem*, that is between administrative departments organised according to subject and according to province respectively. Frederick himself had created this problem by successively adding new subject departments for trade, excise, mining and factories to the old provincial departments. To make matters worse, Silesia formed a separate provincial ministry outside the General Directory which was directly responsible only to the king. A certain amount of confusion was thus unavoidable,[40] especially in view of the fact that the General Directory was organised on a collegial basis: ministers were collectively responsible for the measures taken rather than individually answerable for the departments they headed. This made the decision-making process cumbersome, inefficient and acrimonious in the extreme. Indeed, Frederick William I's complaint that his feuding departments had 'done nothing but feud amongst themselves, as if the Generalkommissariat was not equally the servant of the king of Prussia

---

[39] Von Cölln, *Vertraute Briefe*, I, p. 129: 'Das übelste bei der Sache aber war daß die Kabinettsräthe, dem äußern Schein nach, den Ministern nachstanden, in der Wirklichkeit aber im Hintergrunde, unter der Aegide der königlichen Autorität, ihnen Befehle gaben, ohne dafür verantwortlich zu sein.'
[40] Werner Frauendienst, 'Das preussische Staatsministerium in vorkonstitutioneller Zeit', *Zeitschrift für die gesammte Staatswissenschaft*, 116 (1960), 106.

as the Domänen',[41] might just as well have been made by Frederick William III around the turn of the century.[42] Looking back at the organisation of the Prussian government before 1806, Carl von Clausewitz admitted that the structure of the Generaldirektorium was 'by its very nature likely to produce a contest of different interests'.[43] It was this 'war of all against all' at the highest level which Colonel von Massenbach attacked in his forthright memorandum of 1801.[44] Rather than assist each other, he complained, the departmental heads were in permanent competition; this often led to the blatant obstruction of rivals for personal motives. But the internal frictions resulting from the collegial structure of government were strongest in the Kabinetts-ministerium, in which two or three equal-ranking ministers vied for control of Prussian foreign policy; the losers, in the lament of one minister, risked being reduced to the status of an 'intermediate authority (*Mittelsperson oder Zwischeninstanz*)'.[45] A further flaw in the political system of Prussia was the lack of any overall deliberative body which would mediate between the foreign-political exigencies and the demands of the internal administration. Theoretically, the Staatsrat was intended to provide such a forum, but by the end of the eighteenth century it had fallen into such disuse that it met only once a week, instead of every day, as originally stipulated.[46]

The consequences of these structural flaws were twofold. First of all, a widespread feeling of paralysis permeated most branches of government, especially those concerned with the formulation of foreign policy. One contemporary observer spoke of an 'enervating lethargy (*alle Seelenkräfte abspannende Lethargie*)'.[47] The root cause of this sclerosis was the subversion of rapid decision-making through the emergence of the Kabinett

[41] Quoted in Cosmar and Klaproth, *Staatsrat*, p. 233: 'nichts getan als Kollisones gegen einander gemacht, als wenn das General-Kommissariat nicht des Königs von Preußen sowohl wäre, als die Domänen'.
[42] See *Ressortstreitigkeiten zwischen den Zentralbehörden, 1806*, GStA Rep.96A.134B, unfoliated.
[43] Carl von Clausewitz, 'Nachrichten über Preußen in seiner großen Katastrophe (1825/4). Erstes Buch. Preußen im Jahre 1806. Erstes Kapitel', in Hans Rothfels (ed.), *Carl von Clausewitz. Politische Schriften und Briefe* (Munich, 1922), p. 203: 'ihrer Natur nach geeignet, einen Kampf verschiedener Interessen und Ansichten hervorzurufen'.
[44] Massenbach memorandum, *Memoiren zur Geschichte des preussischen Staates*, III, pp. 268–9.
[45] Schulenburg to Beyme, 2.10.1802, Hildesheim, GStA Rep. 96A.9A1, fo. 32.
[46] On the failure of the Staatsrat to constitute a central focal point of the Prussian executive see also Hintze, 'Das preußische Staatsministerium', p. 531; Hintze, 'Die Entstehung der Ministerien', p. 299: 'regelmäßige Plenarsitzungen hielt er nicht mehr, einen Einigungspunkt für die Geschäfte stellte er nicht dar'; and Hüffer, *Mencken*, p. 21 and p. 5.
[47] Massenbach, *Memoiren zur Geschichte des preußischen Staates*, III, p. 34.

as a deliberative body in tandem with the foreign ministry. The consequence was a babel of opinions clogging up the executive. Instead of proceeding from deliberation to decision, Prussian politicians went into a permanent conclave: no sooner would the white smoke of decision appear than it would be obscured by a grey cloud of uncertainty and equivocation. For the process of decision-making was slowed not merely by the participation of the Kabinett, but also by the need of the competing foreign ministers to reach agreement among themselves. The result was, in the succinct words of one observer, a system in which 'chaque conseiller procède individuellement et contraire le ministre' and which lacked all 'avantages de l'unité, de la concentration, de responsabilité'.[48]

Secondly, the severe structural shortcomings of the Prussian political system imposed a particular strain on the person of the monarch. In the absence of functioning unifying central institutions he was the only focal point of the state, the man without whom the whole edifice would, at least theoretically, dissolve into its component parts. 'The person of the king', Otto Hintze points out, 'was the sole unifying factor.'[49] Inevitably, as the boundaries of the Prussian state itself expanded throughout the reigns of Frederick II and his successors, the monarch and his bureaucrats began to buckle under the weight of business. Thanks to the Polish partitions, Prussia had almost doubled in size by the turn of the century; further gains through the process of secularisation and compensation lay ahead. The task of overseeing the foreign policy and internal administration of the monarchy, which had taxed even such an outstanding figure as Frederick the Great now became impossible. 'No man is universal', was how General Rüchel summed up the problem on the eve of the new century;[50] but just how little the new king shared the abilities of his more illustrious forebears was soon to become apparent.

The monarch and his servants: Frederick William III and the antechamber of power

Since the monarch cannot do everything himself and cannot be equally well informed about the various branches of statecraft and adminis-

---

[48] Laforest to Talleyrand, 11.2.1804, Berlin, in Bailleu (ed.), *Preussen und Frankreich*, II, p. 242.

[49] Hintze, 'Das preußische Staatsministerium', p. 534: 'Die Einheit des Ganzen lag eben in der Person des Königs und nirgend anders.'

[50] Quoted in Hüffer, *Die Kabinetsregierung in Preussen*, p. 83.

tration, he uses advisors and executors of his will, to whom he must necessarily delegate an important part of his power.[51]

'According to the principles of the monarchy your Royal Majesty is invested with the whole power of the state. All authority flows from your Majesty.'[52] These words of the members of the Staatsrat to Frederick William III sum up the theory of politics in pre-Reform Prussia. The king represented his subjects. He controlled and legitimated policies for the material and cultural advancement of those subjects. He alone exercised the political will of the state in its foreign relations. He was responsible to no-one and nothing except to his own conscience before God. He was surrounded by institutions created to facilitate his exercise of absolute power. In the Kabinett there were councillors and secretaries available for advisory or scribal services. The foreign ministry or Kabinetts-ministerium assisted him in the conduct of relations with other states. Military affairs were conducted through two junior adjutants, the Generaladjutantur, who liaised between the king and the army.[53] The day-to-day running of the domestic administration lay in the hands of the Generaldirektorium. All of these institutions were subject to the royal authority which alone gave them legitimacy.

If this was standard absolutist theory, the reality was different. Political power in Prussia was shared between the king and a small number of confidants in his immediate vicinity. On the one hand, the monarch was absolutely central to all political deliberation and decision-making; this has been demonstrated beyond all reasonable doubt by Stamm-Kuhlmann.[54] On the other hand, there was a distinctive antechamber of power which competed for the attention and favour of the king. The composition of this antechamber varied, but its number never exceeded about a dozen at any one time. Membership fell into three categories. First of all, there were the bourgeois cabinet secretaries:

---

[51] Naudé, 'Denkwürdigkeiten des Ministers Grafen von Schulenburg', 414: 'Da aber der Monarch unmöglich alles selbst thun, auch nicht in allen weitläufigen Zweigen der Staatskunst und Staatswirtschaft gleich gut unterrichtet sein kann, so gebraucht er Räte und Vollzieher seiner Befehle, denen er notwendig eine bedeutenden Teil seiner Macht delegieren muß.'

[52] Hermann Granier, 'Ein Reformversuch des preussischen Kanzleistils im Jahre 1800', *FBPG*, 15 (1902), 175: 'Nach den Grundsätzen der Monarchie haben E.K.M. die gantze Macht des Staats. Alle Autorität fließt von E.K.M. aus.'

[53] On the military adjutants see Curt Jany, *Geschichte der königlich-preussischen Armee bis zum Jahre 1807. Dritter Band, 1763–1807* (Berlin, 1929), pp. 400–1.

[54] Stamm-Kuhlmann, *Friedrich Wilhelm III*; see also Dwyer, 'Prussia and the Second Armed Neutrality, 1799–1801', p. 27: Frederick William 'always had the last say'; and Simms, 'Anglo-Prussian relations, 1804–1806: the Napoleonic threat' (unpublished PhD dissertation, University of Cambridge, 1992).

Anastasius Ludwig Mencken,[55] whom Friedrich Gentz described as 'the most important man in the state';[56] Karl Friedrich Beyme,[57] councillor for the internal administration of Prussia, the man who succeeded Mencken to become, in the words of Boyen, the 'concealed minister for foreign affairs';[58] and Johann Wilhelm Lombard,[59] the febrile councillor for foreign affairs, who was later to describe himself as a minister in all but name.[60] Their military counterparts were the adjutants of the Generaladjutantur: Friedrich Wilhelm von Zastrow (1794/7–1801),[61] whom Gentz saw as the 'real head of the army';[62] Johann Hermann von Holtzmann (1801–3);[63] Friedrich Heinrich Kleist von Nollendorf

[55] Anastasius Ludwig Mencken, b. 2.8.1752, d. 5.8.1801, Potsdam. Bourgeois background; made Kabinettssekretär in 1782; Frederick William II appointed him Kabinettsrat in 1786; fell into ill favour during war of intervention against France, possibly because of Jacobinical sympathies; restored to office by Frederick William III, during whose early reign he enjoyed considerable influence in domestic affairs. See Hüffer, *Mencken*; his projected full biography of Mencken (p. 3) was never published.

[56] Paul Wittichen, 'Das preußische Kabinett und Friedrich von Gentz. Eine Denkschrift aus dem Jahre 1800', *HZ*, 89 (1902), 257: 'eigentlich jetzt der wichtigste Mann im Staat'.

[57] Karl Friedrich von Beyme, b. 1765 Königsberg, d. 1838 Berlin, son of a regimental surgeon. Educated at Halle orphanage, entered the Prussian administration through the *Kammergericht*, made a Kabinettsrat in 1798 by Frederick William III, eager reformer and achieved the emancipation of peasants on royal but not noble domains before 1806. Source *ADB*, 2 (1955), p. 208. There is no scholarly biography of Beyme but the brief profile by Werner Beyme, *Carl Friedrich Beyme. Preußische Köpfe* (Berlin, 1987), is useful.

[58] Quoted in Hans Saring, 'Karl Friedrich von Beyme', *Jahrbuch für brandenburgische Landesgeschichte*, 7 (1956), 38: 'versteckter Premierminister für die Civilangelegen-heiten'. Hüffer, *Mencken*, p. 21, calls him 'der eigentliche Regent für die innere Verwaltung'.

[59] Johann Wilhelm Lombard, b. 1767 Berlin, d. 1812 Nice. Son of a wig-maker in the Huguenot colony. First employed in 1786 by Frederick II, he rose rapidly to become a Geheimer Kabinettsrat in 1800 with competence in foreign affairs. Source: *NDB*, 15 (1986), pp. 142–3.

[60] See the withering characterisations of Boyen in F. Nippold (ed.), *Erinnerungen aus dem Leben des Generalfeldmarschalls Herman von Boyen* (Leipzig, 1889), I, p. 127: 'frivoler Wüstling'; and E. Kieseritzky, 'Die Sendung von Haugwitz nach Wien' (PhD dissertation, University of Göttingen, 1895), p. 10: 'eitler seichter Schöngeist'. Hüffer, *Die Kabinettsregierung in Preussen*, attempts a rehabilitation. Bruno Gaide, 'Der diplomatische Verkehr des Geheimen Kabinettsrats Lombard mit den Vertretern auswärtiger Mächte nach den Urkunden und seine Rechtfertigungsschrift' (PhD dissertation, University of Greifswald, 1911), esp. pp. 104–5.

[61] Friedrich Wilhelm von Zastrow, b. 22.12.1752 Ruppin, d. 22.7.1830 Neufchâtel. *Generaladjutant* in 1794; retires for health reasons January 1801. Source: *ADB*, 44 (1898), pp. 721–3. Boyen, *Erinnerungen*, I, says that Zastrow saw everything through the 'alte preußische Exerzierbrille', p. 126.

[62] Wittichen, 'Das preußische Kabinett und Friedrich von Gentz', p. 256: 'wahre Chef der Armee'.

[63] There are no biographical entries for Holtzmann in either the *ADB* or the *NDB*.

(1803-6);[64] and the omnipresent second adjutant Karl Leopold von Köckritz (1797-1806),[65] perhaps the only man who enjoyed the complete confidence of the king. Secondly, there were the foreign ministers of the Kabinettsministerium: Philip Karl von Alvensleben,[66] an old Frederician whose relationship with the king was never warm; Karl Wilhelm Finck von Finckenstein,[67] an increasingly frail octogenarian; Heinrich Christian Kurt von Haugwitz,[68] easily the most dominant figure in Prussian foreign policy during the first seven years of Frederick William's reign; and Karl August von Hardenberg,[69] the man who was to become Haugwitz's most bitter rival after 1804. Thirdly, more peripheral than the previous two groups, but still firmly 'within the fringe', there were those individuals who were not always members of either the Kabinett, the Generaladjutantur or the Kabinettsministerium, but who were periodically summoned to Berlin for consultations: Friedrich

[64] Friedrich Heinrich Kleist von Nollendorf, b. 1762 Berlin, d. 1823 Berlin. From an old Prussian military family; joined Prussian army at very young age; 1793 joined Hohenlohe as General Staff officer; successful participation in the war of the first coalition; end of 1793 became general-adjutant to Field-Marshal Möllendorf; 1803 made vortragender General-Adjutant to Frederick William. *ADB*, 16 (1882), pp. 124-7; *NDB*, 12 (1980), pp. 27-8.

[65] Karl Leopold von Köckritz, d. 1821 Berlin. Joined Prussian army as Junker 1762; 1794 accepted into the suite of the crown prince and later king, Frederick William; remains close to him after his accession as Frederick William III; 1801 given sinecure of Chef des reitenden Feldjägercorps; 1803 made major-general. *ADB*, 16, pp. 416-17.

[66] Philipp Karl von Alvensleben, b. 16.12.1745 Hanover, d. 21.10.1802 Berlin. Legal background; envoy to Saxony until 1787; made Kabinettsminister in 1791; awarded title of count in 1800.

[67] Karl Wilhelm Finck von Finckenstein, b. 11.2.1714 Berlin, d. 3.1.1800 Berlin. Envoy to Sweden and Denmark in 1740s; made Kabinettsminister 1749; sole minister after death of Podewils 1760; gradually pushed aside by Hertzberg; stayed on increasingly unwillingly under Frederick William II and III; almost completely without influence by the time of his death at the turn of the century. For Finckenstein's earlier long career see Melle Klinkenborg, 'Die Stellung des Hauses Finckenstein am preußischen Hofe im 17. und 18. Jahrhundert', *Hohenzollern Jahrbuch*, 17 (1913).

[68] Heinrich Christian Kurt von Haugwitz, b. 1752 Peiche/Silesia, d. 1832 Venice. Of old Junker stock, related to many of the major families, educated at Halle and Göttingen, drawn to court through the favour of Frederick William II, envoy to Vienna 1791, succeeded Schulenburg-Kehnert as Staats- und Kabinettsminister in 1792, solely responsible for the Kabinettsministerium after 1803, retired 1804 on grounds of ill-health, returned in late 1805 as joint foreign minister, sole foreign minister from April 1806. *NDB*, 8 (1968), pp. 94-5.

[69] Karl August von Hardenberg, b. 1750 Nesselrode, d. 1822 Genoa. Of Hanoverian noble stock, studied at Göttingen and Leipzig, after service in the Hanoverian administration took charge of the Prussian bureaucracy in Ansbach-Bayreuth, temporarily foreign minister in 1803, chief minister for foreign affairs 1804 and most of 1805, joint minister from late 1805 until his resignation in April 1806. *NDB*, 7 (1965), pp. 658-63.

Wilhelm von der Schulenburg-Kehnert,[70] a one-time Kabinettsminister under Frederick William II, and Karl Wilhelm Ferdinand, Duke of Brunswick and Lüneburg, former commander of the Prussian army.[71] The antechamber of power thus had a varied social and generational profile; a firm bias towards the East Elbian nobility is, of course, undeniable. What all its members had in common was *access*. In the case of the adjutants and the cabinet secretaries, this access was the unavoidable result of their constant proximity to the king; in the case of the foreign ministers, the right of access to the king – *Immediatrecht* – was both an indispensable privilege of office and the characteristic which distinguished them from the senior bureaucrats of the Generaldirektorium; whereas in the case of particular individuals, such as Schulenberg, this *Immediatrecht* was a mark of royal favour.

One can only speculate as to why Frederick William was so attracted to this arrangement. He may have found the bourgeois councillors more pliable and congenial than his self-confident noble ministers; perhaps he also found them more willing to indulge his frequent changes of course.[72] In this sense, to quote Max Weber, the Kabinett was a 'personal fortress' in which the ruler 'sought refuge in the face of expert knowledge and the impersonal and functional routinization of administrators'.[73] However, there were other, more objective reasons for his extensive use of the Kabinett, which tally with what we know of traditional Hohenzollern practice. Frederick William III's treatise on government, written just before his accession to the throne, contains a revealing sub-section entitled 'What does self-governing mean? An examination of this question.'[74] In it he stressed that it was 'impossible' for anybody to oversee, judge and decide all matters of state. No monarch, not even a Frederick the Great, which in any case he manifestly was not, could

---

[70] Friedrich Wilhelm von der Schulenburg-Kehnert, b. 1742 Kehnert in Magdeburg, d. 1815 Kehnert. Of old noble stock, made Geheimer Etats-, Kriegs- und Dirigierender Minister for Magdeburg and western territories by Frederick II in 1771, retired 1786, recalled for the Revolutionary Wars, 1791 joined Alvensleben as Kabinettsminister, 1798–1802 various posts in financial administration, often called for conferences at Berlin, put in charge of occupied Hanover in 1806. *ADB*, 34 (1892), pp. 742–3.

[71] Karl Wilhelm Ferdinand, Duke of Brunswick-Lüneburg, b. 1735 Brunswick, d. 1806 Ottensen/Denmark. Made Prussian infantry general in 1773; planned the lightning war against Holland in 1787; 1792 commander of coalition armies against the French revolutionaries; author of the severe anti-Revolutionary manifesto of the same year; resigned 1794; took up command of Prussian army again in 1806. *NDB*, 2, pp. 224–5.

[72] Hüffer, *Die Kabinettsregierung in Preussen*, p. 92.

[73] Gerth and Mills (eds.), *From Max Weber*, pp. 236–7.

[74] '*Gedanken über die Regierungskunst zu Papier gebracht im Jahre [17]96–97*', printed in Georg Küntzel and Martin Haß, *Die Politischen Testamente der Hohenzollern nebst ergänzenden Aktenstück* (Leipzig and Berlin, 1920), II, p. 113: 'Was heißt selbst regieren? Zergliederung dieser Frage.'

do everything alone and without any counsel whatsoever. Hence, as he outlined in another sub-section, again significantly entitled 'Choice of councillors and confidants', the real issue was how to choose the *right* men. Councillors would have to be 'righteous, sober, perceptive and disinterested'.[75] Thus, far from abdicating his responsibility to rule, he saw himself as a realist, rejecting the chimera of complete self-government for a role in which, rather like the Great Elector, he fed on the expertise of his advisors before taking the ultimate decision himself.

In practice, this system conferred immense potential power on those in the immediate surroundings of the king. Every day, Köckritz would open the correspondence and – depending on whether the communication related to civil, diplomatic or military matters – pass it on to the relevant cabinet councillor or adjutant.[76] The function of the cabinet councillor was to make a preliminary selection of the correspondence for the king's benefit: 'It is physically impossible', Lombard told the king, 'for you to read or to have read to you all the dispatches' and it was therefore his duty to draw the king's attention to the most important passages.[77] Lombard was of course right: Frederick William could not possibly sift his entire correspondence. However, this fact increased rather than lessened the obvious possibilities for manipulation. Indeed, Lombard's power rested on his complete control over the royal correspondence in foreign affairs. 'C'est à moi que la poste addressera vos dépêches', he reminded one envoy, 'moi qui seul les déchiffrai, et de moi que S.M. les récevra.'[78] Hence, whenever the ministers of the Kabinettsministerium – who received diplomatic dispatches in duplicate – were summoned they faced a monarch who had already been extensively, and perhaps selectively briefed by the Kabinett. By the early 1800s, it was quite common for Lombard to be sent to confer with the foreign ministers in his own right. In domestic policy, the councillor for internal affairs – Beyme – enjoyed a similarly commanding position in the antechamber of power around the king.

Among those not included in the antechamber of power was virtually the whole administrative elite of the monarchy, whose *public* standing was far greater than that of the cabinet councillors. Neither the departmental heads of the Generaldirektorium, nor the ministers of the Justizdepartement, nor even the minister for Silesia, enjoyed the right of

---

[75] Ibid., p. 115: '*Wahl der Räthe und Vertrauten*'.
[76] Bailleu, 'Haugwitz und Hardenberg', p. 271.
[77] Lombard to Frederick William, 2.12.1805, Potsdam, GStA Rep. 92 *Friedr. Wilh. d. Dritte* B.VI.14, unfoliated.
[78] Lombard to Caesar, 1799, GStA Rep. 92 *Caesar* 28, unfoliated.

access to the king.[79] All of their correspondence passed through the cabinet secretaries and was thus vulnerable to manipulation; they were unable to put their case directly to the monarch. This reflected the much lower prestige accorded to domestic affairs by comparison with the foreign relations of the monarchy. Hence, while many of these bureaucrats were powerful regional figures in their own right – one thinks of the vice-grip exercised by Hoym in Silesia – they were non-entities in terms of high politics. Perhaps the best illustration of this rigid distinction between politics and administration is the fact that the turnover among senior bureaucrats was much lower than in the antechamber of power. Thus, between 1797 and 1806 the Kabinettsministerium saw the death of two out of four ministers, and the emergence of another, not to mention various resignations; the Generaladjutantur saw numerous changes in personnel; only the Kabinett remained relatively stable after the death of Mencken. By contrast, even after nearly a decade on the throne, only one third of the fifteen-odd members of the Staatsrat concerned with internal administration were creations of Frederick William III: the Justizminister Massow; von Angern the minister for Kurmark-Magdeburg; von Dietherdt of the military department; von Reden, the minister for mining; and Stein, the minister for customs and excise. Another third were creations of his father: von Voss, the minister for the Kurmark, Neumark, Pommern and South Prussia; the Justizminister Goldbeck; the Justizminister von Thulemeier; von Buchholz, the minister for Southern Prussia; and von Schrötter, the minister for East Prussia. The rest – such as the minister for Silesia, Hoym, and the Justizminister von der Reck – were old Fredericians. In short, high politics and the bureaucracy were two entirely distinct spheres, the one characterised by insecurity and change, the other by continuity and professionalism; the two worlds did not meet, except notionally through the Staatsrat. It was only towards the end of our period that the rigid separation of politics and administration broke down, with spectacular results.

The role of the court was equally peripheral, at least during the first decade of Frederick William's reign. Unlike other European monarchies, court and high politics remained largely distinct.[80] There was no system

---

[79] Hüffer, *Die Kabinetsregierung in Preußen*, p. 47; Meissner, 'Die monarchische Regierungsform', p. 232; Neugebauer, 'Zur neueren Deutung der preußischen Verwaltung im 17. und 18. Jahrhundert', p. 554.

[80] There is no monograph on the court of Frederick William III. The pioneering work of Thomas Stamm-Kuhlmann, 'Der Hof König Friedrich Wilhelms III. von Preußen 1797–1840', in Karl Möckl (ed.), *Hof und Hofgesellschaft in den deutschen Staaten im 19. und beginnenden 2. Jahrhundert* (Boppard, 1990), excepting the caveat entered below, is

of courtly patronage to engineer the appointment of ministers; only in the summer of 1806 did prominent members of the court steel themselves to protest against the course of Prussian policy under Haugwitz and the results were disastrous. Nor did status at court imply political significance. Major figures such as Valentin von Massow, Hofmarschall since 1797, and Ludwig von Jagow, the Flügeladjutant, were politically inconsequential.[81] Only very occasionally did prominent courtiers act in a political capacity – such as the involvement of the chamberlain, Prince Wittgenstein, in the secret policy of 1806. Conversely, the Kabinettsräte, some of the most powerful people in the monarchy, were not acknowledged by the court. The impotence of the court reflected the power and inclination of Frederick William himself. Whenever the court became the focus of Prussian politics, for example during the visits of Tsar Alexander in 1801 and 1805, this was because Frederick William chose to make it so – the court lent itself to the reception and entertainment of foreign royalty. Most of the time, however, Frederick William avoided the court as much as possible. Even the spartan opulence of Potsdam offended his bourgeois tastes and he hated being the centre of attention.[82] Besides, the court was the natural habitat of people like Prince Louis Ferdinand, the king's cousin, a real or imagined rival for the queen's affections. To this extent, it is a little misleading for Stamm-Kuhlmann to refer to the court as a Regierungszentrale;[83] The Regierungszentrale was very firmly focussed on the monarch himself and the men in his immediate vicinity. Wherever Frederick William went, be it to Potsdam, to his residence at Charlottenburg or to his country retreat at Paretz, the antechamber of power moved with him.

If it is true that the antechamber of power influenced the formulation of royal policy, it is equally undeniable that the personality of the monarch left its mark on the antechamber of power.

---

most helpful. David Barclay, 'Ritual, ceremonial, and the "invention" of a monarchical tradition in nineteenth-century Prussia', in Heinz Duchhardt, Richard A. Jackson and David Sturdy (eds.), *European monarchy. Its evolution and practice from Roman antiquity to modern times* (Stuttgart, 1992), pp. 207–20, is very useful for the reign of Frederick William IV, but contains little before 1806. Karl Hammer, 'Die preußischen Könige und Königinnen im 19. Jahrhundert und ihr Hof', in Karl Ferdinand Werner (ed.), *Hof, Kultur und Politik im 19. Jahrhundert* (Bonn, 1985), pp. 87–98, contains little of interest on Frederick William III. For courts elsewhere see also Krüger-Löwenstein, *Rußland, Frankreich und das Reich, 1801–1803*, esp. pp. 20–1.

[81] Stamm-Kuhlmann, 'Der Hof Friedrich Wilhelms III', p. 291.
[82] Ibid., p. 286; Christopher Clark, 'The Frederick Williams of nineteenth-century Prussia', *Bulletin of the German Historical Institute*, 15 (1993), 5.
[83] Stamm-Kuhlmann, 'Der Hof Friedrich Wilhelms III', p. 297.

Frederick William's political temperament can only be described as complex. On the one hand, he was a timid and indecisive monarch: descriptions such as 'passive'[84] and 'inexcusably weak'[85] are commonplace; Franz Mehring characterised him as being 'always the spare wheel and often even the brake on the carriage';[86] and few would dispute Herrmann's assessment of Frederick William as 'undoubtedly one of the less talented Hohenzollern personalities'.[87] 'He was', to quote Marwitz, 'determined to do nothing.'[88] Underlying this passivity was his deep abhorrence of bloodshed. 'I detest war', he told his uncle Prince Heinrich, and added that he knew 'no greater aim on earth than the preservation of peace'.[89] The immobile, almost comatose policy of neutrality was thus, as we shall see, very much Frederick William's own policy. And yet it would be wrong to see Frederick William as a 'weak' monarch in the conventional sense. He was always, in the words of one French envoy, 'très jaloux de son pouvoir'[90] and remained – to quote Max Lehmann – a man 'firm in the preservation of his prerogative'.[91]

The ambiguity of Frederick William's relationship with the men in his immediate vicinity was epitomised by the person of Köckritz. Here was a man who enjoyed the unrivalled confidence of the king, a man to whom Frederick William instinctively looked for advice and support. In the dispatches of foreign diplomats Köckritz invariably features in the

---

[84] Boyen, *Erinnerungen*, I, p. 123; Marwitz, *Ein märkischer Edelmann im Zeitalter der Befreiungskriege*, I, pp. 150–1.

[85] Max Lehmann, *Freiherr vom Stein*, vol. I: *Vor der Reform, 1757–1807* (Leipzig, 1902), p. 302.

[86] Quoted in Thomas Stamm-Kuhlmann, 'Die Rolle von Staat und Monarchie bei der Modernisierung von oben. Ein Literaturbericht mit ergänzenden Betrachtungen zur person König Friedrich Wilhelms III.', in Bernd Sösemann (ed.), *Gemeingeist und Bürgersinn. Die preußischen Reformen*, FBPG NF 2 (Berlin, 1993), p. 270: 'immer nur das fünfte Rad und meistens sogar der Hemmschuh am Wagen'.

[87] Alfred Herrmann, 'Friedrich Wilhelm III und sein Antheil an der Heeresreform bis 1813', *Historische Vierteljahrsschrift*, 11 (1908), 516. There is a useful survey of the earlier literature on Frederick William in Schulze, 'Die Beurteilung Friedrich Wilhelms III', pp. 339–43. F. R. Paulig, *Friedrich Wilhelm III. König von Preussen (1770–1840). Sein Privatleben und seine Regierung im Lichte neuer Forschungen* (Frankfurt/Oder, 1905), is disappointing; Griewank, 'Hardenberg und die preußische Politik', p. 270 and *passim*.

[88] Quoted in Schulze, 'Die Beurteilung Friedrich Wilhelms III', p. 343: 'Er war entschlossen nichts zu tun.'

[89] Quoted in Bailleu, 'Vor hundert Jahren', p. 206; see also the remarks in instructions for Sandoz-Rollin, 18.7.1800, Berlin, in Bailleu (ed.), *Preussen und Frankreich*, I, p. 385. For Frederick William's own early experience of warfare see Fritz Behrend, 'Kronprinz Friedrich Wilhelm (III.) Kampagne in Frankreich 1792', *Hohenzollern Jahrbuch*, 16 (1912), 228–34.

[90] Otto, 25.9.1799, in Bailleu (ed.), *Preussen und Frankreich*, I, p. 513.

[91] Max Lehmann, *Scharnhorst*, vol. I: *Bis zum Tilsiter Frieden* (Leipzig, 1887), p. 354.

background as a kind of bloodless eminence.[92] Yet it would be hard to think of a single occasion upon which he insinuated his own ideas into the formulation of policy, as opposed to simply reinforcing those of his royal master. Indeed, Köckritz was self-confessedly bewildered by the cut and thrust of political debate.[93] His value to the king lay in his function as a sounding board – a *Resonanzkörper* in Stamm-Kuhlmann's words – for the king's own ideas, as an interpreter of the royal will.[94] Köckritz, in the judgment of Friedrich Gentz, was a man who 'counted for nothing' and who 'would always endorse everything'.[95] At the very most, he may have used his position to bestow personal favours;[96] his influence on high politics was negligible. For Köckritz the confidence of the king was an end in itself.

But even those with greater ambitions were forced to work within the parameters of the royal will. This resulted in a peculiarly diffident political mentality. A typical example was Finckenstein. 'His fear of giving offence', Alvensleben observed, 'rendered his contributions so cautious as to render them meaningless.'[97] Nobody was exempt from this fear of offending the king. Indeed, after the defeat at Jena Lombard was to justify his behaviour to Friedrich Gentz with the question: 'Do you know the king?', adding, 'My whole justification [for my conduct] is contained in this question.'[98] We should therefore resist the assumption that Frederick William was the prisoner of his antechamber. For while there was no power in Prussia without royal access, this access alone was no guarantee of power. It may be true that politicians can be divided between those want to 'do' something and those who want to 'be' something. If so, many Prussian politicians were to find that they had to abandon their ambition to do anything substantial, so as to remain being somebody.

---

[92] See Dwyer, 'Prussia and the Armed Neutrality', p. 665; Jackson report, 17.9.1804, Berlin, PROL FO 64/66.

[93] See remarks to Boyen, cited by Leo Hellwig, *Schulenburg-Kehnert unter Friedrich Wilhelm III (1798–1806)* (Berlin, 1936), p. 25.

[94] See the description by Lombard in *Matériaux*, p. 57: 'Il étoit présent à toutes les conférences, sans prendre part dans la règle à la discussion, mais pour que le roi eut, hors des heures du travail, quelqu'un avec lequel il peut rappeler les idées du matin et s'aider à mûrir les siennes.'

[95] Wittichen, 'Das preußische Kabinett und Friedrich von Gentz', p. 256.

[96] Stamm-Kuhlmann, *Friedrich Wilhelm III*, p. 114.

[97] 'Entwurf des Grafen von Alvensleben zu einer Charakteristik des Grafen Karl Wilhelm Finck von Finckenstein (1801)', in Klinkenborg (ed.), 'Geheimen Staatsministers Finckenstein', *FBPG*, 28 (1915), 564: 'Seine Furcht irgendwo anzustoßen brachte es dahin, daß seine Erklärungen, seine Antworten so abgemessen waren, daß das Resultat in nichts zerfiel.'

[98] Quoted in Gaide, 'Der diplomatische Verkehr des Geheimen Kabinettsrats Lombard', p. 100: 'Kennen Sie den König? Meine ganze Rechtfertigung liegt in dieser Frage.'

Alternative power centres? Aristocracy, bureaucracy and the autocratic state

In recent years there has been a tendency to qualify the traditional conception of European absolutism in favour of a more nuanced view of the distribution of power between crown, nobility and bureaucracy.[99] Prussia is no exception. The process of revision began with the work of Eckart Kehr and Hans Rosenberg. They claimed that, far from being omnipotent, the king was increasingly hemmed in by a self-conscious bureaucratic elite; by the end of the eighteenth century, their argument ran, the replacement of royal absolutism by a 'dictatorship of the bureaucracy' was well under way.[100] As a result, power shifted to a cadre of ministerial experts, nominally responsible to the monarch, but in reality largely autonomous. At local level, moreover, the power of the administration was almost unchallenged. Here, bureaucrats could delay, dilute and even frustrate the royal will. This interpretation seemed to be borne out by the historical development of the eighteenth-century Prussian administration: the introduction of competitive examinations; security of tenure against royal caprice; and the independence of the judiciary.

The second stage of historical revision focussed on the persistence of aristocratic power.[101] Far from being eliminated as a political factor, it was argued, the Prussian nobility had simply mutated from a consultative partner of the prince into a socio-political hegemon at local level. The events of the mid-seventeenth century, previously seen as a crucial step in the development of the modern Prussian state at the expense of the nobility, were now re-interpreted as a *Herrschaftskompromiß*, a 'governing compromise' in which the nobility surrendered its share of the political executive in return for total control over the subject peasantry in the countryside. According to this view, relations between crown and nobility were characterised by cooperation, not conflict; this parallels the

---

[99] Paradigmatic: Nicholas Henshall, *The myth of absolutism. Change and continuity in early modern European monarchy* (London and New York, 1992), especially pp. 182–6: 'Estates: crushed or co-operating?'

[100] Kehr, 'Zur Genesis der preußischen Bürokratie', pp. 31–52; Rosenberg, *Bureaucracy, aristocracy and autocracy.* J. R. Gillis, 'Autocracy and bureaucracy in nineteenth-century Prussia', *P&P*, 41 (1968), 105–29, focusses mainly on the period after 1806.

[101] E.g. Schissler, *Preußische Agrargesellschaft im Wandel* and Otto Büsch, *Militärsystem und Sozialleben im Alten Preussen 1713–1807. Die Anfänge der sozialen Militarisierung der preussisch-deutschen Gesellschaft* (Berlin, 1962). The most recent treatment of the 'cultural and political hegemony' (p. 13) of the Junkers is Berdahl, *The politics of the Prussian nobility.* In the same vein more generally see Klaus Vetter, 'Die Stände im absolutistischen Preußen. Ein Beitrag zur Absolutismus-Diskussion', *ZfG*, 24 (1976), 1290–306, especially 1304.

findings of newer studies of French absolutism.[102] Aristocratic power was the pillar upon which princely absolutism rested, and the policies and institutions of absolutism reflected royal indebtedness to the nobility. On this reading, the prince himself was merely a 'super-Junker', or, in the parody of Klaus Deppermann, a 'total feudalist' (*Gesamtfeudalist*).[103] The 're-aristocratisation' of the bureaucracy under Frederick the Great; the resulting tenacious defence of feudal privileges by many administrators; the dominant role of the Junker as simultaneous landlord, magistrate, recruiting-sergeant and commanding officer; all this seemed to underline the importance of noble power in pre-Reform Prussia.

Marxist historians have carried the qualification of royal absolutism a stage further. For them, the Prussian state was merely, to adapt the famous phrase, 'a committee for the administration of Junker interests'.[104] 'The Prussian kings', writes Klaus Vetter, 'could only rule "absolutely" for as long as their policies did not contradict their [i.e. the Junkers'] fundamental interests'; this was guaranteed by the dominance of the nobility and noble interests in the General Directory and the Kabinettsministerium.[105] This theme was developed by Meta Kohnke in her detailed study of the Kabinettsministerium. She saw the foreign ministry as an instrument for the 'external defence of feudal dominance', whose 'conservative stance' was guaranteed by the social background of its members.[106] Kohnke does not claim that these social interests *determined* Prussian foreign policy, but insists that one 'cannot deny' that Prussian foreign policy was 'conducted in the interests of the dominant

---

102 The ur-Henshall is Roger Mettam, *Power and faction in Louis XIV's France* (Oxford, 1988), especially chapter 2: 'Historians and "Absolutism": the illusion and the reality', pp. 13–44 (NB: p. 33) and 'King, court, aristocracy and faction', pp. 45–101.

103 Rosenberg, *Bureaucracy, aristocracy and autocracy*, p. 31. For a general overview of the Prussian administration up to 1803 see Walther Hubatsch, 'Verwaltungsentwicklung von 1713–1803', in K. G. A. Jeserich, Hans Pohl and Georg-Christoph von Unruh (eds.), *Deutsche Verwaltungsgeschichte*. Vol. I: *Vom Spätmittelalter bis zum Ende des Reiches* (Stuttgart, 1983), pp. 892–941; for an idealistic view see Ernst Rudolf Huber, *Deutsche Verfassungsgeschichte seit 1789*. Vol. I: *Reform und Restauration 1789 bis 1830* (Stuttgart, 1957); for a general overview of recent historiography of the German bureaucracy see Bernd Wunder, 'Zur Geschichte der deutschen Beamtenschaft 1945–1985', *Geschichte und Gesellschaft*, 17, 2 (1991), 256–77. Klaus Deppermann, 'Der preußische Absolutismus und der Adel: eine Auseinandersetzung mit der marxistischen Absolutismustheorie', *Geschichte und Gesellschaft*, 8 (1982), 553.

104 Ibid., p. 192.

105 Klaus Vetter, *Kurmärkischer Adel und preußische Reformen* (Weimar, 1979), p. 32: 'Die preußischen Könige', writes Klaus Vetter, 'konnten nur solange "absolut" regieren, wie ihre Politik nicht gegen grundlegende Interessen ihrer Klasse verstieß'; see also p. 89.

106 Meta Kohnke, 'Das preußische Kabinettsministerium. Ein Beitrag zur Geschichte des Staatsapparates im Spätfeudalismus' (unpublished PhD dissertation, University of Berlin/East, 1967), p. 1001. Vetter, 'Die Stände im absolutistischen Preußen', pp. 1304–6, is ambiguous on the relationship between the nobility and foreign policy.

class'; the distinction seems a trifle forced. Typical of this view would be Erhard Moritz's contention that the final partition of Poland was a 'military intervention . . . which the Hohenzollern state undertook in the interests of the nobility'.[107] But it would be wrong to see the Marxist contribution purely in terms of crude socio-economic reductionism. Indeed, it was Klaus Vetter who broke substantial empirical new ground with a study of the nobility of the Kurmark. This revealed a vibrant structure of representative institutions through which aristocratic interests could be articulated.[108] At the bi-annual Kreistage the estates were able to air their grievances and petition the crown for redress.[109] Such representative bodies had also survived in the outlying western province of Cleves-Mark and in East Prussia. In the latter case, the estates used the occasion of Frederick William's *Huldigungslandtag*, the traditional ceremony at which homage was rendered to a new monarch, to present their *gravamina* and have their privileges confirmed;[110] they also put forward a whole programme of reforms involving the re-structuring of the Generaldirektorium, the abolition of internal tariffs, and the free export of grain.

Yet recent research has shown that the 'model of straightforward class domination' by the bureaucracy is untenable. The state was, as Lenore O'Boyle writes, 'within limits, autonomous'.[111] In any case, the limits to noble and bureaucratic power were clearly defined. Thus the bureaucracy could conceal, exaggerate and obfuscate, but it could not – in its own right – prevail against the royal will on major matters of policy.[112] The crucial distinction here is that between administration and politics; in German history, the two are often confused. Frederick the Great summarised this division of responsibilities between the monarch and the General Directory as follows: 'il [the GD] règle toutes les bagatelles et renvoye au prince les choses les plus importantes en lui

[107] Erhard Moritz, *Preussen und der Kosciuzko-Aufstand 1794. Zur preussischen Polenpolitik in der Zeit der Französischen Revolution* (East Berlin, 1968), p. 5.
[108] Vetter, *Kurmärkischer Adel*, pp. 19, 22 and *passim*. Vetter's work has now been supplemented and – in places – superseded by Wolfgang Neugebauer's monumental *Politischer Wandel*; for his critique of Vetter see p. 21.
[109] Vetter, *Kurmärkischer Adel*, p. 30; Neugebauer, *Politischer Wandel*, pp. 65–6.
[110] Hermann Eicke, *Der ostpreußische Landtag von 1798* (Göttingen, 1910), pp. 1–5 and *passim*.
[111] Lenore O'Boyle, 'Some recent studies of nineteenth-century European bureaucracy', *CEH*, 19 (1986), 390; see also Deppermann, 'Der preußische Absolutismus und der Adel'.
[112] See Dorn, 'The Prussian bureaucracy in the eighteenth century', pp. 417–18, 419, who argues that the 'silent contest' between monarch and administration 'never developed into open bureaucratic opposition'.

exposant la chose avec le pour et le contre'.[113] The fact that the king busied himself only with the more important matters was not royal weakness or bureaucratic dictatorship but monarchic *strength*: it was only by ridding himself of the day-to-day clutter of internal administration that he could hope to concentrate on matters of high policy, especially foreign affairs. A striking insight into the political peripherality of most senior bureaucrats is afforded by the comments of Schulenburg during the early reign of Frederick William III. When asked whether Stein or Angern should be promoted into the General Directory he had replied that Stein's political and economic competence made him resemble a British minister more than a Prussian bureaucrat and thus rendered him over-qualified for the post.[114] Angern, on the other hand, was an experienced, well-intentioned and thrifty administrator and thus, in Schulenburg's estimation, well-suited to the General Directory. In short, while there may have been a widespread impatience with monarchic meddling, and ill-disguised contempt for royal favourites, the bureaucracy did not have a significant corporate *political* identity. Instead, the internal administration could serve as a springboard for personal political advancement. The most obvious example here would be Hardenberg, who spent much of his early career empire-building in Ansbach-Bayreuth. As we shall see, this quest for personal power usually transcended any notions of bureaucratic solidarity.

If the political power of the bureaucracy was restricted, that of the aristocracy was equally circumscribed.[115] The representative institutions of the nobility had no significant participatory political rights. They could petition, but they could not demand. Indeed, the aristocracy had long since lost their most effective traditional sanction against princely absolutism: the right to approve taxes. Throughout the eighteenth century, feeble Junker attempts to recover this right met furious royal resistance. The most notorious incident was the outburst of Frederick William I, who dismissed Junker pretences to control taxation with the words: 'After all, we are lord and king, and may do as we please', adding for good measure the threat that 'the authority of the Junkers will be

---

[113] Quoted in Otto Hintze, 'Das preußische Staatsministerium', p. 534.

[114] Lehmann, *Stein*, I, p. 311.

[115] Günter Birtsch, 'Der preußische Hochabsolutismus und die Stände', in Peter Baumgart (ed.), *Ständetum und Staatsbildung in Brandenburg-Preussen. Ergebnisse einer internationalen Fachtagung* (Berlin and New York, 1983), p. 398 and *passim*. Birtsch also speaks of a *begrenzte Mitwirkung* ('limited participation') at local level (p. 402). Wolf-Günther Bennecke, 'Stand und Stände in Preußen vor den Reformen' (unpublished PhD dissertation, University of Berlin, 1935), contains nothing of interest.

ruined *nie pos volam*, but I will stabilise my sovereignty like a *Rocher de Bronze*.[116] By the end of the century little had changed. In 1799, Frederick William III not merely refused a petition of the estates of Lebus and Crossen against the extension of the *Grundsteuer* – the basic land tax – but also issued a *Kabinettsordre* expressly forbidding such protests for the future.[117] In short, unlike their feral Hungarian counterparts in the Habsburg monarchy, the Prussian nobility had been politically neutered. The aristocracy, Otto Hintze argues, 'retained their 'socio-legal' but lost their 'political' privileges.[118] Moreover, the promulgation of the *Allgemeines Landrecht* (*ALR*) in 1794, far from placing legal and corporate restraints on the monarch, actually served to strengthen his hold on the executive. Contrary to widespread belief, the *ALR* did not amount to a Prussian 'constitution'; at most it corresponded to Reinhard Koselleck's description of a 'substitute constitution (*Ersatzverfassung*)'.[119] It is true that the *ALR* confirmed the nobility as the 'first estate'. It is also true that the aristocracy were guaranteed key juridical and social privileges, including the exclusive right to own noble estates and to control local ecclesiastical appointments.[120] But as Günter Birtsch has pointed out, none of this made the *ALR* a *constitution*, for it neither defined nor limited the 'form of government' in Prussia.[121] Indeed, one of its main authors, Suarez, had specifically stated that the *ALR* was not meant to concern 'relations between the regent and the nation as a whole', and Suarez had explicitly excluded anything to do with the 'main rights of the state', such as the right to make war, to sign peace treaties

---

[116] Quoted in ibid., p. 395: 'Wir sind doch Herr und König und können thun was wir wollen . . . Junkers ihre Autorität wird nie pos volam ruinieret werden, Ich aber stabilisire die Souveraineté wie einen Rocher de Bronze.'

[117] Otto Hintze, 'Preußische Reformbestrebungen vor 1806', in Otto Hintze, *Regierung und Verwaltung. Gesammelte Abhandlungen zur Staats-, Rechts-, und Sozialgeschichte Preussens*, edited and introduced by Gerhard Oestreich (Göttingen, 1967), p. 517.

[118] Hintze, 'Staatenbildung und Verfassungsentwicklung', p. 49.

[119] Reinhard Koselleck, *Preußen zwischen Reform und Revolution. Allgemeines Landrecht, Verwaltung, und soziale Bewegung von 1791–1848* (Stuttgart, 1975), p. 31.

[120] See Günter Birtsch, 'Zur sozialen und politischen Rolle des deutschen vornehmlich preußischen Adels am Ende des 18. Jahrhunderts', in Rudolf Vierhaus (ed.), *Der Adel vor der Revolution. Zur sozialen und politischen Funktion des Adels im vorrevolutionären Europa* (Göttingen, 1971), pp. 85–7.

[121] Günter Birtsch, 'Zum konstitutionellen Charakter des preußischen Allgemeinen Landrechts von 1794', in Kurt Kluxen und Wolfgang Mommsen (eds.), *Politische Ideologien und nationalstaatliche Ordnung. Studien zur Geschichte des 19. und 20. Jahrhunderts. Festschrift für Theodor Schieder zu seinem 60. Geburtstag* (Munich, 1968), p. 101. Birtsch's arguments have recently been developed by Andreas Schwennicke, *Die Entstehung des Allgemeinen Landrechts von 1794* (Frankfurt, 1993), especially p. 347.

and to ensure internal security.[122] Instead, the *ALR* was intended to cover only the 'relations of the state with individual citizens or moral persons', in other words anything that could be decided by judicial *fiat*;[123] it did not apply beyond the point where law ended and politics began. For the introduction to the *ALR* not merely defined the purpose of the state as the establishment of the 'internal and external security (*innere und äußere Ruhe*)' of its citizens, it also determined that 'all individual rights of the citizen must be subordinated to the aim of general tranquillity and security'.[124] Crucially, the right to declare such an internal or external emergency lay solely with the monarch; 'he who decides the state of emergency', as Carl Schmitt says, 'is sovereign'.[125]

In fact, the *ALR* can only be properly understood within the context of the traditional primacy of foreign policy. It was firmly rooted in a long-standing Prussian consensus on the virtues of absolute monarchy. Thus Christian Wolff credited monarchy with the 'advantage that one can reach a rapid decision (*Vortheil, daß man geschwinde zu einem Schlusse kommen kann*)'; Christian Ludwig Paalzow praised monarchy for being free of the sectional pressures which so bedevilled 'aristocratic' polities; and Joachim Georg Darjes believed that 'security is best served by monarchic forms [of government] because *una voluntas omnium est*. In an aristocratic polity there are many *rationes* before a *conclusum* is reached. In a democracy much time is lost before a deliberation can even take place. By that time, a monarch will have already dealt many blows.'[126] The extent to which the authors of the *ALR* shared such views is evident from the remarks of Christoph Gößler, a close collaborator of Carmer and Suarez, in the *Berlinische Monatsschrift* of 1792. 'The special

---

122 Quoted in Birtsch, 'Zum konstitutionellen Charakter des preußischen Allgemeinen Landrechts', pp. 100–1; and Schwennicke, *Die Entstehung des Allgemeinen Landrechts von 1794*, p. 299: 'Verhältnisse des Regenten gegen das Corps der Nation im ganzen genommen . . . erste Hauptklasse der Rechte des Staats.'

123 Quoted in Schwennicke, ibid., p. 347: 'Verhältnisse des Staats gegen einzelne Bürger oder moralische Personen.'

124 Quoted in Schwennicke, ibid., p. 299: 'alle einzelne Rechte der Bürger des Staats müssen dem Endzweck der allgemeinen Ruhe und Sicherheit untergeordnet sein'.

125 Schmitt, *Politische Theologie*, p. 9

126 Wolff, Paalzow and Darjes are cited in Eckhart Hellmuth, *Naturrechts-philosophie und bürokratischer Werthorizont. Studien zur preußischen Geistes-und Sozialgeschichte des 18. Jahrhunderts*, Veröffentlichungen des Max-Planck-Instituts für Geschichte 78 (Göttingen, 1985), on pp. 44, 147 and 45 respectively: 'die Sicherheit auch leichter in forma Monarchica erhalten werden, denn una voluntas omnium est. In einer Aristocracie paßiren viele rationes, bis ein Conclusum gemacht wird. In einer Demokratie vergeht auch viel Zeit, bis nur die Zusammenkunft bewürket wird. Ehe diese richtig ist, hat der Monarch schon etliche Prügel ausgetheilet.' See also p. 161 on Georg Friedrich Lamprecht.

[geographic: BS] situation of the Prussian state', he argued, 'makes it necessary not only to maintain Prussian military power, and everything that goes with it, but to increase it.' Prussia, he continued, needs a 'true and strong monarchy', for experience showed 'that states need a supreme head in whom all power is united and who is enabled to set this power in motion instantly, if they are to act with strength and vigour in wartime'.[127]

It is thus hardly surprising that all the privileges and rights enshrined in the *ALR* were contingent. This was not only explicit in the introduction, it was also spelt out by Suarez to the young Frederick William. 'In the event of an emergency', he wrote, 'in which the security of the state is endangered and cannot be ensured in any other way, the exempted estates may be prevailed upon to sacrifice their privileges, and to contribute whatever the state desperately needs, but cannot extract from the rest of society.'[128] In other words, what the monarch granted, the monarch could take away. Aristocratic privileges were held not by inalienable right, but by virtue of services rendered to the state; as von Witzleben has pointed out, such arrangements were only valid until foreign-political changes necessitated their re-negotiation.[129] Clearly, the political role envisaged for the nobility in the *ALR* was that of a *functional*, not a participatory elite.[130]

---

[127] Quoted in Birtsch, 'Zum konstitutionellen Charakter des preußischen Allgemeinen Landrechts', p. 114: 'nach der eigentümlichen Lage des preußischen Staats noch besonders dazu beitragen . . . dem ganzen Körper Festigkeit, Stärke und Spannkraft zu geben: die militärische Macht, und alles was darauf Bezug hat, nicht nur zu erhalten, sondern zu vermehren, zu erhöhen, und in ihren Wirkungen regelmäßig, schnell, und – man erlaube mir den Ausdruck – zermalmend zu machen . . . feste wahre Monarchie . . . daß nur diejenigen Staaten im Kriege mit Kraft und Nachdruck handeln können, die ein Oberhaupt haben, in welchem sich die ganze Macht vereinigt und das dadurch imstande ist, mit weiser Leitung diese ganze Macht auf den ersten Wink in Bewegung zu setzen'.

[128] Quoted in Hellmuth, *Naturrechts-philosophie und Werthorizont*, p. 245: 'In einem solchen äußersten Falle, wo es wirklich um die Erhaltung der Existenz des Staats zu thun ist, und wo dieser auf andere Art nicht gestattet werden kann, sind allerdings die eximierten Stände schuldig auf ihre Privilegien Verzicht zu thun, und zu den Bedürfnissen des Staats dasjenige beizutragen, was der Staat nicht entbehren und doch von den übrigen Classen dessen gänzliche Unterdrückung nicht mehr aufbringen kann.' Hellmuth, pp. 245–6, espouses an oddly minimalist view of this passage, which he takes to be a reference to a possible financial crisis rather than any scenario involving an external threat.

[129] Alexander von Witzleben, *Staatsfinanznot und sozialer Wandel. Eine finanzsoziologische Analyse der preußischen Reformzeit zu Beginn des 19. Jahrhunderts* (Stuttgart and Wiesbaden, 1985), p. 58.

[130] See Birtsch, 'Zur sozialen und politischen Rolle', p. 78, on the transformation of the Prussian nobility into a 'functional' elite; Müller-Weil, *Absolutismus und Außenpolitik*, p. 73, on estates and foreign policy.

The political weakness of the nobility was mirrored in the role of the military. Certainly, the army was a bastion of aristocratic power: the Junkers enjoyed a monopoly of the officer corps; the bourgeoisie paid for its upkeep through taxation; and the peasantry, drawing the shortest straw,[131] were liable to both recruitment and taxation. Certainly, the army was both a repository of conservative values and the focus of an *esprit de corps* to the extent that it constituted, in a well-known phrase, a 'state within a state'.[132] Yet it would be quite wrong to see Prussian politics as being determined by the army: Prussia was very far from being 'militarist' in the conventional twentieth-century sense.[133] Admittedly, Frederick William enjoyed appearing in uniform; it is also true that many of his closest confidants – Zastrow, Köckritz and Kleist – were military men.[134] But Frederick William's emphasis on bourgeois values and his dismissive attitude towards the social pretensions of the officer corps contradicted the traditional Prussian military code of honour.[135] More importantly, the army had no strong sense of corporate political – as opposed to socio-cultural – identity. Attempts to reduce its privileges would be energetically resisted, but in relation to the political executive the army's role was largely functional. The military experts were frequently consulted on points of technical detail, less so on matters of high policy. Moreover, the polycratic chaos of military administration with its competing Militärdepartement, Oberkriegskollegium, and the Generalinspektion der Truppen frustrated the emergence of a coherent military standpoint; besides, all military business had to go through the relatively junior, but potentially *puissant* adjutants in order to reach

---

131 Rainer Wohlfeil, *Vom stehenden Heer des Absolutismus zur Allgemeinen Wehrpflicht (1789–1814)* (Frankfurt/Main, 1964), pp. 81–153.
132 Clausewitz quoted in Helmut Schnitter, 'Revolution und Heer. Reformbestrebungen und Revolutionseinflüsse im preußischen Heer vor 1806. Lernfähigkeit und Lernbereitschaft einer feudal-absolutistischen Armee im Umfeld der französischen Revolution, 1789–1795', in Heiner Timmermann (ed.), *Die französische Revolution und Europa, 1789–1799* (Saarbrücken, 1989), p. 690. See also Gordon Craig, *The politics of the Prussian army* (Oxford, 1955). On the inextricable link between social structure and military organisation see Büsch, *Militärsystem und Sozialleben im alten Preußen.*
133 The classic – but problematic – account of German militarism is Gerhard Ritter, *The sword and the sceptre. The problem of militarism in Germany.* Vol. I. *The Prussian tradition, 1740–1890* (London, 1972), which contains virtually nothing on the Prussian army in politics between 1797 and 1806. The same is true of Gerhard Förster, Heinz Helmert, Helmut Otto and Helmut Schnitter, *Der preußisch-deutsche Generalstab, 1640–1965. Zu seiner politischen Rolle in der Geschichte* (Berlin/East, 1966). Volker Berghahn, *Militarism. The history of an international debate, 1861–1979* (Leamington Spa, 1981) is an anti-Ritter.
134 Stamm-Kuhlmann, *Friedrich Wilhelm III*, p. 114.
135 Paul and Gisela Habermann, *Friedrich Wilhelm III. König von Preußen, im Blick wohlwollender Zeitzeugen* (Schernfeld, 1990), pp. 34, 47.

the king.[136] Where military men – such as the adjutants – were prominent in the antechamber of power, their presence derived from the confidence of the king, not from their military standing. In any case, the will of the monarch was decisive. 'No institution', writes Curt Jany, 'could defy an explicit royal command.'[137]

Corporate interests, be they aristocratic, bureaucratic or military, were thus rigidly excluded from foreign-political decision-making. This had not always been the case. Until the mid-seventeenth-century watershed, the estates had enjoyed the explicit right of participation in foreign affairs;[138] thereafter, the 'governing compromise' abolished any such consultative rights.[139] This redefinition of the relationship was not an amicable arrangement, but was forced upon the weaker party by the victorious Great Elector. Hence, at about the same time as the representative institutions in England found themselves – intentionally or not – in (ultimate) control of the executive, the Prussian nobility had forfeited not only its consultative role but also its ability to control foreign policy through the regulation of taxation. From this point onwards, Prussian foreign policy was conducted without serious regard to sectional interests. As we shall see, there is no evidence that Prussian foreign policy during the Napoleonic period was either directly influenced by the dominant Junker class, or conducted by the king and the foreign ministry on their behalf. Indeed, a desperate and highly unusual protest by the estates of Cleves-Mark against their planned abandonment to France had absolutely no impact on the determination of Prussian statesmen to rid themselves of that exposed and indefensible principality.[140] Similarly, foreign policy was formulated with an almost cavalier disregard for economic interests, for example during the Armed Neutrality of 1800–1, when conflict with Britain threatened economic ruin.[141] Later on we shall

---

[136] For an excellent overview of this polycratic chaos see Schmidt-Bückeburg, *Das Militärkabinett der preußischen Könige*, pp. 7–9; for contemporary observations see Droysen, *York von Wartenburg*, p. 88 and Rothfels (ed.), *Clausewitz. Briefe und Schriften*, p. 210.

[137] Jany, *Geschichte des preußischen Heeres, bis 1807*, p. 400: 'Einem klar ausgesprochenen königlichen Willen hätte sich keine Behörde versagen dürfen.'

[138] Birtsch, 'Preußischer Hochabsolutismus und die Stände', p. 398.

[139] Cosmar and Klaproth, *Staatsrat*, p. 230.

[140] See Wilhelm Steffens, 'Rheingrenze und territoriale Entschädigungsfrage in der preussischen Politik der Jahre 1795–98. Zugleich ein Beitrag zur Steinforschung. Mit drei unveröffentlichten Denkschriften des Freiherrn von Stein', *Westfälische Forschungen*, 6 (1953), 162.

[141] The unsuccessful bureaucratic opposition and merchant protests concerning a breach with Britain are described in Richard Krauel, 'Die Beteiligung Preussens an der zweiten Bewaffneten Neutralität vom Dezember 1801', *FBPG*, 27 (1914), 215–17. See also Dwyer, 'Prussia and the Second Armed Neutrality', p. 121.

be discussing a far more spectacular instance of the primacy of foreign policy over economic rationality in the Hanoverian crisis of 1806.

In any case, with the exception of a few – and usually unsuccessful – attempts to reverse a diplomatic manoeuvre for domestic reasons, bureaucrats such as Auerswald, Dohna, Schrötter and Stägemann remained aloof from foreign affairs.[142] Indeed, when Karl von Altenstein, a senior bureaucrat in Ansbach-Bayreuth, sent his famous memorandum to Hardenberg in December 1805, he apologised for 'venturing into an alien sphere [of activity] (*in eine fremde Sphäre wagte*)';[143] this is an excellent contemporary illustration of the distinction between politics and administration. As for the military, there are only two major incidences of foreign-political activism during the Revolutionary and Napoleonic period, both arising out of blatant insubordination by a senior commander. The first was Field Marshal Möllendorf's peace initiative towards France in 1794,[144] which was undertaken without the approval of Frederick William II; the second was Yorck von Wartenburg's unsanctioned treaty with the Russians at Tauroggen in December 1812. Even if a certain restlessness can be observed among elements of the army by 1806, there were no comparable incidents during the early reign of Frederick William III. Indeed, when one senior military figure criticised Prussian policy in a memorandum, the unanimous response of the politicians was: 'Well! If artillery generals are going to interfere in politics, then we might as well give in'; similarly disparaging remarks about military interference in politics were made by the young Yorck von Wartenburg.[145]

To sum up: the interpretations of Kehr, Rosenberg, Vetter and others, have all undoubtedly added to our knowledge of pre-Reform Prussia; for the purposes of this study, however, they are only of peripheral importance. Even if the bureaucracy controlled the day-to-day administration of the state, even if the aristocracy dominated a still overwhelmingly rural

142 Raumer, *Deutschland um 1800. Krise und Neugestaltung, 1789–1815*, edited by Leo Just (Konstanz, 1961), p. 178.
143 Ernst Müsebeck, 'Fragmentarische Aufzeichnungen Altensteins über die auswärtige Politik Preussens vom 28/29 Dezember 1805', *FBPG*, 28 (1915), 140.
144 See Sidney Biro, *The German policy of Revolutionary France. A study in French diplomacy during the war of the first coalition 1792–1797* (Cambridge, Mass., 1957), I, p. 266. Surprisingly, this under-researched incident is not mentioned in Craig, *The politics of the Prussian army*.
145 Massenbach, *Memoiren zur Geschichte des preussischen Staates*, p. 129 (re the memorandum of General der Artillerie Tempelhoff): 'Ja! Wenn die Artillerie-Generale sich in Politik mischen wollen, so machen wir das Buch zu'; Droysen, *York von Wartenburg*, p. 94. On York see also Peter Paret, *Yorck and the era of Prussian Reform 1807–1815* (Princeton, 1966).

society, the crucial sphere of high politics and foreign policy remained entirely distinct and operated according to its own specific rules. Here the main actors were holders of *personal* – not institutional or social – authority, legitimated by the confidence of the king, from whom all power came and through whom all ambitions could be fulfilled. If – as Hugo Preuß once remarked – the power of the state ended at the *Kreis* level, where it passed to a feudal nobility,[146] then the reverse is also true, namely that the corporate political power of the nobility did not extend beyond the *Kreis*. It was a long way from the East-Elbian estates of the military-agrarian complex to the antechamber of power in Berlin; different explanatory models are required in each instance. As Berdahl has pointed out for the period after 1815, 'The perspective from the centre is always different from that on the periphery.'[147] The Count Haugwitz who lorded it over his Silesian tenants was not the same Haugwitz, whose precarious position as minister of foreign affairs necessitated close collaboration with *bourgeois* cabinet secretaries against his aristocratic colleagues. In short, the interpretation advanced in this study is not necessarily in conflict with the existing historiography, *except* where notions of aristocratic dominance and bureaucratic ambition obtrude into the spheres of high politics, foreign policy and executive reform.

[146] Quoted in Witzleben, *Staatsfinanznot und sozialer Wandel*, p. 59.
[147] Berdahl, *The politics of the Prussian nobility*, p. 203 (concerning Gustav von Rochow specifically). I am grateful to Christopher Clark for drawing my attention to this reference.

3   Problem areas of Prussian policy and
     politics: the centres of attention abroad,
     1797–1804

From intervention to neutrality: A brief outline of
Prussian foreign policy, 1792–1804

All eyes were on eastern Europe in the summer of 1789. It was the anticipated war of the Turkish succession which exercised statesmen in Berlin and throughout Europe, not reports of the breakdown of the *ancien régime* in France.[1] Yet the expected breach between Prussia, Turkey and Poland on the one hand, and Austria and Russia on the other, did not come to pass. Instead, the two German powers patched up their quarrel and went to war against Revolutionary France. But what started out as an opportunist police action against a supposed revolutionary rabble soon turned into a protracted conflict. In the autumn of 1792, the Prussian army under the Duke of Brunswick lumbered into northern France until checked at Valmy. By the end of the year the revolutionary armies had not only cleared the invaders from French soil, but had flooded into western and southern Germany. The following year brought some successes, including the recapture of Mainz: a temporary respite only, as it proved. By late 1793, the French had surged forward again. Mainz changed hands for the third time, Italy was invaded and by 1794–5 the Netherlands were overrun. In the meantime, Britain had joined the coalition, but although it was able and eager to inflict painful defeats on the French at sea, it was unable or unwilling to redress the military balance in continental Europe.

It was in this context of the diminishing returns of a war with France, that the Prussians broke ranks with the coalition. In 1793, Frederick William II turned eastwards to partition Poland with Catherine II of Russia; two years later the Austrians joined the scramble to divide up what was left. By then, however, Prussia had not only *de facto*, but also *de jure* abandoned the common cause. For at the Treaty of Basle in 1795

[1] For the diplomatic situation of Europe in 1789 see Blanning, *The origins of the French Revolutionary Wars*, pp. 36–68, and Schroeder, *The transformation of European politics*, pp. 53–99.

she undertook to maintain a strict neutrality in the continuing war against France. In return the French eventually promised to respect the so-called 'demarcation line' behind which would lie a Prussian-dominated neutrality zone in northern Germany. With the help of semi-voluntary contributions from northern German princes, the Prussians were able to raise and maintain an army of observation. As for those German territories which lay beyond the demarcation line, they were abandoned to the tender mercies of French invasion or salvation at the hands of the Austrians. Indeed, a secret clause of the Treaty of Basle stipulated a later French annexation of the left bank of the Rhine, even though Frederick William hoped to the end that this could be avoided.

In the meantime the war against France continued. Overseas, Britain cleaned up France's colonies, and everybody else's at the same time. On the continent, the very much less glamorous task of defeating the land forces of the French republic devolved to the Austrians, upon whom the brunt of the coalition war effort was to fall for much of the next ten years. Prussia thus escaped the full fury of the French onslaught on Germany in 1796 to 1797. The maintenance of the neutrality zone, however, proved less straightforward than had been hoped. Flagrant Austrian and French violations were to plague the Prussians for at least a year. It was only once a more permanent arrangement had been made with France in August 1796 and the Austrians had been expelled from most of southern Germany, that the integrity of the neutrality zone, for the time being at least, was assured. In fact, towards the end of 1797 the prospects for a lasting peace in Europe looked good. After five years of war, Austria was finally forced to settle at the Treaty of Campoformio; outstanding territorial questions were referred to a Congress convened at Rastatt in 1797. Only Britain fought on.

The hope of the new king of Prussia, Frederick William III, that the neutrality policy could be consolidated, proved shortlived. Relations between Austria and France rapidly deteriorated again; more worryingly, Russia too seemed set against France. Throughout 1798, Prussia became the focus of European diplomacy, as the representatives of Austria, Britain and Russia sought to draw her into the Second Coalition. At the same time, France redoubled her efforts for a Prussian alliance. By October 1798, the French were forced to admit defeat and break off negotiations. During the winter of 1798/9, Franco-Prussian relations then cooled to the verge of conflict. But despite the efforts of leading Prussian politicians, Frederick William refused to take the final step towards joining the coalition; this produced an acrimonious split within the Prussian ruling elite. Within two months negotiations with the coalition powers were also wound up.

Retrospectively, the Prussians felt they had had a narrow escape. After initial reverses, the French rallied to push the Austro-Russian forces out of Italy and Switzerland. A joint Austro-Russian operation against Holland was an ignominious failure. In Paris, the coup by Napoleon Bonaparte in November 1799 promised a more vigorous prosecution of the war. By mid-1800, after decisive French victories at Lodi, Marengo and Hohenlinden, the military defeat of the Second Coalition was evident. For Prussia, however, the break up of the coalition, amidst mutual recrimination, brought dangers of its own. If the Austro-Russian quarrel was welcome enough, the Anglo-Russian breach soon precipitated Prussia into a fresh crisis. For by helping to mediate a Franco-Russian *rapprochement* in 1800, Prussia exposed itself to their demands for joint action against British maritime supremacy. In July 1800 the Peterhof treaty with Russia committed both to mutual support if attacked by a third party. By December 1800, Prussia acceded to the Armed Convention in defence of neutral shipping.

Once Britain had broken off relations with Russia and Denmark in January 1801, pressure began to mount on Prussia to honour her obligations by the Armed Neutrality. Without any naval forces worthy of the name, the only way in which Prussia could effectively come to grips with Britain was by striking at her continental trade and possessions. In March 1801, the Prussians closed the ports of the Elbe and Weser to British shipping, and in the following month they occupied the electorate of Hanover, which was the patrimony of King George III of England. With breathtaking speed, however, Prussia found herself no longer belatedly in step with her allies, but dangerously out on a limb, for the murder of Tsar Paul in St Petersburg led to the accession of Alexander I and a reversal of the former pro-French policy. In June 1801, Russia came to terms with Britain in the Anglo-Russian Maritime Convention; the Armed Neutrality was thus formally at an end. Wrong-footed by the sudden Russian defection, and embarrassed by a semi-public annexation debate over Hanover, the Prussians were left to thrash about in their north German thicket. The autumn brought Franco-British peace preliminaries, and in November 1801 the Prussians finally evacuated the electorate.

After emerging relatively unscathed from the Hanoverian debacle, Prussia moved quickly to mend fences with Russia and France. Frederick William and Alexander met at Memel in June 1802 amidst much acclaim; around the same time, a less publicised agreement with France determined the extent to which Prussia was to be compensated for the loss of her left-bank territories. Although the final judgment of the commission designated to regulate the new territorial complexion of

Germany – the *Reichshauptdeputationsschluss* – did not appear until 1803, the Prussians swiftly took *de facto* possession of their considerable gains. In the meantime, the general political outlook had improved dramatically. Britain and France had concluded a peace treaty at Amiens in 1802 and, with both Russia and Austria quiescent, no new coalitions appeared in the offing.

It was therefore with considerable concern that Prussia observed the breakdown of the Franco-British truce over Malta in 1802 to 1803. Concern turned to outright alarm when Napoleon made clear his intention of striking at Britain by occupying Hanover. A protracted debate ensued in Berlin as to whether Prussia should pre-empt a French invasion. Once again, Frederick William decided in favour of caution and, despite vocal Prussian protests, a large French force took possession of the electorate in May 1803. This move shattered the integrity of the Neutrality Zone as originally conceived. The French troops in Hanover not only represented a direct challenge to Prussian hegemony in north Germany, they were also a potential target of any future British, Austrian or Russian expeditionary force. Further problems were caused by the resulting British blockade of the Elbe, Weser and Ems rivers. But most serious of all were the numerous indications that the occupation of Hanover was merely the overture to more far-reaching ambitions in Germany. In late March 1804, for example, French troops abducted the Duc d'Enghien, a prominent Bourbon exiled in western Germany, in a clear violation of the integrity of the Holy Roman Empire. Two months later, Napoleon fuelled speculation about his imperial designs by proclaiming himself emperor. But Prussia remained passive and continued to thread its way between its two powerful neighbours. In May 1804 she concluded a secret alliance with Russia for the defence of northern Germany. One month later, an agreement with France regulated the size of the garrison in Hanover. There then followed a period of comparative tranquillity. The policy of neutrality had been restored, if not to its former majesty, then at least to working order. Napoleonic hegemony in Europe as a whole was indisputable, but Prussia could still believe herself supreme in the narrower north German sphere. Despite the Franco-British breach there were no obvious signs that either Russia or Austria would take the field against France yet again. In fact, there was nothing – except experience – to suggest the kind of crises which were to hit the Prussian state from the autumn of 1804 onwards.

These are the bare facts of Prussian foreign policy between the First Coalition and the refoundation of the neutrality policy in 1803–4. What follows is an attempt to look behind the bald chronological facade and discuss the background of policy debates and fears, of personal ambitions and animosities against which these events took place.

The role of geopolitical thinking in Prussian foreign policy

As you can see, the geographic location [of the Prussian state] makes us neighbours of all the great rulers of Europe. All of these neighbours are potentially envious of us or secret enemies of our power.

Frederick the Great, 'Political testament of 1752'[2]

'The provinces of the Prussian monarchy', Frederick the Great noted in 1752, 'are nearly all separated from each other.'[3] Forty years later, the Prussia of Frederick William III remained essentially a heterogenous collection of disparate territories in the heart of Europe. Even after the Prussian possessions on the left bank of the Rhine were effectively lost to France, the distance between the western and eastern extremes of the monarchy still exceeded 1000 km. Nor, despite the efforts of Frederick the Great, was Prussia a unified contiguous state. A solid block of Hanoverian and ecclesiastical territory separated the western lands from the main body of the state; to the south, Saxon and Bavarian lands cut off the Prussian enclaves of Ansbach and Bayreuth. As if this were not bad enough, Prussia enjoyed no natural boundaries, save some of those to the south with the Habsburg monarchy. To the east, there lay more than 500 km of indefensible border with Russia. To the west and south there was only a nightmarish patchwork quilt of isolated territories: Emden, Ansbach-Bayreuth and the March, all of them within easy striking distance of French or Austrian forces.

If the geopolitical exposure of their monarchy was an indisputable objective fact, it was also very much a matter of subjective concern among Prussian statesmen. This was evident from the distinctive geopolitical rhetoric developed to describe Prussia's predicament. The phrase 'one only has to look at the map' took on a certain frequency in Prussian debate. 'One glance at the map', wrote one senior diplomat, 'and one immediately sees the disadvantages arising out of our encircled

---

2 Oppeln-Bronikowski (ed.), *Friedrich der Große. Das politische Testament von 1752*, p. 56: 'Wir ihr seht, macht uns diese geographische Lage zu Nachbarn der großen europäischen Herrscher. Alle diese Nachbarn sind ebenso viele Neider oder geheime Feinde unserer Macht'; in a similar vein, p. 105.

3 Ibid., p. 56.

situation.'[4] Prussia was in fact, as the Kabinettsministerium noted simply in January 1801, 'surrounded by three powerful neighbours'.[5] Moreover, she was not only 'placée . . . entre les deux extrêmes' (of France and Russia) but also 'voisine par une longue étendue de frontières d'une puissance toujours redoutable' (Russia).[6] To make matters worse, all three neighbours, even Austria, were individually either actually or potentially more powerful than Prussia. This prompted Hardenberg to describe Prussia as being 'presqu'entourée de deux grandes monarchies infiniment supérieurs en forces physiques'.[7] It was hardly surprising, therefore, that Prussian strategists were obsessed by the undefended borders of the monarchy to the east, south and west. 'Prussia is the only military state in Europe which has no military borders', lamented the Duke of Brunswick, the Prussian commander-in-chief. Indeed, Brunswick spoke of the 'already too extended geographic location' which deprived the Prussian state of secure borders.[8] In the same vein, Colonel Massenbach noted that 'Russia and Austria have offensive borders against us', while France even 'encircles us on three sides'.[9]

These fears were a legacy of the mid-eighteenth century, when Prussia had stood practically alone against an Austrian, Russian and French alliance. Even fifty years later, the French were still able to play on these fears by threatening a 'retour des liaisons politiques de l'an 1756' and adverting to Austrian attempts to 'renouer les liens établis entre la France et l'Autriche par le traité de 1756'.[10] 'Il serait superflu d'observer', the Kabinettsministerium warned, 'combien d'après la position topographique de vos états, sire, une rupture avec les deux cours

---

[4] Memorandum of LeCoq, 'Bemerkungen über Russland in besonderer Rücksicht auf Preussen', 3.10.1801, Potsdam, GStA Rep.92 *Friedr. Wilh. d. Dritte* B.VI.4, fo. 92: 'Ein Blick auf die Karte und man sieht zugleich alle Nachteile einer umklammernden Lage'; see also 'Note remise le 7 avril 1801 au Comte de Panin par le Colonel de le Coq, St Petersburg', Rep.92 *Schöll* 21, fo. 41: 'il suffit de jetter un coup d'oeil sur la carte'.

[5] 'Note des preußischen Ministeriums an Beurnonville', 17.1.1802, Berlin, in Bailleu (ed.), *Preussen und Frankreich*, II, p. 70.

[6] Instruction for Lucchesini, 14–16.10.1800, Berlin, in Bailleu (ed.), *Preussen und Frankreich*, II, pp. 7–8.

[7] Memorandum of Hardenberg, 26.1.1801, Berlin, GStA Rep. 92 *Schöll* 21, fo. 2.

[8] Brunswick to Massenbach, 10.6.1801, in Massenbach, *Memoiren zur Geschichte des preussischen Staates*, III, p. 196: 'Preußen ist in Europa der einzige militärische Staat, der keine militärische Grenze hat . . . bereits zu sehr ausgedehnte geographische Lage.'

[9] Massenbach memorandum of May 1801, in Massenbach, *Memoiren zur Geschichte des preussischen Staates*, III, pp. 175–6; see also Massenbach memorandum of January 1801, in ibid., III, pp. 397–400: 'Russland und Österreich und Frankreich haben Offensivgrenzen gegen uns . . . Frankreich umklammert uns an drei Seiten.'

[10] Lucchesini report, 29.5.1803, Paris, in Bailleu (ed.), *Preussen und Frankreich*, II, p. 150.

impériales [Austria and Russia] serait dangereuse'.[11] Consequently, sensitivity about her undefended borders had always permeated Prussian plans for territorial expansion. Indeed, it is often difficult to determine where legitimate security fears end and expansionism begins. This need for aggrandisement could be expressed in general terms, especially when Austrian or Russian gains required compensatory accretions. However, expansionist demands were also voiced with direct reference to Prussia's specific vulnerability within the European pentarchy. Thus when Colonel Massenbach noted in January 1798 that 'Prussia must remain an expansionist state', he was referring to a general need of European great powers; when he stressed that 'Berlin has no (defensive) outworks, such outworks are only to be found in Bohemia', and that Prussia must therefore 'advance to her natural borders or decline from her present level of power', he was articulating a specifically Prussian geopolitical reflex.[12]

To a certain extent, therefore, Prussian concerns were part of a long-established geopolitical preoccupation going back to the great elector.[13] But by the end of the eighteenth century, political developments had rendered the Prussian predicament even more acutely uncomfortable. First of all, the new French advance into Germany threatened to complete the encirclement of Prussia. Secondly, the final partitions of Poland between 1793 and 1795 fundamentally transformed Prussia's position in eastern Europe. By destroying a crucial buffer between the expanding Russian empire and Prussia's vulnerable eastern border, the elimination of Poland compromised the monarchy still further.[14] Many Prussian politicians were horrified by this violation of the old Frederician maxim that a weak Poland was vital to the security of Prussia; Frederick's brother Prince Heinrich even went so far as to plead for the restoration of Poland.[15] Lombard criticised the elimination of

---

[11] Kabinettsministerium to Frederick William, 13.5.1798, Berlin, in Bailleu (ed.), *Preussen und Frankreich*, I, p. 203.

[12] Massenbach to Brunswick, 21.2.1798, Potsdam, in Massenbach, *Memoiren zur Geschichte des preussischen Staates*, III, pp. 31–3: 'Berlin hat keine Vormauern, Diese Vormauern befinden sich nur in Böhmen . . . bis zu seinen natürlichen Grenzen vorrücken, oder Preußen sinkt von der Stufe der Macht, auf welcher es heute stehet herab.'

[13] See Gregor Schöllgen, 'Sicherheit durch Expansion? Die aussenpolitischen Lageanalysen der Hohenzollern im 17. und 18. Jahrhundert im Lichte des Kontinuitätsproblems in der preußischen und deutschen Geschichte', *Historisches Jahrbuch*, 104 (1984), 22–45.

[14] Köckritz to Hardenberg, 25.11.03, Potsdam, enclosing two memoranda by Massenbach, Rep. 92 *Hardenberg* E3, unfoliated.

[15] Koser, 'Preußische Politik', p. 479; Luise von Preussen, Princess Anton Radziwill (ed.), *Fünfundvierzig Jahre aus meinem Leben (1770–1815)* (Brunswick, 1912), p. 105.

Poland retrospectively in his memoirs,[16] while Queen Louise later openly acknowledged the 'énnervation de la position géographique et politique de la Prusse par l'acquisition de la Pologne'.[17] Finally, the partitions involved the acquisition of huge numbers of Polish subjects, among them a numerous, factious and free-spirited nobility, which severely impaired the internal stability of the monarchy. The result was a sense of 'imperial overstretch',[18] which was aggravated by worries that Polish discontent might be stirred up by France. Indeed, fears of Polish *'Explosionen'* continued to plague Frederick William until they finally materialised in 1806–7.[19]

Under Frederick the Great, the Prussian predicament had led to an aggressive disposition in foreign affairs. Frederick William III, however, reacted in exactly the opposite way. If the neutrality policy had originally been conceived as an expedient to mask the fiscal and political bankruptcy of his father's interventionism,[20] the new king furnished it with a reasoned geopolitical rhetoric. When Frederick William spoke of 'la position géographique de ma monarchie et . . . la double circonspection dont elle me fait la loi',[21] he was justifying his policy of cautious neutrality with direct reference to geography. Prussia, the argument went, could not defend more than 'sa position géographique lui permet de défendre', namely the north of Germany. Such an arrangement was 'dans l'ordre naturel des choses',[22] and would enable Prussia to erect a 'dyke' against French expansion, behind which those German territories selected 'par leur position topographique' could shelter.[23] In short, to borrow Frederick William's own graphic description, the neutrality

---

[16] Lombard, *Matériaux*, pp. 74–5.

[17] Bogdan Krieger, 'Königin Luise und der Geheime Kabinetsrat Lombard', *Deutsche Revue*, 26 (1901), 341.

[18] Klaus Zernack, 'Polen in der Geschichte Preußens', in Büsch (ed.), *Handbuch der preußischen Geschichte*, p. 430; Klaus Zernack, 'Preußen-Frankreich-Polen. Revolution und Teilung', in Büsch and Neugebauer-Wölk (eds.), *Preußen und die revolutionäre Herausforderung*, pp. 22–40; Hagen, 'The partitions of Poland'.

[19] Memorandum by Frederick William marked 'sicher vor 1800' by archivist, GStA Rep. 92 *Friedr.Wilh.d.Dritte* B.VI.21, fo. 1. See also memorandum of Alvensleben, 12.5.1798, Berlin, in Bailleu (ed.), *Preussen und Frankreich*, I, p. 201.

[20] Memorandum of Alvensleben, 1.10.1797, Berlin, in Bailleu, ibid., p. 151; Willy Real, 'Die preussischen Staatsfinanzen und die Anbahnung des Sonderfriedens von Basel 1795', *FBPG*, NF 1 (1991), 53–100.

[21] Frederick William to Haugwitz, 29.8.1799, Charlottenburg, in Bailleu (ed.), *Preussen und Frankreich*, I, p. 334.

[22] 'Contre-Observations sur la réponse des plénipotentiaries Russes remise aux ministres de Prusse dans la conférence du 16 Juillet 1798', GStA Rep. 92 *Schöll* 18, fo. 35; in a similar vein see also Haugwitz memorandum, 30.1.1797, Berlin, in Bailleu (ed.), *Preussen und Frankreich*, I, p. 113.

[23] Haugwitz memorandum, 15.1.1797, Berlin, in Bailleu (ed.), *Preussen und Frankreich*, I, p. 266.

policy was a 'système que ma position géographique et les motifs les plus graves m'imposent imperiéusement'.[24] Or, as he put it in the following year: 'Vous conviendriez, Sire, que la position géographique dans laquelle se trouve une grande partie de mes états et de ceux qui les avoisinent, rend les ménagements indispensables.'[25]

The upshot of this analysis was a ritually affirmed determination to preserve the neutrality of northern Germany.[26] Prussia undertook to resist all 'entreprises qui compromissent la sureté du nord au point d'equivaloir à une aggression'.[27] Everything to the west and south of the neutrality line was abandoned. Already under Frederick William II, the initial demarcation line was redrawn to exclude even such proximate territories as Frankfurt and Hesse-Darmstadt.[28] Nor was the integrity of the neutrality zone always upheld as energetically as Prussian rhetoric suggested. In practice, the caveat 'd'equivaloir à une aggression' allowed for a flexible response to Austrian and French violations. Still, according to its own criteria, the neutrality policy could on balance be viewed as a qualified success. Until 1803, serious French penetration of the north German area had been resisted; thereafter, it was at least contained. The price was a frustrating and often humiliating passivity in the face of events. Thus in May 1804, Queen Louise was forced to curtail her public mourning for the murdered Duc d'Enghien on the grounds that 'notre position épineuse ne semble pas permettre de s'y livrer à l'exemple de la Russie seule, qui se trouve dans une situation bien différente, ou il ne coûte rien de déployer ce sentiment, tandis que nous lui servons de boulevard'.[29]

Prussia's neutrality policy was not confined to preservation of the

---

[24] Frederick William to Lucchesini, 24.9.1803, in Bailleu (ed.), *Preussen und Frankreich*, II, p. 203.

[25] Frederick William to Alexander, 11.4.1804, in Paul Bailleu (ed.), *Briefwechsel König Friedrich Wilhelms III und der Königin Luise mit Kaiser Alexander I* (Leipzig, 1900), p. 52.

[26] Walter Trummel, 'Der Norddeutsche Neutralitätsverband, 1795–1801', *Beiträge für die Geschichte Niedersachsens und Westfalens* 41 (Hildesheim, 1913), is largely preoccupied with the recruitment, supply and payment of the Prussian-led army of observation; it is also heavily weighted towards the period 1795–6.

[27] 'Ordre de cabinet addressé le 12 mars 1799 par le roi de Prusse à son ministère' (copy), Berlin, GStA Rep. 92 *Schöll* 19, fo. 1. In a similar vein see: 'Note remise le 7 avril 1801 au Comte de Panin par le Colonel de le Coq' (copy), St Petersburg, GStA Rep. 92 *Schöll* 21, fo. 41; memorandum of Haugwitz, 2.4.1802, Berlin, GStA Rep. 92 *Friedr. Wilh. d. Dritte* B.VI.12, unfoliated; Hardenberg to Brunswick, 6.6.1803, no place, GStA Rep. 92 *Hardenberg* E3, unfoliated.

[28] P. von Bojanovski, *Niederschriften des Herzogs Carl August von Weimar über den Schutz der Demarkationslinie, den Rennweg (1796) und die Defension Thüringens (1798)* (Weimar, 1902); Biro, *German policy of Revolutionary France*, II, p. 531.

[29] Hardenberg to Lombard, 9.5.1804, Berlin, in Bailleu (ed.), *Preussen und Frankreich*, II, p. 262.

tranquillity of northern Germany through the exclusion of French or coalition forces. There was also a more activist dimension, which was manifested in the desire to achieve a Franco-Russian *rapprochement* through Prussian mediation. First efforts in that direction were made under Frederick William II in 1797,[30] and gathered pace during the final stages of the war of the Second Coalition.[31] If the maintenance of the neutrality zone sought to shield Prussia from the consequences of continued European warfare, the mediation policy was intended to remove its root causes. The geopolitical imperative to avoid a Franco-Russian clash, which threatened to be played out on Prussian territory, was thus self-evident; equally obvious was the related imperative to prevent Franco-Russian relations from achieving real intimacy. This was clearly demonstrated during the Armed Neutrality crisis of 1800–1.[32] For by helping to mediate a Franco-Russian *rapprochement* after the collapse of the Second Coalition, Prussia had inadvertently placed herself back in the international firing line. If she had been the focus of intense Russo-British blandishments in 1798–9, she was now buffeted by Franco-Russian demands for action against Britain. Within a few months, Prussia was transformed from a mediator into a protagonist, not because her own policy or interests had changed, but simply because relations between her two most powerful neighbours had undergone a fundamental change.

In the meantime, a less spectacular, but no less significant policy debate was taking place in Berlin. This concerned the nature and direction of Prussian territorial compensation for her losses on the left bank of the Rhine. In order to maximise these gains, it was essential to remain on good terms with the Russians, but especially with France; the desire to make France and Russia more amenable to Prussian compensation claims had been not the least motivation for Prussian behaviour during the Armed Neutrality, when she allowed a relatively minor maritime quarrel with Britain to escalate to the brink of military

---

[30] Instruction for Sandoz-Rollin (Prussian ambassador in Paris), 23.1.1797, Berlin, in Bailleu (ed.), *Preussen und Frankreich*, I, p. 11.

[31] Frederick William to Haugwitz, 25/27.1.1800, Berlin, in Bailleu (ed.), *Preussen und Frankreich*, I, p. 358; instruction for Sandoz-Rollin, 31.1.01, Berlin, ibid., pp. 361–2; ibid., p. 361, 358, 378, 389 and *passim*; instructions for Lucchesini, 13.1.1801, Berlin, in Bailleu (ed.), *Preussen und Frankreich*, II, pp. 18–20; Lucchesini report, 21.1.01, Paris, ibid., p. 21.

[32] Hugh Ragsdale, 'Russia, Prussia and Europe in the policy of Paul I', *Jahrbücher für die Geschichet Osteuropas*, 31 (1983), 81–118, esp. 102–3; Dwyer, 'Prussia and the Armed Neutrality'; Krauel, 'Die Beteiligung Preussens'.

confrontation.[33] 'France', to quote the words of Baron Görtz, 'was the kitchen where the last supper of the law was prepared.'[34] But which of the enticing dishes should Prussia sample? After nearly three decades of eastern European gains, Prussian politicians were forced to refocus their attention to the west and south and make their choice from the apparent *embarras de richesse* which now presented itself to them. The resulting debate was not, *pace* Aretin,[35] primarily about the Reich and Prussian visions of its future configuration, but rather about Prussia's future geopolitical orientation.

By far the weakest school of opinion were the 'westerners', led by two senior bureaucrats, Stein and Heinitz. They pleaded for the retention of the small but economically vibrant lands on the far side of the Rhine; later they shifted to demanding compensations in Westphalia.[36] In direct contradiction to this policy were the 'southerners', headed by Hardenberg. Ever since his appointment as provincial minister for Ansbach-Bayreuth, he had been consolidating Prussia's position there as a springboard for further southwards expansion.[37] Already in 1796 he had authorised the annexation of the free city of Nuremberg by *coup de main*, an action which a furious Kabinettsministerium promptly reversed.[38] Soon, however, the prospect of compensations and secularisations seemed to offer him a fresh chance to press for Prussian gains in the south, notably the territories of Würzburg, Bamberg, Eichstätt, Nuremberg, Rothenburg and Frankfurt. In a series of memoranda, he argued that expansion towards the south was geopolitically necessary and preferable to Westphalian compensations, if future disputes with France rising out of contiguous borders were to be avoided.[39] If precautionary

[33] Heinrich Ulmann, 'Preußen, die bewaffnete Meeresneutralität und die Besitznahme Hannovers im Jahre 1801', *Deutsche Zeitschrift für Geschichtswissenschaft*, 2 (1897/8), 254.

[34] Johann Eustach Schlitz von Görtz, *Memoiren eines deutschen Staatsmannes aus den Jahren 1788–1816* (Leipzig, 1833), p. 183: 'Frankreich war die Küche, wo das Trauermahl des Rechts bereitet wurde.'

[35] Karl Otmar von Aretin, 'Deutschland und die Französische Revolution', in K. O. von Aretin and Karl Härter (eds.), *Revolution und konservatives Beharren. Das alte Reich und die Französische Revolution* (Mainz, 1990), p. 19.

[36] Steffens, 'Rheingrenze und territoriale Entschädigungsfrage', 172–3 and *passim*.

[37] Karl Süßheim, *Preussens Politik in Ansbach-Bayreuth, 1791–1806* (Berlin, 1902), p. 227 and *passim*. Hausherr, *Hardenberg*, I, pp. 206–7, 223.

[38] Fritz Zierke, *Die deutsche Politik Hardenbergs in der ersten Periode seines Staatsmännischen Wirkens 1770–1807. Ein Beitrag zum Bilde des preussischen Staatskanzlers und zur Geschichte des preussisch-deutschen Problems im Zeitalter der Französischen Revolution* (Gelnhausen, 1932), p. 77.

[39] *Reflexions politiques sur l'intérêt de la prusse à la conservation de ses deux principautés en Franconie, et leur extension territoriale par le moyen des secularisations*, mid-May 1799, GStA Rep. 92 *Schöll* 19, fos. 12–27; 'Mémoire sur les objets d'indemnisation pour les

measures were not adopted, Hardenberg warned that the encirclement of Prussia by Austria and Russia would be completed by the 'contiguité d'une troisième puissance, plus formidable encore'. For this reason alone Prussia should seek to 'écarter en avance, les differens que pourra faire naître le contact avec la République française' and opt instead for compensations which would make 'toutes collisiones moins possibles'.[40] This theme was taken up by Lucchesini, who argued that acquisitions in Franconia would enable Prussia to 'éviter toute occasion de différends entre les deux états, en diminuant autant que possible les points de contact entre les territoires respectifs'.[41]

Ultimately, Hardenberg's visions impaled themselves on the objections of the 'northerners', led by Haugwitz and Alvensleben, who were easily the largest school of thought in the compensations debate. They agreed with Hardenberg that Prussia should pursue a policy of disengagement in the west. Now that the left bank had been abandoned to the French, Haugwitz argued, the retention of lands on the Rhine could only be a 'source éternelle de différens et de chicanes avec cette puissance'.[42] In any case, ever since Frederick the Great's experiences in the Seven Years War, the abandonment of the western provinces had long been an aim of Prussian policy.[43] As Horst Carl has written, 'the increasing lack of interest of the central government in the difficult and exposed provinces led logically to their surrender'.[44] Outlying possessions such as Neufchâtel, after all, had already been cut adrift with a minimum of fuss.[45] Where the northerners differed from Hardenberg,

provinces transrhénanes du roi, surtout sur la préférence qu'on semble devoir accorder à cet égard à la Franconie de même que sur quelques autres points rélatifs aux provinces du roi dans ce cercle' (copy), 26.1.1801, Berlin, GStA Rep. 92 *Schöll* 21, fo. 2. See also Rep. 92 *Hardenberg* E1, 'Das Säcularisations- und Indemnitätsgeschäft in Maasgabe des Luneviller Friedens, 1800–1802': e.g. Hardenberg to Haugwitz, 12.3.1801, fo. 11; Hardenberg to Haugwitz, 4.4.01, Ansbach, fo. 27.

[40] Hardenberg memorandum (copy), 26.1.01, Berlin, GStA Rep. 92 *Schöll* 21, fos. 2–3.
[41] 'Mémoire présenté le 25 mars 1801 par le Marquis de Lucchesini au ministre des affaires étrangères de France' (copy), Paris, GStA Rep. 92 *Schöll* 21, fo. 15.
[42] Haugwitz to Frederick William (copy), 20.2.1801, GStA Rep. 92 *Lucchesini* 31, fo. 122. Passage not cited in Bailleu (ed.), *Preussen und Frankreich*, II, pp. 26–9; see also Beurnonville to Talleyrand, 29.12.1801, Berlin, in Bailleu (ed.), *Preussen und Frankreich*, p. 65.
[43] Lehmann, *Stein*, I, pp. 334–5; Steffens, 'Rheingrenze und territoriale Entschädigungs-frage', 155; Tümpel, *Die Entstehung des brandenburgisch-preußischen Einheitsstaates*, pp. 185–8.
[44] Horst Carl, *Okkupation und Regionalismus. Die preussischen Westprovinzen im Sieben-jährigen Krieg*, edited K. O. von Aretin (Mainz, 1993), chapter 2: 'Die preussischen Westprovinzen als Nebenlande der Monarchie', pp. 20–65, especially, pp. 28–9; quotation on pp. 415–16.
[45] See Ernst Oppliger, *Neuenburg, die Schweiz und Preussen, 1798–1806* (Zurich and Leipzig, 1915).

was in their belief that expansion into southern Germany was geopolitically equally unsound. For one thing, it threatened an unnecessary
and unwinnable conflict with Austria; critics pointed out that the
Emperor was still paramount in the Franconian circle.[46] Furthermore,
southwards expansion was suspect on the grounds that it distanced
Prussia from its centre of gravity to the north and east. 'All acquisitions
which distance Prussia from her focal point', argued the Duke of
Brunswick, 'are harmful.'[47]

Instead, the majority opinion called for compensations in northern
Germany. One possibility was the acquisition of Saxon Lusatia, which
was in danger of reverting to Habsburg control. 'One only has to glance
at the map', wrote Massenbach, 'in order to see what the deleterious
effect of such a move would be on Prussia.'[48] But few Prussians were
convinced of his belief that failure to absorb Lusatia would make
Prussia's demise 'mathematically inescapable'. Another attractive idea
was that of acquiring Hanover or Mecklenburg by exchange; this was
briefly canvassed, but foundered on the objections of the reigning princes
which Frederick William refused to override.[49] Prussian statesmen therefore turned to more modest, but nonetheless enticing prospects:
Hildesheim, Erfurt, Osnabrück and Paderborn. 'Un coup d'oeil sur la
carte', the Kabinettsministerium argued, would show the advantages of
gains in that direction.[50] Some, such as Alvensleben, demanded that all
territories to the west and south, including Franconia, be abandoned in
favour of a more consolidated position in the north between the rivers
Ems, Weser and Elbe. What was lost in revenue, he claimed, would be
made up in geographical consistency. Above all, the argument ran,
disengagement from the south and west would 'also avoid entangled
borders, and thus friction with many neighbours; it would avoid

---

[46] Fritz Tarrasch, *Der Übergang des Fürstentums Ansbach an Bayern* (Munich and Berlin, 1912), p. 6; Haugwitz memorandum, 21.8.1801, Berlin, in Bailleu (ed.), *Preussen und Frankreich*, II, p. 55; instruction for Lucchesini, 14–16.10.1800, Berlin, in ibid., p. 8; Rudolf Endres, 'Die preußische Ära in Franken', in Peter Baumgart (ed.), *Expansion und Integration. Zur Eingliederung neugewonnener Gebiete in den preußischen Staat* (Cologne and Vienna, 1984), pp. 170 and 190–1.

[47] Cited in Massenbach memorandum, 10.6.1801, in Massenbach, *Memoiren zur Geschichte des preussischen Staates*, III, pp. 196: 'Alle Acquisitionen die Preußen von seinem Mittelpunkt entfernen, sind schädlich.'

[48] Massenbach memorandum, May 1801, in Massenbach, *Memoiren zur Geschichte des preussischen Staates*, III, pp. 180–1: 'Nun braucht man nur einen Blick auf die Charte zu werfen um den Nachteil zu sehen, der daraus für Preußen entstehen würde.' Prussian designs on Lusatia went back to Frederick II: Oppeln-Bronikowski (ed.), *Friedrich der Große. Das politische Testament von 1752*, pp. 82–3.

[49] Note of Prussian ministry to Beurnonville, 17.1.1802, Berlin, in Bailleu (ed.), *Preussen und Frankreich*, II, pp. 68–9.

[50] Ibid., p. 70.

immediate contact with France'. Picking up a familiar theme, he added that in this way the Prussian state would acquire 'natural borders in the form of rivers' and thus provide greater security in Berlin's western approaches.[51] Haugwitz endorsed this view when he decreed that while expansion in Franconia had its attractions, 'political circumstances' dictated that Prussia should seek gains in North Germany. Compensations, in short, should be employed to reinforce the neutrality policy, not to over-extend it to the south.[52]

The policy of disengagement from the west and south enjoyed the considerable advantage of being compatible with French views. Already in July 1798, Sièyes had suggested that the Prussians should be contained beyond the Elbe.[53] While this rather drastic prescription was not yet being applied, the French were determined, to quote the words of Talleyrand, to 'éloigner du Rhin toute puissance prépondérante' and ensure that there be 'aucun point de contact' between the two states. Moreover, Talleyrand insisted that Prussia should not be 'limitrophes de la Batavie' – ruling out gains in the west – and should seek compensations in Westphalia instead.[54] In the end, it was the French attitude which proved decisive. If Haugwitz and Alvensleben had on occasion entertained the thought of southwards expansion,[55] French hostility forced them to back off.[56] Hardenberg, who had originally hoped to enlist French support for an active Prussian policy against Austria in southern Germany, was overruled. The result was that Prussia's principal gains under the *Reichsdeputationshauptschluss* included the northern German territories of Osnabrück, Hildesheim,[57] the Eichsfeld and Erfurt; only enclaves such as Essen, Elten and Werden bordered directly on France.[58] The Franconian secularisations fell to Bavaria.

The divide between westerners, southerners and northerners was

[51] Alvensleben memorandum, 26.2.1801, Berlin, GStA Rep. 92 *Lucchesini* 23, fos. 18–19: 'vermeiden ferner, dadurch die sich so oft schneidenden Grenzen, und die daher entstehenden Weitläufigkeiten mit vielen Nachbarn, vermeiden den unmittelbaren contact mit Frankreich . . . natürlicher Grenzen durch Flüsse'.
[52] Haugwitz to Hardenberg, 1.9.1801, Berlin, GStA Rep. 92 *Hardenberg* E1, fo. 29.
[53] Sièyes report, 27.7.1798, Berlin, in Bailleu (ed.), *Preussen und Frankreich*, I, 482.
[54] Talleyrand to Beurnonville, 18.12.1801, Paris, in Bailleu (ed.), *Preussen und Frankreich*, II, p. 64.
[55] Steffens, 'Rheingrenze und territoriale Entschädigungsfrage', pp. 162–3; Haugwitz to Frederick William, 20.1.1801, Berlin, in Bailleu (ed.), *Preussen und Frankreich*, II, p. 27.
[56] Zierke, *Deutsche Politik Hardenbergs*, p. 83; Tarrasch, *Übergang*, pp. 9–10.
[57] J. H. Gebauer, 'Aus der Vorgeschichte der ersten Einverleibung Hildesheims in Preußen (1768–1802)', *FBPG*, 31 (1918), 107–37, especially 130–7.
[58] See F. Körholz, *Die Säkularisation und Organisation in den preußischen Entschädigungsländern Essen, Elten und Werden, 1802–1806* (Münster, 1907).

important and deep-seated. Yet in one crucial sense all three groupings had something in common: they all advocated a policy involving a greater or lesser degree of activism. Pitted against this was what we may call the 'passivist' outlook of the king and some of his immediate entourage. Indeed, 'passive' was the adjective Frederick William himself used to define his policy.[59] The negative implications of this stance for Hardenberg's southern policy are obvious; Frederick William's 'passivism' also made life difficult for the northerners. He raised sentimental objections to the idea of abandoning outlying Prussian territories such as Ansbach-Bayreuth. 'Il repugne à mes principes', he told Hardenberg, 'de renoncer à une partie quelconque de mes ancêtres.'[60] Perhaps the most dramatic altercation between activists and passivists was the highly charged exchange between Massenbach and Mencken in 1798. 'We had a map in front of us', Massenbach wrote later, 'onto which I had outlined the [suggested] new border with red ink. You are right, said Mencken, to have marked the new border in red. It is the colour of the human blood which must be spilt in order to make this conquest. War is a monstrous thing which is fed by blood and treasure.'[61] It was the clash of two entirely differing conceptions of Prussian security needs. On the one hand, the quest for security through expansion; on the other a policy of strict neutrality in pursuit of the same goal. On the one hand the crass and simplistic *Realpolitik* of a Massenbach; on the other, the worthy and no less simplistic humanitarian scruples of a Mencken. Time was to show who was right.

Hanover: the 'neuralgic spot'

If there was one issue on which all strands of Prussian opinion could agree, it was the importance of the electorate of Hanover. As matters stood at the turn of the century, it was by far the largest of the northern German territories separating the Prussian heartland from the outlying western possessions of Emden, Minden-Ravensburg, Tecklenburg and

---

[59] Frederick William to Knobelsdorff, 20.10.1804, Potsdam, in Bailleu (ed.), *Preussen und Frankreich*, II, p. 304 ('nur bei meinem passiven System bleiben kann').

[60] Frederick William to Hardenberg, 2.11.1801, Berlin, GStA Rep. 92 *Schöll* 21, fo. 95; Beurnonville report, 26.2.1800, Berlin, in Bailleu (ed.), *Preussen und Frankreich*, I, p. 523; Tarrasch, *Übergang*, p. 17.

[61] Described in Massenbach, *Memoiren zur Geschichte des preussischen Staates*, III, pp. 32–3: 'Wir hatten eine Landkarte vor uns liegen auf welcher ich die neue Grenze mit einem rothen Strich bezeichnet hatte. Sie haben Recht, sagte Mencken, die neue Grenze mit rother Farbe bezeichnet zu haben. Es ist die Farbe des Menschenblutes, das vergossen werden muß, um diese Eroberung zu machen. Der Krieg ist ein Ungeheuer, das sich von Geld und Blut nährt.'

Cleves-Mark. After the *Reichsdeputationshauptschluss* of 1803, by which Prussia absorbed Hildesheim, Paderborn and Münster, the electorate still neatly divided Prussia in half. It was natural, therefore, that Prussian statesmen should covet Hanover, as they had intermittently throughout the eighteenth century, especially as it was now hemmed in on three sides by Prussian territory. There was, however, a further twist to the Hanoverian problem which was to cause enormous embarrassment to Prussia in the years to come. This was the curious fact that George, Elector of Hanover, was simultaneously George III of England. This meant that the fate of Hanover was inextricably bound up with the Franco-British relationship on the wider world stage. In effect, Hanover served as a potential or actual bargaining counter for any French government which found itself worsted at sea. For Prussia, the resulting threat of a French invasion of Hanover had to be averted at all costs, for its inevitable consequence would be the collapse of the neutrality zone.

Throughout the 1790s, Prussian policy aimed to defuse the danger inherent in the Hanoverian predicament. In 1795, Prussia successfully insisted on the demilitarisation of the electorate and the expulsion of the disruptive French émigrés who had sought sanctuary there. By the following year, Hanover had been successfully integrated into the neutrality zone. This led to the paradoxical situation that George III happily if uneasily coexisted with France as elector of Hanover, while continuing to remain at war as king of England.[62] Towards the end of the 1790s, however, French designs against Hanover gathered pace. Already in 1796, a farsighted French diplomat had stressed that the occupation of Hanover was the only practical way of coming to grips with an 'insular' power such as Great Britain; it would also serve as a useful indemnity to make good colonial losses. In January 1799, Sièyes confirmed this view when he wrote that France could only knock Britain out of the war by 'laying hands' on her continental possession of Hanover.[63] He added the rhetorical question: who is preventing this? – and supplied his own answer: Prussia. The potential for a Franco-Prussian breach was thus obvious and it was registered with increasing alarm in Berlin.[64]

---

[62] Karl Friedrich Brandes, 'Hannover in der Politik der Großmächte 1801–1807', *FBPG*, 51 (1939), 241.

[63] Sièyes to Talleyrand, 8.1.1799, Berlin, in Bailleu (ed.), *Preussen und Frankreich*, I, p. 496.

[64] Kabinettsministerium to Frederick William, 13.5.1798, Berlin, in Bailleu (ed.), *Preussen und Frankreich*, I, p. 204; Haugwitz to Brunswick, 17.5.1798, Potsdam, ibid., p. 206; Haugwitz memorandum, 15.1.1799, Berlin, ibid., p. 266.

It is against this background that the Hanoverian crisis of 1801 must be seen. According to the terms of the Armed Neutrality Prussia found herself ranged with France, Russia and the smaller northern powers against Britain. At first, Frederick William hoped to avert an open breach. 'The conduct of this court', noted Lord Carysfort, the British ambassador in Berlin, 'continues what it has been, full of outward violence and private professions of goodwill.'[65] Frederick William was encouraged in this by the skilful British response, which sought to split the maritime coalition against them by exempting Prussia from reprisals.[66] By early 1801, however, Franco-Russian pressure mounted on Prussia to strike at Hanover, the only practical way in which she could contribute to the war effort. There was also the danger that France would occupy the electorate herself; in mid-March the French threatened to do exactly that and close the Elbe and Weser to shipping, if the Prussians refused to act.[67] At the time it suited the Prussians to argue that they were acting under Franco-Russian duress.[68] But in a persuasive piece of historical revision, Philip Dwyer has argued that the Franco-Russian threats were less immediate than had hitherto been assumed.[69] In particular he shows that the famous Russian 'ultimatum', which was previously assumed to have triggered the Prussian invasion, arrived *after* the decision to occupy Hanover had been taken. There were, indeed, cool considerations of Prussian *raison d'état* for the move against the electorate. If the crucial Franco-Russian goodwill in the *Reichs-deputationshauptschluss* was to be retained, some gesture in the common struggle against Britain had to be made. Moreover, an occupation of Hanover reinforced the neutrality policy and confirmed Prussian

---

[65] Carysfort to Grenville, 1.4.1801, Berlin, in *The MSS of J. B. Fortescue of Dropmore*, VII, p. 1.

[66] Krauel, 'Die Beteiligung Preussens', 209–10.

[67] Haugwitz to Brunswick, 8.2.1801, Berlin, in Bailleu (ed.), *Preussen und Frankreich*, II, p. 25; Lucchesini report, 10.3.1801, Paris, ibid., p. 31.

[68] Hardenberg to Walmoden (draft), 29.3.1801, Berlin, GStA Rep. 92 *Schöll* 21, fo. 38. See also Frederick William to Tsar Alexander, March 1805 (draft: never sent): 'Il y a quatre ans que j'occupai le pais d'Hannovre, à l'instigation de la Russie', Rep. XI.175.155B, fo. 20.

[69] Dwyer, 'Prussia and the Second Armed Neutrality'; Philip Dwyer has kindly also made available to me two longer (unpublished) draft articles upon which the piece in the *IHR* was based: 'Prussia, England and the Second Armed Neutrality' and 'Was Prussia forced to invade Hanover in 1801?'. Typical of older views are Krauel, 'Die Beteiligung Preussens', pp. 222–3; Ulmann, 'Preussen, die bewaffnete Meeresneutralität und die Besitznahme Hannovers', p. 255, stresses the *Zwangslage*, especially pp. 251, 258; Ford, *Hanover and Prussia*, pp. 21, 232; and Heinrich Ulmann, *Russisch-preussische Politik unter Alexander I und Friedrich Wilhelm III, bis 1806* (Leipzig, 1899), p. 3.

hegemony in northern Germany; failure to prevent a French occupation would irreparably damage that policy. In any case, the move could be justifed as the fulfilment of treaty obligations contracted under the Armed Neutrality. Finally, there were the commercial grievances against Britain which were far from decisive, but not negligible either. The fact remains, however, that while the Prussian decision was freely and rationally taken, the broader context was unmistakably coercive. Prussia may not have been literally forced to invade Hanover, but the imperative to forestall a French operation amounted to same thing.

Occupying Hanover in April 1801 was straightforward enough; there was no resistance. Once in possession, however, the Prussians were faced with a set of new dilemmas. The least of these was the resulting breach with Britain. As Philip Dwyer has shown, British attempts to eject the Prussians were rather half-hearted until after the collapse of the Armed Neutrality.[70] In fact, three months into the occupation, Britain suggested an arrangement by which the continued Prussian presence would be endorsed by George III. Frederick William sensibly rejected this on the grounds that it would embroil him with France.[71] Hanover's role as the poisoned pawn of Prussian policy was most strikingly demonstrated, however, by the way in which the occupation inevitably became entangled in the simultaneous compensations debate. It had long been French policy to encourage a Prussian annexation of Hanover, preferably in conjunction with a French alliance.[72] In 1801, the French renewed their offer; the Russians, too, held out the annexation of Hanover as an additional inducement to occupy the electorate.[73] Prussian opinion was divided. Some, such as Lucchesini, regarded the French scheme as a trap and warned against hasty permanent annexation.[74] Massenbach, strangely, also argued against it, suggesting that Prussia should concentrate on the ecclesiastical states instead.[75] Others such as LeCoq were enthusiastically in favour and articulated their views in character- istically geopolitical terms. 'Sans doute', he wrote in mid-April, 'que de toutes les indemnités, celle qui reviendroit à la monarchie Prussienne par l'Electorat d'Hannovre conviendroit le mieux à sa position géographique et ses intérêts; elle augmenteroit surtout ses moyens de défence à l'ouest

[70] Dwyer, 'Prussia and the Armed Neutrality', 683.
[71] Ford, *Hanover and Prussia*, p. 258.
[72] Biro, *German policy of revolutionary France*, II, pp. 531, 829.
[73] Re France: Haugwitz to Lucchesini, 24.5.1801, GStA Rep. 92 *Lucchesini* 31. fo. 139; Lucchesini report, 24.4.1801, Paris, in Bailleu (ed.), *Preussen und Frankreich*, II, p. 39. Re Russia: proposals of Krüdener (March 1801), ibid., pp. 34–5.
[74] Lucchesini reports of 25.1.1801 and 5.4.1801, Paris, ibid., p. 24, 37.
[75] Massenbach memorandum, May 1801, in Massenbach, *Memoiren zur Geschichte des preussischen Staates*, III, p. 180; Selma Stern, *Karl Wilhelm Ferdinand*, p. 307.

de l'Allemagne et contribueroit mieux que toute autre à la sûreté du Nord de l'Europe.'[76]

The logic of this argument was hard to refute. Control of Hanover would clearly bolster the neutrality policy and remove a constant source of friction from northern Germany. For this reason Haugwitz gave a guarded welcome to LeCoq's suggestions and asked that they be explored further.[77] But, as always, it was Frederick William's attitude that was decisive.[78] Already before the occupation he had signalled that he would not countenance the acquisition of Hanover unless it was part of a general compensation deal enjoying the blessing of Britain and the other great powers.[79] Even once in actual possession of Hanover he was adamant that he would not annex any 'hereditary states (erbliche Staaten)', a Jesuitical formula which entitled Frederick William to a share of the ecclesiastical states while at the same time keeping the Hanoverian annexationists at arm's length. In the end, the Prussian dilemma was resolved by unexpected changes in the broader international scene. The death of Tsar Paul and the subsequent volte face in Russian policy, followed by the first Franco-British peace preliminaries, removed any possible justification for a continued occupation. The Prussian withdrawal was carried out in November 1801, thus bringing the annexation debate to an abrupt close.

The evacuation brought some temporary relief to Prussia; the Hanoverian problem itself remained unresolved. Within fifteen months, changes in the broader European political scene once again presented Prussian politicians with unenviable choices. The renewed outbreak of war between France and Britain in 1802–3 thrust Hanover back into the orbit of potential French military action. In early May 1803 Napoleon dispatched General Duroc to Berlin with the task of sounding out the likely Prussian reaction to a French occupation of Hanover.[80] The result was an acrimonious debate about the wisdom of forestalling a French invasion of Hanover by a Prussian occupation. Haugwitz, Möllendorf,

---

[76] 'Note remise le 13 avril 1801 au Comte Panin par le Colonel de le Coq' (copy), St Petersburg, GStA Rep. 92 *Schöll* 21, fo. 43. See also Ulmann, 'Preussen, die bewaffnete Meeresneutralität und die Besitznahme Hannovers', p. 261.

[77] Brandes, 'Hannover in der Politik der Großmächte', pp. 242–3; Ulmann, 'Preußen, die bewaffnete Meeresneutralität und die Besitznahme Hannovers', p. 266.

[78] Ibid., p. 267.

[79] 'Esquisse d'un arrangement préalable et éventuel à conclure entre S.M. le roi de Prusse et la République française . . . ' (copy), February 1801, GStA Rep.92 *Schöll* 21, fo. 47; Lucchesini instruction, 10.7.1801, Berlin, in Bailleu (ed.), *Preussen und Frankreich*, II p. 50.

[80] See now Philip Dwyer, 'Duroc diplomate. Un militaire au service de la diplomatie napoléonienne', *Le Souvenir Napoléonien*, 58 (1995), 21–38.

Schulenburg, Hohenlohe, Struensee and Rüchel were among those pressing for a pre-emptive strike;[81] Beyme, Lombard and Köckritz counselled against. The arguments against tolerating a French presence in Hanover were as strong as they had ever been: the need to keep the French out of northern Germany, the likely effect on the smaller German princes, the commercial losses which would follow the resulting British blockade, and so on. In the end, as ever, it was Frederick William's attitude which was decisive and it was now that the legacy of the events of 1801 proved particularly debilitating. Having had his fingers comprehensively burnt some two years earlier, the Prussian monarch was loath to expose himself over Hanover again.[82] Matters were not helped by the attitude of the Hanoverians themselves,[83] who were plainly divided as to whether they preferred a temporary French occupation to a potentially permanent Prussian one; this did not prevent them from subsequently execrating the Prussians for not coming to their aid. All Haugwitz's attempts to secure Russian and Hanoverian agreement for a new Prussian occupation petered out in the face of royal caution and Hanoverian suspicion.[84] The only positive move to emerge from Berlin was a futile attempt to head off the Franco-British split through a mediation effort.[85]

In May 1803 French troops took possession of Hanover, virtually unopposed. At a blow the geopolitics of northern Germany was utterly transformed. As early as March 1803, Haugwitz had warned against an 'occupation precipitée d'Hannovre par les trouppes françaises'.[86] Subsequently, he lamented that the French occupation of Hanover made a nonsense of the policy of disengagement in the west. If hitherto the argument had been that 'il falloit éviter autant que possible tout *contact de frontières* [original italics]', there was now not only 'un contact de province', but 'ce sont des armées françoises qui se trouvent dans le

---

[81] Ford, *Hanover and Prussia*, p. 301; Haugwitz to Frederick William III, 4.6.1803, Berlin, in Bailleu (ed.), *Preussen und Frankreich*, II, p. 153.

[82] Frederick William to Haugwitz, 9.6.1803, Ansbach, in Bailleu (ed.), *Preussen und Frankreich*, II, p. 160; Ulmann, *Russisch-preussische Politik*, p. 3; Gerhard Aengenyndt, 'Die Okkupation des Kurfürstentums Hannover durch die Franzosen im Jahre 1803', *Zeitschrift des historischen Vereins für Niedersachsen* 87 (1922), 40; Ulmann, 'Preußen, die bewaffnete Meeresneutralität und die Besitznahme Hannovers', 256.

[83] Günther Sieske, *Preussen im Urteil Hannovers, 1795–1806. Ein Beitrag zur Geschichte der politischen Publizistik in Niedersachsen* (Hildesheim, 1959), p. 36 and *passim*.

[84] Ford, *Hanover and Prussia*, pp. 290, 299, 301; Aengenyndt, 'Die Okkupation des Kurfürstentums Hannover durch die Franzosen im Jahre 1803', 57–8.

[85] Instruction for Lucchesini, 6.5.1803, Berlin, in Bailleu (ed.), *Preussen und Frankreich*, II, p. 142.

[86] Haugwitz to Lucchesini, 26.3.1803, Berlin, GStA Rep. 92 *Lucchesini* 31, fo. 180.

centre de la monarchie'.[87] This left Prussia at the mercy of a future Franco-Russian split, which would almost certainly lead to a struggle for Hanover. Indeed, to quote the dramatic description of Friedrich von Cölln, the French presence in Hanover constituted a threat aimed at the 'heart' of the Prussian state.[88] Even more serious was the risk that Napoleon might annex the electorate permanently; this threatened to complete the encirclement of Prussia still further. 'La France garder l'Hannovre!' wrote Lombard, 'Pressés à l'Orient et au Midi comme nous le sommes, il ne nous faudrait plus que cela. On peut en dépouiller l'Angleterre, mais en enrichir sa rivale, c'est que le roi ne peut prévoir.'[89] Finally, there was the considerable loss of Prussian prestige, a point not lost on the wary smaller German princes or on the enormous pamphlet literature spawned by the French occupation.[90]

If Prussian policy in northern Germany wished to be more than a 'chimera', the removal of the French from Hanover was essential. This was pointed out by Baron Brockhausen, the envoy to Saxony, in a blistering memorandum in early 1804.[91] As early as August 1803, Lombard was sent to Napoleon at Brussels. Despite strong initial scepticism, Napoleon convinced him that a satisfactory arrangement concerning Hanover could be reached. His optimism soon evaporated; the French stayed put. There followed many futile Prussian initiatives to persuade the French to evacuate Hanover, or at the very least to limit the size of their garrison.[92] As outright evacuation became more and more improbable, the Prussians turned to other stratagems. One of these was the scheme to acquire the electorate through exchange. To this end Frederick William finally dropped his long-standing moral objections and agreed to the sacrifice of his Westphalian territories in return for Hanover at a general peace agreement. The geopolitical justification for such a change of course was outlined by Lombard. 'Fatigué des éternelles sollicitudes que la position géographique de ses états fait naître pour la conservation de la paix', he wrote, 'il [Frederick William] revient

[87] Haugwitz to Lucchesini, 8.6.1803, Berlin, GStA Rep. 92 *Lucchesini* 31, fo. 186.
[88] Cölln, *Vertraute Briefe*, I, p. 165.
[89] Lombard to Lucchesini, 17.12.1803, no place, in Bailleu (ed.), *Preussen und Frankreich*, II, p. 226.
[90] E.g. GStA Rep. XI 140.Braunschweig-Lüneburg.49.1, *Acta betrf. die französische Okkupation von Hannover, Bremen.* Vol. I: *1803 April–Dezember.*
[91] Brockhausen memorandum, 13.4.1804, Berlin, GStA Rep. 92 *Friedr. Wilh.d.Dritte* B.VI.15, fo. 2.
[92] Instruction for Lucchesini, 18.6.1803, Berlin, in Bailleu (ed.), *Preussen und Frankreich*, II, p. 169; Haugwitz memorandum, 3.11.1803, Berlin, ibid., p. 212, Talleyrand to Laforest, 30.11.1803, Paris, ibid,, p. 221.

à des idées qui lui ont répugné sept ans.'[93] Another exercise in damage limitation was the attempt to bind French hands with regard to the future ownership of the electorate. An agreement to the effect that France would not dispose of Hanover without previously consulting Prussia, even reached draft stage in December 1803; Frederick William justified this request with reference to 'la position géographique de la Prusse' which rendered the future of the electorate more important to her than to any other state.[94] Yet another tactic was the idea of bribing the French to leave Hanover with a substantial indemnity.[95]

By the autumn of 1804, however, the French were still firmly in possession of Hanover, and the threat this posed to Prussian security was no less acute than it had been twelve months before. This prompted the new foreign minister, Count Hardenberg, to put forward a novel proposal: Prussian troops should take possession of Hanover *en dépôt* until its fate was settled at a general peace.[96] At first sight, the plan appeared to kill several birds with one stone. It gave no offence to the Russians or British; it removed the French peacefully from northern Germany and thus held out the prospect of maintaining the neutrality zone, even in the face of a new continental coalition against Napoleon; it might well attract the French, because it allowed them to withdraw their substantial garrison there for operations elsewhere; finally, it left open the possibility of an eventual acquisition of Hanover by exchange at a general peace. Unfortunately, the French turned the offer down. They rejected the neutralisation of northern Germany as insufficient recompense for the surrender of Hanover. Instead, they used the resulting contacts with Prussia to suggest a French alliance in return for the electorate. As matters stood in Berlin in the autumn of 1804, this plan had no chance of success, but the themes thereby opened up were to figure prominently in the debates of the turbulent years ahead.

Hanover was not the only focus of Prussian sensitivities. Many headaches were caused by the problem of Swedish Pomerania, which bordered on Prussian Pomerania to the north of the monarchy. The difficulty here lay in the unpredictable and irrational behaviour of the Swedish monarch, Gustavus IV. His inflexibly legitimist stance against the new regime in France threatened to provoke a French response and thus destabilise the existing tranquillity of that corner of Germany.

[93] Lombard to Hardenberg, 2.10.1804, Potsdam, ibid., p. 296.
[94] Instruction for Lucchesini, 15.12.1803, Berlin, ibid., p. 225.
[95] Haugwitz to Lucchesini, 15.11.1803, Berlin, GStA Rep. 92 *Lucchesini* 31, fo. 19.
[96] Laforest to Talleyrand, 16.10.1804, Berlin, in Bailleu (ed.), *Preussen und Frankreich*, II, p. 297; Hardenberg to Lucchesini, 22.10.1804, Potsdam, ibid., p. 306; Hardenberg to Lucchesini, 7.9.1804, Berlin, ibid., p. 291.

Equally serious was the danger of Russian troops using Pomerania as a base for a future war of coalition against France, with similar results.[97] The breach between France and Sweden in September 1804 was therefore the cause of considerable concern in Berlin; Lombard spoke of Frederick William's 'chagrin de voir sa tranquillité compromise par les Don-Quichottades du roi de Suède'.[98] A projected pre-emptive occupation of Pomerania was only called off in the face of strong Russian protests. But Hanover remained the primary focus of Prussia's geopolitical fears. Hanover was, in the memorable words of Kurt von Raumer, the 'neuralgic spot' of Prussian foreign policy.[99] In short, the obsession with Hanover both reflected and brought into sharp relief the numerous concerns of Prussian policy: the maintenance of the north German neutrality zone; the fear of a Franco-Russian breach; and the need for the consolidation of the far-flung possessions of the Prussian monarchy.

Prussia and her neighbours (1): the French threat

L'Europe et avec elle la Prusse ne connait qu'un seul ennemi. Une seule calamité afflige la terre; un seul danger par conséquent menace la prusse. C'est sur elle aussi que pèse la puissance gigantesque de la France.[100]

'When France has a cold', Metternich remarked, 'all Europe sneezes.' Ever since the early 1790s, events in France had decisively moulded European politics. At the outset, European concern was for the contagious nature of revolutionary ideology; by the end of the decade this had metamorphosed into a terror of French hegemony. It was French power, not French ideas, that Europe really feared.

The Prussia of Frederick William III was no exception. One of his dead father's last dispatches had spoken of France as 'une puissance qui, par l'étendue des ses conquêtes et surtout par la perspective dangereuse qu'offrent sa conduite et ses principes, doit exciter une attention générale';[101] it was not long before the freshly crowned king was to come around to the same view. Indeed, a highly symbolic encounter between

---

[97] Ulmann, *Russisch-preussische Politik*, p. 129.
[98] Lombard to Hardenberg, 2.10.1804, Potsdam, in Bailleu (ed.), *Preussen und Frankreich*, II, p. 295.
[99] Raumer, *Deutschland um 1800*, p. 187.
[100] Haugwitz memorandum, 15.1.1799, Berlin, in Bailleu (ed.), *Preussen und Frankreich*, I, p. 271.
[101] Instruction for Sandoz, 2.10.1797, Berlin, ibid., p. 153.

the old and new worlds took place at the ceremony of homage – *Huldigungsfeier* – for the young monarch in July 1798. Participants were unsettled by the dramatic arrival of the Abbé Sièyes, the infamous regicide and firebrand, now French ambassador to Berlin. Clad in a tricolour toga of white, red and blue, Sièyes struck a posture of severe classical republican virtue which went to the very heart of the involved and deferential ritual taking place around him. It was, in the words of Friedrich August von der Marwitz, who observed the scene as a young man, 'a terrible omen of the time (*Ein schreckliches Omen der Zeit*)'.[102] In some ways, however, Sièyes was already a man of the past. A new force was about to make itself felt on the European stage. 'Qu'un homme de génie et de caractère paraisse', the Prussian ambassador in Berlin, Sandoz-Rollin, had predicted in early 1797, 'et tout sera asservi.'[103] Towards the end of that year, Napoleon Bonaparte had carried out his coup of Fructidor against the Directory; by the end of 1799 he was in undisputed control of France. Incredibly, Sandoz-Rollin's first assessment of Napoleon spoke of his 'goût pour les lettres et la philosophie et son besoin de repos'.[104] This conceit did not last long. Far from bringing the expansionist policy of the Directory to an end, the advent of Napoleon merely ushered in a new phase in the French drive for hegemony in Europe.

Neither the contest with Revolutionary France, which had just ended, nor the struggle against Napoleon, which was about to begin, was primarily about ideology.[105] Contrary to widespread belief, Prussia's initial participation in the war of the First Coalition was not motivated by fear of revolution.[106] Indeed, in the same year as the outbreak of

---

[102] Meusel (ed.), *Friedrich August von der Marwitz*. Vol. I: *Lebensbeschreibung* (Berlin, 1908), p. 153.

[103] Sandoz report, 12.1.1797, Paris, in Bailleu (ed.), *Preussen und Frankreich*, I, p. 110.

[104] Sandoz reports of 11.12.1797, 14.12.1797 and 3.1.1798, Paris, ibid., pp. 163, 165, 167.

[105] See also more generally the insightful observations of Winkler, 'Gesellschaftsform und Außenpolitik', p. 344. Scott and Mackay's contention that 'international relations acquired a new ideological dimension', in which the idea that the war against France was 'a war between conflicting views of society and of political organisation . . . supplemented, though never completely replaced' traditional *raison d'état* is less true for Prussia than perhaps for other European powers, *The rise of the great powers, 1648–1815* (London and New York, 1983), p. 273.

[106] Misleading in this respect are: Ernst Wangermann, 'Preußen und die revolutionären Bewegungen in Ungarn und den österreichischen Niederlanden zur Zeit der Französischen Revolution', in Büsch and Neugebauer-Wölk (eds.), *Preußen und die revolutionäre Herausforderung seit 1789*, p. 85; Steffens, 'Rheingrenze und territoriale Entschädigungsfrage', 151; Heinz Gollwitzer, 'Ideologische Blockbildung als Bestandteil internationaler Politik im 19. Jahrhundert', *HZ*, 201 (1965), 310–11; Bruno Bauer, *Der Einfluß Frankreichs auf die preussische Politik und die Entwicklung*

revolution in France, Prussia had sabotaged the *Reichsexekution* against the rebels in Liège, not because of any ideological common ground, but in order to embarrass the Austrians.[107] Throughout 1789–90, Prussia continued to act according to the primacy of foreign policy. Far from recoiling at the idea of European internal unrest, she actively encouraged it in the Habsburg lands, especially Galicia, Belgium and Bohemia. As for the Revolution in France, this was welcomed on the grounds that it brought the long-standing Franco-Austrian alliance to an end.[108] It was only after the quarrel with Austria was patched up at the Treaty of Reichenbach in 1790, that Prussia turned her attention westwards. Despite a great deal of legitimist rhetoric, the chief motivation here was hope of territorial gain at the expense of the rescued Louis XVI.[109] The Prussians expected the invasion of France to be a richly rewarded walkover – a 'promenade to Paris (*Spaziergang nach Paris*)' in the words of Schulenburg.[110] But once the sobering reality of war against the Revolutionary French had sunk in, ideological imperatives receded.

Just as the original decision to intervene was largely unrelated to ideological considerations, the Prussian disengagement from the war after 1793 reflected a changed perception, not of the French Revolution as such, but of Prussia's own foreign political interests. A severe financial crisis,[111] the collapse of the *rapprochement* with Austria and the prospect of extensive and relatively bloodless gains in the east led Prussian statesmen to break off the campaign in the west and join Russia in the

---

des preussischen Staates. Dargestellt an den Bündnissen, Verträgen und gegenseitigen Beziehungen (Hanover, 1888/reprint Aalen, 1969), p. 143. Even the usually surefooted Günter Birtsch, 'Revolutionsfurcht in Preußen 1789 bis 1794', in Büsch and Neugebauer-Wölk (eds.), *Preußen und die revolutionäre Herausforderung nach 1789*, pp. 89–91, is rather too quick to see ideological factors at work in the intervention against France. A major offender is Kurt Holzapfel, 'Intervention oder Koexistenz. Preussens Stellung zu Frankreich 1789–1792', *ZfG* 25 (1977), 787–802, esp. 794–7. This study is well-grounded in MSS material, but heavily weighed down with concessions to the *Zeitgeist*.

107 Friedrich Carl Wittichen, *Preussen und die Revolutionen in Belgien und Lüttich 1789–1790* (Göttingen, 1905); Möller, 'Primat der Aussenpolitik, pp. 65–81; Monika Neugebauer-Wölk, 'Preußen und die Revolutionen in Lüttich. Zur Politik des Christian Wilhelm von Dohm, 1789/90', in Büsch and Neugebauer-Wölk (eds.), *Preußen und die revolutionäre Herausforderung seit 1789*, betrays considerable uneasiness with the concept of the primacy of foreign policy.

108 Bourel, 'Zwischen Abwehr und Neutralität', p. 48.

109 Kurt Heidrich, *Preussen im Kampfe gegen die französische Revolution bis zur zweiten Teilung Polens* (Stuttgart and Berlin, 1908), *passim*; Aretin, *Heiliges römisches Reich*, I, p. 262; Aretin, 'Deutschland und die Französische Revolution', p. 14.

110 Aretin, *Das Reich*, p. 362.

111 Real, 'Die preussischen Staatsfinanzen, 53–100; Albert Naudé, 'Der preußische Staatsschatz unter König Friedrich Wilhelm II und seine Erschöpfung', *FBPG*, 5, (1892), 205–6.

partition of Poland. One Marxist historian described this as the triumph of the narrow socio-economic interests of the Prussian nobility over international class solidarity.[112] In fact, it was the triumph of a narrow, but entirely coherent, Prussian state interest over the supposed need for international solidarity against French hegemony. Nor is it true to say that Prussian politicians were in fear of French-sponsored internal unrest.[113] Certainly, there was some concern about the infiltration of French principles; one of the purposes of the neutrality line was to keep out revolutionary ideas[114] and to preserve northern Germany from being *sansculottisés*.[115] In no sense, however, was Prussian policy primarily driven by the threat of revolution. When in April 1798, Haugwitz justified the surrender of the left bank of the Rhine by referring to the need to keep out 'der leider sehr um sich greifenden Neuerungsgrund-sätzen',[116] he was merely supplying a *post-hoc* ideological rationalisation for a geopolitically inspired decision. Alvensleben's remark that he was in danger of becoming a pauper through the loss of his estates in the Altmark was a transparent rhetorical device to bolster his demand for a withdrawal in the west;[117] he had opposed the intervention from the very beginning, long before there was any prospect of a French invasion of Germany.

The opposition of Alvensleben, as of many other Prussian statesmen, to the war with France had nothing to do with narrow class interests. Unlike seemingly 'doctrinaire' opponents of the Revolution, such as Schulenburg and Bischoffwerder, Alvensleben regarded the contest as 'une guerre qui nous ne concerne pas'.[118] Even the unreconstructed reactionary Wöllner, whose anti-revolutionary credentials were beyond doubt, rejected intervention.[119] Throughout the 1790s, there was thus no direct or necessary link between ideological preferences and foreign-political attitudes towards France. Nor did this change with the accession of Frederick William III. Certainly, there was widespread hatred of

---

[112] Holzapfel, 'Intervention oder Koexistenz?', p. 801; Kurt Holzapfel, 'La Prusse avant la paix de Bâle. Le torpillage du traités de subsidies de la Haye par le "parti prussien de paix" (1794–1795)', *Annales Historique de la Revolution Française*, 56 (1984), 238–9.

[113] Moritz, *Preussen und der Kosciuzko-Aufstand*.

[114] Biro, *German policy of Revolutionary France*, II, pp. 603–4; Finckenstein to Haugwitz, 22.2.96, Berlin, in Bailleu (ed.), *Preussen und Frankreich*, I, p. 53.

[115] Haugwitz memorandum, 30.1.97, Berlin, in Bailleu (ed.), *Preussen und Frankreich*, I, p. 113.

[116] Steffens, 'Rheingrenze und territoriale Entschädigungsfrage', p. 164.

[117] Moritz, *Preussen und der Kosciuzko-Aufstand*, pp. 127–8.

[118] Holzapfel, 'Intervention oder Koexistenz?', 789.

[119] Friedrich von Oppeln-Bronikowski, *Abenteurer am preußischen Hofe 1700–1800* (Berlin, 1927), p. 157; Max Lehmann, 'Wöllner und die auswärtige Politik Friedrich Wilhelms II', *HZ*, 62 (1889), 285–6.

Sièyes, 'le démon de la Révolution',[120] but there is no evidence beyond Sièyes's own paranoia that it seriously affected Prussian policy. In any case, fear of revolution could cut both ways. This was shown by Alvensleben when he argued that a successful counter-revolutionary crusade against France would require such fundamental changes to Prussian society and the armed forces as to amount to a revolution in itself;[121] given his previous opposition to the war, one suspects that this was yet another rhetorical flourish. Nor did the rise of the Kabinett introduce a significant class factor in Prussian decision-making. While it is true that the bourgeois councillors were ideologically more sympathetic to France, they were no more or less pro-French in foreign policy than their noble counterparts.[122]

In short, as far as Prussia was concerned, the contest with France was no *Weltanschauungskrieg*. Equally importantly, it was no longer regarded as such by the French themselves either. The commitment to help revolutionaries worldwide, issued during the heady days of spring 1792, was revoked by Danton in the following year. This did not go unnoticed. 'On n'a pas ici l'intention d'insurger les peuples de l'Allemagne', Sandoz Rollin reported from Paris.[123] Even if Sièyes's personal preference was for the *républicanisation* of Prussia,[124] his instructions were to achieve an alliance with Frederick William. The Prussians in turn gave no encouragement to the numerous French émigrés in Berlin pressing for a Bourbon restoration. 'Leur crédit', the French ambassador noted with satisfaction, 'est entièrement nul dans les affaires publiques.'[125] Very soon, however, it became clear that the generalised danger of French-sponsored internal unrest had simply given way to a far greater threat: the radical hegemonic pretensions of France. When French armies operating in southern Germany were instructed to cooperate with the local princes, rather than raise the populace against them, this might be welcome in

120 'Extrait d'un Bulletin secret de Paris', *c.* 2.6.1798, in Adler-Bresse, *Sièyes et le monde allemand*, II, p. 311; Dominique Bourel, 'Un régicide ambassadeur à la cour des Hohenzollern', in Hervé Brouillet (ed.), *Contribution à l'histoire de la Révolution et de l'Empire* (Baden-Baden, 1989), pp. 277–286, especially pp. 280–1.
121 Alvensleben memorandum, 12.5.1798, Berlin, in Bailleu (ed.), *Preussen und Frankreich*, I, p. 200.
122 Misleading on this point is Kurt Eisner, *Das Ende des Reichs: Deutschland und Preußen im Zeitalter der großen Revolution* (Berlin, 1907), p. 227.
123 Sandoz report, 7.1.1797, Paris, in Bailleu (ed.), *Preussen und Frankreich*, I, p. 108.
124 See Sièyes to Talleyrand, 29.8.1798, Berlin, in Bailleu (ed.), *Preussen und Frankreich*, I, p. 487 for Sièyes's *plan de républicanisation*; Adler-Bresse, *Sièyes et le monde allemand*.
125 Caillard report, 28.3.1797, Berlin, in Bailleu (ed.), *Preussen und Frankreich*, I, p. 457.

itself;[126] when it was coupled with the obvious intention of eliminating Prussian influence in the south, there was palpable alarm in Berlin. Equally serious was the recourse to the doctrine of the so-called 'natural limits' of France, the drive to secure safe borders on the Rhine, Alps and Pyrenees.[127] By reactivating the expansionist legacy of Louis XIV, which had remained dormant throughout the later Bourbon period, the Directory issued a direct challenge not only to the integrity of the Holy Roman Empire as a whole, but also to the integrity of those states, including Prussia, which held land on the left bank of the Rhine. Prussia responded to this, as we have seen, with a policy of disengagement in the west. Yet under Napoleon French ambitions revealed themselves to be more extensive still than those of the Directory. At the outset of his rule, France already held Holland, Belgium, the left bank of the Rhine and much of north-western Italy. Within two years Napoleon had added Switzerland and Lombardy and showed no signs of letting up.

In Berlin, the extent of the French threat was being registered with increasing disquiet. It was only in early 1799, however, that the full impact of Napoleon on Prussian policy became apparent. In the debate precipitated by the war of the Second Coalition, the main concern of Prussian statesmen was the potentially unlimited nature of French power; this interacted with an underlying – but subordinate – ideological prejudice. The resulting tension between *Realpolitik* and *Weltanschauung* was most evident in the arguments of Haugwitz. On the one hand he condemned the French Revolution as the 'eruption d'un volcan qui embrace aujourd'hui l'Europe' which threatened to 'alarmer le repos de l'Europe'. On the other hand, he stressed that Prussia's aim could only be to 'retrouver l'équilibre que la révolution française et ses progrès alarmants ont menacé de renverser de fond en comble'. It was clearly 'la puissance gigantesque de la France' which worried Haugwitz, not the Revolution itself; this fear prompted him to advise joining the coalition

---

[126] Volker Press, 'Warum gab es keine deutsche Revolution? Deutschland und das revolutionäre Frankreich, 1789–1815', in Dieter Langewiesche (ed.), *Revolution und Krieg. Zur Dynamik historischen Wandels seit dem 18. Jahrhundert* (Paderborn, 1989), p. 80.

[127] Biro, *German policy of Revolutionary France*; Max Braubach, 'Frankreichs Rheinpolitik im Zeitalter der französischen Revolution', *Archiv für Politik und Geschichte* 5 (1927), 172–86, exaggerates the continuity with the *ancien régime*; Eckhard Buddruss, 'Die Deutschlandpolitik der Französischen Revolution zwischen Traditionen und revolutionärem Bruch', in K. O. von Aretin and K. Härter (eds.), *Revolution und konservatives Beharren. Das Alte Reich und die Französische Revolution* (Mainz, 1990), pp. 145–54, and Eckhard Buddruss, *Die französische Deutschlandpolitik, 1756–1789* (Mainz, 1995), are definitive. On the doctrine of 'natural frontiers' see now Peter Sahlins, 'Natural frontiers revisited. France's boundaries since the seventeenth-century', *AHR*, 95, 5 (1990), 1423–51.

against France.[128] Throughout the first eight months of 1799, Haugwitz rehearsed the arguments in favour of action. In May he called upon Prussia to cooperate with Britain and Russia before France had 'consolidé son ouvrage gigantesque' and to suppress 'l'ennemi de tout ordre social'.[129] Two months later Haugwitz repeated his demand that 'the European balance, which has been disturbed by the French Revolution and has only just been threatened with complete upheaval, be restored, and with it the prospect of future peace'.[130]

These arguments found widespread approval among Prussian politicians. One by one senior figures came out in favour of joining the coalition against France. The Duke of Brunswick spoke of the need to return France to 'a firm form of government';[131] his real concern, however, was the 'nécessité de s'opposer avec efficacité au torrent dévastateur qui menace de tout envahir'.[132] General Rüchel went so far as to proclaim that 'Revolutionary France in its subversive manifestation is a threat to the whole of humanity'.[133] Others, such as Zastrow, referred to France as the 'common enemy of all monarchies'.[134] Even Lombard took a – momentarily – rather apocalyptic view of the French threat. 'L'ancienne politique n'existe plus', he wrote, 'Les opinions les plus saintes d'autrefois sont aujourd'hui des préjugés gothiques. Cette vieille haine contre l'Autriche, cette jalousie contre la Russie, cette existence en Empire, tous ces phantômes disparaissent devant une considération plus puissante, et il n'y a plus dans ce moment que deux rivaux en présence: la France et l'Europe.'[135] It was, Lombard stressed, a question of *vaincre ou mourir*; curiously, though, he did not expressly recommend joining the coalition. There were, moreover, many Prussians who were still very much in the grip of the old Gothic prejudices. One of these was General Tempelhoff, who warned against the complete elimination of France as

---

[128] Haugwitz memorandum, 15.1.1799, Berlin, in Bailleu (ed.), *Preussen und Frankreich*, I, pp. 266–272.

[129] Haugwitz memorandum, 5.5.1799, Berlin, ibid., p. 285.

[130] Haugwitz memorandum, mid-July, 1799, ibid., p. 312; Haugwitz memorandum, late-August 1799, Berlin, ibid., p. 331: 'das durch die Französische Revolution gestörte und noch vor kurzem mit dem gänzlichen Umsturz bedrohte Gleichgewicht von Europa wiederherzustellen und dadurch den Frieden für die Zukunft zu sichern'.

[131] Brunswick memorandum, 25.8.1799, ibid., p. 327: 'eine feste Regierungsform'.

[132] As reported by Chevalier Galatin to Baron Reede, 30.4.1798, ibid., p. 545.

[133] Rüchel memorandum, mid-May 1799, ibid., p. 292: 'das revolutionäre Frankreich in seiner boulversierenden Form ist ein allgemeiner Feind der ganzen Menschheit'; see also pp. 294–5.

[134] Zastrow to Frederick William, 27.4.1799, Rep. 92 *Friedr. Wilh. d. Dritte* B.VI.4, fo. 32: 'gemeinsamen Feind aller Monarchien'.

[135] Lombard memorandum, mid-May 1799, in Bailleu (ed.), *Preussen und Frankreich*, I, p. 287.

a great power 'so that Russia and Austria do not oppress the smaller states'.[136] A more prominent opponent of the Second Coalition was Alvensleben. He did not deny the gravity of the French threat, but warned that 'les Français étant déjà au coeur de l'Allemagne, nous serions obligés de nous opposer les premiers au torrent, avant que la Russie ait pris l'idée de faire quelque chose'.[137] It was one thing to be in the vanguard of an avenging European crusade against the Revolution; it was quite another thing to face the full force of French power unsupported. This was also the view of Frederick William, whose innate caution finally decided the debate against the coalition. In the end it was Prussia's uniquely precarious geopolitical situation which ensured Prussia's neutrality. 'Des considérations puissantes, particulières à ma monarchie,' Frederick William told Haugwitz, 'prises surtout de sa position géographique, ne m'ont pas permis de concourir au succès du voeu commun sur le même plan que mes alliés.'[138]

If the ideological dimension to the struggle had been at best of secondary importance during the 1790s, it receded almost entirely after 1800. Haugwitz might make throwaway remarks about the Jacobinical 'freedom-swindle (*Freiheitsschwindel*)',[139] but otherwise his statements are remarkably free of ideological bias. Legationsrath Buch summed up the general feeling when he stressed the impossibility of changing the internal government of France through external intervention.[140] Indeed, the Prussian government was encouraged by the quasi-monarchical character of Napoleon's rule. It explicitly hoped that Napoleon could re-establish a solid government in France and thus 'tranquillise le continent sur les idées subversives de tout ordre social qui guidaient autrefois les gouvernements en France'.[141] 'Bonaparte', Lucchesini reported, 'travaille peu à peu pour la monarchie sous les enseignes

---

[136] Memorandum of General der Artillerie Tempelhoff, 'Gedanken über die Frage: soll Preußen der Coalition gegen Frankreich beitreten?', 21.7.1799, Berlin, in Massenbach, *Memoiren zur Geschichte des preussischen Staates*, III, pp. 91–2: 'damit Rußland und Österreich nicht die kleinen Staaten unterdrücken'.

[137] Alvensleben memorandum, 12.5.1798, Berlin, in Bailleu (ed.), *Preussen und Frankreich*, I, p. 200.

[138] Frederick William to Haugwitz, 21.7.1799, Charlottenburg, ibid., p. 319.

[139] Haugwitz memorandum, 2.4.1802, Berlin, GStA Rep. 92 *Friedr. Wilh. d. Dritte* B.VI.12, unfoliated.

[140] Buch memorandum, 'Was soll aber endlich daraus werden? oder einige Betrachtungen über die jetztige politische Lage von Europa', 28.10.1800, GStA Rep. 92 *Friedr. Wilh. d. Dritte* B.VI.9, unfoliated.

[141] Instruction for Lucchesini, 14–16.10.1800, Berlin, in Bailleu (ed.), *Preussen und Frankreich*, II, p. 5.

républicaines.'[142] By 1801, Haugwitz was prepared to welcome him into the European society of monarchs, to which he *de facto* already belonged.[143] The Prussians were therefore heartened by Napoleon's imperial title which they were among the first to recognise. A reciprocal *Monsieur mon frère* in official communications now became customary.[144]

The hope that Napoleon's firm hand at home would have a calming influence abroad proved shortlived. 'Quelque changement favorable qu'ait subi le gouvernment français en passant des mains de l'anarchie directoriale', Lucchesini warned in July 1801, 'la politique extérieure n'a rien changé des ses plans ambitieux et de ses relations arbitraires.'[145] Indeed, Christian Dohm feared that an internal dynamic was driving France towards external expansion. 'La guerre exterieure', he wrote, 'peut malheureusement être la condition de la paix intérieure; la guerre peut devenir- un besoin des français'; this was a startling departure from the traditional primacy of foreign policy.[146] Prussian worst fears were confirmed when Napoleon strengthened his grip on Italy with the annexation of Piedmont in September 1802. In 1803 he imposed an act of mediation on Switzerland. The distressing occupation of Hanover in the same year thus took place against a background of rampant French expansionism. This was fully appreciated by Prussian statesmen. Some suspected Napoleon of harbouring pretensions to universal monarchy. Lucchesini spoke of him 'recreating Charlemagne', while Clausewitz feared that Napoleon wanted to turn France into a 'second Rome'.[147] Haugwitz railed against Bonaparte's 'continental despotism';[148] Frederick William spoke of his *ambition démesurée*;[149] and even Lombard stressed 'l'intérêt extrême qu'a la Prusse de ne point permettre aux Français de nouvelles extensions'.[150] Yet permit such expansion they did,

---

[142] Lucchesini to Frederick William, 12.1.01, Paris, in Paul Marmottan, 'Lucchesini. Ambassadeur de Prusse à Paris', *RHD*, 43 (1929), 70.

[143] Haugwitz memorandum, 21.5.1801, Berlin, ibid., p. 95; Duroc report, 20–27.3.1803, ibid., p. 132.

[144] E.g. Frederick William to Napoleon, 28.4.1804, Berlin, ibid., p. 273.

[145] Lucchesini report, late July 1801, Paris, ibid., p. 51.

[146] Quotation from Ilsegret Dambacher, *Christian Wilhelm von Dohm. Ein Beitrag zur Geschichte des preußischen aufgeklärten Beamtentums und seiner Reformbestrebungen am Ausgang des 18. Jahrhunderts* (Berne, 1974), p. 377; Olden, *Napoleon und Talleyrand*, p. 91 and *passim* for an ur-Kehrite interpretation of Napoleonic foreign policy.

[147] Clausewitz, 'Historisch-politische Aufzeichnungen 1803–1806', in Rothfels (ed.), *Carl von Clausewitz. Politische Schriften und Briefe*, p. 1; Lucchesini report, 20.7.1801, Paris, in Bailleu (ed.), *Preussen und Frankreich*, II, p. 16.

[148] Ulmann, *Russisch-preussische Politik*, p. 71.

[149] Notes by Frederick William, mid-February 1804, in Bailleu (ed.), *Preussen und Frankreich*, II, p. 245.

[150] Lombard to Hardenberg, 2.10.1804, Potsdam, ibid., p. 295.

and they were to continue doing so for many years. The reason was that fear of French power led to a debilitating urge, not to resist France, but to reach accommodation with her. Resistance was simply no longer an option. Indeed, Massenbach felt that the certainty of defeat in conflict with France was as clear as Pythagoras's theorem.[151] After the fiasco of the second coalition not even Haugwitz advocated defiance. France might be a 'Colossus', he wrote in May 1801, but one should remember that 'si ce torrent déborde, c'est la Prusse ou l'Autriche séparément, ou l'une et l'autre à la fois, qui s'en trouvent menacées les premières et d'une manière effrayante'.[152]

In these circumstances the question of an alliance with France took on a particular importance. The French threat could be an opportunity as well as a danger. If Prussia could enlist France for her compensation demands, then she could steal a march on the Austrians; conversely, there was the danger that the Habsburgs would beat the Prussians into the first place in French affections.[153] Unsurprisingly, the French sought to capitalise on this by seeking an alliance with Prussia. Initial overtures between 1795 and 1797 petered out,[154] but towards the beginning of Frederick William III's reign the French tried again.[155] At this point, something like a genuine partnership was on offer: Hanover and predominance in northern Germany, in return for a recognition of the 'natural limits' and an offensive and defensive alliance.[156] These proposals won support from those Prussian statesmen who believed that Prussia not only had no choice but to accommodate itself to French power, but actually stood to gain substantially from such an agreement. If Alvensleben pleaded in favour of a French alliance on the cogent grounds that the most immediate military threat to the monarchy would thereby be averted,[157] Prince Heinrich articulated a more general imperative towards cooperation with France. Ideological differences,

---

[151] Massenbach memorandum, November 1803, GStA Rep. 92 *Hardenberg* E3, unfoliated: 'Durch einen Krieg gegen Frankreich eilen wir mit beschleunigter Geschwindigkeit unserem Untergange entgegen. Ich habe diesen Satz (der mir die Klarheit des pythagorischen Theorems zu haben scheint) in zwey anderen Aufsätzen . . . auseinandergesetzt.'

[152] Haugwitz memorandum, 21.5.1802, Berlin, in Bailleu (ed.), *Preussen und Frankreich*, II, p. 93.

[153] See Lucchesini letter, 17.1.02, Paris, in Paul Marmottan, 'Lucchesini', *RHD*, 44, 1 (1930), 451.

[154] Biro, *German policy of Revolutionary France*, I, p. 403; Sandoz report, 8.10.1797, Paris, in Bailleu (ed.), *Preussen und Frankreich*, I, p. 154.

[155] Sandoz report, 25.1.1798, Paris, ibid., p. 168.

[156] Biro, *German policy of Revolutionary France*, II, pp. 891–3.

[157] Alvensleben memorandum, 12.5.1798, Berlin, in Bailleu (ed.), *Preussen und Frankreich*, I, p. 199.

Heinrich argued in September 1798, should not stand in the way of an alliance with France. He accused the partisans of the coalition of confusing 'la moralité de la Révolution' and 'la politique. Cette dernière reste toujours la même.' The eternal verity, he claimed, was that Prussia and France were 'géographiquement placées pour être alliées'. Indeed, Heinrich was certain 'que la vaste monarchie de la France, sa population, ses richesses, sa position géographique relativement à la Prusse ont formées le système politique qui rend l'union nécessaire entre les deux états'.[158] Heinrich's pro-French sentiments thus no longer stemmed from his legendary cultural Francophilia or his alleged revolutionary sympathies. 'Cette France que j'aimais', he had told Frederick William II, 'était celle d'autrefois.' The France of today, he continued, was no more than a 'foreign power' which 'la Prusse est intéressée à la seconder'.[159] Neither Haugwitz nor Frederick William III was impressed with these arguments. Alliance with France was regarded as too risky and the French offers were rejected.[160] Instead, the new monarch reaffirmed his *persévérance inébranable* in the neutrality policy;[161] he expressed concern, however, that France might turn to Austria instead. Throughout 1798, Sièyes pushed unsuccessfully for a Prussian alliance, even going so far as to attempt to bypass the uncooperative Haugwitz through General Zastrow. In 1800 the French finally threw their hands up in despair. Talleyrand was forced to recognise that the 'unbelievable apathy' and 'passivity' of the Prussians was no basis for a fruitful relationship.[162]

After 1803, though, the brutal fact of French power made some kind of an arrangement with Napoleon imperative. Renewed French blandishments came hard on the heels of the occupation of Hanover.[163] Given her worsening international position, Prussia was ill-placed to reject these overtures outright. Compared to the late 1790s, the options had narrowed. There was nobody of consequence who advocated open

---

[158] 'Mémoire sur la crise présente, sur les dangers et les seules ressources qu'elle présente', 12.9.98, in Richard Krauel, *Prinz Heinrich von Preußen als Politiker* (Berlin, 1902), p. 287.

[159] Caillard report, 24.3.1797, Berlin, in Bailleu (ed.), *Preussen und Frankreich*, I, p. 456. On Prince Heinrich's relations with France generally see Raymond Tabournel, 'Le prince Henri de Prusse et le Directoire, 1795–1802', *Revue des Etudes Historiques*, 74 (1908), 5–41.

[160] On the evasive Prussian response to French – and Russian – blandishments see Herman Hüffer, 'Der Feldzug der Engländer und Russen in Holland im Herbst 1799 und die Stellung Preussens', *Historische Vierteljahresschrift*, 5, (1902), 168–73.

[161] Memorandum of Kabinettsministerium, 13.8.1798, Berlin, ibid., p. 202; Haugwitz to Finckenstein, 21.8.1798, Berlin, ibid., p. 233.

[162] Adolf Wohlwill, 'Frankreich und Norddeutschland von 1795–1800', 432.

[163] Lucchesini report, 29.5.1803, Paris, in Bailleu (ed.), *Preussen und Frankreich*, p. 150.

resistance to France. Even such stalwarts as Brockhausen, who condemned the French alliance proposals as *inutile, dangereuse* and *impractible*, did not envisage open defiance of France but merely a more rigorous enforcement of the neutrality zone;[164] Friedrich Gentz, a resister of the first hour, had already been forced into exile and was thus no longer a participant in the high-political debate.[165] But there were no forceful partisans of an all-out French alliance either; that tradition had died with Alvensleben and Prince Heinrich in 1802. Instead, Prussian statesmen huddled in the narrow middle ground left to them. Haugwitz rejected a bilateral alliance with France and tried to explore the idea of a triple defensive alliance between Russia, Prussia and France; a *sine qua non* would be the evacuation of Hanover.[166] This in turn was rejected by the French. They refused to leave Hanover, insisted on a Prussian guarantee of their Italian gains and demanded that any arrangement use the word 'alliance' explicitly.[167] Yet, as Lombard pointed out, the word 'alliance' was one that Prussia dare not use for fear of offending Russia. Rather unconvincingly, he argued that the tepid understanding on offer from Prussia almost amounted to the same thing – 'c'est bien à peu près celà' – as an alliance.[168] Clearly, not even the indisputable power of France in 1803 was sufficient to motivate Prussia into giving up her cherished neutrality. Acknowledging the futility of further discussions, Frederick William broke off the negotiations in mid-January 1804.[169]

At root, the debate on the French threat was – like all Prussian foreign-political questions – a debate between activists and passivists. Whereas Haugwitz had been prepared to take active measures to confront Napoleon, Frederick William preferred to stick to the policy of strict neutrality and inaction. This, he believed, gave him greater flexibility to respond to events.[170] Prussian policy, as Haugwitz confided to Hardenberg in 1798, thus rested on 'une conduite absolument passive et

---

164 See Brockhausen's memorandum of 13.4.1804, Berlin and Lombard's comments, GStA Rep. 92 *Friedr. Wilh. d. Dritte* B.VI.15, fos. 2–10, fo. 13.

165 For Gentz see Golo Mann, *Secretary of Europe. The life of Friedrich Gentz, enemy of Napoleon* (New Haven, 1946); Paul Sweet, *Friedrich von Gentz. Defender of the old order* (Madison, Wisc., 1941); Alexander von Hase, 'Friedrich von Gentz "Von dem politischen Zustande von Europa vor und nach der Französischen Revolution" (1801) Analyse und Interpretation' (PhD dissertation, University of Erlangen, 1968).

166 Haugwitz memorandum, 12.8.1803, Berlin, in Bailleu (ed.), *Preussen und Frankreich*, II, p. 196; Haugwitz memorandum, 3.11.1803, Berlin, ibid., pp. 210–12; notes of Haugwitz, 10.3.1803, Berlin, ibid., pp. 213–15.

167 Talleyrand to Laforest, 3.12.1803, Paris, ibid., pp. 230–2.

168 Lombard to Lucchesini, 17.12.1803, ibid., p. 226.

169 Notes, mid-January 1804, ibid., p. 233.

170 Frederick William to Haugwitz, 17.7.1799, Charlottenburg, ibid., I, p. 317.

neutre'.[171] In fact, as Haugwitz later pointed out with considerable prescience, a passive policy, far from making Prussia the arbiter of her own destiny, actually left her at the mercy of events. Indeed, he argued that Prussia's geopolitical position forbade such a policy. 'Vu la position intermédiaire de la Prusse', Haugwitz wrote in the summer of 1803,

ayant d'un côté la France active et exigeante dont les troupes se rouvent ou avancent au milieu des ses provinces, de l'autre la Russie avec laquelle elle ne peut se compromettre sans le plus grand risque, ce parti absolument passif est impracticable pour elle; que plus tôt ou tard la force des événements la précipiterait dans les embarras inextricables, et l'obligerait enfin à prendre les armes pour défendre son existence, probablement isolée alors et placée sous les rapports les plus désavantageux.[172]

Prussia and her neighbours (2): Russia, Austria, Great Britain, the Reich and the smaller German states

Russia: 'the mountain of snow'

The geographical location of the Prussian state makes her defence difficult, especially when she is faced by a number of enemies at the same time; in particular, Prussia's situation has been substantially worsened by the fact that Russia, which had previously been 50 miles and more distant, is now in possession of the greater part of former Poland and thus borders directly on Prussia.[173]

If in the west Prussia faced the resurgent ambition of France, in the east she was confronted with the imponderable power of Russia. Ever since the days of Frederick the Great, Prussian statesmen had been gripped by fear of tsarist expansionism.[174] At that time, there was still a comfortable

---

[171] Hardenberg diary, 12.7.98, GStA Rep.92 *Hardenberg* L24, fo. 3.

[172] Haugwitz memorandum, 28.6.1803, Berlin, ibid., pp. 177–8.

[173] Zastrow to Frederick William, 27.4.1799, GStA Rep. 92 *Friedr. Wilh. d. Dritte* B.VI.4, fo. 32: 'Die geographische Lage des Preussischen Staats macht dessen Verteidigung, wenn derselbe mit mehreren Feinden gleichzeitig zu tun hat, ungemein schwierig, besonders aber ist die Lage derselben dadurch beträchtlich verschlimmert worden, daß sich Russland welches ehedem 50 Meilen und drüber von der Preussischen Grenze entfernt war, jetzt in den Besitz des größten Teils des ehemaligen Polens befindet, und dadurch unmittelbar an Preussen angrenzt.'

[174] Oppeln-Bronikowski (ed.), *Friedrich der Große. Das politische Testament von 1752*, pp. 86–7: 'Krieg mit Russland so lange zu vermeiden als eure Ehre es zuläßt.' In general see Wolfgang Stribrny, *Die Russlandpolitik Friedrichs des Großen (1764–1786)* (Würzburg, 1966). See also H. M. Scott, 'Aping the great powers', 286–307, especially 293–4; Claus Scharf, *Katharina II, Deutschland und die Deutschen* (Mainz, 1995), especially pp. 384–5; Werner Gembruch, 'Prinz Heinrich von Preussen, Bruder Friedrichs des Grossen', in Werner Gembruch, *Staat und Heer. Ausgewählte historische Studien zum ancien régime, zur französischen Revolution und zu den Befreiungskriegen*, edited by Johannes Kunisch (Berlin, 1990), p. 229.

buffer of Polish territory separating the two states. Now, after the partitions of the 1790s, Russian armies were poised to strike at the very heart of the Prussian monarchy. 'The most terrible power on earth (*Die furchtbarste Macht der Erde*)', wrote Baron von Schroetter, had now advanced to Prussia's borders.[175] Schroetter was particularly concerned because his administrative bailiwick of East Prussia was now immediately exposed to possible Russian attack. 'The barbarians are driving us into the sea', he wrote, 'but the sea is driving us back against the barbarians (*die Barbaren treiben uns nach dem See, das Meer aber treibt uns gegen die Barbaren zurück*)'. These sentiments were echoed by the Duke of Brunswick. For political reasons, he argued, East Prussia could not simply be abandoned, but its defence had become a military nightmare after the Polish partitions.[176] Prussia was, as LeCoq put it in October 1801, 'hemmed in' by Russian power.[177] Only half of her 500-mile border with Russia lay behind a natural barrier (the Memel river); the rest was open countryside. Prussia's predicament was aggravated by the fact that Russia herself was impregnable. In the words of Massenbach, Prussia was 'incapable of really damaging Russia'.[178] The result was that fear of Russian power came to dominate Prussian decision-making at least as much as the mounting French threat in the west. This was most strikingly demonstrated by an exchange which took place in 1803, in the context of the renewed French search for a Prussian alliance. When Napoleon dismissed Russia as 'cette montagne de neige',[179] Lombard responded with the following vivid image: 'la montagne de neige a de terribles avalanches, et elles roulent des années, sans que la masse de montagne en diminue, et elles peuvent beaucoup engloutir'.[180]

Avoiding conflict was not enough in itself, however. Prussia's geo-political predicament also made it imperative to forestall a Franco-Russian breach; war between these two flanking powers threatened to crush those states, especially Prussia, which lay in between. 'Je ne connaîtrais pas de situation plus pénible', wrote Frederick William in

[175] Quoted in Colmar von der Goltz, *Von Rossbach bis Jena*, p. 245.
[176] 'Ansichten des Herzogs von Braunschweig über die Verteidigung Ostpreußens', in Massenbach, *Memoiren zur Geschichte des preussischen Staates*, III, p. 441.
[177] Le Coq memorandum, 3.10.1801, Potsdam, GStA Rep. 92 *Friedr. Wilh. d. Dritte* B.VI.4, fo. 92.
[178] Undated Massenbach memorandum, 'Über die Anlegung der neuen Festungen und über die ersten Versammlungslager der Reserve-Schlesischen-Süd- und Ost-preußischen Armee', in Massenbach, *Memoiren zur Geschichte des preussischen Staates*, III, p. 299: 'außer Stande, Rußland eigentlich weh thun zu können'.
[179] Lucchesini report, 29.5.1803, Paris, in Bailleu (ed.), *Preussen und Frankreich*, II, p. 150.
[180] Lombard to Lucchesini, 6.6.1803, Fürth, ibid., p. 156.

June 1803, 'que celle ou la Prusse se trouverait si les deux redoutables voisins . . . se trouvaient décidément en opposition de principes'.[181] It was in order to forestall such a painful situation that the Prussians closely monitored the state of Franco-Russian relations and sought, as we have already seen, to mediate between the two powers whenever the occasion presented itself. On the other hand, Prussia's geopolitical exposure meant that an overly intimate Franco-Russian understanding at her expense had to be avoided at all costs. 'Il est de l'intérêt du roi', Frederick William had instructed Lucchesini in October 1800, 'que la réconciliation entre la Russie et la France ait effectivement lieu par son entremise, afin d'affirmir ainsi de plus le système qui lie la première à la Prusse.'[182] But even a Prussian-sponsored *rapprochement* could lead to embarrassing embroilments. This Prussian dilemma was cruelly exposed during the Armed Neutrality of 1800–1. Hardly had the spectre of a Franco-Russian clash in northern Germany receded, than Prussia found herself stampeded by the new Franco-Russian alliance into open conflict with England. 'Russia and France laid down the law for us', wrote Massenbach in 1801. 'If these two powers were united, then Prussia's independence would be no more; if they were divided, then Prussia would be driven either by France against Russia, or by Russia against France.'[183]

To make matters worse, agreement with one of the two flanking powers was not in itself sufficient to guarantee Prussia's security; good relations with *both* were essential.[184] A French alliance was of doubtful use against a Russian invasion in the east; this was not the least important reason why Napoleon's overtures in 1803–4 came to nothing. An agreement with France without Russian approval, Haugwitz claimed, would be 'un monstre en politique'.[185] On the other hand a Russian alliance alone was equally inadequate to fulfil Prussia's security needs. 'Quelque imposante que soit la réunion des deux monarques du nord', Haugwitz had already noted in 1801, 'elle ne suffit pas pour garantir nos frontières ouvertes du côté de la France.'[186] This acute sense of Prussia's

---

[181] Frederick William to Lucchesini, 15.6.1803, Wilhelmsbad, ibid., p. 166.

[182] Instruction for Lucchesini, 14/16.10.1803, Berlin, ibid., p. 4.

[183] Massenbach, *Memoiren zur Geschichte des preussischen Staates*, III, p. 150: 'Rußland und Frankreich schrieben uns das Gesetz vor. Waren diese beiden Mächte vereiniget; so war es um Preußens Selbstständigkeit geschehen. Waren sie entzweiet; so ward Preußen entweder von Frankreich gegen Rußland, oder von Rußland gegen Frankreich geschoben.'

[184] Frederick William to Lucchesini, 24.9.1803, in Bailleu (ed.), *Preussen und Frankreich*, II, p. 203.

[185] Haugwitz memorandum, 3.11.1803, Berlin, ibid., p. 210.

[186] Haugwitz memorandum, 21.5.1801, Berlin, ibid., p. 94.

vulnerability was reflected in the instructions for Baron von der Goltz, ambassador to Russia: 'C'est la Prusse qui par sa situation est destinée à recevoir et à porter les premiers coups.'[187] Russia was quite simply too remote to be of any immediate assistance to Prussia. Already during the debate about the Second Coalition, Alvensleben had stressed that 'nous serions la première victime, car les Français étant déjà au coeur de l'Allemagne, nous serions obligés de nous opposer les premiers au torrent, avant que la Russie ait pris l'idée de faire quelque chose'.[188] 'We will be the *first* victim [of a coalition against France]', Massenbach warned, 'and Russia, as they say in the proverb, will carry home the bride.'[189] But not only was Russia too remote, she was also too unreliable. Prussia would always be at the mercy of a palace revolution. This had already been painfully demonstrated by the sudden death of Paul in 1801 and the subsequent volte face in Russian policy.[190] To add insult to injury, the new Russian Tsar even joined in the call for an immediate evacuation of Hanover; the final humiliation was the Russian offer to mediate between Prussia and Great Britain to end a quarrel which Russia had substantially helped to create.

On the whole Prussia was quite successful in striking the right balance between France and Russia. By 1804, she had survived nearly ten years, two coalitions and an extremely fraught Armed Neutrality without coming to grief. Indeed, after the uncertainties of the turn of the century, Prussian statesmen might have been forgiven for thinking that calmer times lay ahead. While keeping French blandishments at arm's length, Frederick William succeeded in cultivating what Stamm-Kuhlmann has called a 'special relationship' with Alexander; the Russian foreign minister Czartoryski was later to criticise Alexander for seeing in Frederick William a 'personal friend in relations with whom you were bound by personal obligations'.[191] A highly publicised meeting between the two at Memel in June 1802 paved the way for a potentially far-reaching understanding in May 1804. This arrangement amounted to

---

[187] 'Communications que le Comte de Goltz fut chargé de faire à la cour de St Petersburg le 5 avril 1804', GStA Rep. 92 *Hardenberg* L12, fo. 53.

[188] Alvensleben memorandum, 12.5.1798, Berlin, in Bailleu (ed.), *Preussen und Frankreich*, I, p. 200.

[189] Massenbach, 'Betrachtungen über die politisch-militärische Lage in welcher sich Preußen zu Ende des Jahres 1803 befindet', c. November 1803, GStA Rep. 92 *Hardenberg* E3, unfoliated: 'Wir werden das *erste* Opfer . . . und Rußland wird wie man im Sprichwort zu sagen pflegt, die Braut nach Hause führen.'

[190] Ulmann, *Russisch-preussische Politik*, p. 3.

[191] Stamm-Kuhlmann, *König in Preußens großer Zeit*, p. 180; Stephen Scherer, 'Alexander I, the Prussian royal couple, and European politics, 1801–1807', *The Michigan Academician*, 13, 1 (1980), 37–44.

nothing less than a re-founding of the traditional neutrality policy, for by
its terms Prussia and Russia jointly undertook to guarantee the security
of northern Germany. But May 1804 also saw another development
which threatened to shatter the neutrality zone beyond repair. For it
was in that month that Lucchesini first reported the danger of a Franco-
Russian rupture.[192] In Berlin, Hardenberg shrugged off any such
suggestion; he continued to nourish the conceit that an open breach
between the two could be avoided.[193] Once again, developments on the
wider European stage were about to thrust Prussia back into the international limelight.

Prussia and Austria: the persistence of dualism

> There are certain relationships between neighbouring states which
> arise out of their geographical situation, out of the reciprocal
> influence which each has on the security and welfare of the other;
> so long as these states exist, such relationships are by their very
> nature unchangeable . . . Hence, ever since the conquest of Silesia,
> and the resulting circumstances, it has been a necessity for Prussia
> to resist all increases in Austrian power which might make it too
> powerful.[194]

Hatred of Austria, in the graphic words of Friedrich von Cölln, was a
sentiment which Prussians 'sucked in with their mother's milk'.[195]
Thanks to the Silesian wars, this hatred was the most enduring of
Frederick the Great's protean legacy.[196] It was shared by all Prussian
politicians without exception, from such senior statesmen as Haugwitz,

---

[192] Lucchesini report, 17.5.1804, Paris, in Bailleu (ed.), *Preussen und Frankreich*, II,
p. 263.
[193] Hardenberg to Frederick William, 6.6.1804, Berlin, ibid., p. 272; Hardenberg to
Lombard, 22.10.1804, Potsdam, ibid., p. 306.
[194] Massenbach memorandum, 'Über Preußens politische Lage im Anfange des 1790sten
Jahres', in Massenbach, *Memoiren zur Geschichte des preussischen Staates*, III, p. 71:
'Zwischen benachbarten Staaten giebt es gewisse Verhältnisse, die aus ihrer
geographischen Lage, aus dem wechselseitigen Einfluß, den jeder auf des andern
Wohlfahrt und Sicherheit hat, entspringen, die so lange als diese Staaten aufrecht
stehen, ihrer Natur nach unveränderlich sind . . . So ist, seit der Eroberung Schlesiens,
und den daraus in der Folge enstandenen Begebenheiten, für Preußen die
Nothwendigkeit eingetreten, sich allen Vergrößerungen Österreichs, wodurch es zu
sehr überlegen werden könnte, zu widersetzen.'
[195] Cölln, *Vertraute Briefe*, p. 201: 'sie scheinen ihn mit der Muttermilch eingesogen zu
haben'.
[196] Oppeln-Bronikowski (ed.), *Friedrich der Große. Das politische Testament von 1752*:
'Es ist unser Hauptfeind' (p. 69), 'unversöhnliche Feinde' (p. 105), p. 57, 71 and
passim.

Hardenberg and Lombard[197] to peripheral figures such as General Tempelhoff.[198] Nothing could persuade such a figure as Lucchesini, who boasted of having breathed the air of Sanssouci, that Prussian and Austrian interests were anything other than irreconcilable.[199] This hatred, it should be added, was cordially returned by the Austrians.[200] After all, the period immediately preceding, and indeed following, the French Revolution was characterised by determined Prussian attempts to curb the ambitions of Joseph II.[201] The collapse of Austro-Prussian relations after 1795 should therefore come as no surprise; it is the peculiar period of rapprochement leading to the First Coalition which is in need of explanation. Indeed, a strong anti-Austrian animus is detectable among those Prussian generals, such as Kalckreuth and Möllendorf, who initiated the negotiations which eventually led to the separate peace with France.[202] The creation of the neutrality zone led to further friction with the Austrians, who refused to recognise it until 1800. Indeed, during the early period they showed even less respect for the demarcation line than the French did.[203] Suspicion of Austria also surfaced throughout the debate on the Second Coalition.[204] One of the arguments Brunswick had to counter in his plea for action against France was the charge that this would involve Prussia in the defence of Austrian interests.[205] By the end of the 1790s therefore, as the late Volker Press pointed out, the 'laws of German dualism' had won the upper hand again.[206]

[197] For anti-Austrian sentiment in general, see Theodor Bitterauf, 'Studien zur preussischen Politik im Jahre 1805', *FBPG*, 27 (1914), 515; for Hardenberg, see Max Duncker, 'Graf Haugwitz und Freiherr von Hardenberg. Aktenstücke zu den Denkwürdigkeiten des Fürsten von Hardenberg, Band 5', *PJ*, 42 (1878), 571–2; for Lombard and Haugwitz, see Bruno Gaide, 'Der diplomatische Verkehr des Geheimen Kabinettsrats Lombard', p. 27.

[198] Memorandum of Tempelhoff, 'Gedanken über die Frage: soll Preußen der Coalition gegen Frankreich beitreten', July 1799, in Massenbach, *Memoiren zur Geschichte des preussischen Staates*, III, p. 96.

[199] Koser, 'Preußische Politik', p. 475.

[200] 'Instruction für den Grafen Metternich', in A. Fournier, *Gentz und Cobenzl. Geschichte der österreichischen Diplomatie in den Jahren 1801–5 nach neuen Quellen* (Vienna, 1880), p. 214; Enno Kraehe, *Metternich's German policy*. Vol. I: *The contest with Napoleon, 1799–1814* (Princeton, N.J., 1963), p. 29.

[201] See now T. C. W. Blanning, *Joseph II* (London and New York, 1994), pp. 176–85.

[202] Holzapfel, 'Intervention oder Koexistenz', 800.

[203] Biro, *German policy of Revolutionary France*, II, p. 530.

[204] Paul Schroeder, 'The collapse of the Second Coalition', *JMH*, 59 (1987), 244–90.

[205] Brunswick memorandum, 25.8.1799, in Bailleu (ed.), *Preussen und Frankreich*, I, p. 328. Temporary tactical exceptions to this anti-Austrian mood are: Rüchel memorandum, mid-May 1799, ibid., p. 293; Lombard memorandum, mid-May 1799, ibid., p. 287.

[206] Press, 'Warum gab es keine deutsche Revolution?', p. 7.

The persistence of Austro-Prussian dualism transformed what was at one level a struggle about French hegemony in Europe into merely another phase in the longstanding contest for mastery in Germany. At times it almost seemed as if Prussian statesmen were more concerned about the advance of Austrian than of French power in the Reich; the memoranda of Christian Dohm, the enlightened but rabidly Austrophobic Prussian envoy at Rastatt, certainly give that impression.[207] Indeed, the French threat, far from uniting the two German powers, actually set off a scramble for Napoleon's affections.[208] The French, of course, played to these fears. 'Nos désirs sont pour la Prusse', Talleyrand's argument went, 'qu'elle ne nous force pas de rechercher l'Autriche.'[209] One of those Prussian politicians who sought to use the French for a more activist policy against the Austrians was Hardenberg. His attempts to extend the Prussian foothold in southern Germany were plainly anti-Habsburgist.[210] The treaty of 1802, in which France and Prussia joined to curb Austrian ambitions against Bavaria, is another example. But perhaps the most striking instance of the persistence of dualism was the question of the territorial reorganisation of Germany after the loss of the left bank of the Rhine. Having themselves tried to enlist French support for their compensation plans, the Prussians were understandably fearful that the Austrians would strike a deal with Napoleon first.[211] It was vital, wrote Alvensleben in February 1801, that suitable acquisitions be made 'so as not to lose sight of Prussia's interests and to maintain the equilibrium in Germany'.[212] Hardenberg and Haugwitz spoke of the need to *contrebalancer* Austria through secularisations or other suitable compensations;[213] one Prussian even appealed to Russia to help 'entretenir l'équilibre en Allemagne contre ces projets de la maison d'Autriche'.[214] Prussia, so apparently blind to the growth

[207] Dambacher, *Dohm*, p. 383, 376.
[208] Kabinettsministerium to Frederick William, 13.5.1798, Berlin, in Bailleu (ed.), *Preussen und Frankreich*, I p. 203; Zastrow notes, 12.8.1798, Berlin, ibid., pp. 230–1; Haugwitz memorandum, 12.1.1801, Berlin, ibid., II, p. 17.
[209] Talleyrand to Laforest, 17.3.1803, Paris, ibid., p. 145.
[210] Zierke, *Deutsche Politik Hardenbergs*, p. 76.
[211] Instruction for Sandoz, 4.2.1798, Berlin, in Bailleu (ed.), *Preussen und Frankreich*, I, pp. 170–2; instruction for Lucchesini, 14/16.10.1800, Berlin, ibid., II, pp. 3–4.
[212] Alvensleben memorandum, 26.2.1801, Berlin, GStA Rep. 92 *Lucchesini* 23, fo. 18: 'um den Vorteil Preussens nicht aus den Augen zu verlieren und das Gleichgewicht in Deutschland zu erhalten'.
[213] Hardenberg memorandum, 26.1.1801, Berlin, GStA Rep. 92 *Schöll* 21, fo. 3; 'Rapport addressé le 26 novembre 1802 au roi de Prusse par le comte de Haugwitz' (copy), Berlin, ibid., fo. 78.
[214] 'Note remise par . . . le Colonel de le Coq' (copy), St Petersburg, 7.4.1801, GStA Rep. 92 *Schöll* 21, fo. 41.

of French power in the west, was endowed with the exacting eye of a diamond-cutter when it came to the question of Austrian gains in Germany. Apart from some brief attempts at *rapprochement* between 1801 and 1803,[215] this dualist suspicion endured up to and beyond the collapse of the old Prussia in 1806.

Land *versus* Meer: *Prussia and Great Britain*

Between 1795 and 1806, J. M. Sherwig points out, William Pitt launched no fewer than five missions to Berlin.[216] Their purpose was to win the Prussians for a coalition against France in return for subsidies and generous territorial inducements. Indeed, the centrality of Prussia in Britain's continental strategy is unmistakable.[217] Yet in spite, or perhaps because of this, Anglo-Prussian relations throughout the revolutionary and Napoleonic period were rarely cordial. One of the reasons for this was the ingrained suspicions most Prussians harboured of Britain and British motives. While this feeling never took on the same intensity as hatred of Austria, one can at this stage already identify the themes of later nineteenth-century *Englandhaß*. The acrimonious break up of the Anglo-Prussian coalition in the final stages of the Seven Years War left a legacy which long outlasted the death of Frederick the Great.[218] 'L'expérience de tout ce siècle', Alvensleben claimed of Britain in May 1799, 'doit nous prouver qu'elle ne pense constamment qu'à elle.'[219] There was also a strong intellectual tradition of Anglophobia, represented by figures such as Buchholz and Fichte. They regarded the prospect of Universal Monarchy under Napoleon as preferable to the ravages of a British-

---

[215] Oncken, *Österreich und Preußen im Befreiungskriege*, II, p. 3.

[216] J. H. Sherwig, *Guineas and gunpowder. British foreign aid in the wars with France* (Cambridge, Mass., 1969), p. 347.

[217] Simms, 'Anglo-Prussian relations'; V. R. Ham, 'Strategies of coalition and isolation. British war policy and north-west Europe, 1803–1810' (unpublished DPhil dissertation, University of Oxford, 1977); Sherwig, *Guineas and gunpowder*, pp. 167–9, 172 and *passim*.

[218] Oppeln-Bronikowski (ed.), *Friedrich der Große. Das politische Testament von 1752*, p. 63. H. D. Schmidt, 'The idea and slogan of Perfidious Albion', *Journal of the History of Ideas*, 14 (1953), 604–16; Scott, 'Aping the great powers', 295; Friedrich Carl Wittichen, 'Zur Geschichte der öffentlichen Meinung in Preussen vor 1806', *FBPG*, 23 (1910), 47, 53; anon., 'Preußen und England', *PJ*, 1 (1858); Werner Gembruch, 'Zum England-Bild des Freiherrn vom Stein', in Gembruch, *Staat und Heer*, pp. 534–5; Walther Hubatsch, *Der Freiherr vom Stein und England* (Cologne, 1977).

[219] Alvensleben memorandum, 12.5.1798, Berlin, in Bailleu (ed.), *Preussen und Frankreich*, I, p. 198.

sponsored balance of power in Europe.[220] The only notable exception to this vibrant strain of intellectual Anglophobia was Friedrich Gentz, at this point already in the pay of the British government;[221] his *Englandhaß* was to come later. A particular focus of Prussian resentment was Britain's maritime policies. Britain, it was claimed, exercised a 'despotism over the trade of the continent[s?] (*Despotie über den Continent-Handel*)'.[222] Throughout the struggle against France, British ships reserved the right to stop foreign ships and confiscate suspected contraband. All Prussian attempts to negotiate a less oppressive maritime regime came to nothing.[223] Prussia was not alone in her resentment of British naval high-handedness; similar feelings were also strong not only in Russia, but throughout mainland Europe.[224] Indeed, as far as Britain was concerned, Frederick William even spoke of an *identité d'intérêts* to re-establish *l'équilibre du commerce* between Prussia and France.[225]

Nonetheless, despite all the public and private rhetoric, it would be wrong to see maritime rights as the chief bone of contention between Britain and Prussia. As a power almost entirely without naval ambitions,

---

[220] Werner Gembruch, 'England und Kontinentaleuropa im politischen Denken von Friedrich Buchholz. Ein Beitrag zur Diskussion um die Freiheit der Meere und der kolonialen Expansion in der Napoleonischen Era', in Gembruch, *Staat und Heer*, pp. 277–305; Gärber, 'Politische Revolution und industrielle Evolution: Reformstrategien des preußischen Saint-Simonismus (Friedrich Buchholz)', in Büsch and Neugebauer-Wölk, (eds.), *Preußen und die revolutionäre Herausforderung seit 1789*, pp. 301–29; Theodor Schmalz, *Staatsverfassung Großbritanniens* (Halle, 1806), pp. 233, 276 and *passim*; Roger Dufraisse, 'Die Deutschen und Napoleon im 20. Jahrhundert', *HJ*, 252 (1991), 597–8.

[221] Krauel, 'Die Beteiligung Preussens', p. 201.

[222] Alvensleben memorandum, 26.2.1801, Berlin, Rep. 92 Lucchesini 23, fo. 18; in the same vein the prolonged diatribe of Massenbach, 'Über Preußens politische Lage im Anfange des 1790sten Jahres' in Massenbach, *Memoiren zur Geschichte des preussischen Staates*, III, pp. 72–9; Tempelhoff memorandum, July 1799, in Massenbach, *Memoiren zur Geschichte des preussischen Staates*, III, pp. 100–1; Haugwitz's remarks of May 1803 as quoted in Ulmann, *Russisch-preussische Politik*, p. 71; Krauel, 'Die Beteiligung Preussens', p. 191.

[223] This is covered in some detail by Dwyer, 'Prussia and the Second Armed Neutrality', pp. 40–1. The technical side of maritime affairs is also given an airing in Albrecht Eckhardt, 'Unter Kniphauser Flagge. Zur Neutralitätspolitik des Grafen Bentinck in napoleonischer Zeit (1803–1808), *NJBLG*, 61 (1989), 181–214; Walter Alison Phillips and Arthur H. Reade, *Neutrality: its history, economics and law*. Vol. II: *The Napoleonic period* (Columbia, 1936; reprint New York, 1976), pp. 268, 286, 289.

[224] See Peter Scheibert, '"Quelques changements dans le code maritime". Zur Nachgeschichte der "Bewaffneten Neutralität", 1801–1805', in Peter Classen and Peter Scheibert (eds.), *Festschrift Percy Ernst Schramm zu seinem Siebzigsten Geburtstag von Schülern und Freunden zugeeignet* (Wiesbaden, 1964), II, pp. 145–53; A. D. Harvey, 'European attitudes to Britain during the French Revolutionary and Napoleonic Era', *History*, 63 (1978), 356–66, especially 359–61.

[225] Instruction for Lucchesini, 14–16.10.1800, Berlin, in Bailleu (ed.), *Preussen und Frankreich*, II, p. 5.

maritime rights were very much a secondary concern for Prussia. What did cause Prussian politicians considerable anxiety was Britain's persistent attempts not only to re-create a continental coalition against France, but also to embroil Prussia herself in the struggle. The experience of the First Coalition, its unpaid subsidies and broken promises on both sides, made the Prussians even more sensitive to British blandishments. 'England', Frederick the Great had warned, 'will pay you a subsidy and will regard you as a mercenary whom she can dismiss as soon as you have accomplished the task allotted to you.'[226] All subsequent British attempts to seduce the Prussians into an alliance against France, including a particularly sustained drive during the Second Coalition, came to nothing.[227] Four years later, the British ambassador saw so little chance of obtaining a Prussian alliance, that he did not bother to pass on his government's offer of subsidies.[228] Maritime issues were not even the prime motivation behind Prussia's membership of the Armed Neutrality in 1800–1.[229] It was *one* factor, certainly. The chief purpose, however, was the preservation of good relations between Russia and France; this would both spare northern Germany and help Prussia to make the maximum gains from the *Reichsdeputations-hauptschluss*. At no point did Prussia deliberately seek a confrontation with Britain, she merely accepted it as the lesser of two evils.

Relations with Britain were thus very much subordinate to the general political situation in Europe. A *rapprochement* between France and Russia or a collapse of Franco-British relations had far-reaching consequences for Prussia; the entirely remote quarrel over Malta, for example, led to the French occupation of Hanover and the embarrassments that followed therefrom. 'The inter-connections of politics are now so manifold', wrote Gneisenau, then a junior Prussian officer, 'that no shot may be fired in the Mediterranean without a resulting echo in Germany.'[230] If, in the graphic phrase of Paul Schroeder, the struggle

---

[226] Quoted in Daniel A. Baugh, 'Great Britain's "blue-water" policy 1689–1815', *IHR*, 10, 1 (1988), 54.

[227] Ragsdale, 'Russia, Prussia and Europe', p. 87; 'für Englands Interesse, nicht für Preussens Interesse': Massenbach memorandum, November 1803, GStA Rep. 92 *Hardenberg* E3, unfoliated.

[228] Sherwig, *Guineas and gunpowder*, p. 145.

[229] This is spelt out in Richard Krauel, 'Die Haltung Preussens in Fragen des Seekriegsrechts von 1783–1799', *FBPG*, 24 (1911), 183–226, especially 226; Krauel, 'Die Beteiligung Preußens'; Ulmann, 'Preußen, die bewaffnete Meeresneutralität und die Besitznahme Hannovers', p. 246.

[230] Gneisenau to his wife, 13.5.1801, Erfurt, in Karl Griewank (ed.), *Gneisenau. Ein Leben in Briefen* (Leipzig, 1939), p. 39: 'Die Verkettungen der Politik sind jetzt so mannigfaltig, daß kein Schuß im Mittelländischen Meere geschehen kann, der nicht in Deutschland widerhalle.'

between France and Britain was that between tiger and shark,[231] the Prussian goat could relate more immediately to the former. Of the two hegemonic pretensions, that of France was infinitely more dangerous to Prussia; this made Prussia all the more hostile to British plans for a continental coalition in which Prussia would be the first victim. Whereas the insular power of Britain sought to maintain the balance of power in Europe, while retaining mastery of the seas, Prussia, as a continental power sought only to secure its own survival.[232] This tension was soon to become spectacularly apparent. For in June 1803, in a triumph of hope over experience, the British government authorised the embassy in Berlin to seek an alliance with Prussia.[233] The initiative was stillborn; however, it soon became clear that a new coalition would go ahead, with or without Prussia.

Prussia, the Reich and the smaller German powers

> Il me paroit guère possible que ce fantôme d'organisation qualifié du beau nom de Constitution Germanique puisse être conservé en Entier.[234]

It cannot be said that Prussian statesmen showed any great interest in or respect for the Holy Roman Empire, that venerable bundle of ancient institutions and practices which had provided a framework for political coexistence in Germany since time immemorial. Admittedly, Prussia was probably less quick to surrender the left bank of the Rhine to France than has generally been assumed; Paul Bailleu has long since shown that Frederick William II hoped until the very end that such a move could be avoided.[235] It is equally true that the neutrality zone sheltered the northern half of the Reich from French encroachments. The Hanseatic towns, Bremen, Hamburg and Lübeck even had their independence specifically guaranteed by Prussia.[236] However, this was a by-product of

---

[231] Paul Schroeder, *The transformation of European politics, 1763–1848* (Oxford, 1994), p. 117.

[232] See Brendan Simms, 'Fra *Land* e *Meer*. La Gran Bretagna, la Prussia e il problema del decisionismo (1804–1806)', *Ricerche di Storia Politica*, 6 (1991), 5–34; Roman Schnur, 'Land und Meer – Napoleon gegen England. Ein Kapitel der Geschichte internationaler Politik', in Roman Schnur, *Revolution und Weltbürgerkrieg. Studien zur Ouverture nach 1789* (Berlin, 1983), pp. 33–58.

[233] Hartmut Gembries, 'Das Thema Preußen in der politischen Diskussion Englands zwischen 1792 und 1807' (unpublished PhD dissertation, University of Freiburg, 1988), p. 54.

[234] Hardenberg memorandum, 26.1.1801, Berlin, GStA Rep. 92 *Schöll* 21, fo. 7.

[235] See the views of Paul Bailleu in *Preussen und Frankreich*, I, pp. xxi, xxxiv and *passim*.

[236] Fritz Wiedemann, *Die Aussenpolitik Bremens im Zeitalter der Französischen Revolution, 1794–1803* (Bremen, 1960), p. 71.

Prussia's determination to preserve the security of northern Germany, rather than an attempt to benefit the Reich as a whole; those territories beyond the demarcation line were abandoned to their fate. Indeed, Prussia increasingly withdrew from an active *Reichspolitik* towards the end of the 1790s.[237] She did so, however, not primarily out of hostility for the Reich, but because it was the inevitable consequence of the decisions taken during the compensations debate.

Karl Otmar von Aretin's claim that Frederick William sought to 'destroy' the Roman Catholic territories of the Reich through secularisations at Rastatt may be true;[238] this was not his main object, however. In abandoning southern and western Germany and seeking northern secularisations, the Prussians were making a geopolitical response arising out of the acute French foreign-political threat. The negative consequences for the Reich as a whole were indisputable, but they were also somewhat coincidental. Nor can it argued that Hardenberg's southern policy was an attempt to safeguard broader German interests against the French.[239] Rather, this policy was a transparent attempt to embarrass Austria. In fact, Hardenberg encouraged French incursions into Franconia in the hope of detaching the smaller princes from the emperor.[240] Certainly, neither Hardenberg nor Prussia as whole showed any enthusiasm to take on a 'national' role defending the Reich against French encroachments in the west. His only contribution to the debate about the future of the Reich was to push for a more federal structure which would reduce the influence of the emperor; once again, the anti-Austrian animus is evident. Beyond that, Hardenberg was typical of most Prussian politicians in his contemptuous dismissal of the Reich as a 'phantom'.[241]

There was, however, a price to be paid. At first, the smaller and middling German states scrambled to be admitted to the neutrality zone. Some, such as the electorate of Mainz, the free imperial city of Frankfurt and the principality of Hessen-Darmstadt lay outside of Prussia's self-imposed geopolitical remit and were rejected; Hessen-Darmstadt

---

[237] Karl Härter, *Reichstag und Revolution, 1789–1806. Die Auseinandersetzung des immer-währenden Reichstags zu Regensburg mit den Auswirkungen der Französischen Revolution auf das alte Reich* (Göttingen, 1992), pp. 649–65.

[238] Aretin, 'Deutschland und die Französische Revolution', p. 19.

[239] See the misleading claim by Christian Meyer, *Preußen und Frankreich, 1795–1800* (Munich, 1903), p. 80; also the unusual slip of Bailleu (ed.), *Preussen und Frankreich*, I, p. xv.

[240] Aretin, *Reich*, pp. 471–2.

[241] See Hardenberg memorandum, 26.1.1801, Berlin, GStA Rep. 92 *Schöll* 21, fo. 7 (quoted above, p. 111); Steffens, 'Rheingrenze und territoriale Entschädigungsfrage', pp. 169–70.

appealed against this decision for four years. Even further south, the Hohenzollern principalities in Württemberg appealed to Prussia for help; initially, Hardenberg was happy to exploit them for anti-Austrian purposes in Franconia.[242] Later, many states turned to Prussia for support in their compensation demands.[243] By the turn of the century, however, Prussia's prestige in the *Reich* was in terminal decline. Her policy of disengagement in the south and west forced the smaller powers to leave the Prussian orbit and gravitate towards France.[244] The French for their part, frustrated in their hopes for a full Prussian alliance, turned more and more to the smaller German states.[245] A classic example of this process was the association of tiny lands assembled in the Frankfurt Union, which the Prussians quite rightly interpreted as the result of their failure to protect traditional clients.[246] More distressing for Prussia was the drift of a traditional protégé like Bavaria into alliance with France. At the time of the Second Coalition, Bavaria had unsuccessfully looked to Prussia for protection.[247] The result was a Franco-Bavarian treaty of friendship in 1801; by 1803, in the words of Gmeinwiser, Bavaria had already undertaken a 'fundamental reorientation' towards France which Prussia did nothing to stop.[248] Even such a stalwart supporter as Saxony was unsettled both by the Prussian acquisition of nearby Erfurt[249] and the steady erosion of Prussian power, especially after the occupation of

---

[242] Fritz Kallenberg, 'Die Fürstentümer Hohenzollern im Zeitalter der Französischen Revolution und Napoleons', *Zeitschrift für die Geschichte des Oberrheins*, 111 (1963), 370.

[243] Frederick of Hesse to Hardenberg, 23.8.1804, Hamburg, GStA Rep. 92 *Hardenberg* E2, *Gesuche mehrerer Reichsstände um diesseitige Vermittelung, 1801–1806*, unfoliated.

[244] Eberhard Weis, 'Die außenpolitischen Reaktionen der deutschen Staaten auf die französische Hegemoniepolitik: zwischen Anpassung und Widerstand', in K.O. von Aretin and Gerhard A. Ritter (eds.), *Historismus und moderne Geschichtswissenschaft. Europa zwischen Revolution und Restauration* (Wiesbaden, 1987), pp. 185–200.

[245] Meyer, *Preußen und Frankreich*, p. 88.

[246] Eva Kell, 'Die Frankfurter Union (1803–1806). Eine Fürstenassoziation zur "verfassungsmäßigen Selbsterhaltung" der kleineren weltlichen Adelsherrschaften', *ZfHF*, 18 (1991), 75.

[247] Wilhelm Anders, 'Napoleon Bonaparte und die Beziehungen zwischen Preußen und Bayern. Beiträge zur deutschen Geschichte, vornehmlich im Jahre 1806' (unpublished PhD dissertation, University of Munich, 1921), p. 8; Theodor Santelmann, 'Die Beziehungen zwischen Bayern und Preußen, 1799–1805' (unpublished PhD dissertation, University of Munich, 1906), p. 13; Eberhard Weis, 'Bayern und Frankreich in der Zeit des Konsulats und des ersten Empire (1799–1815)', *HZ*, 237 (1983), 559–95; Eberhard Weis, *Montgelas, 1759–1799. Zwischen Revolution und Reform* (Munich, 1971), pp. 347–8; Montgelas to Prussian diplomat (copy), 5.12.1800, Bayreuth, GStA Rep. 92 *Hardenberg* E1, fo. 9.

[248] Josef Gmeinwiser, 'Die bayerische Politik im Jahre 1805' (unpublished PhD dissertation, University of Munich, 1928), pp. 22, 150.

[249] Fritz Friedrich, *Politik Sachsens, 1801 bis 1803* (Leipzig, 1898), p. 48.

Hanover in 1803.[250] In short, by the beginning of 1804, Prussia's once powerful position among the other German states had collapsed.

Clearly, given the multiplicity of interpretations within the Prussian ruling elite, it would be wrong to see a rigid geopolitical determinism at work. After all, 'a glance at the map' could justify almost anything from disengagement in the west to the absorption of nearby Lusatia. Foreign policy could never be, as Massenbach claimed, a matter of 'mathematical' precision, but an imperfect science; even the strict geopolitical 'laws' which Frederick William professed to follow were relativised by dynastic ties. What is remarkable, however, is the almost instinctive use of geopolitical themes and rhetoric in every major policy debate. The prescriptive remedies may have differed widely: common to all was the sense of geographic vulnerability; of the proximity and danger of French power; and of the simultaneous threat and remoteness of Russia.

---

[250] Hans-Joachim von Brockhusen, *Carl Christian Friedrich von Brockhausen. Ein preußischer Staatsmann um die Wende des XVIII. Jahrhunderts. Ein Lebens- und Kulturbild. Dargestellt auf Grund der Gesandtenberichte des Preußischen Geheimen Staatsarchivs* (Greifswald, 1927), pp. 48–9.

4 Problem areas of Prussian policy and politics: the centres of attention at home, 1797–1804

The primacy of foreign policy: the French threat, fear of revolution and the reform of state and society

For a Prussian patriot it can be nothing less than highly pleasing to perceive the great advantages which his fatherland enjoys by virtue of this system [of neutrality]; this system has also provided the long years of tranquillity with which to restore the inner strengths of the state. While the other great empires exhausted and destroyed themselves in an interminable war, Prussia remained in the fortunate situation of being able to recuperate from her previous military exertions – an advantage which was, relatively speaking, increased by the fact that the other states continued to exhaust themselves. Prussia remained capable of cultivating all branches of her domestic administration and economy, her trades and manufactures. While those of many other countries sometimes entirely stagnated, Prussian trades and manufactures boomed; her trade and shipping flourished under the protection of her neutral flag – the only one in the whole of Europe during the last year.

Haugwitz memorandum, 2.4.1801, Berlin[1]

Throughout the Revolutionary and Napoleonic periods, Prussian statesmen were preoccupied with foreign-political issues; internal affairs were of secondary importance. Indeed, compared to Belgium, Poland and

---

[1] Haugwitz memorandum, 2.4.1802, Berlin, GStA Rep. 92 *Friedr. Wilh. d. Dritte*, unfoliated: 'Insbesondere kann es für dem Preussischen Patrioten nicht anders als höchst erfreulich sein, die großen Vortheile wahrzunehmen, welche sein Vaterland durch dieses System und durch diesen vieljährigen Ruhestand für die inneren Staatskräfte gewonnen hat; während die anderen größten Reiche in einem hartknäckigen Krieg sich erschöpften und zu Grunde richteten, blieb Preußen in der glücklichen Lage, sich von seiner vormaligen Kriegsführung zu erholen, – ein Gewinn, der überdies relativ gegen die anderen Staaten, dadurch, daß diese unterdeß im entgegengesetzten Verhältniß sich schwächten und erschöpften; noch viel wichtiger und unschätzbarer, als schon an und für sich erscheint; er blieb in der Lage alle Zweige der inneren Staatsverwaltung ungestört zu kultivieren, seine Gewerbe und Fabricationen, während die von mehreren anderen Staten durch den Krieg zum Theil gänzlich stockten, immer blühender zu machen, seine Handlung und Schiffarth under dem Schutz seiner neutralen Flagge, welche im letzten Jahre selbst die einzige neutrale in Europa war, immer mehr zu erweitern.'

France herself, Prussia was a haven of domestic tranquillity; the severest threats to the monarchy all came from the outside world. Yet even in Prussia foreign policy did not take place in a vacuum. First of all, there was always the danger that local malcontents would make common cause with the monarchy's external enemies. Secondly, Prussian statesmen found their foreign-political room for manoeuvre painfully limited by a consciousness of their weakness; the more far-sighted among them attributed this to the internal structural flaws of the Prussian state. Thirdly and relatedly, the policy of neutrality provided a protective carapace behind which the necessary reforms could be undertaken.

There was no revolution in Prussia in 1789. In part, this simply reflected the absence of a French-style revolutionary upheaval in Germany as a whole.[2] There was no general 'aristocratic revolt', and even if one assumes the bourgeoisie to be a necessary vehicle of revolution, the German middle class remained firmly tied to the established order. In Prussia, the danger of internal unrest seemed particularly remote. Unlike France, the enlightened elite and the economic bourgeoisie were largely integrated into the state.[3] Even Henri Brunschwig's curious *Gesellschaft und Romantik in Preußen im 18. Jahrhundert,* diagnoses a deep sense of social, political and moral 'crisis', but no revolutionary spirit.[4] Indeed, there was a widespread belief among bureaucrats and the educated public that the progressive Prussian state did not *need* a revolution on the French model. Three decades of enlightened absolutism – which Aretin has called the 'German form of the revolution'[5] – seemed to have pre-empted violent change. Besides, political theory in Prussia had still not advanced much beyond Christian Wolff; Wolff decreed that the ruler must not neglect his duties to his subjects, but that he could not be

---

[2] Press, 'Warum gab es keine deutsche Revolution?'; Epstein, *The genesis of German conservatism,* p. 507, on German immunity to the ideas of the revolution. See also more generally Rudolf Vierhaus, 'Die Revolution als Gegenstand der geistigen Auseinandersetzung in Deutschland, 1789–1830', in Roger Dufraisse and Elizabeth Müller-Luckner (eds.), *Revolution und Gegenrevolution, 1789–1830. Zur geistigen Auseinandersetzung in Frankreich und Deutschland* (Berlin, 1991), pp. 251–62.

[3] Horst Möller, 'Preußische Aufklärungsgesellschaften und Revolutionserfahrung', in Büsch and Neugebauer-Wölk (eds.), *Preußen und die revolutionäre Herausforderung seit 1789,* p. 108; Helga Schultz, 'Gesellschaftliche Strukturen und geistig-politisches Klima in Berlin, 1789–1799', in Timmermann (ed.), *Die französische Revolution und Europa,* pp. 381–92, especially 384, 389. On the complex role of Prussia's 'immature' bourgeoisie before 1789 see Ingrid Mittenzwei, *Preußen nach dem Siebenjährigen Krieg* (Berlin/GDR, 1979), pp. 100, 241–2 and *passim.*

[4] Henri Brunschwig, *Gesellschaft und Romantik in Preußen im 18. Jahrhundert. Die Krise des preußischen Staates am Ende des 18. Jahrhunderts und die Entstehung der romantischen Mentalität* (Frankfurt, 1975).

[5] Aretin, *Das Reich,* p. 108.

removed even if he did. In the realm of high philosophy, Immanuel Kant still believed that even if Prussia was not yet in an enlightened age, she was on the way there. At a considerably lower level of sophistication, Ritter von Gleim and Thomas Abbt continued to propagate their inoffensive ideology of Prussian state patriotism.

Ranged against the established order was a motley crew of idealists, eccentrics and misfits. Even the close scrutiny of Walter Grab was unable to uncover more than a handful of isolated revolutionaries in Prussia.[6] Some, such as the bureaucrats Joseph Zerboni di Sposetti and Hans von Held, accused of Jacobinical subversion in Silesia, merely seem to have fallen foul of its venal governor, Count Hoym.[7] Others, such as the members of the mysterious 'Ordre de vérité', attracted the attention of the authorities primarily because they were believed to be in league with Sièyes, the French ambassador.[8] This threat of foreign subversion spurred the government into action. In October 1798 – nearly ten years after the outbreak of the Revolution – all secret societies or debating clubs devoted to the achievement or discussion of constitutional change were banned. In any case, if there ever had been a real threat of revolution, it receded rapidly in the late 1790s.[9] A conservative pamphleteer such as Gentz might claim that nine-tenths of all state officials were 'committed revolutionaries (*entschiedene Revolutionäre*)',[10] but an investigation of the foreign ministry identified only one bureaucrat, the utterly insignificant court historiographer Kuhn, as a carrier of 'democratic principles (*democratische Grundsätze*)'.[11] It should be added that this operation was more of an efficiency drive than an anti-Jacobin purge; a far greater number were censored on the grounds of incompetence.[12]

Nor did the public sphere present any threat to the established order. Indeed, Prussia was remarkable as a centre of counter-revolutionary

---

[6] Walter Grab, 'Revolutionsfreunde in Preußen im Zeitalter der französischen Revolution', in Büsch and Neugebauer-Wölk (eds.), *Preußen und die revolutionäre Herausforderung seit 1789*, p. 119; see also Boyen, *Erinnerungen*, I, p. 134, on the negligible impact of the Revolution on Prussia. For a general discussion of the German Jacobins see T. C. W. Blanning, 'The German Jacobins and the French Revolution', *HJ*, 23 (1980), 985–1002.

[7] For a more favourable view of Hoym and a less favourable view of Zerboni and Held see Colmar Grünhagen, *Zerboni and Held in ihren Konflikten mit der Staatsgewalt, 1796–1802* (Berlin, 1897), *passim*, especially pp. 285–7.

[8] Adler-Bresse, *Sièyes et le monde allemand*, pp. 175–89.

[9] Birtsch, 'Revolutionsfurcht in Preußen', p. 93.

[10] Wittichen, 'Das preußische Kabinett und Friedrich von Gentz', 271.

[11] Report of Finckenstein, Alvensleben and Haugwitz, *c.* February 1798, GStA Rep. 96A.9A1, fo. 4.

[12] E.g. von Kathe was described as 'ganz unbrauchbar', ibid., fo.8.

118   The structures

propaganda.[13] Of course, as everywhere, critics of the status quo did exist. Direct attacks on the monarchy were hazardous; this may have led to stratagems such as showing up the inadequacy of Frederick William III through exaggerated praise for the queen, Louise, or cultivating the memory of the incomparably more dynamic Frederick II.[14] On the other hand, as Rudolf Vierhaus has suggested, criticism could often replace rather than inflame radical action.[15] Admittedly, the 1790s did bring a sharp rise in state censorship.[16] Here the revolution may have accelerated, but it certainly did not cause an ideological reaction to the enlightenment in church and education; this had already been begun in 1788 by Woellner. The relatively relaxed attitude into which the government had settled back by the late 1790s is shown by Beyme's remarks during a discussion on censorship. 'The absurdities with which the common man is supplied by his writers', he wrote in March 1798, 'belong so to speak to his traditional amusements; these absurdities are read and forgotten, without, at least as far as we are concerned, leaving behind a dangerous impression.'[17] This latitude did not extend to coverage of foreign-policy matters, which continued to be rigorously censored, as they had been since the days of Frederick the Great. Finally, even had considerable pro-revolutionary sentiment existed, there were no institutional mechanisms by which popular opinion would have been enabled to influence high policy.

If disaffection among the educated middle class was politically insignificant, the same cannot be said for the rural and urban poor. On

[13] Otto Tschirch, *Geschichte der öffentlichen Meinung in Preußen im Friedensjahrzehnt vom Baseler Frieden bis zum Zusammenbruch des Staates (1795–1806)*, 2 vols. (Weimar, 1933–4); Heinz-Otto Sieburg, 'Die französische Revolution im Spiegel der Presse und politischen Publizistik Deutschlands (1789–1801)', *Historische Mitteilungen*, 2 (1989), pp. 44–5; Ursula E. Koch, 'Französische Revolution und preußische Tagespublizistik', in Büsch and Neugebauer-Wölk (eds.), *Preußen und die revolutionäre Herausforderung seit 1789*, p. 218. Günter Vogler and Ilonka Egert, 'Stimmen zur französischen Revolution in Preussen 1789–1795. Argumente und Motive für Pro und Contra', in Timmermann (ed.), *Die französische Revolution und Europa*, pp. 360–1 show that most Prussians came to oppose the Revolution despite considerable initial sympathy.

[14] Monika Wienfort, *Monarchie in der bürgerlichen Gesellschaft. Deutschland und England von 1640 bis 1848* (Göttingen, 1993), pp. 12 and 173.

[15] Rudolf Vierhaus, ' "Sie und nicht wir." Deutsche Urteile über den Ausbruch der französischen Revolution', in Rudolf Vierhaus, *Deutschland im 18. Jahrhundert. Politische Verfassung, soziales Gefüge, geistige Bewegung* (Göttingen, 1987), p. 215.

[16] See Wilhelm Lüdtke, 'Friedrich Wilhelm II und die revolutionäre Propaganda (1789–1791)', *FBPG*, 44 (1932), 80–3.

[17] Quoted in Paul Wittichen, 'Friedrich Gentz und Preußen vor der Reform', *FBPG*, 18 (1905), 218: 'Die Absurditäten, womit der gemeine Mann von seinen Schriftstellern bedient wird gehören gewissermaßen zu seinen hergebrachten Vergnügungen, werden gelesen und vergessen, ohne wenigstens bei uns einen gefährlichen Eindruck zurückzulassen.'

numerous occasions the military had to be called in to quell disturbances in the town of Breslau, in the Silesian countryside and in the Altmark. Yet the famous events known as the 'Breslauer Gesellenaufstand' were hardly a serious threat to the established order. Closer examination shows the riot to have been a traditional affray between the guilds and the magistracy, not a radical insurrection. Clashes with the military only ensued because marauding apprentices attempted to storm a bordello defended by soldiers.[18] Fears that the crowd was linked to a group of middle-class conspirators called the *Evergetenbund* proved groundless. Indeed, a subsequent investigation was unable to unearth a single Jacobin.[19] At around the same time, the Altmark experienced a surge of rural discontent. The local peasants were already personally free; they demanded the abolition of certain feudal services. Among the families affected were the Schulenburgs and the Alvenslebens.[20] Interestingly, neither Schulenburg nor Alvensleben allowed this to interfere with foreign policy. Schulenburg had always been an opponent of France and remained so (until 1807); Alvensleben continued to search for an accommodation with France. There is certainly no evidence for Meta Kohnke's claim that these disturbances 'induced fearful panic among the ruling class'.[21]

Peasant unrest continued to plague the authorities during the early reign of Frederick William III. Silesia proved particularly restive: the new king called the province 'mein Sorgenkind'.[22] In 1798 violence exploded in Hirschberg.[23] 'The German who does not unite with the French is a scoundrel', sang the revolting peasants. 'The devil take the nobility and the clergy.'[24] The implied threat of joint action with the Revolutionary

---

[18] Arno Herzig and Rainer Sachs, *Der Breslauer Gesellenaufstand von 1793. Die Aufzeichnungen des Schniedermeisters Johann Gottlieb Klose. Darstellung und Dokumentation* (Göttingen, 1987), p. 19.

[19] Ibid., p. 11; Arno Herzig, *Unterschichtenprotest in Deutschland, 1790–1870* (Göttingen, 1988), p. 100; Arno Herzig, 'Der Einfluß der französischen Revolution auf den Unterschichtenprotest in Deutschland während der 1790er Jahre', in Helmut Berding (ed.), *Soziale Unruhen in Deutschland während der Französischen Revolution* (Göttingen, 1988), p. 205.

[20] Meta Kohnke, 'Bauernunruhen in der Altmark im Sommer 1794', *Jahrbuch für Regionalgeschichte*, 16 (1989), 96.

[21] Kohnke, 'Bauernunruhen in der Altmark', p. 108: 'herrschende Feudalklasse in panische Angst versetzt'.

[22] Adler-Bresse, *Sièyes et le monde allemand*, p. 148.

[23] The classic account here is Johannes Ziekursch, *Hundert Jahre schlesischer Agrargeschichte. Vom Hubertusburger Frieden bis zum Abschluss der Bauernbefreiung* (Breslau, 1915), pp. 241–75, especially pp. 242–5.

[24] Herzig, *Unterschichtenprotest in Deutschland*, p. 91: 'Ein Hundsfott muß der Deutsche sein, der jetzt mit den Franzosen nicht stimmet ein. Der Teufel hole den Adel und Pfaffen.'

French unsettled the government, especially in the light of Sièyes's activities. They need not have worried: As Arno Herzig has pointed out, if the rioters were clearly hostile to noble privilege, they were nevertheless still very monarchic in sentiment. Indeed, they looked to the king for redress of their grievances.[25] A similar picture emerges from the disturbances in Pomerania in 1799 to 1800. Here the military had to be called in to arrest ringleaders and force peasants back to work.[26] Yet the authorities preferred to speak of 'misled people (*irre geleiteten Menschen*)' and 'misbehaviour (*Widersetzlichkeit*)',[27] rather than revolutionaries. If the rural population was far from being the docile and deferential herd of popular – and scholarly – myth,[28] their activism was primarily directed towards traditional concerns, such as the re-establishment of a 'moral economy'. But the resulting unrest, while clearly far from trivial, did not and was not perceived to represent any mortal danger to the security of the Prussian state. First of all, the long-standing – albeit increasingly ramshackle – state policy of intervention in the grain market served to defuse tension.[29] Secondly, despite periodic government paranoia, peasant links to urban middle-class conspiracies were minimal; potentially lethal contacts with the Revolutionary French never took place. *Socially*, the peasants may have been subversive; *politically*, they were biddable. In short, to quote the words of the German Marxist historian Kurt Holzapfel,[30] there was no 'revolutionary situation' in Prussia in the 1790s. Above all, as Günther Birtsch points out,[31] by the mid-1790s, anti-revolutionary motivations had long ceased to influence foreign policy, if indeed they had ever seriously done so.

[25] Ibid., pp. 70–2, 101.
[26] GStA Rep.96A.128E, 'Widerspenthige Unterthanen in Pommern, 1799–1800': Memorandum of Reck, Goldbeck, Thulemeier, Massow and Arnim, 6.5.1799, Berlin, fo. 1; *Kriegs- und Domänenkammer* of Pomerania to Frederick William, 12.6.1800, Stettin, fo. 2; Von Ingersleben, 10.8.1800, Stettin, fo. 6.
[27] Colonel von Lettow to Frederick William, 12.8.1800, Bütow, ibid., fo. 13.
[28] For Prussia in particular see William W. Hagen, 'The Junkers' faithless servants: peasant insubordination and the breakdown of serfdom in Brandenburg-Prussia, 1763–1811', in R. J. Evans and W. R. Lee (eds.), *The German peasantry: conflict and community in rural society from the eighteenth to the twentieth centuries* (London, 1986), pp. 71–101. Hagen criticises Hintze, Meinecke and others for ignoring 'rumblings in the villages'. The report of von Puttnitz, 12.11.98, Berlin, cited in Ziekursch, *Hundert Jahre schlesischer Agrargeschichte*, p. 251, is a graphic instance of the perceived breakdown of peasant deference in Prussia. For Germany as a whole see Helmut Gabel and Winfried Schulze, 'Peasant resistance and politicisation in Germany in the eighteenth century', in Eckhart Hellmuth (ed.), *The transformation of political culture. England and Germany in the late eighteenth century* (Oxford, 1990), pp. 119–46.
[29] August Skalweit, *Die Getreidehandelspolitik und Kriegsmagazinverwaltung Preußens, 1756–1806* (Berlin, 1931), pp. 199–200.
[30] Holzapfel, 'Intervention oder Koexistenz', 789.
[31] Birtsch, 'Revolutionsfurcht in Preußen', p. 93.

The big exception was Poland. In the course of the final partitions in 1793–5, Prussia had slightly more than doubled her total surface area. This not only had the effect of completely altering the geopolitical situation of the state, it also radically changed the internal balance within the monarchy itself. While the Polish gains looked formidable on paper, Prussian politicians surveyed the quality and were not impressed.[32] First of all, the result was a considerable dilution of the German character of the monarchy: about one-third of Frederick William's subjects were now Polish speakers. Secondly, the Prussian bureaucracy was confronted with a new mass of what seemed to them semi-literate and superstitious peasantry.[33] Thirdly and most importantly, the monarchy was now saddled with the separatist pretensions of the Polish nobility. Already during the rising of 1794, the Poles had put patriotic aims before class solidarity.[34] To make matters worse, some insurgents entertained their own variant of France's *Grande Nation*. They aimed to restore Poland within the borders of 1772, with an option on Silesia;[35] this scheme was to re-emerge in 1805–6 as the *Mordplan* against Prussia. It is therefore hardly surprising that Prussian politicians continued to worry about a Polish revolt, especially one fomented by the French to create a diversion in the east.[36] 'Il est très possible', the Kabinettsministerium noted, 'que pour opérer . . . une diversion puissante, la France cherchât à exciter et à sountenir les dispositions révolutionnaires des mécontents en Pologne.'[37] In this way what was essentially a problem of internal security in the eastern provinces contributed to Prussia's sense of encirclement. Indeed, the Prussian state lived in much greater terror of

[32] *Pace* T. C. W. Blanning, 'The French Revolution and Europe', in Colin Lucas (ed.), *Rewriting the French Revolution* (Oxford, 1991), p. 198; Moritz, *Preußen und der Kosciuzko-Aufstand*, p. 192; Meyer, *Preußen und Frankreich*, pp. 73–4. For a radical national (-socialist) critique of Prussian policy in Poland see Manfred Laubert, *Die preußische Polenpolitik von 1772 bis 1914* (Cracow, 1944), pp. 18–38.

[33] Hagen, 'The partitions of Poland'; see also I. C. Bussenius and Walther Hubatsch (eds.), *Die preußische Verwaltung in Süd- und Neostpreußen, 1793–1806* (Heidelberg, 1960), pp. 16–20.

[34] Waclaw Dlugoborski, 'Volksbewegungen im preußisch-polnischen Grenzraum während der Französischen Revolution 1789 bis 1794', in Büsch and Neugebauer-Wölk (eds.), *Preußen und die revolutionäre Herausforderung seit 1789*, p. 149.

[35] Dlugoborski, 'Volksbewegungen im preußisch-polnischen Grenzraum', pp. 155, 167–8.

[36] Hagen, 'The partitions of Poland', p. 122; Massenbach, *Memoiren zur Geschichte des preussischen Staates*, III, p. 87; Alvensleben memorandum, 19.8.1798, Berlin, in Bailleu (ed.), *Preussen und Frankreich*, I, p. 201; memorandum by Frederick William marked 'sicher vor 1800' by archivist, GStA Rep. 92 *Friedr.Wilh.d.Dritte* B.VI.21, fo. 1.

[37] Kabinettsministerium to Frederick William, 13.5.98, Berlin, in Bailleu (ed.), *Preussen und Frankreich* I, p. 204.

the shambolic and backward Polish nobility than it did of any class-based progressive revolutionary movements among its German subjects.

These Polish headaches made Frederick William all the more determined to stick to his policy of neutrality. Only a prolonged period of tranquillity would allow the integration of the territories; a new war of coalition would expose Prussia to terrible dangers on her eastern flank. But the neutrality policy also created the preconditions for reform in the monarchy as a whole. 'La révolution très utile que vous avez faite du bas en haut', Struensee is famously said to have told the French ambassador, 'se fera lentement en Prusse du haut en bas. Le roi est démocrate à sa manière; il travaille sans relâche à réduire les privilèges de la noblesse, et il suivra à cet égard le plan de Joseph II, mais par des moyens lents. Sous peu d'années il n'y aura plus de classe privilégiée en Prusse.'[38] The aim of this 'revolution from above' was twofold. In the first place, the government thereby hoped to stave off possible revolution from below. 'If the estate-owners have to sacrifice something', Beyme wrote in 1798, 'it would be better if they did so voluntarily or at least on orders from above, than if the people are driven by the spirit of the times to take everything.'[39] As the threat of revolution receded, however, internal reform was increasingly seen as a strategy to strengthen Prussia in the crucial sphere of international relations. Even such a partisan of the Second Coalition as General Rüchel acknowledged the need for Prussia to achieve a 'concentration of her internal strength (*Sammlung seiner inneren Kraft*)' while still at peace.[40] This interaction between internal and external factors was in the long Prussian tradition of the primacy of foreign policy. It is generally accepted, for example, that Beyme's opposition to the Second Coalition was at least partly motivated by the need for a period of tranquillity to implement key internal reforms, notably the emancipation of the peasants.[41] Indeed, the argument that Prussia needed peace to consolidate her hold on Poland and reform her finances was one of seven objections to the coalition that Brunswick sought to counter in August 1799.[42] The long-term aim of these

---

[38] As reported by Otto to Talleyrand, 13.8.1799, in Bailleu (ed.), *Preussen und Frankreich*, I, p. 505.

[39] Beyme to Carmer, 15.3.1798, quoted in Möller, 'Der Primat der Aussenpolitik', p. 74.

[40] Rüchel memorandum, mid-May 1799, in Bailleu (ed.), *Preussen und Frankreich*, I, pp. 295–6.

[41] Karl Disch, 'Der Kabinettsrat Beyme und die auswärtige Politik', 337; Hans Saring, 'Karl Friedrich von Beyme', *Jahrbuch für brandenburgische Landesgeschichte*, 7 (1956), 38.

[42] Brunswick memorandum, 25.8.1799, in Bailleu (ed.), *Preussen und Frankreich*, I, p. 325.

measures, of course, was to strengthen the state *vis à vis* her international rivals.

This double imperative powered a reform movement in the early reign of Frederick William III. Its achievements have often been overlooked, but they were not negligible.[43] A royal commission rejected a wealth tax, but it did levy new impositions without the traditional exemptions.[44] In 1800 a *Kabinettsordre* announced the lifting of internal tariffs within the monarchy, at least in principle; five years later Stein had turned intent into reality everywhere except Silesia and Franconia, which lay outside of his control.[45] Impressive strides were made in the crucial area of agrarian reform.[46] Various oppressive labour services such as the *Vorspann* were reduced, though its complete abolition only came later; free-trading bureaucrats – and nobles – also wanted to scrap the restrictive corn and magazine policy, by which the export of grain was restricted until sufficient stocks had accumulated to cover times of dearth.[47] The most important reform, however, was the emancipation of the crown peasants, led by Beyme.[48] If Hartmut Harnisch is right in arguing that agrarian reform after the mid-1790s was an attempt to effect changes without changing the overall structures,[49] then it is also true that between 1798 and 1804 more peasants were emancipated on crown lands than were

---

[43] See especially, Hintze, 'Preußische Reformbestrebungen vor 1806'. Hintze's article, first published in 1896, was something of a historiographical watershed; ur-Hintzian is C. E. Schück, 'Friedrich Wilhelm III und seine Räte für die innere Gesetzgebung Preußens, 1797–1807', *Abhandlungen der Schlesischen Gesellschaft für vaterländische Cultur*, 45 (1867), esp. 69; Hans-Ulrich Wehler, *Deutsche Gesellschaftsgeschichte*, I, p. 352, is not impressed with the achievements of the pre-reform. A recent *Beiheft* on the reforms of the *Forschungen zur brandenburgisch-preussischen Geschichte* neglected the pre-reform: Bernd Sösemann (ed.), *Gemeingeist und Bürgersinn. Die preußischen Reformen*, FBPG NF 2; the exception is Thomas Stamm-Kuhlmann, 'Die Rolle von Staat und Monarchie bei der Modernisierung von oben. Ein Literaturbericht mit ergänzenden Betrachtungen zur Person König Friedrich Wilhelms III.', in Sösemann (ed.), *Gemeingeist und Bürgersinn*, p. 270; for a vulgar Marxist reading of the pre-reform see Eisner, *Das Ende des Reichs*, p. 232.

[44] Horst Petzold, *Die Verhandlungen der 1798 von König Friedrich Wilhelm III eingesetzten Finanzkommission* (PhD dissertation, University of Göttingen, 1911), p. 48; Friedrich Meusel, 'Die Aufhebung der Akzisefreiheit des Adels in Preußen (1799)', *FBPG*, 21 (1908), 559–63.

[45] Wolfgang Radtke, *Die preussische Seehandlung zwischen Staat und Wirtschaft in der Frühphase der Industrialisierung* (Berlin, 1981), pp. 28–9.

[46] Rudolf Stadelmann, *Preußens Könige in ihrer Tätigkeit für die Landeskultur. Vierter Teil. Friedrich Wilhelm III (1797–1807)*. Publicationen aus den K. preussischen Staatsarchiven (Leipzig, 1887), *passim*.

[47] Petzold, *Finanzkommission*, p. 103.

[48] Hintze, 'Preußische Reformbestrebungen vor 1806', p. 509.

[49] Hartmut Harnisch, 'Die agrarpolitischen Reformmaßnahmen der preußischen Staatsführung in dem Jahrzehnt vor 1806/07', *Jahrbuch für Wirtschaftsgeschichte*, (1977), 129 and *passim*.

124   The structures

freed on the *Rittergüter* in the forty years after 1810. In this respect Ernst von Meier is right to argue that 'The edict of 9 October 1807 merely burst open the shell within which the fruit had slowly ripened.'[50] Finally, the first years of Frederick William III's reign saw a vibrant military reform debate.[51] The king himself took a particular interest in military improvements, for it was here that reform was most obviously linked to the external vulnerability of the monarchy.[52] A comprehensive review of such issues as corporal punishment, training, weapons, tactics and officer education now began.[53] But the most pressing question of all was that of conscription; many Prussians, especially townspeople, were exempted from military service. Yet it was only by imitating the radical methods of the revolutionary French that the Prussians could hope to compete. Initial plans for a *levée en masse* foundered, but in time the king came around to the views of men like Scharnhorst and Knesebeck, who saw in every Prussian subject a potential defender of the monarchy. By December 1803 Frederick William had called for a detailed plan for a national militia.

If in 1799 Haugwitz lamented the failure to use the respite provided by

---

50 Ernst von Meier, *Die Reform der Verwaltungsorganisation unter Stein und Hardenberg* (Leipzig, 1881), p. 158: 'Das Edikt vom 9. Oktober 1807 hat nur die Hülle gesprengt, unter der die Frucht langsam herangereift war.' In a strongly revisionist article, Edgar Melton, 'The decline of *Gutsherrschaft*', especially p. 335, argues that the greatest changes were powered by the Junkers themselves rather than the state. Hans-Heinrich Müller, 'Der agrarische Fortschritt und die Bauern in Brandenburg vor den Reformen von 1807', *ZfG*, 12 (1964), 629–48 stresses the role of the peasantry in bringing about agrarian improvements. Wolfgang Neugebauer, 'Krisensymptome und Vorreformen', in Ingo Materna and Wolfgang Ribbe (eds), *Brandenburgische Geschichte* (Berlin, 1995), p. 390, stresses the importance of agrarian developments before 1807.

51 On the debate in general see Goltz, *Von Rossbach bis Jena*; Werner Gembruch, 'Friedrich von Cölln als Publizist vor dem Zusammenbruch Preußens im Jahre 1806', in Gembruch, *Staat und Heer*, pp. 306–33; Paret, *Yorck and the era of Prussian reform*; and Bernhard R. Kroener, 'Aufklärung und Revolution. Die preußische Armee am Vorabend der Katastrophe von 1806', Militärgeschichtliches Forschungsamt (ed.), *Die französische Revolution und der Beginn des Zweiten Weltkrieges aus deutscher und französischer Sicht* (Herford and Bonn, 1989), pp. 45–70. On the limitations of military reform before 1806 see Helmut Schnitter, 'Revolution und Heer. Reformbestrebungen und Revolutionseinflüsse im preußischen Heer vor 1806. Lernfähigkeit und Lernbereitschaft einer feudal- absolutistischen Armee im Umfeld der Französischen Revolution 1789/1795', in Timmermann (ed.), *Die Französische Revolution und Europa*, pp. 689–701 and the very bleak assessment of Johannes Ziekursch, 'Die preussischen Landesreservebataillone, 1805/06 – eine Reform vor der Reform?', *HZ*, 103 (1909), 85–94. For a much more positive view of the Prussian army before 1806 see D. F. Showalter, 'Hubertusberg [*sic*] to Auerstädt', especially 323–33 and Jany, *Geschichte der königlichen-preussischen Armee bis zum Jahre 1807*, p. 365, who speaks of stagnation (*stehengeblieben*) rather than decline (*Rückgang*).

52 Alfred Herrmann, 'Friedrich Wilhelm III und sein Anteil', p. 290.

53 Rainer Wohlfeil, *Vom stehenden Heer des Absolutismus zur Allgemeinen Wehrpflicht*, vol. II, pp. 97–8.

the neutrality policy to effect a financial reform and consolidate Prussia's internal strength,[54] by 1802 he was able to look back on the achievements of the last four years with some satisfaction.[55] While the rest of Europe was riven by war, Prussia experienced an economic boom. There was a roaring export trade with Britain in grain and naval goods;[56] Prussian ports such as Emden benefited very substantially from their neutral status.[57] This helps to account for the widespread popularity of the neutrality policy among Prussian opinion.[58] Moreover, Prussian bureaucrats were now freed from the threat of war to develop manufactures through economic improvements. Increased taxation receipts helped to raise state revenue from 20.5 million Thalers in 1797–8 to 27 million in 1805. The national debt was correspondingly reduced by 7 million;[59] a treasure of 13 million for emergencies was set aside.

Yet there was a limit to what reform could achieve. In both intention and execution the measures adopted before 1806 stopped well short of a complete transformation of Prussian society; whether such a transformation actually took place after the defeat of Jena is another matter. The urban middle class, keen for equal treatment in other areas, resisted the attempt to lift their exemptions from military service; the Kabinettsräte Beyme and Mencken supported them in this.[60] Above all, the attempt to emancipate private peasants failed.[61] This was the result

[54] Haugwitz memorandum, 15.1.1799, Berlin, in Bailleu (ed.), *Preussen und Frankreich*, I, p. 267.

[55] Haugwitz memorandum, 2.4.1802, Berlin, GStA Rep. 92 *Friedr. Wilh. d. Dritte*, unfoliated (cited *in extenso* above, p. 115).

[56] Sven-Erik Astrom, 'Britain's timber imports from the Baltic, 1775–1830. Some new figures and viewpoints', *Scandinavian Economic History Review*, 37 (1989), 57–71. See also the figures in Mahan, *Influence of sea power*, II, p. 28.

[57] Eckhardt, 'Unter Kniphauser Flagge'; Phillips and Reade, *Neutrality*, pp. 268, 286, 289.

[58] Friedrich Carl Wittichen, 'Zur Geschichte der öffentlichen Meinung in Preussen vor 1806', *FBPG*, 23 (1910), 38; Tschirch, *Geschichte der öffentlichen Meinung in Preußen*, I, p. 225 and *passim*.

[59] Leo Hellwig, *Schulenburg-Kehnert unter Friedrich Wilhelm III, 1798–1806*, pp. 57–9; Wilhelm Treue, 'Preußens Wirtschaft vom Dreißigjährigen Krieg bis zum Nationalsozialismus', in Otto Büsch (ed.), *Handbuch der preußischen Geschichte*, II, p. 495.

[60] Schück, 'Friedrich Wilhelm III und seine Räte', p. 60.

[61] Marie Rumler, 'Die Bestrebungen zur Befreiung der Privatbauern in Preußen, 1797–1806', *FBPG*, 37 (1925), 31–76. Hartmut Harnisch, 'Peasants and markets. The background to the agrarian reforms in feudal Prussia east of the Elbe, 1760–1807', in Evans and Lee (eds.), *The German peasantry*, pp. 37–70, emphasises the effect of broader socio-economic changes in the eighteenth century, but insists that the shock of 1806–7 was needed to set real reform in motion (pp. 62–7). For a particularly bleak assessment of agrarian reform before Jena see Ziekursch, *Hundert Jahre schlesischer Agrargeschichte*, 'Das Scheitern der Agrarreform in den ersten Jahren der Regierung Friedrich Wilhelms III', pp. 241–75, especially pp. 257–75.

of furious opposition to agrarian reform from the nobility. They argued that thoroughgoing social change, far from pre-empting unrest or enabling Prussia to take the field against the French, would simply hasten revolution at home. 'Pour combattre les Français avec avantage', Alvensleben argued, 'il faut adopter leurs usages, leurs moyens, sans quoi nous serons toujours inférieurs et aurions constamment le dessous.'[62] But in doing so, he warned, 'on adopte de fait une révolution volontaire, si on peut même parvenir à conserver l'état monarchique en employant des voies si dures; mais ce qui est bien plus à craindre, on amènera peut-être par cette marche une révolution républicaine, précisément le mal qu'on veut éviter, et on l'accélera, au lieu de l'éloigner'. Even if on this occasion Alvensleben was merely adopting a rhetorical posture against the Second Coalition, which he already opposed on the grounds of pure *Realpolitik*, he was still articulating the views of those Junkers who were not prepared to subordinate their own class interests to the primacy of foreign policy.

This primacy was the main driving force behind the reforms. On the other hand, the organs of the state were themselves the first to recognise the constraints which it placed upon reform. If the Prussian administator and thinker Wilhelm von Humboldt defined the purpose of the state as 'the maintenance of security against external enemies as well as internal quarrels', he also insisted that personal freedoms should not 'proceed a step farther than is necessary for the security and protection of citizens against foreign enemies'.[63] This was most strikingly demonstrated by the complex interaction between foreign policy, agrarian relations and military reform. When Major von Knesebeck called for a national militia in early 1803, he justified this in terms of Prussia's acute foreign-political vulnerability. In order to survive, he argued, the monarchy must achieve an exceptional degree of military preparedness; only this could compensate for the numerical superiority of potential enemies.[64] The Duke of Brunswick developed this argument with reference to Prussia's geopolitical exposure. 'It is well known that the Prussian monarchy has no natural borders or fortifications towards the Memel or the Rhine', he

---

[62] Alvensleben memorandum, 12.5.1798, Berlin, in Bailleu (ed.), *Preussen und Frankreich*, I, pp. 200–1. In a similar vein see Goldbeck to Hoym, 23.12.1799, cited in Ziekursch, *Ein Jahrhundert schlesischer Agrargeschichte*, p. 250.

[63] Cited in George Peabody Gooch, *Germany and the French Revolution* (London, 1920; reprinted 1965), p. 110; see also John Gagliardo, *Reich and nation. The Holy Roman Empire as idea and reality, 1763–1806* (Bloomington and London, 1980), p. 122.

[64] Goltz, *Von Rossbach bis Jena*, p. 281; in a similar vein also Clausewitz, *Politische Schriften und Briefe*, p. 209.

wrote, adding that only 'the most accomplished military constitution' could guarantee the security of the monarchy.[65] Yet if timely reform was necessary to maintain Prussia's military capability and thus her external security, precipitate change could endanger it. The unique 'military–agrarian complex' in Prussia was predicated on the assumption that unfree peasants would both till the land and supply the necessary recruits for a noble-officered army.[66] Real agrarian reform would release the peasants and subvert the tried and proven military organisation of the monarchy. 'The Prussian military constitution and administration of the state is a venerable original', warned General Rüchel, '[and] if one interferes with one of its component parts the whole machine is given a jolt'.[67] This was demonstrated during the discussions about the abolition of the *Vorspann*. Senior bureaucrats such as Struensee genuinely agreed that its abolition was 'desirable (*wünschenswürdig*)', but pointed out that it remained crucial to the supply of certain regiments in wartime; his colleague, Werder, pleaded for the retention of the hated *Vorspann* – which required peasants to provide draught horses to the feudal lord – for 'emergency' situations.[68] It therefore became axiomatic that premature and controversial reform should be avoided at a time of acute foreign-political danger. Looking back after the catastrophe, Clausewitz reflected that 'it would have been very risky to have provoked a great discontent through far-reaching changes, which might not be allayed in time, and which could be dangerous in a time when one needed the support of all estates and classes of the people'.[69]

---

[65] Brunswick memorandum, 25.8.1799, in Bailleu (ed.), *Preussen und Frankreich*, I, p. 328: 'Bekanntlich hat die preußische Monarchie gegen die Memel sowie gegen den Rhein keine natürlichen Grenzen noch feste Plätze . . . Nur die vorzüglichste Militärverfassung, die Belebung des Geistes in der Armee . . . kann Preußens fortdauerndes Glück und Sicherheit bestätigen.'

[66] Otto Büsch, *Militärsystem und Sozialleben im alten Preussen*; Hanna Schissler, 'The social and economic power of the Prussian Junkers', in Ralph Gibson and Martin Blinkhorn (eds.), *Landownership and power in modern Europe* (London, 1991), p. 103.

[67] Cited in Wohlfeil, *Vom stehenden Heer des Absolutismus zur Allgemeinen Wehrpflicht*, p. 99: 'Die preußische Militärverfassung und Staatswirtschaft ist ein ehrwürdiges Original, rührt man ein Glied an, so erhält die ganze Maschine einen Schlag.'

[68] GStA Rep.96A.145, *Die Verhandlungen über Abschaffung des Vorspanns, 1799–1805*, unfoliated: Struensee to Frederick William, 8.2.1799, Berlin; Werder to Frederick William, 19.2.1799, Berlin.

[69] See Clausewitz, *Politische Schriften und Briefe*, pp. 216–17; also the contemporary remarks of Gentz quoted in Wittichen, 'Das preußische Kabinett und Friedrich von Gentz', p. 268: 'es wäre sogar sehr gewagt gewesen, durch große Veränderungen eine Unzufriedenheit hervorzurufen, die die Zeit nicht mehr beschwichtigen konnte, und die in einer Lage gefährlich werden mußte, wo man des Beistands aller Stände und Klassen im Volk bedurfte'.

The executive reform debate before 1804

In my opinion, a prime minister is preferable to the *Kabinett* system because he is responsible [for his actions], . . . and because he guarantees unity of direction; but he is nevertheless dangerous, because the monarch transfers to him too large a part of his powers, and receives one-sided briefings in all branches of government without fear of contradiction; and where is the man who is so well-instructed about all branches of statecraft and economy that he can direct them with success?

Count Schulenburg, writing after 1806[70]

During the early reign of Frederick William III, the reform of society, law and the economy was still very much of a sideshow. The main focus of internal reform was the *executive* apparatus of the state; this was often extended to include the Generaldirektorium – the highest level of internal administration – but the chief concern was with the formulation and execution of foreign policy. This order of priorities reflected the prevailing primacy of foreign policy. 'Before one redecorates one's house', wrote Friedrich von Gentz, 'one must first be sure that one will keep it.'[71] Indeed, it was the evident inadequacy of Prussian foreign policy in the face of the mounting French threat that spurred Gentz to launch his famous radical critique of the Kabinett at the turn of the century.

According to Gentz, Prussia's foreign-political predicament was not the result of a coincidental and thus corrigible error of policy. Rather, it was a 'necessary consequence' of the 'radical sickness' of the Prussian state which could not be healed except by a complete overhaul – a *Total-Veränderung* – in the internal organisation of the Prussian system of government.[72] Gentz stressed that he was not referring to the humdrum 'general' internal administration of the monarchy, but rather to the 'organisation of the supreme organs of the state (*Organizasion (sic) der*

---

[70] Count Schulenburg quoted in Naudé, 'Denkwürdigkeiten des Ministers Grafen Schulenburg', p. 415: 'Ein Premierminister ist nach meiner Meinung zwar der Kabinettsregierung wegen seiner Verantwortlichkeit . . . vorzuziehen, auch weil er Einheit bewirkt, aber doch gefährlich, weil der Monarch ihm einen zu großen Teil seiner Gewalt überträgt, nur einseitige Vorträge in allen Zweigen ohne Widerspruch eines anderen erhält, und wo ist der Mann, der in allen Teilen der Staatskunst und Wirtschaft so unterrichtet ist, daß er sie mit Erfolg zu leiten vermag?'

[71] Wittichen, 'Das preußische Kabinett und Friedrich von Gentz', p. 249: 'Ehe man sein Haus neu dekoriert muß man sich erst die Gewißheit verschaffen, daß man es behalten werde.' Note the parallels to Bismarck's later statement that a house had to be made safe from the (external) elements before embarking upon its interior decoration, see chapter 1, pp. 4–5.

[72] Ibid., pp. 246–7.

oberen Staats-Behörden)'; this distinction should be taken as read in all executive reform debates preceding 1807. The root of Prussia's evils was traced to the men of the Kabinett, whom Gentz held responsible for the obstruction of the foreign ministry and the the 'paralysis' of the 'political machinery'. Their influence rested on a commanding role in the ante-chamber of power around the king. 'They alone enjoy the right to brief the king in person', Gentz wrote; 'all ministerial reports, without exception, pass through their hands and the king only perceives these reports in the form in which they are presented to him.'[73] Moreover, he added, the blame for a failed policy could always be pinned on the responsible ministers, while the Kabinett hid behind the authority of the king.

If Friedrich Gentz was easily the most forthright and eloquent critic of the Kabinett, his concern with the question of royal access was widely shared. Around 1798, for example, one member of the Geheime Cabinetts-Expedition stressed the need to 'control' the Kabinettsräte and suggested that the king should try and open at least some if not all of his correspondence himself, so that the secretaries would be 'unable to suppress any letters'.[74] Such recommendations, of course, were the staple of a long-standing Prussian debate on the nature of the ante-chamber of power. But they all impaled themselves on the same practical problem: how to brief the sovereign without exposing him either to the manipulation of his secretaries or to the unsifted and growing mountain of daily correspondence? As far back as 1786, Frederick William II's favourite Wöllner had defined the essence of the Kabinett as lying in secrecy, simplicity and speed.[75] It should execute the king's will. In order to do so the king must be comprehensively informed. However, Wöllner continued, experience had shown that the councillors – especially Frederick the Great's confidant, Eichel – could control the flow of information reaching the king. The solution, he suggested, was to keep all correspondence from the councillors until it had passed through the king's hands. There then followed elaborate proposals on how to prevent the cabinet secretaries and councillors from manipulating the king.[76]

[73] Ibid.: 'Sie sind die einzigen welche dem König unmittelbare und mündliche Vorträge halten; alle Berichte der Minister gehen ohne Ausnahme durch ihre Hände, und der König vernimmt den Inhalt derselben nur in der Form, in welche sie ihn einkleiden.'
[74] Niethe memorandum, *c.* 1798, GStA Rep. 92 *Friedr. Wilh.d.Dritte* B.VII.4, fo. 36: 'keinen Brief zu unterschlagen im Stande ist'.
[75] 'Schreiben Wöllners über die Einrichtung des Kabinets, vermutlich an Bischoffwerder', printed in Hüffer, *Die Kabinetsregierung in Preussen*, appendix VII, p. 503.
[76] Ibid., p. 503.

The accession of Frederick William III gave rise to a renewed discussion. After all, as Hofprediger Sack stressed at Frederick William's *Huldigungsfeier* in 1798, Prussia expected that the new monarch would 'hold the rudder of state with a firm hand'.[77] Already, in the autumn of 1797, the young king-to-be was presented with a memorandum suggesting that 'everything be concentrated on one point' at the highest levels of state decision-making;[78] this involved the appointment of a 'reliable man' who would help the king to sort out the correspondence and save him from being swamped by minor details. It is not clear what the improvement on the existing situation would have been, save that the creation of a single post responsible for incoming business would place its holder in a position similar to that of Eichel and thus help to aggravate the very abuses it was meant to eliminate. Indeed, in October of that same year, just after Frederick William's coronation, the inherent limits of any attempt to reform the existing system were highlighted by Mencken. At the beginning of his memorandum Mencken set out the guiding principle of Prussian politics: 'Most rulers of the Prussian royal house have sought honour in governing their country themselves, without a prime minister.' There thus resulted a need for a Kabinett to execute the royal commands. Under Frederick II, Mencken continued, the Kabinett had been well handled. Frederick was active and vigilant and his subordinates found it difficult to manipulate him. The advantages of such a Kabinett were the old virtues of administrative order, rapidity of execution and vigilance among the servants of the state. Its disadvantages, however, lay in the tendency to deal with matters superficially and out of context. There was also the danger that ignorance of the broader affairs led subordinates to judge wrongly, a frequent occurrence in the old Frederician Prussia, according to Mencken. Finally, the cabinet system was open to abuse by the secretaries who could bend the monarch to their will 'through manipulation of business [and] through sensitivity to the mood of the day'.[79] But when he came to the question of possible remedies Mencken fell back on the now familiar schemes for arranging the conduct of business in such

---

[77] Quoted in Wienfort, *Monarchie in der bürgerlichen Gesellschaft*, p. 136: 'mit starkem Arm das Ruder des Staates festhalten'.

[78] 'Denkschrift einer dem Kronprinzen Friedrich Wilhelm nahestehenden Person "Ueber die Führung der Geschäfte"', printed in Hüffer, *Die Kabinetsregierung in Preussen*, appendix IX, 509.

[79] 'Denkschrift Menckens über die Einrichtung des Kabinets', printed in Hüffer, *Die Kabinetsregierung in Preussen*, p. 512: 'Die meisten Regenten des Preußischen Hauses haben ihre Ehre darin gesucht, die Uebersicht ihrer Landesregierung selbst zu führen, ohne einen Premierminister . . . durch Zusammenstellung der Geschäfte, durch Aufmerksamkeit auf die Laune des Tages.'

a way that the monarch was neither overwhelmed nor exposed to manipulation.

A contemporaneous memorandum by General Rüchel ran up against exactly the same problem. Like Mencken, he began with a forthright summary of the decision-making ideal in Prussia. Indeed, the relative lucidity with which the usually incoherent Rüchel sketches its underlying principles is striking. He refers to 'The spirit of order, – the systematic arrangement of business – the strict and reliable working of this machine – and its *Point Central* [the king] which maintains a constant state of awareness and surveys everything – these factors made for the visible strengths of the Prussian state over the years.'[80] In the same vein he proceeded to explain that the king, that 'mild but also forceful dictator', must know the workings of all the departments and determine the broad outlines of policy within them. However, 'it is impossible for a single individual to deal with everything in detail. From this there follows the need for the so-called Kabinett.'[81] But Rüchel too could provide no better safeguard against abuses than ensuring the employment of 'honest and talented' councillors. As if unconvinced by this he then went on to devote the rest of his memorandum to the practicalities of distributing business without risking manipulation of the monarch.[82] There was, it seems, no escape from the Kabinett.

Where Gentz differed from the long-standing and increasingly sterile debate on the antechamber of power was in his demand for the creation of a new ministerial council including ministers for foreign, military and internal affairs; the Kabinett was to be reduced to its original secretarial function.[83] In so doing Gentz abandoned the narrow focus on royal access and took up a theme introduced by Hardenberg three years earlier. This memorandum seems to have been the first manifesto for ministerial government in Prussia.[84] Like Gentz, Hardenberg had noted

---

80 Rüchel memorandum printed in Hüffer, *Die Kabinetsregierung in Preussen*, p. 520: 'Geist der Ordnung, – der systematische Geschäftsgang- das unverbrüchliche und steife Festhalten dieser regelmäßigen Maschine- und ihr Point Central Ressorts derselben in ewig angespannter Thätigkeit zu erhalten, solche zu übersehen- diese bewürkten durch die Dauer der Zeit die sichtbaren Vorzüge des preußischen Staats!' For a crushing characterisation of Rüchel see Boyen, *Erinnerungen*, I, p. 124.

81 Ibid., p. 520: 'da es einem einzelnen Menschen unmöglich ist, in das jedesmalige Wesen der Details einzudringen, so erwächst nun aus dieser zweiten Nothwendigkeit, das Daseyn des sogenannten Cabinets'.

82 Ibid., p. 521.

83 Gentz memorandum printed in Wittichen, 'Das preußische Kabinett und Friedrich von Gentz', pp. 269–70.

84 'Ideen zur Errichtung eines Conseils die ich den 25 Januar 1797 dem Könige Friedrich Wilhelm III als Kronprinz zugeschickt habe', cited *in extenso* in Stamm-Kuhlmann, *Friedrich Wilhelm III*, pp. 115–16.

the lack of direction in Prussian foreign policy and the detumescence (*Erschlaffung*) of the internal administration; both of these developments he attributed to the lack of any focal point in decision-making. Like Gentz, he saw the remedy in the establishment of a regular council, composed of the ministers for foreign affairs, war, internal affairs and justice, and presided over by the king; this council would be the forum for collective deliberation in which 'all branches of government would have to cooperate'. Hence, unlike the earlier memorialists such as Wöllner, Mencken and Rüchel, both Hardenberg and Gentz came up with a plan for executive reform which went beyond the old fixation on the antechamber of power to propose a new institutional framework which would enable Prussia to face the growing challenge from Napoleonic France.

The notion of a ministerial council, or at least of a single central focus for decision-making, found an almost universally favourable echo among Prussian politicians. Thus, Colonel Massenbach stressed the need to integrate military and political concerns; this required a 'central point from which all instructions radiate as if out of one focus'.[85] In the foreign ministry, the search for a unified executive was also reflected in Alvensleben's demand for 'more unity in the administration and simplification and rationalisation of the affairs of state'.[86] This theme was taken up by Schulenburg when he defended Haugwitz's candidature for sole control over foreign policy in terms of the need for the 'simplification of business and its concentration under a single direction'.[87] Very similar language was used by Beyme when he called for the 'simplification of the highest cogs of state and . . . thereafter the unification of all branches of each department in the hands of a single man'.[88] This focus on executive reform extended to the highest levels of the domestic administration. In a series of memoranda one senior bureaucrat, Borgstede, called for the restructuring of the General Directory to reflect subject matter alone, rather than the traditional mixture of territorial and subject *ressorts*;[89] the

---

[85] Massenbach memorandum, 11.12.1801 in Massenbach, *Memoiren zur Geschichte des preussischen Staates*, III, p. 268: 'ein Centralpunkt aus welchem alle diese Anordnungen, wie aus *einem* Brennpunkte hervorstrahlen'.

[86] Alvensleben memorandum, 'spring 1802', GStA Rep.96A.9A1, fo. 21: 'mehr Einheit in der Administration und Vereinfachung und Abkürzung der Geschäfte'.

[87] Schulenburg to Frederick William III, 30.10.1804, Hildesheim, GStA Rep.96A.9A1, fo. 41: 'Vereinfachung der Geschäfte und Concentrirung derselben in einer Hand.'

[88] Beyme to Schulenburg, 26.10.1802, Potsdam, in Gustav Roloff, 'Die Neuorganisation im Ministerium des Auswärtigen im Jahre 1802', *FBPG*, 7 (1894), 106: 'Vereinfachung der höchsten Triebräder des Staates und . . . darnach alle Zweige eines jeden Departements in eine Hand zu bringen.'

[89] Borgstede memorandum of 20.1.1799, in Petzold, *Finanzkommission*, p. 61; Borgstede memorandum, 1.6.1800, in Hellwig, *Schulenburg-Kehnert*, p. 32.

reformed body would then be chaired by the eldest minister. Only in this way, Borgstede argued, could decision-making be freed from the thicket of competing institutional imperatives. 'If one wants to supervise everything', he wrote, 'one eventually loses sight of everything.'

Several uncoordinated attempts were now made to put the new ideas into practice. The least successful of these was Beyme's proposal to elevate Schulenburg into a kind of Prime Minister for internal affairs.[90] In some ways, this would merely have confirmed Schulenburg's compulsive collection of offices – which included that of Generalkontrolleur der Finanzen, General-Postmeister, Chef der Kassen-, Stempel-, Münz-, Banco-, Medizinial-, und Lotterie Departements; in a display of almost eccentric reticence, however, Schulenburg declined. Much more progress was made in the field of foreign policy. Here Haugwitz's objectives were twofold. First of all, he aimed to concentrate the decision-making process in a single responsible minister (himself); this required the elimination of his co-ministers, Alvensleben and Finckenstein. Secondly, he sought to rid himself of the extraneous business which was traditionally the preserve of the foreign ministry; this meant offloading responsibility for all peripheral matters onto somebody else. These questions were first broached by Haugwitz within a year of Frederick William's accession to power.[91] On that occasion, his plea that he be left in charge of the 'genuinely political part (*eigentliche politische Teil*)' of foreign policy went unheeded. But Haugwitz kept trying, and after the death of Finckenstein in January 1800 he approached the king directly with a critique of the 'extremely mistaken organisation of the Kabinettsministerium'. Only by granting him sole control over foreign policy, Haugwitz argued, could Prussia hope to introduce and maintain 'a unified policy, which would be pursued consistently while maintaining the strictest secrecy'.[92] This time Haugwitz was more successful and when Alvensleben died in 1802 there was no pressure to appoint a new co-minister for foreign affairs.[93]

But the hope that this would end the long-standing confusion in Prussian policy proved mistaken, for by that stage the cabinet secretary

---

[90] See Naudé, 'Denkwürdigkeiten des Ministers Grafen von Schulenburg', pp. 417–18; Schück, 'Friedrich Wilhelm III und seine Räte für die innere Gesetzgebung Preußens, 1797–1807', *Abhandlungen der Schlesischen Gesellschaft für vaterländische Kultur*, p. 58; Hellwig, *Schulenburg-Kehnert*, pp. 20–1.

[91] Haugwitz to Köckritz, 3.10.1798, Berlin, in Gustav Roloff, 'Die Neuorganisation im Ministerium des Auswärtigen im Jahre 1802', *FBPG*, 5 (1892), 268.

[92] Ibid., pp. 270–1: 'Einheit im System, beständige Consequenz in der Behandlung derselben und Geheimniß in Führung der Geschäfte einzuführen und zu erhalten.'

[93] Lombard to Köckritz, 23.10.1802, Potsdam, in Roloff, 'Die Neuorganisation', V, p. 271.

Lombard had already effectively usurped the role of a co-minister of foreign affairs. All attempts by Haugwitz and his successor Hardenberg to restrict the formulation of policy to the responsible minister failed; the result was a continued lack of cohesion in Prussian diplomacy. 'In my opinion', Hardenberg complained, 'Lombard must refrain from conducting official negotiations, as these should be the preserve of one man if the essential requirement of consistency is to be maintained.'[94] In the same letter, Hardenberg insisted that he 'must be quite sure that no parallel negotiations take place without my knowledge, that no royal instructions are sent to our envoys without prior consultation with me'. Indeed, Hardenberg refused to countenance sharing authority with Lombard. 'I have the position of Cabinetsminister with undivided responsibility', he asserted, 'our Lombard is not responsible, once the king has signed.' There could be no more eloquent exposition of the dangers of disunity in the formulation of foreign policy.

If there was widespread agreement among Prussian politicians that a reform of the executive was long overdue, then the king himself was less enthusiastic. From his perspective, the suggested ministerial council, or single responsible ministry in foreign affairs must have seemed like an attempt to circumscribe royal authority. This objection was anticipated by the reformers themselves. 'One should not object', Hardenberg had written in his original memorandum of 1797, 'that the king would find his freedom curtailed by such a council and thus suffer a decrease of power.'[95] Instead, he argued, Frederick William would find his power enhanced, for the elimination of the Kabinett would reduce the chances 'that something would be instigated or some beneficient measure would be frustrated through cabals and personal intrigues (*daß durch Kabalen und persönliche Rücksichten etwas erschlichen oder Gutes verhindert werde*)'. Frederick William does not seem to have seen things this way. In theory, he recognised the danger of a co-ministry;[96] in practice, he was its greatest supporter. While he never explicitly stated his own motivations,

---

[94] Hardenberg to Beyme (draft), 30.8.1804, Berlin, GStA Rep. 92 *Hardenberg* E5, fos. 117–18: 'Meines Erachtens muß sich Lombard der offiziellen Rücksprachen enthalten, da diese wirklich von einem geschehen dürfen, wenn Consequenz – das wesentliche Bedürfnis demselben – darin existieren will; . . . Ich muß darauf rechnen können, daß keine Neben Negociationen stattfinden, die ich nicht kenne, daß keine Immediat Verfügungen an unsere Gesandten abgehen die nicht mit mir concertirt sind; . . . Ich habe die Stelle des Cabinetsministers mit ungeteilter Verantwortlichkeit, unser Lombard hat gar keine, sobald der König unterschrieben hat.'

[95] Stamm-Kuhlmann, *Friedrich Wilhelm III*, p. 116: 'Man wende nicht ein, daß der König durch ein solches Conseil in seinen Entschlüssen geniert und weniger Herr sein würde.'

[96] Kabinetsordre of Frederick William to Hardenberg and Haugwitz, 14.7.04, Charlottenburg, in Ranke (ed.), *Denkwürdigkeiten Hardenbergs*, I, p. 71, speaks of 'gemeinschaftlichen Geschäftsführung, die ich dem Dienste für nachteilig halte'.

we may assume that he pursued a strategy akin to *divide et impera*: a sole foreign minister might try to force his views on the king; a threatened or aspirant co-minister would always try to cast himself as the defender of the royal standpoint. To an indecisive monarch such as Frederick William, the attractions of ruling through and with a Kabinett were thus obvious. Any other system, in the perceptive words of Schulenburg, was suspect to Prussian monarchs 'because it appeared to indicate a restriction on their personal power'.[97]

Such concern was exaggerated. Although they all sought – to a greater or lesser degree – to influence the monarch, Prussian politicians were both instinctively and rhetorically incapable of mounting a sustained challenge to royal authority. Indeed, the centrality of the king in the decision-making process was ritually – and genuinely – affirmed by ministers and cabinet councillors alike. 'Il n'appartient qu' à V.M. seule', the Kabinetsministerium wrote, 'de prendre son parti entre ces deux alternatives difficiles.'[98] 'Malheureusement pour le roi', Lombard told Frederick William, 'c'est lui seul qui doit décider.'[99] 'By submitting the following to the most high approbation, I urgently and humbly dare to ask you for a definitive decision', Haugwitz wrote.[100] The men in the antechamber of power might cajole, influence and manipulate, but the final decision rested indisputably with the monarch. Hence the schemes for executive reform after 1797 were not intended to sideline Frederick William, but – among other things – to *strengthen* royal power and enable – or encourage – the king to make more effective decisions in the face of Napoleonic France.

Admittedly, there was a broad consensus on the need for a 'central focus' of decision-making; on the particular need for a monocratic foreign ministry; and on the need for the right blend of deliberation and decision. But none of this amounted to a serious challenge to royal authority. There was no suggestion that the estates or any other representative assembly should be consulted on foreign policy. Nor was there any attempt at a 'bureaucratic takeover' of the state. In theory, the proposals for a ministerial council and the removal of the Kabinett could be construed as such. In practice, however, the notion of a collective

---

[97] Naudé, 'Denkwürdigkeiten des Ministers Grafen von Schulenburg', pp. 414–15: 'weil sie glauben den Anschein zu haben, nicht allein zu regieren'.

[98] Kabinettsministerium to Frederick William, 13.5.1798, Berlin, in Bailleu (ed.), *Preussen und Frankreich*, I, p. 204.

[99] Lombard memorandum, mid-May 1799, in Bailleu (ed.), *Preussen und Frankreich*, I, p. 289. In a similar vein see Rüchel memorandum, mid-May 1799, in ibid., p. 295.

[100] Haugwitz memorandum, mid-July 1799, in Bailleu (ed.), *Preussen und Frankreich*, I, p. 316: 'Indem ich der höchsten Beurteilung Vorstehendes unterwerfe, wage ich es so dringend als ehrfurchtsvoll um eine definitive Entscheidung zu bitten.'

bureaucratic campaign to wrest the high-political executive from the monarch exceeded the mental horizons of most Prussian politicians; the day-to-day running of the domestic administration was another matter. Of course, ambitious individual politicians sought to impose their will on the king, but this was not related to any broader corporate agenda. Instead, Prussian politicians pursued aims that were both more specific and more general: more general, in that they were engaged in a genuine quest to strengthen the decision-making apparatus in face of the French threat; more specific, in that the resulting reform plans aimed not so much to eliminate the antechamber of power as to dominate it. As we shall see, Prussian politicians wanted not to overcome royal power, but to appropriate it for their own personal advancement.

The struggle for the executive: adversarial politics in Prussia, 1797–1804

. . . ne serais-je pas l'être le plus méprisable, si, lié comme je le suis d'amitié avec le comte Haugwitz, je pourrais avoir un instant l'idée de le supplanter?[101]

Intense though the debates on the French threat or the imperative for reform might have been, they were far surpassed in ferocity by the simultaneous struggles in the antechamber of power at Berlin. The focus of this contest was the person of the monarch; its supreme prize was the control of the foreign-political executive, be it as a responsible minister, or as a Kabinettssekretär behind the scenes. To the politicians of pre-reform Prussia, politics was not primarily about social or economic development. They were no different from the mass of their European colleagues in regarding foreign policy as the paramount activity of the state; the 'eudaemonist-utilitarian function of the state' emphasised by Eckhart Hellmuth[102] was subordinate to external demands. Around 1800, the *Geschichtliche Grundbegriffe* remind us, 'the word "politics" had taken on the meaning of the conduct of external affairs'.[103] Much of what we now consider 'politics' was then deemed to be administration, the

[101] Hardenberg to Bischoffwerder, 9.3.1796, Berlin, in Bailleu (ed.), *Preussen und Frankreich*, I, pp. 56–6.
[102] Hellmuth, *Naturrechts-philosophie und bürokratischer Werthorizont*, pp. 124–5, 150 and *passim*: 'eudämonistisch-utilaristische Staatszweckbestimmung'.
[103] Volker Sellin, 'Politik', in Otto Brunner, Werner Conze and Reinhart Koselleck (eds.), *Geschichtliche Grundbegriffe* (Stuttgart, 1978), p. 843. On the centrality of foreign policy for Frederick II see Müller-Weil, *Absolutismus und Außenpolitik*, p. 77 and *passim*; and Horst Dreitzel, *Monarchiebegriffe in der Fürstengesellschaft. Semantik und Theorie der Einherrschaft in Deutschland von der Reformation bis zum Vormärz* (Cologne, Weimar and Vienna, 1991), I, p. 735.

domain of worthy bureaucrats perhaps, but certainly not a concern of aspiring statesmen. The prestige of the foreign ministry was a function of the high stakes involved. A skilful policy could strengthen the state more than the most patient administration; serious error might mean immediate extinction. As Alvensleben explained to Frederick William in 1799, only the men of the foreign ministry could 'contribuer au bien de l'état ou tendre à sa destruction'.[104] Indeed, it is striking that Hardenberg, chiefly known to posterity as a great Prussian reformer, was most concerned about his reputation in foreign policy. This is obvious in the *Denkwürdigkeiten* – written in 1807–8 as an apologia for his recent diplomacy, but never published in his lifetime – in which the full decade of reforming activity in Ansbach-Bayreuth barely rated a mention. Even after the great period of reforms, Hardenberg remained preoccupied with the idea of a memoir recording only his foreign-political activities.[105] If such a versatile figure as Hardenberg gave a clear precedence to foreign over domestic affairs, this was even truer for politicians such as Haugwitz, whose ignorance of domestic matters was matched only by his indifference. 'Qu'est-ce que la politique? Quel en est le vrai but?', he asked. Politics, he answered, was about 'le grand contrat social qui unit tacitement les peuples civilisés sous les lois du droit des gens naturel et l'art qu'on emploie pour maintenir cette union . . . elle est l'art de maintenir, autant que possible, la paix'.[106] Politics, in short, was about foreign policy; there is no evidence that Haugwitz showed sustained interest in any aspect of domestic policy.

The struggle for the foreign-political executive in the antechamber of power around the king was a long-established feature of Prussian politics. This contest was particularly ferocious whenever, as was the case with Frederick William II and Frederick William III, the monarch was either indecisive or impressionable. During the previous reign, the ministers of the Kabinettsministerium, Alvensleben, Haugwitz, Schulenburg and Finckenstein had been pitted both against each other and against the royal favourites Bischoffwerder and – to a lesser extent – Wöllner in the antechamber of power around the king. The accession of Frederick William III inevitably brought a reversal of high-political fortunes. Some, such as Bischoffwerder, went quietly. Others joined the scramble to accommodate their new master. Some eventually had to be prised loose

---

104 Alvensleben to Frederick William, 13.5.1799, Berlin, GStA Rep. 92 *Alvensleben* 1, fo. 59.
105 Hausherr, *Hardenberg*, I, p. 10. The material assembled by Hardenberg's assistant Schöll is a useful and much-neglected source for this period.
106 Haugwitz memorandum, 21.5.1802, Berlin, in Bailleu (ed.), *Preussen und Frankreich*, II, p. 92.

from the reins of office. In a frantic bid for royal favour, Wöllner rushed
to disown his own campaign against the enlightenment. He declared
himself prepared 'to fulfil all instructions of his master, to obey the will
of the king in all things absolutely'.[107] Wöllner was sacked without a
pension in March 1798. New figures moved to occupy the antechamber
of power: Mencken, and later Beyme replaced Wöllner; in time,
Lombard replaced Bischoffwerder as councillor on foreign affairs. The
senior figures of the Kabinettsministerium – Alvensleben, Finckenstein
and Haugwitz – retained their places, partly no doubt because their
experience was indispensable, but perhaps also because the new king
was confident they would serve him as faithfully as they had his father.
Haugwitz in particular showed remarkable survival skills after the death
of his former patron. Despite the fact that he – much more than his two
colleagues – had been deeply implicated in the Rosicrucian hocus-pocus
of Wöllner and Bischoffwerder, Haugwitz deftly changed horses. It
was he who encouraged Frederick William in his first political move,
the arrest, interrogation and banishment of his father's mistress, the
Countess Lichtenau.[108]

At first sight, the high-political changes after 1797 seem personal
rather than structural. The old system of favourites was merely replaced
by the Kabinett, not abolished as the ministers desired. It is certainly
true that in the sphere of domestic politics a gulf opened up between
Mencken – later Beyme – and the senior bureaucrats of the Generaldirektorium which, in form if not in content, was not unlike the struggle
between Wöllner and his adversaries; these disputes need not concern us
too closely here. In the field of foreign policy, however, the Kabinettsministerium profited from the vacuum left by the departure of
Bischoffwerder. Prussian high politics now focused on the rivalry
between Alvensleben and Haugwitz. Due to ill health, the role of the
third minister, Finckenstein, was minimal after 1798. Of the other
prominent figures, only Schulenburg was a possible contender; he
retained the confidence of the king but, despite widespread speculation,
Schulenburg never made a bid for the foreign ministry.[109] Throughout
the first five years of Frederick William's reign, Haugwitz sought to

[107] Paul Bailleu, 'Johann Christoph Wöllner', in Bailleu, *Preußischer Wille. Gesammelte Aufsätze von Paul Bailleu*, edited by Melle Klinkenborg (Berlin, 1924), pp. 138–53; Oppeln-Bronikowski, *Abenteurer am preußischen Hofe*, p. 158: 'alle Befehle seines Herrn vollstrecken, dem Willen des Königs aufs pünktlichste streng gehorchen zu wollen'.
[108] Oppeln-Bronikowski, *Abenteurer am preußischen Hofe*, p. 170; Radziwill, *Fünfundvierzig Jahre aus meinem Leben*, p. 115.
[109] On Schulenburg's role in high politics see Hellwig, *Schulenburg-Kehnert*, especially pp. 18 and 24.

dislodge Alvensleben and assume sole command of the foreign ministry. As far back as the early- to mid-1790s, Haugwitz had tried to isolate Alvensleben and cut him off both from the flow of diplomatic information and from contact with the king. Alvensleben complained bitterly of being 'peu instruit, comme le département l'était toujours des intentions du roi, connues au comte Haugwitz seul';[110] by 1798 the success of this strategy was becoming evident.[111]

In his campaign to sideline Alvensleben, Haugwitz launched an initiative which was to have far-reaching consequences for Prussian high politics. On the eve of his accession to the throne, Haugwitz had suggested to the crown prince Frederick William in March 1797 that he should take 'un conseiller dont la politique fasse destination essentielle'. This councillor should be the crucial figure in foreign affairs, for all diplomatic business to and from the king would pass through his hands. The man Haugwitz suggested for the job was his protégé, Johann Wilhelm Lombard.[112] In February 1798, Haugwitz renewed his request for such an appointment.[113] The intention was quite plainly to infiltrate Haugwitz's own man into the antechamber of power around the king and thereby consolidate his hold on the conduct of foreign affairs still further. But by far the best opportunity to eliminate Alvensleben presented itself upon the death of Finckenstein in 1800. Haugwitz used the resulting debate about the reform of the foreign-political executive as a weapon in his high-political struggle. Under the previous collegial system, all three ministers had been technically equally responsible for the conduct of affairs; apart from foreign affairs, the Kabinettsministerium was also charged with the relatively unimportant business relating to the royal house. Already in 1798, Haugwitz had attempted to rid himself of this clutter by offloading it on his colleagues, while taking over unfettered control of foreign policy.[114] Alvensleben, however, insisted on retaining the right 'to be kept continuously informed of the progress of political affairs'. After the death of Finckenstein, Alvensleben agreed to confine his main activities to the 'non-political' business of the ministry. As a consolation he was made a count. Alvensleben felt his exclusion

---

110 Alvensleben memorandum, 1.10.1797, Berlin, in Bailleu (ed.), *Preussen und Frankreich*, I, pp. 149–50.
111 Sièyes report, 28.7.98, Berlin, ibid., p. 483.
112 Haugwitz to Frederick William, 3.3.1797, GStA Rep. 92 *Friedr. Wilh. d. Dritte* B.VI.4, fos. 34–5.
113 Hüffer, *Die Kabinettsregierung in Preussen*, p. 89.
114 Gustav Roloff, 'Die Neuorganisation im Ministerium des Auswärtigen im Jahre 1802. Briefe von Haugwitz und Lombard', *FBPG*, 5 (1892), 99. See also Kohnke, 'Das preußische Kabinettsministerium', pp. 346–8.

keenly;[115] thanks to the intervention of Frederick William, however, he retained the right both to be kept informed of developments and to advise the king on foreign policy.

On 21 October 1802, Alvensleben died. Haugwitz's main concern was to avoid the appointment of another Kabinettsminister; at the very least he was determined that any candidate should be his creature.[116] To Haugwitz's delight, no successor was chosen and those of Alvensleben's functions relating to foreign affairs were transferred to him. The tedious dynastic business and other clutter were dumped on an unfortunate bureaucrat, von der Reck. The triumph of Haugwitz now seemed complete. For the first time in two reigns, a single minister now controlled Prussian foreign policy.

Very soon, however, Haugwitz's supremacy was being challenged from within the antechamber of power itself. Indeed, the abandonment of the collegial principle in the foreign ministry ensured that the structural antithesis between ministry and Kabinett became correspondingly more important. For unlike Mencken, who had had no foreign-political pretensions, the man whom Haugwitz had infiltrated into the Kabinett now became a more dangerous adversary than Alvensleben had ever been. In 1799, Lombard was already being described as making 'des progrès rapides dans l'opinion du monarque . . . il pourra devenir sous peu un personnage plus important qu'aucun des membres du cabinet [meaning here the foreign ministry]'.[117] By 1801, another observer noted that 'Il devient chaque jour plus évident que M.Lombard cherche à étendre sa considération et à devenir aussi une puissance.'[118] Public recognition of Lombard's role came in August 1803 with his dispatch to Napoleon in his own capacity as 'conseiller intime de cabinet'.[119] The complete failure of this mission damaged Lombard's standing and dented his self-confidence; his political position with the king, however, remained unshaken. Despite Haugwitz's officially far senior stature, the contest was in many ways an unequal one. Thanks to his commanding role in the antechamber of power, Lombard was progressively able to deny Haugwitz access to the king. It seems that in 1800 Lombard persuaded Frederick William to issue an instruction according to which no decision in foreign affairs could be made on the strength of an oral submission by a minister alone. Even the oral approval of the king was

[115] Alvensleben to Frederick William, 24.4.1802, Berlin, GStA Rep.96A.9A1, fo. 24.
[116] Roloff, 'Neuorganisation im Ministerium des Auswärtigen', pp. 106–8.
[117] Otto report, 25.9.1799, Berlin, in Bailleu (ed.), *Preussen und Frankreich*, I, p. 513.
[118] Bignon report, 15.2.1801, Berlin, ibid., II, p. 124.
[119] Instruction for Lucchesini, 7.7.1803, Charlottenburg, ibid., II, p. 181.

deemed to be insufficient, unless it was accompanied by a written royal instruction.[120] The purpose of this exercise was transparent: whenever Haugwitz gained access to the king, Lombard would subsequently be enabled to subvert whatever had been decided. Admittedly, the existence of this document is disputed and no record is extant in the archives.[121] Yet some such arrangement must have existed, for there is no other way of explaining the steady eclipse of Haugwitz after 1802.

Little by little, Haugwitz saw his functions usurped by Lombard. Prussian diplomats were assiduously courted and left in no doubt with whom real power lay.[122] More seriously, Lombard directly challenged the competency of the foreign minister by taking up contact with the French envoys in Berlin. In March 1802, Bignon reported that he had been invited to 'addresser à lui lorsque je voudrais quelque explication'. The result was, he added, that French diplomats tried to 'trouver auprès de M. Lombard les éclaircissements qui me manqueraient de l'autre côté'.[123] Quick to exploit the personal weaknesses of their hosts, the French pandered to Lombard's literary pretensions by attending his *petits dîners litteraires*;[124] they also flattered him with cultural distinctions.[125] In the meantime, Haugwitz's position was in irretrievable decline. 'M. de Haugwitz', the French ambassador reported, 's'apercevait que M. Lombard en est venu à défendre avec indépendance ses idées vis-à-vis de lui, et il y est d'autant plus sensible qu'il se complaisait dans le rôle prépondérant.'[126] Haugwitz's retreat was accelerated by his failure to convince Frederick William to join the Second Coalition; this has often been traced to the influence of Lombard. A further personal blow came in 1803, when his attempts to forestall the French invasion of Hanover came to nothing.[127] By October of the same year, Laforest was predicting that Haugwitz would 'se retirer avant d'être supplanté'.[128] The announcement of Haugwitz's retirement in July 1804 did not, therefore,

---

[120] Wittichen, 'Das preußische Kabinett und Friedrich von Gentz', p. 252.
[121] Hermann Hüffer, 'Nachträgliche Bemerkungen zum Feldzuge der Engländer und Russen in Holland', *Historische Vierteljahrsschrift*, 5 (1902), 524; Paul Wittichen, 'Zu Gentz's Denkschrift über das preussische Kabinett', *HZ*, 91 (1903), 62.
[122] Lombard to Lucchesini, 28.11.1802, Potsdam, in Bailleu (ed.), *Preussen und Frankreich*, II, pp. 120–1; Lombard to Lucchesini, 6.6.1803, Fürth, ibid., pp. 156–7; Lombard to Lucchesini, 15.6.1803, Wilhelmsbad, ibid., p. 167.
[123] Bignon to Talleyrand, 6.3.1802, Berlin, ibid., p. 78; Otto to Reinhard, 20.9.1799, Berlin, ibid., I, p. 510.
[124] Bignon to Talleyrand, 29.1.1803, Berlin, ibid., p. 123.
[125] Beurnonville to Talleyrand, 25.5.1802, Neuilly, ibid., p. 97;
[126] Laforest to Talleyrand, 17.10.1803, Berlin, ibid., p. 208.
[127] Ford, *Hanover and Prussia*, p. 314.
[128] Laforest to Talleyrand, 14.10.1803, Berlin, in Bailleu (ed.), *Preussen und Frankreich*, II, p. 26.

come as a complete surprise.[129] Anxiety about the condition of his estates and mounting health problems may have been more than a public pretext. The main reason, however, was the humiliating political ascendancy of Lombard. By now, Haugwitz hardly saw the king more than once a fortnight;[130] in order to obtain this audience he had to negotiate with Lombard. This state of affairs led Metternich to dub Lombard the king's *Schildwache*.[131] At one level, Haugwitz's resignation was thus an obvious capitulation. However, the arrangements for his retirement kept open the possibility of a return to high politics. Haugwitz retained the right to participate in policy debates when in Berlin for the winter season; to be kept abreast of developments; and to deputise for his successor.[132] This prompted Schulenburg to warn the new minister, Hardenberg, that 'la part plus ou moins directe ou indirecte que Msr le comte Haugwitz veut garder dans les affaires, menera à des désagreements'; on the other hand, Schulenburg conceded, the relevant clauses might only be a device to increase his pension rights.[133] Only time would tell.

The new minister of foreign affairs was no stranger to the ebb and flow of Prussian high politics. In 1795, Hardenberg had accepted the post of deputy foreign minister to participate in the peace negotiations with Revolutionary France at Basle. He was prominently associated with the resulting treaty and can justly be called an architect of the neutrality policy. Already at this stage, Hardenberg's consuming ambition was evident to his colleagues. Nobody believed his protestations that he was 'incapable d'intriguer' or that he was 'très content du poste que j'occupe'.[134] After 1796, however, he fell out with Lucchesini, Möllendorf and the Lichtenau coterie; this cost him the goodwill of Frederick William II.[135] Frustrated in his first excursion into high politics, Hardenberg returned to the political wilderness as chief administrator of Ansbach and Bayreuth. Throughout the late 1790s, he sought to consolidate his local power-base through a programme of reforms. Many of those who later became prominent during the Prussian reform movement, such as Kircheisen, Altenstein and Nagler, first

---

[129] Beyme to Hardenberg, 9.7.1804, Charlottenburg, GStA Rep. 92 *Hardenberg* E5, fo. 56.
[130] Wittichen, 'Das preußische Kabinett und Friedrich von Gentz', p. 252.
[131] Gaide, 'Der diplomatische Verkehr des geheimen Kabinettrats Lombard', pp. 48–9.
[132] Hüffer, *Die Kabinettsregierung in Preussen*, pp. 139–40; Ranke (ed.), *Denkwürdigkeiten Hardenbergs*, II, 69, 137–38.
[133] Schulenburg to Hardenberg, 23.7.1804, Kehnert, in Ranke (ed.), *Denkwürdigkeiten Hardenbergs*, I, p. 74.
[134] Hardenberg to Bischoffwerder, 3.9.1796, Berlin, in Bailleu (ed.), *Preussen und Frankreich*, I, p. 57.
[135] Hausherr, *Hardenberg*, I, p. 187.

cut their teeth under Hardenberg in Franconia.[136] These men were promoted as much for their loyalty to Hardenberg as for their administrative ability. 'A minister who knows his trade', he confided to the Ritter von Lang, 'will never choose too intelligent a subordinate.'[137] Like Haugwitz, Hardenberg made mistakes; his protégé Altenstein later went on to become a bitter political rival.

Despite banishment to Franconia, Hardenberg continued to maintain his foreign-political ambitions. It is not clear whether his scheme for the annexation of Nuremberg was frustrated by the Kabinettsministerium out of envy and malice; Hardenberg certainly believed this to be the case.[138] Very soon, however, he rejoined the foreign-political debate with his plans for a southern expansion of Prussia. Not least among Hardenberg's motivations during the compensations debate was his personal interest in consolidating the Prussian position in southern Germany. In this respect he resembled the 'westerners'; the opposition of both groups to the policy of disengagement from the west and south was transparently linked to the fear of losing their administrative fiefdoms. Nor – going by the evidence of his diaries – did Hardenberg lose sight of the broader concerns of Prussian foreign policy.[139] It is therefore somewhat misleading to claim, as one of his biographers does, that Hardenberg dropped out of Prussian foreign policy for some years after 1796.[140] What facilitated his return to the foreign-political executive was Hardenberg's connection with Haugwitz, which went back to the latter's invitation to accompany him to Basle. Since then, relations between the two had been cordial, at least in public. Whenever he was in Berlin, Hardenberg made a point of calling on Haugwitz; joint visits to the theatre or dinner engagements were not uncommon.[141] In the privacy of his diary, however, Hardenberg was scathing. Haugwitz was criticised for having gained his decorations 'dishonourably'; on another occasion he was described as having 'hay on his horns', meaning that Haugwitz was a dangerous man and not to be trusted.[142] In 1803 and again in the spring

---

[136] Endres, 'Preußische Ära in Franken', pp. 186–7.
[137] Ibid., pp. 195–6: 'Ein Minister, der sein Handwerk versteht, wird sich niemals einen genialen Kopf zum Handlanger suchen.'
[138] Ranke (ed.), *Denkwürdigkeiten Hardenbergs*, I, p. 365.
[139] See his diary entries criticising Alvensleben: Hardenberg diary, 3.8.1798, Berlin, GStA Rep. 92 *Hardenberg* L24, fo. 6.
[140] Hausherr, *Hardenberg*, I, p. 187; Zierke, *Hardenbergs deutsche Politik*, p. 75.
[141] GStA Rep. 92 *Hardenberg* L24: diary entries 17, 19, and 22 August 1798, fos. 7, 11–14.
[142] Diary entry for 7.7.1798, ibid., fo. 7; entry for 2.7.1798, the original phrase being 'foenum in cornu habet'. I am told by my colleague Dr Philip Pattenden that this is a reference to Horace, *Satires*, 1.4.34; an ox had hay bound around its horns if dangerous.

of 1804, this friendship paid off, when Haugwitz invited Hardenberg to deputise for him.[143] Inevitably, some friction resulted during Haugwitz's absence; he continued to be kept abreast of developments and insisted that Hardenberg delay all important decisions until his return.[144] Nevertheless, the arrangement worked well enough for Haugwitz to recommend Hardenberg as his successor upon his retirement in August 1804.[145] Significantly – and as it turned out ominously – Haugwitz remained free to attend and participate in policy discussions, especially during the winter, when he was not on his Silesian estates.

At the outset, Hardenberg was widely seen as a man who, in the words of the British ambassador, Sir Francis Jackson, lacked a 'sufficiently strong footing in the country or upon the king's affections' to be 'obnoxious' to colleagues.[146] But this was soon to change, as Hardenberg systematically went about consolidating his position with Frederick William.[147] Above all, Hardenberg was determined 'not to allow anybody else to brief the king on an important matter'.[148] This was a significant break with the practice of his predecessor, who had allowed the Kabinett to monopolise the king before belatedly realising his mistake. Even when Lombard was away, Beyme deputised for him in foreign affairs, so that one intermediary was simply replaced by another.[149] Inevitably, Hardenberg's largely successful quest for a direct relationship with the king brought him into conflict with Lombard. If at first he had offered Hardenberg his *respect, docilité* and *reconnaissance*,[150] Lombard soon moved to defend his position in the antechamber of power. Hardly a month after Hardenberg took office, he set out his fears to Beyme, who in turn conveyed them to Hardenberg. Lombard's primary concern, Beyme wrote, was that Haugwitz's 'ill-humour (*Mißvergnügen*)' with him might have encouraged Hardenberg to consider 'changes in the existing

---

[143] Beyme to Hardenberg, 31.3.1804, Berlin, GStA Rep. 92 *Hardenberg* E5, fo. 11.

[144] Haugwitz to Hardenberg, 26.6.1804, Rogau, ibid., fo. 52.

[145] Hardenberg took sole charge of the Kabinetsministerium on 13 August 1804: Ranke (ed.), *Denkwürdigkeiten Hardenbergs*, I, p. 72.

[146] Jackson report, 17.9.1804, PROL F.O. 64/6, unfoliated.

[147] Griewank, 'Hardenberg und die preußische Politik', pp. 236–7; Hüffer, *Die Kabinettsregierung in Preussen*, p. 139.

[148] Hardenberg to Frederick William, *c.* August 1804, paraphrased in Ranke (ed.), *Denkwürdigkeiten Hardenbergs*, I., p. 34: 'in keiner wichtigen Sache den Vortrag einem anderen zu überlassen'.

[149] GStA Rep. 92 *Hardenberg* E5: Beyme to Hardenberg, 3.7.1804, Charlottenburg, fo. 53; Beyme to Hardenberg, 14.7.1804, Charlottenburg, fo. 66; Beyme to Hardenberg, 10.7.1804, Charlottenburg, fo. 57. See also Disch, 'Der Kabinetsrat Beyme und die auswärtige Politik', *FBPG*, 42 (1929), 96.

[150] Lombard to Hardenberg, 30.7.1804, Landeck, in Hüffer, *Die Kabinettsregierung in Preussen*, p. 531.

order of business (*Änderungen in dem bisherigen Geschäftsgange*)' which 'might affect his own sphere of action in a negative manner. He seemed to be particularly struck by the fact that his excellency [i.e. Hardenberg] had personally submitted the dispatches [to the king] last Tuesday.'[151] It would be difficult to find a franker and more succinct description either of the particular contest which now developed between Hardenberg and Lombard, or, by extrapolation, of the nature of the struggle in the antechamber of power as a whole.

Thanks to the considerable social gulf separating Hardenberg from his middle-class adversaries in the Kabinett, some contemporaries and many historians have stressed the element of class-hatred in the high-political struggle in Prussia.[152] Yet one should beware of false polarities. Contrary to what one might imagine, social background played a relatively minor role in Prussian high politics. Indeed, for a state whose social structure was supposedly so ossified, upward mobility among the political elite was not uncommon. Thus, two of the most influential figures of the period, the cabinet counsellors Beyme and Lombard, came from indisputably bourgeois backgrounds. The basis of their high-political power was no different from that of their aristocratic colleagues, namely the confidence of the king. It should therefore come as no surprise to find that high-political alignments bore no relation whatever to class divisions. Thus, on one side of the divide we find Junkers of the purest stock, such as Kleist and Köckeritz in the Generaladjutantur, facing equally long-established aristocrats such as Schulenburg on the other side. Similarly, we find Haugwitz, a Silesian magnate, allied with the bourgeois Lombard and Beyme against Hardenberg, a Hanoverian nobleman and thus notionally sharing the same class interest as his adversary. In short, it is fair to say that all Prussian politicians shed their social identities once they entered the rarified sphere of high politics. Noble origin may have helped, but it was not decisive. Whatever the restrictions in other fields of human endeavour might have been, birth was certainly not an essential qualification for participation in Prussian high politics.

---

151 Beyme to Hardenberg, 21.8.1804, Neisse, GStA Rep. 92 *Hardenberg* E5, fo. 111: 'ihn in seinem Wirkungskreise nachteilig werde dürfte. Besonders schien ihn die Nachricht zu frappieren, daß Exz. [i.e. Hardenberg] selbst die depeches am letzten Dienstag S.M. vorgelegt hätten.'

152 Stamm-Kuhlmann, *Friedrich Wilhelm III*, p. 212; G. P. Gooch, *Germany and the French Revolution* (reprinted London, 1965), p. 409; Cölln, *Vertraute Briefe*, I, p. 129, 145–6. See also the remarks by Clausewitz in Rothfels (ed.), *Clausewitz. Politische Schriften und Briefe*, p. 208, on the 'liberalism' of the bourgeois *Kabinetsräte* versus 'der aristokratische Sinn des adligen Ministeriums'; and Paul Wittichen on the class hatred between Kabinett and ministers, 'Zu Gentz's Denkschrift über das preußische Kabinett', pp. 63–6.

If social background did not substantially influence high-political alignments, then neither did it pre-determine foreign-political orientation. For example, such stalwart Junkers as Alvensleben were also outspoken Francophiles in foreign policy. His noble colleague Schulenburg on the other hand, remained implacably anti-French until a dramatic conversion to Napoleon after 1807. Similarly, while the reforming zeal of Beyme was clearly linked to his bourgeois contempt for aristocratic privilege, the driving force behind the reforms until 1806, and indeed thereafter, was a small number of progressive noble bureaucrats, men such as Stein, Struensee and Schrötter. Yet even they were far from a unified group. Struensee was well-known as both a reformer and a Francophile in foreign policy, while Stein – though no less a virulent critic of the Prussian *ancien régime* – was from the very beginning an opponent both of France and its 'perfidious principles'.[153] Moreover, the very nature of their enterprise often brought the aristocratic reformers into conflict with their own class; a typical instance of this would be Hardenberg's ruthless suppression of the Franconian nobility.[154] But upon closer investigation the picture becomes more differentiated still. High-political alignments were not even primarily linked to policy differences. Thus, a glance at the membership of the Militärische Gesellschaft in Berlin, the intellectual powerhouse of military reform, shows the presence of such allies as Scharnhorst, Boyen and Gneisenau; closer scutiny also reveals the names of their bitter enemies, Zastrow, LeCoq and Kleist von Nollendorf.[155] If we turn to the sphere of social and economic reform, we find that such adversaries as Beyme and Mencken on the one hand, and Stein and Schrötter on the other hand, were all trying to achieve the same thing.[156] As for the debate in foreign policy, the protagonists were either all fundamentally agreed on neutrality, or soon bowed to the prevailing view (see below); what they acrimoniously disputed was the control of that policy. In short, there was no direct or necessary link between birth, high-political loyalty and domestic or foreign-political orientation.

---

[153] Steffens, 'Rheingrenze und territoriale Entschädigungsfrage', p. 171.
[154] Hardenberg to Haugwitz, 12.3.1801, GStA Rep. 92 *Hardenberg* E1, fo. 11; Hardenberg to Haugwitz, 4.4.1801, Ansbach, ibid., fo. 27. See also Fritz Hartung, *Hardenberg und die preußische Verwaltung in Ansbach-Bayreuth von 1792 bis 1806* (Tübingen, 1908), *passim* especially pp. 26–51; Süßheim, *Preußens innere Politik in Ansbach-Bayreuth*, pp. 61–2 and *passim*; and Endres, 'Preußische Ära in Franken', especially pp. 173–5.
[155] Charles Edward White, *The enlightened soldier. Scharnhorst and the 'Militärische Gesellschaft in Berlin, 1801–1805'* (New York and London, 1989), pp. 203–11.
[156] This was noted by Hintze, 'Preußische Reformbestrebungen vor 1806', pp. 507–8; before him by Schück, 'Friedrich Wilhelm III und sene Räte', pp. 68–70.

Indeed, Prussian politics polarised not around issues but around the dominant set of adversarial relationships at a given time. In the first years of Frederick William's reign, attention focussed on the rivalry between Haugwitz and Alvensleben; after 1800 the contest between Haugwitz and Lombard moved increasingly centre stage; and from mid-1804 onwards it was Hardenberg's struggle with Lombard which predominated. The roots of these political enmities were more anthropological than intellectual. 'They are two men', says Leonore in *Torquato Tasso*, Goethe's classic tale of courtly intrigue and disappointed ambition, 'who I have long believed are foes because nature did not make one man out of them.'[157] In fact, political hatred was recognised to be an inescapable fact of political life. 'Thank God I have had many loyal friends, and I still have them', said Schulenburg at the end of his life, 'but I have also had enemies, known and unknown ones, as is always the case.'[158] It was the clash of irreconcilable personal ambitions, not that of contrasting political programmes, which gave the struggle in the antechamber of power its particularly bitter edge.

Neither superior arguments nor public rhetoric could prevail in the antechamber of power; the king's confidence and favour alone was decisive. But in order to secure and maintain that confidence, regular access to the royal person was essential. It was for this reason that the crux of Hardenberg's relationship with Lombard was his successful insistence on direct and regular contact with the king. Inevitably, access to the monarch was a jealously guarded privilege.[159] Those deprived of the oxygen of royal favour simply withered on the vine. The classic instance of this was the elderly Prince Heinrich, brother of Frederick the Great. By the end of the century, this once-respected figure had transmogrified into the ancient mariner of Prussian politics, button-holing harassed foreign envoys before they could make their excuses. Prince Heinrich's misfortune was to have fallen out of favour with Frederick William at the beginning of his reign; henceforth ambitious politicians gave Heinrich's estate at Rheinsberg the widest berth they

---

157 Leonore in Johann Wolfgang Goethe, *Torquato Tasso. Ein Schauspiel* (Stuttgart, 1964), third act, second scene, p. 50: 'Zwei Männer sind's, ich hab es lang gefühlt, Die darum Feinde sind, weil die Natur nicht einen Mann aus ihnen beiden formte.'
158 Naudé, 'Denkwürdigkeiten des Ministers Grafen von Schulenburg', 390: 'Freunde hab ich gottlob mehrere treue, sehr verdiente Männer gehabt, und habe sie noch, Feinde aber auch, bekannte und unbekannte, wie es nicht anders sein kann.'
159 E.g. the bad-tempered exchange between Görtz and Haugwitz recounted in Görtz, *Memoiren eines deutschen Staatsmannes*, p. 615; Massenbach, *Memoiren zur Geschichte des preussischen Staates*, III, pp. 134, 142–4, 295–6 and *passim* on his tribulations in the antechamber of power; for the use of Beyme for purposes of access, see: Von Moser to Beyme, 18.5.1805, Berlin, GStA Rep.96A.18B, fo. 127.

could find.[160] 'Il est nul dans les affaires', Sièyes commented cruelly;[161] 'toujours actif et ne faisant jamais rien', was the description of another observer.[162] Beurnonville spoke of his 'ambition toujours sans effet, mais toujours subsistant';[163] and Hardenberg dismissed him as 'ce vieux fou'.[164]

Inevitably, passions ran high among those who had drawn the shorter straw in the scramble for access and advancement. When Colonel Massenbach swore to 'break the neck' of the rival who had beaten him to the post of personal military adjutant to Frederick William, he was only articulating what many frustrated figures must have thought in similar situations.[165] But the bitterness engendered by disappointed ambition was perhaps most vividly reflected in the notes left by one mortified loser in the unceasing struggle for patronage and recognition which constituted Prussian high politics. 'Est-ce une fatalité du sort qui constamment me prodique la haine et le mépris en public', wrote Legationsrath Cäsar in Vienna, 'et ne m'accorde l'estime et la confiance qu'au secret? Suis-je donc toujours condamné au rôle équivoque d'un bâtard? Ne trouverai-je jamais un ami, un protecteur, un ministre, pas même un roi qui ait le courage de m'avouer?'[166]

The politics of neutrality

BOSWELL: How then, Sir, did he [Shelburne] get into favour with the king?

JOHNSON: Because, Sir, I suppose he promised the king, to do whatever the king pleases.[167]

When the master lets his preference be known, the servants pursue it with a vengeance.

Tian Jiaying (Secretary to Chairman Mao)[168]

---

[160] Radziwill, *Fünfundvierzig Jahre aus meinen Leben*, p. 138. In the kindly words of Chester V. Easum, *Prince Henry of Prussia, Brother of Frederick the Great* (Westport, Conn., 1971), p. 371 he 'became . . . a living legend'.

[161] Sièyes report, 7.7.1798, Berlin, in Bailleu (ed.), *Preussen und Frankreich*, I, p. 481.

[162] Report of Reuß (Austrian envoy in Berlin), 20.6.1797, Berlin, ibid., p. 535.

[163] Beurnonville to Talleyrand, 13.6.1800, Berlin, ibid., p. 525.

[164] Hardenberg diary entry, 17.8.1798, GStA Rep 92. *Hardenberg* L24, fo. 7.

[165] Massenbach, *Memoiren zur Geschichte des preussischen Staates*, III, p. 296; see also ibid., p. 294: 'nun schwor ich, Holtzmann den Hals zu brechen'.

[166] Caesar notes, October 1799, GStA Rep. 92 *Caesar* 28, unfoliated.

[167] Cited in Conor Cruise O'Brien, *The great melody: a thematic biography and commented anthology of Edmund Burke* (London, 1992), p. 231.

[168] Tian Jiaying, cited in *New York Review of Books*, 17.11.94, p. 25.

If I am to know His Majesty's own will and to get to know him better,
if I am to win his confidence and remain capable of adapting the
conduct of affairs to the character and view of the king, then I must see
the king frequently.

Hardenberg to Beyme, 30.8.1804, Berlin[169]

Anticipating the known or suspected will of the monarch had always
been the first concern of Prussian politicians. Until 1786 however, the
dominant personality of Frederick the Great had severely limited the
influence of his advisors. A not untypical example was that of Count
Finckenstein. 'His great respect for Frederick II', wrote one contemporary, 'and the long period which he served under him, had left
him with the habit of not risking the first comment without outside
encouragement; nor did he push through his own views, but rather took
council from the view on high, or at least from those informed of the view
from on high.'[170] In this respect, little changed under Frederick William
II. 'The influence of Frederick William II's civil servants', Reinhold
Koser noted, 'rose and fell according to the degree to which their views
coincided with those of the king.'[171] Their situation, to quote Mencken's
graphic image, resembled that of a ship's passenger who is forced to
synchronise his own movements with the swaying of the vessel.[172] A case
in point would be Count Schulenburg, who had initially taken
Alvensleben's side against war with France. However, once it became
clear that Frederick William's mind was set on intervention, he quickly
changed his tack, and placed himself in the vanguard of the war party;
this enabled him to enhance his standing in Prussian high politics.[173]

---

[169] Hardenberg to Beyme, 30.8.1804, Berlin, GStA Rep. 92 *Hardenberg* E5, fo. 117: 'daß
ich den König oft sehe, um den eigenen Sinn S.M. zu kennen und ihn selbst bekannter
zu werden, um sein Vertrauen zu erwerben und fortwährend im Stande zu sein, die
Leitung der politischen Angelegenheiten dem Charakter und den Gesinnungen des
Königs anzupassen'.

[170] Melle Klinkenborg, 'Materialen zur Geschichte des Geheimen Staatsministers
Karl Wilhelm Finck von Finckenstein', *FBPG*, 28 (1915), 564: 'Seine große Ehrfurcht
für Friedrich II, die lange Zeit welcher er unter ihm gedient, hatten es ihm zur
Gewohnheit gemacht, daß er selten ohne fremde Impulsion die erste Behauptung
wagte, nicht weniger sie aus eigener Überzeugung durchsetzte, mithin hierbei die
höhere Stimmung oder die, welche die höhere Stimmung leiteten, in seiner Art zu
handeln, zu Rate zog' (Alvensleben's words *verbatim*).

[171] Koser, 'Preußische Politik', p. 475: 'Der Einfluß der Beamten Friedrich Wilhelms II
stieg oder fiel, je nachdem sie sich mit den Gesichtspunkten des Königs begegneten
oder nicht.'

[172] Paraphrased in Hüffer, *Mencken*, p. 14: 'in Rücksicht seiner politischen Lage sich
immer in den Verhältnissen eines Menschen betrachtet, der als Passagier eine Seereise
mache und deshalb lernen müsse, seine Bewegungen nach dem Schwanken des Schiffes
abzupassen'.

[173] Ibid., pp. 469–70.

Schulenburg's ascendancy was shortlived, for his standing plummeted with the failure of intervention. Though he remained an important figure until 1806, he was never quite able to shake off his – entirely coincidental – reputation for Austrophilia. The relationship between high politics and foreign policy was thus always a dialectical one. Deft and cynical manoeuvres in Berlin might enable one protagonist to steal a march on his rival, but if a foreign-political gambit failed – as Schulenburg's did – then that political capital was quickly forfeit. Hence, while policy postures were often taken up for purely 'adversarial' reasons, there was always the possibility of a crushing 'objective' judgment delivered in the sphere of international relations. In short, the overriding priority in Prussian policy and politics was the need to find the right balance between royal favour on the one hand, and the exigencies of the foreign-political situation on the other hand.

Like their predecessors, the ministers of Frederick William III strove to reflect the will of the king. According to Schulenburg, ministers might express their own opinions openly, but in the last analysis they owed 'unconditional obedience (*unbedingter Gehorsam*)' to the king. Once the royal will had been made clear, Schulenburg added, the minister 'must act as if the decision came from his own heart. If, in some very important matter, he believes himself incapable of doing so, then he must resign.'[174] Haugwitz gave a similar definition of the minister's task. Speaking of monarchic wishes, he assured Frederick William that 'Le devoir de vos serviteurs, Sire, est de tenter tout pour les remplir autant que leur opposition le permettra.'[175] This was a view with which Hardenberg entirely concurred. 'Un ministre des affaires étrangères', he told Laforest, 'doit avant toutes choses chercher à bien connaître des dispositions positives de son souverain et n'y jamais mêler ses opinions personnelles dans ses relations avec les envoyés des autres cours.'[176] Given this interpretation of ministerial duties, it is easy to understand the universal preoccupation with access to the king; Hardenberg himself stressed the need to 'see the king regularly and know his mind'.[177] To be

---

174 Naudé, 'Denkwürdigkeiten des Ministers Grafen von Schulenburg', p. 395: 'muß handeln, als wenn der Entschluß des Herrn aus seinem Herzen käme. Glaubt er das in sehr wichtigen Dingen nicht zu können, so muß er sich zurückziehen.'
175 Haugwitz to Frederick William, 30.3.1804, Berlin, in Bailleu (ed.), *Preussen und Frankreich*, II, p. 253.
176 Laforest to Talleyrand, 18.8.1804, Berlin, ibid., p. 285. On the importance of guessing Frederick William's intentions see also Stamm-Kuhlmann, *Friedrich Wilhelm III*, p. 169.
177 Hardenberg to Beyme, 30.8.1804, Berlin, GStA Rep. 92 *Hardenberg* E5, fo. 117, cited *in extenso* above (see p. 149). See also in a very similar vein, Hardenberg to Beyme, 'im Winter 1804' (April 1804?), Rep. 92 *Hardenberg* E5, fo. 4; less explicitly in a letter to Frederick William in April 1804, in Ranke (ed.), *Denkwürdigkeiten Hardenbergs*, I, p. 32.

denied this contact by the interposition of the Kabinett threatened to degrade the foreign ministry to a mere executive organ, excluded from the deliberation of policy and ignorant of the wishes of the monarch.

The quest to retain the confidence of the king was to have a powerful effect on the formulation of Prussian foreign policy. As we have seen, the real policy divide during the first years of Frederick William's reign was between activists and passivists. Admittedly, there were few who publicly entertained such extensive aggressive designs as Massenbach – he was an utterly marginal figure. But there were some such as Hardenberg, whose plans for a southern expansion of the Prussian state required a considerably more dynamic approach than Frederick William was prepared to countenance. Even the 'northerners', whose policy of disengagement in the west and south approximated most closely to the views of the king, met his stubborn resistance when they suggested the surrender of exposed Hohenzollern territories whose value was purely sentimental. They were also hampered in their compensation plans by Frederick William's unwillingness to absorb the lands of hereditary princes. In these debates, Haugwitz did not always take the king's side; for example, he risked royal displeasure by suggesting the abandonment of the Prussian holdings in Franconia. But on the whole, he was careful to distinguish himself not only as a champion of the neutrality policy, which he claimed as his *enfant chéri*,[178] but also of the passive line favoured by the king. Hence the lukewarm reception afforded to Sieyès was not simply a reflection of Haugwitz's ideological contempt for the notorious Jacobin, but also an attempt to pander to the king's own obvious dislike of the man; the rather more enthusiastic welcome afforded by Alvensleben and Finckenstein certainly did them no favours.[179] Moreover, Haugwitz's handling of the French alliance overtures was completely in tune with the king's own views. 'Non', Sieyès wrote in exasperation, 'M. de Haugwitz n'est pas du parti français. Il est du parti de rien faire . . . Il finasse pour éviter d'entendre, il finasse pour éviter de répondre.'[180] 'Haugwitz est beaucoup moins le ministre des affaires étrangères', he later added, 'qu'une sentinelle placée à la porte avec la consigne d'empêcher les affaires d'entrer.'[181] Indeed, this studied passivism, which contrasted favourably in the king's eyes with the much less congenial Francophilia of Alvensleben, contributed in no small

---

[178] Cited in Dwyer, 'The politics of Prussian neutrality', p. 356.
[179] Adler-Bresse, *Sièyes et le monde allemand*, pp. 193–5.
[180] Sièyes report, 28.7.1798, Berlin, in Bailleu (ed.), *Preussen und Frankreich*, I, p. 484.
[181] Quoted in ibid., p. 483.

measure to the increasing political ascendancy of Haugwitz throughout 1797–8.

In the summer of 1799, however, Haugwitz threw his weight behind the adherents of the Second Coalition. As we have seen, this decision was taken for 'objective' reasons. Alarmed by the growth of French power, Haugwitz pleaded for a Prussian entry into the coalition. Yet the ensuing debate and especially its consequences must also be understood in terms of Prussian high politics. Throughout the discussions, Frederick William made his opposition to war and his displeasure with Haugwitz's advice unmistakably clear.[182] Even so, after an intensive conference at Petershagen, the king was momentarily persuaded to join the coalition. But before he could send off the necessary orders, Frederick William reverted to his previous stance of strict neutrality. The blame for this volte face has frequently been laid at Lombard's door; the evidential base for such an assertion is slim, however.[183] It is more likely that Frederick William's immediate surroundings merely encouraged him to do what he intended to do anyway. The reported exchange between Köckritz and the king has the ring of truth to it. When Frederick William expressed his unhappiness about the decision to join the coalition, Köckritz is said to have responded: 'Your Majesty is our lord and master; your beliefs are our commands.'[184] It is certainly most unlikely that Lombard or anybody else in the antechamber of power could have persuaded Frederick William to forswear the coalition unless he had already made up his mind to do so.

The high-political consequences of the debate on the Second Coalition were nonetheless far-reaching. Imperceptibly at first, Haugwitz now began a slow slide from power, for the events of 1799 had severely shaken his standing with the king. Another blow came in 1803, when his demand for a pre-emptive occupation of Hanover was ignored; Haugwitz was further mortified in August 1803, when he was passed over for the important mission to Napoleon in Brussels. But Haugwitz's loss was Lombard's gain. He instinctively grasped the opportunity to consolidate his hold on the affections of the king. With disarming frankness, he later penned the following description of the events at Petershagen: 'Frederick William was unreceptive to the arguments of his ministers, to

---

182 Frederick William to Köckritz, 12.5.1799, Charlottenburg, ibid., p. 297; Haugwitz to Finckenstein and Alvensleben, 15.5.1799, Berlin, ibid., p. 298.
183 See Wittichen, 'Zu Gentz's Denkschrift', pp. 58–62; Bailleu (ed.), *Preussen und Frankreich*, I, p. xlix; but see also pp. li–lii. On Lombard's role at Petershagen see Hüffer, 'Der Feldzug der Engländer und Russen in Holland im Herbst 1799 und die Stellung Preussens', pp. 180–5.
184 Massenbach, *Memoiren zur Geschichte des preussischen Staates*, III, p. 90: 'E.K.M. sind Herr und Meister. Ihre Überzeugung ist uns Befehl.'

the pleas of the [foreign] courts and to the stirring news from Italy. In this moment, his confidants divined the mystery of his thoughts and henceforth made them their own.'[185] Lombard thus moved into the vacuum left by Haugwitz's shift towards a more activist policy. Rather than make specific recommendations, Lombard preferred to hone his dialectical skills by presenting both sides of an argument and then leaving the final decision to Frederick William.[186] His good standing with the king was thus entirely a function of his skill in reflecting and buttressing the royal standpoint. In a revealing statement, Lombard wrote that 'unless I have a mistaken view of the duties of a servant of the state, then so long as your royal highness approves the present course of action, the silent fulfilment of the highest orders will be greater evidence of zeal and even honour, than a pride which bristles at any contradiction'.[187] Lombard's actual influence over Frederick William is thus hard to assess, but he certainly was able to shut out the influence of others, and herein lay the essence of his power. For Haugwitz, the experiences of 1799–1803 were both chastening and instructive. Never again would he go out on a limb in pursuit of a risky and activist policy, while his rivals pandered to the king's preference for inaction. Rather than resigning, von der Marwitz observed, Haugwitz stayed and concluded 'that the king was hopeless whenever a firm decision was needed and that one should spare him such an embarrassment at all costs'.[188]

By 1802, the parameters of Prussian policy and politics were clearly defined by two factors. First of all, there was Frederick William's unshakable commitment to a policy of neutrality; this severely cramped the style of those who favoured a more activist policy. Secondly, French power was now unmistakably supreme in Europe; this left Prussia with little choice but to pursue a policy of accommodation. Those who had once counselled resistance – such as Haugwitz – were forced to recognise that defiance of France was both externally suicidal and politically unrealistic at home. Those who still counselled resistance – such as

---

185 Lombard, *Matériaux pour servir*, p. 79: 'Friedrich Wilhelm war den Vorstellungen seiner Minister, der Bitten der Höfe, wie der Verlockung der glänzenden Nachrichten, die aus Italien kamen, unzugänglich. In diesem Augenblick errieten seine Vertrauten das Geheimnis seines Gedankens und sagten sich, daß er fortan der ihrige sein müsse.'
186 Gaide, 'Der diplomatische Verkehr des geheimen Kabinettsrats Lombard', p. 44.
187 Lombard to Frederick William, 2.12.1802, Potsdam, GStA Rep. 92 *Friedr.Wilh.d.Dritte* B.VI.14, unfoliated: 'So lange aber Allerhöchstdieselbe den jetzigen Gang heiligen, habe ich von den Pflichten eines Staatsdieners einen falschen Begriff, oder stille Erfüllung der höheren Befehle beweiset mehr für den Eifer und selbst für das Ehrgefühl, als ein Stolz, den jeden Widerspruch empört.'
188 Meusel (ed.), *Marwitz*, p. 153: 'daß mit dem Könige nichts anzufangen sei, sobald es eines festen Entschlusses bedurfte, und das man ihm diesen also um jeden Preis ersparen müsse'.

Gentz – were a small and utterly marginalised minority. The long debate between activists and passivists had now been decided in favour of the latter, although it was still unclear whether the passivists prevailed because they dominated in the antechamber of power, or whether they predominated there simply because they were passivists. In any case, from now on, foreign-political imperatives and high politics converged. The result was that Prussian politicians crowded into the narrow middle ground of the neutrality policy, not merely because that was the surest route to royal favour, but also because the magnitude of the French threat rendered such a policy inescapable. This tendency was reinforced by the growth of direct French interference in Prussian high politics. The impact of Napoleon was not yet as oppressive as it was to become later, yet it was already tangible enough. Nobody wanted to experience the 'longue et cruelle incertitude' to which Lucchesini had been exposed when he temporarily fell out of favour with Napoleon.[189] Incurring French displeasure increasingly risked high-political oblivion; soon Prussian politicians realised that French wrath could be visited on their personal rivals.

Unconditional support for the neutrality policy thus became the essential prerequisite for political participation in Prussia after 1800. This development was clearly a product of high politics, but it was also a substantial stimulant to it. Given the limited room for political manoeuvre, Prussian politicians now sought to establish themselves as the more faithful interpreters of the king's will. At first, nobody mastered this art better than Hardenberg, the new foreign minister. Given the circumstances of Haugwitz's fall, Hardenberg was hardly likely to jeopardise his position by questioning the neutrality policy. 'The neutrality policy had to be maintained', he subsequently admitted, 'because it would have been quite futile to try and persuade the king otherwise.'[190] In any case, Hardenberg's credentials in this respect were impeccable. It will be recalled that he had acted as midwife to the neutrality policy at Basle, nine years before: 'secure', 'advantageous', 'honourable' were the words he had used then.[191] It should come as no surprise that Hardenberg stressed his continued support for the

---

[189] Haugwitz to Lucchesini, 19.2.1802, GStA Rep. 92 *Lucchesini* 31, fo. 151; Haugwitz to Lucchesini, 14.10.1801, Berlin, fo. 142: 'j'entrevois les plus grandes difficultés à vous conserver'.

[190] Ranke (ed.), *Denkwürdigkeiten Hardenbergs*, II, p. 54: 'Neutralität mußte das System bleiben, denn der Versuch wäre ganz vergeblich gewesen den König zu enem andern zu bewegen.'

[191] Hardenberg memorandum, 6.4.1795, ibid., V, p. 82; Oncken, *Österreich und Preußen im Befreiungskriege*, p. 139.

neutrality policy while deputising for Haugwitz in 1803 and the summer of 1804, thereby increasing his acceptability to Frederick William. 'Your Majesty's political system', he assured Frederick William, 'is based on fundamentally decent values. Duty and inclination command me to bear it in mind at all times.'[192] It was Hardenberg who cooperated with Lombard in refusing to allow the king to express public mourning for the death of the Duc d'Enghien.[193] There were, of course, sound reasons for this. 'Notre système', he stressed, 'ne peut fournir aucun sujet de méfiance ou de mécontentement français.'[194] Hardenberg seemed to have learned well the lessons of the first seven years of Frederick William's reign. So long as he humoured the king with a policy of strict neutrality; so long as he remained acceptable to the French; so long as Haugwitz was off the scene; so long as he could bypass Lombard and deal directly with the king; for so long, Hardenberg was politically as safe as he could ever be.

To sum up: political action in Prussia did not revolve primarily around issues; rather it centred on the retention of royal confidence and the removal of possible rivals for power and favour. Only very occasionally, therefore, did a politician set himself directly against the will of the king, for to do so was to court disfavour. 'One must accept the king as he is, one cannot remould him' was how Hardenberg himself put it. Or, to quote another of his striking insights into the nature of Prussian high politics, 'The will of the king was also law for me; I had to accept it or withdraw from the scene.'[195] Few politicians allowed their better judgment to get in the way of their craving for power and influence. Consequently, the issues of politics themselves became of secondary importance as Prussian politicians strove to align themselves as closely as possible with the known royal standpoint. They adapted their own positions not primarily with reference to the objective march of events but in a dialectic with their adversaries and their relationship with the king at a given time.

Towards the end of 1804, nearly all the themes and personalities of the tumultuous two years preceding Jena were in place: the neutrality policy;

---

192 Ranke (ed.), *Denkwürdigkeiten Hardenbergs*, I, p. 72: 'Höchstdero politisches System ist auf der biedersten Charakter der Redlichkeit gegründet. Aus Pflicht und aus Neigung werde ich es unverrückt vor Augen halten.'

193 Hüffer, *Kabinettsregierung in Preussen*, p. 136; Hardenberg to Lombard, 9.5.1799, Berlin, in Bailleu (ed.), *Preussen und Frankreich*, II, p. 262.

194 Hardenberg to Lucchesini, 25.5.1804, Berlin, ibid., p. 269.

195 'Man muß den König so nehmen wie er ist, man kann ihn nicht umschmelzen'; 'Des Königs Willen war ja auch für mich Gesetz, ich mußte ihn befolgen oder vom Schauplatz abtreten', in Ranke (ed.), *Denkwürdigkeiten Hardenbergs*, p. 316.

the instinctive geopolitical thinking; the French presence in Hanover; the unpredictability of Russia; the ministry of Hardenberg; the pretensions of Lombard and the Kabinett; and finally, the quest for reform, especially executive reform, reflected not least by the promotion of the then little-known Baron Stein to the Generaldirektorium in August 1804. On the face of it, the worst appeared to be over. The neutrality policy had weathered the storms of the Second Coalition and Armed Neutrality more or less intact; Europe and with it Prussia seemed a safer place. Prussia was certainly a larger and more prosperous place. Between 1793 and 1802, she had achieved a greater territorial increase than all the wars of Frederick the Great put together. Even an unsympathetic observer had to admit that the neutrality policy had brought Prussia considerable advantage: while the rest of Europe was at odds, Prussia dominated northern Germany; while her neighbours wasted blood and treasure, Prussia achieved bloodless territorial expansion; while the coalition powers experienced one debilitating defeat after another at the hands of France, Frederick William operated a prestigious mediation policy; while the continent as a whole sank into economic ruin, Prussia enjoyed a commercial boom.[196]

Yet none of this could disguise the essential fragility of Prussia's position in late 1804. When asked what he feared most, Harold Macmillan is said to have answered: 'Events, dear boy, events.' Frederick William, too, feared events. He was the first to acknowledge the danger of a policy which would 'attend les événements pour juger de son devoir et se laisse surprendre par eux'.[197] That same month, his foreign minister had also warned of the threat of being 'prise au dépourvu et se livrer au torrent des événements qui l'attendent'.[198] Even the usually Francophile Prince Heinrich stressed the dangers of inaction. 'Attendre les événements', he wrote, 'c'est laisser la volonté à Buonaparte de faire un second traité de Campoformio; c'est vous placer entre les petits princes de l'Allemagne.'[199] Yet this was exactly what Frederick William was proposing to do. His policy of strict neutrality not only risked, it positively invited the challenge of events.

---

[196] The unsympathetic observer was Baron Hudelist, imperial chargé d'affaires in Berlin: Hudelist report, 31.3.1800, Berlin, in Bailleu (ed.), Preussen und Frankreich, I, pp. 56–62.

[197] Frederick William to Haugwitz, 9.6.1803, Ansbach, ibid., II, p. 159.

[198] Haugwitz memorandum, 28.6.1803, Berlin, ibid., p. 175.

[199] Prince Heinrich to Frederick William (copy), 2.7.1800, Rheinsberg, in Richard Krauel, Prinz Heinrich von Preußen als Politiker, p. 296.

Part II

The events

The failure of neutrality: Prussian policy and
politics, October 1804 – September 1805

We are sleeping over a volcano and shall not awake until the roof over
our heads is burning.

Friedrich von Cölln, 1804[1]

Nord und West und Süd zerplittern, Throne bersten, Reiche zittern.

Johann Wolfgang von Goethe, *West-östlicher Divan*

The Rumbold affair

Mr Jackson avait eu hier un petit diner . . . ; l'événement lui faisait grand
plaisir, il servirait à mêler les cartes, ou nous nous brouillerons avec
la France ou avec la Russie et quoique le premier cas soit préférable le
second amenerait d'autres événements pour transplanter le théâtre de
la guerre sur le continent. Je crois que comme Anglais il a raison.

Schulenburg to Hardenberg, 29.10.1804, Berlin[2]

Count Haugwitz seems to be using this opportunity in order to realise
his plans. I admit that I can have no confidence in him after what has
happened. What has happened and what is now happening teaches me
what I can expect from him in the future. He can remain on his estates
for as long as it pleases and commodes him, . . . and leave all the work
to me, only to come here whenever he feels like it and enjoy broad scope
for intrigue and interference, . . . while I remain completely responsible
for the conduct of affairs, until it pleases him to push me out of office
entirely.

Hardenberg to Beyme, 12.11.1804, Berlin[3]

---

[1] Cölln, *Vertraute Briefe*, I, p. 178: 'Wir schlafen über einem Vulkan, und werden nicht
erwachen wenn uns schon das Haus über dem Kopfe brennt.'
[2] Schulenburg to Hardenberg, 29.10.1804, Berlin, GStA Rep.XI.89.394, fo. 2.
[3] Hardenberg to Beyme, 12.11.04, Berlin, GStA Rep.92 *Hardenberg* E5, fo. 176: 'scheint
Graf Haugwitz diese Gelegenheit zu benutzen um seine Pläne näher zum Ziele zu
führen. Ich gestehe, daß ich, nach dem was vorgegangen ist, kein Vertrauen zu ihm
haben kann. Was geschehen ist und jetzt geschieht lehrt mich, was ich für die Folge von
ihm zu erwarten habe. Nach seinem Gefallen und seiner Bequemlichkeit auf seinen
Gütern abwesend, wird er so lange . . . mir alle Beschwerlichkeiten des Dienstes überlassen, dann so-oft es ihm einfällt hierher kommen . . . und während mir die ganze
Verantwortlichkeit . . . bleibt, ein weites Feld zu Einmischung und Intrigen haben, bis
er es etwa seiner Convenienz gemäß findet mich ganz aus meiner Stelle zu drängen.'

On 24 October 1804 French troops crossed the Elbe at Hamburg and seized the British envoy there, Sir George Rumbold, together with all his papers. Plainly, there was nothing the Hamburg senate could do for Rumbold and so all eyes turned to see how Prussia, the dominant power of northern Germany, would react.[4] Frederick William was under severe pressure to respond for two reasons. First of all, there were his formal duties as director of the Lower Saxon *Reichskreis* (Circle of the Empire) to which Rumbold had been accredited. Admittedly, unlike its more dynamic southern counterparts, this *Kreis* had been entirely moribund since the late seventeenth century and all semblance of *Kreis* cooperation had long since collapsed.[5] Nevertheless, the fact that Rumbold had been personally accredited to the Prussian monarch in his capacity as Duke of Magdeburg placed Frederick William under the obligation to do more than simply join in the general indignation. Secondly, and far more importantly, there were the implications of Napoleon's action for Prussia's policy of neutrality. France's enemies would expect Prussia to punish, or at least react to this flagrant violation of the neutrality zone.[6] Almost immediately, the Russian ambassador in Berlin, Baron Maximilian von Alopeus, invoked the secret Russo-Prussian convention of May 1804 and called upon Prussia to uphold the neutrality of northern Germany. To make matters worse, the King of Sweden inquired as to what had become of Frederick William's much-broadcast determination to defend the neutrality of northern Germany against allcomers.[7]

On 30 October, Hardenberg, Schulenburg, Lombard and the king met at Potsdam to discuss the Prussian response. A strong plea for action against France came from Schulenburg. If Prussia did not make a stand, he argued, she would become entirely dependent on Napoleon. Moreover, there was the risk of offending the tsar, if Prussia failed to honour her commitments under the treaty of May 1804. On the other hand, Schulenburg was fearful of a war with France, especially in view of

---

[4] See copy of letter of senate of Hamburg to Grote (Prussian envoy in Hamburg) in Francis Jackson to Harrowby, 29.10.04, Berlin, PROL FO 64/66.

[5] See Walther Schmidt, 'Geschichte des niedersächsischen Kreises vom Jahre 1673 bis zum Zusammenbruch der Kreisverfassung', *Niedersächsisches Jahrbuch für Landesgeschichte*, 7 (1930), 1–134, especially pp. 132–4. This study, which effectively ends in the early eighteenth century, makes no mention of the Rumbold affair. Griewank, 'Hardenberg und die preussische Politik', p. 246, covers the whole incident very sketchily.

[6] NB: the formal demarcation line ceased to exist after 1801 (Lunéville). For convenience this book will continue to refer to the Prussian sphere of influence in northern Germany as the 'neutrality zone'.

[7] Jackson, *Diaries*, p. 251.

her military presence in Hanover. For this reason, he urged that all diplomatic avenues be exhausted before further action was taken; above all, Napoleon should be left an open door through which he could retreat.[8] Hardenberg's memorandum also painted the effect of Napoleon's action on the Prussian position in northern Germany in stark colours.[9] Not only, he argued, was it a blow to the Prussian neutrality system in general, it was also a specific insult to Frederick William in his capacity as director of the Lower Saxon *Kreis*. Indeed, the whole business was doubly unfortunate because it endangered the chance of a mediation between Russia and France, which could at least delay a breach between the two powers, if not ultimately prevent it. Frederick William could not avoid involvement, Hardenberg stressed: now was the time to decide between France and Russia. Conflict with France, Hardenberg concluded, was the lesser evil because the treaty with Russia covered Prussia's rear. Frederick William would have to stand his ground or else follow Italy and Holland into the Napoleonic orbit.

Yet Hardenberg's analysis was soon contradicted by his political prescription. Because although Hardenberg wanted a show of energy, he did not necessarily want open war. Instead, he advised the dispatch of a firm but not threatening letter, demanding Rumbold's release and simultaneously allowing Napoleon a golden bridge over which he could withdraw. If this demand were not complied with, there should be no immediate escalation but rather a further request, namely a French evacuation of Hanover. This, Hardenberg conceded, would almost certainly lead to war, but it would gain time for military preparations, if only to show that Prussia was in earnest. Yet Hardenberg was far from being the sole – or even the original – driving force behind the hard line against France. It was in fact, as Laforest noted with astonishment, Lombard from whom all the decisive measures originated. It was he who initiated the conference at Potsdam and drafted the summons for Schulenburg,[10] and it was he who recommended the recall of the Duke of Brunswick in case military preparations were needed. For the duration of the crisis Lombard suspended his habitual contact with French diplomats.

---

[8] Schulenburg memorandum, 30.10.04, Berlin, GStA Rep. XI.89.394, fo. 8
[9] Hardenberg memorandum, 30.10.04, Berlin, printed in Adolf Wohlwill, 'Fernere Aktenstücke zur Rumboldschen Angelegenheit', *Zeitschrift des Vereins für Hamburgische Geschichte*, 8 (1886), 200–6.
[10] Laforest to Talleyrand, 30.10.04, Berlin, in Bailleu (ed.), *Preussen und Frankreich*, II, p. 310; Laforest to Talleyrand, 6.11.04, Berlin, in Bailleu (ed.), *Preussen und Frankreich*, II, p. 312; Laforest to Talleyrand, 10.11.04, Berlin, in Bailleu (ed.), *Preussen und Frankreich*, II, pp. 312–13.

Since mid-1804, Hardenberg had pursued two clearly defined objectives: first, the removal of French troops from Hanover and, secondly, the prevention of a Franco-Russian rupture. On the eve of Rumbold's abduction, General Knobelsdorff had been sent to Paris, ostensibly to attend Napoleon's coronation, but also to set negotiations about Russia and Hanover in motion. In order to ease the path of a Prussian-mediated *rapprochement* between Russia and France, Hardenberg expressly wished to avoid international tension at all costs.[11] The kidnapping of Rumbold jeopardised this hope. It was, as Hardenberg wrote to Lucchesini, a 'disastrous affair' especially as it had come at a time when Russia had formally accepted Prussia's mediation.[12] Hardenberg certainly did not seize on the Rumbold crisis as an opportunity to abandon the old neutrality policy and bring the king around to a firm anti-French stance. Rather, he hoped at first that the whole business – which had caused him 'une surprise et une peine impossibles à exprimer' – was a ghastly mistake.[13] 'Cette affaire majeure', Hardenberg complained, 'tient toutes les autres en suspens'; as long as the Rumbold affair lasted, the Prussian mediation between Russia and France could have no hope of success.[14] Thus when Hardenberg claimed that it was now time to choose between Russia and France, this dramatic statement should be seen in its context. It was necessary for Prussia to make a show of energy both in order to maintain her credibility as a mediator and to honour her commitments to Russia under the treaty of the preceding May. Indeed, when the Rumbold affair had been solved to his satisfaction, Hardenberg's first hope was that this would counteract any unfavourable impression in St Petersburg.[15] War with France would have wrecked all hopes of mediation beyond repair; on the other hand, total capitulation risked alienating Russia and undermining Prussia's status as a mediator.

It is surely no coincidence that Hardenberg's memoirs leave out the vital first third of his memorandum for the Potsdam conference, which referred to his concern about the effects of the Rumbold affair on Russia and the proposed Franco-Russian mediation. This deletion transforms his action from a gesture to impress Russia in the ultimate interest of furthering a Franco-Russian *rapprochement* – his true motivation – into an

[11] Hardenberg to Balan (Legationssekretär in London, temporarily replacing Jacobi), 26.10.04, Berlin, GStA Rep.XI.73.178B, fos. 117–18 (All official dispatches were drafted by the minister and countersigned by the monarch.).
[12] Hardenberg to Lucchesini, 1.11.04, Berlin, in Bailleu (ed.), *Preussen und Frankreich*, II, p. 310.
[13] Hardenberg to Jacobi, 2.11.04, Berlin, GStA Rep.XI.73.178B, fos. 124–5.
[14] Ibid.; also Hardenberg to Jacobi, 16.11.04, Berlin, fo. 138.
[15] Hardenberg to Jacobi, 19.11.04, GStA Rep.XI.73.178B, fo. 151.

early manifestation of anti-Napoleonic resistance.[16] The lengths to which Hardenberg went at the time and later to cover his tracks is further shown by his false claim to Francis Jackson that he himself had advised the summoning of Schulenburg so as to have a counterweight to Lombard.[17] The great value which Hardenberg attached to his mediation plan is illustrated by his cordial interview with Laforest, *before* Rumbold's release, in which he blamed the ill-feeling against France on public opinion.[18] This move, which ran contrary to the official Prussian policy, only makes sense in the context of Hardenberg trying to keep the mediation idea alive, an idea which depended on cordial relations with *both* Russia and France for its realisation.

The result of all this was a stiff personal letter from Frederick William to Napoleon demanding Rumbold's instant release.[19] General Knobelsdorff, still under way on his courtesy visit to Napoleon, was instructed to interrupt his journey until further notice or, if already on French territory, to desist from making any political overtures;[20] the Duke of Brunswick was recalled to Berlin to supervise military preparations. In the meantime, the British ambassador in Berlin, Sir Francis Jackson, was working hard to turn the whole affair to his country's advantage. Almost immediately he wrote to Hardenberg reminding him of Prussia's commitment to the neutrality of northern Germany.[21] Three days later he was optimistic that both Frederick William and Napoleon were so far committed that the latter could only 'recede with shame and disgrace'; Jackson felt that 'the more *éclat* is given to the [Prussian] demand, the better'.[22] Indeed, rather than simply waiting passively for the Prussian ultimatum to produce the expected breach with France, Britain now took the initiative. Even before the Rumbold affair became known in Britain, Lord Harrowby, the British foreign minister, had instructed Jackson to try to establish a British-financed Russo-Prussian alliance to guarantee the security of northern Germany. By 18 November Harrowby had gone a step further and urged

---

[16] See Ranke (ed.), *Denkwürdigkeiten Hardenbergs*, II, pp. 89–94; Wohlwill, 'Fernere Aktenstücke', pp. 200–6.

[17] Francis Jackson to Harrowby, 29.10.04, Berlin, PROL FO 64/66.

[18] Laforest to Talleyrand, 6.11.04, Berlin, in Bailleu (ed.), *Preussen und Frankreich*, II, p. 312.

[19] Frederick William to Napoleon, 30.10.04, Potsdam, in Adolf Wohlwill (ed.), 'Aktenstücke zur Rumboldschen Angelegenheit', *Zeitschrift des Vereins für Hamburgische Geschichte*, 7 (1981), 396–9.

[20] Hardenberg to Knobelsdorff, 28.10.04, Berlin, in Bailleu (ed.), *Preussen und Frankreich*, II, p. 307.

[21] Francis Jackson to Hardenberg, 28.10.04, Berlin, PROL FO 64/66 (copy).

[22] Francis Jackson to Harrowby, 2.11.04, Berlin, PROL FO 64/66; Francis Jackson to Harrowby, 10.11.04, PROL FO 64/66.

Jackson to press for a 'defensive concert' between Great Britain and Prussia. This initiative, like so many other British appeals to Prussia before and afterwards, met with no success whatsoever.[23] In any case, hopes of exploiting the Franco-Prussian tension were soon dashed by the prompt release of Rumbold, albeit without his papers. This turn of events, the first time Napoleon had ever backed down, represented a diplomatic triumph for Prussia, the more so since the terms of release made direct reference to the intervention of the Prussian monarch.[24] The Prussians now lost all interest in military measures against France; in particular, they rejected British demands to turn Rumbold's stolen documents into a *casus belli*.[25] Prussia, as Hardenberg remarked in exasperation could hardly be expected to go to war for a 'box of papers'.[26]

If the international ramifications of the Rumbold affair ended largely with his release, the 'high-political' dimension was just beginning to unfold. For only the workings of high politics can explain how Frederick William was pushed into taking a firm stance and how Lombard, usually regarded as a Francophile sycophant, actually pursued a much more radically anti-French course than Hardenberg. At first sight, Lombard, until then and henceforth a firm supporter of the neutrality policy, seems indeed to have departed from his usual stance. Yet seen in the context of his humiliating mission to Brussels in August 1803, Lombard's behaviour seems less puzzling. Laforest, usually a reliable and perceptive observer of the Prussian high-political scene, suggested that Lombard was not opposed to a Franco-Prussian alliance in principle but was simply working off his pique at having been deceived by Napoleon in Brussels about his intentions towards Hanover. In addition, Lombard was concerned to recapture the influence lost to Hardenberg since the departure of Haugwitz from the foreign office. The Rumbold affair was thus an opportunity to *mortifier* Hardenberg.[27] Of course, this adversarial instinct was equally well-developed in Hardenberg. His initial

---

23 Harrowby to Jackson, 4.11.04, London, PROL FO 64/66; Harrowby to Jackson, 18.11.04, Bath, PROL FO 64/66; Francis Jackson to Harrowby, 22.12.04, Berlin, PROL FO 64/66.
24 Lucchesini report, 12.11.04, Paris, in Bailleu (ed.), *Preussen und Frankreich*, II, p. 313; Napoleon to Frederick William III, 10.11.04, Paris, in Wohlwill, 'Fernere Aktenstücke', p. 399.
25 Hardenberg to Jacobi-Kloest, 28.12.04, Berlin, GStA Rep.XI.73.178B, fo. 184; Harrowby to Jackson, 18.11.04, Bath, PROL FO 64/66. See also Francis Jackson's dispatches nos. 117 and 118, 1.12.04, Berlin, PROL FO 64/66.
26 Francis Jackson to Harrowby, 27.12.04, Berlin, PROL FO 64/66.
27 Laforest to Talleyrand, 10.11.04, Berlin, in Bailleu (ed.), *Preussen und Frankreich*, II, pp. 312–13; Hüffer, *Kabinettsregierung in Preussen*, pp. 143–5, is unenlightening about Lombard's role during the Rumbold crisis.

concern had been fear of being supplanted by Schulenburg, whom he and Haugwitz had effectively sidelined in foreign policy some time before. As Laforest remarked, the summoning of Schulenburg must have been 'extremely embarrassing (*extrêmement gênant*)' for Hardenberg.[28] To a certain extent therefore, his strong stance at the Potsdam conference can be explained by the desire not to be overshadowed by Schulenburg – a known exponent of firmness towards France at this point – in his defence of Prussia's neutrality policy. Hardenberg also had to fend off Lombard's attempts to wrest the initiative in foreign policy making. Indeed, as the Austrian ambassador Prince Metternich observed, Hardenberg was anxious to use the Rumbold affair to 'reduce Lombard's influence (*réduire le faction de Lombard*)'.[29]

The most fundamental threat to Hardenberg's position was, however, to come from another quarter. Once free of the influence of his advisors, Frederick William began to regret the extent to which he had committed himself. Right from the beginning, though furious, he had been unwilling to undertake anything concrete. At first he had maintained that the kidnapping of Rumbold had not been an insult to himself but to the British. Then, having issued an ultimatum to Napoleon and with open war a real possibility, he showed an inclination to panic. Suddenly terrified by his commitments to the Russians, he even briefly (but unsuccessfully) attempted to throw doubt on the validity of the May treaty by rejecting the exchange of presents which customarily accompanied ratification. So, temporarily isolated among his usual advisors, Lombard, Schulenburg, Hardenberg and Brunswick, Frederick William turned to his former foreign minister Haugwitz, then still in retirement in Silesia.[30] 'There are many who are in favour of war but not I (*Il y a plusieurs qui votent en faveur de la guerre, moi pas*)' he wrote.[31] It was this *moi pas* which gave Haugwitz the opening to re-enter the high-political sphere on the king's side against his other advisors. From this moment onwards, of course, Hardenberg's fear for his own position in government far exceeded his concern with the matter at hand, that is, the release of Rumbold.

---

[28] Laforest to Talleyrand, 30.10.04, Berlin, in Bailleu (ed.), *Preussen und Frankreich*, II, p. 310.

[29] Metternich to Colloredo, 5.12.04, Berlin, in Alfons von Klinkowström (ed.), *Aus Metternichs nachgelassenen Papieren. Erster Teil. Von der Geburt Metternichs bis zum Wiener Congreß 1773–1815* (Vienna, 1880), pp. 31–2.

[30] Ranke (ed.), *Denkwürdigkeiten Hardenbergs*, II, pp. 95–6. Bailleu's contention, 'Haugwitz und Hardenberg', p. 291, that Haugwitz was not involved in high politics between his retirement in mid-1804 and his return in August 1805 is thus in need of revision.

[31] Ranke (ed.), *Denkwürdigkeiten Hardenbergs*, II, pp. 95–6.

Doubtless this fear was well justified. Once back in Berlin Haugwitz referred to Hardenberg's presence in the foreign ministry as merely a *zwei-jähriges Vikariat* – a two-year 'deputyship'.[32] To make matters worse, Haugwitz was quite out of touch with the current state of Prussia's foreign-political activities – and thus also with Hardenberg's mediation plan. The first thing Haugwitz did was to complain that important dispatches had not been communicated to him, in spite of prior agreement at his retirement. Such insolicitude on Hardenberg's part, Haugwitz added, 'm'étonne et me blesse'.[33] As a result, Haugwitz was compelled to spend valuable time familiarising himself with the diplomatic exchanges of the last weeks. Unsettled, Hardenberg decided to approach the king through Beyme, whom both parties seem to have accepted as an honest broker at this stage. Hardenberg claimed that Haugwitz was using the Rumbold affair to 'realise his plans'. Moreover, while Hardenberg would be left to carry the burden of office, Haugwitz was reserving to himself 'a broad field of intrigue and interference until it suits him [Haugwitz] to push me out of my post altogether'.[34] Finally, Hardenberg demanded that the king confirm his confidence in him, grant him a monopoly of Prussia's political correspondence, and banish Haugwitz. Failing this, Hardenberg would tender his resignation. But Beyme refused to pass on the message to the king; instead, he invited Hardenberg to his estate in Steglitz for a private discussion. Indeed, Beyme and Lombard were inclined to smooth over the differences between Haugwitz and Hardenberg so as not to burden the king with their quarrel. The effect would simply be to put Hardenberg in bad odour.[35] There the matter rested, at least for the time being.

The Prussians did not go to war 'for a box of papers' as the British had hoped: the Rumbold affair had illustrated – once again – that the geopolitical situations and interests of Britain and Prussia were fundamentally different. Prussia had always to be concerned that relations between Russia and France remained neither too cordial *nor* too hostile. A Franco-Russian alliance, as Talleyrand observed, would constitute such a concentration of power that it could never be in Prussia or

[32] Hardenberg to Beyme, 12.11.04, Berlin, GStA Rep. 92 *Hardenberg* E5, fo. 174; Ranke (ed.), *Denkwürdigkeiten Hardenbergs*, II, p. 100.

[33] Haugwitz to Hardenberg, 8.11.04, Rogau, GStA Rep. 92 *Hardenberg* E5, fo. 166. See also Hardenberg to Haugwitz (draft), 17.11.04, GStA Rep. 92 *Hardenberg* E5, fo. 184.

[34] Hardenberg to Beyme, 12.11.04, Berlin, GStA Rep. 92 *Hardenberg* E5, fo. 176, cited *in extenso* above (p. 159).

[35] See Lombard to Hardenberg in which Hardenberg is asked to tone down the polemic in his letter against Haugwitz, GStA Rep. 92 *Hardenberg* E5, fo. 187.

Austria's interest to see it come about. Equally, however, Talleyrand continued, Prussia would not welcome a complete rupture between the two states.[36] Hardenberg was convinced, and this was indeed the logical consequence of the king's strict neutrality policy, that the only way of preserving the peace of northern Germany was a Franco-Russian *rapprochement* or at least the prevention of open war between the two powers. Due to the French presence in Hanover, right in the heart of Prussia, such a conflict would wreck the cherished neutrality policy once and for all.

'Let us cast our eyes on the map (*jetons les yeux sur la carte*)' – Hardenberg enjoined Lucchesini. For the map of northern Germany dictated an iron logic which Prussia could only ignore at her peril. Hardenberg's reasoning followed the same lines as Talleyrand's: Prussia must prevent a Franco-Russian alliance to share the domination of Europe, but so long as this was a remote possibility it would be safe to initiate a reconciliation. Inside Germany itself the French must be eased out of Hanover; at the very least it should not be allowed to fall to a third party as part of a compensation arrangement. The ideal solution would be an exchange for the dangerously exposed western provinces. In short: 'More concentration, a modified frontier which avoids all collision with France whom we want to make our friend, which tightens our links and unites our interests [with France], territorial increases proportional to those of our neighbours – this is what we must aim for if we are not to lose ground rapidly.'[37] Similar arguments were made by Lombard. 'Il faut à la Prusse une frontière sûre', he wrote, 'et surtout le Hanovre qui peut la lui donner.'[38] In the meantime, Prussia's first concern had always to be the tranquillity of northern Germany. 'Notre intérêt', Hardenberg confirmed at the height of the crisis, 'est toujours le même: le maintien de notre neutralité et de la tranquillité du nord de l'Allemagne.'[39] Great Britain, on the other hand had precisely the opposite interest, namely to push Prussia into an anti-French alliance. The attempted British manipulation of the Rumbold affair is one example of this policy. As

---

[36] Talleyrand to Laforest, 4.12.04, Paris, in Bailleu (ed.), *Preussen und Frankreich*, II, p. 322.

[37] Hardenberg to Lucchesini, 25.12.04, Berlin, in Bailleu (ed.), *Preussen und Frankreich*, II, p. 328: 'Plus de concentration, une autre frontière qui écarte toute collision avec la France dont nous voulons faire notre amie, qui resserre nos liens et unisse nos intérêts, des aggrandissements proportionnés à ceux de nos voisins – voilà à quoi nous devons tendre si nous ne voulons reculer rapidement.'

[38] Lombard memorandum, 24.10.04, Berlin, in Ranke (ed.), *Denkwürdigkeiten Hardenbergs*, I, p. 312.

[39] Hardenberg to Haugwitz (draft), 17.11.04, GStA Rep. 92 *Hardenberg* E5, fo. 184.

Schulenburg pointed out, Britain's sole interest in the Rumbold affair had been to 'brouiller les cartes dans le nord, qu'il lui est presque indifférent que ce soit nous en nous brouillent avec la France ou la Russie, bien que les choses n'en restent pas là et que le feu de la guerre s'étend plus loin'.[40]

By the beginning of November 1804 the Rumbold crisis was largely over, although British attempts to revive it persisted until the end of the year. For reasons of tact, Knobelsdorff and Lucchesini were instructed to play down the Prussian triumph, and very soon both men had reported the resumption of normal relations with France.[41] This restored the preconditions for the old plan to reconcile Russia and France and to manoeuvre the French out of Hanover. By mid-December the mediation was well under way again. A Franco-Russian *rapprochement*, Hardenberg argued, 'seroit le plus sûr garant du maintien de la paix sur le continent'.[42] This time there were good grounds for optimism: in London Jacobi was optimistic that the Tsar's special envoy Novosiltzov had come with the intention of communicating Russia's assent to the mediation proposal;[43] in Paris Talleyrand expressed a willingness in principle to accept the Prussian mediation;[44] and between Christmas and New Year Knobelsdorff even reported some French movement on the Hanover question.[45]

The beginning of a new policy towards Prussia

In January 1805 the future of Europe was still undecided. Only in the west, where Great Britain and Napoleonic France were once again locked in a struggle which had lasted intermittently since 1793, were the battle lines of the coming two years clearly to be discerned. To the south, in Italy, to the east, in Russia, and especially in the German Empire, everything was still in a state of flux. By no means all the obstacles, most of them in the Mediterranean, to a British–Russian alliance had been

---

[40] Schulenburg memorandum, 30.10.04, Berlin, GStA Rep.XI.89.394, fo. 9.
[41] Knobelsdorff report, 18.11.04, Paris, in Bailleu (ed.), *Preussen und Frankreich*, II, p. 314; Frederick William to Lucchesini, 21.11.04, Berlin, in Bailleu (ed.), *Preussen und Frankreich*, II, p. 317.
[42] Hardenberg to Jacobi, 17.12.04, Berlin, GStA Rep.XI.73.178B, fo. 178. See also Francis Jackson to Harrowby, 8.12.04, Berlin, PROL FO 64/66; Francis Jackson to Harrowby, 27.12.04, Berlin, PROL FO 64/66.
[43] Jacobi to Hardenberg, 23.11.04, London, GStA Rep.XI.73.178B, fo. 169; Jacobi to Hardenberg, 14.12.04, London, GStA Rep.XI.73.178B, fo. 188.
[44] Talleyrand to Laforest, 4.12.04, Paris, in Bailleu (ed.), *Preussen und Frankreich*, II, p. 323.
[45] Knobelsdorff report, 29–30.12.04, Paris, in Bailleu (ed.), *Preussen und Frankreich*, II, pp. 329–31.

eliminated. Britain seemed preoccupied with its war against Spain while a Franco-Prussian war against Sweden seemed as likely as any continental agreement against France. There was, in short, nothing inevitable about the Third Coalition of Britain, Austria and Russia against France or the war of the same name which was soon to bring yet more of the European continent under the immediate control of Napoleonic France.[46]

At the beginning of 1805, Prussian policy was the same as it had ever been. On the one hand, it sought to reassure France 'qu'elle seroit l'abri de toute attaque dans le nord de l'Allemagne, pourvuqu'elle s'abstienne, qu'elle n'augmente pas sa armée dans le pais d'Hannovre'. On the other hand – and relatedly – it sought to save northern Germany from the ravages of the Franco-British quarrel. If forced to choose, Hardenberg would opt for Russia, but in the meantime Prussia should persist with the neutrality policy.[47] So the developing rift between France and Russia and the British attempts at coalition-making on the continent had two possible consequences for Prussia. The first, and least desired, was the crystallisation of Swedish, Russian and Austrian grievances against Napoleon into a full-blown coalition against France, financed with British gold and subordinated to British interests. The second, and entirely preferable, alternative was a Franco-Russian *rapprochement* through the mediation of Prussia, followed hopefully, but not necessarily, by a Franco-British understanding at a later stage. Prussian statesmen felt that if such an agreement could be set in train, then all the other troubles assailing the Prussian state, from hyperactive legitimist Swedes to the fragile peace of northern Germany, would fall into place, allowing Prussia to maintain her long-standing policy of neutrality. But these hopes were soon to be dashed. The demands of geopolitics meant that Prussia could not escape embroilment in the developing Third Coalition of Britain, Russia and Austria against France. First of all, the territories of the Prussian crown straddled much of the area in which the struggle with Napoleon was expected to take place. Allied armies could not reach Swedish Pomerania and the Electorate of Hanover without Prussia's support or at least passive acquiescence. Secondly, and most importantly for the future of Europe, both Russia and Great Britain were agreed that a substantial increase of territory for Prussia was necessary to form a bulwark against French expansion in the west. It was therefore only to be

---

[46] On the Third Coalition in general see Hildegard Schaeder, *Die dritte Koalition und die heilige Allianz* (Königsberg and Berlin, 1934).

[47] *Copie de la note verbale remise . . . par Hardenberg à M. d'Alopeus, 17.3.1805*, GStA Rep. 92 *Hardenberg* L13, fo. 12; Hardenberg memorandum, 12.3.1805, GStA Rep. XI.89.400, fo. 7.

expected that both Russia and Great Britain would attempt to obtain Prussian cooperation in the next coalition against France.

This cooperation was to be gained by persuasion if possible, by compulsion if necessary. Already in September 1804, Francis Jackson had suggested 'in strong and unequivocal terms, the alternative of a close alliance . . . [between Prussia and the Anglo-Russian coalition], or of a decided enmity and total separation of interests'.[48] On the Russian side, the foreign minister, Prince Adam Czartoryski, first aired the idea of coercing Prussia in late December 1804.[49] Very soon, Granville Leveson Gower, the British ambassador in St Petersburg, was speaking of the 'policy of forcing Prussia to become a party in a general coalition against France'.[50] Britain and Russia were agreed that Prussia must be forced and that a system of possible rewards and certain penalties be devised to effect this aim.[51] It was not long before this policy began to take on a very tangible and worrying shape for Prussia. At this point, the main impulse came from the Russians. As 'fear [was] the predominating motive which influenced the conduct of that cabinet', Czartoryski hoped that three-power hostility would cause Prussia to abandon her neutrality. Britain, Czartoryski suggested, could interrupt Prussian commerce at sea, while Russia and Austria menaced her by land.[52] Beforehand, however, one last attempt to bring Prussia to reason was to be made before this coercive machinery was set in motion. This was entrusted to the Russian diplomat Baron von Wintzingerode, whose mission to Berlin as envoy of the Tsar took place in early February 1805.[53] From the Prussian point of view the choice of Wintzingerode was hardly auspicious. By background a Hessian, he had seen service in the Austrian army and was known for his anti-Prussian orientation. To make matters worse, Wintzingerode was reckoned among those who believed that Prussia's

[48] Francis Jackson report, 17.8.1804, Berlin, PROL FO 64/66. See also Gembries, 'Das Thema Preussen in der politischen Diskussion Englands', p. 57, on the new *Freund–Feind* alternative towards Prussia. Griewank, 'Hardenberg und die preussische Politik', p. 257.

[49] Ulmann, *Russisch-preussische Politik*, p. 127, is wrong to say that the idea originated in Russia.

[50] Gower to Harrowby, 24.12.1804, St Petersburg, in J. H. Rose (ed.), *Select Dispatches from the British Foreign Office Archives relating to the Formation of the Third Coalition against France, 1804–5*, p. 80.

[51] E.g. Mulgrave to Gower, 21.11.1805, London, in Rose (ed.), *Select dispatches*, pp. 88–92; Mulgrave to Gower, 29.1.1805, London, in Rose (ed.), *Documents relating*, pp. 98–101.

[52] Gower to Harrowby, 24.12.04, St Petersburg, in Rose (ed.), *Documents relating*, p. 81.

[53] Most of the background material for the following paragraphs has been taken from 'Acta touch. la Mission du Général de Wintzingerode aux affaires politiques avec la Russie', GStA Rep.XI.175.155B, especially Frederick William to Alexander (draft), March 1805, Berlin, fos. 2–22. See also Zawadzki, *Czartoryski*, p. 126.

hand would have to be forced; very probably, he was resigned to the failure of his mission from the beginning. Once in Berlin, Wintzingerode proved unable to make any headway on the two objectives of his mission – the winning of Prussia for an anti-French coalition and the ending of Prusso-Swedish tension over Swedish Pomerania.

Indeed, it was in Prussia's relations with Sweden that her extremely precarious political position was exemplified once more.[54] Sweden's ultra-legitimist and possibly slightly deranged monarch Gustavus IV had broken off diplomatic relations with France in September 1804 – much to Prussia's horror. The problem was that Gustavus's German possessions fell, by any reckoning, within the proclaimed Prussian neutrality zone and were thus entitled to her protection. As a result Frederick William III felt bound to forbid any Swedish operations from Pomerania in order to avoid provoking France. Ideally, the Prussians would have liked to occupy the province as a preventive measure but were deterred by fear of extreme Russian displeasure and the accusation of partiality towards France.[55] After all, in a similar situation in 1803, when George III's possessions had been threatened by Napoleon, Frederick William had not undertaken a pre-emptive occupation of Hanover to deny it to France. Clearly, the trouble with Gustavus was in many ways simply a function of Prussia's relationship with Russia and Great Britain. Whenever Prussia was on bad terms with the latter two powers, Sweden was activated to put pressure on Frederick William. Conversely, Prussia rarely attempted to deal directly with the troublesome Swedes, but preferred to go over Gustavus's head and address the root causes of the conflict in London or St Petersburg. In early 1805, however, this rather simple pattern was complicated by rumours of an impending sale of Swedish Pomerania to Russia. Not surprisingly, in view of the complete change in the geopolitical situation of northern Germany that such an event would have entailed, these rumours caused considerable alarm in Berlin until they were proved to be groundless.[56]

The Prussian reaction to the Swedish and Russian threats was along the lines of her traditional neutrality policy. In late February 1805 Haugwitz drew attention to the *double objet* of Wintzingerode's mission, namely the clarification of the situation in Swedish Pomerania, and the establishment of an Austrian–Prussian–Russian understanding on

---

[54] For Gustavus and Prussia in general see K. Ullrich, 'Die deutsche Politik König Gustavus IV von Schweden, 1799–1806 (PhD dissertation, University of Erlangen, 1914), pp. 16, 49, 94–5 and *passim*.

[55] Jackson to Harrowby, 1.1.05, Berlin, PROL FO 64/67 (unfoliated); Jackson to Harrowby, 22.1.05, Berlin, PROL FO 64/67.

[56] Hardenberg to Jacobi, 15.6.05, Alexandersbad, GStA Rep.XI.73.179A, fo. 155.

the future of Europe.[57] As Haugwitz saw it, Prussia had three options. It could accept the Russian proposals, it could reject them or it could pursue a third course which allowed Prussia both to maintain her own security and to remain on good terms with the two imperial courts. On no account, Haugwitz argued, must Prussia commit herself to the defence of non-Prussian interests. If one simply accepted the Russian overtures one ran the risk of being exposed to the hazards of her policies and being caught up in the British and Russian strategy against France: 'Without knowing the threats, the links which interconnect them [the powers of Europe], she [Prussia] risks that which has happily guided her through the labyrinth in which Europe has lost herself.'[58] Thus, while Haugwitz thought it inadvisable to reject the Russian overtures entirely, he was anxious that Prussia should not become involved in areas outside of North Germany. She should certainly not enter into any commitments concerning the rest of the French empire, the Batavian and Swiss republics, Italy and the Porte. Not for Prussia the global, all-embracing strategic view of Britain, France or Russia. 'No event which takes place in Europe', Haugwitz conceded, 'is in the last analysis irrelevant to Prussia but the interest which she takes in it differs according to the amount of influence which it has on its own existence.' So: 'The aim which we propose for ourselves [must be] not to tie our hands beyond the extent dictated by our own convictions.'[59]

Meanwhile, Britain had thrown its weight behind the policy of coercion. In Berlin, Francis Jackson pressed Wintzingerode to force Prussia to decide for or against the coalition. Given that 'fear is (as I have often had occasion to observe) the main hinge upon which the operations of this government turn', it was quite pointless, Jackson argued, to expect anything from 'the best logical reasons that can be employed in support of [the allied] cause'.[60] When Wintzingerode adverted to the danger of driving Prussia into the French camp, Jackson replied that '[Wintzingerode's] negotiation would be fruitless if it was not prepared to put it in motion by some violent impulse, and to the chance of which cause it would ultimately embrace.'[61] By mid-March this attitude had hardened into a distinct policy of using the weight of Russian arms to

---

[57] 'Denkschrift von Haugwitz über die politische Lage im Anschluss an die Mission des Barons von Wintzingerode 1805', 27/II., GStA Rep.XI.89.399 (unfoliated).

[58] Ibid.

[59] Ibid. See also Hardenberg to Jacobi, 25.1.05, Berlin, GStA Rep.XI.73.179A, fo. 20; Hardenberg to Lucchesini, Potsdam, 20.2.05, in Bailleu (ed.), *Preussen und Frankreich*, II, p. 333.

[60] Jackson to Mulgrave, 23.2.05, Berlin, PROL FO 64/67.

[61] Ibid.

make up Prussia's mind for her. Francis Jackson despaired of 'obtaining the willing acquiescence of this court. It remains to be seen whether the Russian government will of itself come forward and exert the only means by which such a system can be effected.'[62] Under these circumstances Prussian policy towards Britain could only be aimed towards bringing Britain and France together and keeping Great Britain and Russia as far apart as possible.

But while it was still too early to judge the outcome of the negotiations between the two powers, Hardenberg saw that the *dénouement de la crise* was now approaching.[63] Everything would depend on what was decided for Italy; until then judgment would have to be suspended. If it did come to a Russian–French éclat, however, Prussia's policy of neutrality was going to be put to a severe test. It was thus important to move quickly, before the final obstacles to British–Russian agreement, such as the future of Malta, had been overcome.[64] The Prussians decided to send a mission to the tsar in order to present the case for Prussian neutrality to him. The choice of envoy – Zastrow rather than Haugwitz – was calculated to mollify Russia. In a letter originally drafted to accompany Zastrow, Frederick William stated his determination 'neither to permit French oppressions nor to fight for England and her allies'.[65]

While acknowledging the threat to the whole of Europe from Napoleon, Frederick William wished to base his relationship with Alexander solely on the agreement of May 1804; this guaranteed the neutrality of northern Germany, but no more.[66] Frederick William moved on to explain why he could not join the grand coalition against Napoleon. Russia, he pointed out, could afford to espouse her noble and unselfish cause for the good of all Europe without putting herself in serious danger. Even if she did not succeed, all that was at stake for her was a little more or a little less honour. There then followed the classic Prussian geopolitical argument, which contrasted the exposed location of Prussia with the eternal security enjoyed by Russia:

From the shelter of an invulnerable rampart she [Russia] defies the ambition which she would have vainly combated for others and from one epoch to another

---

[62] Jackson to Mulgrave, 2.3.05, Berlin, PROL FO 64/67.
[63] Hardenberg to Jacobi, 1.4.05, Berlin, GStA Rep.XI.73.179A, fo. 87.
[64] Jacobi to Hardenberg, 24.5.05, London, GStA Rep.XI.73.179A, fo. 142.
[65] This letter to Alexander was drafted in March but never sent, presumably because such frankness about one's fears was considered unbecoming for a Prussian monarch. Some passages were incorporated into the instructions for General Zastrow: GStA Rep.XI.175.155B, fos. 21–2.
[66] See the instructions for General Zastrow in Ranke (ed.), *Denkwürdigkeiten Hardenbergs*, V, pp. 137–45.

she resumes her congenial role. It is a different matter for a state like my own which [is] without secure frontiers, has no other guarantee of its survival than its army, its thrift and its wisdom . . . Such are the demands of my geographical position and the need which I would have of all my resources in the event that she [Prussia] is faced by incalculable dangers.[67]

In St Petersburg, Zastrow found the Russians unimpressed by these arguments.[68] The foreign minister, Czartoryski, seemed possessed by an *idée fixe* of war against France;[69] even the tsar was fervently anti-French. Both tsar and foreign minister were eager to win Prussia over to the coalition quickly, for it was clear that this would sway the still vacillating Austrians. The promise of *dédomagements suffisants* was held out. But, in spite of Zastrow's warnings that Frederick William would defend it against allcomers, the Russians showed little respect for the idea of the neutrality of North Germany. This Russian attitude did not change fundamentally throughout Zastrow's stay.[70] But there was still one ground for optimism in Russia. For in spite of his commitment to force Prussia into the coming war, Czartoryski believed that his task would be greatly simplified by proving that Napoleon had refused all reasonable peace projects.[71] To this end, the experienced diplomat and favourite of the tsar, Baron Novosiltzov, was to be dispatched to Paris with proposals for the resumption of negotiations. The Prussians were elated at this prospect of a Franco-Prussian *rapprochement* and gladly complied with the Russian request for assistance in obtaining the passports necessary to Novosiltzov's mission.[72]

By the time Novosiltzov had reached Berlin it was already clear that he had failed in the true aim of his exercise, which was to impress Frederick William with the Russian determination to confront France and hold out some territorial bait for the Prussians.[73] Prussia refused either to be wooed or to be convinced that all possible avenues for a peaceful settlement had been explored. What Prussia did not realise was that Great Britain and Russia were preparing to coerce Prussia once Novosiltzov

[67] Ibid., pp. 142–3.
[68] See 'Acta touchant la Mission du Gen. Maj. de Zastrow à Peterbourg', GStA Rep.XI.175.155C, *passim*.
[69] Report of General Zastrow, 13.5.05, St Petersburg, GStA Rep.XI.175.155C, fo. 33.
[70] Report of General Zastrow, 16.5.05, St Petersburg, GStA Rep.XI.175.155C, fo. 40.
[71] Gower to Mulgrave, 12.4.05, St. Petersburg, in Rose (ed.), *Select dispatches*, p. 135.
[72] See Jackson to Mulgrave, 23.5.05, Berlin, PROL FO 64/67; Hardenberg to Jacobi, 23.5.05, Berlin, GStA Rep.XI.73.179A, fo. 133.
[73] See 'Propositions que Mr. de Novosiltzoff (*sic*) sera autorisé à faire' in 'Acta touch. Les bases de pacification arretées entre la Russie et l'Angleterre pour la négoçiation dont Mr. de Novosiltzoff a été chargé avec le Chef du Gouvernement Français', GStA Rep.XI.175.155D, fos. 57–63.

had returned from Paris. British–Russian patience with the Prussian neutrality policy was now being stretched to its very limit. On 25 June Francis Jackson expressed the need to force Prussia but 'only in a distant view and in terms as little likely as possible to create offence'.[74] Any 'undisguised menace' should be reserved until *after* Novosiltzov's mission was over.[75] That such menace should be applied was, however, no longer in doubt. Two weeks later Francis Jackson noted with satisfaction that 'Upon this part of the subject M. de Novosiltzov seems to accede to the opinion which I gave him very soon after his arrival that nothing short of actual force will bring the King of Prussia to stir from the ground he has taken as the basis of his political conduct.'[76] But before he could proceed with his cosmetic exercise, Novosiltzov's mission was aborted by the French annexation of Genoa. In Britain the news of this new provocation was received with relief. There was now hope that it would prod at least Russia and possibly even Austria into action.[77] The Prussians, on the other hand, were aghast.[78] On the one hand, they had long realised that the Italian question would be decisive,[79] and had feared that the failure of the Novosiltzov mission would mean war.[80] On the other hand, they had long ignored Napoleon's Italian policy, partly out of fear or indifference, but also because they wanted to wait for the Austrian reaction.[81] Now, with the resumption of European hostilities staring her in the face, Prussia still clung obstinately to the hope of a successful mediation. Indeed, by a curious logic, she argued that a quick peace was needed to put an end to further Napoleonic moves. Hence, to quote Hardenberg, Prussian policy must take the line that 'the conquest of Genoa was not sufficient cause to restart the war on the continent'.[82]

By late July, however, such hopes had become increasingly detached from reality. The April treaty between Great Britain and Russia had already set the tone of how Prussia was to be treated. In it Russia and Britain undertook 'to make common cause against every power, which by too close an union with France, may impede the objects of the present

[74] Jackson to Mulgrave, 25.6.05, Berlin, PROL FO 64/67.
[75] Gower to Mulgrave, 22.3.05, St Petersburg, in Rose (ed.), *Select dispatches*, p. 123.
[76] Jackson to Mulgrave, 10.7.05, Berlin, PROL FO 64/68.
[77] Jacobi to Hardenberg, 25.6.05, London, GStA Rep.XI.73.179B, fo. 7.
[78] Hardenberg to Jacobi, 12.7.05, Berlin, GStA Rep.XI.73.179B, fo. 13.
[79] Jacobi to Hardenberg, 15.3.05, London, GStA Rep.XI.73.179A, fo. 85; Hardenberg to Jacobi, 8.4.05, Berlin, GStA Rep.XI.73.179A, fo. 94.
[80] Jacobi to Hardenberg, 21.6.05, London, GStA Rep.XI.73.179B, fo. 3.
[81] Hardenberg to Jacobi, 22.4.05, GStA Rep.XI.73.179A, fo. 109.
[82] Hardenberg to Zastrow (draft), 7.6.05, Fürth, GStA Rep.XI.175.155C, fos. 47–8.

alliance'.[83] In concrete terms this meant the march of the northern Russian armies through Prussian Poland to 'obtain' the cooperation of Berlin.[84] The plan, Francis Jackson explained, was to start operations in North Germany, partly to crush the French in Hanover, but mainly in order to encourage Frederick William 'in the course of these operations to emerge from his present state of indifference and inactivity'.[85] To this end a Russian landing in Mecklenburg seemed to Francis Jackson the most efficacious measure 'likely to bring his [Frederick William's] court into action as the establishment of the war on a theatre so near and interesting to the Prussian dominions'. Clearly, to quote Hardenberg's own words, the *moment critique* had now come.[86]

The French alliance overtures

'The departure of M. Novosiltzov has taken place and since then we have had a total political calm which might well be followed by a tempest', Hardenberg observed towards the end of July 1805.[87] For much of the following August and September such a tempest was in the air. Interestingly, the metereological metaphor was also one that occurred to the French: 'Une fermentation sourde annonce une orage, et l'Angleterre le souffle',[88] Laforest told the Prussian government. If the previous months had been characterised by British and Russian blandishments and French threats, Prussia was now to be caught between the threat of a Russian invasion and France's tempting offers of territorial aggrandisement.

On 8 August 1805, the French envoy in Berlin, Laforest, made a set of proposals which was to dominate Prussian politics for the next two months.[89] Bombastic in tone, by turns insulting, sneering, flattering and cajoling in approach, the proposals were intended to win a Prussian alliance, or at least a guarantee of France's Italian gains, in return for the electorate of Hanover. The specific arguments employed to seduce the Prussians from their cherished neutrality were ones that they could

---

[83] Gower to Mulgrave, 7.4.05, St Petersburg, in Rose (ed.), *Select dispatches*. See also Ulmann, *Russisch-preussische Politik*, pp. 185–6, on the policy of forcing Prussia.

[84] Gower to Mulgrave, 22.7.05, St Petersburg, in Rose (ed.), *Select dispatches*, p. 190.

[85] Jackson to Mulgrave, 20.7.05, Berlin, PROL FO 64/68.

[86] Hardenberg to Jacobi, 12.7.05 Berlin, GStA Rep.XI.73.179B, fo. 13.

[87] Hardenberg to Lucchesini, 26.7.05, in Bailleu (ed.), *Preussen und Frankreich*, II, p. 356.

[88] Ranke (ed.), *Denkwürdigkeiten Hardenbergs*, V, p. 154.

[89] 'Französische Denkschrift, welche Laforest am 8. August 1805 Hardenberg über-reichte', in Ranke (ed.), *Denkwürdigkeiten Hardenbergs*, V, pp. 145–60.

ill afford to ignore. Laforest stressed the importance of the Prussian northern German neutrality zone because it had enabled the French to hold the area with few troops. Now the French feared that Prussia would permit the allies to attack the lightly held electorate. Should this happen, Laforest warned, the French would chase them out and the ensuing pursuit would probably wreck the northern German neutrality zone. Even in the unlikely event of an allied victory, Prussia's position would be no better. She would then be 'hemmed in (cernée)' by Russian forces on both sides, those in Hanover and those in western Poland.

Moving back again from specifics, the note then drew attention to the general question of Prussia's relative weakness. Compared to her neighbours, the argument ran, Prussia just did not have the resources for grandeur nor much chance of acquiring them under her own steam. Austria, Frederick William was reminded, had emerged from the last war much strengthened. She had exchanged the exposed Austrian Netherlands for much better situated Italian territories. Russia, too, had made enormous gains in Poland and the Baltic, not to mention the Black Sea and Central Asia. Unless she were to fall behind, Prussia needed accretions. Laforest spelled this out with brutal clarity:

If, in the midst of a continual process which has recently been accelerated, in which the great powers have not ceased to aggrandise themselves more and more, the Prussian monarchy remains stationary and is as if immobile, it is inevitable that her relative power will become smaller and smaller, so that she will find herself eventually at a stage at which she is no longer counted as being among the first-ranking powers.

Since she could not achieve such accretions on her own, the French plea continued, what better course of action than a French alliance? All Prussia would have to do in return was to guarantee France's Italian gains.

The bait was to be the electorate of Hanover. Napoleon not only offered the whole province by right of conquest, he also played on old Prussian fears for the security of northern Germany. Openly admitting that Hanover was a useful *point d'appui* against George III, the French threatened to remain there in peacetime as well. In order to assuage Prussian worries of offending Britain by an occupation of Hanover, the note claimed that such a move would certainly anger George but actually please the British government – 'toute administration anglaise croira gagner pour la Grande-Bretagne ce que le souverain perdra personelle-ment'; this argument was to have curious resonances later on. Then, towards the end of the note, after piling argument upon argument, the French asked:

The events

What could make the king hesitate? Would it be a spirit of moderation? But the spirit of his forbears, the glory of his children, the interest of his peoples, the geographic situation of his monarchy (*l'assiette géographique de sa monarchie*), the necessity of maintaining a certain equilibrium with his neighbours, the evident danger of falling into a situation of relative inferiority, all invite him [Frederick William] to analyse the nature of a sovereign's moderation. It does not at all consist in remaining immobile while all around him aggrandise themselves. This [policy] is not so much one of conservation [of power] but the neglect of the means of keeping his state at the level of the others. One often says that a state which no longer increases decreases.[90]

It would be difficult to find a more succinct summary of the perils and temptations facing Prussia in the late summer and early autumn of 1805. Indeed the logic of the French solicitation, the appeal to tradition and the dictates of her central location was not lost on her statesmen. The next two months saw a complex and often acrimonious debate among them on the best course of action in response to French blandishments and allied threats. Should Prussia take sides before being coerced by one side, or thereby driven involuntarily into the arms of the power that did not force her? Should she take the poisoned pawn of Hanover? Did the territorial and above all strategic gain of the electorate outweigh any possible public odium and British opposition? Perhaps more to the point was the attitude of the king: was it realistic to ask him to abandon his cherished neutrality scheme in favour of increased foreign political activism? Could the strengthened international position of Prussia compensate for any resulting loss of favour with the king? These were the central questions facing Prussian statesmen in the autumn of 1805 as they wrestled with the great dialectic between professional judgment and personal political advancement.

A cautious 'yes' to the French proposals came from Beyme, the king's trusted privy councillor.[91] He argued that since the main aim of Prussia was the prevention of a Franco-Russian war,[92] a limited alliance with France would most probably deter the allies. An essential measure to this end was the removal of the French from Hanover. Indeed, he believed that the possession of Hanover 'was too important, not to risk something

---

[90] Ibid., pp. 158–9.
[91] Memorandum by Beyme, 16.8.05, Tempelberg, in Bailleu (ed.), *Preussen und Frank-reich*, II, pp. 362–4; memorandum by Beyme, 18.8.05, in Bailleu (ed.), *Preussen und Frankreich*, II, pp. 364–6. On Beyme's stance see Disch, 'Der Kabinettsrat Beyme und die auswärtige Politik', 347.
[92] Memorandum by Beyme, 16.8.05, in Bailleu (ed.), *Preussen und Frankreich*, II, p. 363. On the need to prevent a Franco-Russian rupture and the resulting destabilisation of northern Germany see Hardenberg to Haugwitz, 17.8.05, Tempelberg, GStA Rep.XI.89.394, fo. 19.

for it'.[93] As for the wider issue of a full French alliance, however, Beyme felt that the conditions attached were too onerous to permit outright acceptance.[94] He was especially wary of the French demand for a guarantee of their Italian gains and made a series of elaborate counter-proposals designed to diminish Prussian commitments outside of Germany.[95] Hardenberg was a great deal more enthusiastic about the French proposals. This is, or has been, a matter of some historiographical debate,[96] but it seems clear that Hardenberg was aiming for a limited French alliance in the autumn of 1805. His main motive was the acquisition of Hanover, if necessary through some exchange of Prussia's western territories.[97] During a meeting with Laforest, Hardenberg identified the steps necessary for the implementation of a Franco-Prussian alliance. The general scruples of Frederick William would have to be overcome, as would his private unease about the spoliation of the related and allied house of Brunswick-Lüneburg. He would also have to be persuaded to set aside his cherished policy of neutrality.[98] But the conversion of the king to a policy of activism and alliance with France, however desirable it might be for the interests of the Prussian state, was fraught with personal political risks for Hardenberg; any attempt at converting Frederick William also risked alienating him. The relevant passage in Laforest's dispatch, in which Hardenberg's dilemma is described, is a classic example of the dialectic between personal ambition and *raison d'état* so common in Prussian high politics: 'Il m'a entretenu avec la dernière confiance de sa position personelle. Il est sensible a l'ambition de signaler son ministère par une opération qui redresserait la défectuosité la plus monstreuse de l'assiette géographique de la Prusse, mais il est sûr d'une disgrace s'il s'obstine à violenter les idées tenaces du roi.'[99]

The instructions sent to Lucchesini in Paris show that Frederick William had been at least partially impressed by the French arguments. They stressed the need to pre-empt a Russian–British–Swedish attempt on Hanover, which would revive all of Prussia's troubles in northern Germany; if necessary, Prussia should enter into an agreement with

---

[93] Ibid.
[94] Memorandum by Beyme, 18.8.05, in Bailleu (ed.), *Preussen und Frankreich*, II, p. 364.
[95] Ibid., p. 365.
[96] Summarised in Carl Hansing, *Hardenberg und die dritte Koalition* (Berlin, 1899), pp. 4–5. See the equivocations in Ranke, *Denkwürdigkeiten Hardenbergs*, II, pp. 191, 206.
[97] Hardenberg memorandum, 25.8.05, Berlin, GStA Rep.XI.89.394, fo.40.
[98] Laforest to Talleyrand, 10.8.05, Berlin, in Bailleu (ed.), *Preussen und Frankreich*, II, pp. 357–9.
[99] Ibid., p. 358.

France to forestall the allies.[100] In a separate letter written the same day, Beyme outlined the reasoning behind these instructions. The king would act on Laforest's offer, but the primary reason was not the acquisition of Hanover *per se* but its neutralisation as a potential source of danger to Prussia. Beyme also emphasised the king's unease about a guarantee of French possessions in Italy. Yet Frederick William was prepared to undertake just such a guarantee if it was the only way of preserving the peace of northern Germany.[101] Hardenberg's comments on Beyme's letter are illuminating. Despite the often carping tone of his marginalia, it is clear that Hardenberg agreed with the broad thrust of the argument – limited alliance with France, occupation of Hanover – but called for more activism and less hesitation throughout.[102] 'Of course the whole matter is not without risk, but where is now the least risk and where will the least risk be in the near future? This is what matters.'[103] The king himself was loath to take the necessary risks for the sake of Hanover. 'Can I', he asked Hardenberg, 'without violating moral rules, without losing the esteem of good men in Europe, without being noted in history as a prince without faith, depart from the stance which I have maintained hitherto in order to have Hanover?'[104] Hardenberg and Brunswick believed that he could and should, if only to keep the electorate out of French hands.[105]

The policy advocated by Hardenberg and Brunswick emerges clearly from the protocol of the Halberstadt conference, attended by Hardenberg, Brunswick and Schulenburg.[106] All three recommended acceptance of the French proposals. Like Beyme, they stressed that the long-term acquisition of the electorate was not the main aim behind the occupation of Hanover. Rather, Prussia's intention should be the consolidation of the neutrality of northern Germany. Pious hopes were expressed that the measure would help to keep the continental peace and encourage Britain to resume negotiations. Apart from the enormous strategic benefits of an occupation, the participants also welcomed some

---

[100] Instructions for Lucchesini, 17.8.05, Berlin, in Ranke (ed.), *Denkwürdigkeiten Hardenbergs*, V, p. 161; ibid., p. 162.
[101] Beyme to Lucchesini, 17.8.05, Charlottenburg, in Ranke (ed.), *Denkwürdigkeiten Hardenbergs*, V, pp. 164–7.
[102] See Hardenberg's marginalia, ibid., pp. 164–7.
[103] Ibid., p. 165.
[104] As reported in Laforest to Talleyrand, 14.8.05, Berlin, in Bailleu (ed.), *Preussen und Frankreich*, II, p. 361.
[105] Brunswick to Hardenberg, 30.8.05, Brunswick, GStA Rep.XI.89.Frankreich.394, fo. 57.
[106] Protocol of the Halberstadt conference, 22.8.05, in Ranke (ed.), *Denkwürdigkeiten Hardenbergs*, V, p. 168.

lesser advantages such as an end to the 'inconveniences' of the French presence and an end to the blockade of the Elbe and Weser. Though outright annexation was ruled out, the conference was fearful of the likely Russian reaction, especially in view of Prussia's realisation of her own military weakness.[107] However, though the risk of war was not considered great, it had to be countenanced. Interestingly enough, despite Frederick William's often-stated scruples, very little consideration was given to the likely British reaction to the occupation of the electorate. Beyme had probably had British sensibilities in mind when he wanted any clauses on Hanover to be kept secret in an eventual French–Prussian agreement. By and large, however, the Prussians seem to have accepted the French distinction between electoral and governmental interests in Great Britain; this was to have important long-term consequences. But for the moment Hardenberg argued that although one would have to reckon with a certain amount of British and Russian hostility, George III was not in actual possession of the electorate in any case. 'We don't want to take it from him', as Hardenberg put it, 'but rather to occupy it for him, so-to-speak.'[108]

As the Prussians pondered the arguments for and against an alliance with France, Napoleon became more and more impatient. Grand Marshal Duroc was dispatched to Berlin to speed things up;[109] however, he found the going unexpectedly difficult. Duroc rehearsed the usual French demands and arguments: Prussia must take Hanover, put pressure on Austria to remain neutral and join in alliance with France. Having found Hardenberg reserved at their first meeting, Duroc soon became frankly pessimistic about the outcome of his mission.[110] Frederick William, he complained, was quite happy to ally with France provided he did not actually have to do anything. By mid-September, there was the unmistakable tone of despair in Duroc's communications: there was no longer any hope of bringing Prussia into a defensive and offensive alliance.[111] This pessimism was justified, for on 9 September Frederick William had informed Lucchesini of his rejection of the guarantee plan: it would 'enchain me, feet and fingers tied, to the cause

---

[107] Ibid., pp. 169–71.
[108] Hardenberg memorandum, 10.9.05, Berlin, in Bailleu (ed.), *Preussen und Frankreich*, II, p. 382.
[109] Duroc to Talleyrand, 3.9.05, Berlin, in Bailleu (ed.), *Preussen und Frankreich*, II, p. 372. On Duroc's (second) mission to Berlin see G. Dwyer, 'Duroc diplomate', 32–7.
[110] Duroc to Talleyrand, 8.9.05, Berlin, in Bailleu (ed.), *Preussen und Frankreich*, II, p. 377.
[111] Duroc to Talleyrand, 18.9.05, Berlin, in Bailleu (ed.), *Preussen und Frankreich*, II, p. 387.

and interests of France' and thrust him into a dangerous and offensive war.[112]

The Russian threat

> Je vois avec douleur approcher le moment que nous avons jusqu'ici seulement aperçu dans le lointain, quand les deux terribles rivals, la France et la Russie, cherchant des points de combat pour s'atteindre, ne laisseront plus à la Prusse, leur voisine respective, que la liberté du choix du parti à prendre entr'elles.
>
> Lucchesini to Hardenberg, 29.7.05, Paris[113]

By the time the proposed French alliance had finally fallen through, Prussia's statesmen were already more concerned with the new threat taking shape in the east. Britain and Russia had not remained passive throughout the events outlined above. Acting on the policy of coercion agreed in the early summer, these two powers used the eight weeks of August and September to win Prussia over, before the military logic of the Russian advance made further negotiations pointless. The latest date by which a Prussian–Russian agreement could be reached was 28 September, for it was then that the first Russian troops would be ready to cross the Prussian border. Meanwhile, the political pressure on Prussia mounted. In early September Mulgrave judged the moment propitious for the resumption of negotiations for a subsidy treaty; in anticipation, Russia had already offered Prussia the same subsidy terms a few days before.[114] At the same time the Russians were preparing themselves for the worst. Alopeus was issued with instructions just in case Frederick William did not come round. The passage of Russian troops through Prussian territory was to go ahead on 28 September, with or without Prussian consent. As Czartoryski stressed, Russia 'preferred to have Prussia against us than to leave her neutral'.[115]

Prussia's statesmen were, of course, well aware of the implication of the approach of the Russian army and the ever closer cooperation between the tsar, Great Britain, Austria and Sweden. The mounting Russian pressure now supplanted the French alliance proposals as the main topic of high-political debate in Prussia. Beyme rejected the

---

[112] Instructions for Lucchesini, 9.9.05, Berlin, in Bailleu (ed.), *Preussen und Frankreich*, II, p. 379.

[113] Lucchesini to Hardenberg, 29.7.05, Paris, in Bailleu (ed.), *Preussen und Frankreich*, II, p. 353.

[114] Mulgrave to Jackson, 'September 1805', London, PROL FO 64/68; Francis Jackson to Mulgrave, 20.9.05, Berlin, PROL FO 64/68.

[115] Czartoryski to Alopeus, 1.9.05, St Petersburg, in *Vneshnaya Politika*, p. 549.

Russian request, but acknowledged that there was a real danger of an invasion;[116] in consequence, he recommended a show of strength, such as ostentatious military manoeuvres. This would help to maintain neutrality towards Russia in the east; in the west Hanover should be occupied until a general peace. This was 'worth risking something for'. Frederick William, however, baulked at the thought of military demonstrations against Russia and, obviously unhappy with the advice offered, requested the recall of Haugwitz.[117] Unlike Beyme, Hardenberg tended to play down any possible Russian threat.[118] He believed, or professed to, that the Russians were unlikely to march through Prussian territory without permission, and more likely to occupy Swedish Pomerania and Mecklenburg to increase the pressure on Prussia.[119] In his own memorandum, drawn up two days later, Hardenberg maintained this optimistic line: the threat of Russian invasion was not acute and thus no military demonstration was necessary.[120] In the meantime, Haugwitz and Zastrow should be dispatched to Vienna and St Petersburg, respectively, there to put the Prussian case to the Russian and Austrian governments. Frederick William's reply to Alexander was a compromise between Beyme's caution and Hardenberg's optimism. He refused the tsar's demand for active Prussian participation in the coalition and announced the mobilisation of one army corps, but expressed the hope that Duroc's mission would facilitate a peaceful settlement. A severe warning against any Russian designs on Swedish Pomerania was also issued.[121]

Even as Frederick William penned his reply to Alexander, the Russians were stepping up their diplomatic campaign against Prussia. On 1 September Alopeus once again demanded Prussian cooperation against France. As a long-term reward for her participation Prussia was to be offered a 'considerable aggrandisement' on the left bank of the Rhine, an offer which, as Hardenberg commented, had no other purpose than to involve Prussia in the defence of Holland against France.[122] So

---

[116] Beyme memorandum, 30.8.05, no place, printed in Disch, 'Der Kabinettsrat Beyme und die auswärtige Politik', *FBPG*, 42 (1929), 124–8. See also Disch, ibid., *FBPG*, 41 (1928), 344–7.

[117] Beyme to Hardenberg, 31.8.05, Berlin, in Bailleu (ed.), *Preussen und Frankreich*, II, p. 370.

[118] Hardenberg's comments on Alexander's letter, 31.8.05, Berlin, GStA Rep.XI.175.155D, fo. 107; Disch, 'Der Kabinettsrat Beyme', p. 125.

[119] Ibid.

[120] Hardenberg memorandum, 1.9.05, Berlin, in Bailleu (ed.), *Preussen und Frankreich*, II, p. 370.

[121] Frederick William to Alexander, Berlin, 6.9.05, in Bailleu (ed.), *Briefwechsel Alexanders*, p. 75.

[122] 'Propositions dont M. d'Alopeus est chargé et qu'il m'a enoncées le 1 sept. au soir', in Hardenberg's handwriting, GStA Rep.XI.175.155D, fo. 116.

184   The events

Hardenberg continued to advise caution. At the very beginning of his 10 September memorandum he affirmed that: 'The system of your Royal majesty is the neutrality of your monarchy and of the neighbouring states in northern Germany.'[123] Apart from the occupation of Hanover, the only activist measures Hardenberg felt confident enough to recommend were the possible occupation of Mecklenburg and the Hanseatic ports as part of the larger northern German neutrality scheme.[124] This was a militarily and politically sound move, as it both demonstrated Prussian determination to defend the neutrality zone and made physical violations of it more difficult. However, the main issue of whether to side with Russia or France in the imminent war of the Third Coalition was hardly addressed, let alone solved, by such an action. Yet Hardenberg's room for manoeuvre was limited: his former activism was muted by pessimism about getting the king to agree to any kind of decisive action and a consequent unwillingness to compromise his standing at court by advocating such action. It is surely no coincidence that in a memorandum of mid-September, Hardenberg specifically asked whether Frederick William was prepared to risk war before he offered any further advice.[125]

Hardenberg's problems with Frederick William's lack of foreign political drive were exacerbated by the recall of Haugwitz. As during the Rumbold affair, Hardenberg had now every reason to fear that Haugwitz would use the opportunity to ingratiate himself with the king by counselling a less active, and consequently less risky, policy closer to the king's own convictions. Indeed, it is unlikely that Frederick William had summoned Haugwitz for any other purpose than that of balancing the bellicose advice offered by Hardenberg. Sure enough, Haugwitz's memorandum of 22 August stressed that the French proposals, though seductive, especially with respect to Hanover, could never balance the risk of war with Russia.[126] In a passage which was obviously directed towards Frederick William's known fears, he drew attention to the danger of committing oneself to the French interest in Italy. Instead, Hardenberg advised Frederick William to 's'en tenir constamment à notre système de neutralité, le rendre assuré et veritablement imposant par la, le modifier peut-être d'après les circonstances du temps'.[127]

---

123 Hardenberg memorandum, 10.9.05, Berlin, in Bailleu (ed.), *Preussen und Frankreich*, II, p. 380.
124 Ibid., p. 381.
125 Hardenberg to Frederick William, 15.9.05, Berlin, in Bailleu (ed.), *Preussen und Frankreich*, II, p. 386.
126 Haugwitz to Frederick William, 22.8.05, Rogau, GStA Rep.XI.89.394, fo. 46.
127 Haugwitz memorandum, 22.8.05, Rogau, GStA Rep.XI.89.394, fo. 51.

Hardenberg's response to this danger was twofold and not without ingenuity. In the first instance, as we have just seen, he toned down his ostentatious activism of early August and harmonised his own policy with the known preferences of the king. Hardenberg's second tactic was to have Haugwitz removed from Berlin. This was done by dispatching him on a supposedly prestigious, but in reality entirely fruitless, mission to Vienna. Hardenberg was careful to point out that Haugwitz had in fact called for such an assignment himself.[128] However, it seems clear that Hardenberg was anxious that Haugwitz's mission should take place 'in any case', as he wrote to the Duke of Brunswick.[129] Foreign ambassadors were certainly in no doubt that Haugwitz was being sent to Vienna to get him out of the way, though they also accepted Hardenberg's stated purpose of gaining time.[130] Haugwitz's first mission to Vienna was thus a neat example of Hardenberg's continuing need to combine personal political ambition with the objective demands of policy. Metternich was doubly right when he condemned the Haugwitz mission as being 'just another manoeuvre'.[131]

Manoeuvre alone, however, could not prevent the Russian armies from crossing the Prussian border at the end of the month, if they so wished. As 28 September, the scheduled date of invasion, loomed, Prussia's statesmen were increasingly forced to consider the option of armed resistance. At the Berlin conference on 18 September, attended by all senior military men and a select group of politicians, it was decided to resist Russia with all available strength; total mobilisation was recommended.[132] On the political side, Frederick William was advised to accept the personal meeting with Alexander offered in the last letter, in order to delay the Russian invasion as long as possible.[133] These recommendations were immediately acted upon. The following day Hardenberg warned Alopeus against any infringement of Prussian territory and took up the tsar's idea of a personal rendezvous between the two monarchs.[134] In so doing Hardenberg seized on a throwaway remark

---

[128] Hardenberg to Haugwitz, 1.9.05, Berlin, GStA Rep.XI.89.394, fo. 29.
[129] Hardenberg to Brunswick, 8.9.05, Berlin, in Bailleu (ed.), *Preussen und Frankreich*, II, p. 376.
[130] Francis Jackson to Mulgrave, 20.9.05, Berlin, PROL FO 64/68; Metternich to Colloredo, 20.9.05, Berlin, in Klinkowström (ed.), *Metternichs nachgelassenen Papieren*, p. 47.
[131] Ibid., p. 52.
[132] Grosser Generalstab, Kriegsgeschichtliche Abteilung (eds.), *Die preußischen Kriegsvorbereitungen und Operationspläne von 1805*, Kriegsgeschichtliche Einzelschriften 1 (Berlin, 1883), especially pp. 59–60.
[133] Protocol of the Berlin conference, 19.9.05, in Ranke (ed.), *Denkwürdigkeiten Hardenbergs*, V, pp. 176–8.
[134] Hardenberg to Alopeus (draft), 23.9.05, GStA Rep.XI.175.155D, fo. 157.

of the tsar's, which had originally been intended as an invitation to discuss the details of military cooperation, as a delaying tactic.[135] Frederick William's own letter followed similar lines: the passage of Russian troops was flatly rejected, but the prospect of a personal meeting with the Tsar was warmly welcomed.[136] Alexander's reply was cordial but even more desperate in tone.[137] Once again he departed from Czartoryski's principle of forcing Prussia towards a decision by saying that he knew it was 'simply a matter of providing your Majesty [Frederick William] with an occasion to declare himself without fearing the effects of Napoleon's vengeance'.[138] The tsar, in other words, was prepared to acknowledge Prussia's precarious international position and the consequent policy constraints it imposed upon her.

In so doing Alexander had, somewhat belatedly, put his finger on the Prussian dilemma of August–September 1805. Running through all the deliberations of her high-political elite was the central theme of Prussia's exposed geographical position and its resulting political logic. This was most evident in her rejection of Anglo-Russian offers of territorial gain in the west, and her intense interest in the acquisition, or at least occupation of Hanover. The Prussians argued that a territorial bird in the hand was worth any number in the bush. Significantly, Lucchesini used the French offers in August 1805 to remind Hardenberg of the old Frederician maxim that a village on one's own borders was more valuable than the most lucrative overseas possessions.[139] Indeed, Hardenberg himself, to quote Francis Jackson's own words, was not interested in western gains, which 'by bringing the king his master in contact with France would expose him to endless disputes with that power, and that in general it was not for His interest to make distant and insulated (*sic*) acquisitions, which would rather tend to weaken than to consolidate his means of defence'.[140] Conversely, this same logic made the acquisition of Hanover all the more attractive. Lombard used similar geopolitical arguments when he referred to the electoral territories 'whose geographic position places them automatically under the protection of Prussia'.[141] Indeed, he argued, Hanover was so important

[135] Hardenberg to Jacobi, 23.9.05, Berlin, GStA Rep.XI.81.231, fo. 53; Alexander to Frederick William, 4.9.05, St Petersburg, in Bailleu (ed.), *Briefwechsel Alexanders*, p. 72.
[136] Frederick William to Alexander, 21.9.05, Potsdam, ibid., pp. 76–7.
[137] Alexander to Frederick William, 27.9.05, Brzest, ibid., p. 78.
[138] Alexander to Frederick William, 30.9.05, Poulavy, ibid., p. 80.
[139] Lucchesini to Hardenberg, 6.8.05, Paris, in Bailleu (ed.), *Preussen und Frankreich*, II, p. 356.
[140] Francis Jackson to Mulgrave, 25.9.05, Berlin, PROL FO 64/68.
[141] Lombard note, 17.9.05, Berlin, in Ranke (ed.), *Denkwürdigkeiten Hardenbergs*, V, p. 174.

to Prussia that 'it was worth making some sacrifice in order to obtain it'.[142]

This was, as we have seen, the consensus view. But action on Hanover and the associated prospect of a French alliance was complicated by the equally consensual fear of Russia's response. Frederick William, as Duroc repeatedly noted, 'fears war with Russia above all else because of the dangers his provinces bordering on that power would run'.[143] Fear of Russia was also the motivation behind Prussia's concern for the future of Swedish Pomerania. One of her constant fears – Hardenberg had already touched on it earlier – was the appearance of a Russian army at Stralsund, thus both surrounding Prussia with Russian forces and ruining her north German neutrality scheme. Not surprisingly, Prussia had reacted violently to rumours of a Russian purchase of Swedish Pomerania, especially in view of the evasiveness of the Swedes on the matter, and it was only in mid-September that these fears were laid to rest.[144] On the other hand, alliance *with* Russia was a no less hazardous business than her enmity. It would expose Prussia to the wrath of France without any guarantee of sufficient support. 'An alliance with Russia', Frederick William had told an Austrian envoy in late September, 'is an awkward business because it could withdraw at the flimsiest of pretexts, even without making peace, as it had already done before.'[145] This was to become a familiar theme in Prussian rhetoric in the weeks to come.

In the meantime, the consequences of Prussian passivity were making themselves felt in southern and western Germany. 'A state resembles a bank', Scharnhorst had warned in December 1804, 'once it has lost its credit, the end cannot be far off.'[146] Nowhere was this more obvious than in Prussia's deteriorating relations with Baden, Nassau, Hesse-Darmstadt and Hesse-Cassel, Württemberg and Bavaria. These states were coming under increasing French pressure to declare themselves

---

[142] Lucchesini to Hardenberg, 6.8.05, Paris, in Bailleu (ed.), *Preussen und Frankreich*, II, p. 356.

[143] Duroc to Talleyrand, 3.9.05, Berlin, ibid., p. 374. See also Duroc to Napoleon, 8.9.05, Berlin, ibid., p. 377.

[144] Instructions for Lucchesini, 17.8.05, Berlin, in Ranke (ed.), *Denkwürdigkeiten Hardenbergs*, p. 163; Francis Jackson to Mulgrave, 24.8.05, Berlin, PROL FO 64/68; Francis Jackson to Mulgrave, 8.9.05, Berlin, PROL FO 64/68; Jacobi report, 9.8.05, London, GStA Rep. XI.73.179B, fo. 49; Jacobi report, 10.9.05, London, fo. 80.

[145] Merveldt's 'Précis d'une conversation . . . avec le roi de Prusse, Berlin, 22 sept.', quoted in Ulmann, *Russisch-preußische Politik*, p. 221.

[146] Scharnhorst memorandum, 2.12.04, in Lehmann, *Scharnhorst*, I, p. 341: 'Ein Staat gleicht einer Handelskasse, hat er den Credit verloren, so ist er seinem Falle nahe.'

after the summer of 1805.[147] The steady erosion of Prussian power and prestige, in combination with Frederick William's manifest unwillingness to engage beyond the narrow limits of northern Germany left them no choice but to seek an accommodation with France. Württemberg, Hessen-Darmstadt and and Nassau repeatedly sought Prussian protection, but without success.[148] 'This means fairly clearly', one Nassau diplomat observed, 'that we are being left to our fate.'[149] Clearly, Prussia was unable to provide any substantial protection for the smaller German princes because she herself was too weak to resist French demands on her own. The Prussian experience and her policy was thus in many ways a variant of theirs. When Lombard criticised Austria for having confronted Bavaria with an ultimatum to join the Third Coalition the strong note of empathy is apparent: 'She (Austria) is forcing, for her own interests, a weak prince, to whom the new struggle is of no concern, to choose between equal dangers.'[150] Was this not Prussia's situation in August and September of 1805? Is this not the same sentiment which ran through Frederick William's plea to the tsar not to leave him only the choice between 'dishonour' and 'despair'?[151] This was the rhetoric of the middle-ranking, centrally located power, caught between the ambitions of its powerful neighbours.

But Prussia's weakness was also her strength. If the international situation put Prussia in considerable danger, it equally held out the prospect of substantial gain. By taking the right decisions, her statesmen felt, she could both weather the storm and carry off the acquisitions necessary to prevent her from slipping into a position of relative inferiority. Beyme had said as much in his memorandum of 30 July, on the eve of the autumn crisis: Prussia should remain neutral and commit herself as her interest dictated.[152] Prussia, in other words, should act as a

---

147 See Hans Karl von Zwehl, *Der Kampf um Bayern 1805. I. Der Abschluss der bayerisch-französischen Allianz* (Munich, 1937); Marcel Dunan, 'La naissance de l'Allemagne Napoléonienne. L'alliance franco-bavaroise de 1805. A propos d'un livre récent', *Revue Historique*, 188 (1940), 105–11; Richard Ledermann, *Der Anschluss Bayerns an Frankreich im Jahre 1805*, Forschungen zur Geschichte Bayerns 9 (Berlin, 1901), especially, p. 207.

148 Bernath, 'Die auswärtige Politik Nassaus 1805–1812. Ein Beitrag zur Geschichte des Rheinbundes und den politischen Ideen am Mittelrhein zur Zeit Napoleons', *Nassauische Annalen*, 63 (1953), 106–91, 115–132 and *passim*.

149 Ibid., p. 123: 'Das heißt also ziemlich klar, wir werden unserem Schicksal überlassen.'

150 Lombard note, 17.9.05, Berlin, in Ranke (ed.), *Denkwürdigkeiten Hardenbergs*, V, p. 175.

151 Frederick William to Alexander, 21.9.05, Potsdam, in Bailleu (ed.), *Briefwechsel Alexanders*, p. 77.

152 Beyme memorandum, 30.7.05, Berlin. Quoted in Disch, 'Kabinettsrat Beyme', pp. 339–40.

'trimmer', making up for what she lacked in military strength with political manoeuvre. A judicious display of neutrality was quite compatible with this policy and throughout much of the autumn months it seemed as if Prussian policy was working. She had managed to remain neutral while both sides had rushed to court her with territorial inducements. Prussia seemed poised to assume a pivotal position in the affairs of Europe. 'The fate of Europe is in your hands', Alexander told Frederick William in early September; his accession would 'tip the balance'.[153] 'If the king succeeds in maintaining his neutrality for just a little longer', the duke of Brunswick argued a fortnight later, 'the time will come when he can decide the fate of Europe.'[154]

In the meantime, the imperative to act on Hanover became ever stronger for Prussia. The long-awaited French withdrawal brought with it a new set of problems. It was, as Hardenberg put it, a *positive* development insofar as it eased Russian pressure on the Prussian eastern border; it was a *negative* development insofar as British, Russian and Swedish forces were now likely to move into the vacuum.[155] Such fears were confirmed by Jacobi's report that there was a British expedition in the offing, possibly to Swedish Pomerania.[156] For this reason the Duke of Brunswick even went so far as to say that the continued presence of a strong French force was desirable to keep the allies out.[157] But the French withdrawal was now irrevocable and by mid-September a Prussian liaison officer in the electorate reported that French forces in the area were few and far between.[158] Given the fact that Hanover was now almost completely unguarded, save for a small French force of 2,000 men at Hameln under General Barbou and a few scattered detachments, a successful allied invasion of the province with all its attendant complications was a real possibility. This was the news that Hardenberg had been waiting for. The occupation of the electorate, decided at the Berlin conference, would have to go ahead immediately to prevent the allies from getting there first.

To the east, there still remained the problem of the impending Russian invasion to be addressed. In early September, when the first military measures – partial mobilisation – were ordered, Frederick

---

153 Alexander to Frederick William, 4.9.05, St Petersburg, in Bailleu (ed.), *Briefwechsel Alexanders*, p. 73.
154 Brunswick to Hardenberg, 22.9.05, Sanssouci Berlin, GStA Rep.XI.89.394, fo. 110.
155 Hardenberg memorandum, 10.9.05, Berlin, in Bailleu (ed.), *Preussen und Frankreich*, II, p. 380.
156 Jacobi report, 30.8.05, London, GStA Rep.XI.73.179B, fo. 72.
157 Brunswick to Hardenberg, 10.9.05, Brunswick, GStA Rep.XI.89.394, fo. 85.
158 Copy of Wedel to Brunswick, dated mid-September by the archivist, GStA Rep.XI.89.394.

William had still been confident that war could be avoided and that he could continue his policy of neutrality.[159] But by the end of the month this optimism had evaporated. Though the Russian ambassador in Berlin, Alopeus, sympathised with the Prussian position and made every effort to avoid conflict,[160] a clash seemed unavoidable. The policy of 'forcing Prussia' seemed about to be forced through to its logical conclusion. Prussia and the diplomatic community in Berlin braced itself for the impending shock. But on 27 September a Russian messenger arrived with the news that the progress of the Russian troops had been halted until the outcome of the proposed royal rendezvous with Alexander was known. Frederick William was not going to have to decide, just yet, after all.

[159] Hardenberg to Jacobi, 9.9.05, Berlin, GStA Rep.XI.73.179B, fo. 70.
[160] Notes of the Duke of Brunswick, 16.9.05, GStA Rep.XI.89.394, fo. 96.

6 Delayed decisions: Prussian policy and politics, October 1805–February 1806

Ansbach, Potsdam and after: the ascendancy of Hardenberg

The news that French troops under Marshal Bernadotte had flagrantly violated Prussian neutrality by marching through Ansbach and Bayreuth on their way south completely transformed the Central European political scene in early October 1805.[1] Among the allied envoys resident in Berlin the mood was one of jubilation. Metternich reckoned that the affair had 'thrown the king into the allied camp by hitting him at his most sensitive point',[2] that is by infringing his neutrality zone. His British colleague, Francis Jackson, believed that the Prussians, those 'repentant sinners', were on the verge of joining the allied cause.[3] This did not happen. The tension which had been building up in the shadow of the threatened Russian violation of Prussia's neutrality, did not, as might reasonably have been expected, unload itself over the heads of the offending French. Instead, Prussia only inched very slowly towards accession to the Third Coalition and swung back to the old neutrality stance with alacrity after the disastrous allied defeat at Austerlitz. But the policy of mediation and neutrality resumed was in many ways a mask for Prussia's increasingly client status and had been purchased at the price of an inbuilt conflict with Great Britain which was to erupt with considerable violence in the spring of 1806.

Frederick William reacted to the news of the French action at Ansbach-Bayreuth with uncharacteristic fury and determination. It was, he said, 'un événement qui peut changer la face des affaires'.[4] Laforest reported

---

[1] Eberhard Mayerhoffer von Vedropolje, *1805. Der Krieg der dritten Koalition* (Vienna, 1905), p. 11.
[2] Metternich to Colloredo, 7.10.1805, Berlin, in Klinkowström (ed.), *Metternichs nachgelassenen Papieren*, p. 55.
[3] Francis Jackson to Pitt (marked 'private'), 17.10.05, Berlin, PROL FO 64/69, not foliated; Francis Jackson to Mulgrave, 7.10.05, Berlin, PROL FO 64/69.
[4] Instructions for Jacobi, 8.10.05, GStA, Rep.XI.81.231, fo. 55.

that 'Le Roi s'est laissé allé à un grand excès de colère', while Duroc found the king so angry that he would not even listen to explanations.[5] Allied observers could be forgiven for hoping to make political capital out of this. The events of the last days, Frederick William told Alexander, had given him a 'new but decisive' way of looking at things. 'Tous mes devoirs vont changer', he continued and announced his intention to act against Napoleon, the wrecker of his eight-year-old neutrality scheme.[6] But by the time the letter to Alexander was penned, Frederick William had already drawn back from really decisive measures against France. In the first flush of anger he had intended to expel the French envoys, Duroc and Laforest, a move which, as Hardenberg said, would have been 'tantamount to a declaration of war'.[7] It was for this very reason that Hardenberg counselled against the move, however astonishing that may seem to those accustomed to see in him the single-minded proponent of an anti-French policy.[8]

On 7 October, a preliminary conference was convened to discuss Prussia's response to the French provocation.[9] Hardenberg himself, Schulenburg, Brunswick and Field Marshal Möllendorf[10] were present. Their findings were grim: the French, who had actually done what the Russians had only threatened to do, had treated Prussia like one of the smaller Italian or German states. The old neutrality system had thereby been rendered null and void. To ignore what had happened or to remain inactive would be incompatible with the honour and security of the state; it would also court allied suspicions. The participants therefore advised that the Russians be allowed a controlled passage through Prussian territory; Hanover was to be occupied and the local French forces expelled. That, however, was the limit of the anti-French measures which the participants were prepared to advise. They represented a definite swing to the coalition and marked a departure from the policy of August and September. But they were still a far cry from the king's

---

⁵ Laforest to Talleyrand, 9.10.05, Berlin, in Bailleu (ed.), *Preussen und Frankreich*, II, p. 394; Duroc to Napoleon, 9.10.05, Berlin, in ibid., p. 396. For a more positive view of the violations see Tarrasch, *Übergang*, pp. 37–45.

⁶ Frederick William to Alexander, 9.10.05, Potsdam, in Bailleu (ed.), *Briefwechsel*, p. 81.

⁷ Ranke (ed.), *Denkwürdigkeiten Hardenbergs*, I, p. 263.

⁸ Theodor Bitterauf, 'Studien zur preußischen Politik', *FBPG*, 27 (1914), 468. See also Gaide, 'Der diplomatische Verkehr', pp. 63–4.

⁹ Conference protocol in Ranke (ed.), *Denkwürdigkeiten Hardenbergs*, I, pp. 268–75. See also Disch, 'Der Kabinettsrat Beyme', *FBPG*, 41 (1928), 354–5.

¹⁰ Wichard Joachim Heinrich von Möllendorf, b. 1724 Lindenberg in der Priegnitz, d. Havelberg, 1816. Prussian Field Marshal. Joined army of Frederick the Great at a very early age; distinguished himself in battle; made general 1757; made field marshal 1793; succeeds Brunswick as commander of the coalition troops on the Rhine 1794; in favour of Treaty of Basle (1795); generally pro-French. *ADB*, vol. XXII, pp. 120–1.

own radical and spontaneous desire to send the French diplomats home.

These recommendations were elaborated and affirmed at a full Council of State held at Potsdam two days later[11] which was attended by Kalckreuth,[12] Köckritz, Kleist and Lombard. But while certain key features of the 7 October meeting such as the transit of Russian troops remained undisputed, a definite note of equivocation, perhaps not unrelated to the king's own second thoughts, had crept into the protocol. If the allies were prepared to reduce their demands to such an extent as to make Napoleon's rejection of them odious in the eyes of Europe, Frederick William should offer an armed mediation in favour of that party which accepted the conditions; Frederick William described this as his 'grand ouvrage, sa médiation active'.[13] In so doing, the conference argued, the king would pursue his current policy to the end. No matter the outcome, the argument continued, the winter – and thus a respite from campaigning – still lay ahead. Honour would have been satisfied and security guaranteed. Above all, the protocol stressed, 'No war has been declared yet, all dice remain to be cast and we are free to take advantage of any circumstances which may arise in the meantime.' In one important sense, however, the Council of State at Potsdam went further than the earlier meeting: Prussia's cooperation with the coalition would have to be paid for by what the participants called 'present means' and 'future means'. 'Present means' meant subsidies, while 'future means' referred to territorial gains. Prussia, they counselled, must seek 'a less involved border, . . . which would not be compromised in every new continental or maritime war, as is the case today. With one word: Hanover: in return for an exchange or some other arrangement.'[14]

---

[11] Ranke (ed.), *Denkwürdigkeiten Hardenbergs*, I, p. 275.
[12] Friedrich Adolf von Kalckreuth, b. 1737 Sottenhausen bei Sangerhausen, d. 1818 Berlin. Prussian field marshal. Adjutant of Prince Henry; in disfavour with Frederick the Great; ennobled by Frederick William II; distinguished himself as Lieutenant-General by capturing Mainz in 1793; brief prominence as chief negotiator with the French after Jena; anti-Austrian, pro-French and the enlightenment; protagonist of the Treaty of Basle. *NDB*, 11, p. 50.
[13] Hardenberg to Duroc and Laforest, 14.10.05, Berlin, in Klinkowström (ed.), *Metternichs nachgelassenen Papieren*, p. 67; Hardenberg to Köckritz, 15.10.05, Berlin, in Bailleu (ed.), *Preussen und Frankreich*, II, p. 399.
[14] Ranke (ed.), *Denkwürdigkeiten Hardenbergs*, I, p. 275: 'spinnt der König sein bisheriges System bis auf den letzten Faden ab . . . und, was auch der Erfolg sei, wir haben den Winter vor uns. Die Attitude hat der Ehre genügt, hat für die Sicherheit gesorgt. Noch ist kein Krieg erklärt, noch liegen alle Würfel, und jeder Gebrauch der Zwischen-begebenheiten steht in unserer Macht'. And: 'eine weniger verwickelte Grenze . . . , die es nicht bei jedem neuen Continental oder Seekriege so wie heute compromittierte. Nicht Ambition, sondern Sicherheit. Mit einem Wort: Hannover: gegen irgend einen Tausch oder sonstiges Arrangement.'

Concrete steps were now undertaken. On 11 October contact was made with the Saxons as part of the traditional policy of integrating the smaller North German powers into Prussian strategy.[15] Three days later, Hardenberg informed Frederick William that Prussian troops would be in the city of Hanover by 18 October.[16] But even now geopolitical considerations dictated military restraint. Indeed, Brunswick's queries about his orders show the extent of ambiguity in the Prussian plan about the use of force in the occupation.[17] This was largely due to the need – dictated by Prussia's exposed position – to avoid being overrun while unprepared. Admittedly, Lombard's suggestion that the situation of *de facto* war be concealed from France until Prussia's armies were in place may have been simply an excuse for further equivocation.[18] But even Metternich, not usually an observer sympathetic to Prussian needs, conceded that Prussia could not declare herself until all her forces were assembled and ready to strike;[19] and Hardenberg told the Hanoverian ambassador in Berlin, Count Ompteda, that Prussia wanted to avoid the 'error of the Austrian court' of breaking off negotiations while militarily unprepared.[20]

There were, however, other reasons for Hardenberg's cautious response to the events in Ansbach-Bayreuth. Hardenberg's own explanation was that Frederick William, after the first wave of indignation, was unlikely to follow his initial determination, thus rendering the whole exercise pointless.[21] This may well have been one reason, but on closer examination a more subtle and far-sighted motive emerges. In order to ensure Prussia the maximum gain from her policy of 'trimming', Hardenberg had to determine the price of her cooperation in advance. The Ansbach affair was thus welcome, in the sense that it paved the way for much greater political activism than Frederick William was prepared to countenance in August and September, but it was also potentially counterproductive, insofar as it seemed to compel Prussia to act of her

---

[15] Hardenberg to Frederick William 11.10.05, Berlin, 'Generalia betr. die politischen Unterhandlungen in den Jahren 1804, 1805 und 1806', GStA Rep.XI.89.394, fos. 169–70.

[16] Hardenberg to Frederick William, 14.10.05, Berlin, in Bailleu (ed.), *Preussen und Frankreich*, II, p. 399.

[17] Brunswick note (marked 'about 14th October'), GStA Rep.XI.89.394, fo. 189.

[18] Lombard to Hardenberg, 19.10.05, Potsdam, in Bailleu (ed.), *Preussen und Frankreich*, II, p. 401.

[19] Metternich to Colloredo, 15.10.05, Berlin, in Klinkowström (ed.), *Metternichs nachgelassenen Papieren*, p. 58.

[20] Ompteda to Münster, 24.10.05, Schwerin, in Ludwig von Ompteda, *Politischer Nachlaß des hannoverschen Staats- und Cabinettsministers, Ludwig von Ompteda aus den Jahren 1804 bis 1813*, 3 vols. (Jena, 1869), p. 91.

[21] Ranke (ed.), *Denkwürdigkeiten Hardenbergs*, I, p. 263.

own accord and thus substantially reduced any allied incentive to offer a bribe. The king's first angry reaction almost resulted in just that and so Hardenberg had to bring him back from the brink and negotiate Prussia's accession to the Third Coalition at her own pace and on her own terms. In order to do so he had to make clear to the foreign envoys that there was nothing automatic about Prussian military action against France. This he did with considerable skill and discretion. His first task was to prevent Frederick William from being stampeded into war by Russia. When Alopeus wanted to resume his pressure for Prussian action, Hardenberg recommended that he remain quiet 'and let the event work its own way in the mind of the king of Prussia'.[22] In fact, of course, that was exactly what Hardenberg did not allow for, for with every passing day he knew Frederick William's resolve to be growing weaker not stronger. Alopeus does not seem to have seen through Hardenberg's manoeuvre. Nor for that matter did Francis Jackson, who noted with some surprise that the Prussians did not seem at all keen on subsidies, whereas, as we shall soon see, Hardenberg was simply trying to drive up the subsidy bribe.[23] In an especially disingenuous move, Hardenberg then proceeded to blame the 'French faction' for what he himself had initiated.[24] Metternich, too, was upset by Hardenberg's insistence that the infringement of Prussian territory alone was insufficient reason for war. He countered with some force that this had not been Prussia's attitude towards Russia in September,[25] but does not seem to have spotted the logic behind the altered Prussian stance, namely that of extorting the maximum possible gain from her alignment with the allied cause. Only Laforest recognised that Hardenberg had to show determination to avenge the French infringements while simultaneously bringing the king back to a more measured course of action.[26] In order to do so he promised not to see the French delegation for a few days, though the French envoys themselves were under no doubt that he wished to keep the door to France open. Indeed, when Laforest asked to see Hardenberg at a particularly intense moment of the crisis, the latter replied *verbally* that he would let them know when he wanted to see them and asked them to keep a low profile until that time.[27]

22 Francis Jackson to Mulgrave, 8.10.05, Berlin, PROL FO 64/69.
23 George Jackson to Mulgrave, 16.10.05, Berlin, PROL FO 64/69.
24 Francis Jackson to Mulgrave, 16.10.05, Berlin, PROL FO 64/69.
25 Metternich to Colloredo, 16.10.05, Berlin, in Klinkowström (ed.), *Metternichs nachgelassenen Papieren*, p. 61.
26 Laforest to Talleyrand, 9.10.05, Berlin, in Bailleu (ed.), *Preussen und Frankreich*, II, p. 394.
27 Ibid., p. 396.

By mid-October it was clear that Hardenberg had both judged the royal mood correctly and found general acceptance for his ideas on Ansbach. Only a week after wanting to expel the French envoys, Frederick William was back to his usual role of dragging his heels on active measures against France,[28] while insisting that all specific references to military action be removed from the protest note to Duroc and Laforest.[29] Having saved Prussia from what he considered a premature break with France, Hardenberg was now free to implement his policy of controlled accession to the coalition, a policy which rested on a broad consensus within the Prussian elite. This consensus had come about as a direct result of the Ansbach infringements. Lombard and Beyme, both previously staunch adherents of strict neutrality and passivity, had followed the royal lead of initial bellicosity, to the extent that both of them considered Prussia *de facto* at war with France after Ansbach.[30] This caused some amazement to outside observers,[31] but it came as no surprise to those attuned to the high-political practice of pandering to the king's will. Once the royal mood had swung back to its accustomed passivity and the cabinet councillors followed suit, the way was clear for Prussian policy to be channelled into the narrow programme set out in the conferences of 7 and 9 October. The unmistakable hand of Hardenberg can be found in the resolution 'not to ally with Russia and Austria unconditionally but only insofar as it corresponds with [Prussia's] true interest'. Exactly the same sentiments were voiced by Beyme a week later: Prussia should only join the coalition insofar as her interest coincides with that of the coalition partners.[32]

The wisdom of Hardenberg's strategy was soon borne out by the course of the subsidy negotiations. Back in September, Hardenberg had responded to one of Francis Jackson's periodic subsidy overtures by 'let[ting] it rest for the moment'.[33] After Ansbach, Hardenberg realised, such indifference would be difficult to affect and yet the pretence was essential to Prussian interests. But the need for subsidy was great,[34]

---

[28] This emerges from Hardenberg to Frederick William, 13.10.05, Berlin, in Bailleu (ed.), *Preussen und Frankreich*, II, p. 398.
[29] Lombard to Hardenberg, 14.10.05, Potsdam, in Bailleu (ed.), *Preussen und Frankreich*, II, p. 398.
[30] Lombard to Hardenberg, 19.10.05, Potsdam, in Bailleu (ed.), *Preussen und Frankreich*, II, p. 401; Beyme memorandum of 18.10.05, in Disch, 'Der Kabinettsrat Beyme und die auswärtige Politik', p. 128.
[31] Metternich to Colloredo, 18.10.05, Berlin, in Klinkowström (ed.), *Metternichs nachgelassenen Papieren*, p. 65.
[32] Disch, 'Der Kabinettsrat Beyme und die auswärtige Politik', p. 128.
[33] Hardenberg to Jacobi, 20.9.05, Berlin, GStA Rep.XI.81.231, fo. 51.
[34] See Hardenberg to Jacobi, 17.10.05, Berlin, GStA Rep.XI.81.231, fos. 57–8; Mulgrave to Francis Jackson (draft), 16.10.05, London, PROL FO 64/69.

and so a conference held on 17 October, at which only Hardenberg, Haugwitz, Brunswick and the king were present, gave the final go-ahead for a subsidy overture to Jackson.[35] These first soundings of the British envoy showed that a level of subsidy acceptable to the Prussians was going to have to be fought for.[36] When approached by Hardenberg, Francis Jackson professed himself happy to support the Prussian war effort but argued that the question of subsidising Prussia was different in principle from Russia and Austria. This was because 'the two imperial courts were making war from motives long since recognised by them as essential to the welfare and independence of Europe, whilst Prussia had an offence of the gravest nature to avenge'.[37] In London, Jacobi was being confronted with the same ploy: while Mulgrave was content to subsidise Prussia along with her smaller North German allies, Saxony, Hesse-Cassel and Brunswick, the Prussian ambassador thought it likely that Britain would haggle over the amount of subsidy in view of the fact that Prussia had already taken up arms to avenge the insult of Ansbach.[38] This was an argument which Hardenberg had foreseen but which he desperately had to refute. The same day he instructed Jacobi to inform the British government that Prussia needed subsidies both because she lacked resources and because she was fighting 'for a cause in which [she] was far less interested than the other powers'.[39]

By mid-October, once the clamour over Ansbach had died down and the royal fervour had completely evaporated, Prussia was in an increasingly powerful bargaining position *vis à vis* Russia and Britain. For, in the meantime, British policy had swung away from that of coercion, as practised in August and September, and back to the old strategy of wooing Prussia into the allied camp through bribery. On 8 October 1805, though still prepared to countenance hostility in conjunction with Russia, Mulgrave instructed Jackson not to take the lead in 'anything like menace' and expressed the hope that Prussia would be 'induced by considerations of a different nature, to unite with the allies'.[40] In Berlin, Francis Jackson now described Prussia as 'a chief bulwark against the overthrow of the whole continent',[41] while in London the war office decided to capitalise on the new opportunities by dispatching a British

---

[35] Ranke (ed.), *Denkwürdigkeiten Hardenbergs*, I, p. 300.
[36] Hardenberg to Frederick William (draft), 18.10.05, Berlin, GStA Rep.XI.89.394, fo. 205.
[37] Francis Jackson to Mulgrave, 17.10.05, Berlin, PROL FO 64/69.
[38] Jacobi report, 25.10.05, London, GStA Rep.XI.73.179B, fo. 148.
[39] Hardenberg to Jacobi, 17.10.05, Berlin, GStA Rep.XI.81.231, fo. 57.
[40] Mulgrave to Francis Jackson, 8.10.05, London, PROL FO 64/69.
[41] Francis Jackson to Pitt, 17.10.05, Berlin, PROL FO 64/69.

expeditionary force to northern Germany.[42] There was now yet another element to be added to the already confused North German political scene, yet another variable in the increasingly complex picture of Prussian foreign policy, a variable that was to take on a peculiar and unforeseen importance in the months ahead.

For the time being, however, Prussian attention was firmly centred on the leisurely imperial progress of Alexander I towards the Prussian border and his personal meeting with Frederick William. Originally suggested by the tsar in order to coordinate military operations against the French in September, the meeting had taken on a new significance in the light of recent events. The forced French passage through Ansbach-Bayreuth had two important consequences for the approaching Russo-Prussian negotiations. First of all, the Prussian fury made the chances of an alliance against Napoleon an infinitely more realistic prospect than it had been the month before. Secondly, the rapid and entirely unexpected French *coup de main* at Ansbach had caught the Austrian troops in Southern Germany under the inept General Mack off balance, leading to their shattering defeat and humiliating surrender at Ulm in October 1805. The loss of this army did not, as yet, mean the military end of the coalition, but it did make the task of gaining Prussian support even more pressing than had hitherto been the case.

For Hardenberg the impending meeting was of great personal as well as general political importance. Ever since late August his arch-rival, Count Haugwitz, had been creeping back into his former position of authority with the king, thus putting Hardenberg's sole responsibility for foreign affairs in question. On 22 October Hardenberg's worst fears were confirmed when on returning from some days in the country, he found a royal *Cabinetsordre*, formalising Haugwitz's position as joint minister for foreign affairs.[43] Hardenberg immediately offered his resignation; the offer was rejected by the king on the grounds that he needed advice from all quarters, especially during the present crisis and the days of negotiation which lay ahead.[44] As a result, Hardenberg seems to have decided to exploit the exceptional circumstances of the next week to make one last attempt to ward off the threats to his competency

---

[42] Jacobi report, 15.10.05, London, GStA Rep.XI.73.179B, fos. 140–1; Jacobi report, 18.10.05, London, GStA Rep.XI.73.179B, fo. 144. 'Memorandum relative to the Projected Expedition, for the consideration of the Cabinet', 21.10.05, Downing Street; Castlereagh to Don, 24.10.05, Downing Street; Castlereagh to Harrowby, 19.11.05, Downing Street, all in Vane (ed.), *Castlereagh*, pp. 25, 29, 43.

[43] Frederick William to Hardenberg and Haugwitz, 19.10.05, Potsdam, in Ranke (ed.), *Denkwürdigkeiten Hardenbergs*, I, p. 302.

[44] Ibid., p. 305.

and consolidate his crumbling position as Prussian foreign minister. With this aim in mind, Hardenberg succeeded in frustrating Frederick William's attempts to wriggle out of the meeting with Alexander; the king was even prepared to simulate illness in order to avoid meeting Alexander.[45]

As Alexander approached Berlin, Prussia's senior politicians steeled themselves for the forthcoming jockeying for position and intrigue to come by loading the dice as heavily as possible in their favour. Thus, when it was suggested that Haugwitz be sent to meet Alexander after Ansbach, Hardenberg insisted on his being kept in Berlin, ostensibly for political consultations, but more probably because he feared that he might influence the tsar.[46] As regards location, one astute observer noted that, after Ansbach, Hardenberg, Möllendorf, Brunswick and Schulenburg tried to draw Frederick William away from his country retreat at Paretz 'where in this moment of crisis the manoeuvres of the cabinet secretaries retain him and exercise on him an influence more extensive than would be the case in Berlin or even Potsdam'.[47] Perhaps it was for this reason that Frederick William left Berlin to meet the tsar at Potsdam, which represented a kind of middle ground between the mounting anti-French patriotic fever in Berlin[48] and the confines of a Paretz dominated by the cabinet secretaries.

The man whose active cooperation Alexander won, and whose name was henceforth to be inextricably bound up with the allied cause, was Hardenberg.[49] Through his wholehearted and public conversion to the coalition, Hardenberg was able to use the tsar's presence to tip the high-political balance against Haugwitz.[50] Thanks to Alexander's complete domination of the social and political scene in Berlin, the so-called 'French Party' – the sweeping generalisation used to describe a whole spectrum of views from unabashed Francophilia to cautious neutralism – was utterly eclipsed. At dinner, on parade, indeed on almost every occasion during the social whirl accompanying the tsar's stay,

---

[45] Ibid., pp. 252–3; p. 260; Bailleu, 'Vor hundert Jahren', p. 215.

[46] Ranke (ed.), *Denkwürdigkeiten Hardenbergs*, I, pp. 275–6.

[47] Metternich to Colloredo, 16.10.05, Berlin, in Klinkowström (ed.), *Metternichs nachgelassenen Papieren*, pp. 62–3.

[48] Tschirch, *Geschichte der öffentlichen Meinung in Preußen*, II, pp. 189–90 for a judicious assessment of anti-French feeling in autumn 1805; Duroc to Napoleon, 27.10.05, Berlin, in Bailleu (ed.), *Preussen und Frankreich*, II, p. 401.

[49] On background see Bailleu, 'Vor hundert Jahren', esp. 217–21.

[50] See his manipulation of the negotiations, in Ranke (ed.), *Denkwürdigkeiten Hardenbergs*, I, p. 317. See also the astute comments of Kieseritzky, 'Die Sendung von Haugwitz nach Wien', p. 14 and Olden, 'Napoleon und Talleyrand', pp. 72–3, who stresses Hardenberg's 'Antagonismus zu seinem Kon-Aussenminister'.

Francophobe sentiment became the norm.[51] It was particularly marked in court circles, especially with Prince Louis Ferdinand and the queen, whose increased activism the French envoy later noted with alarm.[52] Admittedly, as Metternich complained, Haugwitz was able to maintain some influence with the king while the 'hand of Lombard' was still often to be recognised.[53] The presence of the tsar did, however, cramp the style of Hardenberg's adversaries. On most occasions they argued in favour of the coalition even if, in Francis Jackson's judgment, this was only because they did not dare oppose those who had already aligned themselves with Russia and Austria.[54] Nonetheless, though he was unable to eliminate the subterranean influence of his rivals Hardenberg could, and did, use the tsar's presence to override open obstruction of the negotiations. Whatever the cabinet secretaries and Haugwitz may have said in private, it was Hardenberg who dominated the joint sessions with the Russians, and who was instrumental in steering Prussia away from a course of strict neutrality.

Once established as the principal Prussian negotiator, Hardenberg drove a hard bargain with the Russians. The treaty that finally emerged from the negotiations at Potsdam was thus, both in fact and in the public perception, Hardenberg's work. Signed on 3 November 1805 between Russia, Prussia and the Holy Roman Emperor, the Treaty of Potsdam laid down the terms for what at least two of the signatories believed to be Prussia's imminent accession to the allied cause. By articles I and II, Frederick William undertook an armed mediation between France and the coalition on the basis of the treaty of Lunéville: this included compensation for the king of Sardinia, the independence of Naples, Holland, Switzerland, the German empire and a guarantee of the integrity of the Porte.[55] Article III stipulated the dispatch of an envoy to Napoleon's headquarters to present the terms of mediation. In the meantime, Prussian troops would move into suitable positions in the west and south-west in the event of a rupture (article VII). A strict military timetable was drawn up and the provisions of the article are worth quoting in full, for they were to be become the subject of con-

---

[51] For Prussian public opinion and Alexander's visit, see Tschirch, *Geschichte der öffentlichen Meinung in Preußen*, II, pp. 187–97. See also Paul Seidel, 'Parade am Berliner Schlosse vor Kaiser Alexander I und König Friedrich Wilhelm III am 25 Oktober 1805', *Hohenzollern Jahrbuch*, 16 (1912), 242–3.
[52] 'Copie d'une apostille du Sieur de Laforest à Son Excellence Monsieur de Talleyrand du 26 janvier', in Ranke (ed.), *Denkwürdigkeiten Hardenbergs*, I, p. 448.
[53] Metternich to Colloredo, 4.11.05, Potsdam, in Klinkowström (ed.), *Metternichs nachgelassenen Papieren*, 76.
[54] Francis Jackson to Mulgrave, 2.11.05, Berlin, PROL FO 64/69.
[55] *Traité du 3 novembre 1805*, in Ranke (ed.), *Denkwürdigkeiten Hardenbergs*, I, p. 325.

siderable dispute in the weeks to come: 'Durant la négociation, les armées prussiennes continueront à avancer vers les points d'où elles devront agir en cas de rupture, et la négociation sera conduite de manière à être terminée dans l'espace de quatre semaines, à compter du jour du départ du négociateur qui aura lieu incessamment.'[56] It was article IX, however, which was to cause the most bitter controversy. It concerned the extent and direction of the bribe for Prussia's active participation in the coalition effort and, at least in the public version of the treaty, was couched in suspiciously vague terms. Prussian gains were to be justified by the geographical imperative – 'impérieusement dictées par la position géographique de ses [Frederick William's] Etats' – so as to give him an increase in strength and to save him from harm resulting from exposed possessions.[57] The article went on to specify Prussia's need for British subsidies and a more secure border: 'Qu'à la paix on procurera à la Prusse une frontière plus sûre que celle qu'elle a actuellement, soit par des acquisitions, soit par des échanges.'[58] What this meant was spelt out in the first separate and secret article accompanying the treaty in which the Russian emperor undertook to use his good offices to acquire Hanover for Prussia.

Not surprisingly, allied enthusiasm for the treaty was muted. It was not, as Metternich wrote to Colloredo, the 'nec [sic] plus ultra', but it was the best one could hope to attain in the circumstances.[59] 'La Prusse', he added, 'est habituée à ne travailler que pour du profit tout clair, c'est lui seul qu'elle calcule.'[60] Indeed, if one compares the terms of Potsdam with the negotiating position outlined in the conferences of 7 and 9 October and later summarised in a memorandum on the eve of the negotiations,[61] the treaty was a triumph of Prussian policy. She had gained Russian backing not only for a generous British subsidy, but also for the annexation of Hanover.

The Harrowby mission: Hanover or the Netherlands?

If Prussia's statesmen could congratulate themselves on having driven a hard bargain, there was an explosive irony built into the agreement they

---

[56] Ibid., p. 328.
[57] Ibid., p. 329.
[58] Ibid., p. 330.
[59] Metternich to Colloredo, 4.11.05, Potsdam, in Klinkowström (ed.), *Metternichs nachgelassenen Papieren*, p. 75.
[60] Ibid.
[61] Hardenberg and Haugwitz to Frederick William, 23.10.05, Berlin, GStA Rep.XI.175.155E, fo. 1.

signed at Potsdam. 'The treaty of 3 November contains two questions which can only be decided by England',[62] noted Metternich, thereby putting his finger on the crux of the problem facing Prussia and the continental allies in November 1805. The first question was that of subsidies, which Prussia had stipulated as a *conditio sine qua non* of her cooperation. The second was the future of Hanover which the treaty had assigned to Prussia. Both clauses of the Potsdam treaty were, by their very nature, only conceivable either with British consent or, in the case of the electorate, at her expense. This fact was not lost on the Prussians, though as later events were to show, they had seriously underestimated its importance. Just after concluding the treaty, Hardenberg wrote to Jacobi stressing the need to gain British agreement both to the subsidy for *all* of Prussia's armaments and to Prussia's need for 'a more secure frontier', in other words Hanover.[63] But Prussian illusions were soon to be shattered by the dispatch to Berlin in late November 1805 of a special British envoy – Lord Harrowby – whose presence led to much-needed but painful clarification of the ramifications of Potsdam.[64] In fact, Harrowby was now the only man who could enable the treaty of Potsdam to be fulfilled. Being equipped with plenipotentiary powers, only he could authorise the subsidies and Hanoverian arrangements around which the whole accord was structured.[65]

Prussia's statesmen were not, at this point, proposing simply to despoil the British monarch of his German possessions. Over the previous months, they had repeatedly affirmed their intention of acquiring Hanover with British consent, preferably through barter.[66] Now, in November 1805, they proposed an exchange for Prussian territories in Westphalia.[67] In purely material terms, this was not disadvantageous to George III, as a comparative table helpfully compiled by the Prussians

[62] Metternich to Colloredo, 22.11.05, Berlin: Ranke (ed.), *Denkwürdigkeiten Hardenbergs*, V, pp. 198–9.

[63] Hardenberg to Jacobi, 5.11.05, Berlin, GStA Rep.XI.81.231, fos. 64–5.

[64] See the very full accounts – from the British perspective – in G.B. Fremont, 'Britain's role in the formation of the Third Coalition against France, 1802–1805' (DPhil dissertation, University of Oxford, 1991), pp. 291–310; Ham, 'Strategies of coalition and isolation', pp. 51–64; Sherwig, *Guineas and gunpowder*, pp. 168–71 on the Harrowby mission.

[65] Hardenberg to Jacobi, 8.11.05, Berlin, GStA Rep.XI.81.231, fo. 73.

[66] Lombard memorandum, 24.10.05, in Ranke (ed.), *Denkwürdigkeiten Hardenbergs*, I, p. 312; protocol of the Charlottenburg conference, 1.10.05, in Ranke (ed.), *Denkwürdigkeiten Hardenbergs*, I, p. 252: 'Die Besetzung von Hannover sollte mit Einwilligung aller Theile geschehen.' See also StaH 110 A 47, 'Preussens Plan die Kurbraunschweigischen Lande durch Tausch an sich zu bringen'.

[67] 'Mémoire relatif à l'acquisition du pays de Hanovre, à la suite du traité de Potsdam du 3 Novembre 1805' (dated end of November 1805), in Ranke (ed.), *Denkwürdigkeiten Hardenbergs*, V, p. 179.

showed.[68] By surrendering Calenberg, Spiegelberg, Grubenhagen, Lüneburg, Celle, Bremen, Verden, Lauenburg, Hohenstein and Hoya in return for Cleves and Mark, Essen, Elten, Paderborn, Münster, East Frisia, Lingen and Tecklenburg he might lose about 190,000 inhabitants but stood to gain nearly 300,000 écus in additional revenue in return. Moreover, this calculation did not consider the extensive war damage to the electorate, which made her more of a liability than an asset to George III. The Prussians also pointed out that, while the two objects of exchange were far apart in terms of surface area, most of the electorate was uncultivated heath. As an additional inducement George III was to be allowed to take his electoral title with him to the new possessions in the west. Great play was made of the cession of Emden, which Hardenberg believed to be highly valued by British commercial circles. In short, the Prussians claimed that the exchange was in the interests of both parties, not least for geographic and strategic reasons: 'Hanover divides his [Frederick William's] possessions and compromises his security; but Hanover is itself divided and surrounded [through the Prussian enclave of Hildesheim] by Prussian provinces', the argument ran.[69] The Prussians genuinely seem to have believed that such an exchange could be agreed, if not with George III, then at least over his head with the British government.[70]

There was a rude awakening in store. Harrowby refused to discuss Hanover, partly because he knew George III to be bitterly opposed to Prussian designs, and partly because electoral affairs were beyond the remit of a British minister.[71] But there was another reason for Harrowby's lack of enthusiasm; this was the desire to direct Prussian expansion into different channels. For the concept of the balance of power itself and the long-term strategic needs of the age-old struggle against France imposed its own logic on British policy. It demanded, first of all, the strengthening of Prussia through the addition of territory, not simply because this would bribe her to join the Third Coalition, though that too played a role, but because the explosion of French power required a corresponding bolstering of Prussia *irrespective of any short-term political calculations*. It also, secondly and consequently, called for a re-orientation of Prussian interests away from the east and towards the

---

[68] GStA Rep.XI.81.231, fo. 72.

[69] Ranke (ed.), *Denkwürdigkeiten Hardenbergs*, I, p. 182.

[70] Jacobi report, 19.11.05, London, GStA Rep.XI.73.179B, fo. 194.

[71] Brendan Simms, '"An odd question enough". Charles James Fox, the crown and British policy during the Hanoverian crisis of 1806', *HJ*, 38, 3 (1995), 572; Simms, 'Anglo-Prussian relations', pp. 69–71. See also Richard Krauel, 'Preußen und England vor hundert Jahren', *Deutsche Revue*, 31 (1906), 7–8.

preservation of Dutch independence, a reversal, in other words, of the policy of disengagement practised since Basle in 1795.

Harrowby was instructed that British interests 'would render the increase of Prussian power on the side of the Low Countries preferable to any other measure'. The aim, to quote Mulgrave's own words, was 'an effectual check to the future encroachments of France. With this view, and more especially for the future security of Holland, it would be desirable to assign to Prussia a military line of frontier from Antwerp to Luxemburg with such a proportion of territory as may be found sufficient to induce Prussia to occupy that line.'[72] Additional territory could also be offered for the purposes of linking the new possessions with the Prussian heartland in the east. To satisfy Russia, she could be assigned Austrian and Prussian territories in Poland. Britain was thus envisaging changes of considerable magnitude, all in the interests of maintaining, or rather re-establishing, the balance against France. Time and again, Mulgrave reiterated this policy in his communications with Harrowby. In his summary of the latter's mission on 31 October 1805, he referred not only to the aim of bringing Prussia into the coalition and of liberating Holland, but also to the need 'to induce Austria and Russia to consent to propose such territorial acquisition to Prussia (especially on the side of Holland) as may make that court hearty in the cause'.[73] Almost one month later, he saw in the Potsdam treaty a first step towards the implementation of the British programme for Prussian aggrandisement.[74] He was happy with the public articles, adding in the case of article IX/3 concerning Prussian expansion, that it should be 'on the side of France'.[75] It was this desire, not any disagreement about the size of the bribe, which divided Britain and Prussia in November and December of 1805.

News of British plans to involve Prussia in the defence of Holland had

---

[72] Mulgrave to Harrowby, 27.11.05, Downing Street, in Rose (ed.), *Select dispatches*, p. 211; for British policy to induce Prussia to occupy Holland see also Fremont, 'Britain's role in the formation of the Third Coalition', p. 230. For the origins of the need to strengthen Prussia see Pitt's memorandum of January 1805, 'On the deliverance and security of Europe', in Harold Temperley and Lilian M. Penson (eds.), *Foundations of British foreign policy from Pitt (1792) to Salisbury (1902) on documents, old and new, selected and edited with historical introduction* (Cambridge, 1938), pp. 12–16. See also Edward Ingram, 'Lord Mulgrave's proposals for the reconstruction of Europe in 1804', *HJ* 19 (1976), especially 516–19 and Schroeder, *The transformation of European politics*, p. 162.

[73] Mulgrave to Harrowby, 31.10.05, Downing Street, PROL FO 64/70 (not in Rose (ed.), *Select dispatches*).

[74] Mulgrave to Harrowby, 23.11.05, Downing Street, in Rose (ed.), *Documents relating*, pp. 230–5.

[75] Ibid., p. 231.

already reached Berlin before Harrowby's arrival. On 5 November Jacobi reported a rumour 'that the cabinet of St James is proposing to declare to His Prussian Majesty that one seriously wishes to obtain for him an extension of his territories towards Holland or considerable acquisition in the Netherlands'.[76] But when Harrowby finally put the idea to Hardenberg in a draft treaty, one of whose clauses stipulated a Prussian guarantee of Dutch independence against French expansion,[77] Prussian objections proved insurmountable. These objections stemmed from what Prussia's statesmen believed to be the supreme law of the state: territorial gains, but above all, security. The first secret and separate article of Potsdam had encapsulated this need: Prussia was 'to obtain a secure frontier with France'.[78] In the circumstances of 1805, this meant putting as much distance as possible between a resurgent France and Prussia's western border. As Metternich observed, the Hanoverian clause at Potsdam fulfilled a double purpose by both implementing long-term Prussian aims towards the electorate and showing 'que cette Puissance redoute de jour en jour plus le contact avec la France'.[79] 'Un coup d'oeil sur la carte', Hardenberg observed, 'fait voir l'urgence de procurer à la monarchie prussienne des arrondissements et des frontières plus sûres, surtout du côté de la France';[80] only Hanover, in exchange for the exposed Westphalian possessions, could satisfy both criteria. He explicitly rejected British offers of gains in the west. 'Il est aisé de prouver', Hardenberg wrote, 'que le véritable intérêt de la Prusse ne peut admettre ni les acquisitions lointaines et détachées du corps de la monarchie, ni dans les provinces, séparées d'elle par des pays étrangers et ne forment même aucun ensemble.'[81]

Britain's offers, in other words, ran contrary to the very essence of Prussian geopolitics. During the Potsdam negotiation Czartoryski had noted 'l'éloignement marqué du roi à accepter pour prix de sa coopération des acquisitions qui le rapprocheraient d'avantage de la France'.[82] Prussia was thus hardly likely to take the British bait and thereby place herself in the front line against France. Try as he might, Harrowby could find no suitable alternative bribe to the electorate. As he noted sadly to Mulgrave, 'none of them could be executed, except upon

[76] Jacobi report, 5.11.05, London, GStA Rep.XI.73.179B, fo. 172.
[77] Harrowby proposal for an Anglo-Prussian treaty, GStA Rep.XI.73.180B, fo. 42.
[78] *Traité du 3 novembre 1805*, in Ranke (ed.), *Denkwürdigkeiten Hardenbergs*, I, p. 331.
[79] Metternich comments on the first secret article of the Potsdam treaty, in Klinkowström (ed.), *Metternichs nachgelassenen Papieren*, p. 79.
[80] Ranke (ed.), *Denkwürdigkeiten Hardenbergs*, V, p. 178.
[81] Ibid., p. 181.
[82] Czartoryski to Vorontsov, 5.10.05, Potsdam, in *Vneshnaya Politika*, pp. 629, 631.

the conclusion of a successful war'.[83] The Hanoverian bird in hand was worth two Dutch birds in the bush. Britain might be generous with territories yet to be reconquered (by Prussia!), but Prussia had to look to where her realistic interest lay. As a last resort, Harrowby indicated that Prussia could hold Holland until a general peace, 'the future disposition of Holland being to remain in such case an object of negotiation'.[84] Not unreasonably, in view of the ambiguous language and context of this statement, Hardenberg took this to be a coded offer of *Holland itself* as an inducement to join the coalition.[85] In view of the immense value of the province, Hardenberg gave the idea careful consideration. But the same objections still applied, and once Frederick William had come out against it, on the grounds that it had been Frederick II's principle that Prussia should never become a sea-power, the idea was laid to rest.[86]

Clearly an impasse in the negotiations on Hanover had been reached. This made the need to come up with some kind of short-term accord which would bring Prussia into the coalition all the more pressing. The issue of Hanover, in other words, was to be by-passed in the interest of immediate agreement. Some days later, Mulgrave expanded on this theme when he spoke of 'reserving the question of territorial acquisition for future discussion'.[87] This British flexibility corresponded to a similar Prussian short-term need. Even as Mulgrave's message was *en route* to Berlin, Harrowby noted that although Hardenberg was still insisting on the exchange of Hanover, he was prepared to enter an agreement for 'temporary cooperation'.[88] The question of subsidy could now be addressed. But the issue of Hanover had only been shelved, not solved; it was to remain so until the events of spring 1806 led to a spectacular denouement.[89]

---

[83] Harrowby to Mulgrave, 24.11.05, Berlin, in Rose (ed.), *Select dispatches*, p. 236.
[84] Ibid.
[85] Ranke (ed.), *Denkwürdigkeiten Hardenbergs*, I, p. 352.
[86] Ibid.
[87] Mulgrave to Harrowby, 5.12.05, Downing Street, in Rose (ed.), *Select dispatches*, p. 250.
[88] See: Harrowby to Mulgrave, 1.12.05, Berlin, in Rose (ed.), *Documents relating*, p. 249; Hardenberg to Harrowby, 11.12.05, Berlin, GStA Rep.XI.73.180B, fos. 68–70; D'Abaye memorandum on an Anglo-Prussian alliance, 11.12.05, Berlin, GStA Rep.XI.73.180B, fo. 36; Haugwitz to Harrowby, 11.11.05, Brunswick, PROL FO 64/70; 2 letters from the Duke of Brunswick to Henry Addington complaining that subsidies had not been paid for troops in 1802, GStA Rep.XI.73.180B, fos. 24–6; Harrowby to Mulgrave, 7.12.05, Berlin, in Rose (ed.), *Select dispatches*, p. 25; Mulgrave to Harrowby, (draft), 20.12.05, Downing Street, PROL FO 64/70; Mulgrave to Harrowby, 10.1.06, Downing Street, PROL FO 64/70.
[89] Hardenberg to Jacobi, 2.12.05, Berlin, GStA Rep.XI.81.231, fo. 8; Hardenberg to Haugwitz, 3.12.05, Berlin, GStA Rep.XI.89.402, unfoliated.

Schönbrunn: the issues of the ratification debate

In the meantime, Prussia pressed ahead with her policy of armed mediation. Haugwitz was sent with full plenipotentiary powers to Napoleon's headquarters, where he was to present him with the terms of the Potsdam agreement.[90] To Russian, Austrian and British observers, as well as to his Prussian critics, Haugwitz was intolerably slow in getting on his way. Indeed, his modest progress during the first half of the journey seemed to them to indicate a less than wholehearted commitment to the strategy agreed at Potsdam. This was, as we shall soon see, not an entirely unfair assessment. But it should be stressed that the speed of Haugwitz's voyage south had already been agreed upon in advance. This agreement had been a consensus decision among Prussian politicians and stemmed from the need to synchronise the political mediation with her military preparedness. The instructions which Haugwitz drew up for himself beforehand make this quite clear. Given that the Duke of Brunswick had stipulated 5 December as the best date for a truce and 15 December for a possible Franco-Prussian rupture,[91] Haugwitz unsurprisingly stressed that 'Il serait dangereux de s'exposer à la rupture avant cette date.' This was a point to which he returned repeatedly in his original instructions:[92] 'je compte toujours', Haugwitz wrote from Prague, 'y être rendu [chez Napoléon] le douzième jour de mon départ de Berlin',[93] and which even such a hostile commentator as Francis Jackson was prepared to concede. Though he chiefly attributed the delay in Haugwitz's journey to 'that gentleman's habitual spirit of procrastination', Jackson was fair-minded enough to point out that 'it is wished here to combine the period at which his negotiation is to be concluded, with that at which the Prussian armies will be at their respective stations – vizt. [sic] – the 15th December – that is also the time fixed by the Austrians for resuming offensive operations'.[94] Indeed, as a detailed subsequent investigation by military experts showed, Haugwitz's delay was entirely justified from a military point of view.[95]

This is not the place to take up the historiographical debate about

---

[90] See the plenipotentiary powers and assurances of safe passage for Haugwitz in GStA Rep.XI.89.403, unfoliated.

[91] 'Second mémoire militaire du Duc de Brunswick, novembre 1805', in Ranke (ed.), *Denkwürdigkeiten Hardenbergs*, I, p. 324.

[92] 'Mémoire du Comte de Haugwitz pour lui servir d'instruction lors de son voyage à Vienne en novembre 1805', in Ranke (ed.), *Denkwürdigkeiten Hardenbergs*, pp. 185–7.

[93] Haugwitz to Hardenberg, 20.11.05, Prague, GStA Rep.XI.89.402, unfoliated.

[94] Francis Jackson to Mulgrave, 16.11.05, Berlin, PROL FO 64/69.

[95] *Kriegsgeschichtliche Einzelschriften*, pp. 25–6; Noack, *Hardenberg und das geheime Kabinett*, p. 24.

Haugwitz's real intentions, and whether he had been given secret instructions by the king to avoid war at all costs.[96] What seems beyond dispute, however, is that Haugwitz left for Vienna with more of an open mind than was strictly compatible with the treaty of Potsdam. For example, he made no secret of his hostility to an Anglo-Russian expeditionary force in north Germany which would 'détruit peut-être le dernier espoir qui nous restait pour la paix';[97] these were hardly the sentiments of a man wholeheartedly committed to an armed mediation with Napoleon. Rather, in accordance with the classic 'continental' political outlook, Haugwitz sought to pull off an extremely delicate balancing act. In the instruction which he gave himself, important questions were deliberately left open. He was always meant to judge on the spot. 'Les événements en décideront', his instruction ran, 'et c'est sur les lieux qu'il faudra en juger.'[98] With remarkable prescience, he had predicted a possible defeat and separate peace and reformulated the Prussian response to such a development. 'Dans un tel cas', Haugwitz wrote, 'il conviendrait, je pense, de redoubler de soin afin de calmer l'humeur que l'empereur des Français aura conçue de l'armement de la Prusse et qu'il ferait doublement éclater alors. Il faudrait surtout s'appliquer à gagner du temps.'[99] That this was Haugwitz's preferred outcome cannot be doubted. In a letter to his confidant Count Hoym in Silesia he admitted that he would welcome it if 'l'autriche pressée de près ait déja fait sa paix particulière',[100] because that would release Frederick William from all obligations while simultaneously showing his commitment to the welfare of Europe. In any case, Haugwitz wanted to keep all options open for Prussia.[101] This policy of equivocation and balance was one that Haugwitz genuinely believed to be in the best interests of the state, but as should soon be clear, it was also fully reconcilable with his own

[96] See Kieseritzky, 'Die Sendung von Haugwitz nach Wien'. Kieseritzky's study is based on printed sources only; it is far from being a rehabilitation of Haugwitz. Rudolfine Freiin von Oer, *Der Friede von Pressburg. Ein Beitrag zur Diplomatiegeschichte des napoleonischen Zeitalters*, p. 75 criticises Haugwitz's 'slowness'; Treitschke, *Deutsche Geschichte*, I, p. 219 speaks of Haugwitz's *Eigenmächtigkeiten*. For a good account of the mission by an historian of the 'heroic' school of Prussian history see Gerhard Ritter, *Stein. Eine politische Biographie* (3rd edn, Stuttgart, 1958), p. 145. Tarrasch, *Übergang*, advances a lot of circumstantial evidence that Frederick William *did* give Haugwitz a secret instruction to wriggle out of the obligations of Potsdam, if necessary, pp. 58–64.
[97] Haugwitz to Hardenberg, 16.11.05, Dresden, GStA Rep.XI.89.402, unfoliated.
[98] 'Mémoire du Comte de Haugwitz', in Ranke (ed.), *Denkwürdigkeiten Hardenbergs*, V, p. 186.
[99] Ibid., pp. 188–9.
[100] Haugwitz to Hoym, 17.11.05, Dresden, GStA Rep.XI.89.403.
[101] Haugwitz report, 2.12.05, Vienna, in Bailleu (ed.), *Preussen und Frankreich*, II, p. 411; Haugwitz report, 5.12.05, Vienna, in Bailleu (ed.), *Preussen und Frankreich*, II, p. 413.

personal high political agenda. Meanwhile, Prussian military measures went ahead as planned. In the Generaldirektorium Baron von Stein and others set about mobilising the economic resources for the forthcoming campaign. As yet there was no open hostility with France. For although the Russians never ceased to express their displeasure at Haugwitz's slowness and to press for quick action,[102] the Duke of Brunswick was adamant that Prussian intentions generally, and the projected Prussian expedition against Holland in particular, should be masked for as long as possible.[103] What Brunswick needed was time, and all his measures after Potsdam were designed to use the time gained by Haugwitz's mission to maximum effect. By the end of October, Prussian troops had occupied the Hanoverian electorate unopposed; at this stage there was no public or secret plan to annex the province outright.[104]

It was against this background of uncharacteristic Prussian activity that the news of the allied disaster at Austerlitz in early December 1805 burst upon the high-political scene in Berlin.[105] This was followed closely by rumours and then the certainty of a separate Franco-Prussian treaty concluded in the wake of the battle by Haugwitz at Schönbrunn. Prussian statesmen, lulled by Haugwitz's earlier gushing dispatches and Napoleon's conditional acceptance of the mediation plan,[106] were numbed to discover that the agreement seemed to run contrary to all principles of neutrality and disengagement to which Prussian policy had hitherto adhered.[107] The salient terms were: a Prussian recognition and guarantee of all French possessions in Italy; the annexation of Hanover by Prussia under French guarantee in return for a Prussian cession of Ansbach and sundry western territories;[108] and a joint Franco-Prussian

[102] Czartoryski to Alopeus (copy), 24.11.05, November, GStA Rep.XI.175.155E, fo. 106; 'Memoire très reservé pour sa majesté le Roi' (apparently from Alopeus), 27.11.05, Berlin, GStA Rep.XI.175.155E, fos. 111–12.
[103] 'Premier mémoire militaire du Duc de Brunswick, sorti de sa propre plume', in Ranke (ed.), Denkwürdigkeiten Hardenbergs, I, pp. 317–22.
[104] Francis Jackson to Mulgrave, 10.10.05, Berlin, PROL FO 64/69; Mulgrave to Francis Jackson (draft), 19.10.05, Downing Street; Hardenberg to Jacobi, 17.10.05, Berlin, GStA Rep.XI.81.231, fo. 57; Francis Jackson to Mulgrave, 17.10.05, Berlin, PROL FO 64/69; Francis Jackson to Mulgrave, 2.11.05, Berlin, PROL FO 64/69; Ompteda to Münster, 24.10.05, Schwerin, in Ompteda, Politischer Nachlaß, pp. 92, 96.
[105] Hardenberg's 'diary' indicates 7 December as the day that news of Austerlitz arrived; 10–14 December is simply marked incertitudes, GStA Rep. 92 Hardenberg L25, fo. 10. See also Hermann Hüffer, 'Haugwitz nach der Schlacht bei Austerlitz', Deutsche Zeitschrift für Geschichtswissenschaft, 6, 1 (1891), 102–4; Noack, Hardenberg und das geheime Kabinett, p. 1.
[106] Haugwitz to Brunswick (copy), 2.12.05, Vienna, GStA Rep.XI.89.403.
[107] The terms of the Treaty of Schönbrunn are in GStA Rep.XI.89.403.
[108] On the loss of Ansbach and Bayreuth in 1806 see Süßheim, Preussens Politik in Ansbach-Bayreuth, pp. 373–415.

undertaking to maintain the Ottoman and reduced Austrian empires. Even if, as a balance sheet showed, the treaty gave Prussia a notional net gain of 500 square miles and 614,000 inhabitants,[109] its specific commitments to French interests in Italy and the Balkans conjured up a nightmarish vision of precisely those entanglements which Prussia had been desperately trying to avoid. To make matters worse, it stipulated a defensive and offensive alliance between Prussia and France in the event of military action arising out of the enforcement of the terms of the agreement.

In order to understand the dilemmas posed by Schönbrunn, it should be added that at first it seemed as if the Prussians would honour the commitments contracted at Potsdam. Military operations proceeded as planned, even after news of Austerlitz had reached Berlin.[110] In a letter of 10 December, that is, *well after* news of Austerlitz, Frederick William reassured the Tsar that Prussian military measures were proceeding apace, though paranoia about Austrian attempts to make a separate peace – which was soon to corrode this firm stance – was already evident.[111] Nor was this adherence to the terms of Potsdam mere rhetoric. The dispatch of Colonel Phull to liaise with the Russians, *after* Austerlitz, and the belief of the monarch, expressed in a confidential communication with Haugwitz, that Prussian troops would be operational in Bohemia in the new year,[112] testify to that. Moreover, a conference, held on 9 December to discuss Haugwitz's first report of Austerlitz, and attended by Hardenberg and numerous senior military figures, showed, as yet, no signs of defeatism.[113] They advised adherence to the Potsdam agreement; the diversion of troops southwards to the endangered Bohemian theatre of war; and coordination of Prussian military movements with those of the allies. But the strongest statement in favour of honouring Potsdam came from Field Marshal von der Schulenburg in a trenchant memorandum presented to the con-

---

[109] Table of territories won and lost for Prussia, GStA Rep.XI.89.403.

[110] Hardenberg to Alopeus, 7.12.05, Berlin, GStA Rep.XI.89.394, fos. 215–17. Von Oer, *Der Friede von Pressburg*, p. 151, says that Haugwitz signed the Treaty of Schönbrunn *before* Austria signed her armistice. This is beside the point (a) because such an armistice had been in the offing for some time, and (b) because Frederick William was still standing by Potsdam in Berlin.

[111] Frederick William to Alexander, 10.12.05, Berlin, in Bailleu (ed.), *Briefwechsel Alexanders*, pp. 90–1.

[112] Frederick William to Haugwitz (copy), 11.12.05, Berlin, GStA Rep.XI.89.402 (especially passages not printed in Bailleu (ed.), *Preussen und Frankreich*, II, pp. 417–19).

[113] Conference protocol in Ranke (ed.), *Denkwürdigkeiten Hardenbergs*, I, p. 357.

ference.[114] In it he counselled against the policy of equivocation, 'nager entre deux eaux' as he described it,[115] and called for Prussia to be at war with France by 11 December. Should Prussia persist in her dilatoriness, he warned in stark but as it turned out prophetic terms, her likely fate would be as a client of France, daily exposed to her insults and humiliations.[116] One only had to look to Spain, the field marshal pointed out, to see that this picture was not exaggerated. Whatever course was taken, though, it should be *decisive*. 'I well know that history contains instances of broken alliances', Schulenburg argued, 'and that King Frederick II himself wrote that they may be justified by reason of state. But a consequence of such a decision must then be alliance with France and instant war with the allies. Great deeds and successes have at times erased the injustice of a cause. Indecision and ambiguity, however, leads to inevitable disaster.'[117]

By the end of the month, however, Prussia had opted for a course of action that was neither in keeping with Schulenburg's own prescription nor *decisive* in any way: conditional ratification of the Schönbrunn accord and thus her own exit from the coalition with all the consequences that entailed. The debate from which this decision emerged deserves to be treated in some detail. But before doing so, it is necessary to draw attention to some of the factors underlying this debate. First of all, there was the progressive loss of nerve on the part of the Prussian military as the full implications of Austerlitz began to sink in.[118] Secondly, there were the well-founded fears of Austrian plans for a separate peace with France to stave off total annihilation at Napoleon's hands,[119] which Prussia's statesmen were soon to advance in justification of their actions.[120] These fears were soon confirmed by news of an Austrian armistice and predictions of a *paix separée* in which 'les deux parties se

---

114 Schulenburg memorandum of 10.12.05, in Ranke (ed.), *Denkwürdigkeiten Hardenbergs*, V, p. 210.
115 Ibid., p. 211.
116 Ibid., p. 212.
117 Ibid.: 'Ich weiß wohl, daß die Geschichte Beispiele gebrochener Allianzen kennt, und daß König Friedrich II selbst geschrieben hat, daß höhere Staats-Rücksichten dazu berechtigen können; dann müßte aber nach einem solchen Entschluß auch die Allianz mit Frankreich und der Krieg mit den Allierten die augenblickliche Folge sein. Große Thaten und Successe haben zuweilen das Unmoralische der Sache verlöscht. Wanken und Zweideutigkeit bringt aber unausbleibliches Verderben.'
118 From the memoirs of Ompteda (beginning of December 1805), *Politischer Nachlaß*, p. 107.
119 Hardenberg to Jacobi, 29.11.05, Berlin, GStA Rep.XI.81.231, fo. 84; Hardenberg to Jacobi, 13.12.05, Berlin, GStA Rep.XI.81.231, fo. 87; Hardenberg (and Frederick William) to Haugwitz, 12.12.05, Berlin, GStA Rep.XI.89.402.
120 Hardenberg to Jacobi, 27.12.05, Berlin, GStA Rep.XI.89.231, fo. 89.

dispensèrent de réclamer la médiation de V.M.'.[121] Moreover, a visiting Austrian general, Stutterheim, felt unable to provide Frederick William with a guarantee that Austria would not make a separate peace with Napoleon.[122] Interestingly enough, Metternich was sufficiently honest to acknowledge – privately – that 'la certitude que nous étions effectivement en négociation pour une paix séparée, a arrêté toutes les mesures du roi relatives aux secours directs à nous porter'.[123] Thirdly, and relatedly, there was the feeling of betrayal at the behaviour of the other continental coalition partner. After Austerlitz, Russia made some perfunctory attempts to get Frederick William to intercede on Austria's behalf,[124] while the tsar himself withdrew with the bulk of his army to the relative safety of Russian Poland; Haugwitz's reports spoke of 'la retour des trouppes russes par étapes'.[125] Though Alexander did offer his troops in northern Germany to Frederick William, it was clear that he expected Prussia to fend for herself. 'J'espère que par la sagesse de vos déterminations, Sire', Alexander wrote, 'vous parviendriez à vous arranger avec la France, et que les démarches que V.M. a faites uniquement pour moi ne la compromettrent pas.'[126] What else could Frederick William do but wholeheartedly agree: 'Il faut s'arranger, je me le dis avec vous.'[127]

The ratification debate raged throughout December 1805 and early January 1806. In his apologia, penned between Christmas and New Year, Haugwitz countered his critics' charge of culpable delay in reaching Napoleon by recourse to the letter and spirit of his original instructions: since a breach with France should not take place any earlier than 15 December, there was little point, indeed great danger, in arriving at Napoleon's headquarters much sooner than that date. He portrayed the Schönbrunn treaty as an extension of this approach. 'En signant', Haugwitz said, 'je gagnais de temps.' He had thereby left all options open to Frederick William. The king, in the classic phrase, 'reste maître de choisir' between ratification and war. If Frederick William wished to choose the latter, he should do so and only Haugwitz himself

---

[121] Addendum to Haugwitz to Frederick William, 6.12.05, Vienna, GStA Rep.XI.89.403, unfoliated.
[122] Bailleu, 'Vor hundert Jahren', p. 224.
[123] Metternich to Stadion, 10.1.06, Berlin, in Metternich, *Memoirs*, p. 103. See also Kraehe, *Metternich's German policy*, p. 42. Schroeder, *The transformation of European politics*, pp. 283–5, makes no mention of Austria abandoning Prussia at Pressburg.
[124] Czartoryski to Alopeus (copy), 8.12.05, GStA Rep.XI.175.155E, fo. 120.
[125] Addendum to Haugwitz to Frederick William, 6.12.05, Vienna, GStA Rep.XI.89.403, unfoliated.
[126] Alexander to Frederick William, 24.11.05, Hollitsch, in Bailleu (ed.), *Briefwechsel Alexanders*, p. 88.
[127] Frederick William to Alexander, 17.12.05, Berlin, ibid., p. 92.

would be compromised. A 'third alternative' was, however, explicitly ruled out. The choice was 'la ratification du traité telle que je la propose, ou la guerre'. Haugwitz was careful not actually to rule out war, leaving the question instead for Frederick William to decide. What was important was Prussia's true interest. 'Quelle est la loi que cet intérêt nous dicte?', he asked. 'C'est là la seule question qui nous reste à discuter.' Towards the end of his self-justification, Haugwitz did advance an opinion, in favour of ratification, as indeed he had to if he was to avoid political suicide. The treaty, he argued, gave Prussia the best of both worlds on Hanover: France would secure it for her and guarantee it for the future, while Russia would prefer it to be in Prussian rather than French hands, as had hitherto been the case. In any case, acceptance was the only means of avoiding war.[128]

Hardenberg's memorandum on Schönbrunn threw the threats and temptations of the Prussian position in late 1805 into stark relief.[129] There were three arguments, he wrote, which could justify the complete change of policy involved in the proposed treaty. The first was the need for Prussian territorial gains and the realisation that only France could provide these. The second was anti-British sentiment, especially that relating to the latter's commercial monopoly which made her 'l'ennemi la plus dangereuse du continent'. Thirdly and finally, the change of policy could be justified by the need for a French alliance to forestall annihilation at her hands. Hardenberg agreed that Prussia needed territorial increases, even if this desire was somewhat at odds with conventional morality, especially in the case of the proposed treaty. By way of justification Hardenberg restated the old maxims of the need for territorial gains to balance those of other European powers, but above all, the pressing geopolitical need for security against the expansion of French power. 'La Prusse doit s'aggrandir pour ne pas rétrograder', he claimed, 'elle doit surtout se procurer une frontière plus sûre, et en faisant l'acquisition du pays de Hanovre, écarter l'objet qui, à chaque coup de canon entre la France et l'Angleterre, menace sa tranquillité et rend sa neutralité presque impossible.' At the present moment, Hardenberg argued, this aim could only be attained through alliance with France, by attaching oneself to the power and genius of Napoleon. Compared to this imperative, anti-British feeling was quite secondary.

Having analysed the possible arguments in favour of Schönbrunn, the

---

[128] Haugwitz's report on his mission to Napoleon, 26.12.1805, Berlin, in Ranke (ed.), *Denkwürdigkeiten Hardenbergs*, V, pp. 222–40.
[129] First Hardenberg memorandum on the Schönbrunn treaty, 30.12.05, Berlin, ibid., V, pp. 243–56.

memorandum moved on to review Prussia's general political situation and her relationships with other powers. These passages throw light on the broader considerations informing Prussian policy and are a key to understanding the Prussian dilemma after Austerlitz. Austria, Hardenberg wrote, was 'practically annihilated' and Prussia had no obligation towards her. Nor was Prussia in any way bound to Britain. Indeed, Hardenberg expressed resentment at the way in which Britain sought to keep a conflict alive from which 'elle en sortira toujours sans essuyer de grandes pertes'. As for Russia, she had 'abandonné au roi de s'arranger avec la France'; later in the same document he was to speak of 'l'éloignement de secours suffisantes de la part de la Russie'. The agreement of Potsdam was thus defunct. France, Hardenberg concluded, dominated everything. Yet after outlining the stark realities as he saw them, Hardenberg did not explicitly advocate a French alliance. Instead, he postulated a choice between three courses of action. He would examine the 'pour et contre, mais sans me permettre aucune détermination pour l'un ou pour l'autre. C'est au roi à la prendre.' These courses were: first of all, the middle way of no war, no gains, no alliance; secondly, war; and thirdly, alliance. At first sight, he argued, the middle way seemed the most attractive. It could even, at that juncture, be reconciled with the tsar's views. If the French re-occupied Hanover, however, this course would become problematic, and in such an event war should be considered. Pure neutrality (*simple neutralité*) on the other hand was rejected as depriving Prussia of any opportunity of making gains, a variation on Hardenberg's old argument that complete neutrality meant complete loss of influence. Prussia would be unable to balance Napoleon's drive towards Universal Monarchy (*monarchie universelle*). Indeed, in the last analysis neutrality would mean renouncing all territorial gains and the likelihood of having to defend the neutrality without foreign assistance. While appearing to rule out any offensive action *against* Napoleon, he pointed out that alliance *with* France might be the only way of securing Prussia's position. But if such an alliance were to be undertaken, he stressed that it should be done wholeheartedly, that is 'au dessus de toute autre considération'.

What followed was implicitly a plan for temporary but enthusiastic alliance with France: Prussia should allow Napoleon to control the south of Europe while she herself dominated the north. Hence Prussia should not simply accept the Schönbrunn treaty as it stood, and become a French 'satellite'. Rather, she should re-negotiate the treaty as an equal and become a partner of France. In other words, Hardenberg's remedy was to *deepen* the relationship with France. Hand in hand with this policy of alliance with France, he envisaged a strategy of disengagement in the west, coupled with territorial gains in the north and centre of Germany. Dispersed possessions, especially in Westphalia, were to be jettisoned. Prussia, Hardenberg insisted, should 'cesse d'être limitrophe de la France' and try to 'céder le reste du duché de Clève pour éviter tout contact avec la France'. Ansbach, surprisingly enough in view of its relative geographic remotenesss, was to be retained. The Hanseatic towns of Hamburg, Lübeck and Bremen with dependent territories were to be incorporated into Prussia as part of her plan for domination of the north.

Hardenberg's scheme seems to have found little resonance among his more narrow-minded colleagues in the Prussian high political scene. Military opinion was divided between those like Field Marshal von der Schulenburg, to whom ratification constituted a betrayal of the terms of Potsdam, and those like the Duke of Brunswick, for whom the catastrophic military situation after Austerlitz annulled whatever had been agreed through sheer force of necessity. To Schulenburg, acceptance of Schönbrunn would not only lead to Prussian isolation among the other powers, but also leave the monarchy in a state of 'absolute dependence' on France. Instead, Prussia should try to take Hanover *en dépôt* until a general peace, rather than annexing it outright.[130] Yet, even though he was plainly opposed to ratification of the treaty, Schulenburg shrank from pushing his own opinion and left the ultimate decision to Frederick William: 'Entre ces deux alternatives dures', he wrote, 'il n'y a que le sentiment intérieur du roi qui puisse décider, un serviteur n'oserait proposer un choix.'[131] The Duke of Brunswick, on the other hand, argued that the defeats of Austria and Russia had made ratification of Schönbrunn inescapable;[132] added to this was the fear that Austria or some third party might be offered Hanover by the French.[133] Brunswick did, however, express the desire to restrict the alliance to *defensive* purposes. He also stressed the need to avoid friction with George III, by portraying the occupation of Hanover as 'plus une mesure de nécessité que de simple convenance'.[134]

Frustrated by opposition to his first, more ambitious plan, Hardenberg submitted a second memorandum soon after.[135] In the introduction, he

---

[130] Memorandum of Schulenburg, 31.12.185, Berlin, in Ranke (ed.), *Denkwürdigkeiten Hardenbergs*, V, pp. 257–9.
[131] Ibid.
[132] Memorandum of the Duke of Brunswick, 31.12.05, Berlin, in Ranke (ed.), *Denkwürdigkeiten Hardenbergs*, V, pp. 259–61.
[133] Ibid., p. 260.
[134] Ibid., p. 261.
[135] Second Hardenberg memorandum on the Schönbrunn treaty, 1.1.06, Berlin, in Ranke (ed.), *Denkwürdigkeiten Hardenbergs*, V, pp. 263–71.

paraphrased his earlier arguments, noting that 'je ne suis pas permis de décider pour aucun, mais j'ai manifesté l'opinion qu'une fois déterminé à l'alliance avec Napoléon, il ne faudrait pas de demi-mesure'. However, after seeing Haugwitz's memorandum, as well as those of Schulenburg and Brunswick, and after discussion with the king, Hardenberg had been led to 'more mature reflection'. This mature reflection caused Hardenberg to counsel rejection of the treaty on four grounds. First, because it would isolate Prussia from other powers. Secondly, because it would embroil her with Russia. Thirdly, because it provided no guarantee of avoiding war, since one might have to fight in alliance *with* the French. Fourthly, because the treaty would make Prussia a dependancy of France. Clearly, Hardenberg had adapted his former plan to take account of the known wishes of the king. He invoked the rhetoric of the 'third way' by rejecting the straight choice between 'the treaty as it stands, or war'. The tranquillity of northern Germany was to be achieved by taking Hanover *en dépôt* until a general peace, by convincing the French to evacuate the fortress of Hameln which they still held, and by arranging the evacuation of British, Russian and Swedish troops from the area. Only once a general peace settlement had been reached did Hardenberg plan an offensive and defensive alliance with France. Thus, in response to intense scepticism towards his initial plan, Hardenberg had come up with an alternative whose short-term provisions were geared towards royal acceptance, while simultaneously leaving the door open for the implementation of more far-reaching designs in the long run. The emphasis on the tranquillity of the north, the delaying of an alliance with France until a general peace and his support for a modified ratification of the treaty were all intended to secure royal approval. Yet Hardenberg had not given up, but merely disguised, his long-term adherence to the scheme of Prussian domination of the north of Germany. This is quite clearly demonstrated in his plan for a new imperial constitution which was mooted in January and drawn up in February. Here the assumption that Napoleon had conclusively won the struggle for supremacy in central and southern Germany and that Prussia must consolidate her position in the north and east, formed the point of departure for any reorganisation of the *Reich*.[136]

The ratification document drawn up in early January represented a consensus of Prussian high-political opinion, a synthesis of the views of Frederick William, Haugwitz, Schulenburg, Brunswick and Hardenberg, even if the latter's agreement was tactically motivated with

---

[136] Hardenberg's plan for a new constitution of the Holy Roman Empire, 5.2.1806, ibid., V, pp. 294–300.

a completely different long-term policy in mind. In the *mémoire explicatif* accompanying the ratification all reference to an *offensive* alliance was dropped, while Prussia would only cede her western territories if Hanover were guaranteed to her after a general European peace and if British consent were forthcoming.[137] The purpose of these modifications, Frederick William subsequently explained, was to render the content of the treaty 'hypothétique et éventuel'.[138] On 4 January Haugwitz exchanged the ratifications with Laforest.

Even without the commitment to a French alliance and the seizure of Hanover, the agreement which Prussia had just ratified still represented a breach of the letter and spirit of Potsdam. To the outside world, and indeed to themselves, the Prussians justified the decision in terms of pure necessity arising out of their abandonment by the other two signatories, Austria and Russia. 'Since Austria is apparently on the verge of making a separate peace no matter what sacrifices it costs her', Hardenberg wrote in late December, 'and as according to some indications she may well be forced to unite herself to France, Russia for her part having quitted the game, it is clear that Prussia must avoid a war in which she would carry the chief burden.'[139] It would be difficult to find a more succinct statement of Prussia's position after Austerlitz. Some days after the modified ratification had been sent off to Paris, Frederick William justified his policy to his envoy in St Petersburg in almost exactly the same terms.[140] Should he, he asked rhetorically, put the fate of the *patrie* at risk, once the Russian troops had withdrawn? Surely not. These arguments were rehearsed once again in mid-January, when the Duke of Brunswick was being briefed on his mission to St Petersburg, which was intended to show the Prussian change of course in as favourable a light as possible.[141] Separate Austrian negotiations, the instructions claimed, had annulled Potsdam: Prussia had been in extreme danger of fighting alone and to avoid this she had had to come to terms with France. Lombard's memorandum for the duke was even more forthright. 'The defection of Austria' had relieved Prussia of all obligations towards her.[142] Besides which, he argued, Russia had urged Prussia to look after herself: 'Elle a invité le roi à pourvoir à son sûreté par un arrangement qui convînt aux

137 'Mémoire explicatif', ibid., I, p. 392.
138 Instructions for Jacobi, 24.3.06, Berlin, GStA Rep.XI.73.180C, fo. 106.
139 Hardenberg to Jacobi, 27.12.05, Berlin, GStA Rep.XI.81.231, fo. 89.
140 Frederick William to Goltz, 8.1.06, Berlin, in Ranke (ed.), *Denkwürdigkeiten Hardenbergs*, V, p. 275.
141 Memorandum for the duke of Brunswick on the occasion of his dispatch to St Petersburg, 17.1.06, Berlin, in Ranke (ed.), *Denkwürdigkeiten Hardenbergs*, V, p. 278.
142 Memorandum of Lombard for the duke of Brunswick on the occasion of his dispatch to St Petersburg, no date, in Ranke (ed.), *Denkwürdigkeiten Hardenbergs*, V, p. 288.

circonstances.'[143] Small wonder then that practically the whole of the Prussian political establishment seemed to cry with von Kleist: 'Peace, peace! is to be wished-for under the present circumstances.'[144] To Alexander, Frederick William wrote with less flourish but equally bleak honesty: 'les malheurs publics [sic] ne me laissent plus maître de mon choix'.[145]

Schönbrunn: the high politics of the ratification debate

FOOL: Sirrah, you were best take my foxcomb!
KENT: Why fool?
FOOL: Why for taking one's part that is out of favour.

King Lear, Act 1, scene 4, lines 99–101

The discussions in Berlin of mid- to late December and early January were clearly not just about the objective merits of the treaty of Schönbrunn. What emerges from the analysis of the respective standpoints of Hardenberg, Haugwitz, Schulenburg and Brunswick undertaken above, is the degree to which they achieved a consensus on certain key issues: the occupation of Hanover, the neutrality of northern Germany and the need to disengage in the west, even if much of this consensus stemmed from tactical posturing *vis à vis* the king. Such posturing was particularly marked in Hardenberg's case, as is demonstrated by his second memorandum on Schönbrunn, in which he tamely advanced all the old arguments in favour of neutrality he had so mercilessly criticised in the earlier document. He did so with explicit reference to the opposition of the king and others to his initial ideas. In part, no doubt, this was, as outlined above, an attempt to slip the rest of his programme in through the back door. But it also reflected something else: the fundamental concern of Hardenberg, the politician, to maintain the royal favour on which his increasingly shaky tenure in office depended.

This hidden high-political agenda had always existed alongside objective considerations of policy. But in the autumn and winter of 1805 the conflict between Haugwitz and Hardenberg for political influence had reached its most intense level so far. Haugwitz's return to the high-political scene must strictly speaking be dated from his recall in late August. However, it was only two months later, with the *Kabinetsordre* of

---

143 Ibid., pp. 291–2.
144 Kleist to Hoym, 28.12.05, Berlin, in Bailleu (ed.), *Preussen und Frankreich*, II, p. 429: 'Friede, Friede! ist unter den Umständen das wünschenswerthe!'
145 Frederick William to Alexander, 7.1.06, Berlin, in Bailleu (ed.), *Briefwechsel*, p. 94.

19 October, briefly mentioned above (p. 198), that the threat to Hardenberg's authority reached crisis proportions. In what must surely rank as one of the crucial documents to an understanding of Prussian high politics during the period, Hardenberg explained his fears to Beyme, a man whom at that point he still considered a friend. The letter is worth paraphrasing in some detail here.[146] In it Hardenberg confided what a great blow the *Kabinettsordre*, in which he was instructed to share the foreign ministry with Haugwitz, had been to him.[147] He drew Beyme's attention to the earlier royal instruction in which 'joint responsibility had been declared disadvantageous for the conduct of [foreign] affairs and expressly added that the count [Haugwitz] should refrain from behaviour which might lead to such a situation'.[148] Indeed, the king had expressly noted that a joint ministry would hamper negotiations with foreign envoys.[149] Now, under the new arrangement, this wisdom had been overturned and joint conduct of foreign affairs was deemed wise, 'particularly in respect to the conduct of affairs with the [foreign] envoys because everything depended on it in these important times'.[150]

Since there was no objective logic to the king's volte face on joint ministries ('unmöglich auf die Sache selbst gegründet sein'), Hardenberg could only conceive of the change of mind in terms of 'personal considerations (*es bleiben also nur persönliche Rücksichten übrig*)'. In any case, he remained utterly opposed to the whole idea of shared responsibility. Not only would negotiations with foreign envoys be complicated, but inevitable misunderstandings would throw the door open to friction and intrigue.[151] In a powerful passage which exposes the sheer paranoia rampant in Prussian high politics at the time, Hardenberg made his fears explicit. Joint management would mean that while Haugwitz would bask in the glory of the successes, Hardenberg would be left to answer for the failures.[152] He illustrated this point with reference to precedent, denying that there had been many examples of joint ministries: 'Only one man was really in power. The other remained in the background and

---

[146] Hardenberg to Beyme, 7.12.1805, Berlin, in Ranke (ed.), *Denkwürdigkeiten Hardenbergs*, I, p. 403. See also Disch, 'Der Kabinetsrat Beyme und die auswärtige Politik Preussens', 42 (1929), p. 98.

[147] Ibid., p. 404.

[148] Ibid.: 'eine gemeinschaftliche Geschäftsordnung für den Dienst nachtheilig erklärt und ausdrücklich hinzugesetzt: daß der Graf sich alles dessen enthalten müsse, was dazu führen könnte'.

[149] Ibid.

[150] Ibid., p. 405: 'besonders in Absicht auf die Verhandlungen mit den Gesandten, weil in dieser wichtigen Periode alles davon abhänge'.

[151] Ibid., p. 406.

[152] Ibid.

only affected to rule.'[153] The erstwhile joint ministry of Haugwitz, Alvensleben and Finckenstein served as a case in point to Hardenberg. During that ministry Haugwitz had often overturned agreed joint policy by going to the monarch separately and then pleading his verbal orders. Hardenberg obviously feared that this was going to happen to him, and not without reason, as it turned out.[154] He refused, as he put it, to become 'ministre en peinture'.[155]

During the crisis leading up to the treaty of Potsdam, Hardenberg had decided to let the matter rest until a more propitious moment. But in early December the moment of high-political truth was fast approaching. 'Now the moment when Count Haugwitz returns is imminent. He will be totally available for the king. This will be the moment when the most important political questions will be decided.' Should the king choose to take Haugwitz into the field with him as minister, Hardenberg would resign.[156] There were thus two related imperatives driving Hardenberg in the weeks immediately following Potsdam. First of all, there was the need to use Haugwitz's absence to strengthen his own position. Secondly, there was the need to belittle whatever the latter might achieve at Napoleon's headquarters. In the words of Metternich: 'Il aura encore une époque à mettre à profit, celle de l'absence de son collègue . . . s'il la manque, on ne saurait se flatter, à moins d'evenements très favorables pour lui, que son Ministère soit encore de longue durée.'[157] Or, as the French envoy Laforest put it, the return of Haugwitz seemed to 'prépare la retraite de M. de Hardenberg, si M. de Haugwitz réussit dans sa mission'.[158] This was an interpretation to which he returned two weeks later, when he noted that Hardenberg 'peut-être songe pour son intérêt personnel à défendre un poste qu'il sait ne pouvoir garder, si M. de Haugwitz réussit'.[159]

Hardenberg therefore strained every nerve to ensure that Haugwitz did not succeed, first by committing Prussia ever more irretrievably, as he

---

[153] Ibid., p. 407: 'Einer nur hatte die Wirklichkeit, der andere stand im Hintergrunde, paradirte nur.'
[154] Ibid.
[155] Ibid.: 'Ministre en peinture kann und will ich nicht sein, und Haugwitz wird es ebensowenig wollen.'
[156] Ibid.: 'Nun nähert sich der Augenblick wo Graf Haugwitz zurückkommt und für den König ganz disponibel ist, wo die wichtigen politischen Hauptfragen für uns entschieden sein werden.'
[157] Metternich to Colloredo, 6.11.05, Berlin, in Klinkowström (ed.), *Metternichs nachgelassenen Papieren*, p. 81.
[158] Laforest to Talleyrand, 14.11.05, Berlin, in Bailleu (ed.), *Preussen und Frankreich*, II, p. 405.
[159] Laforest to Talleyrand, 5.12.05, Berlin, in Bailleu (ed.), *Preussen und Frankreich*, II, p. 415.

thought, to the coalition cause, and then by sniping at the treaty which his adversary brought back from Schönbrunn. That this sniping was not primarily motivated by objective policy considerations should now be beyond doubt. The main charges against Haugwitz were that he had delayed too long in setting off for Napoleon's headquarters; that his progress was deliberately and malignantly slow; that he had reneged on the terms of Potsdam; and that, after the rejection of the conditional ratification of Schönbrunn, his fatal optimism about French intentions had led to the demobilisation which left Prussia defenceless in the New Year.[160] Hardenberg's vitriolic marginalia to Haugwitz's justificatory memorandum were certainly unfair.[161] Even if he himself did not agree with the Duke of Brunswick's timetable for action, Hardenberg knew that it represented considered consensus opinion, not simply Haugwitz's inclination to delay a breach with France as long as possible. Indeed, Hardenberg is on record as having stated to foreign envoys that Prussian troops could not move until Haugwitz's negotiation had failed.[162] As for the treaty of Schönbrunn, once the triumph of France was clear for all to see, Hardenberg's main criticism, as outlined above, was that the agreement was not aggressive and far-reaching *enough*.[163] Finally, Hardenberg himself subsequently admitted that he believed that the French would accept the conditional ratification of the treaty[164] and this is sufficiently documented by the sources.[165]

Seen from this perspective, Hardenberg's position during the ratification debates appears in a very different light from that of a man bent on bringing Prussia into the Third Coalition. His stance was determined in the first instance by considerations of personal political survival. This does not rule out espousal of a policy based on objective criteria of state security and aggrandisement, but this policy was only conceivable within

---

[160] See especially Friedrich Thimme, 'Die Okkupation des Kurfürstenthums Hannover durch die Preussen im Jahre 1806' (DPhil dissertation, University of Göttingen, 1893), pp. 6–7, for a detailed discussion of the Haugwitz mission, the charges made against him and possible exonerations; Hüffer, 'Haugwitz nach der Schlacht bei Austerlitz', 102–4; good assessments are also found in Ritter, Stein, p. 145 and Griewank, 'Hardenberg und die preußische Politik', p. 294. Re Prussian demobilisation see Hardenberg's 'diary', 21.1.06, 'résolution de renvoyer l'armée dans ses quartiers à mon inscu- j'étais très malade', GStA Rep. 92 Hardenberg L26, fo. 1.

[161] Report of Haugwitz on his mission to Napoleon, 26.12.05, Berlin, in Ranke (ed.), Denkwürdigkeiten Hardenbergs, V, pp. 222, 224, 235.

[162] Ibid., p. 241.

[163] First Hardenberg memorandum on the Schönbrunn treaty, 30.12.05, Berlin, in Ranke (ed.), Denkwürdigkeiten Hardenbergs, V, p. 254.

[164] Ibid., I, p. 436.

[165] Hardenberg to Haugwitz (draft), 27.1.06, Berlin, GStA Rep.XI.89.406, unfoliated; Hardenberg (and Frederick William) to Haugwitz (draft), 31.1.06, Berlin, GStA Rep.XI.89.406.

the framework of a strategy of personal survival and was always subordinate to it. It has already been noted that Hardenberg used the tsar's presence and his own embrace of the Third Coalition to consolidate his position against Haugwitz. During the first weeks after Potsdam Hardenberg was able to maintain this supremacy. He became the hero of the rising anti-French feeling in the Prussian capital, which intensified after the departure of Haugwitz. He began to pay particular attention to the court, especially to the queen. This placed him even more in the coalition camp, for the queen was known to be dominated by the radical firebrand of the war party, the young Prince Louis Ferdinand. As a result, figures such as Köckritz and Lombard were so eclipsed that they did not dare communicate openly with the French envoy. Hardenberg, by contrast, became the darling of the allied missions, to whom he had expressed his 'disgust' at Haugwitz's mission and by whom he was described as 'indefatigable in his exertion for the success of the good cause', a man whose retirement would be a 'veritable calamity'.[166] The treaty of Potsdam was, both in terms of high-political prestige and in the public eye, *his* work.

The allied defeat at Austerlitz, and the resulting demolition of the arrangements of Potsdam, thus created a whole new set of high-political realities. Accession to the coalition was no longer both the way to national aggrandisement and personal political advancement for Hardenberg. The approval of the allies, so central to his predominance during and just after Potsdam, now became the kiss of death for Hardenberg.[167] The change in the international situation brought, as we have seen, a change in Prussian foreign policy, but it also fundamentally transformed the relationship between the high-political actors in Berlin. Hardenberg had overreached himself in the glow of Alexander's temporary ascendancy and associated himself too closely with the Russian alliance. When the Russian alliance policy fell, Hardenberg threatened to fall with it. In no instance is the dialectic between foreign policy and personal political advancement more clearly demonstrated.

Exactly what happened at Schönbrunn is unclear. Haugwitz may or may not have consciously used the triumph of France to topple Hardenberg: this was certainly the long-term objective result of what

[166] Francis Jackson to Mulgrave, 10.10.05, Berlin, PROL FO 64/69; Metternich to Colloredo, 6.11.05, Berlin, in Klinkowström (ed.), *Metternichs nachgelassenen Papieren*, p. 81.
[167] E.g. the letter of Prince Alexander Kourakin to Hardenberg, 27.12.05, St Petersburg, awarding him the order of St Andrew, St Anne and Alexander Nevsky, GStA Rep. 92 *Hardenberg* J2, fo. 134.

passed there. We do know, from Haugwitz's own account, that when he finally caught up with Napoleon, the latter bitterly accused him of having signed the Potsdam accord.[168] What could be more plausible than that he blamed everything on his co-signatory, at the same time lessening the wrath of France against himself, facilitating Prussia's volte face and preparing the way for the removal of his worst adversary? Upon his return to Berlin, Haugwitz found public and court opinion against him, but the logic of the international situation ran in his favour. It was this logic which brought the partisans of a French alliance and the neutralists out of their boltholes in support of Haugwitz. Lombard, Köckritz and Möllendorf were now able to communicate directly with the French envoy, enabling them to dispense with the services of the dubious banker, Ephraim, who had been the only link between them for some weeks.[169] Most importantly of all, the king gave his approval: 'Mon ministre a saisi l'esprit du moment.'[170] The triumph of Haugwitz seemed at hand.

But Hardenberg was not going to exit without a struggle. His first instinct had been to resign, but royal favour, and especially the intervention of the queen, persuaded him to hang on.[171] Indeed, he now made every effort to adapt to the new circumstances. But his attempts to approach the French envoys were rebuffed. The French envoys would only treat with Haugwitz.[172] Unlike Lombard and Brunswick, both of whom rushed to mend fences with the French delegation,[173] Hardenberg had over-exposed himself during the heady days of Potsdam. Just as he had once used the dominant Russian influence against his personal political opponents, so Hardenberg was in turn subjected to a concerted French campaign to oust him. On 20 December Talleyrand laid down that Hardenberg was to be isolated and forced into retirement; French envoys were henceforth to have no contact with him.[174] He also wanted Lucchesini recalled and replaced by Knobelsdorff. Simultaneously, a French press campaign was launched, in which it was insinuated that

---

[168] Report of Haugwitz on his mission to Napoleon, 26.12.05, Berlin, in Ranke (ed.), *Denkwürdigkeiten Hardenbergs*, V, p. 228.

[169] Laforest to Talleyrand, 13.12.05, Berlin, in Bailleu (ed.), *Preussen und Frankreich*, II, pp. 419–20.

[170] Instructions for Lucchesini, 9.1.06, Berlin, ibid., II, p. 432.

[171] Metternich to Stadion, 10.1.06, Berlin, Klinkowström (ed.), *Metternichs nachgelassenen Papieren,* p. 99.

[172] Francis Jackson to Mulgrave, 18.1.06, Berlin, PROL FO 64/71, fos. 33–9.

[173] Laforest to Talleyrand, 18.12.05, Berlin, in Bailleu (ed.), *Preussen und Frankreich*, II, p. 422.

[174] Talleyrand to Laforest, 20.12.05, in Bailleu (ed.), *Preussen und Frankreich*, II, p. 426.

Hardenberg was in the pay of Britain and should be replaced by Haugwitz.[175]

This turn of affairs was not without bitter irony for Hardenberg. It was half-measures to which he had been opposed, not to France *per se*. 'Que de revirements pendant cette époque!' he wrote to Lucchesini. 'Vous savez que ces demi-mesures ne sont pas mon ouvrage sans que je vous le dise.'[176] Indeed, the charge of Francophobia sat ill with the man who had spent most of August and September preaching a French alliance, and on far better terms, as he was quick to point out, than were offered at Schönbrunn.[177] But it was all to no avail. Associated in Napoleon's and the public mind with the work of Potsdam, Hardenberg's days were numbered. The sheer injustice and perversity of this development is best seen in Hardenberg's own summary of his relationship with France: 'C'est toujours un caprice du sort', he complained, 'que le ministre sous lequel la Prusse s'empressa la première à reconnaître la dynastie Bonaparte, article cité par l'Empereur dans sa dernière lettre au Roi – que celui qui en août a voulu l'alliance avec la France et poussé les armements contre la Russie, devienne l'objet d'un mécontentement peu équitable.'[178]

The Prussian dilemma after Austerlitz

The Prussian situation in the winter of 1805–6 may be summarised as follows: having departed from her previous policy of strict neutrality in favour of an armed mediation which was clearly orientated towards accession to the coalition against France, Prussia found herself dangerously exposed by the allied defeat at Austerlitz. Once she had been deserted, as she saw it, by her continental allies, Austria and Russia, Prussia felt free to make her own arrangements with France. This policy prepared the way for the return to power of those who, whether through coincidence or better insight, had read the international situation correctly. In the short term, however, while the effect of the allied disaster had still to make itself felt on the high-political struggle in Berlin, Prussia's politicians were in remarkable agreement about the policies needed to extricate the Prussian state from the implications of Potsdam.

---

[175] Extract from *Journal Politique* published at Leyden, 31.12.05; same in *Journal Politique*, published at Mannheim 23.12.05, both in GStA Rep.XI.89.402, unfoliated.
[176] Hardenberg to Lucchesini, 22.12.05, Berlin, in Bailleu (ed.), *Preussen und Frankreich*, II, p. 428.
[177] Ranke (ed.), *Denkwürdigkeiten Hardenbergs*, I, p. 387.
[178] Hardenberg to Lucchesini, 29.1.05, Berlin, in Bailleu (ed.), *Preussen und Frankreich*, II, p. 438.

At the same time, Hardenberg scrambled to improve his standing with Napoleon by jettisoning his erstwhile allies. This immediately became obvious during the subsidy negotiations between Harrowby and Hardenberg. Hardenberg now sought two things. First, to dissociate himself personally from his disastrous link with the allies; secondly, to extricate Prussia from any arrangement with the coalition which might give offence to Napoleon. 'I was struck', wrote Harrowby, 'with something like hesitation in his manner, – with a sort of reference to the future orders of the king, and with an expression which dropped from him, that circumstances might possibly arise, in which Prussia could only look to her own defence and security.'[179] Within the space of a few weeks, the subsidy negotiations were allowed to peter out. The motives behind this policy were transparent enough. In order to escape French wrath it was essential both to distance oneself from Britain and to ensure the removal of the combined Anglo-Hanoverian force from northern Germany. This emerges very clearly from Hardenberg's attitude towards Lord Harrington, Harrowby's replacement in the special mission to Prussia. Writing to Haugwitz in Paris, he expressed the fear that Harrington's mission would be misunderstood by France ('qu'on representait la mission de Lord Harrington dans un faux jour').[180] For this reason he wanted Harrington out of the country as soon as possible. It was with considerable relief (*grand joye*) that he noted that he was not going to present his letters of credence, and thus embarrass the Prussian government with further alliance overtures.[181] These, it should be noted, are not the actions of a committed partisan of the anti-French cause, but rather the policy of a man driven by the immediate needs of the state and the desire to mend fences with France for personal political reasons.

Terminating the subsidy negotiations and distancing oneself from Britain was one thing, ensuring the withdrawal of the Anglo-Hanoverian forces from northern Germany was quite another. As the Duke of Brunswick pointed out, the allied defeat at Austerlitz had left these troops in an exposed position.[182] They also constituted a considerable embarrassment for the Prussian government, because their presence could serve to justify the return of French troops to flush them out, something that had to be avoided at all costs. In Berlin, Harrowby saw his main purpose after Austerlitz in bringing the troops home, to which end

---

179 Harrowby to Mulgrave, 8.12.05, Berlin, in Rose (ed.), *Select dispatches*, p. 260.
180 Hardenberg to Haugwitz (draft), 30.1.06, Berlin, GStA Rep.XI.89.406, unfoliated.
181 Hardenberg to Haugwitz (draft), 6.2.06, Berlin, GStA Rep.XI.89.406, unfoliated.
182 Brunswick to Hardenberg, 11.12.05, Berlin, GStA Rep.XI.89.402, unfoliated.

he sought and obtained reluctant Prussian assurances for their safety.[183] But the fate of the north German expedition was not decided by military criteria alone. Rather, the question of withdrawal was linked to the broader political question of British policy towards Prussia after Austerlitz. Central to this policy was the continuing British hope that Prussia would lead a renewed coalition against France. One way of achieving this was territorial bribery. This had, of course, been tried by Harrowby without success. But by early 1806, the British were prepared to improve on their offers of November 1805. 'A strong sense of obvious and impending danger is not alone sufficient to determine the Prussian government,' Mulgrave wrote, and continued: 'The powerful means of a general coalition has not been sufficient; an increase of territory has been its leading, and indeed only influencing object . . . Holland therefore, under present circumstances seems to me alone likely to purchase vigorous and immediate exertions on the part of Prussia.' The Dutch Stadtholder should be suitably compensated and the Prussians put in his place. Mulgrave does not seem to have been troubled by the questionable ethics of such a transaction. 'No bribe seems to me too high for Prussia at the moment', he argued. But the cession of Holland to Prussia was to have a purpose beyond the purely short-term need to win Prussian support: Prussia was to be brought into contact with France. 'Holland must become a province of France or of some other power', Mulgrave wrote:

Can it be placed in any other hands capable of defending it except Prussia? Is there any other acquisition which can by its value tempt Prussia to come into contact with France,and which by its frontier will enable that kingdom to keep the French force at bay, except Holland? As long as Prussia shall hold its connection with this country, the United Provinces in her hands will secure all the northern and eastern parts of Great Britain against the dangers of invasion.[184]

The other approach was to use the presence of the Anglo-Hanoverian force in north Germany to embroil Prussia in the conflict against her will.

---

[183] Hardenberg to Harrowby, 15.12.05, Berlin, PROL FO 64/70; Harrowby to Cathcart, 20.12.05, Berlin, PROL FO 64/70; 'Extract of a letter from Lord Harrowby to Baron Hardenberg, dated Berlin, 13 December', PROL FO 64/70; Harrowby to Mulgrave, 23.12.05, Berlin, PROL FO 64/70; Harrowby to Cathcart (copy), 7.1.06, Berlin, PROL FO 64/70; Mulgrave to Harrowby (draft), 8.1.06, Downing Street, PROL FO 64/70; Hardenberg to Jacobi, 16.12.05, Berlin, GStA Rep.XI.81.231, fo. 88; Hardenberg to Harrowby (draft), 15.12.05, Berlin, GStA Rep.XI.73.180B., fo. 81; Hardenberg to Harrowby, 22.12.05, Berlin, GStA Rep.XI.73.180B, fo. 86.

[184] Mulgrave to Pitt, 6.1.06, Fulham, in A. W. Ward and G. P. Gooch (eds.), *The Cambridge history of British foreign policy, 1783–1919*, vol. I (Cambridge, 1922), p. 588; see also Fremont, 'Britain's role in the formation of the Third Coalition', p. 39, on continued British attempts to get Prussia involved in the struggle against Napoleon.

While this had not been the original purpose of the mission, which was more narrowly military in conception, it soon became so. Once embarked, the British force might help to stiffen Prussian resolve against Napoleon.[185] 'I should be sorry', wrote Castlereagh, 'that any thing was done on our part which might have the appearance of either weakening Prussia, or leaving her in the lurch at a critical moment, if she either chooses or is forced to fight.'[186] The troops were to remain in Hanover until Prussia had made her decision. Political considerations had clearly taken precedence, for Harrowby was instructed that the continued presence of the troops gave him 'an instrument for bringing the Court of Berlin to a precise decision with respect to the north of Germany'.[187] This had always been Pitt's view of the expedition, to whom it had been meant as an encouragement for Prussia to come forward. When it was proposed to withdraw them he objected that 'By bringing them away now, I fear we should hardly give a fair chance to the good disposition of Prussia, if any such really exists.'[188] This was a view shared by the foreign minister, Lord Mulgrave, to whom the presence of the troops was a welcome 'chance of stirring up something' as he put it. 'Nothing', he thought, 'seems more likely to decide the hostility of France against Prussia than a junction of British troops with those of Prussia',[189] and it seemed reasonable to assume that the longer these remained in north Germany, the greater the chances of widening the conflict aganst Napoleon. This policy was abandoned in mid-January when Castlereagh realised that 'whatever risk we may run by keeping our troops longer on the Continent, we are not likely to influence thereby the conduct of Prussia' and thus issued the orders for withdrawal.[190]

The reasons why Prussia refused either to be drawn by the territorial bribe or to be influenced by the British force in northern Germany are not hard to see. They are the familiar arguments of the ratification debates of December 1805. Prussia had no intention of committing herself to a disastrous war with France, especially not to serve the interests of the power whom she increasingly held responsible for the perpetuation of conflict on the continent. Even before Austerlitz Haugwitz had pointed out that all that had been agreed at Potsdam was to concert military measures according to a particular situation. As that

185 See Simms, 'Anglo-Prussian relations', p. 9.
186 Castlereagh to Pitt, 5.1.06, Downing Street, in Vane (ed.), *Castlereagh.*, p. 104.
187 Castlereagh to Harrowby, 10.1.06, Downing Street, ibid., p. 112.
188 Pitt to Castlereagh, 6.1.06, Bath, ibid., p. 69.
189 Mulgrave to Pitt, 5.1.06, Speenhill, in full in Ward and Gooch (eds.), *British foreign policy*, p. 587.
190 Castlereagh to Harrowby, 11.1.06, Downing Street, in Vane (ed.), *Castlereagh*, p. 117.

situation had now utterly changed, Prussia must look to the security of her own state.[191] Even before Austerlitz, Haugwitz had strongly disapproved of the British expedition, because he feared that it would destroy the last hope of peace.[192] Now, with France triumphant, the British presence in northern Germany was not merely embarrassing, but potentially catastrophic for Prussia. Rather than allow herself to be embroiled in Britain's quarrel with France, Frederick William now offered to mediate between France and her adversaries.[193] The main object of Prussian policy reverted to being 'the maintenance of the peace of north Germany and, to that end, the prevention of the reoccupation of Hanover by French forces'.[194] The return to the traditional – pre-Potsdam – mediation policy based on strict neutrality was now complete.

When rebuffing the British overtures, Prussian statesmen did not hesitate to point to Prussia's particularly exposed position. In late December Hardenberg stressed the uncertainty of the situation, the need for 'circumspection' and his fear that the weight of the war would fall on Prussia.[195] Frequent reference was made to Prussia's 'exposure' and the 'paralysis' which the Russian defection had caused. British assistance was deemed impractical and rejected because of the 'geographical state of his [Frederick William's] dominions'.[196] Nor was this just public rhetoric, for these familiar themes were also rehearsed in the confidential communications between Berlin and the Prussian ambassador in London, Jacobi-Kloest. Perhaps the best instance of this would be the dispatch of 25 January 1806 which was intended to be communicated confidentially to the British government as an apologia for Prussia's change of course.[197] The events of the last two months and especially those of the 26 December treaty at Pressburg between Austria and France, the Prussians argued, had completely changed the political face of Europe. Austria had not consulted Frederick William before concluding the Treaty of Pressburg, causing Prussia severe embarrassment. All Frederick William had desired was to keep the war as far away as

---

[191] Haugwitz to Frederick William, 21.11.05, Prague, GStA Rep.XI.89.402, unfoliated.
[192] Haugwitz to Hardenberg, 16.11.05, Dresden, GStA Rep.XI.89.402, unfoliated.
[193] Hardenberg to Jacobi, 24.1.06, Berlin, GStA Rep.XI.73.180C, fo. 23. See also Franco-British mediation: Haugwitz to Alopeus (draft), 22.12.05, Berlin, GStA Rep.XI.175.155E, fo. 131.
[194] Hardenberg to Jacobi, 27.12.05, Berlin, GStA Rep.XI.81.231, fo. 89.
[195] Hardenberg to Harrowby (copy), 22.12.05, Berlin, PROL FO 64/70.
[196] Hammond to Mulgrave, 3.1.06, Berlin, PROL FO 64/70; Harrowby to Mulgrave, 7.1.06, Berlin, PROL FO 64/70.
[197] Frederick William to Jacobi (copy), 25.1.06, Berlin, PROL FO 64/71, fos. 56–7; copy in Prussian hands: Hardenberg to Jacobi, 25.1.06, Berlin, GStA Rep.XI.73.180C, fos. 24–6.

possible from Prussia's own borders and bring about a general peace through his intervention. However, events had overtaken all the arrangements made to this end. One consequence, the dispatch continued, was obviously going to be the return of French troops to the electorate where Hameln was still holding out. Prussia, menaced by the victor of Austerlitz on the Silesian border, and by troops massing in Holland and the north of Germany, was thus ill-placed to prevent Napoleon from reclaiming the Hanoverian electorate by what he called his right of conquest. Prussia had therefore only three options. The first was passively to watch the return of the French troops to Hanover and suffer the consequences. The second was to resist by force and risk a catastrophic war. The third was to attempt a 'middle way (*terme moyen*)', which would both conciliate French demands and spare north Germany the dangers of a bloody war. In view of the grim military situation and the remoteness of outside help, the first two options were ruled out. The Prussians pleaded for British understanding. Surely, they asked, Britain would not want to see the last bulwark against Napoleon in north Germany flattened in a hopeless struggle? Surely, they argued, neither reason, nor political sanity nor duty obliged Frederick William to enter a quarrel which he was not otherwise obliged to enter?[198]

[198] Ibid.

7 The Hanoverian crisis: Prussian policy and politics, March–June 1806

In 1806 the 'Second Hundred Years War'[1] entered into a crucial phase. The great Third Coalition of Great Britain, Austria and Russia against France, mobilised by Pitt, had been crushed by successive French victories at Ulm and Austerlitz. Napoleon now stood astride central Europe. To the south and east the Austrians, cowed, had sued for a separate peace, which they obtained at Pressburg in December 1805. To the east, the shattered Russian armies were in full retreat. In the north of Germany the small body of Anglo-Hanoverian troops, so hastily dispatched to take advantage of the French evacuation of the electorate of Hanover the preceding autumn, awaited their re-embarkation by the Royal Navy. All over Europe, Napoleonic puppets had been installed or were on the verge of being so. French influence stretched from the Channel to the north of Germany, from the Hook of Holland to the heel of the Italian boot. Although the political situation was, territorially speaking, to get a great deal worse yet, there was no doubt among contemporaries that Napoleon's power was at its zenith. But if Prussia's troubles with France had now come to a temporary end, those with Britain were only about to begin.[2] For in the Treaty of Paris Prussia committed herself to the closure of the North Sea ports to ships of the British flag as well as to the permanent annexation of the electorate of Hanover which she had occupied in the previous October. The British reaction was swift. An embargo was placed on Prussian vessels in March.

[1] J. S. Bromley, 'The Second Hundred Years War (1689–1815)', in Douglas Johnson, François Crouzet and François Bédarida (eds.), *Britain and France. Ten centuries* (Folkestone, 1980), pp. 164–72.

[2] The best accounts of the British–Prussian war of 1806 are the two articles by Richard Krauel: 'Preußen und England vor hundert Jahren' and 'Stein während des preussisch-englischen Konflikts im Jahre 1806', *PJ*, 137 (1909), 429–57. Gembries, 'Das Thema Preußen in der politischen Diskussion Englands', pp. 66–70, is handicapped by the lack of Prussian documentation. Ham, 'Strategies of coalition and isolation', pp. 70–86, sees things from the British angle only. For the Hanoverian perspective see Sieske, *Preußen im Urteil Hannovers*, pp. 56–84 and Brandes, 'Hannover in der Politik der Großmächte', *FBPG*, 52 (1940), esp. 26–39; Simms, 'An "odd question enough"'.

This was followed by the issue of royal letters of marque and reprisal and finally by the declaration of war in June 1806. All Prussian attempts to negotiate a lifting of the embargo in return for an end to the closure of the North Sea ports failed. Britain insisted on the unconditional return of Hanover as the *sine qua non* for the resumption of normal relations.

The Treaty of Paris: the ratification debate and the hegemony of France

At the beginning of 1806, Prussia's most pressing need was to clarify her relationship with Napoleon. In particular, she had to secure acceptance of the modified ratification of the terms of Schönbrunn. At first it seemed as if all would go well. The belief that the ratifications would go through appears to have been universal[3] and the consequent decision to demobilise for financial reasons cannot be blamed on Hardenberg's high political enemies alone. There is certainly no evidence either that Haugwitz advised such a step or, more importantly, that Hardenberg took any steps to prevent it.[4] Disillusionment came in early February. Haugwitz's reports told of bruising interviews with Napoleon in which he was bombarded with accusations of Prussian bad faith. Napoleon, in short, would not accept the modified ratifications. Haugwitz, it should be noted, called for the continuation of military preparations. But there was worse to come. In his meetings with Talleyrand it soon emerged that not only the modifications, but the whole treaty of Schönbrunn itself was now being rejected by the French. The French foreign minister even issued thinly veiled threats of a possible Austro-French alliance.[5] Finally, on 22 February 1806 Haugwitz arrived back in Berlin with the new agreement which Napoleon had dictated in place of the defunct arrangements of Schönbrunn. The only concession to Prussian wishes was the dropping of the expression 'offensive alliance'. But it remained that in all but name, for the territorial clauses and the mutual guarantees remained essentially in force. Most importantly, however, the new proposed treaty contained a further French demand which was calculated to integrate Prussia into Napoleon's plans for Europe: the closure of the ports under Prussian control to British shipping. Haugwitz counselled immediate acceptance: the alternative would be the military confrontation with

[3] Frederick William to Alexander, 26.1.06, Potsdam, in Bailleu (ed.), *Briefwechsel Alexanders*, p. 95.
[4] Brandes, 'Hannover in der Politik der Großmächte', p. 26.
[5] Haugwitz report, 8.2.06, Paris, in Ranke (ed.), *Denkwürdigkeiten Hardenbergs*, I, pp. 463–9; Haugwitz report, 12.2.06, Paris, in ibid., pp. 471–5; Haugwitz report, 15.2.06, Paris, in ibid., pp. 475–82.

France that Prussia was so anxious to avoid. 'Une seconde fois', he wrote, 'j'ai arrêté l'épée dans le fourreau pour le cas où le roi ratifié le nouveau traité.'[6] There followed a much shorter though essentially similar debate to that which followed Schönbrunn. The arguments advanced were much the same; the big difference lay in the fact that the room for manoeuvre, at least in the subjective view of the participants, had shrunk.

The conference of 24 February demonstrated just how limited Prussia's room for manoeuvre was. Hardenberg's memorandum summed up the question before Prussia's decision-makers: war or the treaty.[7] He claimed that he had always been against 'half measures', and that it was impossible to sustain the neutrality policy. Whatever decision was taken, it should be taken with 'consequence, promptitude and energy'. Roundly condemning Napoleon's plans to subject Prussia, Hardenberg proceeded to an analysis of the mistakes of Prussian policy since the violations at Ansbach. He criticised Haugwitz's mistaken belief that one could use the ratification process to slip in changes to the Schönbrunn treaty, while Napoleon used the disbandment of the Prussian forces to put crushing pressure on Haugwitz. Turning back to the main question – the treaty or war – Hardenberg rejected any idea of a 'middle way'.[8] He specifically said that to reject the treaty and to evacuate Hanover to the French would be 'the worst course of all'. Yet his own recommendation was to abandon Hanover and hold on to Ansbach, as a way of saving face. To accept the treaty would be to affirm client status with France, he continued. This was a negative view which fitted ill with his previous claim that a rejection of the treaty would be 'the worst' possible course. One is therefore forced to assume that client status, though hardly ideal, was preferable to Hardenberg than the sure extinction or irrelevance which would accompany rejection of the treaty. In any case, Hardenberg made no suggestion of an anti-French stand on principle which one might have expected to have accompanied his forthright condemnation of France at the outset of the memorandum. Instead, he left the question to the ultimate decision of Frederick William.

The protocol of the ratification debate shows that most Prussian statesmen followed Hardenberg's reasoning, though they rejected his

---

[6] Haugwitz to Schulenburg (copy), 16.2.06, Paris, GStA Rep.XI.89.407, unfoliated. (The first time had been Schönbrunn.)
[7] 'Mémoire de Hardenberg sur le traité du 15 février 1806', in Ranke (ed.), *Denkwürdigkeiten Hardenbergs*, I, pp. 490–7.
[8] Ibid., p. 493.

polemical intent.[9] Like Hardenberg, the conference, which was attended by Rüchel, Lucchesini, Köckritz, Kleist, Lombard, Beyme and Hardenberg, posed the choice: acceptance of the treaty, war or some third course of action. Along with Hardenberg they rejected the third option outright: the 'middle way' had been exhausted. The worst-case scenario was judged to be a French return to Hanover. This could only be prevented by ratification or by force of arms. By ratifying, Prussia would acquire a superb, well-positioned province; she would also avoid the sacrifices of a bloody war with France. On the debit side, Prussia would have to face a Britain that considered itself attacked. What damage could she do? She could attack Prussian commerce: this could cause serious problems. The best that could be hoped for was that Britain would think twice before pushing things to the brink. The attitude of Russia was also unclear, but she was likely to be displeased. This displeasure, however, was unlikely to lead to war, while rejecting the treaty would *definitely* lead to war with France. Though the authors were obviously in favour of immediate ratification, the document shied away from making a specific recommendation, just as Hardenberg had done. The decision was left to Frederick William: 'Ce sont là réflexions dont tout le monde est convenu. En abandonnant au Roi la décision tous les soussignés portent à ces pieds le voeu de décider à l'instant même, mais pour l'un ou l'autre partie sans moyen terme.'

The decision to ratify the treaty of Paris without reservation was duly taken. It was justified in terms of pure necessity of state. In a dispatch to the Duke of Brunswick, to whom the task of explaining Prussian policy in St Petersburg was to fall, Frederick William stressed the almost complete absence of choice. Following the arguments offered in the conference protocol, he maintained that war would have been a calamity, that a return of French troops to the electorate would be no less, and that consequently only ratification of the new treaty was feasible. Only the removal of the offensive clause in the alliance had been achieved. Nobody in Berlin was happy with the turn of events, least of all the king. But there had been no choice: 'Le choix du moindre mal, c'était là ce qui me restait.'[10] So Frederick William was forced to justify himself towards Alexander with the old Prussian rhetorical device which was to become all too familiar in months to come: 'mais l'empereur de Russie se mettra-t-il à ma place?'[11]

[9] See e.g. conference protocol, in Ranke (ed.), *Denkwürdigkeiten Hardenbergs*, I, pp. 488–9.
[10] Ibid., p. 303.
[11] Frederick William to Duke of Brunswick, Berlin, 28.2.06, in Ranke (ed.), *Denkwürdigkeiten Hardenbergs*, V, pp. 301–4.

War with Britain did not come as a complete surprise to Prussia. In his memorandum of 24 February, Hardenberg had stressed that the Paris treaty would probably provoke conflict with Britain, because the dignity of George III – Hanover – and the self-interest of the nation – the closure of the ports – demanded it.[12] Though Britain could not seriously threaten Prussian territory, he continued, the consequences of an Anglo-Prussian war would be grave, indeed 'the ruin of commerce' would result. On the other hand rejection of the treaty would *certainly* lead to war with France. It was, as Francis Jackson put it, 'a very embarrassing dilemma',[13] but the path to be taken by Prussia was never in any doubt. All the economic arguments in favour of *rapprochement* with Britain advanced during the Harrowby negotiations, such as the lifting of the Elbe blockade and the importation of East Indian saltpetre, went by the wayside.[14] Haugwitz was at least partly aware of the likely consequences of the Paris treaty,[15] but the immediate deliverance of the state from possible extinction at the hands of France overrode all misgivings. Added to this was the belief, or self-deception, that Britain would draw back at the brink from a breach with Prussia.[16] However, though this complete misjudgment of the British reaction was undoubtedly a contributory factor to the ratification of Paris, it followed from, rather than underlay the fundamental decision made in February 1806.

Central to Prussian policy in early 1806 were two factors. First and foremost was fear of France. 'On dit toujours', Queen Louise lamented, 'il ne faut pas se brouiller avec la France, avec ce monstre de pouvoir.'[17] 'If Russia were located in Denmark', Beyme argued, 'then Prussia would be able to choose between a Russian or a French alliance; at the moment the former is ruled out by our geographic situation and for other reasons.' The alliance with France, in short, was the fruit of stark geopolitical necessity. 'A French alliance', Beyme continued, 'is certainly inconvenient insofar as it is dictated by necessity; but one must try to lessen its oppressive nature by establishing our value as an ally and coordinating the Prussian state interest with that of France with as much intelligence

---

[12] Hardenberg memorandum of 24.2.06, Berlin, ibid., I, p. 495.
[13] Francis Jackson to Mulgrave, 25.1.06, Berlin, PROL FO 64/71.
[14] D'Abaye memorandum on an Anglo-Prussian alliance, 11.12.05, Berlin, GStA, Rep.XI.73.180B, fo. 36.
[15] Haugwitz report of 15.2.06, Paris, in Ranke (ed.), *Denkwürdigkeiten Hardenbergs*, I, pp. 476–82.
[16] Protocol of the conference of 2.3.06, Berlin, in Ranke (ed.), *Denkwürdigkeiten Hardenbergs*, I, pp. 503–5.
[17] Notes made by Louise, c. March 1806, cited in Tessa Klatt, *Königin Luise in der Zeit der Napoleonischen Kriege* (Berlin, 1937), p. 207.

as possible.'[18] If this meant that Prussia was, in Metternich's words, 'momentanément accolée à la marche dévastrice de Bonaparte', so be it.[19] 'Voici quel était son raisonnement', the Prussians argued, 'la France est puissante et Napoléon l'homme du siècle; uni à lui, que pourrai-je jamais avoir à craindre?'[20] These thoughts, attributed by Haugwitz to Frederick William but more likely those of Haugwitz himself, sum up the arguments behind the ratification of Paris. Others, including the king, believed that ratification had taken place out of necessity, not choice and certainly not out of wholehearted approval of a French alliance. There was, according to the consensus view, simply no other viable course for Prussia to take, even if this meant acquiescing in the French domination of Europe. When reminded that Napoleon was inexorably extending his control over Europe, Jacobi spoke for almost all Prussian statesmen when he replied that 'tout cela devoit servir de motif puissant pour se hâter de faire la paix'.[21] In a similar vein, the instructions to Jacobi in mid-March argued that the longer Britain delayed in finding ways to end the war, 'plus il joue le jeu de la France, en lui faisant l'occasion d'étendre de plus en plus et sous toutes sortes de prétextes, sa domination sur le continent'.[22]

Second only to fear of France in motivating Prussia to ratify the treaty of Paris was her long-standing ambition to annex the electorate of Hanover. Even those – such as Stein and Hardenberg – who professed to 'abhor' the manner in which the electorate had been acquired, stressed that possession of Hanover was 'extremement importante et éssentielle'.[23] Most importantly, the king, initially sceptical about the exchange of Ansbach for Hanover,[24] recognised the crucial importance of such a move. Prussia, in the judgment of Francis Jackson, was thus 'in the dilemma either of giving up Ansbach without an equivalent, or of

---

18 Beyme memorandum, 4.7.06, cited in Dehio, 'Beyme', p. 332: 'Läge Rußland wo Dänemark liegt, so würde Preußen zwischen einer russischen oder französischen Allianz wählen können; jetzt ist die erstere vermöge unserer geographischen Lage drückend und in andrer Hinsicht unwirksam . . . Eine französische Allianz! Sie hat freilich ihre Unbequemlichkeiten insofern sie durch die Notwendigkeit diktiert wird; aber man muß das drückende dadurch zu mindern suchen, daß man sich einen Wert als Alliierten verschafft und das preußische Staatsinteresse dem französischen mit möglicher Klugheit koordiniert wird.'
19 Metternich memorandum, 12.4.06, Berlin, in Klinkowström (ed.), *Metternichs nachgelassenen Papieren*, p. 117.
20 Haugwitz to Lucchesini, 15.6.06, Berlin, in Bailleu (ed.), *Preussen und Frankreich*, II, p. 468.
21 Jacobi report, 28.2.06, London, GStA Rep.XI.73.180C, fo. 80.
22 Instructions for Jacobi, 21.3.06, Berlin, GStA Rep.XI.73.180C, fo. 90.
23 Hardenberg to Jacobi, 25.3.06, Berlin, GStA Rep.XI.81.241, fo. 52. Re Stein see Lehmann, *Stein*, I, p. 396.
24 Frederick William to Haugwitz, 3.2.06, Berlin, GStA Rep.XI.89.406, unfoliated.

forfeiting the pledge that has been given to His Majesty and to the emperor of Russia that Hanover shall not be alienated without his Majesty's consent'.[25] So the annexation went ahead, partly to avoid a net loss through the cession of territories in Franconia, but mainly in order to secure the north of Germany from further French encroachments, a security which only actual possession of Hanover would provide. 'Its value to Prussia', to use Frederick William's own words, 'lies in its geographical situation which is so essential to its own defence and that of the whole of the north, [that] I cannot let it fall into the hands of anybody else.'[26] The Prussian king also pointed out that in the event of a British–French war Hanover was always involved at the 'first cannon shot' which endangered Prussian security. In any case he stressed, 'A glance at the map shows the urgency of providing for the Prussian monarchy acquisitions and more secure frontiers, especially with France.'[27]

From now on, Prussian policy towards Britain could only be one of damage limitation. Against all the odds, Britain would have to be persuaded that Prussia had no choice but to align herself publicly with Napoleon; that Prussia would do her utmost to alleviate the practical effect of her commercial measures against Britain; and that reprisals against Prussia would merely drive her even further into the French camp. 'La tache n'est pas facile . . . ', Hardenberg told Jacobi. 'Vous devez être l'avocat d'une très mauvaise cause . . . Hélas.'[28] In accordance with this policy, Prussian captains were given orders to avoid confrontation at all costs and it was hoped that Britain would do the same. Furthermore, Jacobi assured the foreign office that the closure of the four northern ports was not being strictly observed;[29] this Prussian moderation, he argued, merited British moderation in return. In Berlin, Hardenberg promised that all measures would be generously interpreted in return for which he hoped that Russia and Great Britain 'would make some allowances for the situation of this country'.[30] In early April Hardenberg went so far as to say that Schulenburg's declaration concerning the closure of the ports was *pro forma* only and that British

[25] Francis Jackson to Fox, 26.2.06, Berlin, PROL FO 64/71, fo. 111.

[26] Instructions for Jacobi, 24.3.06, Berlin, GStA Rep.XI.73.180C, fo. 106.

[27] 'Propositions of Prussia to the Elector of Hanover relative to an exchange of territory for the purpose of arrondissement and rendering his frontier more secure against that of France, 1806', PROL FO 64/71, fos. 59–62.

[28] Hardenberg to Jacobi, 25.3.06, Berlin, GStA Rep.XI.81.London.241, fo. 51. See also Instructions for Jacobi, 25.3.06, Berlin, GStA Rep.XI.73.180C, fo. 110; Instructions for Jacobi, 31.3.06, Berlin, Rep.XI.73.180C, fo. 112.

[29] Jacobi to Schulenburg (draft), 2.3.06, London, GStA Rep.XI.81.241, fo. 3.

[30] Francis Jackson to Fox, 27.3.06, Berlin, PROL FO 64/71, fo. 161. See also Francis Jackson to Fox, 28.3.06, Berlin, PROL FO 64/71, fos. 170–1.

merchandise was not in danger provided it was brought by neutral vessels.[31] Indeed, Haugwitz wrote, Britain should be assured that the Prussian action was only 'une mesure de police un peu rigoreuse. Elle n'est pas tant en s'en faut ce qu'elle paroit au premier coup d'oeil.'[32]

This policy of playing down the effects of the blockade on Britain had been conceived even before the first British countermeasures set in. Thus, Beyme had opposed including Emden in the Prussian measures against Britain, on the grounds that the town was not included in the relevant clause of the Paris treaty. His intention – in Lombard's words – was to 'laisser du vague dans la phrase pour diminuer l'odieux de la première impression' so that one would have 'moins à craindre de la première passion'.[33] In accordance with this policy, Schulenburg was instructed to exercise utmost restraint in the application of his orders.[34] British ships should preferably be warned and taken into custody rather than bombarded. All in all there was some justification for the Prussian claim that British trade was not suffering greatly from the Prussian action. Indeed, British ships used the same outlets as during the French occupation of Hanover: via Tonningen and Husum to Hamburg or Lübeck. Only the path through Oldenburg to Bremen remained closed.[35] But the British remained unimpressed, partly because the Prussian signals in the direction of conciliation were occasionally contradicted by excessive zeal against British commerce on the ground,[36] but mainly because Hanover, not the ports, was the real issue.[37] This was not at all clear, however, to Prussia's statesmen during the early stages of the crisis. They saw 'above all the need to distinguish well in this affair between the royal house, the British government . . . and the personal attachment of the king to his estates in Germany'.[38] 'La fermeture des ports est le principal grief de l'Angleterre', Haugwitz argued, 'et celui auquel il faut s'attacher surtout à repondre.'[39] It was not until much later

[31] Francis Jackson to Fox, 8.4.06, Berlin, PROL FO 64/71, fo. 200.
[32] Instructions for Jacobi, 21.4.06, Berlin, GStA Rep.XI.73.190C, fo. 133.
[33] Lombard to Schulenburg (?), c. end of March 1806, GStA Rep.XI.140.c.3.50.fasc.1., fo. 179.
[34] Brandes, 'Hannover in der Politik der Großmächte', p. 31.
[35] Thimme, 'Die Okkupation des Kurfürstentums Hannover', p. 19. See also Instructions to Jacobi, 30.4.06, Berlin, GStA Rep.XI.73.180C, fos. 152–1.
[36] 'D' (obviously a British agent) to Lord Moira, 8.4.06, Hamburg, BL Add MSS 51460, fo. 130.
[37] See Simms, '"An odd question enough"'.
[38] Instructions for Jacobi, 7.2.06, Berlin, GStA Rep.XI.73.180C, fo. 45. See also Doerries, 'Ce qui m'est arrivé', p. 28 and passim, who perpetuates Jacobi's errors about Prussian policy being geared towards the ports.
[39] Instructions for Jacobi, PS to 30.4.06, GStA Rep.XI.73.180C.

that the importance of Hanover to British policy in its own right was recognised.[40] This British commitment to Hanover doomed all Prussian attempts at conciliation to failure.

The resulting Prussian dilemma was a peculiarly *continental* phenomenon, the predicament of a central power caught in the crossfire of their more peripherally located neighbours, in this case Britain and France. Unable to appease Britain in any way, the Prussians were reduced to the rhetoric of necessity. 'It is a case of everyman for himself', Goltz told the Hanoverian envoy in St Petersburg, 'in times such as these, one must only think of guaranteeing one's own existence.'[41] The justificatory note to Jacobi and the *Note Verbale* to Britain itself were shot through with such rhetoric,[42] which was to characterise almost every Anglo-Prussian diplomatic encounter for the next month. Thus in May 1806, Haugwitz expressed surprise that Britain could not 'put himself in our position and see things from the right point of view, that of a more or less temporary state of affairs, the result of irresistible events for which we are certainly not to blame'.[43] Not long after Jacobi begged him to consider 'la situation pénible de la Prusse'.[44] On another occasion Frederick William expressed his own personal abhorrence of annexing Hanover, adding, however, in a memorable phrase, 'But am I in control of circumstances?'[45] In short, the Prussians attempted to portray the move, in Francis Jackson's characterisation of Haugwitz's pleas, as 'an affair of necessity, not of choice'.[46]

The rhetoric of necessity was given force by the always implicit and sometimes explicit threat that further British action would only serve to drive Prussia finally into the French camp. Prussia's statesmen saw this as their strongest card and they played it to the full. To press Prussia any further, Frederick William argued, would be to 'me jetter dans un système contraire',[47] or 'nous jetter entièrement entre les bras de sa

---

[40] For the British insistence on Hanover see: Jacobi report, 18.7.06, London, GStA Rep.XI.73.181A, fos. 30–1; Jacobi report, 22.7.06, London, GStA Rep.XI.73.181A, fos. 33–4; Jacobi report, 1.8.06, London, fos. 53–4.

[41] Cited in Möller report, 31.1.06, F. von Ompteda (ed.), *Politischer Nachlaß des hannoverschen Staats- und Cabinettsministers, Ludwig von Ompteda aus den Jahren 1804 bis 1813. Abtheilung I. Aus den Jahren 1804 bis 1809* (Jena, 1869), p. 131. 'Ein jeder ist sich selbst der nächste, in Zeiten wie diese sind, muß man nur auf eigene Existenz und deren Erhaltung und Sicherstellung denken.'

[42] *Note Verbale*, PROL FO 64/71, fo. 166; Instructions for Jacobi, 24.3.06, Berlin GStA Rep.XI.73.180C, fos. 104–7.

[43] Haugwitz to Jacobi, 13.5.06, Berlin, GStA Rep.XI.73.180C, fo. 191.

[44] Jacobi report, 16.5.06, Berlin, GStA Rep.XI.73.180C, fo. 209.

[45] Instructions for Jacobi, 4.3.06, Berlin, GStA Rep.XI.73.180C, fo. 74.

[46] Francis Jackson to Fox, 25.4.06, Berlin, PROL FO 64/71, fo. 236.

[47] Haugwitz to Jacobi, 13.5.06, Berlin, GStA Rep.XI.73.180C, fo. 191.

rivale'[48] or 'me jetter lui même dans le système de la France',[49] or some other such formulation.[50] This rhetoric, it should be stressed, was adopted by *all* Prussian politicians, even those critical of the policy towards Britain. Schulenburg complained that if Britain wanted to maintain a bulwark in northern Germany her policy was calculated to achieve exactly the opposite by driving Prussia into the arms of France.[51] The same thoughts, expressed in almost exactly the same words, were recorded by Hardenberg and Goltz;[52] all three were bitter opponents of Haugwitz.

War with Britain was thus something that Prussia had very much hoped to avoid, but it was the lesser of two evils. Offered the choice between instant destruction at Napoleon's hands and economic strangulation by Great Britain she chose the latter. At first, as we have seen, Prussia's statesmen were confident that Britain could be appeased, and they went to considerable lengths, such as the relaxation of the closure of the ports to achieve this. Once it had become clear that Britain, for motives entirely beyond their comprehension, was going to insist on the restitution of the electorate, Prussia's statesmen had no choice but to weather the storm. They were not unaware of the questionable ethics of their actions, but, as Frederick William asked his ambassador in London: 'in the stormy times in which we live, when it is a matter of saving the ship, without regard to other losses, should we allow ourselves to be bound by a simple point of honour or a personal affection, however just it may be?'[53] The question was rhetorical, the answer clear to all Prussians: a 'simple point of honour' should not obstruct the task of the statesman, which was to 'sauver l'essentiel quoi qu'il peut coûter'.[54] When Jacobi protested against the Prussian action on ethical grounds, he was informed that 'tout ce que vous pouvez me dire, a été pesé et senti. Mon parti est pris.'[55]

In short, war with Britain was not actively sought, nor was it unforeseen, though the extent of its consequences took everybody by surprise. Rather war with Britain was taken into account, and finally accepted, as a part of the calculated risk of Prussian policy. If Hanover was annexed for its strategic value, the ports were closed because, as we have seen,

---

[48] Instructions for Jacobi, 1.5.06, Berlin, GStA Rep.XI.73.180C, fo. 156.
[49] Instructions for Jacobi, 30.4.06, Berlin, GStA Rep.XI.73.180C, fo. 156.
[50] Haugwitz to Jacobi, 1.5.06, Berlin, GStA Rep.XI.81.241, fo. 19.
[51] Schulenburg to Jacobi, 18.6.06, Hanover, GStA Rep.81.241, fo. 10.
[52] Hardenberg to Brunswick, 28.2.06, Berlin, GStA Rep.92 *Hardenberg* E9, fo. 5; Goltz to Jacobi, 15.5.06, St Petersburg, GStA Rep.XI.81.241, fos. 6–7.
[53] Instructions for Jacobi, 24.3.06, Berlin, GStA Rep.XI.73.180C, fo. 105.
[54] Ibid.
[55] Instructions for Jacobi, 23.5.06, Berlin, GStA Rep.XI.73.180C, fo. 204.

offending Britain seemed less hazardous than offending the French. 'Je dois m'y soumettre . . . ', Frederick William wrote. 'C'est une conséquence de l'occupation du pays de Hannovre, et je m'y soumettrai sans regrets, pourvu que je puisse compter sur la garantie de la France qui m'en assure la propriété.'[56] The concomitant ruin of her trade and grain economy, though regrettable, was a price which the Prussian political leadership was prepared to pay, even when the full devastation of the British measures could no longer be ignored. Surveying the likely destruction of her economy, Francis Jackson had this to say about Prussian policy:

I was at first inclined to think that this step was taken without a due consideration of its probable consequences, and by way of experiment to try how far it might be possible to go in submission to France without the risk of rupture with Great Britain. But I have now ascertained that the two sides of the question have been duly weighed and that the choice has been finally made upon principle and with a clear understanding of the embarrassments to which it may lead.[57]

The triumph of Haugwitz. High politics and foreign policy in Prussia during the early stages of the Hanoverian crisis

Engrossing though the events outlined above were for the statesmen in Berlin, they did not represent the sum, or in some cases even the essence, of political life in the Prussian capital and the royal residences surrounding it. For the momentous happenings of the new year on the foreign political scene ran parallel to and interacted with the temporary denouement of the old struggle between Haugwitz and Hardenberg for control of the executive. We have already seen how the latter had enlisted the aid of Britain and Russia in that struggle. By the beginning of 1806, however, allied support hung like a millstone around Hardenberg's neck; in the same way, Hardenberg himself was an embarrassment to a Prussian state intent on weathering the storm which broke after Austerlitz. The treaty of Schönbrunn had dealt his position a body blow and the treaty of Paris had only confirmed this. Hardenberg's adversaries, on the other hand, basked in French approval and they now moved to convert that capital into personal political gain.

First attempts at removing Hardenberg proved, however, counter-productive. The overt French campaign to influence Prussia's domestic

---

[56] Instructions for Lucchesini, 26.5.06, Berlin, in Bailleu (ed.), *Preussen und Frankreich*, II, 1, pp. 463–4.

[57] Francis Jackson to Fox, 3.4.06, Berlin, PROL FO 64/71, fos. 183–4.

affairs ran up against the ill-will of the king. Indeed, Haugwitz even found it expedient to profess to defend Hardenberg against the French press, partly no doubt in order to appease Frederick William.[58] But after the Treaty of Paris this situation could not last for long. Indeed, Haugwitz's high-political move against Hardenberg came on the very same day. It took the form of a separate letter to the king assuring him of his affection for Hardenberg but urging his removal as foreign minister; Napoleon, having conceived a great dislike for Hardenberg, would not accept a ratification countersigned by him. For this reason Lucchesini, rather than Hardenberg, was being dispatched to Paris, ostensibly to provide further information on the treaty, but in reality to sign the ratification in Hardenberg's place.[59] In this way Haugwitz made full use of the altered circumstances after Austerlitz to further his personal political ends. There is, however, no evidence that he directly enlisted French help in the way that Hardenberg had deployed the Russian connection, and was increasingly to do.

It was not until the end of March that Hardenberg finally offered his resignation, which was made public about two weeks later.[60] His demand that he be kept *au courant* of business indicated that he had not given up all hope of political participation.[61] The demand was granted and, in a somewhat perfunctory way, actually honoured during the coming months.[62] In any case he was to stay on as a member of the General-direktorium to supervise the transfer to Bavarian control of the Franconian provinces, where he had cut his administrative teeth as a young bureaucrat.[63] Hardenberg's departure caused widespread regret among many Prussian politicians.[64] In some cases, as in that of Schrötter, the expressions of regret were accompanied by cryptic but unmistakable references to the loss suffered thereby by 'true patriots'.[65]

[58] Haugwitz to Laforest (draft), 7.12.05, GStA Rep.XI.89.402, unfoliated.
[59] Postscript to Haugwitz's report of 15.2.06, Paris, in Ranke (ed.), *Denkwürdigkeiten Hardenbergs*, I, pp. 485–6.
[60] Copy of the *Berlinische Nachrichten* of 15 April with the announcement of Hardenberg's leave-taking, GStA Rep.92 *Hardenberg* E8, fo. 15. For a good analysis of the high-political background to Hardenberg's resignation see Schroeder, *Transformation of European politics*, p. 304.
[61] Hardenberg to Frederick William, 30.3.06, Berlin, in Ranke (ed.), *Denkwürdigkeiten Hardenbergs*, I, p. 588.
[62] Thus Haugwitz to Hardenberg, 28.6.06, Berlin, keeping Hardenberg informed of developments with Sweden and commerce in the Baltic, GStA Rep.92 *Hardenberg* E8 fo. 64.
[63] For Hardenberg's activities concerning Franconia see the report of the General Oberkriegs- und Domänen Direktorium, Stein, Voss, Reden, Schrötter, Dietherdt, 22.4.06, Berlin, GStA Rep. 92 *Hardenberg* J2, fo. 139.
[64] Reck to Hardenberg, 15.4.06, Berlin, GStA Rep.92 *Hardenberg* E8, fo. 11.
[65] Schrötter to Hardenberg, 16.4.06, Berlin, GStA Rep.92 *Hardenberg* E8, fo. 24.

Others, like Schulenburg, envied his chance to find peace 'loin de tourbillion des affaires'.[66] Others again, such as Brockhausen, the ambassador in Dresden, were overcome by pessimism at the news and the general situation, and regarded 'les affaires de l'état comme gâtés sans retour'.[67] However, in at least one case – that of Count Hoym, a long-standing crony of Haugwitz and the notoriously venal governor of Silesia – the expressions of regret had a hollow ring to them.[68]

There were certainly many who were not sorry to see him go. One of these was of course Haugwitz himself. But it was with the normally reclusive cabinet secretaries that Hardenberg's acrimonious dispute spilled over into the public sphere. The trigger proved to be an episode in Anglo-Prussian relations of the previous year. Hardenberg's note to Harrowby of 22 December 1805, concerning a projected Anglo-Prussian alliance, had been presented, along with numerous other documents, to the British parliament in the new year. It had then been reproduced in English translation in the British newspaper *The Sun* and eventually ended up, retranslated into French, in the official organ of the French government, the *Moniteur* of 21 March 1806.[69] Quite apart from being a classic example of the dangers of lax British security, the event was a severe embarrassment to Hardenberg. For in the note he had still been operating on the assumption that some kind of agreement would be reached with Britain to finance the armed mediation stipulated at Potsdam. This accorded ill with the new policy which Haugwitz had inaugurated at Schönbrunn ten days earlier and opened the door to French accusations of bad faith on the part of Hardenberg who was accused of 's'être prostitué aux éternels ennemis du continent', that is the British.[70] Hardenberg had a simple line of defence in that he could fairly claim to have been ignorant of Haugwitz's actions at the time of writing, but the affair could not but provide his adversaries with further ammunition against him. To make matters worse, Hardenberg responded by publishing the original letter, with some alterations, in the *Berlinische Nachrichten*.[71] Appended was a statement that he had been acting with the full knowledge of the king. This move infuriated many, partly because it jeopardised the fragile relationship with France and partly because it was considered an attempt at self-justification at the

---

[66] Schulenburg to Hardenberg, 16.4.06, Berlin, GStA Rep.92 *Hardenberg* E8, fo. 25.
[67] Brockhausen to Hardenberg, 204.06, Dresden, GStA Rep.92 *Hardenberg* E8, fo. 38.
[68] Hoym to Hardenberg, 19.4.06, Breslau, GStA Rep.92 *Hardenberg* E8, fo. 37.
[69] Quoted in Ranke (ed.), *Denkwürdigkeiten Hardenbergs*, I, pp. 590–2.
[70] Ranke (ed.), *Denkwürdigkeiten Hardenbergs*, I, p. 591.
[71] Ibid., p. 593.

king's expense, unfitting for a ministerial servant.[72] The net result was a further polarisation of Prussian high politics. During the affair Hardenberg's relationship with Beyme, whom he had hitherto regarded as an ally and confidant, deteriorated to such an extent that an altercation took place on the eve of his retirement. The squabble was broken up by the king but, to quote Hardenberg's own words, 'From that moment on, Beyme became my declared enemy. We neither saw, nor spoke to each other from then on.'[73]

But the triumph of Haugwitz was not yet complete. With Hardenberg gone, Frederick William instinctively looked to replace him with another Kabinettsminister to assist – or balance – Haugwitz in the formulation of Prussian foreign policy. Three senior diplomats were considered, Jacobi in London, Lucchesini in Paris and Keller[74] in Vienna; after some debate, Keller was chosen and summoned to Berlin in late April. At once, Haugwitz moved to eliminate this threat to his exclusive control of the foreign ministry. According to Keller's own account, Haugwitz stressed his determination to retain the 'direction *principale* [original italics] de la partie politique'. Keller was to be specifically debarred from conferring with foreign envoys or opening any ministerial correspondence; the very most he could hope for was to deputise in Haugwitz's absence. Indeed, Keller soon realised that what Haugwitz wanted was essentially a clerical assistant, not an equal colleague. If one subtracted 'political affairs' and the dynastic affairs left to von der Reck since the changes of 1802, then, Keller complained, this left only matters relating to 'unimportant business relating to individual subjects, the personal affairs of envoys and the issuing of passports (Die Besorgung unbedeutender Unhterthanenbedürfnisse, die persönlichen Reclamationen der Gesandten und die Ausfertigung der Pässe)'. What Haugwitz wanted, Keller noted with frustration, was not merely the *direction principale*, but the *direction seule* of foreign affairs.[75]

---

[72] Lombard to Lucchesini, 12.4.06, Berlin, in Bailleu (ed.), *Preussen und Frankreich*, II, p. 453.

[73] Ranke (ed.), *Denkwürdigkeiten Hardenbergs*, I, p. 596: 'von dem Augenblick an wart Beyme mein erklärter Gegner; wir sahen und sprachen uns nicht mehr'. See also Hardenberg's 'diary', 14.4.06: 'scène avec Beyme', GStA Rep. 92 *Hardenberg* L26, fo. 2; Disch, 'Der Kabinetsrat Beyme und die auswärtige Politik', *FBPG*, 41 (1929), 93–5.

[74] Dorotheus Ludwig Christoph Count von Keller, b. Gotha, 1757, d. Stetten, 1827. Enters Prussian service 1777; ambassador to Sweden 1779; ambassador to Russia, 1786–9; ambassador to the Hague, 1790–5; ambassador to Vienna, 1797–1805; temporary retirement May 1805 due to financial difficulties. *ADB*, 15 (1882), p. 563.

[75] See 'Vertraute Eröffnungen des Grafen von Keller über seine Ernennung zum Cabinetsminister' (in German), in PROL FO 353/80, fos. 523–8.

A brief glance at Haugwitz's own communications shows that these suspicions were entirely justified. He feared that Keller would be under the influence of *quelques personnes* who would establish 'dans le cabinet un parti opposé, je ne dirai pas au mien, puisque je n'ai jamais ambitioné d'en avoir, mais à mes principes'.[76] In particular, Haugwitz was determined to retain 'la direction principale des affaires politiques', 'la direction exclusive des affaires politiques', and that 'la direction des affaires fût réservée à moi seul', or some other such unambiguous formulation. By mid-June, Haugwitz was assuring Lucchesini that 'pour le moment au moins, il ne sera pas question de nommer un second ministre du cabinet; mais dans tous les cas il sera sans aucune influence quelconque pour la politique'.[77] By the end of that month, after increasingly acrimonious disputes about money and his radius of action, the challenge from Keller had finally been seen off.[78] Except for some minor administrative changes to lighten his burden, Haugwitz assured Lucchesini, 'tout le reste continuera à subsister sur l'ancien pied'.[79]

Yet even with Keller out of the way, Haugwitz was unable to celebrate the defeat of Hardenberg for long. Public opinion had finally swung against him after the humiliation of the Treaty of Paris.[80] This in itself would not have been worrying, but opposition extended well beyond the newspapers and flysheets of Berlin to the army, the court, especially the queen, and even the diplomatic service. When the residents of Ansbach petitioned the king to allow the province to remain in the Prussian monarchy, they not only played on Frederick William's emotions, they were also registering a veiled protest against the official foreign policy.[81] Public discussion of public affairs in the army could be, and was,[82] forbidden. Yet such measures merely provoked Haugwitz's

---

[76] Haugwitz to Lucchesini, 15.6.06, Berlin, in Bailleu (ed.), *Preussen und Frankreich*, II, p. 469.

[77] Haugwitz to Lucchesini, 25.4.06, Berlin, ibid., II, p. 457; Haugwitz to Lucchesini, 15.6.06, Berlin, ibid., II, p. 467.

[78] Keller to Hardenberg, 27.6.06, GStA Rep. 92 *Hardenberg* E8, fo. 57; Frederick William to Keller (copy), 17.6.06, Charlottenburg, ibid., fo. 58; Frederick William to Keller (copy), 24.1.06, Charlottenburg, ibid., fo. 60.

[79] Haugwitz to Lucchesini, 30.6.06, Berlin, in Bailleu (ed.), *Preussen und Frankreich*, II, p. 478.

[80] Tschirch, *Geschichte der öffentlichen Meinung in Preußen*, II, p. 385, has very little to say about this.

[81] 'Petition of the inhabitants of Ansbach to the King of Prussia', translation, PROL FO 64/71, fos. 126–8. See also Tarrasch, *Übergang*, p. 107; and Endres, 'Preußische Ära in Franken', p. 191, who lists a cross-section of the flood of petitions and pamphlets.

[82] Francis Jackson to Fox, 19.3.06, Berlin, PROL FO 64/71, fo. 145.

opponents to more extreme actions. At the end of March the windows of his town house were smashed twice by carbine bullets during the night.[83] This was almost certainly the work of the local garrison. As a result, a police guard was placed around the house. In vain Haugwitz attempted to distance himself from some of the more unfortunate features of the Paris treaty, such as the 'precipitate' closing of the ports, the 'importunate' declaration made to London concerning Hanover and the 'premature' demobilisation of the army in the new year.[84] The same factors which he had employed to eject Hardenberg and consolidate his hold on power, had irretrievably damned him in the public eye. As yet, however, Haugwitz retained the confidence of the only man who ultimately counted, the king himself. Haugwitz, Frederick William argued, 'a crû agir d'après son devoir et en bon patriote, mais il n'a pu changer les circonstances et il a crû devoir choisir le seul parti que lui paraissait le moins funeste'.[85]

The role of economic interest groups in Prussian policy

To risk or to countenance war with Britain was one thing, to prepare for it was quite another. Unlike the British, who had been very quick to notify their merchants of the dangers of war, Prussian statesmen neglected to do so until very late in the day. The chief reason for this was that the threat to Prussian commerce, though acknowledged, played a very minor role in the formation of policy. The ferocity of the British response thus came as a shock, the more so as Prussia's own naval forces were pathetically inadequate: the merchants of Danzig even tried to hire their own protection.[86] By mid-April measures against Prussia in the Baltic already amounted to a partial blockade.[87] To make matters worse,

---

[83] Francis Jackson to Fox, 27.4.06, Berlin, PROL FO 64/71, fos. 244–5.
[84] Francis Jackson to Fox, 25.4.06, Berlin, PROL FO 64/71, fo. 235; Haugwitz to Brunswick, 28.8.06, Berlin, in Bailleu (ed.), *Preussen und Frankreich*, II, p. 545; Haugwitz to Jacobi, 1.5.06, Berlin, GStA Rep.XI.81.241, fos. 19–21.
[85] Frederick William to Alexander, 23.6.06, Charlottenburg, in Bailleu (ed.), *Preussen und Frankreich*, II, p. 475. In a similar vein, Lucchesini to Frederick William, 27.3.06, Paris, in Bailleu (ed.), *Preussen und Frankreich*, p. 448.
[86] Szymanski, *Brandenburg-Preussen zur See*, p. 145. On the importance of British trade in the Baltic see Astrom, 'Britain's timber imports from the Baltic', pp. 57–71; Wolfram Fischer, 'Wirtschaft und Wirtschaftspolitik in Deutschland unter den Bedingungen der britisch-französischen Blockade und Gegenblockade (1797–1812)', in Aretin and Ritter (eds.), *Historismus und moderne Geschichtswissenschaft*, pp. 248–50; Martin Kutz, 'Die deutsch-britischen Handelsbeziehungen von 1790 bis zur Gründung des Zollvereins', *VSWG*, 56 (1969), 178–214.
[87] Jacobi report, 18.4.06, London, GStA Rep.XI.73.180C, fo. 161.

the Swedes joined in the blockade, thus effectively closing the Baltic to Prussian shipping.[88]

What aggravated the impact of the British measures was the fact that they came as a complete surprise. In 1801, at least, Jacobi had been informed in time to warn Prussian ships to leave British ports.[89] When, in mid-February 1806, the Prussian consul in London had asked Jacobi whether there could be any consequences for Prussian shipping as a result of the occupation of Hanover, the latter ridiculed the suggestion *en riant*.[90] But Jacobi's smile was soon to fade. Incredibly, Berlin had neglected to inform him of the clauses in the Paris treaty relating to the closure of the northern ports to British shipping. It was not until 24 March, over a month after the signing of the treaty, that Hardenberg brought him up to date rather sheepishly, adding, almost as an afterthought, that he should be on his guard for possible retaliatory measures against Prussian shipping[91] Jacobi, in a rare burst of initiative, had in fact already discreetly instructed his consuls to take action to enable Prussian captains and cargoes at least to reach the relative safety of the high seas.[92] But the warning came too late: the pessimistic predictions of his consuls were soon fulfilled. By 11 April, 150 ships had been seized by the Royal Navy, although half of them may have been Dutch vessels trading fraudulently with Britain's enemies.[93] Soon the total had reached 300 with no signs of any respite.[94] An absurdly optimistic declaration from Hardenberg in mid-March, assuring traders that there was nothing to fear,[95] had not helped matters. Jacobi complained that had he known of the plan to close the ports, he could have prevented 'enormous losses'.[96] 'My blood freezes', he wrote, 'at the sombre prospect of possible future misfortunes.'[97]

[88] Schrötter to Frederick William, 19.5.06, 'Acta des Kabinets König Friedrich Wilhelms III. Der Handelskrieg mit England und Schweden', GStA Rep.96A.4Aa2, fo. 58; copy of letter from Otto Petersen, captain of the Swedish frigate *Zarasmus*, before Pillau, 25.8.06, GStA Rep.96A.4Aa2, fo. 72. See also Immediatbericht of Stein, 1.9.06, Berlin, in Hubatsch and Botzenhart (ed.), *Stein*, vol. II/I (Stuttgart 1957–74), p. 263; Immediatbericht of Stein, 3.9.06, Berlin, ibid., p. 265.
[89] Krauel, 'Preussen und die zweite bewaffnete Meeresneutralität', p. 211.
[90] Jacobi report, 18.2.06, London, GStA Rep.XI.73.180C, fo. 69.
[91] Instructions for Jacobi, 24.3.06, Berlin, GStA Rep.XI.73.180C, fo. 107.
[92] Jacobi report, 25.3.06, London, GStA Rep.XI.73.180C, fo. 122.
[93] PS to Jacobi report, 8.4.06, London, GStA Rep.XI.73.180C, fos. 140–1; Jacobi report, 11.4.06, London, GStA Rep.XI.73.180C, fos. 142–3.
[94] Jacobi to Schulenburg (draft), 2.3.06, GStA Rep.XI.81.241, fo. 3.
[95] Jacobi report, 11.4.06, London, GStA Rep.XI.73.180C, fo. 142.
[96] Jacobi report, 24.4.06, London, GStA Rep.XI.73.180C, fo. 149.
[97] Jacobi report, 29.4.06, London, GStA Rep.XI.73.180C, fo. 185. For the importance of the Prussian timber trade with Britain see Astrom, 'Britain's timber imports from the Baltic', 58–59, 70.

But the damage was not confined to shipping alone. The Anglo-Prussian war of 1806 had potentially disastrous consequences for her largely agrarian economy. A very substantial amount of Prussian exports passed by way of the Danish Sound, now blockaded against her by British frigates. In 1805 Prussian exports from the Baltic ports of Danzig, Elbing, Stettin, Königsberg and Memel totalled over 27 million Reichstaler; this was 25 per cent more than in the previous year. The largest single item of export was grain, nearly all of which went to Britain. To the agrarian economy of East Elbia, this trade was of crucial importance, especially in years of record harvests such as 1806.[98] Even at the best of times the grain trade was a risky business, dependent on low customs dues and high British prices.[99] The same applied to the important wood trade, which was subject to huge price fluctuations.[100] In early April Stein predicted the likely results of a conflict with Britain: first, a glut of products from the Polish provinces, especially grain, in the ports, which would depress prices, and secondly, a crisis in the thread and yarn industry dependent on British raw materials and the lack of colonial produce.[101] It was not very long before these predictions were to be fulfilled.

Almost at once, the traders of the Baltic ports sought to bring their influence to bear upon the government. In late April, still comparatively early on in the crisis, grain merchants from Königsberg presented a cautiously worded petition to the crown. They were disquieted by the intense activity of the local British consuls and the rumours of British reprisals against Prussia. They could not fail to be alarmed by the warnings sent to British shipping as far afield as Memel and Pillau. How, they asked, could they reconcile the notices of British measures in newspapers from Hamburg with the assurances only recently given by the Prussian government? Should these fears of British reprisal come to pass, the petitioners emphasised, a great many trading houses would be threatened with ruin, indeed trade would be given a 'deadly blow'. In view of the fact that there were a large number of cargoes on their way to Prussia, numerous Prussian ships in British ports and many Prussian goods awaiting sale stored in British depots, the petitioners requested

---

[98] Struensee memorandum with enclosed figures, 8.2.1801, Berlin, GStA Rep.96A.4Aa1 *Preußischer Seehandel 1799–1806*, fo. 7. On the general background see Neugebauer, *Politischer Wandel*, ch. 5: 'Europäischer Markt und "Zweite Verwestlichung"', pp. 152–94.

[99] Kutz, 'Die Deutsch-Britischen Handelsbeziehungen', *VSWG*, 56 (1969), 197. See also Dwyer, 'Prussia and the Second Armed Neutrality', p. 10, on the grain trade.

[100] Kutz, 'Die Deutsch-Britischen Handelsbeziehungen', pp. 203–5.

[101] Francis Jackson to Fox, 3.4.06, Berlin, PROL FO 64/71, fo. 185.

enlightenment and reassurance as quickly as possible. In response, Beyme gave an assurance that His Majesty would do his very best to induce the British government to reverse their hostile measures against Prussian commerce and shipping, but that the supplicants 'should take their own precautions as best they could as further hostile measures were to be expected'.[102]

But it was now much too late to take effective precautions. This was explained by a Stettin merchant called Schultz, who warned that 'millions' would be lost and many traders ruined in the event of open war with Britain. No preparations could be made because most Prussian ships were already locked up in British ports and, in any case, insurance premiums had risen to dizzy heights.[103] To make matters worse, he added, the British measures had come at a bad time of the year. Four weeks ago the traders could have cancelled those orders made in faraway countries. Worrying too were the unconfirmed reports that British frigates were on their way to intercept Prussian shipping in the Baltic. The consequence, Schultz warned, was that Prussian commerce would be unable to move freely even in the Baltic. He instanced the case of several ships loaded with salt for the Danish navy and bound for Copenhagen which dared not risk leaving Swinemünde. There were also huge quantities of rye at Riga, which had already been paid for by Stettin merchants and which could not be collected. Indeed, so precarious had the situation become that Hamburg merchants had begun to refuse credit to Prussian traders. While denying any intention to interfere with state policy, the petition attempted precisely that, albeit couched in deferential terms. Whereas Frederick William was simply turning British ships away, Schultz pointed out, the British were seemingly detaining ships as well. Should Prussia not respond in kind, he asked? Attention was drawn to the valuable British goods stored in Hamburg, Lübeck, Bremen and even East Frisia, Frankfurt/Oder and Stettin. Schultz called for a royal proclamation of confiscation against them. Indeed, he even went so far as to advocate pressurising the Saxon government about the huge British depots in Leipzig if developments took a further turn for the worse.

These two instances are representative of the flood of similar petitions to the king which swamped the government between April and June

---

[102] Petition of the Königsberg traders Maulbars, Schultz, Rühser and Woltra to Frederick William, 23.4.06, Königsberg, GStA Rep.96A.4Aa2, fos. 12–13.

[103] Petition from the Stettin trader Schultz, 24.4.06, Stettin, GStA Rep.96A.4Aa2, fos. 14–15.

1806.[104] Though they were not all as forthright in prescriptive remedy as trader Schultz, they all outlined actual or feared commercial loss with the intention of influencing policy. 'The financial losses of its subjects', senior merchants in Berlin pointed out, 'are also a loss for the state itself, which cannot draw any revenue from impoverished subjects; it is therefore in every respect highly urgent that decisive measures be taken.'[105] The responsible privy councillor, Beyme, did his best to reassure the supplicants. On 5 May he wrote to another group of Königsberg petitioners: 'The supplicants may rest assured that everything that is any way compatible with the dignity of the state is being done to avert danger from the shipping and trade of his majesty's subjects.'[106] But by this stage the number of captured Prussian ships had climbed to the 300 mark and there was no sign of *rapprochement* with Britain. Clearly, the Prussian state was not going to change its policy in response to this kind of pressure.

The most powerful challenge to the policy which had led to war with Britain did not come from the grain merchants and shipping magnates of the Baltic. Instead, it came from inside the government, from the bureaucrats of the Generaldirektorium for whom the rapid collapse of Prussian commerce not only affected private interests but also constituted a body blow to the welfare of the state. These bureaucrats were, moreover, aggrieved that while at the highest levels of decision-making war with Britain had been weighed and taken into account, nobody had bothered to inform them, still less to ask their opinion.[107] If Jacobi could consider himself ill-informed by being notified a month after the signing of the Treaty of Paris, Baron von Stein, at that time the minister responsible for

---

104 See the more than forty petitions in GStA Rep. 96A.4A.a2, 'Der Handelskrieg mit England und Schweden 1806', fos. 5–71 (*passim*). Curiously, the relevant works on Prussian grain policy make no mention of the war with Britain and the events of 1806: Wilhelm Naudé, 'Die brandenburgisch-preußische Getreidehandelspolitik von 1713–1806', in [Schmoller's] *Jahrbuch für Gesetzgebung, Verwaltung und Volkswirtschaft*, 29 (1905), 161–90, especially 185–6; Skalweit, *Die Getreidehandelspolitik*.

105 Die ältesten der Kaufmannschaft, 27.4.06, Berlin, GStA Rep. 96A.4A.a2, fo. 21: 'Species facti über die gegenwärtige Lage der Handlung der königl. Preußischen Unterthanen.' This document contains the best account of the incompetence and indifference with which the political leadership treated commercial concerns during the Hanoverian crisis, especially fos. 16–20: 'Der Verlust des Vermögens der Unterthanen ist es zugleich für dem Staate selbst, der von verarmten Unterthanen keine Einkünfte ziehen kann; es ist also in jeder Hinsicht höchst dringend, daß entscheidende Maaßregeln genommen werden.'

106 Beyme's marginal note on the petition of the Königsberg traders Hoegg and Böhm, 'Leading representatives of the local shipping owners', 5.5.06, Königsberg, GStA Rep.96A.4Aa2, fo. 39.

107 See the very detailed account in Krauel, 'Stein während des preußisch-englischen Konflikts im Jahre 1806', pp. 431–2.

trade and excise could be forgiven his frustration at hearing, officially, a month later.[108] When the news of conflict with Britain finally did percolate through, the bureaucracy reacted at once.[109] However, it was only in early May, when the crisis was in full swing, that Stein began to receive anything like the level of information he needed.[110] By this time Stein had already initiated a private correspondence with Jacobi, bypassing Haugwitz, in order to obtain the intelligence vital to Prussian trade and shipping. He also asked Jacobi to make special representations on behalf of the Seehandlung in London for the export of rye, though without any success. It was one of many such secret relationships which were to take on an increasingly conspiratorial character as the Prussian state slipped further and further into humiliating impotence during the course of the summer.[111]

The bureaucracy now mounted a concerted campaign to reverse, or at the very least moderate, Prussian policy towards Britain. By the end of March, Friedrich von Schrötter, responsible for East Prussia, had sent Beyme an assessment of the likely effects of a British blockade.[112] In the following month Schrötter noted that: 'The complaints and the wailing of all classes practising a trade in Prussia are increasing all the time. In the meantime I am trying to calm the protesters by holding out the hope of better times.'[113] By the end of the month, he was being buried by a flood of petitions, protests and pleas for information coming in from the provinces. It should be remembered that these were in addition to those made directly to the crown. Since matters of government policy were not within Schrötter's competence, he passed them on to Haugwitz. In the meantime, he instructed the regional presidents, Auerswald in Pillau and Buddenbrock in Marienwerder, not to take any measures against British shipping until the outcome of further deliberations in Berlin had become

---

[108] Copy of Frederick William's letter informing Angern and Stein of the closure of the ports, 25.3.06, Berlin, GStA Rep.XI.140.c.3.50.fasc.2, fos. 187–8; Stein to Angern, 26.3.06, Berlin, in Hubatsch and Botzenhart (eds.), *Stein*, pp. 188–9; Ranke (ed.), *Denkwürdigkeiten Hardenbergs*, I, p. 527.

[109] E.g. the warning of Angern to the *Ostfriesische Kriegs- und Domänenkammern zu Aurich*, 27.3.06, Berlin, GStA Rep.96A.4Aa2, fo. 3.

[110] Immediatbericht of Stein, 18.4.06, Berlin, in Hubatsch and Botzenhart (eds.), *Stein*, p. 201; Circular of Stein to the *Kammern* of Stettin, Marienwerder, Königsberg and Aurich, 2.5.06, Berlin, ibid., p. 221; Stein to Haugwitz, 2.5.06, Berlin, ibid., p. 219.

[111] Stein to Jacobi, some time in late March/early April, Berlin, GStA Rep.XI.81.242, fo. 1.

[112] 'General Übersicht des gesamten Handels-Verkehrs in den preußischen Häfen Danzig, Elbing, Königsberg, Braunsberg und Memel', enclosed with letter from Schrötter to Beyme, 31.3.06, GStA Rep.96A.4Aa2, fos. 5–7.

[113] Schrötter to Frederick William, 5.5.06, GStA Rep.96A.4Aa2, fo. 35: 'Die Klagen und das Geschrey aller gewerbetreibenden Klassen in Preußen nehmen immer mehr zu; ich suche indeß die Klagenden mit der Hoffnung auf beßere Zeiten zu beruhigen.'

known. Clearly then, while the bureaucracy could and did attempt a damage limitation exercise, real disaster could only be averted by entering the political sphere.

The man who made this move into the political sphere was Baron von Stein himself. As minister for trade and excise his department was most affected by the blockade and he was best placed to assess its devastating consequences. Though he initially registered the closure of the ports without comment, the issue soon came to dominate his correspondence.[114] He was among the first to become aware of the consequences: 'Everywhere the greatest consternation (*Überall die größte Bestürzung*)' in the trading ports; the flight of British shipping to the protection of British warships at Cuxhaven; the collapse of the Silesian linen trade; and the enormous reluctance of brokers to insure Prussian goods.[115] In mid-April he made an approach to the king, outlining the effects of the blockade. The situation, he stressed, was much worse than in 1801, the immediate point of comparison. At present Britain could do without Prussian wood and grain because the Russian ports were open to them and because grain was cheaper in London than in Danzig. In other words, Stein argued, Britain was no longer under the same obligation to spare Prussian trade as she had been during the 1801 crisis. The worst should therefore be expected. He then went on to give the now familiar outline of Prussian trade and its likely losses.[116] The yearly profits of shipping owners totalled 21,282,230 Reichstaler; these would be lost. Worse still, Prussian manufacturers would be deprived of crucial British raw materials such as colouring agents, cotton and even salt. Reserves of these commodities were very low. Open war with Britain would mean that neutral traders would take over; there would be a massive loss of taxes and excise to the Prussian state. Stein's forceful recommendation at the end of the report thus came as no surprise: 'It is therefore of the greatest importance for the national wealth and for the whole internal economy and administration of the Prussian state, that a maritime war with Britain be avoided.'[117]

When the following week brought no response from the government, Stein decided to force the issue by calling for an extraordinary conference

---

114 Stein to Angern, 26.3.06, Berlin, in Hubatsch and Botzenhart (eds.), *Stein*, pp. 188–9; Immediatbericht of Stein, 18.4.06, Berlin, ibid., pp. 200–1; Stein to Haugwitz, 20.4.06, Berlin, ibid., p. 201.
115 Immediatbericht of Stein, 4.4.06, Berlin, ibid., pp. 190–1.
116 Immediatbericht of Stein, 18.4.06, Berlin, ibid., p. 200.
117 Immediatbericht of Stein, 18.4.06, Berlin, ibid., p. 200: 'Es ist also von der größten Wichtigkeit für das Nationalvermögen und für die ganze innere Oekonomie und Administration des preußischen Staates, einen Seekrieg mit England zu vermeiden.'

to discuss the 'total destruction of our important shipping industry, the stagnation in our import and export trade, the greatly impeded supply of the eastern provinces of the monarchy with salt [and] the significant losses in the collection of duties on imports by sea'.[118] It is perhaps not altogether remarkable that Haugwitz, who was responsible for all this, excused himself on the grounds of a 'sudden indisposition'. The conference, however, went ahead and it proved every bit the indictment of current Prussian policy that Haugwitz seems to have feared. To the participants, who in Haugwitz's absence were predominantly bureaucrats, the consequences of open war with Britain were 'incalculable'. They saw the only escape from the 'destruction of the state' in fresh negotiations with France, either to reverse completely the measures against Britain or at least to restore the circumstances of the 1803 occupation of Hanover. Further reprisals against Britain were to be avoided.[119]

By themselves these resolutions were worth nothing. Stein knew that real policy changes could only be achieved by bringing pressure to bear on the foreign minister, Count Haugwitz. Before the conference Stein had tried to persuade him to effect some 'modifications' in the Prussian stance, such as allowing trade in wood, linen and grain with the Baltic ports which could then be used to wrest concessions from the British.[120] When Haugwitz had obviously not bothered to reply, Stein pressed him, demanding to know what he had done about the 'political part' of the plan.[121] Stressing, once again, the dire consequences that a war would have for the welfare of state and subjects,[122] Stein demanded conciliatory moves towards Britain. It was not enough quietly to tolerate British shipping, as official policy prescribed; rather one should publicly proclaim the neutrality of the Baltic.[123] Some days later he was calling for the opening of the port of Emden to British shipping.[124] Despite all his efforts, however, Stein, and with him the Prussian bureaucracy as a

---

[118] Stein to Haugwitz, 20.4.06, Berlin, in Hubatsch and Botzenhart (eds.), *Stein*, p. 201: 'gänzliche Vernichtung unserer bedeutenden Reederei, Stockung in unsren Aus- und Einfuhrgeschäften, äußerst erschwerte Versorgung der östlichen Provinzen der Monarchie mit Salz, bedeutender Verlust an der Einnahme von Seezöllen'.

[119] Protocol of the conference of 25.4.06 at Berlin, attended by Voss, Schrötter, Angern and Stein, in Hubatsch and Botzenhart (eds.), *Stein*, pp. 204–5. See also Krauel, 'Stein während des preussisch-englischen Konflikts im Jahre 1806', pp. 437–8.

[120] Stein to Jacobi, written in late April, arrived 6.5.06, in Hubatsch and Botzenhart (eds.), *Stein*, pp. 203–4.

[121] Stein to Haugwitz, 4.5.06, Berlin, ibid., p. 222.

[122] Stein to Haugwitz, 5.5.06, Berlin, ibid., p. 223.

[123] Immediatbericht of Stein, 6.5.06, Berlin, ibid., p. 225; Stein to Haugwitz, 6.5.06, Berlin, ibid., p. 225.

[124] Stein to Haugwitz, c.10.5.06, Berlin, ibid., p. 231.

whole, was only able to effect minor changes in government policy. These included the decision not to confiscate British property in Prussia and the opening of Lübeck to British shipping.[125] Apart from the reciprocal lifting of the blockade on the Trave, no relaxation of the British grip on Prussian commerce resulted. By the following month Stein was forced to admit the futility of hoping that 'les personnes qui mènent ici les affaires extérieures' would manage to change the mind of the British government.[126]

This disregard of the economic consequences of the conflict with Britain was not simply due to pure indifference to the interests of Prussia's traders. After all, Jacobi was frequently instructed to make special representations on behalf of trading interests, most notably in the case of the Emden herring fishers.[127] The point is that though the protests of merchants and bureaucracy were not ignored, they were given low priority. While the government was eager to provide underhand assistance, for example through secret assurances to Britain or by trying to re-route Prussian shipping under Russian convoy cover,[128] any wavering in the public stance could bring an instant and fatal response from France. Haugwitz had set the tone in his memorandum of 19 April in which he preferred compensation of the traders to any change in policy.[129] This approach was formalised in a joint statement with Stein to a Memel trader: 'In view of the stagnation which has resulted for Prussian trade as a result of British measures, the whole trading community has equal right to support by the state.'[130]

The limits of bureaucratic and economic pressure group action are thus clear. While Stein could help traders to search for ways around the blockade and ways to minimise hardship,[131] in the last analysis their demands had to be referred to the high-political sphere. The merchants

---

[125] Stein to the trader F. L. MacLean in Danzig, 2.5.06, Berlin, ibid., p. 221; Immediatbericht of Haugwitz and Stein, 9.5.06, Berlin, ibid., p. 229.

[126] Stein to Jacobi, 6.6.06, Berlin, GStA Rep.XI.81.242, fo. 7.

[127] Jacobi report, 13.5.06, London, GStA Rep.XI.73.180C, fo. 207; Jacobi report, 27.5.06, London, Rep.XI.73.180C, fo. 233; Jacobi to Grenville, 27.5.06, London, BL Dropmore MSS 59059, fos. 52–3; Jacobi to Auckland, 26.5.06, London, BL Dropmore MSS 59059, fo. 54; Grenville to Jacobi, 29.5.06, London, BL Dropmore MSS 59059, fos. 55–6.

[128] Immediatbericht of Haugwitz and Stein, 9.5.06, Berlin, in Hubatsch and Botzenhart (eds.), Stein, p. 227.

[129] Haugwitz to Frederick William, 19.4.06, Berlin, GStA Rep.96A.4Aa2, fo. 11.

[130] Stein to the trader Moire in Memel, 9.5.06, Berlin, in Hubatsch and Botzenhart (eds.), Stein, p. 229: 'bei der Stockung, in welche der preußische Handel durch die von England ergriffenen Maßregeln gesetzt worden ist, hat der ganze Handelsstand gleiche Ansprüche auf die Unterstützung des Staates'.

[131] Stein to the state bank and the Seehandlung, 8.5.06, Berlin, ibid., p. 226.

of Stettin, for example, were told to expect 'that an amelioration of the present problems will be achieved by the Department of Foreign Affairs'.[132] In so doing the petitions left the domain of economic rationality and entered the political sphere. Here different rules applied and the petitioners were turned away. This was summed up by Haugwitz's response to a petition from the merchants of Stettin: 'If they [the traders] are trying to comment on political matters', he wrote to Stein, 'then this is not something that is fitting for traders to raise in a supplication to his majesty.'[133] His report of 26 April, penned to accompany, and nullify, the conclusions of the conference demanded by Stein, epitomises this process in other ways.[134] In it Haugwitz accepted that the situation was economically disastrous and should be ameliorated as much as possible. He also noted the call for negotiations with France to change policy towards Britain, but reserved to himself the right to make a separate report to the king on the matter in due course. In short, Haugwitz pleaded for a strict adherence to the pro-French policy, for *political* reasons. This course was not without an inner logic in the circumstances of 1806. In her precarious position Prussia could afford neither to allow the fury of some traders, who demanded reprisals against Britain, nor the calls of the vast majority for an end to the closure of the ports, to affect what was perceived to be the vital interests of the state. Further reprisals would have clashed with the secret policy of conciliation towards Britain in the aftermath of Paris, while a revocation of all measures against her would have destroyed the essential goodwill of France.

Secret du Roi: Frederick William and the parallel foreign policy

Isolated and practically friendless, Prussia now sought an understanding with Russia. In his letter to Alexander of 9 March, Frederick William drew attention to the universal monarchist pretensions of Napoleon, 'qui tendit à régner seul en Europe',[135] and stressed the need for an alliance to put an end to them. The difficulty was that such an alliance would be

---

[132] Stein to the elders of the Stettin traders, 23.4.06, Berlin, ibid., p. 204: 'daß durch das Departement der auswärtigen Angelegenheiten eine Ausgleichung der subsistierenden Mißverhältnisse wird bewirkt werden'.
[133] Quoted in Krauel, 'Stein während des preussisch-englischen Konflikts im Jahre 1806', p. 452.
[134] Haugwitz to Frederick William, 26.4.06, Berlin, GStA Rep.96A.4Aa2, fos. 22–3.
[135] Frederick William to Alexander, 9.3.06, Berlin, in Ranke (ed.), *Denkwürdigkeiten Hardenbergs*, I, pp. 544–6.

interpreted by France as a breach of the Paris treaty. Indeed it was strongly objected to on these and other grounds by Lombard, so that it needed all of the king's willpower to force the communication through.[136] From this realisation it was but a short jump to the idea that there should be a *secret* arrangement with Russia, known only to the king and selected politicians, which would serve as a kind of insurance policy against the day when the fragile understanding with France broke down. Through a stroke of good fortune one agent of such a policy was already on the spot in St Petersburg. This was the Duke of Brunswick, who had been dispatched in January with the thankless task of making the treaty of Paris palatable to the Russians and of offering Prussian mediation between Napoleon and the tsar.[137] His mission was now transformed into one of achieving a secret alliance with Russia.

Fortunately for Prussia, her desires were reciprocated by a tsar equally anxious for a 'most intimate union'.[138] In early March the Russians presented Brunswick with a set of proposals whose essence was to form the basis of the engagements contracted later in the summer. In order to pave the way for an immediate understanding, the Russians made four concrete suggestions. First of all, Prussia must not interpret her treaties with France in such as way as to act against Russia. That is, Prussia must refrain from intervening in a war arising out of either a Russian defence of the Ottoman Empire against French aggression, or a conflict occasioned by Russian attempts to remove the French from the Adriatic. Secondly, Prussia should guarantee the possessions of the Russian and Austrian emperors, the Ottoman empire, Sweden and the north of Germany. Thirdly, French troops were to be ejected from Germany within three months. Fourthly and lastly, no commercial restrictions were to be admitted apart from those in force during the French occupation of Hanover. In return the Russians undertook three things: to employ the largest part of their forces to defend Europe and Prussia against French attack; to remain 'disinterested', that is not to harbour any territorial ambitions; and finally to allow Prussia to continue her mediation policy between Napoleon and the tsar, and simulate good relations with France. Above all the Russians promised to keep the arrangement strictly secret.[139]

[136] Ibid., p. 546.
[137] Ibid., pp. 533–7; pp. 338–40.
[138] Alexander to Frederick William, 10.3.06, St Petersburg, in Bailleu (ed.), *Briefwechsel Alexanders*, p. 99; Goltz report, 8.3.06, St Petersburg, in Ranke (ed.), *Denkwürdigkeiten Hardenbergs*, I, p. 547.
[139] 'Mémoire pour S.A. le Duc de Brunswick', in Ranke (ed.), *Denkwürdigkeiten Hardenbergs*, I, pp. 552–63.

At a second conference held in the duke of Brunswick's townhouse and attended only by Frederick William, Hardenberg and the duke himself. The protocol shows that the Russian suggestions were accepted with only very minor alterations.[140] Some days earlier, Hardenberg had anticipated this result in his reply to Goltz's dispatch.[141] In it he set out the principles of a secret policy with Russia, which were to apply until the volte-face of the official policy in August rendered it defunct. Frederick William, Hardenberg wrote, was on course for a concert with Russia, but the matter was to remain a complete secret. Goltz was urged not to make any mention of it in his letters to Haugwitz or in his official reports to Frederick William. Hardenberg even suggested that Goltz should provide a sanitised version of Alexander's proposals to the king, in order to deceive Haugwitz. Hardenberg then went on to spell out the high political consequences of this strategy. In order to ensure the smooth functioning of the alternative foreign policy, Hardenberg would simulate his withdrawal from public affairs. This would conceal the secret policy from France: 'La France me croira dehors et son système d'autant plus affermi.'[142] In secret, however, Hardenberg would continue to see and advise the king. Thus his resignation in mid-April was far from being the beginning of a long spell in the political wilderness. Rather it formed part of an elaborate deception by which Hardenberg secretly maintained his grip on power and prepared the ground for his triumphal return. Indeed, it was only one day after he formally stepped down from his post as foreign minister that he received a coded summons to coordinate the next step in the secret policy with Russia.[143] Through an ironic twist it was now Hardenberg who moved 'behind the curtain' while his adversaries in the Kabinett, previously lambasted for exercising power without responsibility, were left with the meaningless shell of the official policy.

To compound the irony, Lombard, Beyme and Haugwitz were not even aware of the negotiations going on with Russia, let alone able to influence them. Elaborate and often somewhat comic security arrange-

[140] Hardenberg memorandum of 24.3.06, Berlin, in Ranke (ed.), *Denkwürdigkeiten Hardenbergs*, I, pp. 577–80.

[141] Hardenberg to Goltz, 20.3.06, Berlin, in Ranke (ed.), *Denkwürdigkeiten Hardenbergs*, I, pp. 565–8.

[142] Ibid., p. 566. Hardenberg 'diary', 18.3.06: 'Estaffete du Duc de Br[unswick] et de Golz sur la négociation secrette- écrit à la reine', GStA Rep. 92 *Hardenberg* L26, fo. 1. For the secret policy see also diary entries 19 March, 24 March (both fo. 1) and 20 April/13 June (both fo. 2). For a detailed account of the modalities of the secret policy see also the description in Alopeus to Czartoryski, 21.3.06, Berlin, in *Vneshnaya Politika*, pp. 88–90.

[143] Frederick William, 15.4.06, Berlin, GStA Rep. 92 *Hardenberg* E8, fo. 23.

ments ensured this.[144] Communications between Goltz and Hardenberg, or between Alopeus and the latter, went via von Seegebarth, president of the general post office and a man who could be trusted.[145] The crucial letters between the tsar and Frederick William passed via Alopeus and Hardenberg directly into the king's hands;[146] other avenues of communication were strictly forbidden.[147] Repeatedly, the recipients of letters were instructed, or asked, to destroy them.[148] Meetings between the leading protagonists were generally called through an intermediary such as the queen or her lady-in-waiting and were held well out of the public eye to avoid unwelcome publicity.[149] In this way the number of people in the know in Berlin was kept down to a bare minimum, including Hardenberg, Rüchel, Brunswick,[150] Alopeus, the queen and Frederick William. Of these only the king himself had a full picture of the state of play. While every communication to Frederick William passed via Hardenberg[151] he was not authorised to open them, with the result that he was left in the dark whenever a copy was not returned for his perusal.[152] On occasion he was to complain of a particular document or initiative, saying: 'je ne l'ai pas vue. S.M. m'a dit qu'elle n'était qu'en termes généraux'[153] or, asked whether somebody was privy to the secret,

---

[144] Alopeus to Hardenberg, 28.6.06, Berlin, GStA Rep.92 *Hardenberg* E9, fo. 55; Alopeus to Hardenberg, 17.8.06, Berlin, GStA Rep.92 *Hardenberg* E9, fo. 69; Goltz to Hardenberg, 4.4.06, St Petersburg, GStA Rep.92 *Hardenberg* E9, fo. 26.

[145] See Hardenberg diary 20.4.06: 'Parlé à Seegebarth ordre du roi la manière de me faire parvenir les lettres de la négociation secrette', GStA Rep. 92 *Hardenberg* L26, fo. 2. Covering note of von Seegebarth, 21.3.06, Berlin, GStA Rep.92 *Hardenberg* E9, fo. 11; Goltz to Seegebarth, 27.6.06, St Petersburg, GStA Rep.92 *Hardenberg* E9, fo. 64; Alopeus to Czartoryski, 21.3.06, Berlin, in *Vneshnaya Politika*, pp. 88–90; Hardenberg to Goltz, 2.7.06, Tempelberg, in Ranke (ed.), *Denkwürdigkeiten Hardenbergs*, II, p. 52.

[146] Hardenberg to Frederick William (copy), 3.10.06, Berlin, GStA Rep.92 *Hardenberg* E9, fo. 94.

[147] Hardenberg to Goltz (copy), 11.5.06, Cassel, GStA Rep.92 *Hardenberg* E9, fo. 38.

[148] Frederick William to Alexander, 23.6.06, Charlottenburg, in Bailleu (ed.), *Preussen und Frankreich*, p. 475; Alexander to Frederick William, 12.5.06, St Petersburg, in Bailleu (ed.), *Briefwechsel Alexanders*, p. 104; Alexander to Frederick William, 5.7.06, St Petersburg, ibid., p. 114. Fortunately for the historian, this injunction was not heeded in most cases.

[149] Griewank, 'Hardenberg und die preussische Politik', p. 196.

[150] For Brunswick's role in the secret policy and the duping of Haugwitz see Stern, *Karl Wilhelm Ferdinand*, pp. 321–30. Wilhelm Müller, 'Zur Geschichte des Herzogs Karl Wilhelm Ferdinand in den Jahren 1792 und 1806', *Braunschweigisches Jahrbuch*, 38 (1957), 95–115, is exclusively concerned with Brunswick's military activities in 1806.

[151] See Alopeus to Hardenberg, 3.6.06, Friedrichsfelde, in Ranke (ed.), *Denkwürdigkeiten Hardenbergs*, V, p. 322.

[152] See Hardenberg's complaints in Hardenberg to Frederick William (copy), 3.10.06, Berlin, GStA Rep.92 *Hardenberg* E9, fo. 94; Ranke (ed.), *Denkwürdigkeiten Hardenbergs*, II, p. 144.

[153] Ibid., V, p. 321.

'Le roi m'en dit rien.'[154] To Hardenberg this was a matter of great resentment and anxiety, especially in those cases when his opinion was not asked during a critical stage of the negotiations with Russia.[155]

The extreme secrecy surrounding the whole alternative policy with Russia was most evident whenever Great Britain was concerned. When first organising the *rapprochement* with Russia Hardenberg had stressed that 'Le secret est de toute nécessité.'[156] But with garrulous parliamentary Britain, no secret could be guaranteed. This fact severely complicated one of the aims of the Russian alliance, which was to gain the mediation of the tsar at London. The simplest way of ensuring a successful mediation, the Russians pointed out, was for the Prussians to give a secret written guarantee that Hanover would be returned. However, the Prussians were terrified that word of their secret understanding would leak out and place them in extreme jeopardy with France. As Hardenberg put it to Goltz on 11 May 1806:

l'indiscretion avec laquelle on publie à Londres les négociations les plus secrètes, dont nous avons des preuves récentes à l'égard de celles avec la Russie et l'Autriche et nouvellement avec la Prusse nous serons courir le plus grand danger et serons échouer le but commun si Napoleon, plus que jamais attentif à nos liaisons avec la Russie et ayant encore 200 h/m en Allemagne s'appercevait de notres intelligence secrètes, s'il se pressoit d'en prévenir les effets.[157]

These sentiments were repeated, in as many words, to the king himself. To inform Britain of the secret negotiation with Russia 'me paraissait très dangereuse, surtout dans les circonstances du moment, parce que les Anglais s'expliqueraient en plein Parlement et dans leur gazettes avec une très grande discretion sur les négociations très secrètes'.[158] This could prove fatal if it came to Napoleon's attention, as it surely would. In this respect the Prussian situation seemed only to differ in degree from that of another minor statelet, the duchy of Brunswick, whose prince, being privy to the secret negotiation with France, asked Hardenberg to return his letters, so as to ensure his 'existence politique'.[159]

Meanwhile, the official policy under Haugwitz persisted in its attempts to achieve some sort of amelioration in the Prussian position. These

---

[154] Hardenberg to Goltz, 2.7.06, Tempelberg, in Ranke (ed.), *Denkwürdigkeiten Hardenbergs*, II, p. 57.

[155] Ibid., II, pp. 91, 103, 40.

[156] Hardenberg to Queen Luise, 19.3.06, in Ranke (ed.), *Denkwürdigkeiten Hardenbergs*, I, p. 563.

[157] Hardenberg to Alopeus (copy), 11.5.06, Cassel, GStA Rep.92 *Hardenberg* E9, fo. 36.

[158] Hardenberg to Frederick William, 11.5.06, Cassel, in Ranke (ed.), *Denkwürdigkeiten Hardenbergs*, II, p. 7.

[159] Brunswick to Hardenberg, 31.3.06, Berlin, GStA Rep.92 *Hardenberg* E9, fo. 20.

efforts met with little success,[160] and by early July Jacobi was recalled, leaving behind only his assistant, Balan. Haugwitz's failure in his official attempts to obtain Russian mediation in the conflict with Britain can be put down to the workings of the secret policy. Goltz had, in fact, managed to secure the good offices of the tsar at a relatively early stage, but Haugwitz was kept ignorant of this. 'Ma dépêche officielle annonce un refus', Goltz wrote, 'il faut avoir l'air de s'en tenir à cela.'[161] Similarly, Hardenberg explained to Frederick William in mid-May that: 'Quoique dans une dépêche officielle, qui sans doute aura été communiqué au comte de Haugwitz, on rejette, pour mieux cacher l'intelligence secrète avec la Prusse, l'idée que la Russie puisse engager le ministère à agir avec modération, on s'empresse cependant de recommander aux employés russes à Londres de tâcher d'y disposer le gouvernement anglais.'[162] It is small wonder therefore that Haugwitz's efforts came to naught, and that by the summer he could still offer no visible improvement in the foreign-political predicament of Prussia.

Perhaps the most striking, though not the most serious, manifestation of Prussia's impotence in 1806 was the Swedish problem.[163] Relations with Sweden were essentially a subplot of the wider alienation from Britain and Russia, but during the summer they were to take on an autonomous importance. It is not clear whether Gustavus IV's decision to back George III over Hanover was his own initiative or solely under-taken at the instigation of Britain. The Prussians certainly believed the latter to be the case; in consequence, they initially refused to negotiate with Gustavus directly. Why talk to the Swedish monkey when you could deal with the British organ-grinder?[164] Relations with Sweden's fanatically anti-French king had always been poor, but the roots of this particular crisis went back to February 1806 when Gustavus had put

---

[160] Haugwitz to Goltz, 21.4.06, Berlin, GStA Rep.XI.175.156B, fo. 110; Haugwitz to Goltz, 25.4.06, Berlin, GStA Rep.XI.175.156B, fo. 112; Budberg report on meeting with Goltz, 5.6.06, St Petersburg, in *Vneshnaya Politika*, p. 210; Immediatbericht der Minister Haugwitz und Stein, 9.5.06, in Hubatsch and Botzenhart (eds.), *Stein.*, p. 227; Goltz report, 11.4.06, St Petersburg, GStA Rep.XI.175.156B, fo. 117; Goltz report, 21.4.06, St Petersburg, GStA Rep.XI.175.156B, fos. 131–3; Goltz report, 29.4.06, St Petersburg, GStA Rep.XI.175.156B, fo. 151; Balan report, 12.8.06, London, GStA Rep.XI.73.181A, fo. 59.
[161] Secret message attached to Goltz to Hardenberg, 4.4.06, St Petersburg, GStA Rep.92 *Hardenberg* E9, fo. 26.
[162] Hardenberg to Frederick William, 11.5.06, Cassel, in Ranke (ed.), *Denkwürdigkeiten Hardenbergs*, II, p. 4.
[163] Ullrich, *Die deutsche Politik König Gustavus*, pp. 98–9, does not cover 1806 in any detail.
[164] Instruction for Jacobi, 3.6.06, Berlin, GStA Rep.XI.73.180C, fos. 240–3; Jacobi report, 17.6.06, London, GStA Rep.XI.73.180C, fo. 262.

Hanover under Swedish protection[165] and announced his intention of occupying the province to the east of the Elbe.[166] Apart from the Swedish contribution to the blockade in the Baltic, the posturings of Gustavus posed little threat to Prussia in military terms. Indeed, when the two sides came to blows at Lauenburg during the summer, the Swedes beat a hasty retreat. Politically, however, the conflict was a considerable embarrassment to Berlin, for Russian protection, which the Prussians dared not disregard, enabled Gustavus to continue his provocations well into the autumn. To Frederick William, the perceived manipulation of Sweden by Britain was the cause of some bitterness.[167] 'L'Angleterre', wrote the Bavarian ambassador in Berlin, 'est bien aise de souffler encore sur ce petit reste de l'incendie du continent et elle voudrait encore au moins à bon marché des sottises des autres.'[168]

Far more significant, however, than the differences with Sweden was the question of Hanover itself. Here the secret policy proved no more successful than the public one in separating the issues of Hanover and the ports.[169] In order to have any chance of success, the Russians repeatedly argued that an intervention at London needed to be accompanied by a – secret – Prussian guarantee to return Hanover.[170] But surrender Hanover was one thing that the Prussians were determined not to do. The conference of 24 March, which had inaugurated the secret policy, had stressed that Hanover must be retained for strategic reasons.[171] In early June Frederick William had affirmed that while Hanover could not yet be officially considered Prussian territory, its acquisition was desirable on strategic grounds for purposes of consolidation and in order to secure her western border. In view of this uncharacteristically strong statement on the part of the king, it should come as no surprise that Hardenberg expressed himself in similar terms. 'Je déteste la manière dont nous avons fait l'acquisition du Hanovre', he told Goltz, 'mais je n'en sens pas moins

[165] Hardenberg to Haugwitz (draft), 6.2.06, Berlin, GStA Rep.XI.89.406, unfoliated.
[166] Hardenberg to Haugwitz, 16.2.06, Berlin, GStA Rep.XI.89.406, unfoliated.
[167] Frederick William to Alexander, 23.6.06, Charlottenburg, in Bailleu (ed.), *Preussen und Frankreich*, p. 474.
[168] Bray report on the Swedish–Prussian dispute, 22.7.06, Berlin, cited in Anders, 'Napoleon Bonaparte und die Beziehungen zwischen Preußen und Bayern', p. 45.
[169] Goltz to Hardenberg, 23.4.06, St Petersburg, GStA Rep.92 *Hardenberg* E9, fo. 27.
[170] Czartoryski dispatches and memoranda of 24 May, in Ranke (ed.), *Denkwürdigkeiten Hardenbergs*, II, pp. 12, 13, 17; Alopeus to Czartoryski, 15.6.06, Berlin, in *Vneshnaya Politika*, pp. 194–6; Czartoryski's report on a meeting with Goltz (26.6.06, St Petersburg, in *Vneshnaya Politika*, p. 203).
[171] Hardenberg memorandum of 24.3.06, Berlin, in Ranke (ed.), *Denkwürdigkeiten Hardenbergs*, I, pp. 578–9.

l'importance.'[172] The arguments for the annexation of Hanover were unchanged from the previous year and they remained essentially geopolitical. As Frederick William explained to the tsar, so long as the French held Holland, the fortified places on the Rhine and part of Westphalia, possession of Hanover was 'indispensable à la sûreté de la Prusse'.[173] It was needed, in short, to protect his dangerously exposed western territories. 'On n'a qu'à jeter un coup d'oeil sur la carte', he continued, 'et bien peser la position où la France se trouve et l'éloignement des forces puissantes que V.M. pourrait lui opposer.' He added that although annexation was of questionable legitimacy, it could not be foregone 'sans compromettre le salut de ma monarchie'.[174]

But there was one issue which could not be evaded for long: Russia or France? It should come as no surprise that Hardenberg counselled the former, both because he was aware of Frederick William's personal inclination towards the tsar and because to opt for France would have finally put an end to all hopes of a return to public office and favour. Yet Hardenberg was careful to conceal his preferences behind a cloud of deferential 'decisionist' rhetoric. It was the need to *decide*, not the direction of the decision with which he professed to concern himself. In his letter to Frederick William of 18 June, Hardenberg summed up the situation of Prussia in the following striking terms: 'Votre Majesté a été placé dans la situation singulière d'être à la fois l'allié de la Russie et de la France, de ce qu'il y a dans ce moment de plus hétérogène en politique . . . ', he wrote, 'Cet état ne peut pas durer.'[175] Consequently, the document continued, the king must opt between the two alliances and pursue that course to its logical conclusion. Hardenberg went on to put the case for this with astonishing emphasis on the act of *decision* itself: 'Je ne me permets aucune opinion sur ce choix important; mais j'ose énoncer celle qu'il faut bien décidément prendre l'un des deux et de suivre dès lors avec le plus grand zèle, que ce ne sera qu'après avoir pris cette décision d'une manière ferme et inébranlable.' Leaving all options open to the very end, Hardenberg did not rule out alliance with France, but stressed that it must be accompanied by further territorial gains and

---

172 Hardenberg to Goltz, 2.7.06, Tempelberg, in Ranke (ed.), *Denkwürdigkeiten Hardenbergs*, I, p. 53. See also the views expressed in Hardenberg to Frederick William, 7.6.06, Wolfsburg, 'copy' GStA Rep.92 *Hardenberg* E9, fo. 46; same letter in 'Acta betreffend die geheime Verhandlung mit Russland, 1806' GStA Rep.92 *Friedr. Wilh. d. Dritte* B.VI.18, fo. 18.
173 Frederick William to Alexander, 1.7.06, Charlottenburg, in Bailleu (ed.), *Briefwechsel Alexanders*, p. 110.
174 Ibid., p. 111.
175 Hardenberg memorandum of 18.6.06, Tempelberg, in Ranke (ed.), *Denkwürdigkeiten Hardenbergs*, II, p. 35.

an awareness of the danger of falling into a state of dependency on Napoleon. If, on the other hand, one opted for Russia, a conciliation with Britain must be sought. It was this logic which was the basis for the subsequent attempted *rapprochement* of September 1806.

Despite this effort at balance, however, it is clear from the context and the appended project of an alliance with Russia, that Hardenberg favoured the Russian option. This was not least because, as he put it to Frederick William, he knew an alliance with France to be 'contre le voeu de son coeur'. With this in mind it is remarkable that in retrospect, looking back over the document in 1807, Hardenberg still stood by its decisiveness and the possibility of an alliance with France. Even then, he stressed that *decision* for or against was more important than whether one decided for France or not.[176] Perhaps even more remarkably, he noted that Haugwitz had simultaneously begun to pursue the same policy in June, though ignorant of the secret agreement with Russia. For some days the decision was in abeyance. Finally on 26 June, after much prodding from Hardenberg,[177] Frederick William made his final decision to throw in his lot with Russia, as Hardenberg had always hoped he would. The amended Russian alliance project, the substance of which had been accepted by the king, went off on 1 July with an accompanying letter stressing that his commitments were dependent on his possession of Hanover.[178]

It remains a remarkable fact that the secret of the parallel foreign policy was kept until the deterioration of relations with France made it unnecessary to conceal it any longer. There were occasions, however, when the whole enterprise nearly came to grief. One such instance is best exemplified by the following letter from Haugwitz to Hardenberg in early May:

On returning from dinner I find two packets and a letter addressed to Count Goltz. I ask from whom? One tells me that they are from Mr Alopeus. Without a letter for me? No. In that case bring these packets back and say 'I couldn't accept them; I am sorry'. In view of the behaviour which Mr Alopeus has shown towards me what other response could I give? But you, my dear friend, could you think for a moment that the letter was addressed to you?[179]

He could, in fact, for Haugwitz had just inadvertently stumbled upon the secret foreign policy at work. But, seemingly confident in his own

---

[176] Ibid., p. 40.
[177] Ibid., p. 43.
[178] Frederick William to Alexander, 1.7.06, Charlottenburg, ibid., II, pp. 48–51.
[179] Haugwitz to Hardenberg, 2.5.06, Berlin, Rep. 92 *Hardenberg* E8, fo. 50 (not in any of the printed source collections).

ascendancy, he failed to realise the significance of the event. Later on in the summer he nearly discovered the scheme again by inquiring at the general post office about estaffetes which Hardenberg had been receiving. Seegebarth tried to fob him off by saying that it was just a communication relating to Franconian affairs, but it was clear that Haugwitz had become suspicious.[180]

Not only did the secret policy demand an enervating vigilance on the part of its practitioners, running parallel, as it did, to the official policy; it also exposed the Prussian state to perils of its own. Czartoryski seems to have been the first to put his finger on this when he pointed out 'que pendant qu'on expliquait avec le ministère secret, celui officiel allait toujours son train; qu'il entraînait la Prusse de faux pas en faux pas, et qu'a la fin les deux espèces sous lesquelles la Prusse paraissait alternativement s'embrouilleraient tellement, que ni la Russie, ni la Prusse ne sauraient en dernière analyse où elles sont l'une envers l'autre'.[181] This is a graphic description of the situation of Prussia in 1806. While the secret policy ran its course, the official policy dug Prussia into a deeper and deeper hole. Perhaps the most difficult task was faced by Goltz as ambassador in St Petersburg. He had to run the secret policy, in which he was responsible to Hardenberg, and purposely keep Haugwitz in the dark, while in his official capacity he was instructed to protest publicly at Russian criticisms of Haugwitz. Hardenberg played down these problems, arguing that, though they undoubtedly existed, Prussian official policy 'n'est pas en opposition avec cet accord secret et que par conséquent il s'agira bien rarement d'un double langage, qu'il sera question plutôt de réticences dans les dépêches ordinaires'.[182] As the summer wore on, however, it became clear that not only were the two policies increasingly incompatible, but that it was becoming more and more impractical to run them simultaneously without the involvement of Haugwitz. By late July the strain on Goltz had become very marked. In the long run, he argued, the contradiction between the official and the secret policies could only lead to great inconveniences. Indeed, he now often found himself in the situation of not knowing 'quel bois faire flèche'[183] and warned that he would need to be very fortunate indeed if he were not to end by compromising himself.

---

[180] As reported by Alopeus to Hardenberg, 17.8.06, Berlin, GStA Rep.92 *Hardenberg* E9, fo. 69.

[181] Protocol of a meeting between Czartoryski and Goltz, 9.5.06, in Ranke (ed.), *Denkwürdigkeiten Hardenbergs*, V, p. 325.

[182] Hardenberg to Goltz (copy), 11.5.06, Cassel, GStA Rep.92 *Hardenberg* E9, fo. 38.

[183] Goltz to Hardenberg, 27.7.06, St. Petersburg, in Ranke (ed.), *Denkwürdigkeiten Hardenbergs*, II, p. 100; similar arguments in Goltz to Hardenberg, 21.8.06, St Petersburg, ibid., II, pp. 129–132.

A closer look at the details and subplots of the secret policy shows why Hardenberg was so keen to maintain it. Deprived of control of the 'ostensible' policy by Haugwitz and the enmity of France, he seized upon the Russian initiative in March 1806 to further his own personal political ends. These were to undermine the position and policy of his rival and to prepare the way for his own return to power. The secret policy, which cut across the designs of Haugwitz's official policy, and brought Hardenberg back into direct and frequent contact with the king, was ideally suited to this purpose. If, on the face of it, Haugwitz appeared to have the stronger hand in his enjoyment of French support, Hardenberg used his Russian connection to counteract this.[184] In some cases, such as the mediation in London, the Russians willingly conceded to Hardenberg what they had refused to Haugwitz, thus undermining the latter still further. Indeed, on more than one occasion the Russians indicated an unwillingness to help Prussia *vis à vis* Britain as long as Haugwitz was in power.[185] According to Goltz, the motivation behind this was the desire to boost Hardenberg by refusing to help Haugwitz out of the predicament into which he had manoeuvred himself and the Prussian state. But the enthusiastic support of the Russians for Hardenberg manifested itself most strikingly in the increased pressure on Frederick William for Haugwitz's removal. When Count Stackelberg was sent to mediate between Prussia and Sweden, Czartoryski pointedly wanted him presented to Count Keller, who was at the time being considered as a possible co-foreign minister, rather than to Haugwitz.[186] In early June Alopeus went so far as to suggest that Haugwitz be replaced by Count Keller.[187]

Although this strategy was one that corresponded, in any case, to the objective needs of Russian foreign policy, it is equally true that Hardenberg actively encouraged and coordinated the moves being made on his behalf. This had been agreed in early May, when Alopeus wrote to Hardenberg that the only way to *conjurer l'orage* was 'en éloignant Haugwitz fut-ce même sous un pretexte'.[188] Several months later, Hardenberg wrote a revealing marginal note on a letter from Alopeus: 'NB: l'éloignement de Cte de Haugwitz dont il doit être question dans la

---

[184] For Hardenberg's relations with Russians see the warm and flattering letter of Alexander to Hardenberg, 12.4.06, St Petersburg, GStA Rep. 92 *Hardenberg* J2, fo. 138.

[185] Protocols of two meetings between Czartoryski and Goltz, 9.5.06 and 18.5.06, both St Petersburg, in Ranke (ed.), *Denkwürdigkeiten Hardenbergs*, V, pp. 326, 329.

[186] Ibid., pp. 330–1.

[187] Czartoryski to Alopeus, 24.5.06, St Petersburg, in Ranke (ed.), *Denkwürdigkeiten Hardenbergs*, V, p. 322.

[188] Alopeus to Hardenberg, 5.5.06, Berlin, GStA Rep.92 *Hardenberg* E9, fo. 34.

lettre de l'empereur au roi.'[189] This demonstrates beyond all doubt the way in which Hardenberg attempted to turn the Russian connection to his own advantage. Ultimately, however, these stratagems were frustrated by the obduracy of the king who clung to his foreign minister despite mounting pressure throughout the summer. The numerous Russian overtures to have Haugwitz dropped, made either directly or via Goltz, and often coupled to express requests for the re-employment of Hardenberg, went unheeded.[190] Thus in late August Hardenberg attempted to use a laudatory report from Goltz to press his case for an official recall, though he stressed that he did not want to be reinstated by an outside agency.[191] However, though Frederick William took the approach in good heart, Hardenberg got nowhere. Indeed, the king was so upset by the long-standing feud between Haugwitz and Alopeus[192] that he pressed for the recall of the latter, something which put Goltz in the deeply embarrassing situation of delivering an official protest against a pillar of the secret policy. One problem for Hardenberg lay in the fact that, by its very nature, the secret policy ruled out his public return to power, for that would have been to give the game away to France. It stands to reason, therefore, that it was in Hardenberg's interest ultimately to steer for a public breach with Napoleon, for, as he himself noted in a letter to Goltz, he could not be recalled while Prussia was still publicly on good terms with France.[193] By the end of September the secret policy had outlived its purpose and it should be no surprise to find Hardenberg among those pressing for a confrontation when the time came. War with France thus became simply the continuation of high politics by other means.

---

[189] Hardenberg's marginal note on Alopeus to Hardenberg, 2.10.06, Berlin, GStA Rep.92 *Hardenberg* E9, fo. 91.
[190] Alopeus to Hardenberg, 4.9.06, Berlin, GStA Rep.92 *Hardenberg* E9, fo. 77; Alexander to Frederick William, 5.7.06, St. Petersburg, in Bailleu (ed.), *Briefwechsel Alexanders*, p. 114; Alexander to Frederick William, 12.9.06, St Petersburg, in Bailleu (ed.), *Briefwechsel Alexanders*, p. 125; Goltz to Hardenberg, 21.8.06, St Petersburg, in Ranke (ed.), *Denkwürdigkeiten Hardenbergs*, p. 132.
[191] Hardenberg to Frederick William, 31.8.06, Tempelberg, ibid., II, p. 134.
[192] Haugwitz to Goltz (draft), 9.5.06, Berlin, GStA Rep.XI.175.156B, fo. 146; Alopeus to Hardenberg, 3.6.06, Friedrichsfelde, in Ranke (ed.), *Denkwürdigkeiten Hardenbergs*, V, p. 322.
[193] Hardenberg to Goltz, 11.9.06, Tempelberg, ibid., II, p. 141.

Part III

The responses

8 Facing Napoleonic France: Prussian responses to the French threat, 1804–1806

The primacy of foreign policy and the 'imperious dictates of geography': Prussia confronts the French threat, October 1804 to June 1806

Throughout the period 1804 to 1806 Prussian statesmen remained preoccupied by foreign affairs; domestic matters continued to be entirely subordinate. Indeed, in times of extreme external peril Prussian foreign policy was formulated without consulting, and without reference to, sectional interests. Reinhard Koselleck's contention that the monarch could not undertake anything against the will of the bureaucracy,[1] is thus in need of revision. As the events of the Hanoverian crisis demonstrated, the protests of powerful interest groups such as the Baltic grain merchants and the bureaucracy could be overridden when the higher interests of the state were at stake.[2] It may be, to borrow the vulgar Marxist characterisation of Fritz Eisner, that Prussian bureaucrats were motivated by the 'patriotism of the grain trade', or were merely serving the 'economic interests' of the nobility when they demanded a *rapprochement* with Britain.[3] But the patriotic instincts of Prussian statesmen – estate-owners almost to a man – told them that commercial ruin was a small price to pay when faced with immediate extinction at the hands of France. Moreover, despite looming economic disaster, the grain-producing East Elbian agrarian elites do not seem to have made any attempt to reverse the policy of confrontation with Britain;[4] if they did, it was entirely unsuccessful.

The extreme reluctance of the Junkers to challenge the state over foreign policy was highlighted by the fate of von der Marwitz's philippic

[1] Reinhard Koselleck, *Preußen zwischen Reform und Revolution*, p. 278.
[2] Neither Schissler, *Preußische Agrargesellschaft im Wandel*, nor Berdahl, *The politics of the Prussian nobility*, refer to the importance of the Hanoverian crisis in defining the relationship between state and socio-political interest groups in pre-Reform Prussia.
[3] Eisner, *Das Ende des Reichs*, p. 250.
[4] Neither Vetter, *Kurmärkischer Adel*, nor Neugebauer, *Politischer Wandel*, nor the records of the Kabinettsministerium, make any mention of such a challenge.

against the policy of appeasement towards France. This remonstrance was drafted in the summer of 1806 and read to the assembled Landschaft of the Kurmark by the local Landrat.[5] The preamble was carefully worded. Under normal circumstances, Marwitz wrote, it would be 'an impertinence to try to anticipate the decisions of the monarch'. But even this was too radical for the Landschaft. 'There was no sense [among the assembled state-owners]', Marwitz noted sadly, 'that such a measure might be necessary and admissable (Es ist gar kein Begriff davon anzutreffen gewesen daß so eine Maßregel notwendig und erlaubt sein könne)'. In short, while the nobility possessed a network of local committees in which their socio-economic interests could be aired, there were no representative fora through which foreign policy could be criticised; the notion of converting existing institutions into such a mechanism still exceeded the mental horizons of most Junkers. In this respect the governing compromise of the seventeenth century, the strict separation between the socio-political and high-political spheres, persisted.

At the same time, Prussian statesmen were largely untroubled by the threat of popular unrest. This is not to say that the rural and urban lower orders remained quiescent; far from it. In the provincial town of Halle, for example, food riots erupted during the early summer of 1805. For several days the mob – largely artisans – rampaged unchallenged through the streets, looting warehouses and attacking suspected profiteers; the local police and military found themselves overwhelmed.[6] Within a fortnight the disturbances had spread to nearby Aschersleben and Halberstadt.[7] These events caused the authorities considerable concern. 'The matter itself causes me no disquiet', wrote Schrötter in an initial report, 'but the way in which people behaved and the resulting consequences do unsettle me.'[8] One month later Goldbeck stressed that the matter should be dealt with severely 'because a popular tumult of this sort constitutes a blatant attack on the basis of every political order and constitutes such an attack on persons and property that any extenuating

---

[5] Friedrich August von der Marwitz, 'Entwurf einer Vorstellung der Kurmärkischen Stände an den König, Sommer 1806', in Meusel (ed.), *Marwitz*, II; pp. 132–4.
[6] See the vivid description of the senior citizens Steltzer, Lichotius, Goldhagen, Heisler, Heydrich et al., 15.6.1805, Halle, GStA Rep. 96A.128E, fo. 4. For the extreme poverty caused by the grain shortage of 1804–5 see W. Naudé, 'Brandenburgisch-preußische Getreidehandelspolitik von 1713–1806', pp. 185–6.
[7] On Aschersleben: Schrötter and Dietherdt to Frederick William, 27.6.1805, Berlin, ibid., fo. 7; on Halberstadt: Goldbeck report, 6.12.1805, ibid., fo. 48.
[8] Schrötter report, 20.6.1805, Ibid., fo. 1: 'Die Sache selbst beunruhigt mich nicht, wohl aber die Art wie man sich dabey genommen . . . und wegen die daraus zu besorgenden Folgen.'

circumstances – however valid they may be in any other case – are not applicable here'.[9] Moreover, Goldbeck believed that the investigative commission had placed too much emphasis on the 'crushing poverty (erdrückende Armuth)' in Halle, whereas in fact the situation there was no worse than in other parts of the monarchy equally affected by rising prices. Yet worrying though these events may have been, the impact on 'high' policy was minimal. The developments in Halle-Aschersleben were undoubtedly a spectacular example of a spontaneous moral economy in the Prussian province, but when measured against the incomparably greater foreign-political perils of the state, they constituted little more than a minor irritation.

The same could not be said of Poland, where internal unrest continued to possess a strong foreign-political dimension. As in the previous decade, there was a strong likelihood that conflict with Napoleon would be accompanied by a French-inspired Polish revolt. In November 1805, for example, Haugwitz noted the arrival of the Polish patriot Kosciuzko at the French headquarters with some concern. 'Tout semble être préparé', he warned Frederick William, 'pour jetter le bradon de la Revolution.'[10] Haugwitz would have been even more alarmed had he known of the well-advanced Russian project to expand Poland at Prussia's expense. This scheme – known to a later generation of Prussian historians as the 'murder plan' (Mordplan) – was the brainchild of the Tsar's Polish-born foreign minister, Count Czartoryski; his long-term aim was the creation of an independent Poland, albeit under Russian tutelage.[11] In its most extensive form, the Mordplan envisaged not merely

---

9 Goldbeck report, 1.8.1805, Berlin, ibid., fo. 12: 'weil durch einen Volksaufstand dieser Art, die Basis jeder Staatsordnung aufs gröbste verletzt und Sicherheit der Person und des Eigenthums dergestalt angegriffen ist, daß jeder in anderen Fällen noch so gültige Milderungsgrund – bey den Anstiftern und Haupttheilnehmern wenigstens – von dieser Rücksicht verschwinden muß'. See also Herzig, Unterschichtenprotest in Deutschland, p. 75. For disturbances in Silesia see Ziekursch, Hundert Jahre schlesischer Agrargeschichte, p. 247.

10 Haugwitz to Frederick William, 21.11.1805, Prague, GStA Rep.XI.89.402, unfoliated. In a similar vein see also Hardenberg's memorandum of 12.3.1805, GStA Rep.XI.89.400, fo. 7.

11 The best recent discussion of the Mordplan is to be found in W.H. Zawadzki's judicious new biography: Czartoryski, especially pp. 126, 131, 130 (re Königsberg) and pp. 148–50 (re 1806). For older German views see Oncken, Das Zeitalter der Revolution, II, p. 157 and Ulmann, Russisch-preussische Politik, pp. 252–61. For the subsequent history of the Mordplan see Hans Delbrück, 'Die Frage der polnischen Krone und der Vernichtung Preussens in Tilsit', Studien und Versuche zur neueren Geschichte. Max Lenz gewidmet (Berlin, 1910), pp. 315–36. Curiously the polonophile Zernack makes no mention of the scheme in his 'Polen in der Geschichte Preussens', in Otto Büsch (ed.), Handbuch der preussischen Geschichte. Vol. II: Das 19 Jahrhundert und große Themen der Geschichte Preußens (Berlin and New York, 1992), pp. 377–448.

the restoration of the old Polish borders of 1772, but also the annexation of such old areas of German settlement as Königsberg in East Prussia. As it happened, the plan came to nothing, largely because it was only relevant in the event of a Russo-Prussian war, which was averted by the Treaty of Potsdam. This did not prevent Czartoryski from periodically trying to resuscitate the scheme throughout 1806, with some British encouragement, when the Anglo-Prussian commercial war seemed to offer an opportunity for a joint British–Russian–Swedish campaign against Prussia. All this goes to show that just because the Prussians were paranoid does not mean that neighbouring states were not out to get them.

The greatest threat to Prussian security, of course, continued to be Napoleonic France. This danger was conceived in purely power-political terms; any ideological antipathy had long since receded.[12] 'We don't want to interfere in the internal affairs of France',[13] Hardenberg stressed and there is no evidence that any senior Prussian statesmen harboured restorationist aims towards France in the years 1804 to 1806. Indeed, the Prussians noted with relief that neither the British, nor the Russians had such (Bourbon) restorationist ambitions towards France and were simply concerned for 'le rétablissement de l'ordre general et de l'équilibre nécessaire pour le repos durable de l'Europe'.[14] Rather, they were alarmed at the lack of any obvious limits to Napoleonic ambitions. After a relatively tranquil year, the shock of the Rumbold affair in late October 1804 was a portent of things to come. 'It is clear', Hardenberg told Metternich, 'that the fool, who leads the most powerful empire on the continent is aiming for world domination; he wishes to accustom us all to regard ourselves as his subjects who must accommodate his every whim.'[15] Indeed, fears that Napoleon was planning to establish a 'universal monarchy' – already present before 1804 – began to multiply among Prussian statesmen. In Dresden, the Prussian envoy Brockhausen warned of Napoleon's plans to become a 'new Charlemagne'.[16] In

---

[12] See also Simms, 'Fra Land e Meer', pp. 18–19.

[13] Hardenberg memorandum, 12.3.1805, Berlin, GStA Rep.XI.89.400, fo. 9: 'In die inneren Angelegenheiten Frankreichs will man sich nicht mischen.'

[14] Jacobi report, 23.10.04, London, GStA Rep.XI.73.England 178B, fo. 126. In the same vein the instructions for Jacobi, 12.11.04, Berlin, ibid., fo. 130.

[15] Metternich dispatch of 18.10.1804, cited in Oncken, Das Zeitalter der Revolution, p. 10: 'Es ist klar, der Narr, der sich an der Spitze des mächtigsten Reiches auf dem Festlande befindet, geht auf die Weltherrschaft los, er will uns alle daran gewöhnen, uns als Angehörige seiner Domäne zu betrachten, die sich jedem seiner tollen Einfälle zu beugen haben.' See also Hardenberg's memorandum of 30.10.1804, in Wohlwill, 'Fernere Aktenstücke', p. 204.

[16] Brockhusen, Carl Christian Friedrich von Brockhausen, p. 48.

London, the shock of the Rumbold affair prompted Jacobi to warn of the danger of being treated 'comme un des vassaux couronné de l'Empereur Napoléon';[17] almost two years later he once again cautioned against the 'torrent du système de domination universelle du Cabt. des Tuilleries'.[18] In Berlin, Hardenberg spoke of the 'extension progressive et tout à fait incalulable, de ses vues de conquête et de domination'.[19] These fears were not allayed by Napoleon's own rhetoric: in February 1806 he informed the pope that he was now effectively the new Charlemagne, as he held the crown of France conjointly with that of the Lombards.[20]

French hegemonic pretensions generated three distinct responses in Prussia. First of all, there was the initially small and politically impotent, but growing number of figures demanding outright resistance to Napoleon; of them, more presently. Secondly, there was a vociferous but uninfluential group of 'Napoleonists', who enthusiastically embraced the notion of a French-dominated universal monarchy. Typical among them were such figures as Friedrich Buchholz and Colonel Massenbach, who confessed that 'Napoleon seemed a superior being to me . . . the military greatness of Napoleon had seduced me.'[21] In Germany as a whole such views were typified by the imperial arch chancellor Reichserzkanzler Dalberg, who looked to Napoleon as the new protector of the Reich.[22] Thirdly, there was the majority school of thought, which registered French hegemony with pragmatic resignation. If Haugwitz, Hardenberg,

---

[17] Jacobi to Hardenberg, 16.11.04, London, GStA Rep. 92 *Hardenberg* E5, fos. 182–3.
[18] Jacobi report, 22.7.06, London, GStA Rep.XI.73.181A, fo. 33.
[19] Instructions for Jacobi (Hardenberg), 22.2.1806, Berlin, GStA Rep.XI.73.180C, fo. 62. See also Hardenberg to Haugwitz, 3.12.1805, Berlin, GStA Rep.XI.89.400, unfoliated; Hardenberg to Haugwitz, 6.2.1906, Berlin, GStA Rep.XI.89.406; Hardenberg to Goltz, 2.7.1806, in Ranke (ed.), *Denkwürdigkeiten Hardenbergs*, II, p. 51.
[20] Burgdorf, 'Redundanz und Regression verfassungspolitischer Bemühungen. Die Deutschlandpläne des Erzbischofs von Taurus' (MSS in possession of author), p. 19; Stuart Woolf, *Napoleon's integration of Europe* (London and New York, 1991), especially p. 25; Simms, 'Fra *Land* e *Meer*', pp. 20–1. For the extent of French ambitions see Kurt von Raumer, 'Politiker des Maßes? Talleyrands Strassburger Friedensplan, 17 Oktober 1805', *HZ*, 193 (1961), p. 286 and *passim*; on the clash between universal monarchist pretensions and the *Kaiseridee* see Heinrich Ritter von Srbik, 'Das Österreichische Kaisertum', pp. 151, 331–3; Schroeder, *Transformation of European politics*, p. 291. On universal monarchy see also Dreitzel, *Monarchiebegriffe*. Vol. I: *Semantik der Monarchie*, pp. 182–93.
[21] Massenbach, *Memoiren zur Geschichte des preussischen Staates*, III, p. 132: 'Napoleon erschien mir ein Wesen höherer Art . . . Die militärische Größe Napoleons hatte mich bestochen.' On Buchholz see Kurt Bahrs, *Friedrich Buchholz. Ein preussischer Publizist 1768–1843* (Berlin, 1907). For the extent to which German admiration for Napoleon endured see Roger Dufraisse, 'Die Deutschen und Napoleon im 20. Jahrhundert', *HZ*, 252 (1991), 587–625. See also Hans Schmidt, 'Napoleon in der deutschen Geschichtsschreibung', *Francia*, 14 (1980), 530–60, on German historiography of Napoleon.
[22] See Burgdorf, 'Redundanz und Regression', *passim*.

Lombard and Beyme all harboured various degrees of personal admiration for Napoleon, they were in no doubt that Frederick William's temperament – and Prussia's own geopolitical position – did not allow for more than an unenthusiastic policy of accommodation with France. A good example of this stance was Altenstein's memorandum of December 1805, which was also a précis of Hardenberg's own views.[23] Napoleon, he argued, had 'taken up the old idea of Universal Monarchy with the irresistible force of a genius'; Altenstein also spoke of the 'fruitlessness' of opposing him. Indeed, Altenstein continued, the old balance of power in Europe was wrecked beyond repair. Prussia should therefore recognise French supremacy and try to carve out her own niche in northern Europe, within the wider framework of a Napoleonic universal monarchy. By early 1806 the need to appease France was undisputed. It was pointless, Haugwitz argued, to continue to 'lutter contre le torrent' of Napoleonic power.[24] This meant that each new French encroachment, far from provoking determined resistance, merely accelerated the desire for a quick settlement in Europe, however advantageous to Napoleon.[25] It was this same basic fear of French power that lay behind the decision to risk war with Britain in 1806. To contemporary critics in the bureaucracy it seemed like bumbling incompetence; in retrospect it was clearly the fruit of a cold-blooded assessment of available options. Everything, as Frederick William had assured Jacobi, had been 'pesé et senti. Mon parti est pris.' Given the magnitude of the French threat it is difficult to see what else Prussian statesmen could do, but 'sauver l'essentiel quoi qu'il peut coûter'. Theirs may not have been an honourable choice, but it was certainly a rational one.

If Prussian statesmen found themselves increasingly embattled throughout 1804 to 1806, it was because the fundamental geopolitical situation of the monarchy had remained unchanged. Prussia continued to be 'surrounded by the larger, more powerful empires of Russia, Austria and France'.[26] So nobody disputed Lombard's view that 'Les conditions du concours de la Prusse sont impérieusement dictées par sa position

---

23 Printed in Ernst Müsebeck, 'Fragmentarische Aufzeichnungen Altensteins über die auswärtige Politik Preussens vom 28/29 Dezember 1805', *FBPG*, 28 (1915), 139–73.
24 Instructions for Jacobi, 18.4.1806, Berlin, GStA Rep.XI.73.180C, fo. 132.
25 Frederick William to Alexander, 14.7.1805, in Bailleu (ed.), *Briefwechsel*, p. 67; Jacobi report, 28.2.1806, London, GStA Rep.XI.73.180C, fo. 80; Instructions for Jacobi, 10.3.1806, Berlin, ibid., fo. 79.
26 Anon. memorandum, 'Über Preußens politische Lage', 16.6.1806, GStA Rep. 92 *Friedr. Wilh. d. Dritte* B.VI.22, fo. 27: 'von den Staaten der Größeren, mehr mächtigeren Kayserthümer Rußland, Oesterreich und Frankreich umschloßen'.

géographique.'[27] Just how imperious these dictates were is proved by the omnipresence of geopolitical themes in every major Prussian foreign policy debate before Jena, most notably during the Rumbold affair, during the Anglo-Russian alliance overtures of 1805, and at the time of the treaties of Potsdam and Schönbrunn. Time and again we have seen Prussian statesmen enjoin each other 'to look at the map'; time and again, these statesmen emphasised Prussia's geopolitical 'exposure' and its resulting 'paralysis'; and time and again they revealed a deep-seated fear of losing themselves in the 'labyrinth' of European politics. The continuing policy of neutrality was a direct reflection of these fears. By nailing his colours firmly to the fence, Frederick William hoped to steer a 'middle way' – a *terme moyen* – between Napoleon and the allied powers. To this end he ritually affirmed his determination 'neither to permit French oppressions nor to fight for England and her allies'; at the same time he vowed not to allow Napoleon to 'enchain [him] feet and fingers tied, to the cause and interests of France'.

But if the policy of neutrality were to be sustained, two geopolitical imperatives had to be fulfilled. The first imperative – as ever – was the demilitarisation of northern Germany. 'The main purpose of my policy', Frederick William had written to General Knobelsdorff on the eve of the Rumbold affair, 'is to maintain the tranquillity of the north.'[28] Throughout 1805 this concern underlay Prussian reservations towards the Third Coalition, her extraordinary sensitivity towards rumours of an impending exchange of Swedish Pomerania, and her objections to any allied military activity in Hanover. Indeed, eighteen months after his letter to Knobelsdorff, the king was still searching for 'ce terme moyen . . . pour obtenir mon grand but: la sûreté du Nord de l'Allemagne'.[29] But in order to achieve that security, Prussia had to confront a second imperative arising out of her central geographic location. This was the need to monitor and, if possible, manage the Russo-French relationship. On the one hand, there was the obvious danger that Prussia would be caught in the crossfire in the event of a Franco-Russian split. It was for this reason, as Lucchesini had put it, that Prussia tried to avoid a

---

[27] Lombard memorandum, 24.10.1804, in Ranke (ed.), *Denkwürdigkeiten Hardenbergs*, I, p. 312.

[28] Frederick William to Knobelsdorff, 20.10.1804, Potsdam, in Bailleu (ed.), *Preussen und Frankreich*, II, p. 303: 'Die Ruhe im Norden zu erhalten, ist der Hauptzweck meiner Politik.' See also Hardenberg to Haugwitz (draft), 17.11.1804, GStA Rep. 92 *Hardenberg* E5, fo. 184.

[29] Instructions for Jacobi, 24.3.1806, Berlin, GStA Rep.XI.73.180C, fo. 106. See also 'Denkschrift Haugwitz über den Schönbrunner Vertrag nebst einem Projekt einer Konvention zur Sicherung der Ruhe von Norddeutschland', 26.12.1805, GStA Rep.XI.89.404, unfoliated.

situation where 'les deux terribles rivales, la France et la Russie, cherchant des points de contact pour s'atteindre, ne laisseront plus à la Prusse, leur voisine respective, que la liberté du choix du parti à prendre entr'elles'.[30] On the other hand, Franco-Russian relations might become *too* cordial, at Prussia's expense. Both fears were forcefully articulated by Hardenberg in March 1805. 'Prussia', he argued, 'is less powerful than France, Russia, Austria and is under pressure from the first two and is embarrassed by a quarrel between them. The friendship of both powers is necessary for her security and tranquillity.'[31] Yet if France and Russia were to unite, they would be able to lay down the law for the whole of Europe ('Vereint würden beide Europa Gesetze machen'); this would be equally disastrous. In short, the maintenance of the neutrality policy continued to require a very delicate balancing act between Prussia's two powerful neighbours.

This balancing act was sustained until late 1804; thereafter, it progressively began to break down. The chief reason for this was that Prussian statesmen had been set an impossible task. As Haugwitz had pointed out in March 1803, they were both to avoid war with France, and to prevent further French encroachments; they were neither to make military preparations to prevent such encroachments, nor were they to antagonise Russia to the extent of jeopardising any future Russian assistance; and they were not to tie Frederick William's hands by entering into any fixed agreement with the tsar.[32] If through a combination of manoeuvre and sheer good fortune, all of these objectives had been – more or less – realised before 1804, then the relentless surge of events commencing in the winter of that year began to corrode and subvert long-established policies and assumptions. As Beyme pointed out in February 1806, Prussia's difficulties were directly attributable

---

[30] Lucchesini to Hardenberg, 29/30.7.1805, Paris, in Bailleu (ed.), *Preussen und Frankreich*, II, p. 353.

[31] Hardenberg memorandum, 12.3.1805, Berlin, GStA Rep.XI.89.400, fos. 3–4: 'Preußen, minder mächtig als Frankreich, Rußland Österreich, wird von den beiden ersten . . . gedrückt und durch den ? Streit zwischen solchen in eine sehr schwierige Lage versetzt. Die Freundschaft beider Mächte ist für seine Ruhe und Sicherheit wichtig.' The document is extensively paraphrased, but not printed verbatim, in Ranke (ed.), *Denkwürdigkeiten Hardenbergs*, I, pp. 142–8.

[32] Haugwitz to Frederick William, 30.3.1804, Berlin, in Bailleu (ed.), *Preussen und Frankreich*, II, p. 253: 'V.M. si je ne me trompe, ne veut ni faire la guerre à la France, ni souffrir que ses usurpations s'entendent plus loin, ni recourir, pour en s'assurer, à des armements, ni dégouter la Russie des secours qu'on pourrait attendre, ni cependant se lier les mains sur l'application du principe en entrant avec l'empereur dans un concert trop déterminé. Ce n'est plus le moment d'examiner si tant de conditions délicates peuvent se remplir à la fois .' See also Schroeder, *Transformation of European politics*, p. 254.

to the fact 'that we want to harmonise our movements with both St Petersburg and Paris in equal measure'.[33] Indeed, the very geopolitical impulses that had originally spawned the policy of neutrality now began to tear it apart.

The disintegration of the traditional Prussian foreign policy began with the Rumbold affair in October to November 1804. It was the first incursion into northern Germany since the French occupation of Hanover in May 1803; unlike that event it was entirely unexpected and unprovoked. Napoleon's coup was doubly unwelcome at a time when delicate negotiations to remove, or at least to neutralise, the French presence in Hanover, were afoot. Moreover, the affair threatened to wreck the cherished Prussian plans for a mediation between Russia and France; the risk of being caught in the crossfire of a subsequent dispute was correspondingly greater. Finally, although the affair was resolved by an uncharacteristic and transient Prussian show of strength, the damage to the neutrality policy in northern Germany had been done. 'The neutrality of a state resembles the honour of a woman', Heinrich Ulmann points out, 'once it has been doubted or even tampered with, it no longer commands the necessary respect.'[34] Indeed, the flagrant violation of Prussia's north German sphere of interest could not but publicly subvert her whole policy of neutrality. This accelerated the continuing collapse of Prussian prestige among the smaller and middling German powers. These were the states whose rulers, in Frederick William's vivid description of the landgrave of Darmstadt, 'flotte également entre la crainte et l'espérance'.[35] If in early 1805 many of them still looked to Berlin for protection, they were increasingly unable to elicit satisfactory Prussian guarantees of their own security.[36] By late 1805, the re-orientation of Bavarian foreign policy away from Prussia had culminated in a treaty of alliance with France.[37]

---

[33] Quoted in Disch, 'Der Kabinettsrat Beyme', *FBPG*, 42 (1929), 98: 'daß wir unsere Schritte gleich angenehm in St Petersburg und in Paris machen wollen'.

[34] Ulmann, *Russisch-preussische Politik*, p. 237: 'Mit der Neutralität eines Staates ist es wie mit der Ehre eines Weibes, einmal angezweifelt oder gar angetastet, flößt sie nicht mehr gebührende Achtung ein.'

[35] Frederick William (draft) to Haugwitz, 17.3.1806, Berlin, Rep. Rep.XI.89.406, unfoliated. On the security needs of the smaller German states in 1804–6 see: Kell, 'Die Frankfurter Union', esp. 87–97; Möller, 'Zur Politik der Hansestädte im Jahre 1806', pp. 330–51; and Weis, 'Die außenpolitischen Reaktionen der Deutschen Staaten auf die französische Hegemonialpolitik', pp. 185–99. On the collapse of Frederick William's standing in Germany as a whole see Otto Tschirch, 'Die Flugschrift: "Deutschland in seiner tiefen Erniedrigung" und ihr Verfasser', *HZ*, 165 (1942), 51, 63.

[36] Santelmann, 'Die Beziehungen zwischen Bayern und Preußen', p. 111.

[37] See Anders, 'Napoleon Bonaparte und die Beziehungen zwischen Preussen und Bayern', *passim*.

But Napoleonic penetration of north Germany was not Prussia's only fear in 1805; there was also a growing concern that the emerging Third Coalition would thrust Prussia into the front line against her own will. The simple facts of geography made this inevitable. As in the preceding decade – especially during the Second Coalition – Prussia was once again caught between French blandishments and Anglo-Russian entreaties. Unlike 1800 to 1801, however, Prussia could no longer propitiate Franco-Russian wrath at Britain's expense; she had to choose between them. In the late summer of 1805 it seemed as if this choice would be made in favour of France, partly because of the tempting bait of Hanover, partly because it was dictated by geopolitical considerations, and partly because the Russian determination to 'force' Prussia into an alliance with France produced the opposite effect. Indeed, the same geopolitical arguments which had long justified neutrality were now seen by many Prussian statesmen – among them Hardenberg and Beyme – to make a French alliance both desirable and inescapable. But once again, Frederick William resisted activist councils and recalled Haugwitz, from whom he expected – and received – backing for a continued policy of neutrality.

In the event, the French violations at Ansbach and Bayreuth defused the impending conflict with Russia and set Prussia on confrontation course with France instead. Hardenberg now sought to use Prussia's central location to her advantage. Prussia, he hoped, could act as a 'trimmer': by skilfully distributing her weight she could expect to achieve territorial rewards. If in August Hardenberg had sought these gains from an alliance with France, in October–November he sought to extract the maximum advantage from the allied powers in return for an armed Prussian mediation. Both Hardenberg and the allies themselves expected this to be but a first step towards active membership of the coalition against France. However, this was not the policy of Frederick William and Haugwitz, nor was it what was actually agreed at Potsdam. Rather, the terms of the agreement with Russia reflected a deep-seated Prussian geopolitical *Angst*. For Haugwitz's famous voyage to present the armed mediation to Napoleon at Vienna was delayed, not – as we have seen – because of any dilatoriness on his part, but because of the need to synchronise political measures with military preparations. After all, the Austrian disaster at Ulm had just provided a graphic illustration of the dangers of taking the field unprepared: Prussian statesmen spoke of the need to 'avoid the error of the Austrian court'. At the same time, Haugwitz's instructions had explicitly kept Prussian options open. 'Les événements en décideront', they stressed, 'et c'est sur les lieux qu'il faudra en juger.'

If there were any doubts about the necessity of such a caveat, they were soon dispelled by the dramatic French victory at Austerlitz. Prussia now found herself facing Napoleon militarily unsupported. The dangers of Prussia's 'trimming' role could not have been more vividly exposed. This policy was particularly vulnerable to changes in the general European balance. What had been the potential straw to break the Corsican's back, became merely a drop in the Napoleonic ocean after Austerlitz. Yet contrary to widespread belief, Prussia remained prepared to take the field in support of her armed mediation. The Austrian armistice and the Russian withdrawal made these plans irrelevant; both emperors now urged Frederick William to 'make his own accommodation' with Napoleon. Faced with this, Prussia had no choice but to accept the terms which Haugwitz had negotiated at Schönbrunn and later at Paris. Similarly, the subsequent 'secret policy' with Russia epitomised the Prussian *Mittellage*. It was a direct reflection of Prussia's painful geo-political dilemmas in 1806: how to appease France while at the same time maintaining amicable relations with Russia. If this policy was ultimately doomed to collapse under its own contradictions, then it is remarkable that it held as long as it did.

The events of late 1805 and 1806 confirmed longstanding Prussian beliefs about Great Britain and Russia. For the second time in three years Russia had first encouraged Prussia to act – and then left her in the lurch. Frederick William's prediction that Russia might 'withdraw on the flimsiest of pretexts, even without making peace', was thus amply fulfilled. In that instance he was speaking of 1801, but he might just as easily have been referring to 1805. Well might Prussian statesmen envy the 'congenial role' of Russia, ensconced as she was behind the 'shelter' of a geographically remote 'invulnerable rampart'. This suspicion was even more marked in the case of Britain.[38] Not without reason, the Prussians believed that Britain aimed to 'brouiller les cartes dans le nord' at the expense of her neutrality policy.[39] During the Rumbold affair British attempts to inveigle Prussia into a war 'for a box of papers' were rejected; early in the following year Frederick William vowed not to be used by a power which 'dangled a purse in the air before him'. Indeed, throughout 1805 Prussian statesmen believed that it was not so much French hegemony – which was inescapable – that threatened European stability, as British determination to subvert it. Britain was urged to 'descendre pour un moment de son cheval, afin de faire au moins un essay en combien il seroit possible de se rapprocher sérieusement avec la

---

[38] For more detail on this see Simms, 'Fra *Land* e *Meer*'.
[39] Schulenburg memorandum, 30.10.1804, Berlin, GStA Rep.XI.89.394, fo. 9.

France'.[40] Moreover, the 'prépondérance maritime Britannique', was spoken of in the same breath as the 'puissance de l'empire français'. As Anglo-Prussian relations went from bad to worse, from the sour exchanges of the Harrowby mission to open conflict in 1806, so did references to Britain's 'one-sided money-grubbing policy (*einseitige kaufmännische Politik*)' multiply.[41] But – as ever – maritime concerns were largely peripheral to Prussia. Far more important was the fear that geographically remote Britain would renew the conflict on mainland Europe and thus needlessly endanger the security of all those powers – particularly Prussia – who were unfortunate enough to be situated in the middle of that turbulent continent.

Redressing 'la défectuosité la plus monstrueuse de l'assiette géographique de la Prusse'. Hanover and the annexation debate, 1804–1806

If there was one issue which focussed geopolitical thinking in Prussia before Jena, it was Hanover. Throughout the subsequent three years, Prussian statesmen were to rue the day that they had failed to pre-empt the French occupation of the electorate in May 1803. 'Ah', Lucchesini exclaimed in December 1804, 'que l'on devra longtemps de reprocher de n'avoir pas pris.'[42] It is not hard to see why: the French presence in Hanover continued to be the single greatest obstacle to the preservation of the neutrality of northern Germany. First of all, the Prussians were plagued by resulting commercial and other disruptions throughout 1804 and 1805.[43] Secondly, and much more importantly, it was over Hanover that the general Prussian fears of being dragged into an Anglo-Russian war against France were most acute. If this fear had been largely latent in 1803 and 1804, it burst into the open with the Third Coalition in 1805. For, as we have seen, the Anglo-Russian expedition to Hanover now threatened not merely the political but also the military encirclement of

---

[40] Jacobi report, 15.3.1805, London, GStA Rep.XI.73.179A, fo. 85.; see also Frederick William to Brunswick, 28.2.1806, Berlin, in Ranke (ed.), *Denkwürdigkeiten Hardenbergs*, V, p. 303.

[41] Anon. memorandum, 'Über Preußens politische Lage', 17.6.1806, GStA Rep. 92 *Friedr. Wilhelm.d.Dritte* B.VI.22, fo. 27; 'Erste Denkschrift Hardenbergs über den Vertrag vom 15.12.05', 30.12.05, Berlin, in Ranke (ed.), *Denkwürdigkeiten Hardenbergs*, V, pp. 244, 247.

[42] Lucchesini to Hardenberg, 10.12.1804, Paris, GStA Rep. 92 *Hardenberg* E5, fo. 212. In the same vein see Ranke (ed.), *Denkwürdigkeiten Hardenbergs* I, p. 112; Scharnhorst memorandum, 2.12.04, in Lehmann, *Scharnhorst*, I, p. 342.

[43] Hardenberg to Lucchesini (draft), 9.3.1805, Berlin, GStA Rep. XI.140.49, unfoliated (and *passim*).

Prussia. As Hardenberg had pointed out in September 1805, a 'glance at the map' showed that with an allied army in the electorate, the Swedes on the Baltic, the Austrians to the south, and an overwhelming Russian force to the east, the monarchy was hemmed in on all sides.[44] Even if the coalition powers had not been set upon 'forcing' Prussia to join them, their determination to come to grips with the skeletal French garrison in Hanover might have wrecked the neutrality of northern Germany beyond repair. In short, Lucchesini's assessment that Hanover 'est et demeura la source des tous les embarras et de toutes les inquiétudes qui troublent la neutralité de l'Allemagne', could not be disputed.[45]

As in the period before October 1804, the Prussian response to the Hanoverian problem was to try to persuade the French to withdraw from the electorate. These efforts were intensified in the aftermath of the Rumbold affair, as Prussia strove to restore confidence in her neutrality policy; at the very least, the Prussians wanted to limit the size of the French garrison to the barest minimum.[46] But after mid-1805 the continuities with another strand of Prussian thinking on Hanover began to predominate. This was the demand for the annexation of the electorate, either outright, or as part of a territorial exchange.

The annexation debate in Prussia between 1804 and 1806 had both a general and a specific dimension. Easily the most powerful advocate of the general imperative towards aggrandisement was Hardenberg. Prussia, he stressed in March 1805, must make territorial gains 'if it is not to lose ground (*wenn es nicht Rückschritte machen will*)';[47] 'La Prusse doit s'aggrandir pour ne pas rétrograder', he had told his colleagues during the Schönbrunn debate; and in January 1806 he argued that: 'La Prusse ne peut pas encore s'arrêter dans ses aggrandisements sans tomber en décadence.'[48] Moreover, in their alliance overtures of August 1805 the French specifically played on Prussian fears of 'falling behind' in territorial terms. Indeed, this need to keep pace with a changing world explains much of the restlessness behind Hardenberg's foreign policy.

But if Prussian statesmen were agreed on the need for territorial gains, the specific direction of any future expansion was still a matter of some

---

[44] *Note verbale* of Hardenberg to Laforest, 16.9.1805, in Ranke (ed.), *Denkwürdigkeiten Hardenbergs*, I, pp. 215–17. See also ibid., p. 210.

[45] Quoted in Ranke (ed.), *Denkwürdigkeiten Hardenbergs*, I, p. 107.

[46] See e.g. Wohlwill, 'Fernere Aktenstücke', pp. 203–5. *Copie de la note verbale remise* . . . *par Hardenberg à Mr d'Alopeus*, 17.3.1805, GStA Rep. 92 Hardenberg L13, fo. 12.

[47] Hardenberg memorandum, 12.3.1805, Berlin, GStA Rep. XI.89.400, fo. 4.

[48] Hardenberg memorandum, 11.1.1806, Berlin, in Ranke (ed.), *Denkwürdigkeiten Hardenbergs*, I, p. 423.

dispute. Compared to before 1804, however, the debate had moved on considerably. For a start, any suggestion of consolidating Prussia's position in the west had entirely evaporated. Indeed, the consensus in favour of a complete disengagement in the west was constantly reaffirmed throughout 1804 to 1806. On numerous occasions, as we have seen, Prussian statesmen had spoken of the need to 'cesse d'être limitrophe de la France', to be 'außer Beziehung mit Frankreich selbst',[49] and to 'éviter tout contact avec la France'. The logical consequence of this was a determination to jettison the outlying western provinces of the monarchy. This was most tellingly demonstrated in Hardenberg's memorandum of January 1806: Cleves was 'limitrophe de la France, et ceci entraîne des collisions et des inconvénients qu'il est essentiel d'écarter pour se ménager l'amitié de cette puissance', and would have to be abandoned; Neufchâtel would also have to go as 'son éloignement et sa position gégraphique empêchent le roi de le protéger'; and the same applied to the Westphalian provinces, which were *trop près* to France.[50] In fact, the only exception that Hardenberg made to this grim geo-political determinism was his continued commitment to a Prussian presence in exposed Ansbach and Bayreuth. This was supposedly in order to strengthen Prussia's hold on southern Germany in anticipation of the collapse of the *Reich*, but it might equally have been in deference to the known reluctance of the King to 'abandonner une ancienne . . . province, le berceau de ma maison'.[51]

By far the greatest shift in the annexation debate, however, was the increased – almost exclusive – focus on Hanover. Indeed, the incor-poration of the electorate promised to kill several birds with one stone. First of all and most obviously, it would remove the French from north Germany. Secondly, it would satisfy the ritual demand for 'more secure frontiers', especially if the western territories were surrendered in exchange. Thirdly and relatedly, the acquisition of Hanover corre-sponded to the old Frederician maxim that even the most modest village nearby constituted a bigger gain than the large but indefensible accretions far from the Prussian frontier. As we have seen, these themes recurred during the many debates on Hanover throughout 1804 to 1806. 'Un coup d'oeil sur la carte', Prussian statesmen argued with recourse to the standard geopolitical rhetoric, showed the necessity of providing the

---

[49] Altenstein memorandum, 28.12.1805, in Müsebeck, 'Fragmentarische Aufzeichnun-gen', pp. 154–5.
[50] Hardenberg memorandum, 11.1.1806, in Ranke (ed.), *Denkwürdigkeiten Hardenbergs*, I, p. 417.
[51] Ibid., p. 423; Tarrasch, *Übergang*, pp. 92–4; instruction for Haugwitz, 3.2.1806, Berlin, GStA Rep.XI.89.406, unfoliated.

monarchy with more secure frontiers. The acquisition of Hanover would serve to redress 'la défectuosité la plus monstrueuse de l'assiette géographique de la Prusse'; conversely, 'les acquisitions lointaines et détachées du corps de la monarchie' would not be in Prussia's 'true interests'. If Frederick William had told Napoleon during the Rumbold affair that 'geography' meant that he could not let the electorate fall into 'd'autres mains que dans les miennes', then eighteen months later he was still insisting that Hanover was so 'geographically' valuable that he could not 'let it fall into the hands of anybody else'. In short, as Frederick William had stressed at Potsdam, the acquisition of Hanover was 'impérieusement dictée par la position géographique'.

In spite of this, the French offer of the electorate in return for an alliance met a very mixed response in August 1805. For the apparent consensus on Hanover had masked a dangerous ambiguity throughout the debate. All Prussian statesmen were agreed that the French had to be ejected from Hanover; they also agreed that the acquisition of the electorate was highly desirable. What they *did not* agree upon was the need for the forcible annexation of Hanover, either outright or by means of a territorial exchange. Indeed, the French overtures had the effect of highlighting the deep divide between 'activists' and 'passivists' in Prussia. Hardenberg – and to a much lesser extent Beyme – now argued that Hanover was 'worth risking something for', and advocated a French alliance; even after Jena, Hardenberg was to mount a vigorous defence of this counsel.[52] Absolute neutrality, Hardenberg realised, might be rewarding in high-political terms, but it condemned Prussia to a complete loss of influence on the international stage. In August 1805, therefore, the Hanoverian bait was sufficient to tempt Hardenberg into a more activist policy.

Frederick William, on the other hand, was firmly opposed both to the idea of a French alliance, and to the notion of annexing the electorate by naked force. The neutrality policy continued to rule out any kind of alliance; moreover, Frederick William feared that any such arrangement would burden Prussia with a guarantee of the Italian settlement and other areas well outside of her own narrow sphere of influence. The king's objections to the seizure of Hanover were no less powerful. First of all, there was the known opposition of the Russians, who at that time preferred Prussian expansion in the west.[53] Secondly, Frederick William's natural caution had been accentuated by his unfortunate

---

[52] Ranke (ed.), *Denkwürdigkeiten Hardenbergs*, I, pp. 188, 191, and *passim*.
[53] Zawadzki, *Czartoryski*, p. 125, on Russian objections to a Prussian annexation of Hanover.

experiences during the first occupation of Hanover in 1801. Last but not least, Frederick William had formidable moral scruples. If Frederick William had had moral objections to abandoning his *own* western territories before 1804, he had even greater moral objections to seizing the lands of a fellow monarch. The electorate was still legally the property of George III; outright annexation would not only strain relations with Britain, it would also put Prussia unquestionably in the wrong. 'Puis-je', Frederick William had asked, 'sans manquer aux règles de la morale, sans perdre en Europe l'estime des gens de bien, sans être noté dans l'histoire comme un prince sans foi, me départir, pour avoir le Hanovre, du caractère que j'ai maintenu jusqu'ici?'[54] On balance, he thought not. Instead, Frederick William sought to pursue his traditional policy of neutrality by offering to take Hanover *en dépôt* until a general peace. As Hardenberg had predicted, this drew a frosty response from the French; the Prussians, they insisted, would not be rewarded merely for remaining neutral. To Frederick William, however, the sacrifice of lucrative territorial gains seemed a small price to pay for the release from potentially hazardous political commitments.

Within three months, Hanover was once again the subject of intense discussions. At the Treaty of Potsdam Prussia was promised the electorate as a reward for her armed mediation with Napoleon; Russian objections were dropped. But Prussia was now faced with the furious opposition of Britain, upon whose subsidies the military preparations against France depended. In part, the British stance reflected George III's concern for his German dominions. Far more important, however, were the long-term British plans for the resurrection of the European balance of power. As we have seen, these dictated Prussian gains not in northern Germany, but in the west, so as to constitute a formidable bulwark against France. The result was a fundamental clash between Prussian and British conceptions. For Prussia's own imperative was towards disengagement in the west, and a completion of the fundamental geopolitical reorientation of the monarchy towards the north and east; she certainly saw no profit in fulfilling the role within the broader European context envisaged for her by Britain.

Yet Frederick William remained extremely reluctant to seize the electorate by force. Just as he had always seen the armed mediation as an extension of his neutrality policy, he interpreted the Hanoverian clauses of the treaty of Potsdam more as a basis for negotiations with Britain than as a *fait accompli*. As we have seen, Frederick William continued to hope

---

[54] As quoted in Laforest to Talleyrand, 14.8.1805, Berlin, in Bailleu (ed.), *Preussen und Frankreich*, II, p. 361.

that the electorate might be incorporated with George III's blessing; to this end elaborate and not unfavourable exchange schemes were drawn up. Until consent had been given, Frederick William regarded the occupation of Hanover as merely a temporary expedient. In fact, the decision to annex the electorate outright was only taken after the treaties of Schönbrunn and Paris in the winter of 1805–6. This time Frederick William overrode British protests, not because the possession of Hanover had become any more desirable, but because the overwhelming power of France no longer left him any choice but to indemnify himself for his own losses at the expense of a third party.

The uses of adversity:[55] the French threat and high politics in Prussia, 1804–1806

Intense though the debates on Prussian foreign policy might have been, they were accompanied by a no less vigorous struggle for supremacy in the antechamber of power around the king. As ever, the focus of this contest was the monarch himself; the highest prize continued to be the control of the foreign-political executive. Inevitably, the protagonists sought to use the changing international situation between 1804 and 1806 to further their own personal ends. Foreign-political adversity thus opened up high-political opportunities.

At first, there was nothing to suggest that high politics after 1804 would differ fundamentally from the previous decade. Anticipating the known or suspected will of the king remained the key to personal advancement; this continued to encourage a 'passivist' tendency. Indeed, during 1804 and most of 1805, high-political manoeuvre was confined within the very narrow parameters of the king's neutrality policy. Time and again, Prussian statesmen found themselves compelled to weigh the 'objective' imperatives of the international situation against the 'subjective' demands of high politics. Hardenberg himself had confessed that, though he might wish to distinguish his ministry through territorial expansion, he would be 'sûr d'une disgrace s'il obstine à violenter les idées tenaces du roi'. In this sense, Prussian statesmen were indeed 'seizing the king's wind'.[56] But the debate on foreign policy did not merely serve to retain royal favour; it could also be used to wrong-foot political adversaries. As we have seen, the Rumbold affair was characterised at least as much by Lombard's desire to *mortifier* Hardenberg and Hardenberg's desire to *réduire le faction de Lombard*, as it was by any

---

[55] With apologies to Timothy Garton Ash!
[56] Ranke (ed.), *Denkwürdigkeiten Hardenbergs*, I, p. 99: 'Auram regiam captans.'

objective concern at French encroachments. Similarly, by opposing the 'activist' counsels of their rivals, Prussian statesmen could wrest royal favour from them. This was vividly demonstrated by the recall of Haugwitz during the Rumbold affair. The lesson was repeated in the following August (1805) when Hardenberg was lured into an activist stance by the French alliance overtures. Here the Hanoverian bait proved to be a poisoned pawn for Hardenberg. Unnerved by demands for action, Frederick William summoned Haugwitz for a second time. As a result Hardenberg – who had already conducted a tactical retreat on the French alliance – now found himself outflanked by Haugwitz's passivist prescriptions. If before 1804 Haugwitz had been challenged by Lombard whenever he attempted to deviate from the neutrality policy, Hardenberg confronted the same threat from Haugwitz after 1804. In short, while some of the roles might have been reversed, the fundamental pattern of Prussian high politics remained unchanged.

In October 1805 Hardenberg's worst fears were confirmed when Frederick William reinstated Haugwitz as co-foreign minister. But Hardenberg was determined not to submit to the cyclical caprices of Prussian high politics. Instead, he embarked on an innovative, ambitious and risky course of action. First of all, Hardenberg broke with the traditional policy of neutrality to advocate a Russian alliance, not merely tentatively, as with the French overtures in August, but wholeheartedly. Secondly, Hardenberg used his resulting credit with Russia to neutralise Haugwitz and the Kabinett. For one glorious month, culminating in the Treaty of Potsdam, this strategy succeeded, but it backfired spectacularly after Austerlitz. There could be no more vivid illustration of the dialectic between high politics and foreign policy in Prussia. For the very strategy that had secured Hardenberg's ascendancy at Potsdam – that of tarring his enemies with the French brush – now made Haugwitz's breeze to blow. Because whereas Hardenberg was remarkably successful in making the transition from France to Russia between August and October, he proved unable – despite frantic attempts – to switch horses back to France. Instead, Hardenberg was reduced to sniping at Haugwitz's policy of appeasement towards France, to which he inwardly agreed there was no alternative, for purely adversarial reasons. Having learned the lessons of August–September, when the king had turned down his plans for a French alliance as too dangerous, Hardenberg used the Schönbrunn debates to play on Frederick William's preference for the 'third way' and the policy of neutrality. The ingenuity of this strategy should not be underestimated, especially as Haugwitz was now arguing explicitly against the 'third way' – and in favour of a limited alliance with France – thus ceding that valuable high ground to Hardenberg. But this could only put off the final reckoning. Haugwitz now enlisted French power against Hardenberg, just as Hardenberg had once used the coalition powers aginst him. Objective foreign-political realities now took over. The French refused to accept Hardenberg's (re-)conversion to their cause, and from that moment on his position as official foreign minister became untenable. In a revealing letter, Hardenberg condemned this outcome as 'unjust (*peu équitable*)', but it was the inescapable price of his failed diplomatic and high-political gamble.

The ascendancy of Haugwitz was thus complete. Hardenberg had retired in apparent disgrace; the belated challenge of Count Keller was fought off. For the first time since 1803, Haugwitz enjoyed the sole direction of the Kabinettsministerium. His policy of accommodation with France was hardly popular, but it was undisputed. Yet, unbeknownst to Haugwitz, Hardenberg never left the antechamber of power. The 'secret policy' which Hardenberg, Frederick William and a select few conducted with Russia served not only to subvert the official policy towards France, but also to undermine Haugwitz personally. His attempted policy of conciliation with Britain, for example, was frustrated by the Russians, at least partly at Hardenberg's behest. At the same time, Hardenberg sought to use the Russian connection to *éloigner* Haugwitz. To make matters worse, Haugwitz was now assailed, rather more publicly, from another quarter. This was the 'war party' of soldiers, diplomats and courtiers for whom the alliance with France was an unacceptable humiliation.

Before 1804, those who had consistently counselled outright resistance to France were an insignificant minority. There was Friedrich Gentz, whose strident support for the coalitions against Napoleon had led to disfavour and ultimately exile.[57] In the army, there were Scharnhorst and Gneisenau who had long been convinced that a war with France was inevitable.[58] There was also that resolute opponent of France, Baron Stein, then still a comparatively junior figure in Prussian politics, who in 1802 lamented the 'perfidy of our basic principles, for our spineless

---

[57] On the role of Gentz see *inter alia* Sweet, *Frederick von Gentz*; Mann, *Secretary of Europe*; Paul Wittichen, 'Die Dritte Koalition und Friedrich von Gentz. Eine Denkschrift Gentz's vom Oktober 1804', *Mitteilungen des Instituts für österreichische Geschichte*, 23 (1902), 461–80; Alexander von Hase, 'Friedrich Gentz. Vom Übergang nach Wien bis zu den "Fragmenten des Gleichgewichts" (1802–1806)', *HZ*, 211 (1970), 589–615; Alexander von Hase, 'Das konservative Europa in Bedrängnis: zur Krise des Gleichgewichtspublizisten Friedrich von Gentz (1805–1809)', *Saeculum*, 29 (1978) 385–405, especially 394.

[58] Gneisenau to his wife, 12.6.1801, Treuenbrietzen, in Gneisenau, *Ein Leben in Briefen* ('immer einen Krieg mit Frankreich vorausgesehen'); Lehmann, *Scharnhorst*, I, pp. 330–1.

behaviour is making us the object of general contempt and revulsion'.[59] Similar sentiments were expressed by Prince Ferdinand when he returned from a visit to Gentz in Vienna full of plans for an Austro-Prussian *rapprochement* against France; some months later he warned Kleist of the need to contest Napoleon's pretensions to 'universal monarchy'.[60] It was only in October–November, however, with the tsar's visit, the French violations in Franconia and the Treaty of Potsdam that the ranks of the war party really began to swell. There were now many younger and middle-ranking officers who agreed with Gneisenau that the 'storm' would hit Prussia sooner or later; better to fight now, he argued, than to face France without allies at a future date.[61]

More importantly, the queen – hitherto largely politically passive – threw her weight behind the war party. If in years gone by, Louise was inclined to defend the neutrality policy as a 'pardonable egoism', the French violations at Ansbach transformed her into an enthusiastic advocate of the Third Coalition.[62] 'Je suis persuadée', Louise wrote of the Treaty of Paris, 'que chaque Prussien versera plutôt la dernière goutte de son sang, que de s'avilir du point de souscrire l'infamie de devenir les Alliés ou les esclaves'; 'Napoleon', she subsequently added, 'is a rascal.'[63] As resentment at Prussia's subordination to Napoleon mounted, her belligerence was matched by that of a growing number of diplomats and military men. In April 1806, Scharnhorst spoke for many when he said that 'humiliations' inflicted upon the king had turned his bitterness towards France into 'hatred'; trenchant remarks were also made by Generals Rüchel and Blücher.[64] But perhaps the most powerful

---

[59] Lehmann, *Stein*, I, p. 234: 'Perfidie unserer Grundsätze, denn die Charakterlosigkeit unseres Benehmens macht uns zum Gegenstand allgemeiner Verachtung und allgemeinen Abscheus.'

[60] E. Poseck, *Louis Ferdinand. Prinz von Preussen. Eine Biographie* (Berlin, 1938), pp. 276–283; Poseck, *Louis Ferdinand* (1943 edn), p. 286. Poseck's study is well-grounded in MSS and far from hagiographical. For a very unsympathetic description of Prince Louis Ferdinand see Stamm-Kuhlmann, *Friedrich Wilhelm III*, p. 224.

[61] Gneisenau to his wife, 7.11.1805, Datten bei Pförten i.d. Niederlausitz, in Gneisenau, *Ein Leben in Briefen*, p. 46.

[62] The best treatment of Louise's political role is Tessa Klatt, *Königin Luise*, which is a curious blend of national socialism and mild feminism. On neutrality policy: pp. 36–7; on Ansbach as turning point: p. 46; on role in war party: p. 131; neutrality policy as 'pardonable egoism': '*Aufzeichnung*' 1799, pp. 204–5. See also Princess Anton Radziwill, *Fünfundvierzig Jahre aus meinem Leben*, p. 164; Bailleu, 'Vor hundert Jahren', pp. 217, 220.

[63] Notes of Queen Louise, March 1806, in Klatt, *Königin Luise*, p. 207; Queen to Frederick William, 30.7.06, in Karl Griewank (ed.), *Königin Luise. Briefe und Aufzeichnungen* (Leipzig, 1924): 'Napoleon ist ein Schuft.'

[64] Scharnhorst to Rüchel, 16.4.1806, in Lehmann, *Scharnhorst*, p. 369; Blücher report, 25.7.1806, Münster, in Winter (ed.), *Die Reorganisation*, I, p. 27; Blücher report, 28.7.1806, Münster, in Bailleu (ed.), *Preussen und Frankreich*, II, p. 493.

protest was made by Jacobi, then still ambassador in London. Prussia, he stressed, might have gained 'physically' by the annexation of Hanover, but only at the price of a loss of 'honour'. A month later, Jacobi added that he had no objections to territorial expansion provided it was 'par des arrondissements sanctionnés par les loix des nations', but he condemned the annexation of Hanover as 'un exemple funeste pour la posterité'. Despite reprimands from Berlin, Jacobi persisted with his critique. 'Silence', he wrote, 'would be criminal.' Indeed, towards the end of May, Jacobi returned to the attack with the argument that 'le parti de se défendre les armes à la main contre les demands humiliantes du Cabinet des Thuilleries aurait été préférable à celui de se laisser dicter des conditions comme celles du traité d'alliance de Paris'.[65] It must be stressed, however, that none of this amounted to an organised 'opposition' to royal policy. The army, the court and the bureaucracy had no *corporate* viewpoint in high politics; the war party was merely a collection of disparate, albeit increasingly cohesive, individuals.

Hardenberg's relationship with this group was one of loose association only; their interests were not entirely identical. First of all, as Erich Müsebeck and Karl Griewank have suggested, Hardenberg himself had been partially responsible for the foreign policy now being execrated.[66] Though he had shared a foreign-political platform with the war party in the autumn of 1805 and consistently since April 1806, his record before and in between was unlikely to survive serious scrutiny. As Griewank and Max Duncker have pointed out, Hardenberg's policy differed from that of his rivals not so much in its sympathy, or hostility, to France but in the degree of activism he was prepared to advocate.[67] Secondly, as an experienced politician, Hardenberg was fearful both of antagonising the king through association with his critics – especially the hated Prince Louis Ferdinand[68] – and of appearing to challenge his conduct of affairs. After all, the summer of 1806 marked the apotheosis of Frederick William's own personal control over the conduct of Prussian policy. As

---

[65] Jacobi report, 21.3.1806, London, GStA Rep.XI.73.180C, fo. 114; Jacobi report, 22.4.1806, London, fo. 164; Jacobi to Haugwitz (draft), 29.4.1806, London, GStA Rep.XI.81.241, fo. 18; Jacobi report, 23.5.1806, London, GStA Rep.XI.73.180C, fo. 228.

[66] Ernst Müsebeck, 'Zur Geschichte der Reformbestrebungen vor dem Zusammenbruche des alten Preussens 1806', *FBPG*, 30 (1917), 120; Griewank, 'Hardenberg und die preussische Politik', p. 31: 'Ein Teilhaber der preußischen Fehler und Halbheiten'.

[67] Griewank, 'Hardenberg und die preussische Politik', p. 269; Duncker, 'Die Denkwürdigkeiten', p. 609.

[68] On Frederick William's suspicion of Prince Louis Ferdinand see Poseck, *Louis Ferdinand*, p. 282.

Thomas Stamm-Kuhlmann has shown, all of the threads of the 'secret policy' now converged in Frederick William's hands, making him the 'focal point' of Prussian politics.[69] Although Hardenberg, Goltz, the queen and a number of others were in the know, only the king enjoyed a complete overview; indeed, by drafting letters in his own hand, Frederick William was able to dispense with the scribal services of the previously ubiquitous Kabinett. But the king was not merely jealous of his own authority, he was also loath to see his delicate balancing act between Russia and France jeopardised by war-party rhetoric. Jacobi's protests, for example, had been met with a tart reminder that 'c'est à mes serviteurs à savoir respecter mes resolutions et à s'y conformer'.[70] To have laid himself open to that kind of rebuke would have been counter-productive for Hardenberg.

The real political significance of the war party lay in its manipulation by Hardenberg. For the war party was not merely anti-French, it was also committed to the removal of Haugwitz and the Kabinett. Hardenberg on the other hand – though scarcely less implicated in the debacle of Prussian policy of 1805–6 – was successful in dissociating himself from the policy of accommodation with France. 'Toutes mes dernières mesures', he averred, 'sont absolument contraires à mes sentiments et à ma conviction.'[71] Thanks to his skilful manoeuvres in October–November 1805, Hardenberg not only persuaded the war party of his anti-French credentials, he was also uniquely well-placed to use this credit against his personal rivals in the new year. Throughout the spring and early summer of 1806, therefore, Hardenberg moved to orchestrate the campaign of vilification and intimidation which was now unleashed on Haugwitz, Beyme, Lombard and all those scapegoated for Prussia's foreign-political predicament.[72] 'Now is the time', Stein wrote in early May, 'to eliminate this notorious cabal.'[73] General Blücher fulminated

[69] Stamm-Kuhlmann, *Friedrich Wilhelm III. König in Preussens großer Zeit*, pp. 216–18.

[70] Instruction for Jacobi, 23.5.1806, Berlin, GStA Rep.XI.73.180C, fo. 204.

[71] Hardenberg to Jacobi, 23.3.1806, Berlin, GStA Rep.XI.81.241, fo. 52.

[72] E.g. Hardenberg diary entry 20.4.1806: 'dîner chez Schroetter avec Rüchel, Stein – leur plans . . . ', in Winter (ed.), *Die Reorganisation*, I, p. 3; Hardenberg to Rüchel, 30.4.1806, Berlin, in Winter (ed.), *Die Reorganisation*, p. 4. For Stein's campaign against Lombard see also Richard Krauel, 'Eine Denkschrift des Freiherrn von Stein aus dem Jahre 1806', *HZ*, 102 (1909), 559, citing Stein's memorandum of late May 1805. Ironically, Stein himself may have been implicated in the fiascos of 1805 to the extent of advising Frederick William to accept the treaty of Schönbrunn: see Otto Hintze, 'Stein und der preußische Staat. Eine Besprechung von Max Lehmann's Stein-Biographie I–II', *HZ*, 94 (1905), 412–46.

[73] Stein to Rüchel, 5.5.1806, Berlin, in Hubatsch and Botzenhart (eds.), *Stein*, II/I, p. 223.

against 'these wicked base layabouts, these cursed villains'.[74] Beyme, Lombard and Haugwitz were pilloried – falsely – as 'vile sycophants', as corrupt and effete traitors.[75] The windows of Haugwitz's townhouse were repeatedly smashed.[76] In short, by June 1806 the existence of a war party could no longer be doubted; their most concerted onslaught on Haugwitz and the Kabinett, however, still lay ahead.

The decision against France, June–July 1806

Prussia, Frederick William reminded Napoleon in late September 1806, had been the first state to recognise his imperial title; in deference to his wishes, Prussia had expelled the brother of Louis XVI, the Bourbon claimant to the French throne; and three times the two powers had been on the verge of an alliance. The same themes were to recur a fortnight later in the 'Erfurt Manifesto', which accompanied the public breach with Napoleon.[77] Clearly, no major European power had gone to such lengths to accommodate France as the Prussia of Frederick William III. Yet in September 1806, the Prussians were – all of a sudden – openly prepared to confront Napoleon. What had happened?

The key to Prussian policy – as ever – lay in northern Germany. Here the aim continued to be 'la tranquillité et la paix dans le nord de l'Allemagne'.[78] At least, Frederick William argued in the humiliating aftermath of the Treaty of Paris, northern Germany had been 'sauvé, du moins pour le moment'.[79] Not surprisingly, therefore, Prussia interpreted the revolutionary changes in the European landscape during the summer of 1806 very narrowly in terms of their implications for the security of northern Germany. When Napoleon assembled a Rheinbund

---

[74] Quoted in Rudolf Usinger, *Napoleon, der rheinische und der nordische Bund*, p. 14: 'diese boßhafte niedere Faull Thiere, diese verfluchte, diese bösewigter'.

[75] For example Friedrich von Cölln was a bitter critic of the old Prussia, but he considered the honesty of all three men to have been beyond reproach: Cölln, *Vertraute Briefe*, I, pp. 149–50. But see also the very critical assessment of Lombard in Gaide, 'Der diplomatische Verkehr des Geheimen Kabinettsrats Lombard'.

[76] Hardenberg diary entry 24.4.1806: 'les vitres cassées . . . à Haugw. 3 fois répété', GStA Rep. 92 *Hardenberg* L26, fo. 2; Büsching to Jacobi, 19.5.1806, Berlin, in Rep.XI.81.240, 'Acta betr. den gegen das Haugwitzsche Palais verübten Anschlags . . . 1806'.

[77] Frederick William to Napoleon, 26.9.1806, Naumburg, in Ranke (ed.), *Denkwürdigkeiten Hardenbergs*, II, p. 179; a copy of the Erfurt Manifesto, 9.10.1806, is to be found in GStA Rep. 92 *Hardenberg* E8, fos. 76–83.

[78] Instructions for Jacobi, 25.1.1806, Berlin, GStA Rep.XI.73.180C, fo. 24. In the same vein see also Instructions for Jacobi, 31.1.1806, Berlin, GStA Rep.XI.73.180C, fo. 41. Instructions for Jacobi, 30.4.1806, Berlin, GStA Rep.XI.73.180C, fo. 154.

[79] Frederick William to Alexander, 19.3.1806, Berlin, in Bailleu (ed.), *Briefwechsel*, p. 100.

of biddable German princes in July 1806, Frederick William was under no doubt that this meant the end of the 'edifice de la Constitution Germanique', which would 'entraîner dans sa chute plus d'un état auquel je m'intéresse vivement'. This assessment proved correct, for on 6 August Francis renounced his imperial title, and on 10 August he pronounced the Holy Roman empire to be dissolved. 'Mais mon attention principal', Frederick William continued, 'a dû se porter tout de suite, sur la necessité, de former le plus promptement possible, le reste de l'Allemagne compris sous la dénomination du Nord de l'Empire, une association pareille sous mes auspices'.[80] The roots of this plan for a North German League – which Napoleon initially supported – can be seen in Massenbach's memoranda of 1800–1, in which he unsuccessfully called for a Prussian-led federation in northern Germany; this, he argued, would guarantee Prussian security far more effectively than any territorial gains.[81] There were also obvious parallels with the Fürstenbund of 1785, in which Frederick the Great had assembled many middling German states against the hegemonic pretensions of Joseph II. In the mid-nineteenth century there were predictable, but unpersuasive, attempts to locate the projected North German League within the heroic grand narrative of a Prussian-inspired unification of Germany.[82] In fact, the League was a negation of German nationalism, for it abandoned the rest of Germany to its fate, the better to ensure Prussian security.

At first sight, the league resembled a reduced version of the old Reich, comprising Prussia, Saxony, Hesse and a number of smaller territories, but not Austria nor any of the southern states. The king of Prussia was to be its titular head with the same authority as the erstwhile German emperor had had in the whole empire; the possibility of an imperial dignity for northern Germany was kept open. The council of the League – a kind of surrogate Reichstag – would meet at Hildesheim, and there would also be a system of federal courts, largely copied from the old Reich. Unlike the deceased empire, the military constitution was intended to furnish a serious deterrent – no less than 250,000 men under

---

[80] Instructions for Jacobi, 4.8.1806, Berlin, GStA Rep.XI.73.181A, fo. 45. In a similar vein see Lucchesini to Haugwitz, 22.7.1806, Paris, in Bailleu (ed.), *Preussen und Frankreich*, II, p. 488. The Prussian initiative seems to have predated any French suggestions, see R. Usinger, 'Napoleon und der nordische Bund', *Preussische Jahrbücher*, 14 (1864), 36.

[81] See Usinger, 'Napoleon und der norddeutsche Bund', p. 5; Adolf Schmidt, *Preußens deutsche Politik, 1785.1806.1849.1866* (3rd edn Leipzig, 1867) pp. 82–90; and Heinz Duchhardt, *Protestantisches Kaisertum und altes Reich. Die Diskussion über die Konfession des Kaisers in Politik, Publizistik und Staatsrecht* (Wiesbaden, 1977), pp. 322–3.

[82] See Schmidt, *Preußens deutsche Politik*, especially p. 80.

Prussian leadership – against potential transgressors.[83] But many of the smaller northern German states, especially Waldeck, Lippe-Detmold, the Hanseatic towns and Mecklenburg-Schwerin, were unable to summon much enthusiasm for such thinly disguised Prussian tutelage; and it was ultimately Saxon resistance that delayed ratification of the league until it was overtaken by events.[84]

For although the desire for peace or even an alliance with France had been a prime consideration in official Prussian policy in the early stages of the Hanoverian crisis, events in northern and western Germany soon began to corrode all belief in the value of friendship with Napoleon. The first striking sign of this was the row over the three abbeys of Essen, Elten and Verden, claimed by the French, but regarded by the Prussians as their rightful possession.[85] Throughout April, May, June and much of July French and Prussian forces faced each other in a tense stand-off. Matters were not helped by the fact that the local Prussian commander – General Blücher – was a notorious and outspoken member of the Prussian war party. But the most significant impact was on Haugwitz himself. On the one hand, he was quite prepared to settle the matter with a Prussian climbdown[86] and emphasised that Prussia's destiny was tied to France. On the other hand, he saw in the French behaviour 'procédés presqu'outrageants';[87] from Paris, Lucchesini warned that success had rendered Napoleon *presque intraitable*.[88]

It was the mounting evidence that the French intended to challenge Prussian supremacy in northern Germany that finally propelled Haugwitz towards a policy of resistance to Napoleon. Indeed, his three

[83] Details in Usinger, 'Napoleon und der norddeutsche Bund', pp. 39–51; Schmidt, *Preußens deutsche Politik*, p. 100.

[84] Usinger, 'Napoleon und der norddeutsche Bund', pp. 62–4. See also Schmidt's withering critique of Saxon policy, *Preußens deutsche Politik*, pp. 121–4; Heinrich von Treitschke, 'Zur Geschichte der sächsischen Politik im Jahre 1806', *HZ*, 42 (1879), 566, has a predictably strong anti-particularist bias. For pro-Prussian voices in Hamburg see Möller, 'Hansestädte', p. 332. 'Vereinigungstraktat zwischen den Höfen von Berlin, Dresden und Cassel', August 1806, GStA Rep.92 *Friedr. Wilh. d. Dritte* B.VI.22, fos. 40–3; Prussian plans for the North German League, undated and unsigned, GStA Rep. 92 *Friedr. Wilh. d. Dritte* B.VI.22, fo. 54; 'Entwurf eines Bündniß-Vertrags zwischen Preußen und den Kurfürstenthümern Sachsen und Hessen', in Ranke (ed.), *Denkwürdigkeiten Hardenbergs*, V, pp. 383–7; 'Entwurf eines Bündniß-Vertrags zwischen Preußen und dem Kurfürstenthum Hessen', in Ranke (ed.), *Denkwürdigkeiten Hardenbergs*, V, pp. 387–91.

[85] Lucchesini report, 9.4.06, Paris, in Bailleu (ed.), *Preussen und Frankreich*, II, pp. 450–1.

[86] Note of Haugwitz accompanying the memoranda submitted at Charlottenburg, 10.7.06, GStA Rep.XI.89.407, unfoliated.

[87] Haugwitz to Lucchesini, 15.6.06, Berlin, in Bailleu (ed.), *Preussen und Frankreich*, II, p. 467.

[88] Lucchesini to Haugwitz, 22.7.1806, Paris, in Bailleu (ed.), *Preussen und Frankreich*, II, p. 489.

memoranda of late June and early July 1806 seem to represent a kind of political 'road to Damascus' experience for Haugwitz. If French hegemony had been a fact of diplomatic life since the 1790s, the sheer boundless scale of Napoleonic ambition now hit Haugwitz like a blinding flash of light. What, Haugwitz demanded in an uncharacteristic outburst, had got into Napoleon? Was he challenging Prussia? Was he looking for a quarrel or a pretext for another war?[89]

Just over a week later, these misgivings found further expression in Haugwitz's memorandum of 7 July. Annoyed by French attempts to involve Hesse in the *Rheinbund* and detach her from Prussia, Haugwitz believed that Napoleon's aim was gradually to reduce the sole barrier to his absolute domination of Germany. In response, Haugwitz recommended that Prussia should form alliances with those German states threatened in this manner. As ever, Prussia's vital interest was defined as lying in the preservation of her predominance in the north of Germany. Hence Prussia must have a federal system in northern Germany 'qui lui était assigné par sa position géographique au nord de l'Allemagne, et qui était tellement lié à ses intérêts les plus essentiels'; it would be difficult to find a more succinct geopolitical justification for the northern League. A correspondingly dim view was taken of perceived French attempts to prevent the construction of such a system.[90] 'En effet', Haugwitz continued, 'porter atteinte à la prusse dans le nord de l'allemagne, c'est aller au coeur, c'est menacer, non plus sa prospérité et son bien-être, mais son existence.' Peace would be too expensive at that price, he stressed. For this reason Prussia would have to be prepared for the worst: 'tout doit être prévu, conçu, préparé sur le papier, de manière que le danger existant, il n'y ait qu'à mettre la main à l'oeuvre pour l'exécution du plan combiné'.[91]

There were other reasons for being prepared. Haugwitz foresaw that France would seek active Prussian cooperation against Britain and Russia once their negotiations with France had finally collapsed.[92] This point was not far off, Haugwitz argued, and so Prussia must soon decide to back either Russia or France, a decision which could not be avoided. No decision at all, Haugwitz added, would be the worst decision: 'le pire de tous les partis serait de n'en prendre aucun'. Moreover, the decision

[89] Haugwitz to Lucchesini, 30.6.06, Berlin, ibid., II, pp. 478–9.
[90] For French attempts to sabotage the North German League by discouraging Saxony and Hesse from joining see Usinger, 'Napoleon und der norddeutsche Bund', p. 58; Schmidt, *Preußens deutsche Politik*, p. 123.
[91] [Haugwitz's] 'Zweite Denkschrift', 10.7.06, Berlin, in Ranke (ed.), *Denkwürdigkeiten Hardenbergs*, V, pp. 350–1.
[92] [Haugwitz's] 'Dritte Denkschrift,' July 1806, ibid., V, pp. 356–64.

must be taken *in advance*, albeit *in secret*, so that the state could effect preparations and avoid the worst. Central to the Prussian decision, Haugwitz continued, was the question of Hanover. Clearly, Britain would never surrender it of her own free will. On the other hand, Napoleon could guarantee Hanover, but only at the price of an open Russo-Prussian rupture. If Prussia was prepared to forego Hanover, then the possibility of a Russian alliance was open. The dangers of war with Napoleon, he emphasised, were considerable so long as there were such large numbers of French troops in Germany. In case of war, however, Saxony, Hesse and Russia would be required as allies. The benevolent neutrality of Austria and financial assistance from Britain, far exceeding that offered by Harrowby, would also be needed. While his own views were quite clear, Haugwitz characteristically left the final decision – for or against France – to the king. 'La sagesse du roi', he concluded, 'peut seule décider sur cette grande alternative.' Nor was Haugwitz alone in pressing this policy. General von Rüchel, a man long known for his war-party sympathies, set out similar views in a memorandum during mid-August.[93] The Napoleonic peril, he argued, knew no limits: now his plan for 'Universal Monarchy', as Rüchel called it, was threatening the north of Germany. It was to be feared that the French would force Prussia into a military alliance against her friends and best interests. Thus, for reasons of 'geography' and of common sense, Prussia would have to dig in her heels and fight against French encroachments in north Germany. Rüchel did not deny that such a course would be an adventure – a *Hazardspiel* – but it was also a calculated risk which had to be taken.

In short, contrary to widespread belief, the (official) decision to resist was taken between the end of June and the beginning of July, not between the end of July and the beginning of August.[94] This distinction is important, for it shows that the decision was not taken in the panic arising out of an imminent restitution of Hanover to Britain, nor out of the breakdown of the secret policy occasioned by the rejection of the Oubril treaty, but represented a clearly thought out recognition of

[93] Rüchel, *Skizze des Augenblicks*, 14.8.06, Berlin, ibid., V, pp. 377–83.
[94] Ritter, *Stein*, p. 161, describes Haugwitz's behaviour as '*gänzlich kopflos*'; Friedrich Heinrich Leopold von Schladen, *Preußen in den Jahren 1806 und 1807. Ein Tagebuch. Nebst einem Anhange verschiedener in den Jahren 1807 bis 1809 verfasster politischer Denkschriften* (Mainz, 1845), speaks in his foreword of a 'mit großem Leichtsinne und höchst unvorbereitet' drift into war; Noack, *Hardenberg und das geheime Kabinet*, pp. 88–9 and Doerries, 'Ce qui m'est arrivé', pp. 19–22, puts the decision to go to war down to the Oubril treaty. Treitschke, *Deutsche Geschichte im neunzehnten Jahrhundert*, I, pp. 234–5; Disch, 'Der Kabinettsrat Beyme', p. 107; Cölln, *Vertraute Briefe*, I, pp. 216–17, and Lombard, *Matériaux*, p. 157, see fear of the loss of Hanover as the motivating factor.

the danger that French ambition posed to vital Prussian interests in the north of Germany. Some existing interpretations of Prussia's turn against Napoleon after June 1806 are thus in need of revision. According to Wilhelm Anders, the resulting Franco-Prussian war was 'not brought about by any conscious human will', but was 'decided by a higher power'.[95] In fact, a *considered* Prussian decision to risk war with Napoleon was taken as early as June–July. Thomas Stamm-Kuhlmann correctly insists that Prussia had decided on war by 1 July 'at the latest', but – somewhat contradictorily – sees the deteriorating relations with France as the result of 'irrational' mutual mistrust which ended in a conflict that neither side desired.[96] In fact, the Prussian decision – when seen within the narrow contemporary geopolitical mindset – was entirely rational, though perhaps rather belated and inopportune. If, as Paul Schroeder argues, the Prussians ultimately pursued 'an offensive strategy out of desperation',[97] then they did so on the basis of rational calculation.

'Now or never': the road to Jena, August–September 1806

The most remarkable fact about Prussian policy in 1806 is that just as Hardenberg and Frederick William were secretly preparing for a complete break with France in late June 1806, Haugwitz was trying to execute the same manoeuvre. At both the 'secret' and the 'ostensible' levels, the policy of the 'middle way' had now been exhausted. If the 'imperious dictates of geography' had once forced her to accommodate Napoleon and maintain equidistance between France and Russia, the same dictates now compelled war with Napoleon and alliance with Russia.

But the fundamental fear underlying Prussian policy had remained unchanged. This fear was most vividly expressed by Lucchesini's dispatch of 6 August, which, despite all its obvious hyperbole and even paranoia, provides a penetrating insight into the Prussian political mind under pressure.[98] In it he expressed the fear that the Oubril treaty would herald a new era of wholehearted Franco-Russian cooperation. Indeed, he had been told that the French and Russians were planning to deprive

---

[95] Wilhelm Anders, 'Napoleon Bonaparte und die Beziehungen zwischen Preußen und Bayern', pp. 46–7. In a similar vein see Max Lenz, 'Napoleon I und Preußen', *Cosmopolis: Internationale Revue*, 9 (1898), 589.

[96] Stamm-Kuhlmann, *Friedrich Wilhelm III*, pp. 217–19. See F. M. Kircheisen, 'Pourquoi la guerre éclata en 1806 entre la France et la Prusse?', *Revue d'histoire diplomatique*, 43 (1929), 237–50.

[97] Schroeder, *Transformation of European politics*, p. 304.

[98] Lucchesini to Haugwitz, 6.8.06, Paris, in Bailleu (ed.), *Preussen und Frankreich*, II, p. 505.

Prussia of Pomerania and her Polish territories, which were to be given to Sweden and Russia, respectively. Explicitly raising the spectre of 1756, that perpetual Prussian nightmare of a *renversement des alliances*, Lucchesini continued: 'la haine des quelques ministres, les espérances interessées de quelques courtisans, les intrigues d'une maîtresse polonaise et d'un frère ambitieux et violent, peuvent en 1806 faire taire la raison d'état à Petersburg, comme de pareils motifs lui imposèrent silence en 1756 à Versailles'. While many in Berlin did not share the more manic aspects of Lucchesini's interpretation, the mood was grave. Smooth and devious perhaps in the eyes of his younger patriotic critics, Lucchesini was no gushing Lombard, but a professional diplomat with long years in the Prussian service. When, as an old Frederician, he spoke of '1756' he touched a deep chord in the Prussian political psyche.

Hard upon Lucchesini's dispatch followed news of the tsar's refusal to ratify the peace treaty concluded by his envoy Oubril and the French at Paris on 20 July 1806. This had repercussions for Prussian policy at both the secret and official levels. To Hardenberg and Frederick William, it threatened to expose the contradiction between the guarantees given to Russia in early July and those given to France at the beginning of the year. To Haugwitz, the news of the non-ratification seemed to jeopardise the continuing surreptitious preparations against France. It was now to be feared that Napoleon would see them as 'le germe d'une quatrième coalition',[99] coupled as it was with the extreme difficulties encountered in the peace negotiations with Britain and the simultaneous Prussian troop movements in the west. These fears were confirmed by Lucchesini, who was warned by Napoleon in his final audience that while no hostile Prussian intent was suspected as yet, the troop movements were, in the context of the non-ratification of Oubril, potentially dangerous to France; corresponding precautions were thus justified.[100] The crucial fact, however, is that while the impending Franco-Russian clash, heralded by the Oubril affair, made the continuation of the balancing act between Napoleon and the tsar impossible, the news of non-ratification *followed* rather than provoked the ultimate decision against France. Besides, Haugwitz was at least as worried by the possibility of a Russian acceptance, which would deprive Prussia of Russian backing when the breach with France finally came, as he proved alarmed by the consequences of its rejection. Both outcomes were potentially fatal to the Prussian state. All of this highlighted Prussia's eternal dilemma between

[99] Haugwitz to Brunswick, 28.8.06, Berlin, in Bailleu (ed.), *Preussen und Frankreich*, II, p. 545.
[100] Lucchesini report, 8.9.06, Paris, ibid., II, p. 557.

France and Russia. If Lucchesini's dispatch had conjured up the night-mare of an intimate Franco-Russian understanding at Prussia's expense, the rejection of Oubril's treaty raised the spectre of being caught in the crossfire of a renewed Franco-Russian conflict.

To make matters worse, the Prussians were now horrified to hear that Napoleon was planning to return Hanover to George III as part of a general European peace settlement. Hitherto, the Franco-British peace negotiations were welcome to the Prussians, for only a *rapprochement* between Britain and France could release them from their own specific Anglo-Prussian quarrel, and allow any hope for a more general European pacification.[101] Once again Prussia found herself wrong-footed by changes in the international scene that were largely beyond her control; in this case there was the added irony that the Franco-British negotiations had been not only encouraged but facilitated by Prussia.[102] Yet, the news that France had offered to return Hanover during the discussions at Paris, conveyed in late July by Lucchesini, cannot have come as a complete surprise to the Prussians; rumours to that effect had been circulating since the early summer.[103] In fact, Frederick William's letter to Alexander shows that while the news that Hanover was to be returned to George III had struck a raw nerve in Berlin, the root cause of the Franco-Prussian estrangement lay far deeper than that. Clearly, Frederick William wrote, Napoleon would try to buy peace with Britain by offering the electorate in exchange, but far more serious was his obvious general intention to eliminate Prussia. Prussia, he stressed, was now isolated, and was becoming more so as Napoleon tried to detach her traditional allies in the Reich.[104] In short, the simple desire for survival, not the fear of losing territorial gains, motivated Prussia's stand in 1806.

Last but not least, Haugwitz's turn against France seems to have been at least partly influenced by narrow personal considerations. In late August, his old ally Kleist had bitterly attacked what he considered the

101 Jacobi report, 21.2.06, London, GStA Rep.XI.73.180C, fo. 72; Instructions for Jacobi, 4.3.06, Berlin, GStA Rep.XI.73.180C, fo. 74; Jacobi report, 28.2.06, London, GStA Rep.XI.73.180C, fos. 80–1; Instructions for Jacobi, 21.4.06, Berlin, GStA Rep.XI.73.180C, fos. 133–4; Instructions for Jacobi, 7.7.06, Berlin, GStA Rep.XI.73.181A, fo. 1.

102 E.g. Hardenberg to Haugwitz, 1.3.1806, Berlin, GStA Rep.XI.89.406.

103 Jacobi report, 29.4.06, London, GStA Rep.XI.73.180C, fo. 186; Jacobi report, 17.6.06, London, GStA Rep.XI.73.180C, fo. 262; Jacobi report, 20.6.06, London, GStA Rep.XI.73.180C, fos. 264–6; Jacobi report, 24.6.06, London, GStA Rep.XI.73.181A, fo. 4; Instructions for Jacobi, 18.7.06, Berlin, GStA Rep.XI.73.181A, fo. 22.

104 Frederick William to Alexander, 8.8.06, Charlottenburg, in Bailleu (ed.), *Preussen und Frankreich*, II, p. 509.

lack of direction in Prussian policy.[105] By mid-September Laforest noted that Kleist had gone over to the war party.[106] On the following day he reported that pro-war sentiment was rampant even among former peace-party men, indeed, that Haugwitz and Lombard would soon have to submit to this mood.[107] Such a submission had in fact taken place some time ago, for once the king had (officially) agreed to opt for Russia in late June or early July, as outlined above, there was little to be gained in high-political terms from persevering with the pro-French policy, except in order to delay the breach until all preparations had been completed. 'M. de Haugwitz et les amis de l'alliance française', Laforest observed, 'autour du roi ont bridé jusqu'ici le parti des militaires en se mettant à la tête du mouvement et en se prononçant pour la mise sur pied de guerre des forces de la monarchie.'[108] Indeed, as Hardenberg observed retro-spectively: 'Count Haugwitz had taken a quite different stance for some time. He was ultra-anti-French in order to remain in office, just as he had previously been pro-French in order to recover office.'[109] From what we know of Haugwitz and political practice in Prussia this element of high-political opportunism in his decision to confront France should not be underestimated.

Whatever the reasons, almost all Prussian statesmen had made their minds up by the beginning of September 1806. 'Quoi qu'il en soit, le parti du roi est irrévocablement pris', Haugwitz wrote to Brunswick in mid-September[110] and, indeed, at that point preparations for the ultimate breach had been in full swing for over one month. Political and military overtures were made to Austria and Russia.[111] Orders for Prussian troops to concentrate in Westphalia and Hanover, and to with-draw from the over-exposed positions in the extreme west of Germany, had gone out early the previous month.[112] A smokescreen of frenzied accusations and displays of suspicion, accompanied by professions of

[105] Kleist to Massenbach, 23.8.06, Charlottenburg, in Bailleu (ed.), *Preussen und Frank-reich*, II, pp. 537–8.
[106] Talleyrand to Laforest, 12.9.06, Paris, ibid., p. 567.
[107] Laforest to Talleyrand, 15.9.06, Berlin, ibid., p. 569.
[108] Laforest to Talleyrand, 3.9.06, Berlin, ibid., p. 548.
[109] Ranke (ed.), *Denkwürdigkeiten Hardenbergs*, II, p. 136: 'Der Graf Haugwitz hatte seit einiger Zeit eine ganz andere Rolle angenommen. Er war ultra-antifranzösisch, um sich in seinem Posten zu erhalten, so wie er vorher französisch gewesen war, um sich wieder in solchen hinein zu drängen.'
[110] Haugwitz to Brunswick, 18.9.06, Berlin, in Bailleu (ed.), *Preussen und Frankreich*, II, p. 570.
[111] Doerries, 'Ce qui m'est arrivé', pp. 44–5; Usinger, 'Napoleon und der norddeutsche Bund', pp. 69–70.
[112] Talleyrand to Laforest, 12.9.06, Paris, in Bailleu (ed.), *Preussen und Frankreich*, p. 567.

peaceful intent, was thrown up to cover these movements,[113] while in Berlin Frederick William and his ministers resigned themselves to war.[114] The curious schizophrenia of Haugwitz's language between July and September 1806, on the one hand ritual affirmations of the need for accommodation with France,[115] on the other hand the cool geopolitically based realisation that conflict with Napoleon was inevitable, was a direct result of the Prussian *Mittellage*.

By the late summer of 1806 Prussian policy was thus in a very complicated situation indeed. Prior to July, she had run a secret policy based on the assumption that friendship with France was a matter of necessity which the concealed link with Russia was meant to circumvent, while the parallel official policy centred on the idea that the warm relationship with France was a matter of choice and should therefore be broadened into a complete and wholehearted alliance. Once Haugwitz had decided to confront France, however, the situation, involved enough as it was, became even more complicated. For now there was not only a secret and an ostensible policy, but a secret policy *within* the official policy. It was, so to speak, a deception within a deception in which Haugwitz deceived the French and was in turn deceived by Hardenberg, Frederick William and the Russians. In objective terms therefore, the secret and official policies had converged, to the point that Hardenberg could truthfully assure Goltz in mid-September 1806 that his instructions would be 'no longer contradictory'.[116] If Prussia's geopolitical exposure had temporarily necessitated a 'secret' policy, the same 'imperious dictates of geography' soon forced these parallel policies to converge.

Perhaps the most striking example of the convergence between the 'secret' and 'official' Prussian policies was the attempted *rapprochement* with Britain in September 1806. Conflict with Britain, which had been neither intended nor desired in the first place, though it was certainly

---

[113] Laforest to Talleyrand, 12.8.06, Berlin, in Bailleu (ed.), *Preussen und Frankreich*, II, p. 522; Laforest to Talleyrand, 30.8.06, Berlin, in Bailleu (ed.), *Preussen und Frankreich*, II, pp. 546–7.

[114] Memorandum of Frederick William with ministerial response, 6/7.9.06, Berlin, in Bailleu (ed.), *Preussen und Frankreich*, II, pp. 553–6. On the Prussian mobilisation and Napoleon's reaction see Jay Luvaas, 'Napoleon's use of intelligence: the Jena campaign of 1805 [*sic*]', *Intelligence and National Security*, 3 (1988), 46–53.

[115] E.g. Haugwitz to Lucchesini, 31.7.06, in Bailleu (ed.), *Preussen und Frankreich*, II, p. 498; Haugwitz to Lucchesini, 12.8.06, ibid., p. 516; Haugwitz to Kleist, 29.7.06, ibid., p. 495; Frederick William to Blücher, 2.8.06, ibid., p. 500. Frederick William may have hoped that France would accept his conditions – and leave him Hanover: Paul Bailleu, 'Sitzungsberichte des Vereins für Geschichte der Mark Brandenburg 9. November 1898', *FBPG*, 12 (1899), 574.

[116] Hardenberg to Goltz, 11.9.06, Tempelberg, in Ranke (ed.), *Denkwürdigkeiten Hardenbergs*, II, p. 140.

consciously risked, now seemed doubly pointless; besides, British subsidies would be needed to finance the war against France. Haugwitz was, of course, unaware that negotiations with Britain had already begun at the end of August as part of the secret policy. The first move, surprisingly enough, had come from the British side, via their ambassador in Vienna, Robert Adair. In keeping with the new 'maritime' policy of the Ministry of All the Talents, Prussia was offered not a general coalition in the old Pittite style, but a *defensive* alliance to safeguard the status quo.[117] To a Prussia faced with the full weight of Napoleonic France, the aid thus extended was hopelessly inadequate. The problem about the Adair overture, as Hardenberg pointed out immediately to Frederick William, was that, ironically, at the exact moment when Prussia needed an offensive coalition, which Britain had attempted to ram down her throat in years gone by, all that was on offer was a defensive 'holding' arrangement.[118]

Soon, however, the Adair overture, originally part of the secret policy, was made redundant by the convergence of that policy with the secret dimension of the 'official' Prussian policy. The first real official move towards *rapprochement* with Britain came on 2 September 1806, when Balan, whom Jacobi had left behind as his deputy, was instructed to make overtures in London.[119] There were essentially two parts to the message. The first was that while Prussia would not attempt to hold on to Hanover without British consent, its occupation was crucial to Prussia's security. The second was the assurance that once open war broke out with France, Frederick William would lift the closure of the northern ports to British shipping. In return the Prussians asked for proof of Britain's friendly intentions towards Prussia: the lifting of the blockade of the North Sea rivers; the release of detained Prussian vessels; and entry into further communications about the future. A separate letter of the same date spelt out that what the Prussians expected from these 'further communications' was subsidies.[120] By way of encouragement Haugwitz announced the following week that Prussia was unilaterally opening the ports of Hamburg, Emden and Bremen to British trade and shipping.[121] The note of desperation in Prussian communications was now unmistakable. If Britain failed to subsidise

---

[117] Ranke (ed.), *Denkwürdigkeiten Hardenbergs*, II, pp. 124–5. On the idea of a maritime policy in Britain in 1806 see Simms, 'Anglo-Prussian relations, 1804–1806', pp. 104–9.
[118] Hardenberg to Frederick William, 31.8.06, Tempelberg, in Ranke (ed.), *Denkwürdigkeiten Hardenbergs*, II, p. 126.
[119] Instructions for Balan, 2.9.06, Berlin, GStA Rep.XI.81.238, fo. 76.
[120] Instructions for Jacobi, 2.9.06, Berlin, GStA Rep.XI.81.238, fo. 81.
[121] Haugwitz to Balan, 9.9.06, Berlin, GStA Rep.XI.81.238, fo. 105.

Prussia and allowed her to be overrun, she would subsequently face France alone. Time was now running out: 'Le temps presse.' It was, as the briefing put it with dramatic flourish, a question of now or never: 'Or à présent, ou jamais.'[122]

Predictably, the Prussian overtures met with a cool response in London.[123] In response to Balan's call for conciliatory measures such as the lifting of the blockade of the North Sea rivers, Grenville offered no more than a temporary respite. As for the question of an alliance with Prussia, Grenville wanted the continental powers to adopt a *confédération defensive*, with Russia, Great Britain and Prussia as the major elements. This was far short of what was needed to confront Napoleon in Germany. The Prussian occupation of Hanover continued to be, as Grenville put it to Stuart in mid-September, 'an insurmountable ban to any community of interest between Great Britain and Prussia'.[124] But the continuing Anglo-Prussian estrangement was not just due to the unsolved Hanoverian question. The logic of the Prussian arguments employed at the outset of the negotiations would have been quite sufficient to convince British statesmen guided by the old Pittite orthodoxy of continental intervention, irrespective of Hanover. However, the Prussian overture was unfortunate enough to have been made at a time when this orthodoxy had fallen into disfavour. Disengagement from Europe, not yet another coalition was the foreign-political principle of the Talents' ministry. The brutal fact was that the adoption of a 'maritime policy' had made Prussia all but redundant in British calculations.

Meanwhile Prussian anxiety mounted. Despite the temporary lifting of the blockade of the Ems and Elbe,[125] the British were continuing to detain Prussian ships;[126] the necessary financial assistance had not materialised. On 25 and 28 September, at that point already with the army at Naumburg, Frederick William spurred on his envoy in Hamburg. 'Le moment décisif est venu . . . ', he wrote. 'Je vais parler à la France le langage énergique que ma dignité et l'intérêt commun m'imposent le devoir de lui tenir, or rompre avec elle'.[127] 'Peut-être',

---

[122] Instructions given to Jacobi for mission by Haugwitz, 14.9.06, Berlin, GStA Rep.XI.81.238, fos. 87–94; Instructions for Balan, 15.9.06, Berlin, GStA Rep.XI.81.238, fo. 109.
[123] Balan report (draft), 16.9.06, London, GStA Rep.XI.81.237, fos. 16–20.
[124] Grenville to Jacobi, 3.10.06, Downing Street, BL Dropmore MSS 59059, fos. 179–81.
[125] Howick to Münster, 25.9.06, Downing Street, Niedersächsisches Hauptstaatarchiv Hannover 92 XLI 7, vol. II, fo. 13; Balan report, 30.9.06, London, GStA Rep.XI.81.237, fo. 29.
[126] Jacobi report, 27.9.06, Hamburg, GStA Rep.XI.81.244, fo. 14.
[127] Instructions for Jacobi, 25.9.06, Naumburg, GStA Rep.XI.81.238, fo. 95.

Frederick William concluded, 'qu'avant même le retour du courrier chargé de ma délibération, de grands coups auront déjà été portés'.[128] These words proved prophetic. On 1 October the ultimatum to France to withdraw her troops from Germany was issued.[129] It was ignored. Not long afterwards the Prussian army was on the road to the disasters of Auerstädt and Jena.

---

[128] Instructions for Jacobi, 25.9.06, Naumburg, GStA Rep.XI.81.238, fo. 95.
[129] Printed in Ranke (ed.), *Denkwürdigkeiten Hardenbergs*, II, pp. 188–90.

9   The search for decision: Prussian reform attempts immediately before Jena[1]

> The more power is concentrated in one place and in the hands of one person, the more the question of access to that place and that individual becomes the most important political, organisational and constitutional problem. The struggle for access to the absolute monarch, for the right to brief and advise him, for the right of direct access and suchlike is the real object of the constitutional history of absolutism.
>
> Carl Schmitt[2]

By the spring and early summer of 1806 the magnitude of the French threat to Prussia had become clear for all to see. The resulting debate about policy and personalities has been examined at length in the previous chapters. However, the Prussian response to the mounting French threat did not exhaust itself in those controversies. It was articulated at a level other than that of international relations, namely the related, though nonetheless discrete, area of the reform of the state and its highest institutions. This chapter will prove that the Reform debate and its associated politics form part of a continuous narrative of the Prussian response to Napoleon and follow naturally from the methodology employed to explain this response throughout the book. The crisis in Prussia's foreign political situation and her system of government

---

[1] Due to the very intensive interest of Prussian historians and archivists in the pre-history of the Reform Movement, this chapter has been able to rely almost entirely on printed source material. A thorough search of the relevant material in GStA Rep.96A turned up some additional documentation, mostly relating to the 'adversarial' context of reform. The following source collections were used: Winter (ed.), *Die Reorganisation des preussischen Staates unter Stein und Hardenberg*, vol. I; Hubatsch and Manfred Botzenhart (eds.), *Stein.* II/I; Ranke (ed.), *Denkwürdigkeiten Hardenbergs*, I, II and V. The appendices in Hüffer, *Die Kabinettsregierung in Preussen*.

[2] Schmitt, 'Der Zugang zum Machthaber', p. 430: 'Je mehr sich die politische Macht an einer einzigen Stelle und in der Hand einer einzigen Person konzentriert, um so mehr wird der Zugang zu dieser Stelle und dieser Person das wichtigste politische, organisatorische und verfassungsrechtliche Problem. Der Kampf um den Zugang zum absoluten Monarchen, um seine Beratung und Informierung, um den Immediat-Vortrag und dergleichen ist der eigentliche Inhalt der Verfassungsgeschichte des Absolutismus.'

which resulted from the British war and the preceding humiliations at the hands of France triggered a reform process which, though it did not come to fruition until after the catastrophe of Jena/Auerstädt, should more properly be considered in the context of the crises and political enmities of the early part of the year. What follows is thus a natural extension of the preceding chapters. First, by examining the high-political and adversarial context of the reform debate, an insight from the rest of the work is applied to the area of domestic politics. The demonstration of how 'objective' plans for change concealed a hidden high-political agenda and were indeed influenced and distorted by their passage through the 'antechamber of power' complements what we know about foreign policy during the same period. Secondly, just as the previous chapters stressed the degree to which the geographic exposure of Prussia influenced her political elite, this chapter seeks to complete the picture by demonstrating the effects of the French threat on her decision-making structures.

The historiography of the (pre-)Reform movement in Prussia

Ever since Otto Hintze's seminal article in 1896,[3] historians have been sensitive to the degree of reforming activity in the old Prussia, *before* the disasters of Jena and Auerstädt.[4] Broadly speaking the historiography of the Prussian Reform period divides between older, or at least more 'old-fashioned', interpretations which one might call 'idealistic-constitutional' and newer approaches which one might call 'sceptical-societal'. This book is firmly in the older tradition of the primacy of foreign policy, in that it sees the impulse for reform coming from the catastrophic international situation of the state, and the deficiencies in the executive that it had exposed, rather than any intention to stave off revolution from below with pre-emptive reforms. However, in common with the newer works the book is sceptical of the idealistic motivations of the early reformers. But rather than seeing the prime motivation of these men in their supposed bid for bureaucratic supremacy within the state or seeing them as primarily engaged in a pre-emptive reform out of a fear of revolution, the aim here is to put them back into the high-political – and that means essentially adversarial – context of the time.

[3] Otto Hintze, 'Preußische Reformbestrebungen vor 1806'. Similarly, Huber, *Deutsche Verfassungsgeschichte*, I, p. 102.
[4] See most recently, T. C. W. Blanning, 'The French Revolution and the modernisation of Germany'.

In an article which might justly be said to have fathered the 'critical' approach to the history of the Prussian Reform Movement in general and that of the Prussian bureaucracy in particular, Eckart Kehr set out the arguments which Hans Rosenberg subsequently elaborated.[5] They run something like this: although the bureaucracy had enjoyed what Rosenberg calls a certain 'hierarchical self-government' and 'organisational autonomy'[6] even under the great Frederick, the death of this last exponent of forceful personal rule opened the way for their political ambitions.[7] According to the Kehr/Rosenberg view, Frederick's death in 1786 inaugurated a period lasting until 1806 in which the bureaucracy exhibited their will to become 'masters of the state'.[8] An important success in this direction was achieved in 1794 when the *Allgemeines Landrecht* gave Prussian administrators a kind of security of tenure. This principle of *Unabsetzbarkeit* meant that, as Rosenberg put it, 'Only the "political" ministers, the chiefs of the managerial power machine, could be ousted without legal protection.'[9] Faced with this self-confident, self-recruiting and self-perpetuating elite, the monarchy was increasingly powerless against the 'collective drive of the bureaucratic functionaries and pillars of power for more freedom and independence'.[10] The result was an unrelenting 'battle for an end to royal absolutism and the whims of royal meddling [in the business of the bureaucracy]'.[11]

On this reading the events of 1806 were just the culmination of the long process of what Rosenberg termed 'The emancipation from monarchical authority', or a touch more stridently in the German edition, '*Die Überwindung der monarchischen Autokratie.*' It was an attempt to consolidate the gains of the preceding twenty years in legal form, in effect a bid for supremacy in the state. To paraphrase Rosenberg's own description, the aim of Baron Stein and his colleagues when leading the 'revolt' of 'ambitious senior bureaucrats' against Frederick William and his Kabinett, was to become 'masters of the

---

5 Eckhart Kehr, 'Zur Genesis der preußischen Bürokratie'; Hans Rosenberg, *Bureaucracy, Aristocracy, and Autocracy.* See also William W. Hagen, 'Descent of the *Sonderweg*: Hans Rosenberg's history of Old-Regime Prussia', *CEH*, 24, 1 (1991), 24–50.

6 Rosenberg, *Bureaucracy, aristocracy, and autocracy*, pp. 176–7.

7 Kehr, 'Zur Genesis der preußischen Bürokratie', p. 35.

8 Rosenberg, *Bureaucracy, aristocracy, and autocracy*, p. 199.

9 Ibid., pp. 190–1.

10 Hans Rosenberg, 'Die Überwindung der monarchischen Autokratie (Preußen)', p. 182: 'kollektiven Drang der bürokratischen Funktions- und Herrschaftsträger nach mehr Freiheit und Unabhängigkeit'.

11 Ibid., p. 182: 'Kampf um Ablösung königlicher Willkürherrschaft und launenhafter persönlicher Einmischung'.

state'.[12] A very similar picture was painted by Kehr almost thirty years earlier. He too saw an 'ever more power-hungry bureaucracy (*immer machthungriger werdende Bürokratie*)' attempting to storm the last barricade which the embattled monarchy had inserted between them: the Kabinett.[13] Again, Kehr sees Stein in a pivotal role: '[in] 1805 and 1806, as the battle of the bureaucracy was nearing its decisive stage, Stein was the vanguard of this dictatorship [of the bureaucracy] which was intended to replace the existing distribution of power in late absolutism'.[14] Moreover, Rosenberg saw this contest not merely as an institutional, but also as a class struggle; indeed he speaks of 'an unavoidable struggle for political control between the non-noble cabinet secretaries on the one hand and the aristocratic ministers and senior civil servants of the central administration on the other hand'.[15]

Not surprisingly, this interpretation was anathema to an earlier generation of German historians. Gerhard Oestreich condemned Rosenberg for bringing the age of absolutism into 'dubious nearness to totalitarianism';[16] this was the same Oestreich who had once praised seventeenth-century Prussia as a *Führerstaat*. Yet although it became customary to bemoan the silence with which Kehr and Rosenberg's work was initially received, at least in Germany,[17] their arguments have permeated the recent historiography of the period. Indeed, as Wilhelm Berges has pointed out, Rosenberg established the legitimacy (*Eigenrecht*) of social history in general and the social history of bureaucracies in particular.[18] His model of a 'triangular contest' between the highest level of government, the bureaucracy and the ruling upper class (*Regierungsspitze, Bürokratie* and *herrschende Oberschicht*), that 'sociological dynamic' behind the development of bureaucratic absolutism, has found

---

12 Ibid., p. 200. Otto Hintze, 'Die Entstehung der Ministerien', p. 313, speaks of Stein's plans for a Staatsrat before 1806 as an attempt at 'die Beschränkung der königlichen Selbstregierung [the limitation of royal personal rule]'.
13 Kehr, 'Zur Genesis der preussischen Bürokratie', p. 36.
14 Ibid.: '1805 und 1806, als der Kampf der Bürokratie zur Entscheidung reifte, war Stein der Vorkämpfer dieser Diktatur, die die Herrschaftsverteilung des ausgehenden Absolutismus ersetzen sollte'.
15 Rosenberg, 'Die Überwindung der monarchischen Autokratie (Preußen)', p. 199: 'ein unvermeidlicher Kampf um die politische Führung zwischen den nichtadeligen Kabinettsräten auf der einen Seite und den adligen Ministern und Oberbeamten der Zentralverwaltung auf der anderen Seite'.
16 Gerhard Oestreich review of Hans Rosenberg, *Bureaucracy, aristocracy, and autocracy*, in *VSWG*, 52 (1965), 277: 'die Epoche des Absolutismus, den R[osenberg] bedenklich nahe an den Totalitarismus heranrückt'.
17 Wilhelm Berges and Hans Herzfeld, 'Bürokratie, Aristokratie und Autokratie in Preussen'. Das Werk von Hans Rosenberg', *Jahrbuch für die Geschichte Mittel- und Ostdeutschlands* (1962), pp. 282–6.
18 Berges and Herzfeld, 'Bürokratie, Aristokratie und Autokratie in Preussen', p. 289.

widespread acceptance: Willerd Fann speaks of a personal absolutism of the monarch being limited by a modernised 'bureaucratic absolutism',[19] with the bureaucracy emerging as 'the most important political force' after 1806 to execute a successful 'revolution from above'; Wilhelm Bleek sees the reform period as the 'high point in the struggle between monarchic and bureaucratic autocracy ('Höhepunkt in den Auseinandersetzungen zwischen monarchischer und bürokratischer-Autokratie');[20] and Wolfgang Radtke's study of the *Seehandlung* repeatedly refers to a 'primacy of the bureaucracy'.[21] Of course, this is not to say that Kehr and Rosenberg's interpretations are unchallenged today. Paul Nolte, for example, argues against the notion of 'bureaucratic absolutism' partly because the administration was only a functional elite, and partly because it was riven by factionalism. Similarly, William Hagen criticised Rosenberg's view of the state apparatus as 'an executive committee of the aristocracy' on the grounds that it underplays 'the political factionalisation within the governing establishment'.[22] Others, such as Bernd Wunder, have expressed doubts whether the bureaucracy either intended or managed to supplant the monarchy in government.[23]

The 'critical' school of historians led by Hans-Ulrich Wehler is historiographically related to Kehr and Rosenberg. But instead of adopting their undifferentiated notions of bureaucratic absolutism, the 'critical' school has taken up Kehr and Rosenberg's view of the Reform and pre-Reform era as a period of *internally-generated* change.[24] To be sure, the French Revolution is accorded a decisive role in this process, but the impulse towards social, economic, legal and – most importantly for this book – administrative reform was seen to come from the example of French ideas and models, rather than fear of French hegemony. Thus in his seminal *Deutsche Gesellschaftsgeschichte* Wehler

---

[19] Willerd R. Fann, 'The rise of the Prussian ministry, 1806–1827', in *Sozialgeschichte Heute. Festschrift für Hans Rosenberg zum 70. Geburtstag*, edited by Hans-Ulrich Wehler (Göttingen, 1976), p. 119.

[20] Wilhelm Bleek, *Von der Kameralausbildung zum Juristenprivileg. Studium, Prüfung und Ausbildung der höheren Beamten des allgemeinen Verwaltungsdienstes in Deutschland im 18. und 19. Jahrhundert* (Göttingen, 1985), pp. 83 and *passim*.

[21] Radtke, *Die preussische Seehandlung zwischen Staat und Wirtschaft*, introduced by Otto Büsch (Berlin, 1981), pp. 12ff.

[22] Nolte, *Staatsbildung als Gesellschaftsform*, p. 27; Hagen, 'Descent of the Sonderweg', pp. 47–8.

[23] Bernd Wunder, 'Rolle und Struktur staatlicher Bürokratie in Frankreich und Deutschland', in Helmut Berding, Etienne François and Hans-Peter Ullmann (eds.), *Deutschland und Frankreich im Zeitalter der Französischen Revolution* (Frankfurt, 1989), p. 148.

[24] E.g. Schissler, *Preußische Agrargesellschaft*, p. 21. On p. 105 she does make brief reference to external impulses for change.

speaks of the 'Challenge of the (French) Revolution' which produced a 'qualitative impulse for development (*Entwicklungsschub*)' in the German states.[25] It was not enough, Wehler argues, simply to stick it out in a kind of 'policy of perseverance (*Beharrungspolitik*)'. Rather it was necessary to preserve the old order against Revolution from below, a process which Wehler has termed 'defensive modernisation'. The purpose of this defensive modernisation, Barbara Vogel argues with respect to Hardenberg's reform programme after 1810, was 'modernisation for the purpose of increasing economic efficiency and social mobility (*Modernisierungspolitik zur Steigerung wirtschaftlicher Effizenz und sozialer Mobilität*)'; this corresponds to M. R. Lepsius's definition of modernisation as a 'process of conscious and planned development to increase the efficiency of social systems'.[26] Part and parcel of this programme, so the argument runs, was – or should have been – a catalogue of political rights, most notably the granting of a constitution and the creation of a representative assembly.[27] This view may be tenable for the period after 1807; in the period *before* 1806, however, constitutional reform was much more narrowly conceived. We shall see that the political-administrative reform debate preceding Jena was restricted to the improvement of the executive.

Ironically, the teleology of the 'critical' approach is shared by the more old-fashioned school of historians, which Kehr and Rosenberg sought to refute, but which has flourished in various guises until the present day.[28] The difference lies primarily in the value judgment. Where one school sees a self-interested bureaucracy encroaching upon the king with modernising results for society as a whole, the other sees a noble band of patriots who had absorbed idealistic thought, the principles of the French Revolution and Adam Smith, and who sought to brush aside an ineffectual king to save the country from the oppressor before it was too late. This school also sees the triangle of crown, aristocracy and bureaucracy as a sublimated class struggle, with the *Beamtentum* as a kind of surrogate bourgeoisie. Werner Frauendienst's characterisation of the bureaucracy – 'They embodied progress (*Sie verkörperten den Fortschritt*)'[29] might, stripped of its positive implications, have come from

---

[25] Wehler, *Deutsche Gesellschaftsgeschichte*, I, pp. 341–5.
[26] Vogel, *Allgemeine Gewerbefreiheit*, pp. 12–13: 'Prozeß bewusster und geplanter Entwicklung zur Erhöhung der Leistungsfähigkeit sozialer Systeme.'
[27] Wehler, *Deutsche Gesellschaftsgeschichte*, I, pp. 445–54.
[28] E.g. Walther Hubatsch, 'Stein and constitutional reform in nineteenth-century Germany: pre-conditions, plans and results', *Studies in Medieval and Modern German history* (Oxford, 1985), pp. 93–108.
[29] Frauendienst, 'Das preussische Staatsministerium', p. 111.

the pages of a Kehr or Rosenberg. Conversely, Rosenberg's tribute to the intellectual influences on the pre-Reform bureaucrats bears an uncanny resemblance to Frauendienst's eulogies on the idealistic motivations of the early reformers whose 'self-reliant personalities and superior professional knowledge called for recognition, participation and responsibility'.[30]

More concretely, the old school saw in the events and aspirations of 1806 both a response to the dire international situation of the state and the origins of the familiar ministerial structure of later years. Thus Friedrich Meinecke argued that 'the strongest impulses for genuine internal reforms came from the external situation of the state';[31] this is indisputable. But Meinecke also saw in Stein's memorandum of April 1806 (see pp. 318–20 below), 'a first preparatory step to a constitutional monarchy';[32] as we shall see, this was a much more dubious proposition. More recently, Fritz Knemeyer has suggested that the Prussian plans of the years 1797 to 1806 show a 'clear line of development to ministerial responsibility'.[33] Similarly, Werner Frauendienst saw Stein's memorandum as a programme to 'take the leadership of the state out of the hands of the king and transfer it to a *Staatsministerium*', a move which, in an astonishingly Kehrite phrase, he saw as 'a kind of emancipation of the highest levels of the administration (*eine Art Emanzipation der obersten Spitzen der Verwaltung*)'.[34] Finally, Dieter Grimm's standard *Deutsche Verfassungsgeschichte* sees already in the pre-Reform period a 'small circle of liberal civil servants' ('*kleiner Kreis liberaler Beamten*'),[35] which overcame the 'aristocratic opponents of reform' to push for constitutional change. The purpose of this constitutional change, following Grimm's

[30] Ibid., pp. 104–5: 'Kraft der auf sich selbst gestellten Persönlichkeit sowie überlegenes Fachwissen, verlangten nach Geltung, Teilnahme und Verantwortlichkeit'; in similar vein Rosenberg, 'Die Überwindung der monarchischen Autokratie (Preußen)', p. 192.

[31] Friedrich Meinecke, *The age of German liberation, 1795–1815* (Berkeley, 1977), p. 40. For a more recent recognition of the importance of the primacy of foreign policy for administrative reforms generally see Wunder, 'Rolle und Struktur staatlicher Bürokratie in Frankreich und Deutschland', p. 145.

[32] Friedrich Meinecke, *Das Zeitalter der deutschen Erhebung, 1795–1815* (Bielefeld, 1913), p. 74: 'einen ersten vorbereitenden Schritt zum konstitutionellen Königtum'; in a similar vein see also Herbert von Borch, *Obrigkeit und Widerstand. Zur politischen Soziologie des Beamtentums* (Tübingen, 1954).

[33] Franz-Ludwig Knemeyer, 'Beginn der Reorganisation der Verwaltung in Deutschland', in K. G. A. Jeserich, Hans Pohl and Georg-Christoph von Uruh (eds.), *Deutsche Verwaltungsgeschichte*. Vol. II: *Vom Reichsdeputationshauptschluss bis zur Auflösung des Deutschen Bundes* (Stuttgart, 1983), p. 137: ('*eine klare Entwicklungslinie zum verantwortlichen Ministerium*').

[34] Frauendienst, 'Das preussische Staatsministerium', pp. 112–14.

[35] Dieter Grimm, *Deutsche Verfassungsgeschichte, 1776–1866* (Frankfurt, 1988), p. 77.

general model, was to establish a 'problem-solving mechanism'[36] which
would serve to reconcile a social order based on individual freedom with
a political power which was located outside and above society.[37]

This chapter cannot refute these interpretations conclusively, nor does it
wish to. It *cannot* refute them, because the scope of the study is too
limited chronologically and the focus too foreign-political to mount a
serious challenge to models which purport to explain a broad sweep of
Prussian history from the death of the great Frederick to the Prussian
Reform Movement and even beyond. The bulk of this book is not
concerned with the Prussian bureaucracy as a whole but with the much
smaller group of leading politician-administrators whose security of
tenure was not guaranteed by law. It is with developments in this all-
important area, where administration ended and politics began, that this
chapter is concerned. It is only by studying the aspirations and political
posturing of these men that we will be able to test the Kehr–Rosenberg
hypotheses, and indeed other hypotheses, for their validity for a well-
defined period. Do we really, to conflate the critical and idealistic
interpretations, have a group of self-confident, self-aware bureaucrats,
driven by a collective desire for 'recognition, participation and responsibility (*Geltung, Teilnahme und Verantwortlichkeit*)' baying for their rightful
place at the head of the Prussian state in 1806? Can we really speak of a
concerted attempt, be it ministerial or bureaucratic in origin, to limit the
power of the monarch? Must we, as Dieter Grimm and Kehr/Rosenberg
do, see the process of constitutional change, or *Staatsreform*, as powered
entirely by an internal dynamic? What if – as I shall argue – the attempted
constitutional changes of 1806 were not part of a 'problem-solving
mechanism', but rather, on the one hand, a means of concentrating all
the internal resources of the state to guarantee the executive cohesion so
essential to its survival, and on the other hand, part of a long-standing
high-political feud in which constitutional issues were manipulated for
personal political gain?
   The chapter does not *wish* to refute completely the two existing
approaches to the pre-Reform period, because both contain much that
is valuable. Though it is the contention of this book that the Kehr–
Rosenberg, and to a lesser extent the Wehler, interpretations essentially
distort the motivations of the actors, they have enriched our perspective
of pre-Reform Prussia, at least in the methodological sense. Nonetheless
I hope that what follows will at least dent the applicability of the Kehr–

36 Grimm, *Deutsche Verfassungsgeschichte*, p. 29.
37 Ibid., p. 30: 'Die Verfassung als adäquates Problemlösungsmodell'.

Rosenberg–Wehler view for the time before 1806, especially for the period immediately preceding Jena. Though the alternative offered bears a close resemblance to earlier, 'Primacy of Foreign Policy', views of the pre-Reform period, it is a view shorn of the more anachronistic teleologies. This perspective will be achieved by sketching in the 'adversarial' context without which all these early reform initiatives cannot be properly understood.

The Prussian executive in crisis, 1804–1806

Throughout the period 1804 to 1806, the foreign-political debate in Prussia continued to stress the centrality of the monarch in the decision-making process. 'I consider it my bounden duty', Hardenberg had written during the Rumbold affair, 'to subordinate my own humble opinion to your supreme scrutiny and decision.'[38] The Schönbrunn debate of the following year gave rise to a similar rhetoric: Haugwitz had stressed that Frederick William 'reste maître de choisir'; Hardenberg did not allow himself 'aucune détermination pour l'un ou pour l'autre [course of action], c'est au roi à la prendre'; and General Schulenburg went so far as to say that it was 'le sentiment intérieur du roi qui puisse décider, un serviteur n'oserait proposer un choix'. In early 1806 Hardenberg stressed that 'c'est à sa majesté a prendre les déterminations qu'elle jugera convenables à son caractère, à sa dignité et à l'intérêt de sa monarchie. Toutefois je crois de mon devoir de soumettre les réflexions suivantes à sa haute décision';[39] and a month later he ended with a flourish that neatly summed up the relationship between monarch and councillor: 'Sa Majesté se consultera Elle même, Elle prendra l'avis de militaires experimentales et pénétrés d'un vrai patriotisme; Elle prononcera!'.[40] Even as late as July 1806, when he was arguing in favour of action against France, Haugwitz was careful to disclaim 'aucune opinion sur ce choix important'; 'la sagesse du roi', he added, 'peut seule décider sur cette grande alternative'.

Yet for all the decisionist rhetoric, in reality Prussian policy was characterised by uncertainty and indecision. This was not new, but the

[38] Hardenberg memorandum, 30.10.1804, Berlin, in Wohlwill, 'Fernere Aktenstücke', p. 205: 'Ich halte es für unnachlässliche Pflicht meine unmaasgebliche Meinung hierüber der allerhöchsten Prüfung und Entscheidung zu unterwerfen.'

[39] 'Zweite Denkschrift Hardenbergs über den Vertrag vom 15 December 1805', 1.1.06, Berlin, in Ranke (ed.), Denkwürdigkeiten Hardenbergs, V, p. 265. For similar sentiments see Beyme to Massenbach, 20.7.06, Berlin, in Winter (ed.), Die Reorganisation des preußischen Staates, p. 27.

[40] Hardenberg Memorandum of 24.2.1806, Berlin, in Ranke (ed.), Denkwürdigkeiten Hardenbergs, I, pp. 490–6.

mounting international crisis between 1804 and 1806 made it more dramatic. The roots of this malaise in the Prussian executive were essentially threefold. First of all, there were the complications of a shared foreign ministry. The resulting threat to the coherence of Prussian foreign policy had already been pointed out by Hardenberg in 1804. 'Foreign affairs', he warned,

are intrinsically more difficult to conduct than financial, welfare and judicial matters because unlike these matters, foreign affairs do not depend on certain rules but rather on rapidly changing circumstances . . . But it is impossible to act consistently if parallel plans and negotiations are taking place without the knowledge of the chief minister and if others than he deal with foreign envoys in an official capacity.[41]

Hardenberg's fears were soon to be borne out in October–November 1804, when the recall of Haugwitz complicated his handling of the Rumbold crisis. This concern turned into outright alarm when Haugwitz was recalled for a second time in August 1805; this impelled Hardenberg to make his representations against a joint ministry in October 1805.

But the most graphic illustration of the perils of a split executive was the contradictory – and confused – policy in the winter of 1805–6. While one Prussian foreign minister sought an accommodation with Napoleon, the other had cast his lot for the coalition. While Haugwitz surrendered Prussian territories in Franconia, Hardenberg refused to sign the document of ratification. This prompted Metternich to observe that Frederick William was in the 'étrange situation d'avoir deux ministres des affaires étrangères, dont l'un négocie et dispose à son insu de ses provinces, et dont l'autre refuse d'ajouter son nom au sien'.[42] While one minister reversed the mobilisation of the army in February 1806 so as not to provoke France, the other claimed not to have been consulted. 'Dieu sait', Lombard complained, 'tout le mal qui résulte tous les jours de ce

---

[41] Hardenberg to Beyme, c. March 1804, in GStA Rep. 92 Hardenberg E5, fo. 2: 'Die Auswärtigen Angelegenheiten sind schon an und für sich schwerer zu behandeln als Finanz und Policzey und Justiz-Gegenstände, da sie bei weitem nicht so wie diese, auf bestimmten Regeln sondern mehr auf einer schnellen Veränderlichkeit der Umstände . . . Unmöglich ist es aber, consequent zu handeln, wenn Pläne und Neben-Negociationen stattfinden, von denen derjenige, welcher die Geschäfte leitet nichts weiß und wenn andere als er in officieller Eigenschaft mit den fremden Gesandten traitiren.'

[42] Metternich to Stadion, 28.2.1806, Berlin, in Klinkowström (ed.), *Metternichs nachgelassenen Papieren*, p. 108.

manque d'unité dans ce travail';[43] 'it is', Major-General von Kleist lamented, 'a confusion without parallel'.[44]

The second root cause of the Prussian *misère* lay in the adversarial nature of Prussian high politics itself; the third cause was the indecisive nature of the monarch, Frederick William III. These two factors were not only related and mutually reinforcing, they also fundamentally subverted the principles upon which the Prussian executive was constructed. Ideally, the monarch was supposed to proceed from a well-informed discussion to decisive action. In practice, however, the innate caution and hesitancy of Frederick William made Prussian policy anything but decisive. Instead of *acting*, Frederick William responded to external crisis by indefinitely extending the deliberative process. A certain circularity thus crept into decision-making, for the royal advisors, eager to realise their personal ambitions, merely confirmed the king in his caution; the result was a permanent state of consultation and indecision. And whenever a minister – such as Hardenberg, or Haugwitz before 1804 – counselled a more activist policy, the king turned to his rivals for more palatable advice. This arrangement, to quote the neat description of Paul Schroeder was designed 'not to help him [Frederick William] to reach a decision but to help him avoid one'.[45]

Prussian statesmen had long been well aware of the weakness of their executive. If Friedrich von Cölln had demanded that the commands of the sovereign should 'resonate through all strings of the instrument (of state)', then the reality of Prussian policy was more a discordant cacophony than a harmonious melody. In the place of rational debate, it seemed, there was only the frantic babble of self-serving councillors, in which extensive consultation was bought at the expense of clarity. 'An object', Haugwitz confessed, 'when it is seen from all sides and through many eyes, consequently often seems unclear.'[46] The policy of the 'middle way' – pursued by Prussia so tenaciously until mid-1806 – was the logical outcome of the structure of the Prussian executive. But by 1805–6, Prussian politicians were becoming increasingly restless at the lack of any sense of direction in the formulation and execution of foreign policy. 'Indecision and ambiguity', Schulenburg had warned during the

[43] Lombard to Hardenberg, 12.2.1806, Berlin, in Ranke (ed.), *Denkwürdigkeiten Hardenbergs*, I, pp. 462–3.
[44] Kleist to Massenbach, 27.8.1806, Charlottenburg, in Bailleu (ed.), *Preussen und Frankreich*, II, pp. 544–5: 'Es ist eine Confusion, die ihres gleichen nicht hat.'
[45] Schroeder, *The transformation of European politics*, p. 280.
[46] Ranke (ed.), *Denkwürdigkeiten Hardenbergs*, V, p. 262: 'Ein Gegenstand von allen Seiten und durch mehrere Augen betrachtet, erscheint deswegen schon, wenigstens ist es oft der Fall, wenig klar.'

Schönbrunn debate of December 1805, 'leads to inevitable disaster.' In February 1806, Hardenberg had demanded that decisions should be taken with 'consequence, promptitude and energy'. And in the following July, Haugwitz called for decisions to be taken 'd'une manière ferme et inébranable'; 'le pire de tous les partis', he had stressed, 'serait de n'en prendre aucun'.

Any reform of the executive had to address itself to two problems. In the first place, it had to replace the 'collegial' system of multiple ministers with a monocratic foreign ministry.[47] Secondly, the 'antechamber of power' around the king had to be replaced by a formal council of state, in which policy could be discussed among responsible ministers and then rapidly executed. In this way, Frederick William would be enabled – or forced – to take the necessary decisions with due dispatch. What the reformers did *not* intend – and was never at issue – was to dislodge the monarch from the executive, still less to submit him to any kind of constitutional restraints. Political reform in Prussia before 1807 was thus very narrowly focussed on improving the deliberative and executive mechanisms of the highest organs of state; at no time did the reformers envisage extending the consultative process to the traditional estates, still less to the population as a whole. Indeed, most Prussians were agreed that the exposed geographical location of the monarchy precluded parliamentary structures on the British model. 'The supporter of popular sovereignty should consider', wrote Theodor Schmalz in 1806, 'that only an island can afford Great Britain's parliament and electoral system. Where there is no fleet to defend against external enemies, this function falls to a standing army. But a military constitution is only compatible with an absolute monarchy.'[48] Instead Schmalz called for 'Simplicity in all things! Simplicity in government, simplicity in administration! Only one man should be king and master.'[49] Similarly, Immanuel Kant argued that monarchy might be the best form of government in those states whose geographic situation exposed them to

---

[47] This demand had been articulated by Justi well before the French Revolution: Ernst Klein, 'Johann Heinrich Gottlob Justi und die preußische Staatswirtschaft', *VSWG*, 48 (1961), 195.

[48] Theodor Anton Schmalz, *Staatsverfassung Großbritanniens*, p. 131: 'Der Anhänger der Volksmacht aber bedenke, daß nur eine Insel Großbritanniens Parlament und Volkswahl haben könne. Wo nicht eine Flotte vor äußeren Feinden sichert, da muß es ein stehendes Heer. Die kriegerische Verfassung ist aber unverträglich mit anderen als unumschränkt-monarchischen.' Marion Gray's belief (*Prussia in transition*, pp. 38–9) that Schmalz praised the British constitution as a model for Germany seems to rest on a misunderstanding.

[49] Schmalz, *Staatsverfassung Großbritanniens*, p. iv: 'Einfachkeit in Allem! Einheit der Regierung, Einfachkeit ihrer Verwaltung! Nur einer sei König und Herr.'

the attentions of powerful neighbours.[50] This instinctive link between geography and political structure was typically Prussian.

But Frederick William continued to resist a reform of the executive. For although most memorialists ritually affirmed their intent to 'strengthen the king',[51] the monarch saw in the erection of a formal advisory council of state a clear threat to his own authority. Such a body, Schulenburg warned, was 'the least popular among rulers . . . because they believe it to appear as if they are not in control themselves'.[52] But Frederick William also genuinely seems to have believed that the existing system of extensive consultation and measured, not to say ponderous, decision-making enabled him to maximise the expertise available to him. This preoccupation with 'balance' expressed itself in December 1805, when Hardenberg's attempted resignation was rejected on the grounds that it would lead to 'one-sidedness' in royal counsels;[53] later, in January 1806, Frederick William pleaded with Hardenberg to stay – 'you are surely not going to abandon me (Sie wollen mich doch nicht verlassen)' – for the same reasons.[54]

At first, the executive reform debate of 1805 to 1806 differed little from that of 1797 to 1804. The impulse for reform continued to be the primacy of foreign policy. When Hardenberg's collaborator, Altenstein, proposed a new activist stance in December 1805, he demanded that the whole 'internal constitution [of the state], especially the military constitution', be reformed accordingly; this link between internal cohesion and external threats was being forcefully made by Fichte in his influential lectures on the Grundzüge des gegenwärtigen Zeitalters, which Altenstein attended.[55] While there were some – like Altenstein himself – who

[50] Immanuel Kant, 'Der Streit der Fakultäten. Zweiter Abschnitt. Der Streit der philosophischen Fakultät mit der juristischen', in Hermann Cohen, Artur Buchenau, Otto Buek, Albert Görland, B. Kellermann, O. Schöndorffer and Ernst Cassirer (eds.), Immanuel Kant. Werke VII. Die Metaphysik der Sitten. der Streit der Fakultäten (Hildesheim, 1973), p. 398: 'Es ist aber hiermit nicht gemeint, daß ein Volk, welches eine monarchische Konstitution hat, sich damit das Recht anmaße, ja auch nur in sich geheim den Wunsch hege, sie abgeändert zu wissen; denn seine vielleicht sehr verbreitete Lage in Europa kann ihm jene Verfassung als die eigene anempfehlen, bei den es sich zwischen mächtigen Nachbarn erhalten kann.'
[51] Clausewitz, 'Nachrichten über Preußen in seiner großen Katastrophe', in Rothfels (ed.), Clausewitz. Politische Schriften und Briefe, p. 212.
[52] Naudé (ed.), 'Denkwürdigkeiten des Ministers Grafen Schulenburg', p. 325: 'bei den Herrschern am wenigsten beliebt . . . , weil sie glauben, den Anschein zu erwecken, nicht selbst zu regieren'.
[53] Quoted in Ranke (ed.), Denkwürdigkeiten Hardenbergs, I, p. 412.
[54] Hardenberg Diary 1.1.1806, GStA Rep. 92 Hardenberg L26, fo. 1.
[55] Altenstein memorandum, 28.12.1805, printed in Müsebeck, 'Fragmentatische Aufzeichnungen', 149, 158. See Johann Gottlieb Fichte, Die Grundzüge des gegenwärtigen Zeitalters. Dargestellt von Johann Gottlieb Fichte in Vorlesungen gehalten zu Berlin,

demanded reforms 'following the example of the French (*nach dem Beispiel der Franzosen*)', the attention was still largely focussed on the reform of the executive. 'The decline of which we have spoken', Clausewitz was to observe retrospectively, 'was chiefly a decline of the apparatus of government (*Regierungsmaschine*), not of society as a whole.'[56] There was – as yet – no widespread sense that such deep-seated societal reforms were necessary to counter the mounting French threat. 'During this period', Mathew Levinger writes, 'proponents of reform did not seek drastic changes; instead, they hoped gradually to rationalize the state apparatus and the social order.'[57] 'Pity the ruler', the Prussian jurist Suarez had warned the young Frederick William, 'whose land goes into such a deep decline that he is left with no other means of preserving the state itself than to interfere with the rights and privileges of whole classes of citizens.'[58] The clear implication of this sentiment was that necessity of state could justify any reform, including thoroughgoing societal change. Before 1806 this time had not yet come, but it was not far off.

'The shaky edifice', Struensee had observed of the jungle of competing governmental structures in Prussia before Jena, 'will probably hold another while'.[59] But during the Hanoverian crisis of 1806, the weakness in the executive became too obvious to overlook. The failure to coordinate policy between the Kabinettsministerium and the senior

im *Jahre 1804–5* (Berlin, 1806), pp. 363–4: 'Erst nachdem der Staat vollkommene äußere Sicherheit haben wird, sagte ich, wird ihm die Frage enstehen, worauf die, für seine bisherigen Zwecke, überflüssige Volkskraft gerichtet werden solle'; p. 451: 'Ein mindermächtiger Staat vermag, eben weil er dies ist, nicht, durch auswärtige Eroberungen sich zu vergrößern. Wie soll er denn also, au seinem beschränkten Zustande heraus, zu einem bedeutenderem Gewichte kommen? Es ist ihm kein Mittel übrig als die innere Verstärkung.' See also: Günther Roß, 'Das Leben des Freiherrn von Altenstein bis zum Jahre 1807', *FBPG*, 53 (1941), 120–1, which does not go beyond Müsebeck, and Eduard Spranger, 'Altensteins Denkschrift von 1807 und ihre Beziehungen zur Philosophie', *FBPG*, 18 (1905), 471–517, on the philosophical basis for the primacy of foreign policy with Fichte and Müsebeck, 'Fragmentarische Aufzeichnungen Altensteins', pp. 137, 140 and 142.

56 Clausewitz, 'Nachrichten über Preußen in seiner großen Katastrophe', in Rothfels (ed.), *Clausewitz. Politische Schriften und Briefe*, p. 215: 'Der Verfall von dem wir gesprochen haben, war hauptsächlich ein Verfall der Regierungsmaschine, nicht des ganzen gesellschaftlichen Zustandes.'

57 Mathew Levinger, 'Imagining a nation: the constitutional question in Prussia, 1806–1815' (unpublished DPhil dissertation, University of Chicago, 1992), p. 68. Levinger' s work is almost entirely concerned with the period after 1806–7.

58 Cited in Stamm-Kuhlmann, *Friedrich Wilhelm III*, p. 159: 'Wehe dem Regenten, dessen Land in einem so tiefen Verfall gerät, daß ihm, um den Staat selbst zu konservieren, kein anderes Mittel übrig bleibt, als die Vorrechte und Privilegien ganzer Klassen seiner Staatsbürger anzutasten.'

59 C. Bornhak, 'Die Entstehung der preußischen Ministerien', *FBPG*, 51 (1939), p. 54: 'Einige Zeit wird die Pastete wohl halten.'

administrators of the Generaldirektorium – not to mention the failure to warn the diplomatic service overseas of the threat to Prussian shipping – highlighted the lack of a unified council in which policy could be deliberated and coordinated; the existing Staatsrat, which was supposed to synchronise foreign affairs and internal administration, was not summoned in 1806.[60] If the disregard of bureaucratic opinion reflected Prussian *strengths*, that is the determination of the state to place *raison d'état* above commercial considerations, the failure to keep the administration abreast of diplomatic developments simply reflected the structural *weaknesses* of the Prussian executive. It was, in fact, the shock of international isolation, public humiliation and a disastrous war with Britain that prompted senior Prussian bureaucrats to look beyond their parochial administrative horizons. If in the 1790s such figures as Schrötter, Auerswald and Stein had prided themselves on their 'almost programmatic lack of interest in foreign policy',[61] by 1806 they were forced to confront the reality of the Napoleonic threat.[62] Most importantly of all, the Hanoverian crisis, as Richard Krauel has pointed out, provided the immediate impulse for Stein's memorandum on executive reform.[63]

The substance of Reform: decision, not discussion

In his capacity as minister for trade and excise, Baron Stein had long been a 'root and branch' reformer, committed to a total renewal of the state in the agrarian and economic spheres. It was only in the spring of 1806, however, after the catastrophic experience of war with Britain that Stein turned his attention to the specific problem of executive reform. During this period Stein had witnessed the complete breakdown of communications between the various branches of government through the lack of either a strong ruler or a central political institution to replace him. He had also seen the way in which, as he believed, the professional expertise of the responsible ministers was ignored while the supposedly subordinate clique of cabinet councillors and adjutants precipitated the state into an ill-considered and commercially disastrous war.

---

60 Cosmar and Klaproth, *Der brandenburgisch-preußische Staatsrat*, p. 236.
61 Zernack, 'Polen in der Geschichte Preußens', p. 428.
62 On Stein's increased interest in foreign policy in 1805–6 see Lehmann, *Stein*, I, p. 379 and Werner Gembruch, 'Krieg und Heerwesen im politischen Denken des Freiherrn vom Stein', in Werner Gembruch, *Staat und Heer. Ausgewählte historische Studien zum ancien régime, zur Französischen Revolution und zu den Befreiungskriegen*, edited by Johannes Kunisch (Berlin, 1990), p. 502.
63 Krauel, 'Stein während des preussisch-englischen Konflikts in Jahre 1806', pp. 435, 439.

The essence of Stein's remedy was summed up in the subtitle given to the main section of his April memorandum: 'Description of the faulty organisation of the Kabinett and the need for the creation of a ministerial conference'.[64] Stein set out, as he put it, to 'examine the deficiencies of the present governmental constitution'. He described his motivation in so doing as the 'danger which threatens it [the monarchy], and which threatens to take away its independence and the sources of its national prosperity'. This was a clear reference to the collapse of commerce and shipping resulting from the war with Britain. In order to put things right, Stein continued, it was necessary to tackle the evil at its root and remove it. There followed a short description of the political structure of Prussia which has since become famous: 'The Prussian state has no constitution, the supreme power is not divided between the head and the representatives of the nation.' Admittedly, Stein wrote, the estates of some provinces had certain participatory duties, but only, as he stressed, in 'local' not in 'general' or national affairs. Stein explained that this was in order to prevent the 'conduct of general, [that is national] affairs from being hampered or paralysed'. In other words, limited participation was justified by the need for secure and rapid decision; representative assemblies with potentially retardative effects were rejected.

Stein identified the root of the Prussian problems in the Kabinett, that is, the group of people who as secretaries or as adjutants surrounded the person of the king and who, according to Stein, to all intents and purposes determined the formulation of Prussian policy, despite their non-responsible positions. Together, these cabinet secretaries and military adjutants formed an 'antechamber of power' which Stein described in the following graphic terms:

The king himself lives in complete isolation from his ministers. He is neither in professional communication with them, nor does he meet them, nor does he correspond with them personally. One consequence of this situation is one-sidedness in the impressions which he receives, in the decisions which he takes and in his complete dependence on his surroundings.[65]

Carl Schmitt himself could not have provided a more succinct description of the 'antechamber of power' in action. In order to remedy this situation Stein suggested the creation of a Staatsrat, or Council of State, of five ministers, who would be individually responsible for the following

[64] 'Entwurf eines Immediatberichts des Ministers Freiherr vom Stein nebst einem Promemoria "Darstellung der fehlerhaften Organisation des Kabinetts der Notwendigkeit der Bildung einer Ministerialkonferenz"', Berlin, late April/early May, in Winter (ed.), *Die Reorganisation des preußischen Staates*, I, pp. 4–13.
[65] Ibid., p. 8.

areas: War, Foreign Affairs, Public Security, Public Revenue and two departments for legal affairs. In addition, the cabinet secretaries should be forbidden to brief the king. The final decision should always rest with the king. Stein ended with the warning that if these reforms were not carried out then it should be expected that the state would either dissolve itself or lose its independence. Executive reform was thus a direct response to the dire external situation of the state.

Count Hardenberg, at this point ostensibly in the political wilderness, but in fact conducting the secret policy with Russia behind the backs of the French and his high-political adversaries, did not yet commit his views to paper in the same systematic way as Stein. However, in various audiences with the king and in his private correspondence he was pushing a very similar analysis. Even before Stein penned his memorandum, Hardenberg had warned the king of the real distribution of power in the Prussian state, whose most important business was conducted by two adjutants, two cabinet councillors and a very subordinate, indeed dependent cabinet minister, who was constantly subject to their paralysing and contradictory instructions.[66] To make matters worse, Hardenberg continued, these men exploited the trust of the king. By right they were to do no more than present the reports and petitions of the highest branches of government. Instead, Hardenberg complained, in a phrase which sums up the classic dialectic between absolute power and the inescapable antechamber of power around it, the Kabinett 'insinuated their own ideas on every occasion (*allenthalben ihre eigenen Ideen unterschöben)*', indeed 'they themselves encouraged the belief that they controlled the king (*sie selbst den Glauben verbreiteten: sie leiteten den König)*'.[67]

The solution to these abuses, Hardenberg argued, lay in a change of the 'arrangement of business and the personnel (*Geschäftsverfassung und das Personal*').[68] What he meant by a change in personnel was straightforward enough. This was the removal of his personal enemies, Lombard, Beyme, Haugwitz and the military adjutants. The proposed changes in the structure of decision-making resembled those of Stein in important respects. Part of the problem was the fact that it was impossible for the monarch to 'read and go to the bottom of everything [indeed] how under the existing arrangements, unimportant details made inroads on his time and deprived him of an overview of the whole

---

[66] Ranke (ed.), *Denkwürdigkeiten Hardenbergs*, I, p. 603.
[67] Ibid., p. 604.
[68] Ibid., p. 605.

picture and the more important matters'.[69] This is what Hardenberg meant when he spoke of 'the disadvantages which resulted from the present structure of government and the lack of a central point in the government, whose soul should be [the king] himself'.[70] Clearly, the remedy lay in establishing such a central point at the heart of the Prussian political system, and it was in this sense that he wrote to Rüchel of the need 'to concentrate all the business of government in a central point and entrust it to a council'.[71] This body would be subordinate to the king whose 'branches would work in conjunction with him [the king], receive his instructions and then implement them with responsibility. In this way the king will be even more in charge than he is already.' In a letter to Wittgenstein more than two months later, Hardenberg returned to this theme: he called for a 'responsible council of a few ministers' which would meet not much more than twice a week. Its purpose was to guarantee that all civil and military matters 'converged on a single point (*in einem Centralpunkte zusammentreffen*)'.[72] The intention behind this measure was not to limit the power of the monarch. Rather, Hardenberg maintained, 'The king would be even more in charge with such a council than is the case at present.'[73] Moving from the general to the particular, Hardenberg explained how such a focal point would have prevented some of the more striking disasters of recent times: 'Then the sort of things I have experienced will no longer be possible. In January of this year [1806], for example, the army was demobilised and sent home without so much as a single word in my direction.'[74]

Interestingly enough, Hardenberg's rival Haugwitz shared his reforming demands.[75] If Hardenberg's testimony is to be believed, and in this case there is no reason whatever to doubt it, Haugwitz envisaged a

---

[69] Ibid., p. 604: 'alles lesen und ergründen . . . ; wie ihm gerade bei dem angenommenen Geschäftsbetrieb Kleinigkeiten die Zeit raubten und Uebersicht des Ganzen und der wichtigeren Gegenstände stehen müsse'.

[70] Ibid., p. 603: 'Nachteile, die aus der bisherigen Verfassung und dem Mangel eines Zentralpunktes der Regierung, dessen Seele er selbst sein sollte, entständen'.

[71] Hardenberg to Rüchel, 30.4.06, Berlin, in Winter (ed.), *Die Reorganisation*, I, pp. 3–4: 'die Staatsgeschäfte jeder Art in einem Zentralpunkt zusammenzufassen und einem Konseil zu übergeben'. Also: 'Glieder mit ihm selbst vereint arbeiten, seine Befehle vernehmen und dann mit Responsabilität ausführen. Der König wird dadurch mehr Herr, als er es jetzt ist.'

[72] Hardenberg to Wittgenstein, 4.7.06, Tempelberg, in Ranke (ed.), *Denkwürdigkeiten Hardenbergs*, II, p. 110.

[73] Ibid., p. 111: 'Der König würde mehr Herr bei einem solchem Conseil sein, als jetzt.'

[74] Ibid.: 'Dann würden dergleichen Dinge nicht möglich sein, als ich erlebt habe, daß man z.B. die Armee im Januar d.J. demobilisierte und nach Haus schickte ohne daß ich ein Wort davon erfuhr.'

[75] Ranke (ed.), *Denkwürdigkeiten Hardenbergs*, I, p. 591.

Council of State which the king would chair and in which all reports (*Vorträge*) were to be made. This idea was remarkably close to Hardenberg's own project. As for the all-important question of personnel, Haugwitz suggested that he himself take charge of foreign affairs, Hardenberg be made minister of the interior and a war minister be appointed to take care of military affairs. The two cabinet councillors, both allies of Haugwitz, should be made Assistenzräthe and equal members of the said Council of State. Not surprisingly, Hardenberg would have none of it, replying that though he approved the whole plan 'in principle', the continued presence of the two cabinet councillors rendered its supposed advantages 'illusory'. Indeed, under such an arrangement these men would be the 'true ministers' with Haugwitz and Hardenberg the 'secretaries'.

Perhaps even more surprisingly, Karl Friedrich Beyme had long believed that the system of decision-making in Prussia was in need of reform.[76] As far back as September 1804 he was known to have thought that

it is improper that the country should be governed by those who are not subjected to any responsibility; that he and his Lombard, who in fact transact all the business of the state, are in comparatively obscure situations; whilst ministers have the ostensible responsibility without the power of influencing the decisions of the sovereign. From this he infers that it would be proper to establish a council to which the king should confide the affairs of the country and of which he [Beyme] and Lombard should be the leading members.[77]

Whether Beyme pursued this line of argument at the time is unclear, but he was sufficiently shaken by the events of 1805 to 1806 to rejoin the executive reform debate with a memorandum prescribing 'order, speed, and precision in the conduct of the affairs of state'.[78] Admittedly, the bulk of the argument concerned narrower questions of military reform, but striking parallels with Stein's ideas are evident nonetheless. As Beyme pointed out, once all decisions were no longer taken directly by the monarch, the existing system lost 'concentration', that is, speed of deliberation and execution. By way of remedy, Beyme proposed a 'supreme ministerial council' consisting of a chief cabinet minister – for foreign affairs, a minister for war, and a minister of the interior. No

---

[76] Disch, 'Der Kabinettsrat Beyme und die auswärtige Politik Preussens', *FBPG*, 41 (1928), p. 332.
[77] Francis Jackson to Harrowby, 17.9.04, Berlin, PROL FO 64/66, unfoliated.
[78] 'Aus des geh. Kabinettsrats Beyme "Bemerkungen über einige Punkte, welche bei der militärischen Organisation eines Staats zu berücksichtigen"', 4.7.06, Charlottenburg, in Winter (ed.), *Die Reorganisation*, I, p. 18: 'Ordnung, Schnelligkeit und Genauigkeit in der Verhandlung der Staatsangelegenheiten'.

mention was made of the cabinet secretaries, from which it may be deduced that they – and Beyme – were to maintain their existing role. As Ludwig Dehio has pointed out, these suggestions were a written record of what must have been counselled verbally on more than one occasion; it may even be that Beyme planned to take the wind out of Stein's sails, by anticipating his proposals.[79] Beyme was certainly not opposed to executive reform, as such, provided he was not the loser by it.

The lack of unity in the conduct of state affairs was also criticised by Colonel von Massenbach,[80] a man deeply distrusted by Stein.[81] Like Beyme, he suggested entrusting the affairs of state to three highly esteemed figures of unimpeachable personal and political probity; unlike Beyme, he named those he had in mind: General von Phull as minister for war, Count Keller as minister for foreign affairs and Baron Stein as minister in charge of the state economy. But Massenbach's main concern was the need thereby to capture the 'antechamber of power' around the king:

These three men will work under the eyes of your Majesty and near to your rooms. They will be inseparable from your person. They will be your immediate surroundings. Your Majesty shall be the president of this assembly; you shall chair all their deliberations; you shall attend meetings; you shall sign all their decisions; and this signature shall only sanction that which has been decided in your presence. In this way your Majesty shall constitute a centre, a *Brennpunkt*, from which all the rays of your power shall emanate which affect foreign affairs. In this manner you shall elevate yourself to true sovereignty.[82]

All of these efforts were isolated and uncoordinated. It was not until the end of August that any high political faction in Prussia succeeded in approaching the king with a fully integrated plan for governmental reform and a change in personalities. This initiative, known to history as 'the petition of the princes', was a war-party document which unashamedly sought the removal of the supposedly Francophile cabinet secretaries and official Kabinettsminister from the antechamber of power and their replacement therein by men of true patriotic credentials.

---

[79] See Dehio, 'Eine Reform-Denkschrift Beymes aus dem Sommer 1806', 321–5.

[80] Christian von Massenbach, b. 1758 Schmalkalden, d. Bialokosz (Posen) 1827. Prussian colonel and military theorist. Southern German background; entered Prussian service in 1782; taught the young Frederick William (III) mathematics and remained close to the king thereafter; 1787 wounded in the Dutch campaign; action in the French Revolutionary Wars; quartermaster-general of Hohenlohe in 1806 campaign; author of scurrilous memoirs; ended days in disgrace. *NDB*, 16, pp. 358–9.

[81] *Immediateingabe des Oberst von Massenbach*, 2.7.06, Berlin, in Winter (ed.), *Die Reorganisation*, I, pp. 15–17.

[82] Ibid., p. 16.

Among the signatories of this explosive plea were Stein, senior army figures such as Phull and Rüchel, as well as the princes of the blood, Henry, William, Louis Ferdinand and William Frederick of Orange. The duke of Brunswick had refused to sign the document itself, but wrote an accompanying letter in support of its aims.[83] Rather like Stein's earlier memorandum, the opening passages described the current parlous foreign-political situation of the Prussian state. This was followed by personal attacks, which highlighted the suspicion of the army, the general public and foreign courts against the Kabinett 'as it is organised at present'.[84] Surprisingly little polemic was employed, especially when compared with Stein's original document; nonetheless, the petitioners were adamant that the pro-French Kabinett must be removed. Indeed, their elimination was given precedence over executive reform. 'In fact', the petition ran, 'it is easily possible to lighten and to simplify the whole arrangement of business. But the main thing is that only the removal of Kabinettsminister Count Haugwitz and the two Kabinettsräte Beyme and Lombard will enable anxieties to be allayed and justified confidence in a happy outcome of affairs to be promoted.'[85]

The king's response to this overture was, as we shall see below, very negative indeed. Undeterred, the stalwarts of the war party drew up another document in justification. It was intended to be signed by Generals Blücher and Schmettau and Prince Hohenlohe in addition to the original petitioners, although some of these were now getting distinctly cold feet.[86] This time the language employed against the men of the existing Kabinett was much stronger and the call for action against the Napoleonic threat correspondingly shrill, backed up as it was by the highly unusual threat of collective resignation. The proposed remedy had three parts to it. In the foreign-political sphere there was the need for an 'open and powerful policy, [for] an agreement with other powers and a firm insistence on justice and dignity'. But, given the internal political situation of Prussia, this first demand led naturally to two others, namely the now familiar calls for the 'removal of these people (*Entfernung dieser Menschen*)' and 'the creation of an orderly, legal and responsible

[83] *Immediateingabe Stein und anderer*, 25.8.06, Brunswick and 31.8.06, Berlin, in Hubatsch and Botzenhart (eds.), *Stein*, II/I, p. 260.
[84] Ibid., pp. 260–1.
[85] Ibid., p. 262: 'Es ist sogar leicht möglich, den ganzen Gang der Geschäfte zu erleichtern, zu simplifizieren. Aber die Hauptsache ist, daß nur durch die Entfernung des Kabinettsministers Grafen von Haugwitz und der beiden Kabinettsräte Beyme und Lombard Zutrauen, Festigkeit und Ruhe in die Gemüter und eine gegründete Hoffnung des guten Ausgangs der Sachen zu erzielen möglich ist.'
[86] 'Prinz Wilhelm von Preussen an (einen Unterzeichner der Immediateingabe vom 25/31 August)', 3.9.06, Berlin, in Winter (ed.), *Die Reorganisation*, I, p. 44.

ministerial body, as had formerly existed and was always to be found under the best rulers of other states at all times'.[87]

In the meantime, Hardenberg had been upholding the cause of reform, or his version of it, in the background. Though his name was attached to neither of the two princely petitions, his trusted colleague Altenstein drew up a justificatory memorandum in support of them.[88] The main effort was, however, reserved for another memorandum, drawn up one month later by Altenstein, but heavily annotated and clearly approved by Hardenberg. This document is an invaluable source for an understanding of Hardenberg's role in the whole early reform process.

The rhetoric of decision which lay at the heart of Hardenberg's suggestions was set out forcefully right at the beginning. 'In a monarchy', the argument ran, 'it is undoubtedly the best if the King rules in person' if at all capable. 'Only the personal rule of the King can guarantee a strong government. At least in the most important matters, such a form of government can secure unity of decision, secrecy and rapid execution.'[89] Any intention of replacing the will of the monarch with an institution (*Behörde*) was expressly rejected; the aim was solely to ease the business of government for the King. 'It is only an expedient', the memorandum continued, 'if an administrative body rules instead of the regent (*Es ist nur ein Notbehelf, wenn statt des Regenten eine Behörde regiert*)'. Clearly, there was no sense here – yet – of an encroaching bureaucracy bidding for supremacy in the state. Rather, Frederick William was to be transformed from an indecisive monarch, subject to the whims and fancies of a capricious Kabinett, into a decisive monarch, capable of leading the Prussian state out of the great crisis in which it found itself.

The memorandum expressed optimism that the 'greatest part of these

---

87 'Entwurf einer zweiten Immediatvorstellung, "so von denselben Personen und dem General Blücher, Schmettau und Prinz Hohenlohe übergeben werden soll"', before 9.9.06, in Winter (ed.), *Die Reorganisation*, I, p. 47: 'offene, kraftvolle Politik, ein Einverständnis mit anderen Mächten und eine unüberwindliche Beharrlichkeit auf Recht und Würde', and: 'die Bildung einer ordentlichen gesetzmäßigen, responsablen Ministerialbehörde, wie sie auch ehemals gewesen und unter den besten Regenten anderer Staaten allezeit war'.
88 'Entwurf einer Immediateingabe zur Rechtfertigung der Vorstellung vom 25./31. August 1806', no date, approx. 11–15 September, in Winter (ed.), *Die Reorganisation*, I, pp. 47–55.
89 'Des Geh. Oberfinanzrats Freiherr von Altenstein Entwurf einer Denkschrift (Hardenbergs) über "die des Königs Majestät vorzuschlagende Veränderung in der Verfassung betreffend"', no date, approx. end of September, beginning of October, in Winter (ed.), *Die Reorganisation*, I, p. 62: 'Nur dadurch, dass der König selbst regiert, lässt sich eine kräftige Regierung bewirken. In den wichtigen Angelegenheiten wenigstens lässt sich bei einer solchen Regierung Einheit der Entschliessung, Verschwiegenheit und rasche Ausführung erwarten.'

mistakes would solve themselves, once the king was forced to rule himself, and these mistakes would be of no consequence when the constitution simplified the task of ruling and helped him to rule'. At present however, the memorandum continued, the Kabinett was an obvious brake on clear and sensible decision-making. The year before, in a similar memorandum,[90] Hardenberg and Altenstein had warned that these shackles on political activity had been bad enough in peacetime but could be fatal in a crisis 'when rapid and decisive action is so incredibly important'. By way of remedy they suggested a new structure of political decision-making. The Generaldirektorium and the Kabinetts-ministerium should be abolished and replaced by five ministries with responsibility for foreign affairs, justice, war, finance and the interior. These five ministers should not, however, report simultaneously to the king, but rather enjoy the desired *Immediatrecht*, that is the right of access to the king, individually. The significance of this will soon become clear.

But how could the king be won for this form of government, and how should the intermediate stage between the existing and the suggested constitution be managed? Here Hardenberg – for the thoughts expressed are clearly his own – recommended two measures. The first was the removal of the so-called 'damaging people' (Lombard, Beyme, Haugwitz). The second was the appointment of a foreign and internal minister as a temporary stopgap measure. It does not require too much imagination to see that the first was plainly intended to be Hardenberg himself. This scheme was based on the realisation, which Altenstein expressed towards the end of his memorandum, that Frederick William was attached to his cabinet secretaries primarily because 'he could hope to deal with them'. Altenstein therefore concluded that:

He [Frederick William] can be induced to accept several ministers, if he can hope to remain completely independent of them. He can hope this if they make their reports singly, and he is allowed to keep his cabinet secretaries. Apart from that, he will be doubly suspicious of a council, partly because its existence might appear to give the impression that he had been forced to accept a control on his actions, and partly because he fears that he might not push through his own opinion against strong opposition and might be forced to act against his own better judgment.[91]

The Prussian reformers of April to September 1806 have often been misunderstood. According to Thomas Stamm-Kuhlmann, Stein and

---

[90] Ernst Müsebeck, 'Fragmentarische Aufzeichnungen'.
[91] 'Die des Königs Majestät vorzuschlagende Veränderung in der Verfassung', in Winter (ed.), *Die Reorganisation*, I, p. 67.

Hardenberg were 'basically aiming for the constitutionalisation of the state';[92] and according to Karl Griewank, the proposals were the dawn of a 'new age' of ministerial responsibility over monarchic self-government.[93] In fact, there was no intention – as yet – to 'constitutionalise' the state, nor – for the time being – did anybody envisage 'ministerial responsibility' towards a representative assembly. Instead, the aim of the reformers was to *strengthen* royal decision-making and thus the efficiency of the executive as a whole. They sought, as Fritz Knemeyer has pointed out, to put the monarch at the centre of the political system, not to marginalise him.[94] This view tallies with the interpretation of Mathew Levinger, who has described the post-1815 Hardenberg as neither a 'reactionary' nor a 'revolutionary', but as a man intent on enhancing, rather than contesting, monarchical authority.[95] In short, the proposed reforms were meant to streamline, not overcome absolutism. 'They [were] intended', as Kurt Eisner has said, 'to effect an improved external organisation of absolutism.'[96]

The misunderstanding is a result of taking the concepts of *Verfassung* – constitution – and *Verantwortung* – responsibility – out of their specific historical context. In pre-nineteenth-century continental Europe, *Verfassung* was more likely to be descriptive of the way in which a particular territory was governed, rather than connotating a written, legally binding document which sets out the various political rights, duties, checks and balances customary in modern western societies.[97] When Prussian reformers spoke of *Verfassung* before November 1806, they meant the structure of the executive and decision-making; sometimes *Verfassung* was extended to include the military organisation of the state and even the civil administration as a whole. What they were *not* talking about was any kind of broader political participation – this only surfaced after 1807 – still less any sort of written constitution, as promised in 1815. *After* 1807 *Verfassungsreform* may well have meant 'the attempt to fulfil the participatory demands of "society", of these subjects,

---

92 Stamm-Kuhlmann, *Friedrich Wilhelm III*, pp. 230–1.
93 Griewank, 'Hardenberg und die preußische Politik', pp. 307–8.
94 Knemeyer, *Verwaltungsgeschichte*, p. 137.
95 Mathew Levinger, 'Hardenberg, Wittgenstein and the constitutional question in Prussia, 1815–1822', *German History*, 8 (1990), 260.
96 Eisner, *Das Ende des Reichs*, p. 233: 'Sie zielten, auf eine verbesserte äußere Organisation des Absolutismus ab.'
97 Heinz Mohnhaupt, 'Verfassung I: Konstitution, Status, Lex Fundamentalis', in Otto Brunner, Werner Conze and Reinhart Korelleck (eds.), *Geschichtliche Grundbegriffe* (Stuttgart, 1990), pp. 832, 858; Dieter Grimm, 'Verfassung II: Konstitution, Grundgesetze', in Brunner, Conze and Korelleck (eds.), *Geschichtliche Grundbegriffe*, p. 863.

the governed';[98] *before* November 1806 it meant no such thing. Similarly, 'responsibility', despite its proto-liberal connotations, signified something quite different in pre-Reform Prussia. Unlike their nineteenth-century heirs, these Prussian reformers were offended not by the lack of a parliamentary check on ministerial, or monarchical authority, but by the divergence between ministerial responsibility – or *liability* – and actual *power*, which was said to reside with a shadowy – and thus non-liable – clique of royal advisors.[99]

A particular focus of misunderstanding has been Stein's memorandum of April/May 1806. Max Lehmann saw this document rather prematurely as the 'birth of the Prussian constitution (*Geburtsstunde der preußischen Constitution)*'; Werner Gembruch saw the memorandum as an example of how Stein looked to British history and politics for inspiration to solve Prussia's political problems; Fritz Hartung agreed that Stein had Britain in mind when he spoke of *Verantwortlichkeit*;[100] and even the usually surefooted Stamm-Kuhlmann credits Stein with 'dreaming of the constitutional monarchy . . . he struck at the cabinet, but his real target was the king'.[101] Yet a textual – and contextual – analysis of the memorandum shows that no representative assembly or formal written constitution (in the modern sense) was being suggested; that – if anything – the British example was regarded as either not applicable or as a negative model; that Stein was specifically concerned with the improvement of the executive and the enhancement of monarchic power; and that his endeavours were motivated by an acute sense of the external exposure of the Prussian monarchy. In this respect a considerable gulf separates this document from the even more famous Nassau memorandum of 1808, by which time Stein – and most other reformers – had abandoned the narrow focus on the executive in favour of a much more thoroughgoing reform to activate the hidden strengths of Prussian society against the Napoleonic menace. Similarly, Paul Nolte

[98] Barbara Vogel, 'Verwaltung und Verfassung als Gegenstand staatlicher Reformstrategie', in Sösemann (ed.), *Gemeingeist und Bürgersinn*, p. 25: 'das Bemühen, Partizipationsansprüche der "Gesellschaft", der Untertanen, der Regierten, zu erfüllen'.

[99] For a good definition of '*Verantwortung*' before 1807, see Hans Schneider, *Der preußische Staatsrat* (Munich, 1952), p. 7. See also Bornhak, 'Die Entstehung der preußischen Ministerien', 54.

[100] Fritz Hartung, 'Studien zur Geschichte der preußischen Verwaltung. Erster Teil. Vom 16. Jahrhundert bis zum Zusammenbruch des alten Staates im Jahre 1806', *Abhandlungen der preußischen Akademie der Wissenschaften Jg. 1941 Phil.-hist. Klasse* (Berlin, 1942), no. 17, p. 43.

[101] Max Lehmann, *Stein*, I, p. 411; Gembruch, 'Zum England-Bild des Freiherrn vom Stein', in *Staat und Heer*, p. 538; Stamm-Kuhlmann, *Friedrich Wilhelm III*, p. 211: 'Stein träumte die konstitutionelle Monarchie herbei; . . . Stein schlug das Kabinett, aber er meinte den König.'

appears to have misread Stein's famous remark that the 'Prussian state has no state constitution [because] supreme power is not shared between the sovereign and representatives of the nobility.' Nolte argues that Stein's assessment was *schlichtweg falsch* because the monarchy and bureaucracy still 'shared supreme power with the nobility',[102] In fact, Stein was right, because in the relevant passage he was referring explicitly to the *executive*, not to socio-political or administrative power. It was for this reason that Stein demanded a reform of the Prussian *Regierungsverfassung* – *nota bene*: not of her non-existent *Staatsverfassung* – that is the creation or restoration of an efficient executive capable of confronting Napoleon.[103] In short, the political aspects of the pre-Reform in Prussia were far more limited than the participatory and emancipatory movements which emerged after 1807.

The adversarial context of Reform

Clearly, more than purely objective considerations were at work in the various Reform suggestions. Indeed, one could almost say that the plans described above, which are a representative cross-section of the whole pre-Reform debate, differed very little in substance. All the would-be reformers emphasised the need for *decision* and attributed the final word in decision-making to the king. They all recommended the simplification and rationalisation of high political decision-making as a response to the external threat of Napoleonic France. This is as true for the cabinet secretaries, such as Beyme, and thus theoretically part of the problem, as it is for members of the 'real' bureaucracy, such as Stein and Hardenberg. Yet in high-political terms men like Hardenberg and Beyme, whose standpoints on executive reform were rarely far apart, cultivated intense personal hostility. Conversely, where Reform plans diverged substantively, as in the case of Hardenberg and Stein, this did not interfere with a burgeoning high-political alliance against the Kabinett. One is therefore tempted to conclude that the bitter political enmities of the pre-Reform period, which then went on to mould political life after 1806 in important ways, were primarily 'adversarial' as opposed to 'objective' in nature. Even differences about 'objective' questions of reform could, as we shall soon see, be partly explained with reference to personality clashes. It is thus no coincidence that the Reform

---

102 Nolte, *Staatsbildung als Gesellschaftsreform*, p. 31.
103 Stein, 'Darstellung', in Winter (ed.), *Die Reorganisation der preußischen Staatsverwaltung*, pp. 1, 6: 'Da der preußische Staat keine Staatsverfassung hat, so ist es um so wichtiger, daß seine Regierungsverafssung nach richtigen Grundsätzen gebildet sei.'

plans sketched above differed very little in their fundamental direction, but very much in their personal political recommendations and consequences.

The all-important context to the executive reform debate of 1806 was not just the increasing French threat, but also the continuing struggle for supremacy in the antechamber of power around the king. As a result the reform argument became virtually indistinguishable from the personal ambitions of the various protagonists. In this respect, Kuhlmann misleads when he writes that 'Stein struck the Kabinett, but he meant the king'; as we shall see, one of the main points of the whole exercise was to hit personalities, not monarchic power *per se*. This was most obvious in Hardenberg's case, where executive reform complemented the secret policy with Russia, as an instrument for the elimination of his chief personal political rival. But – as we have seen – the Reform argument could also be deployed by and in defence of those, such as Haugwitz and Beyme, who have been regarded as its bitterest opponents; the aim here was clearly to pre-empt the schemes of their adversaries and to consolidate their own grip on the executive.

At first, it might seem as if Hardenberg's Reform plan placed him in the same camp as those of the war party: the superficial resemblance of his suggestions to those of the 'petition of princes' are obvious. Yet their interests were not identical: for both tactical and strategic reasons, Hardenberg was far less forthright in his demands for the re-organisation of the executive.

The tactical reason for Hardenberg's reticence was his realisation that the attitude of the king was crucial to the success of any reform plan or high-political manoeuvre. 'If this were not changed (*Wurde dieses nicht geändert)*', as Hardenberg said of the royal stance 'then all other changes would be pointless (*so waren alle andern Verbesserungen vergeblich)*'.[104] Thus the reform plans not only put the king at the centre, but their very success was dependent on his approval. It was for this reason, Hardenberg explains in his memoirs, that he stayed aloof from Stein's initiative in April, believing that he could achieve more on his own.[105] Thanks to his years of close personal contact with Frederick William, Hardenberg knew his extreme sensitivity to the adversarial instincts of his servants. When Hardenberg tried to wean the king away from his dependence on the Kabinett, the King replied that Hardenberg's

---

[104] Hardenberg to Wittgenstein, 4.7.06, Tempelberg, in Ranke (ed.), *Denkwürdigkeiten Hardenbergs*, II, p. 105.
[105] Ibid.

accusations against Lombard, Beyme and Haugwitz 'would probably not have more weight than those to which everybody who was so close to the person of the king would be subjected';[106] this was an astute insight into the character of high politics in Prussia. Hardenberg also knew of Frederick's aversion to intrigue, especially organised intrigue. 'Jamais je ne prête l'oreille ni à l'intrigue, ni à la cabale'[107] were the king's very own words and they boded ill for any concerted attack on the Kabinett such as Stein and the war-party were undertaking. Indeed, Hardenberg observed that such efforts had the opposite effect of driving monarch and Kabinett closer together.[108]

Perhaps the best illustration of the complexities of the Prussian scene at the time and Hardenberg's ambiguous relationship with the war-party scheme is to be found in the letter he wrote to his confidant Wittgenstein[109] in early July 1806. In it he acknowledged the need for radical change in Prussian policy, but added that the most important question was how to achieve it (*wie dazu gelangen*). This consideration coloured his attitude to Stein's April memorandum. 'The content', he acknowledged, 'is unfortunately quite true, but regrettably the language is so strong and crass, so that far from achieving its purpose, it is sure to make matters worse.' Hardenberg feared that Frederick William would see in the move nothing but the voice of 'passion and a wounded personal vanity (*Leidenschaft und irgend eines beleidigten heftig aufgereizten Privatgefühls*)'. Thus, he continued, when he spoke with the king, he had 'communicated much of the content [of Stein's memorandum], but in a deferential and quiet tone'. The best approach, Hardenberg felt, was to 'consider how the truth could *successfully* [italics in original] be brought to the king. Part of this endeavour must certainly be first to convince him and then, in the very moment that he recognises the flaws [in the

---

106 Ranke (ed.), *Denkwürdigkeiten Hardenbergs*, I, p. 604: 'wohl nicht mehr Gewicht haben möchten, als solche, die jeden treffen würden, der so nahe um die Person eines Monarchen wäre'.
107 Frederick William to Hardenberg, 29.8.06, Charlottenburg, in Ranke (ed.), *Denkwürdigkeiten Hardenbergs*, II, p. 120.
108 Ibid., II, p. 135.
109 Wilhelm Ludwig Georg, Count of Sayn-Wittgenstein-Hohenstein, b. 1770, d. 1851. Early service at the Bavarian court; close to the Prussian court after 1794; used for special missions; 1797 became Oberhofmeister of the Queen and envoy to Hesse-Cassel; after accession of Frederick William III taken into confidence by Queen Luise and the king; made *Fürst* in 1804; lost his post as Oberhofmeister with the death of the queen mother in 1805, but continued to be in good grace; very active in Prussian politics in 1806 when he acted as a conduit between Louise and Hardenberg. *ADB*, 43, pp. 626–7. On Wittgenstein's role in 1806 see also Hans Branig, *Fürst Wittgenstein. Ein preußischer Staatsmann der Restaurationszeit*, Veröffentlichungen aus den Archiven Preußischer Kulturbesitz 17 (Cologne and Vienna, 1981), pp. 20–1.

existing arrangements], to offer the means and personnel with which
these flaws can be eradicated at their roots.'

The chief vehicle through which Hardenberg hoped to eradicate 'these
flaws' – that is to say, his personal enemies – was the queen. For Louise
was not only proving a dependable ally in the campaign against the
official, supposedly pro-French policy of the state, she also promised
to be a useful conduit for the attack on the Kabinett itself. Hence,
Hardenberg's letter to Wittgenstein – who was acting as intermediary –
stressed that he would be 'entirely guided by her'. 'I shall be quite silent',
Hardenberg continued,

if she thinks we would achieve nothing, and shall act if she instructs me to, if there
is hope. Will it help to approach the king in writing, naturally with measured and
not too strong language? Is it better if a number of people do this simultaneously,
or should it be done individually? What would be the most opportune moment?
Most importantly, will it be possible to achieve a change in personnel? Can the
queen participate or must she avoid compromising herself?[110]

As it turned out, Hardenberg's caution – and that of the queen – was
justified by events. Louise had thought Stein's first memorandum of
April–May 1806 so unsuitable for presentation to the king that she
helped to suppress it;[111] this temporarily saved him from the consequences of his outspokenness. But the queen could not or would not
prevent the 'petition of the princes' going ahead later in the summer,
though she – and Hardenberg – wisely refused to be associated with it.[112]
Predictably, the petition proved to be entirely counterproductive.
Indeed, Frederick William condemned the very notion of a coordinated
demand for the removal of his trusted advisors as 'mutiny' and as a
Fronde. This reference to the seventeenth-century French revolt of the

---

[110] Hardenberg to Wittgenstein, 4.7.06, Tempelberg, in Ranke (ed.), *Denkwürdigkeiten
Hardenbergs*, II, pp. 105–12: 'Der Inhalt ist leider durchaus wahr, aber die Sprache so
stark und grell, daß der Zweck dadurch gar nicht erreicht, vielmehr gewiß dadurch das
Uebel noch ärger . . . mündlich sehr vieles gesagt, was mit dem Inhalt übereinstimmt,
aber in einem ehrerbietigen, glimpflichen, herzlichen Tone . . . überlegen, wie man mit
ERFOLG die Wahrheit an den König bringen könne, wozu durchaus gehört, daß man
bei ihm Ueberzeugung hervorbringe, und in demselbigen Augenblick, wo er das Uebel
einsieht, auch die Mittel und Personen darbiete, wodurch dasselbe mit der Wurzel
ausgerottet werde . . . welche Schritte sie für nützlich hält. Ich werde mich lediglich
danach richten, ganz still sein, wenn sie meint, wir würden nichts bewirken, handeln,
wie sie es vorschreibt, wenn sie Hoffnung hegt. Wird es helfen, wenn man dem König
die Sache schriftlich vorstellt, vertsteht sich, mit wahren, nicht zu heftigen Ausdrücken?
Ist es besser, daß Mehrere zugleich es thun, oder Einzelne? Welches ist der beste
Zeitpunkt? Wird es insonderheit möglich sein, eine Aenderung der Personen zu Wege
zu bringen? Kann die Königin mitwirken oder darf sie sich nicht compromittieren?'
[111] Lehmann, *Stein*, I, pp. 413–14.
[112] Klatt, *Königin Luise von Preussen*, p. 53.

nobility is significant, not so much for its connotations of aristocratic power *per se*, but for its suggestion that it was faction, not class or any principle of abstract institutional organisation which underlay the acrimonious political divide of 1806. In any case, when it came to defending his own prerogative, Frederick William had no hesitation in showing the very forcefulness and self-confidence which he so fatally lacked in foreign policy. The signatories were summoned individually and bawled out; the princes were temporarily banished from Berlin.[113]

But the need to 'manage' the king not only determined the approach to reform, it also permeated the substance of the reform debate itself. It is no coincidence that Altenstein prefaced his memorandum with the remark that it was only sensible to suggest that 'which the king is likely to adopt'.[114] This had a constraining effect on any overt attempts to limit the power of the monarch. In part, the gulf between Stein's ideas and those of Hardenberg can be explained by this. Traditionally, the antithesis between the two has been seen as one between the 'abolition' (Stein) and mere 'restriction' (Hardenberg) of absolutism[115] or the difference between a new style French–Napoleonic ministry and the traditional Brandenburg–Prussian model of collegial administration.[116] Certainly, if we look only at the content of the proposals, the Stein–Hardenberg divide forms part of a long debate in the Prussian administration about the respective virtues of a departmental structure based on a monocratic – *präsidial-monokratische* – and a collegial – *kollegialisch-gremialer*[117] – principle. But if we look at the question from the perspective of the letter quoted above the antithesis was to an important extent tactical, at least from Hardenberg's point of view. Contrary to the strident tones of Stein, the Altenstein–Hardenberg memorandum was tailored to convince the king. It was not only deferentially worded, but went out of its way to allay royal fears of a ministerial take-over. Hence the call for five independent ministries which would report separately to the king, rather than Stein's block of ministers which might intimidate the king in a new Council of State.[118]

---

[113] For accounts of this episode see Lehmann, *Stein*, I, pp. 413–18; Kuhlmann, *Friedrich Wilhelm III*, pp. 230–1; Ranke (ed.), *Denkwürdigkeiten Hardenbergs*, II, p. 117.

[114] 'Die des Königs Majestät vorzuschlagende Veränderung in der Verfassung', in Winter (ed.), *Die Reorganisation*, I, p. 62.

[115] Frauendienst, 'Das preussische Staatsministerium', pp. 112–13.

[116] Müsebeck, 'Zur Geschichte der preussischen Reformbestrebungen', p. 131.

[117] Meissner, 'Die monarchische Regierungsform', p. 220; Hans Hausherr, *Verwaltungseinheit und Ressorttrennung vom Ende des 17. bis zum Beginn des 19. Jahrhunderts* (Berlin/East 1953).

[118] Müsebeck, 'Zur Geschichte der preussischen Reformbestrebungen', p. 131. For astute comments on Hardenberg's superior political sense to Stein in summer 1806 see

There was, however, another reason for the distance between the two men, probably the most important one. This was their differing personal political interests and points of departure. For Stein, a relatively humble senior bureaucrat on the Generaldirektorium, who enjoyed access to the king only once a year, the reform of the whole structure of decision-making made eminent sense. Hardenberg, on the other hand, was *already* at the apex of the Prussian state, or at least close to the throne, even after his resignation. To him the first priority was the elimination of his political rivals, not the structural transformation of a system which had served him well on occasion and might do so again. Indeed, wholescale reform on the Stein model would mean sharing power with the other four ministers, which effectively meant exchanging the old set of rivals for a new one. It is for this reason that we find the Altenstein memorandum so merciless in its personal attacks on the Kabinett, but so willing to compromise on substantive issues.[119] Similarly, we find no 'self-denying ordinance' with Hardenberg, as we do with Stein, who undertook to refuse any personal advancement which might result from his programme. If Reform could be employed to effect his aims, then so much the better, but it made very little sense in the abstract. Stein himself, perhaps inadvertently, put his finger on the essence of the Hardenberg Reform plan. He criticised it for allowing Frederick William to make his decisions without consultation with the full council of five ministers, as Stein had suggested. 'This', Stein observed, 'will leave scope for a state of affairs in which the council of ministers would be circumvented and influence would be exercised by the back door.' This would almost certainly have been the case, except that according to that particular plan Hardenberg himself would have controlled the back door; indeed, thanks to his conduct of the secret Russian negotiation, Hardenberg already controlled the 'back door' to the king.

Hardenberg's correspondence with the queen during the summer of 1806 provides further evidence of an unmistakable 'adversarial' thrust to his Reform plans. For, to his great chagrin, Hardenberg found that while the queen supported his initiative against the Kabinett, she also wanted Haugwitz, against whom the whole scheme was in no small measure aimed, to be associated with it.[120] 'Haugwitz must by all means sign as well (*Haugwitz muß nothwendig mit unterschreiben*)', she insisted, '[and] he will do so once he believes himself secure (*er thut es auch sobald er von*

Griewank, 'Hardenberg und die preußische Politik, 1804–1806', p. 31 (re the revolt of the princes).
[119] Historians have noted this, but never really understood it, Müsebeck, 'Zur Geschichte der Reformbestrebungen', pp. 120–1.
[120] Klatt, *Königin Luise von Preussen*, p. 53.

einer Seite gedeckt ist)';[121] indeed, Louise envisaged that Haugwitz would be appointed to the proposed new ministerial council.[122] The queen's determination to reconcile Haugwitz and Hardenberg, and bring the former into the Reform process, was undoubtedly tactically motivated. If the king would ever accept Reform, he would be more likely to do so if Haugwitz were involved. In this case the personalities issue was to be sacrificed for the substance of reform. The plan was a crafty one, for it proceeded according to the principles laid down by Hardenberg, namely the need to come up with a Reform programme likely to convince the king. But while Hardenberg was well aware of Haugwitz's reform plans[123] – and thus presumably of their similarity to his own – the idea of cooperation was poison, and he said so. It would negate the most important aim of *his* reform programme, the removal of his rival; the strategy of using the queen for high-political purposes now threatened to backfire on him. In his reply to the queen he refused outright to share office with Haugwitz on the grounds that he could not be trusted, adding, somewhat implausibly, 'Believe me, I am not saying this because I wish to supplant him (*Glauben Sie mir, ich sage das nicht, um seine Stelle zu haben)*'.[124] Wittgenstein and the queen continued to try to effect a reconciliation between the two men throughout late July, August and early September, but Hardenberg refused to be swayed.[125]

Even Stein, who was in other ways the most detached and 'objective' of the memorialists of 1806, was not free of personal considerations and ambitions. This is illustrated both by his bitter enmity towards Beyme, whose direct access to Frederick William Stein bitterly resented, but to whom he was 'objectively' very close on many Reform issues,[126] and by his surprising plea against the complete dissolution of the General-direktorium. Given the notorious inefficiency of that body and the vast improvement to be expected from the transfer of business to a council of ministers, Stein's desire seems odd; it certainly puzzled later historians.[127] He justified his stance with the resulting reduced pressure of business on the Staatsrat, but it is at least as likely that Stein feared

[121] Wittgenstein to Hardenberg, 13.7.06, Pyrmont, in Ranke (ed.), *Denkwürdigkeiten Hardenbergs*, II, pp. 112–13.
[122] Krieger, 'Königin Luise un der Geheime Kabinettsrat Lombard', 200–2; Poseck, *Louis Ferdinand*, p. 350.
[123] Hardenberg's diary, 13.4.1806: 'Vu Haugwitz – ses propositions touchant un conseil – avec Beyme, Lombard', GStA Rep. 92 Hardenberg L26, fo. 2.
[124] Hardenberg to Wittgenstein, 19.8.06, Tempelberg, in Ranke (ed.), *Denkwürdigkeiten Hardenbergs*, II, p. 115.
[125] Ibid., p. 136; Ibid., p. 147.
[126] Saring, 'Karl Friedrich von Beyme', 38.
[127] Conrad Bornhak, 'Die Entstehung der preussischen Ministerien', 54.

losing his seat on the General Directory without winning one of the smaller number of new ministerial posts when the political musical chairs of structural change was set in motion.

Clearly, the deep fissures in Prussian high politics had nothing to do with class divides or the antithesis between crown and bureaucracy or bureaucracy and non-responsible secretaries. The struggle against the Kabinett, as Hans Hausherr has stressed, 'was no struggle between bourgeois and aristocrats (*war kein Kampf zwischen Bürgerlichen und Adligen*)'.[128] It may well be that the lower echelons of the bureaucracy were possessed of a strong sense of class, or rather *Stand*, consciousness. They were too far away from the seat of power, however, to have any impact. Social class, in fact, gives no indication of likely political allegiance, nor does occupation, be it membership of the 'real' bureaucracy or of the Kabinett. Haugwitz was a nobleman and a responsible minister. His most intimate allies were bourgeois cabinet secretaries such as Beyme and Lombard, while his bitterest enemy, Hardenberg, was also a nobleman and a responsible minister. What divided these men from one another was not primarily differing views of the state, though these may have played a role, nor diverging backgrounds and training, though these too must be taken into account, but conflicting ambitions and loyalties.

Kehr and Rosenberg were therefore wrong to attribute far-reaching plans to the bureaucracy as a whole, or at least to the senior bureaucrats during the pre-Reform and early Reform period. There was no concerted bureaucratic attempt to wrest control of the highest affairs of the state from the crown. Quite the reverse: the rhetoric and reality of the plans, if implemented, were to strengthen the decision-making powers of the king and thus the state as a whole. This did not mean, as we have seen, that personal political agenda were not being pursued simultaneously, but they were not related to a wider programme of bureaucratic self-advancement. Similarly, if the arguments summarised above are a representative sample of the early executive reform debate, then it is misleading to conceive of a divide between a 'party of reform' and a 'party of reaction'. Rather, there were at least two Reform parties, separated largely by personal political enmity. This was because the sharpest political conflict in Prussia leading up to and during 1806 was not that between reform and reaction, but the struggle for control of the

---

128 Hausherr, 'Stein und Hardenberg', p. 272. On the role of the nobility in the Prussian bureaucracy see further: Henning von Bonin, 'Adel und Bürgertum in der höheren Beamtenschaft der preußischen Monarchie, 1794–1806', *Jahrbuch für Geschichte Mittel- und Ostdeutschlands*, 15 (1966), 146; Nikolaus von Preradovich, *Die Führungs-schichten in Öesterreich und Preußen (1804–1918)* (Wiesbaden, 1955), pp. 115–16.

conduct of Prussian foreign policy. Both sides availed themselves of the rhetoric of reform; Hardenberg did so with most success in the long run. The greater the distance of a memorialist from the centre of power – Stein is the classic instance here – the greater the 'objectivity' of his proposals, but also the less their immediate political importance.

In short, the objects and contents of the executive Reform debate triggered by the catastrophic war with Britain in 1806 are inseparable both from the objective foreign political need of the state – that is: simple survival – and the high-political manoeuvres which accompanied it. An unquestioned need for *decision*, preferably monarchic decision, is to be found all round, while the plenitude of power thereby vested in the monarch led to an inevitable struggle among his ministers and advisors in the antechamber of power. If as *Prussians*, the politicians in Berlin wanted to eliminate all limitations on monarchic 'decisionism', of which the antechamber of power was one instance, as *politicians* they wanted to occupy that antechamber themselves.

10 Conclusion

Machiavelli says that a selfless power which is located between two ambitious powers is doomed to extinction. I am afraid I must admit that Machiavelli is right.

Frederick the Great, 1752[1]

During the period 1797 to 1806, Napoleon Bonaparte emerged as the constitutive force in Prussian politics. His radical hegemonic pretensions shaped Prussian foreign policy; this self-same threat powered the intense executive reform debate before Jena; by 1805–6, his favour could make or break Prussian statesmen in the antechamber of power; and the tide of events he unleashed in 1804 was to have a powerfully solvent effect on policies, politics and structures in the old Prussia.

The impact of Napoleon on Prussian policy was a direct reflection of the geopolitical situation of the monarchy. Their geographical exposure to French power made Prussian statesmen both more sensitive to Napoleonic ambitions and less inclined to oppose them. Unlike Great Britain and Russia, they took a very narrow view of European security. So long as Prussia's immediate sphere of influence in North Germany remained inviolate, she was prepared to permit those French encroachments in western Germany, Italy and elsewhere which she was powerless to stop in any case. This policy of strict neutrality – the 'middle way' – was repeatedly and explicitly justified with reference to the 'imperious dictates' of geography. But the Prussians were concerned not merely to stay out of any Franco-Russian dispute; they also aimed to mediate a limited *rapprochement* between the two powers. This would save them from being caught in the inevitable crossfire as French and Russian forces advanced to do battle in northern Germany. Yet at the same time,

---

[1] von Oppeln-Bronikowski (ed.), *Friedrich der Große*, p. 81: 'Machiavelli sagt, eine selbstlose Macht, die zwischen ehrgeizigen Mächten steht, müßte schließlich zugrunde gehen. Ich muß leider zugeben, daß Machiavelli recht hat.'

Prussia was anxious to prevent Russia and France from becoming too close at her expense. This was the traditional *cauchemar des coalitions* which had dogged Prussian thinking since 1756: it forms a strong undercurrent in the debates after 1797 and is most strikingly manifested in Lucchesini's dramatic dispatch in the summer of 1806.

Prussia's geopolitical position entailed great dangers, but it also provided exceptional opportunities. She could act as a 'trimmer', tipping the balance where appropriate in return for territorial gains. In particular, Prussia could steal a march on her Austrian rival in the struggle for mastery in Germany; this motivation was most pronounced leading up to and during the *Reichsdeputationshauptschluss* of 1803. The success of this strategy was reflected in the fact that until 1806, Prussia was – as a scavenger rather than a predator – a net territorial beneficiary of the Revolutionary and Napoleonic upheavals, having traded her exposed western lands for much more substantial tracts of Poland and northern Germany. Moreover, these increases and exchanges were made in accordance with a conscious reorientation of the monarchy away from French-dominated western Germany and towards the north and east. Similarly, the deep-seated Prussian obsession with Hanover was couched in unambiguously geopolitical terms

Yet – to borrow a phrase – the laws of geopolitics were not engraved on stone tablets; their specific interpretation varied with a changing situation. In 1797, for example, the revival of France and the elimination of the Polish buffer with Russia meant that the geopolitical situation of the monarchy was different – and even more precarious – than it had been at the beginning of Frederick the Great's reign. The main threat was now no longer Austrian dualist ambitions, but the acute Franco-Russian pressure on her eastern and western borders. By 1803, Prussia's slender room for manoeuvre had been further eroded by the French occupation of Hanover. Similarly, the rapid pace of events in the autumn and winter of 1805 saw geopolitics wheeled out by Hardenberg to justify first continued neutrality, then a French alliance, then a Russian alliance, followed by a French alliance again, all within the space of four months. Moreover, if the dictates of geography were imperious, they were also contradictory. Prussia's central location meant good relations with both Russia *and* France were essential. By the summer of 1806 this had resulted in the schizophrenic secret policy in which Prussia contracted mutually exclusive obligations to the two powers. Once France and Russia fell out over the Ottoman empire, this policy instantly came to grief. For despite being the most parochial of all the great powers, Prussia was highly sensitive to shifts beyond her borders. But none of this changes the fact that Prussian policy throughout this period was conditioned by geopolitical thinking, both objectively and in the subjective consciousness of her statesmen. The resulting interpretations might differ and the relevant variables might change, often with breathtaking suddenness, but the guiding principles remained the same.

As we have seen, Prussian policy in the shadow of Napoleon was not primarily due to any ideological objection to the new regime in France, nor was it fundamentally influenced by sectional interests. Indeed, the Hanoverian crisis of 1806 showed that the Prussian monarchy could disregard the protests of powerful bureaucratic and socio-economic lobbies if the greater good of the state so required. Nevertheless, it would be wrong to say that Prussia's response to Napoleon was governed by purely 'objective' considerations. For the most intense political conflict in Prussia before Jena – and perhaps thereafter – was not that between appeasers and resisters, let alone between traditional monarchists and advocates of the 'ideas of 1789', but between Prussian politicians struggling to dominate the antechamber of power around the king. The prize of this contest was control of the foreign-political executive; the focus was the person of the monarch himself. Regular access to the king was an essential prerequisite for power and influence; yet at the same time, royal confidence was dependent on close alignment with the known royal standpoint. The resulting circularity in Prussian decision-making was not merely facilitated, but actively encouraged by Frederick William. Far from being a passive object in high politics, he was in fact an active player. This was clearly demonstrated on numerous occasions: staying out of the Second Coalition in 1799 to 1800, the recall of Haugwitz in October 1804 and August 1805 and his control of the secret policy with Russia, to name but the most obvious. Indeed, through his insistence on a co-foreign ministry and the retention of the Kabinett, Frederick William safeguarded his authority against potentially overmighty councillors. As result Prussian politicians were often forced to subordinate 'objective' policy to the need to anticipate the king's will. This does not mean that all Prussian politicians simply sought power for its own sake, though many did and most came perilously close to doing so. Figures such as Haugwitz, Hardenberg and Beyme – Lombard perhaps less so – held sincere views on the monarchy's *raison d'état*. Once safely established in office they genuinely wanted to *do* something, rather than just *be* something. But in order to achieve and retain office they first had to master the antechamber of power and play by its rules.

The impact of Napoleon meant that high politics in Prussia was never discrete from or impervious to the world outside. As we have seen, the French threat increasingly helped to determine the parameters of high-political manoeuvre; at the same time, the antechamber of power fundamentally shaped perceptions of the French threat. Indeed, the process by whch high politics influenced and interacted with 'objective' foreign policy was very complex. On the one hand, high politics tended to accentuate neutralist counsels, as Prussian statesmen sought to portray themselves as the best interpreters of Frederick William's notoriously passive inclination and thus wrong-foot their political rivals. This was the standard pattern of Prussian high politics after 1797, and it is the key to the essential circularity of Prussian decision-making before 1806. On the other hand, there was also an in-built dynamic to Prussian high politics, in which the adversarial imperative or the changing diplomatic scene prompted an ambitious politician to break the mould. One instance of this was Haugwitz's advocacy of the Second Coalition, a high-political miscalculation for which he paid with a haemorrhaging of royal favour; he did not make the same mistake again. But the classic example was Hardenberg's gambit of autumn 1805, in which he harnessed his own genuine fear of Napoleonic hegemony to his personal political ambitions. Hardenberg was thus not so much the man who 'stopped the rot', as a man who decided that resisting Napoleon was the only way of stopping Haugwitz.[2] His open breach with France was to a considerable extent self-generated within Prussian high politics, rather than being purely a response to the external context; this was the same Hardenberg, after all, who had counselled a French alliance two months earlier. In Prussian high politics, no less than foreign policy, the French threat could be an opportunity as well as a danger.

The same dialectic between foreign-political necessity and personal political advancement is also evident in the executive reform debate before Jena. On the one hand, the attempt to reorganise the executive was an extension of the struggle in the antechamber of power. The proponents of reform saw it not least as a means of eliminating their adversaries; its putative opponents were concerned not so much to block reform as to occupy the newly created institutions themselves. On the other hand, fear of France focussed Prussian politicians on the shortcomings of their decision-making apparatus; this is a clear example of the link between foreign policy and domestic structure postulated by Otto Hintze. A similar debate was taking place in Austria and Russia, which suggests that the Prussian experience may simply have been part of a much broader 'crisis of the executive' in the eastern autocracies.[3] Yet at

---

[2] With apologies to Cowling, *The impact of Hitler*, p. 9.
[3] Karl A. Roider, 'The Habsburg foreign ministry and political reform', *CEH*, 22 (1989), esp. 166.

no point did the reformers challenge royal authority, still less did they intend any kind of 'bureaucratic takeover'. On the contrary: the rhetoric and the content of the debate shows that they aimed to enhance not emasculate the power of the king, by liberating him from the retardative effects of the antechamber of power. Nor was the ritual affirmation of royal supremacy mere camouflage, a late example of the classic early modern *topos* of the 'evil advisor', which merely cloaks criticism of the prince himself. In fact, Prussian politicians were unable to conceive of concerted insubordination, let alone treason. When the 'petition of the princes' openly flouted the royal will, it was not only ruthlessly suppressed by Frederick William, but opposed by such key figures in the antechamber of power, especially Hardenberg and the queen.

Very few of the reformers of the period 1797 to 1806 were – yet – ready to accept that the French threat justified radical changes to Prussian society. With a few exceptions, they understood governmental reform to mean the reorganisation of the executive, no more. It was only after 1806–7, as Mathew Levinger points out, that the impulse for societal reform became irresistible. 'No longer', he writes, 'did the reformers simply call for the rationalisation of the state; now they spoke of regenerating through the political mobilisation of the "nation".'[4]

On 14 October 1806, the Prussian army was crushed at Auerstedt and Jena; only Russian intervention saved Prussia from total dismemberment at the Treaty of Tilsit some eight months later. Not for the first or last time, the Hohenzollern monarchy had almost paid the supreme penalty for political weakness in the predatory world of European great power politics. 'Just because a people no longer has the strength or the will to survive in the political sphere', Carl Schmitt wrote, 'does not mean that politics disappears from the world, but merely that a weak people disappears.'[5] High politics and the shortcomings of the executive were undoubtedly a contributory factor in the Prussian failure to formulate an adequate response to the Napoleonic threat. But the root cause was the character and behaviour of Frederick William himself. To quote Treitschke, he 'seemed as if made to lead a well-ordered middling state honourably through quiet times'.[6] But these were not quiet times, and the Prussian monarch was punished for his reticence rather than his

---

[4] Levinger, 'Imagining the nation', p. 68.
[5] Schmitt, *Begriff des Politischen*, p. 35: 'Dadurch, daß ein Volk nicht mehr die Kraft oder den Willen hat, sich in der Sphäre des Politischen zu halten, verschwindet das Politische nicht aus der Welt. Es verschwindet nur ein schwaches Volk.'
[6] Treitschke, *Deutsche Geschichte*, I, p. 141: 'schien wie geschaffen, einen wohlgeordneten Mittelstaat in Ehren durch eine ruhige Zeit hindurchzuführen'.

hubris. 'More than one King went under', Frederick William lamented almost prophetically in September 1805, 'because he loved war; I shall go under because I loved peace.'[7]

---

[7] Cited in Bailleu, 'Vor hundert Jahren', p. 214: 'Mehr als ein König ist untergangen, weil er den Krieg liebte; ich, ich werde untergehen, weil ich den Frieden liebte.'

Bibliography

MANUSCRIPT SOURCES

BRITISH LIBRARY, LONDON

Additional MSS Holland House Papers 51457–61
Additional MSS Dropmore Papers 58923; 58953; 59059; 59281

PUBLIC RECORD OFFICE, LONDON

FO 64 Prussia, General Correspondence 66–71
FO 353 Jackson Papers 46

GEHEIMES STAATSARCHIV PREUSSISCHER KULTURBESITZ, BERLIN-DAHLEM [GStA]

Rep. XI.73 England 178–81
Rep. XI.81 London 228–44
Rep. XI.89 Frankreich 394–411
Rep. XI.140 Braunschweig-Lüneburg 49–50
Rep. XI.175 Russland 154–7
Rep. 92 Nachlaß Alvensleben 1–6
Rep. 92 Nachlaß Caesar 28; 39
Rep. 92 Nachlaß Friedrich Wilhelm der Dritte B.VI.4–22; B.VII.4
Rep. 92 Nachlaß Hardenberg E1–5; E8–9; K10; L12; L24
Rep. 92 Nachlaß Lucchesini 23; 31
Rep. 92 Nachlaß Schöll 18–21
Rep. 96A Geheimes Zivilkabinett, 1797–1806 4A a1–2; 85–96; 128E; 134A–134B; 145

NIEDERSÄCHSISCHES HAUPTSTAATSARCHIV, HANNOVER

Dep. 110 A Nachlaß Ernst Friedrich Herbert Graf Münster 47, Preussens Plan die Kurbraunschweigischen Lande durch Tausch an sich zu bringen, 1805

PRINTED SOURCES

Allgemeines Landrecht für die preussischen Staaten von 1794. Textausgabe (-Register), introduced by H. Hattenhauer, 2 vols. (Frankfurt, 1970–3)

Auckland, William Eden, First Baron, *The journal and correspondence of William, Lord Auckland*, with a preface and introduction by the Bishop of Bath and Wells, 4 vols. (London, 1861–2)

Bailleu, Paul (ed.), *Publicationen aus den königlichen preussischen Archiven. Vol. 8. Preussen und Frankreich 1795 bis 1807. Diplomatische Correspondenzen*, 2 vols, (Leipzig, 1881–7)

'Aus einem Stammbuch der Königin Luise', *FBPG*, 8 (1895), 251–3

Briefwechsel König Friedrich Wilhelms III und der Königin Luise mit Kaiser Alexander I, Publicationen aus den K. Preußischen Archiven 75 (Leipzig, 1900)

Beyme, Karl Friedrich von, 'Eine Reform-Denkschrift Beyme's aus dem Sommer 1806', communicated by Ludwig Dehio, *FBPG*, 18 (1926), 321–38

Blücher, Leberecht von, *Ausgewählte Briefe des Feldmarschalls Leberecht von Blücher* (Leipzig, no date)

'Ein ungedruckter Brief Blüchers aus dem Jahre 1798', *FBPG*, 29 (1916), 267–70

Bojanovski, P. von (ed.), *Niederschriften des Herzogs Carl August von Weimar über den Schutz der Demarkationslinie, den Rennweg (1796) und die Defension Thüringens* (Weimar, 1902)

Botzenhart, Erich (ed.), *Stein. Briefwechsel, Denkschriften und Aufzeichnungen im Auftrag der Reichsregierung, der Preussischen Staatsregierung und des Deutschen und Preussischen Städtetages*, 7 vols. (Berlin, 1931–7)

Brandes, Ernst, 'Ernst Brandes in den Jahren 1805 und 1806. Fünf Briefe an den Grafen Münster [edited by Carl Haase]', *Niedersächsisches Jahrbuch für Landesgeschichte*, 34 (1962), 194–223

Branig, Hans (ed.), *Briefwechsel des Fürsten Karl August von Hardenberg mit dem Fürsten Wilhelm Ludwig von Sayn-Wittgenstein, 1806–1822*, Veröffentlichungen aus dem Geheimen Staatsarchiv Preußischer Kulturbesitz 9 (Berlin and Cologne, 1982)

Bray, François Gabriel de, *Aus dem Leben eines Diplomaten der alten Schule* (Leipzig, 1901)

Cölln, G. F. W. von, *Vertraute Briefe über die inneren Verhältnisse am preussischen Hofe seit dem Tode Friedrichs II*, vol. I (Amsterdam and Cologne, 1807)

Cosmar, Carl Wilhelm and Klaproth, C. A. L., *Der Königl. Preußische Churfürstl. Brandenburgische Wirklich Geheime Staatsrath* (Berlin, 1805)

Czartoryski, Prince Adam, *Memoirs of Prince Adam Czartoryski and his Correspondence with Alexander*, edited by A. Gielgud, 2 vols. (London, 1888)

Deutschland und die Französische Revolution, 1789–1806, edited by Theo Stammen and Friedrich Eberle (Darmstadt, 1988)

Die politischen Testamente der Hohenzollern, edited by Richard Dietrich (Cologne, 1986)

Dohm, Christian Wilhelm von, *Denkwürdigkeiten meiner Zeit* (Lemgo, 1819)

Dropmore, *The MSS of J. B. Fortescue of Dropmore Esq., preserved at Dropmore (1892–1927)* (Hist. MSS. Commission), vols. II–VIII (1894–1910)

Eckardt, Hans von (ed.), *Friedrich von Gentz in der Zeit deutscher Not, 1799–1813* (Munich, 1921)

Eylert, R. F., *Charakterzüge und historische Fragmente aus dem Leben des Königs von Preussen Friedrich Wilhelm III*, 4 vols. (Magdeburg, 1843–6)

Fichte, Johann Gottlieb, *Die Grundzüge des gegenwärtigen Zeitalters. Dargestellt von Johann Gottlieb Fichte in Vorlesungen gehalten zu Berlin, im Jahre 1804–5* (Berlin, 1806)

Gentz, Friedrich von, 'Das preußische Kabinett und Friedrich von Gentz. Eine Denkschrift aus dem Jahre 1800', communicated by Paul Wittichen, *HZ*, 89 (1902), 239–73

Fragmente aus der neuersten Geschichte des politischen Gleichgewichts in Europa (Leipzig, 1806)

George III, King of England, *The later correspondence of George III* edited by Arthur Aspinall, vol. IV (Cambridge, 1968)

Gneisenau. Ein Leben in Briefen (Leipzig, 1939)

Goethe, Johann Wolfgang von, *Torquato Tasso. Ein Schauspiel* (1790 Stuttgart, 1964)

Görtz, Johann Eustach von, *Historische und politische Denkwürdigkeiten, aus dessen hinterlassenen Papieren entworfen*, 2 vols. (1827/8) (Stuttgart and Tübingen, 1827)

Memoiren eines deutschen Staatsmannes aus den Jahren 1788–1816 (Leipzig, 1833)

Graf Thurnheim, A. (ed.), 'Briefe von Friedrich v. Gentz an den Grafen Louis Starhemberg', *Mitteilungen des Instituts für Österreichische Geschichte*, 7 (1886), 119–55

Griewank, Karl (ed.), *Königin Luise. Briefe und Aufzeichnungen* (Leipzig, 1924)

Briefwechsel der Königin Luise mit ihrem Gemahl Friedrich Wilhelm III, 1793–1810 (Leipzig, 1929)

Königin Luise. Ein Leben in Briefen (Leipzig, 1943)

Grösser Generalstab (ed.), Carl von Clausewitz *Nachrichten über Preußen in seiner großen Katastrophe*, Kriegsgeschichtliche Einzelschriften no. 10 (Berlin, 1882)

Handbuch über den Preußischen Hof und Staat, für das Jahr 1805 (Berlin, 1805)

Handbuch über den königlich preussischen Hof und Staat für das Jahr 1806 (Berlin, 1806)

Haugwitz, Christian Kurt von, 'Notiz über die Memoiren des Grafen von Haugwitz', in Leopold von Ranke, *Hardenberg und die Geschichte des preußischen Staates von 1793–1813*, Vol. II, Sämtliche Werke vol. 47 (Leipzig, 1880), pp. 273–318

Hubatsch, Walter and Botzenhart, Erich (eds.), *Briefe und amtliche Schriften*. Vol. II, part 1. *Minister im Generaldirektorium. Konflikt und Entlassung. Stein in Nassau- Die Nassauer Denkschrift. Wiederberufung (1804–1807)* 10 vols., edited by Peter G. Thielen (Stuttgart, 1957–74)

Huber, Ernst Rudolf (ed.), *Dokumente zur Deutschen Verfassungsgeschichte*. Vol. I: *Deutsche Verfassungsdokumente 1803–1850* (Stuttgart, 1961)

Hueser, *Denkwürdigkeiten aus dem Leben des Generals der Infanterie von Hueser, größtenteils nach dessen hinterlassenen Papieren* edited by M(athilde) Q(uedow) (Berlin, 1877)

Jackson, Lady, *The diaries and letters of Sir G. J. Jackson, from the Peace of Amiens to the Battle of Talavera*, 2 vols. (London, 1872)

Jahrbücher der preussischen Monarchie unter der Regierung Friedrich Wilhelms des Dritten (Berlin, 1798)

Kant, Immanuel, *Die Metaphysik der Sitten. Der Streit der Fakultäten. Immanuel Kant's Werke*, vol. vii, edited Benzion Kellermann (Hildesheim, 1973). Overall series edited by Herman Cohen, Artur Buchenau, Otto Buek, Albert Görland, B. Kellermann, O. Schöndorffer and Ernst Cassirer

Klinkenborg, Melle (ed.), 'Materialen zur Geschichte des Geheimen Staatsministers Karl Wilhelm Finck v. Finckenstein', *FBPG*, 28 (1915), 563–74

Klinkowström, A. von, *Aus Metternich's nachgelassenen Papieren. Erster Theil. Von der Geburt Metternich's bis zum Wiener Congreß, 1773–1815*, edited by A. von Klinkowström, vol. II (Vienna, 1880)

Küntzel, Georg and Haß, Martin (eds.), *Die politischen Testamente der Hohenzollern nebst ergänzenden Aktenstücken*, vols. I and II (Leipzig and Berlin, 1920)

Lehmann, Max (ed.), 'Ein Regierungsprogramm Friedrich Wilhelms III', *HZ*, 61 (1889), 441–60

Linnebach, Karl (ed.), *Scharnhorsts Briefe. Erster Band, Privat-Briefe* (Munich and Leipzig, 1914, reprinted, 1980)

Lombard, Johann Wilhelm, *Matériaux pour servir à l'histoire des années 1805, 1806, 1807 dédié aux Prussiens par un ancien compatriote* (Frankfurt and Leipzig, 1808)

Lucchesini, Girolamo, *Historische Entwicklung der Ursachen und Wirkungen des Rheinbundes*, 3 vols. (Leipzig, 1821–5)

History of the Confederation of the Rhine translated by J. D. Dwyer (London, 1821)

Marmottan, Paul (ed.), 'Lucchesini. Ambassadeur de Prusse à Paris (1800–1801)', *RHD*, 42 (1928), 323–48; 43 (1) (1929), 65–87; 44, 1 (1930), 450–61

Massenbach, Christian von, *Rückerinnerungen an große Männer* (Amsterdam, 1808)

Memoiren zur Geschichte des preußischen Staates unter den Regierungen Friedrich Wilhelm II. und Friedrich Wilhelm III, vol. III (Amsterdam, 1809)

Historische Denkwürdigkeiten zur Geschichte des Verfalls des preußischen Staats seit dem Jahre 1794 nebst meinem Tagebuche über den Feldzug von 1806 (Amsterdam, 1809)

Historische Denkwürdigkeiten, edited by H.-W. Engels (Frankfurt, 1969)

Meissner, H. O. (ed.), *Vom Leben und Sterben der Königin Luise. Eigenhändige Aufzeichnungen* (Berlin, 1926)

Meusel, Friedrich (ed.), *Friedrich August von der Marwitz. Ein märkischer Edelmann im Zeitalter der Befreiungskriege*. Vol I: *Lebensbeschreibung* Vol. II: *Erster Teil. Tagebücher, politische Schriften, und Briefe* (Berlin, 1908–13)

Naudé, Albert (ed.), 'Die Denkwürdigkeiten des Ministers Grafen von Schulenburg', *FBPG*, 15 (1902), 385–419

Nippold, F. (ed.), *Erinnerungen aus dem Leben des Generalfeldmarschalls Hermann von Boyen Erster Theil, 1771–1809*, 3 vols. (Leipzig, 1889–90)

Ompteda, Ludwig von, *Politischer Nachlaß des hannoverschen Staats- und Cabinettsministers, Ludwig von Ompteda aus den Jahren 1804 bis 1813. Abtheilung I. Aus den Jahren 1804 bis 1809*, edited by F. von Ompteda (Jena, 1869)

Irrfahrten und Abenteuer eines Mittelstaatlichen Diplomaten: Ein Lebens- und Kulturbild aus den Zeiten um 1800 (Leipzig, 1894)

Notizen eines deutschen Diplomaten, 1804–1813, edited by Roderich von Ompteda (Berlin, 1935)

Oppeln-Bronikowski, Friedrich von (ed.), *Friedrich der Große. Das politische Testament von 1752* (Stuttgart, 1974)

Paget, Arthur, *Correspondence, 1794–1807*, 2 vols., (London, 1896)

Preußen, Friedrich der Große von, *Politisches Testament von 1768, Regierungssystem*, Klassiker der Politik, vol. 5 (Berlin, 1922)

Preussens Staatsverträge, edited by F. W. von Röhrscheidt (Berlin, 1852)

Preußische Finanzpolitik 1806–1810: Quellen zur Verwaltung der Ministerien Stein und Altenstein, collected by Eckart Kehr and edited by Hanna Schissler and Hans-Ulrich Wehler (Göttingen, 1984)

Radziwill, Princess Anton (ed.), *Fünfundvierzig Jahre aus meinem Leben (1770–1815)* (Brunswick, 1912)

Ragsdale, Hugh (ed.), 'Documents on the foreign policy of Paul I from the former Prussian archives', *Canadian-Slavic Studies*, 7, 1 (1973), 106–11

Ranke, Leopold von, *Denkwürdigkeiten des Staatskanzlers Fürsten von Hardenberg*, 5 vols. (Leipzig, 1877)

Roloff, Gustav von (ed.), 'Die Neuorganisation im Ministerium des Auswärtigen im Jahre 1802. Briefe von Haugwitz und Lombard', *FBPG*, 5 (1892), 265–73; 7 (1894), 97–111

Rose, J. H. (ed.), *Select Dispatches from the British Foreign Office archives relating to the formation of the Third Coalition against France, 1804–5*. Royal Historical Society, Camden Third Series, 1904

Rothfels, Hans (ed.), *Carl von Clausewitz, Politische Schriften und Briefe* (Munich, 1922)

Rothkirch, Malve Gräfin von (ed.), *Königin Luise von Preußen. Briefe und Aufzeichnungen 1786–1810* (Munich, 1985)

Rühl, Franz, *Briefe und Aktenstücke zur Geschichte Preussens unter Friedrich Wilhelms III*, edited by F. A. von Stägemann, 3 vols. (Leipzig, 1902)

Russell, Lord John (ed.), *Memorials and Correspondence of Charles James Fox*, 4 vols. (London, 1853–7)

Sbornik Imperatoskago Russkago. Diplomaticheskiia snosheniia Rossi Frantsiei v epokhu Napoleona I (Sammelband der kaiserlichen russischen historischen Gesellschaft) 82. Die diplomatischen Verhandlungen Russlands mit Frankreich in der Epoche Napoleons I. edited by Alexander Tracerskij (St Petersburg, 1892)

Scheel, Heinrich (ed.), *Das Reformministerium Stein. Akten zur Verfassungs- und Verwaltungsgeschichte aus den Jahren 1807/8*, 3 vols. (Berlin/East, 1966)

Schladen, Friedrich Heinrich Leopold von, *Preußen in den Jahren 1806 und 1807. Ein Tagebuch. Nebst einem Anhange verschiedener, in den Jahren 1807 bis 1809 verfasster politischer Denkschriften* (Mainz, 1845)

Mitteilungen aus den nachgelassenen Papieren eines preussischen Diplomaten (Schladen), edited by L. v. L.(edebour) (Berlin, 1868)

Schlesier, Gustav (ed.), *Ungedruckte Denkschriften, Tagebücher und Briefe von Friedrich von Gentz* (Mannheim, 1840)

Schmalz, Theodor, *Staatsverfassung Großbritanniens* (Halle, 1806)

Schoeps, Hans Joachim (ed.), *Aus den Jahren preußischer Not und Erneuerung: Tagebücher und Briefe der Gebrüder Gerlach und ihres Kreises 1805–1820* (Berlin, 1963)

Stadelmann, Rudolf, *Preußens Könige in ihrere Thätigkeit für die Landeskultur. Vierter Teil. Friedrich Wilhelm III (1797–1807)* Publicationen aus den K. Preussischen Staatsarchiven (Leipzig, 1887)

Temperley, Harold, and Penson, Lilian M., *Foundations of British foreign policy from Pitt (1792) to Salisbury (1902) on documents, old and new, selected and edited with historical introductions* (Cambridge, 1938)

Vane, Charles (ed.) *Robert Stewart, Viscount Castlereagh, Memoirs and Correspondence*, 12 vols. (London, 1850–3)

Vneshnaya Politika Rossii XIX ee Nachala XX Veka, edited by Ministerstuo inostrannykh, vols. V and VI (Moscow, 1961)

Voss, Sophie Marie Gräfin von, *Neunundsechzig Jahre am Preussischen Hofe* (Leipzig, 1876)

Wahl, Hans (ed.), *Prinz Louis Ferdinand von Preußen. Ein Bild seines Lebens in Briefen, Tagebuchblättern und zeitgenössischen Zeugnisen* (Weimar, 1917)

Weil, Maurice (ed.), *D'Ulm a Jena. Correspondance inédite du Chevalier de Gentz avec Francis James Jackson, ministre de la Grande Bretagne à Berlin (1804–6)* (Paris, 1921)

Weimar, Carl August von, *Politischer Briefwechsel des Herzogs u. Grossherzogs Carl August von Weimar*, edited by Willy Andreas (Stuttgart, 1958)

Winter, Georg (ed.), *Die Reorganisation des preussischen Staates unter Stein und Hardenberg. Erster Teil. Allgemeine Verwaltungs- und Behördenreform.* Vol. I: *Vom Beginn des Kampfs gegen die Kabinettsregierung bis zum Wiedereintritt des Ministers vom Stein* (Leipzig, 1931)

Wittichen, Friedrich Carl and Salzer, Ernst (eds.), *Briefe von und an Friedrich von Gentz*, 3 vols. (Berlin, 1909–13)

Wittichen, Paul von (ed.), 'Die dritte Coalition und Friedrich von Gentz. Eine Denkschrift Gentz's vom Oktober 1804', *Mitteilungen des Instituts für Österreichische Geschichte*, 23 (1902), 461–80

Wohlwill, Adolf, 'Aktenstücke zur Rumboldschen Angelegenheit', *Zeitschrift des Vereins für Hamburgische Geschichte*, 7 (1881), 387–400

'Fernere Aktenstücke zur Rumboldschen Angelegenheit', *Zeitschrift des Vereins für Hamburgische Geschichte*, 8 (1886), 192–207

Zwehl, Hans von, *Der Kampf um Bayern 1805.* Vol. II: *Die Bayerische Politik im Jahre 1805. Urkunden* (Munich, 1964)

SECONDARY WORKS

Adler-Bresse, Marcelle, *Sièyes et le monde allemand*, 2 vols. (Lille-Paris, 1977)

Aengenyndt, Gerhard, 'Die Okkupation des Kurfürstentums Hannover durch die Franzosen im Jahre 1803', *Zeitschrift des historischen Vereins für Niedersachsen*, 87 (1922), 1–79; 88 (1923), 1–40

Allgemeine Deutsche Biographie, edited by Historische Kommission bei der Königlichen Akademie der Wissenschaften (Bavaria), 56 vols. (Leipzig, 1875–1912)

Anders, Wilhelm, 'Napoleon Bonaparte und die Beziehungen zwischen Preußen und Bayern. Beiträge zur deutschen Geschichte, vornehmlich im Jahre 1806' (unpublished PhD dissertation, University of Munich, 1921)

Anon., 'Preußen und England', *PJ*, 1 (1858), 23–30

Anon., 'St. Petersburger Briefe vom Jahre 1806', *Deutsche Revue*, 26 (1901), 300–15

Aretin, K. O. von, *Das Reich: Friedensgarantie und europäisches Gleichgewicht 1648–1806* (Stuttgart, 1986)

Heiliges römisches Reich 1776–1806. Reichsverfassung und Staatssouveränität, Veröffentlichungen des Instituts für europäische Geschichte Mainz, vol. 38 Abteilung Universalgeschichte, 2 vols. (Wiesbaden, 1967)

'Deutschland und die französische Revolution', in Aretin and Härter (eds.), *Revolution und konservatives Beharren*, pp. 6–20

Aretin, K.O. von and Härter, Karl (eds.), *Revolution und Konservatives Beharren. Das Alte Reich und die Französische Revolution* (Mainz, 1990)

Aretin, K. O. von and Ritter, Gerhard A. (Ralph Melville and Claus Scharf), *Historismus und Moderne Geschichtswissenschaft. Europa zwischen Revolution und Restauration 1797–1815* (Wiesbaden, 1987)

Arnheim, Fritz, 'Zur Charakteristik Friedrichs des Grossen und seines Grossneffen, des nachmaligen Königs Friedrich Wilhelm III', *FBPG*, 18 (1905), 229–36

Astrom, Sven-Erik, 'Britain's timber imports from the Baltic, 1775–1830. Some new figures and viewpoints', *Scandinavian Economic History Review*, 37 (1989), 57–71

Attar, Frank, *1792, la Révolution française déclare la guerre à l'Europe. Géopolitique de l'Europe de 1792* (Paris, 1992)

Bahrs, Kurt, *Friedrich Buchholz. Ein preussischer Publizist 1768–1843*, Historische Studien LVII (Berlin, 1907)

Bailleu, Paul, 'Haugwitz und Hardenberg', *Deutsche Rundschau*, 20 (1879), 268–98

'Die politische Haltung Friedrich Wilhelms III. vor Ausbruch des Krieges von 1806', *FBPG*, 12 (1899), 250

'Sitzungsberichte des Vereins für Geschichte der Mark Brandenburg. 9 November 1898', *FBPG*, 12 (1899), 574

'Preußen und Rußland im ersten Viertel des neunzehnten Jahrhunderts', *Deutsche Rundschau*, 54 (1900), 427–37

'Sitzungsbericht des Vereins für Geschichte der Mark Brandenburg, 10. Oktober 1900 bis 12. Juni 1901', *FBPG*, 12 (1901), 14

'Vor hundert Jahren. Der Berliner Hof im Herbst und Winter 1805', *Deutsche Rundschau*, 125 (1905), 203–27

Königin Luise. Ein Lebensbild (Berlin, 1908)

'Johann Christoph Wöllner', in *Preußischer Wille. Gesammelte Aufsätze von Paul Bailleu*, edited by Melle Klinkenborg (Berlin, 1924), pp. 134–53

Barclay, David, 'Ritual, ceremonial, and the "Invention" of a monarchical tradition in nineteenth-century Prussia', in Heinz Duchhardt, Richard A. Jackson and David Sturdy (eds.), *European monarchy. Its evolution and practice from Roman antiquity to modern times* (Stuttgart, 1992), pp. 207–20

Frederick William IV and the Prussian monarchy, 1840–1861 (Oxford, 1995)

Bauer, Bruno, *Der Einfluß Frankreichs auf die preussische Politik und die Entwicklung des preussischen Staates. Dargestellt an den Bündnissen, Verträgen und gegenseitigen Beziehungen* (Hanover, 1888, reprinted Aalen 1969)

Baugh, Daniel, 'Great Britain's "Blue-water" policy, 1689–1815', *IHR*, 10, 1 (1988), 33–58

Baumgart, Peter, 'Zur Gründungsgeschichte des Auswärtigen Amtes in Preussen, 1713–1728', *Jahrbuch für die Geschichte Mittel- und Ostdeutschlands*, 7 (1958), 229–48

Baumgart, Winfried, *Der Friede von Paris 1856* (Munich and Vienna, 1972) translated as *The peace of Paris. Studies in war, diplomacy and peace-making* by Ann Pottinger Saab (Santa Barbara, 1981)

Beales, D. E. D. and Blanning, T. C. W., 'Prince Kaunitz and the primacy of domestic policy', *IHR*, 2 (1980), 618–24

Behrend, F., 'Kronprinz Friedrich Wilhelm (III.) Kampagne in Frankreich 1792', *Hohenzollern Jahrbuch*, 16 (1912), 228–34

Behrens, C. B. A., *Society, government and the Enlightenment. The experiences of eighteenth-century France and Prussia* (London, 1985)

Bennecke, Wolf-Günther, 'Stand und Stände in Preußen vor den Reformen' (unpublished PhD dissertation, University of Berlin, 1935)

Bentley, Michael, *Politics without democracy. Great Britain, 1815–1914. Perception and preoccupation in British government* (Oxford, 1984)

Berdahl, Robert M., *The Politics of the Prussian Nobility 1770–1848* (Princeton, N.J., 1989)

Berding, Helmut (ed.), *Soziale Unruhen in Deutschland während der Französischen Revolution*, Geschichte und Gesellschaft Sonderheft 12 (Göttingen, 1988)

Berding, Helmut, François, Etienne and Ullmann, Hans-Peter (eds.), *Deutschland und Frankreich im Zeitalter der Französischen Revolution* (Frankfurt, 1989)

Berges, Wilhelm and Herzfeld, Hans, 'Bürokratie, Aristokratie und Autokratie in Preußen. Das Werk von Hans Rosenberg', *Jahrbuch für die Geschichte Mittel- und Ostdeutschlands*, 11 (1962), 282–96

Berghahn, Volker, *Militarism. The history of an international debate, 1861–1979* (Leamington Spa, 1981)

Bernath, Mathias, 'Die auswärtige Politik Nassaus 1805–1812. Ein Beitrag zur Geschichte des Rheinbundes und den politischen Ideen am Mittelrhein zur Zeit Napoleons', *Nassauische Annalen*, 63 (1952), 106–91

Beyme, Werner von, *Carl Friedrich von Beyme. Preußische Köpfe* (Berlin, 1987)

Bindschedler, Rudolf L., 'Zum Primat der Außenpolitik', in Urs Altermatt and Judith Garamvölgyi (eds.), *Innen- und Aussenpolitik. Primat oder Interdependenz? Festschrift zum 60. Geburtstag von Walter Hofer* (Berne and Stuttgart, 1980), pp. 27–36

Biro, Sidney Seymour, *The German policy of Revolutionary France. A study in French diplomacy during the war of the First Coalition 1792–1797*, 2 vols. (Cambridge, Mass., 1957)

Birtsch, Günter, 'Zum konstitutionellen Charakter des preußischen Allgemeinen Landrechts von 1794', in Kurt Kluxen and Wolfgang Mommsen (eds.), *Politische Ideologien und nationalstaatliche Ordnung. Studien zur Geschichte des*

19. und 20. Jahrhunderts. Festschrift für Theodor Schieder zu seinem 60. Geburtstag (Munich, 1968), pp. 97–115

'Zur sozialen und politischen Rolle des deutschen vornehmlich preußischen Adels am Ende des 18. Jahrhunderts', in Rudolf Vierhaus (ed.), *Der Adel vor der Revolution. Zur sozialen und politischen Funktion des Adels im vorrevolutionären Europa* (Göttingen, 1971), pp. 75–95

'Der preußische Hochabsolutismus und die Stände', in Peter Baumgart (ed.), *Ständetum und Staatsbildung in Brandeburg-Preussen. Ergebnisse einer internationalen Fachtagung*, Veröffentlichungen der Historischen Kommision zu Berlin 55 (Berlin and New York, 1983), pp. 389–408

'Revolutionsfurcht in Preußen 1789 bis 1794', in Büsch and Neugebauer-Wölk (eds.), *Preußen und die revolutionäre Herausforderung nach 1789*, pp. 87–101

Bissing, W.M. von, *Friedrich Wilhelm II, König von Preussen: ein Lebensbild* (Berlin, 1967)

Bitterauf, Theodor, *Geschichte des Rheinbundes*. Vol. I: *Die Gründung des Rheinbundes und der Untergang des alten Reiches* (Munich, 1905)

'Studien zur preussischen Politik im Jahre 1805', *FBPG*, 27 (1914), 431–515

Blanning, T. C. W., *Reform and Revolution in Mainz 1743–1803* (Cambridge, 1974)

'The German Jacobins and the French Revolution', *HJ*, 23 (1980), 985–1002

The French Revolution in Germany. Occupation and resistance in the Rhineland, 1792–1802 (Oxford, 1983)

The origins of the French Revolutionary Wars (London, 1986)

'The death and transfiguration of Prussia', *Historical Journal*, 29, 2 (1986), 433–59

'The French Revolution and the modernisation of Germany', *CEH*, 22 (1989), 109–29

'The French Revolution and Europe', in Colin Lucas (ed.), *Rewriting the French Revolution* (Oxford, 1991), pp. 183–207

Joseph II (London and New York, 1994)

Bleek, Wilhelm, *Von der Kameralausbildung zum Juristenprivileg. Studium, Prüfung und Ausbildung der höheren Beamten des allgemeinen Verwaltungsdienstes in Deutschland im 18. und 19. Jahrhundert*, Historische und Pädagogische Studien 3 (Göttingen, 1985)

Bleich, Erich, *Der Hof des Königs Friedrich Wilhelm II und des Königs Friedrich Wilhelm III* (Berlin, 1914)

Bock, Helmut, 'Reform und Revolution. Zur Einordnung des preußischen Reformministeriums Stein in den Kampf zwischen Forschritt und Reaktion', in Seeber and Noack (eds.), *Preußen in der deutschen Geschichte seit 1789*, pp. 54–81

Boguslawski, A. von, *Aus der preußischen Hof- und diplomatischen Gesellschaft* (Stuttgart/Berlin, 1903)

Bojanovski, P. von, *Niederschriften des Herzogs Carl August von Weimar über den Schutz der Demarkationslinie, den Rennweg (1796) und die Defension Thüringens (1798)* (Weimar, 1902)

Bonin, H. von, 'Adel und Bürgertum in der höheren Beamtenschaft der preußischen Monarchie, 1794–1806', *Jahrbuch für Geschichte Mittel- und Ostdeutschlands*, 15 (1966), 139–74

Bonnal, Edgar, *La Diplomatie prussienne depuis la paix de Presbourg* (Paris, 1880)

Borch, Herbert von, *Obrigkeit und Widerstand. Zur politischen Soziologie des Beamtentums* (Tübingen, 1954)

Bornhak, Conrad, 'Die Entstehung der preußischen Ministerien', *FBPG*, 51 (1939), 52–65

Botzenhart, Manfred, *Metternichs Pariser Botschafterzeit* (Münster, 1967)

Botzenhart, Manfred and Raumer, Kurt von, *Deutschland um 1800. Krise und Neugestaltung 1789–1815*, Handbuch der deutschen Geschichte, edited by Leo Just, vol. III/Ia (Wiesbaden, 1980)

Bourel, Dominique, 'Zwischen Abwehr und Neutralität. Preußen und die Französische Revolution 1789 bis 1795/ 1795 bis 1803/6', in Büsch and Neugebauer-Wölk (eds.), *Preußen und die revolutionäre Herausforderung nach 1789*, pp. 43–57

'Un régicide ambassadeur à la cour des Hohenzollern: Sieyès à Berlin', in Hervé Brouillet (ed.), *Contribution a l'histoire de la Révolution et de l'Empire* (Baden-Baden, 1989), pp. 277–8

Bracher, Karl Dietrich, 'Über das Verhältnis von Innen- und Außenpolitik', in Bracher, *Deutschland zwischen Demokratie und Diktatur* (Berne, Munich and Berlin, 1964), pp. 337–72

Brandes, Karl Friedrich, 'Hannover in der Politik der Großmächte 1801–1807', *FBPG*, 51 (1939), 239–74; 52 (1940), 27–51

Branig, Hans, *Fürst Wittgenstein. Ein preußischer Staatsmann der Restaurationszeit*, Veröffentlichungen aus den Archiven Preußischer Kulturbesitz, 17 (Cologne and Vienna, 1981)

Braubach, Max, 'Frankreichs Rheinlandpolitik im Zeitalter der Französischen Revolution', *Archiv für Politik und Geschichte*, 5 (1927), 172–86

Braun, R., 'Taxation, sociopolitical structure and state-building: Great Britain and Brandenburg-Prussia', *The Formation of National States in Western Europe*, ed. Charles Tilly (Princeton, 1975), pp. 243–327

Brent, Richard, 'Butterfield's Tories: "high politics" and the writing of Modern British Political History', *HJ*, 30, 4 (1987), 943–54

Brill, Heinz, *Geopolitik heute. Deutschlands Chance?* (Frankfurt, 1994)

Brockhusen, Hans-Joachim von, *Carl Christian Friedrich von Brockhausen. Ein preußischer Staatsmann um die Wende des XVIII. Jahrhunderts. Ein Lebens- und Kulturbild. Dargestellt auf Grund der Gesandtenberichte des Preußischen Geheimen Staatsarchivs* (Greifswald, 1927)

Bromley, J. S., 'The Second Hundred Years War (1689–1815)', in Douglas Johnson, François Crouzet and François Bédarida (eds.), *Britain and France. Ten centuries* (Folkestone, 1980), pp. 164–72

Brooke, John, 'Namier and Namierism', *History and Theory*, 3 (1964), 331–47

Broszat, Martin, *Der Staat Hitlers. Grundlegung und Entwicklung seiner inneren Verfassung* (Munich, 1969)

Brunner, Otto, Conze, Werner and Koselleck, Reinhart (eds.), *Geschichtliche Grundbegriffe. Historisches Lexikon zur politisch-sozialen Sprache in Deutschland*, vol. VI (Stuttgart, 1990)

Brunschwig, Henri, *Gesellschaft und Romantik in Preußen im 18. Jahrhundert. Die Krise des preußischen Staates am Ende des 18. Jahrhunderts und die Entstehung der romantischen Mentalität* (Frankfurt, 1975)

Buddruss, Eckhard, 'Die Deutschlandpolitik der Französischen Revolution zwischen Traditionen und revolutionärem Bruch', in Aretin and Härter (eds.), *Revolution und konservatives Beharren*, pp. 145–54

Die französische Deutschlandpolitik, 1756–1789 Veröffentlichungen des Instituts für Europäische Geschichte Mainz 157, edited by Karl Otmar von Aretin (Mainz, 1995)

Burgdorf, Wolfgang, 'Redundanz und Regression verfassungspolitischer Bemühungen. Die Deutschlandspläne des Erzbischofs von Tarsus' (unpublished MSS in author's possession)

Burke, Peter, *The French historical revolution. The 'Annales' school, 1929–89* (Oxford, 1990)

Büsch, Otto, *Militärsystem und Sozialleben im Alten Preußen 1713–1807. Die Anfänge der sozialen Militarisierung der preussisch-deutschen Gesellschaft* (Berlin, 1962)

Büsch, Otto (ed.), 'Zur "preußischen Antwort" auf die revolutionäre Herausforderung seit 1789. Paralipomena aus einer Diskussion', in Büsch and Neugebauer-Wölk (eds.), *Preußen und die revolutionäre Herausforderung seit 1789*, pp. 365–71

Handbuch der preußischen Geschichte. Vol. II: *Das 19. Jahrhundert und große Themen der Geschichte Preussens* (Berlin and New York, 1992)

Büsch, Otto and Neugebauer, Wolfgang (eds.), *Moderne preußische Geschichte, 1648–1947. Eine Anthologie*, 3 vols. (Berlin, 1981)

Büsch, Otto and Neugebauer-Wölk, Monika (eds.), *Preußen und die revolutionäre Herausforderung nach 1789*, Forschungen zur preußischen Geschichte, 78 (Berlin, 1991)

Büschleb, Hermann, *Westfalen und die preußischen Truppen, 1795–1802. Ein Kapitel Militärpolitik und Landesgeschichte*, Studien zur Militärgeschichte, Militärwissenschaft und Konfliktforschung (Osnabrück, 1987)

Bussenius, I. C. and Hubatsch, Walther (eds.), *Die preußische Verwaltung in Süd- und Neuostpreußen, 1793–1806*, Studien zur Geschichte Preußens, 6 (Heidelberg, 1960)

Urkunden und Akten zur Geschichte der preussischen Verwaltung in Südpreussen und Neuostpreussen, 1793–1806 (Frankfurt, 1961)

Butterfield, Herbert, *The peace tactics of Napoleon, 1806–1808* (Cambridge, 1928)

Caemmerer, H. von, 'Rankes große Mächte und die Geschichtsschreibung des 18. Jahrhunderts', in *Studien und Versuche zur neueren Geschichte, Max Lenz gewidmet* (Berlin, 1910), pp. 263–312

Carl, Horst, *Okkupation und Regionalismus. Die preussischen Westprovinzen im Siebenjährigen Krieg*, Veröffentlichungen des Instituts für Europäische Geschichte Mainz, edited by K. O. von Aretin (Mainz, 1993)

Carsten, F. L., *History of the Prussian Junkers* (Aldershot, 1989)

Clark, Christopher, 'The Frederick Williams of nineteenth-century Prussia', *Bulletin of the German Historical Institute*, 15 (1993), 3–13

Clarke, Peter F., 'Political history in the 1980s', *Journal of Interdisciplinary History*, 12, 1 (1981), 45–7

Clement-Simon, M., 'La politique de la Prusse en Orient (1736–1871)', *RHD*, 22 (1908), 383

Conde, Alexander de, 'Essay and reflection: On the nature of international history', *IHR*, 10 (1988), 282–301

Cooke, A. B. and Vincent, John, *The governing passion. Cabinet government and party politics, 1885–1886* (Brighton, 1974)

Coupkova, Anna, 'Über das Familienarchiv Haugwitz in Namiest', *Adler. Zeitschrift für Genealogie und Heraldik*, 17/3 (1993), 81–7

Cowling, Maurice, *1867. Disraeli, Gladstone and revolution. The passing of the second Reform Bill* (Cambridge, 1967)

The impact of Labour, 1920–1924. The beginning of modern British politics (Cambridge, 1971)

The impact of Hitler. British politics and British policy, 1933–1940 (Chicago and London, 1975)

Craig, Gordon A., *The politics of the Prussian army* (Oxford, 1955)

The end of Prussia (Madison, Wisc., 1984)

Czempiel, Ernst-Otto, 'Der Primat der Auswärtigen Politik. Kritische Würdigung einer Staatsmaxime', *Politische Vierteljahresschrift*, 4 (1963), 266–87

'Strukturen absolutistischer Außenpolitik', *ZfHF*, 7 (1980), 445–51

Dambacher, I., *Christian Wilhelm von Dohm. Ein Beitrag zur Geschichte des preußischen aufgeklärten Beamtentums und seiner Reformbestrebungen am Ausgang des 18. Jahrhunderts* (Berne, 1974)

'Eine Reform Denkschrift Beymes aus dem Sommer 1806', *FBPG*, 18 (1926), 321–38

The precarious balance: the politics of power in Europe 1494–1945 (London, 1963)

Delbrück, Hans, 'Die Frage der polnischen Krone und der Vernichtung Preussens in Tilsit', in *Studien und Versuche zur neueren Geschichte. Max Lenz gewidmet* (Berlin, 1910), pp. 312–36

Demandt, Alexander (ed.), *Deutschlands Grenzen in der Geschichte* (Munich, 1990)

Deppermann, Klaus, 'Der preussische Absolutismus und der Adel: eine Auseinandersetzung mit der marxistischen Absolutismustheorie', *Geschichte und Gesellschaft*, 8 (1982), 538–53

Deuerling, Edward, *Das Fürstentum Bayreuth unter französischer Herrschaft und sein Übergang an Bayern 1806 bis 1810* (Erlangen, 1910)

Deutsch, Harold C., *The genesis of Napoleonic imperialism* (Philadelphia, 1975, reprint)

Dietrich, Richard, 'Vom alten Reich bis zum neuen Reich, 1789–1848', in *Die deutsche Einheit als Problem der europäschen Geschichte* (Stuttgart, 1960), pp. 141–55

Dilthey, Wilhelm, 'Friedrich der Grosse und die deutsche Aufklärung', in Wilhelm Dilthey, *Studien zur Geschichte des Deutschen Geistes*, Collected Works, vol. III (Göttingen, 1959), pp. 176–205

Dippel, Horst, 'Austritt aus dem Ghetto? Deutsche Neuerscheinungen zur Französischen Revolution', *HZ*, 258 (1991), 339–94

Disch, Karl, 'Der Kabinettsrat Beyme und die auswärtige Politik Preußens in den Jahren 1805/06', *FBPG*, 41 (1928), 331–66; 42 (1929), 93–134

Dlugoborski, Waclav, 'Volksbewegungen im preußisch-polnischen Grenzraum während der Französischen Revolution 1789 bis 1794', in Büsch and Neugebauer-Wölk (eds.), *Preußen und die revolutionäre Herausforderung seit 1789*, pp. 145–211

Doerries, Heinrich, 'Friedrich von Gentz "Journal de ce qui m'est arrivé de plus marquant . . . au quartier-general de S.M. le roi de Prusse" als Quelle Preussischer Geschichte der Jahre 1805–1806', (DPhil dissertation, University of Greifswald, 1906)

Dorn, W. L., 'The Prussian bureaucracy in the eighteenth century', *Political Science Quarterly*, 46 (1931), 402–23 and 47 (1932), 75–94; 259–73

Dotzauer, Winfried, *Die deutschen Reichskreise in der Verfassung des alten Reiches und ihr Eigenleben (1500–1806)* (Darmstadt, 1989)

Drabek, Anna M., Leitsch, Walter and Plaschka, Richard G. (eds.), *Russland und Österreich der Napoleonischen Kriege* (Vienna, 1989)

Dreitzel, Horst, *Monarchiebegriffe in der Fürstengesellschaft. Semantik und Theorie der Einherrschaft in Deutschland von der Reformation bis zum Vormärz*, 2 vols. (Cologne, Weimar and Vienna, 1991)

Droysen, Johann Gustav, *Das Leben des Feldmarschalls Grafen York von Wartenburg* (Leipzig, 1850/1913, 10th edn 1897)

Droz, Jacques, 'L'idéologie, facteur de la politique internationale. La neutralité prussienne et l'opinion publique de 1795 a 1806', *Mélanges Pierre Renouvin. Etudes d'Histoire des Relations Internationales* (Paris, 1966), pp. 97–106

Duchhardt, Heinz, *Gleichgewicht der Kräfte, Convenance, Europäisches Konzert. Friedenskongresse und Friedensschlüsse vom zeitalter Ludwig XIV bis zum Wiener Kongreß* (Darmstadt, 1976)
  Protestantisches Kaisertum und altes Reich. Die Diskussion über die Konfession des Kaisers in Politik, Publizistik und Staatsrecht, Veröffentlichungen des Instituts für Europäische Geschichte Abteilung Universalgeschichte (Wiesbaden, 1977)
  Deutsche Verfassungsgeschichte, 1495–1806 (Stuttgart, 1991)

Dufraisse, Roger, 'Die "hegemoniale" Integration Europas unter Napoleon I', *Wirtschaftliche und politische Integration in Europa im 19. und 20. Jahrhundert*, edited by Helmut Berding, Geschichte und Gesellschaft Sonderheft 10 (Göttingen, 1984), pp. 34–44
  'Die Deutschen und Napoleon im 20. Jahrhundert', *HZ*, 252 (1991), 587–625
  L'Allemagne à l'époque napoléonienne. Questions d'histoire politique, économique et sociale, Pariser Historische Studien 34 (Berlin, 1992)

Dufraisse, Roger and Müller-Luckner, Elisabeth (eds.), *Revolution und Gegenrevolution, 1789–1830. Zur geistigen Auseinandersetzung in Frankreich und Deutschland* (Berlin, 1991)

Dunan, Marcel, 'La naissance de l'Allemagne napoléonienne. L'alliance franco-bavaroise de 1805. A propos d'un livre récent', *Revue Historique*, 188 (1940), 105

Duncker, Max, 'Die Denkwürdigkeiten des Staatskanzlers Fürsten von Hardenberg', *PJ*, 39 (1877), 606–43

'Graf Haugwitz und Freiherr von Hardenberg. Aktenstücke zu den Denkwürdigkeiten des Fürsten von Hardenberg, Band 5', *PJ*, 42 (1878), 571–625

Dwyer, Philip, 'Prussia and the Second Armed Neutrality, 1799–1801' (unpublished PhD dissertation, University of Western Australia at Perth, 1992)

'Prussia and the Armed Neutrality: the invasion of Hanover in 1801', *IHR*, 15 (1993), 661–87

'The politics of Prussian neutrality, 1795–1806', *German History*, 12 (1994), 351–74

'Duroc diplomate. Un militaire au service de la diplomatie napoléonienne', *Le Souvenir Napoléonien*, 58 (1995), 21–40

Easum, C.V., *Prince Henry of Prussia, brother of Frederick the Great* (Madison, 1942, repr. Westport, Conn., 1971)

Eckhardt, Albrecht, 'Unter Kniphausener Flagge. Zur Neutralitätspolitik des Grafen Bentinck in napoleonischer Zeit (1803–1808),' *NJLG*, 61 (1989), 181–214

Eicke, Hermann, *Der ostpreußische Landtag von 1798* (Göttingen, 1910)

Eisner, Kurt, *Das Ende des Reichs: Deutschland und Preußen im Zeitalter der großen Revolution* (Berlin, 1907)

Eley, Geoffrey, 'The view from the throne: the personal rule of Kaiser Wilhelm II', *HZ*, 28, 2 (1985), 469–85

Elias, Norbert, *Die höfische Gesellschaft. Untersuchungen zur Soziologie des Königstums und der höfischen Gesellschaft*, Soziologische Texte 54 (Neuwied, 1969)

Endres, Rudolf, 'Die preußische Ära in Franken', in Peter Baumgart (ed.), *Expansion und Integration. Zur Eingliederung neugewonnener Gebiete in den preußischen Staat*, Neue Forschungen zur brandenburg-preußischen Geschichte 5, edited Oswald Hauser (Cologne and Vienna, 1984), pp. 169–94

Engelberg, Ernst, 'Preußische Militärs und das antinapoleonisch-bürgerliche Reformwerk', in Seeber and Noack (eds.), *Preußen in der deutschen Geschichte nach 1789*, pp. 49–53

Epstein, Klaus, *The genesis of German conservatism* (Princeton, N.J., 1966)

Fann, Willerd R., 'The rise of the Prussian ministry, 1806–1827', in Hans-Ulrich Wehler (ed.), *Sozialgeschichte Heute Festschrift für Hans Rosenberg zum 70. Geburtstag* (Göttingen, 1976), pp. 119–29

Faulenbach, Bernd, *Ideologie des deutschen Weges. Die Deutsche Geschichte in der Historiographie zwischen Kaiserreich und Nationalsozialismus* (Munich, 1980)

Fehrenbach, Elizabeth, 'Verfassungs- und sozialpolitische Reformen und Reformprojekte in deutschland unter dem Einfluß des napoleonischen Frankreich', in Aretin and Ritter (eds.), *Historismus und Moderne Geschichtswissenschaft*, pp. 291–311

Feuchtwanger, E. J., *Prussia: myth and reality. The role of Prussia in German history* (London, 1970)

Fischer, Wolfram, 'Wirtschaft und Wirtschaftspolitik in Deutschland unter den

Bedingungen der britisch-französischen Blockade und Gegenblockade (1797–1812)', in Aretin and Ritter (eds.), *Historismus und moderne Geschichtswissenschaft*, pp. 243–54

Fisher, H. A. L., *Napoleonic statesmanship in Germany* (Oxford, 1903)

Förster, Gerhard, Helmert, Heinz, Otto, Helmut and Schnitter, Helmut, *Der preußisch-deutsche Generalstab 1740–1965. Zu seiner politischen Rolle in der Geschichte* (Berlin, 1966)

Ford, Guy Stanton, *Hanover and Prussia: a study in neutrality, 1795–1803* (New York, 1903)

Fortescue, J. W., *British statesmen of the great war, 1793–1814* (Oxford, 1911)

Fournier, A., *Gentz und Cobenzl. Geschichte der österreichischen Diplomatie in den Jahren 1801–5 nach neuen Quellen* (Vienna, 1880)

Frauendienst, Werner, 'Das preussische Staatsministerium in vorkonstitutioneller Zeit', *Zeitschrift für die gesammte Staatswissenschaft*, 116 (1960), 104–77

Fremont, Gregory B., 'Britain's role in the formation of the Third Coalition against France, 1802–1805' (unpublished DPhil dissertation, University of Oxford, 1991)

Friedrich, Fritz, *Politik Sachsens, 1801 bis 1806. Ein Beitrag zur Geschichte der Auflösung des heiligen römischen Reichs*, Leipziger Studien aus dem Gebiet der Geschichte 4 (Leipzig, 1898)

Gabel, Helmut and Schulze, Winfried, 'Peasant resistance and politicisation in Germany in the eighteenth century', in Eckhart Hellmuth (ed.), *The transformation of political culture. England and Germany in the late eighteenth century* (Oxford, 1990), pp. 119–46

Gablentz, Otto von der, 'Die Maßstäbe der politischen Entscheidung (Prologema zu einer politischen Ethik', in *Faktoren der politischen Entscheidung. Festgabe für Ernst Fränkel zum 65. Geburtstag*, edited G. A. Ritter and Glibert Ziebura (Berlin, 1963), pp. 11–38

Gärber, Jörn, 'Politische Revolution und industrielle Evolution: Reformstrategien des preußischen Saint-Simonismus (Friedrich Buchholz)', in Büsch and Neugebauer-Wölk (eds.), *Preußen und die revolutionäre Herausforderung seit 1789*, pp. 301–30

Gagliardo, John, *Reich and nation. The Holy Roman Empire as idea and reality, 1763–1806* (Bloomington and London, 1980)

Gaide, Bruno, 'Der diplomatische Verkehr des geheimen Kabinettsrats Lombard mit den Vertretern auswärtiger Mächte nach den Urkunden und seine Rechtfertigungsschrift', (PhD dissertation, University of Greifswald, 1911)

Gebauer, J.H., 'Aus der Vorgeschichte der ersten Einverleibung Hildesheims in Preußen (1768–1802)', *FBPG*, 31 (1918), 107–37

Geh, Hans-Peter, *Insulare Politik in England vor der Tudors* (Lübeck and Hamburg, 1964)

Geiss, Immanuel, 'Geographie und Mitte als historische Kategorien. Anmerkungen zu einem Aspekt des "Historikerstreits"', *ZfG*, 10 (1991), 979–94

Gembries, Hartmut, 'Das Thema Preußen in der politischen Diskussion Englands zwischen 1792 und 1807', (unpublished PhD dissertation, University of Freiburg, 1988)

Gembruch, Werner, *Staat und Heer. Ausgewählte historische Studien zum ancien régime, zur Französischen Revolution und zu den Befreiungskriegen*, edited by Johannes Kunisch, Historische Forschungen, 40 (Berlin, 1990)

'Bürgerliche Publistik und Heeresreform in Preußen (1805–1808)', in Gembruch, Kunisch, ed., *Staat und Heer*, pp. 334–68

'England und Kontinentaleuropa im politischen Denken von Friedrich Buchholz. Ein Beitrag zur Diskussion um die Freiheit der Meere und der kolonialen Expansion in der Napoleonischen Era', in Gembruch, Kunisch (ed.), *Staat und Heer*, pp. 277–305

'Friedrich von Cölln als Publizist vor dem Zusammenbruch Preußens im Jahre 1806', in Gembruch, Kunisch (ed.), *Staat und Heer*, pp. 306–33

'Krieg und Heerwesen im politischen Denken des Freiherrn vom Stein', in Gembruch, Kunisch, ed., *Staat und Heer*, pp. 499–533

'Prinz Heinrich von Preussen, Bruder Friedrichs des Grossen', in Gembruch, Kunisch, ed., *Staat und Heer*, pp. 207–38

'Zum England-Bild des Freiherrn vom Stein', in Gembruch, Kunisch, ed., *Staat und Heer*, pp. 534–56

'Zum Verhältnis von Staat und Heer im Zeitalter der Großen Französischen Revolution', in Gembruch, Kunisch, ed., *Staat und Heer*, pp. 257–76

'Zur Diskussion um Heeresverfassung und Kriegführung in der Zeit vor der französischen Revolution', in Gembruch, Kunisch, ed., *Staat und Heer*, pp. 239–56

Gerth, H. and Mills, C. Wright (eds.), *From Max Weber. Essays in sociology* (New York, 1970)

Gillis, John R., 'Aristocracy and bureaucracy in nineteenth-century Prussia', *P&P*, 41 (1968), 105–29

Gmeinwiser, Josef, 'Die bayerische Politik im Jahre 1805', (unpublished PhD dissertation, University of Munich, 1928)

Görlitz, Walther, *Der deutsche Generalstab: Geschichte und Gestalt, 1657–1945* (Frankfurt, 1950)

Goldschmidt, Paul, 'Altenstein', *ADB*, 35, 645–60

Gollwitzer, H., 'Ideologische Blockbildung als Bestandteil internationaler Politik im 19. Jahrhundert', *HZ*, 201 (1965), 306–33

Goltz, Colmar von der, *Von Roßbach bis Jena und Auerstädt: ein Beitrag zur Geschichte des preußischen Heeres* (Berlin, 1906)

Gooch, George Peabody, *Germany and the French Revolution* (London, 1920, reprinted 1965)

'Henry of Prussia. Statesman and diplomatist', in *Studies in German History* (London, 1948), pp. 119–65

Grab, Walter, 'Revolutionsfreunde in Preußen im Zeitalter der französischen Revolution', in Büsch and Neugebauer-Wölk (eds.), *Preußen und die revolutionäre Herausforderung seit 1789*, pp. 119–44

Granier, Hermann, 'Ein Reformversuch des preussischen Kanzleistils im Jahre 1800', *FBPG*, 15 (1902), 168–80

Gray, Marion W., *Prussia in transition: society and politics under the Stein reform ministry of 1808*, Transactions of the American Philosophical Society, 76 (Philadelphia, 1986)

'The rise of German nationalism and the wars of liberation (1803–1814)', in

Donald D. Horward (ed.), *Napoleonic military history: a bibliography*, Military History bibliographies 9, Garland Reference Library of Social Science 194 (New York and London, 1986), pp. 435–78

Griewank, Karl, 'Hardenberg und die preußische Politik, 1804 bis 1806', *FBPG*, 47 (1935), 227–308

'Hardenberg 1750–1822', in *Die Großen Deutschen*, edited W. Andreas and W. von Scholz, vol. III (Berlin, 1936), pp. 28–41

Grimm, Dieter, *Deutsche Verfassungsgeschichte, 1776–1866* (Frankfurt, 1988)

'Verfassung II: Konstitution, Grundgesetze', in Otto Brunner, Werner Conze and Reinhart Koselleck (eds.), *Geschichtliche Grundbegriffe*. Historisches Lexikon zur politisch-sozialen Sprache in Deutschland 6 (Stuttgart, 1990), pp. 863–99

Groote, Wolfgang von (ed.), *Napoleon I und die Staaten seiner Zeit* (Freiburg, 1969)

Grosser Generalstab, Kriegsgeschichtliche Abteilung (eds.), *Die preussischen Kriegsvorbereitungen und Operationspläne von 1805*, Kriegsgeschichtliche Einzelschriften 1 (Berlin, 1883)

1806. Das preussische Offizierkorps und die Untersuchung der Kriegsereignisse (Berlin, 1906)

Grünhagen, C., *Zerboni und Held in ihren Konflikten mit der Staatsgewalt, 1796–1802* (Berlin, 1897)

Gruner, Wolf, D., *Die deutsche Frage. Ein problem der europäischen Geschichte seit 1800* (Munich, 1985)

Deutschland mitten in Europa. Aspekte und Perspektiven der deutschen Frage in Geschichte und Gegenwart, Beiträge zur deutschen und europäischen Geschichte 5, edited Klaus Arnold, Wolf Gruner and Kersten Krüger (Hamburg, 1992)

Haase, Carl, 'Ernst Brandes in den Jahren 1805 und 1806. Fünf Briefe an den Grafen Münster', *NJBLG*, 34 (1962), 194–223

'Graf Münster, von Lenthe und die Katastrophe Kurhannovers 1803', *NJBLG*, 53 (1981), 279–87

Habermann, Paul and Gisela, *Friedrich Wilhelm III. König von Preußen im Blick wohlwollender Zeitzeugen* (Schernfeld, 1990)

Habermas, Jürgen, 'Eine Art Schadensabwicklung. Die apologetischen Tendenzen in der deutschen Zeitgeschichtsschreibung', in *Historikerstreit. Die Dokumentation der Kontroverse um de Einzigartigkeit der national-sozialistischen Judenvernichtung* (Munich and Zurich, 1987)

Härter, Karl, *Reichstag und Revolution, 1789–1806. Die Auseinandersetzung des immerwährenden Reichstags zu Regensburg mit den Auswirkungen der Französischen Revolution auf das alte Reich*, Schriftenreihe der historischen Kommission bei der bayerischen Akademie der Wissenschaft, 46 (Göttingen, 1992)

Hagen, William W., 'The partitions of Poland and the crisis of the Old Regime in Prussia 1772–1806', *CEH*, 9 (1976), 115–28

'The Junkers' faithless servants: peasant insubordination and the breakdown of serfdom in Brandenburg-Prussia, 1763–1811', in R. J. Evans and W. R. Lee (eds), *The German peasantry: conflict and community in rural society from the eighteenth to the twentieth centuries* (London, 1986), pp. 71–101

'Descent of the *Sonderweg*: Hans Rosenberg's history of Old-Regime Prussia', *CEH*, 24, 1 (1991), 24–50

Hallgarten, George, *Imperialismus vor 1914. Die soziologischen Grundlagen der Aussenpolitik europäischer Grossmächte vor dem ersten Weltkrieg*, 2 vols. (Munich, 1963)

Ham, V. R., 'Strategies of coalition and isolation. British war policy and northwest Europe, 1803–1810 (unpublished DPhil dissertation, University of Oxford, 1977)

Hammer, Karl, 'Die preußischen Könige und Königinnen im 19. Jahrhundert und ihr Hof', in Karl Ferdinand Werner (ed.), *Hof, Kultur und Politik im 19. Jahrhundert* (Bonn, 1985), pp. 87–98

Hansing, Carl, *Hardenberg und die dritte Koalition*, Historische Studien 12 (Berlin, 1899)

Harnisch, Hartmut, 'Die agrarpolitischen Reformmaßnahmen der preußischen Staatsführung in dem Jahrzehnt vor 1806/07', *Jahrbuch für Wirtschaftsgeschichte*, 3 (1977), 129–53

'Peasants and markets. The background to the agrarian reforms in feudal Prussia east of the Elbe, 1760–1807', in Lee and Evans (eds.), *The German peasantry*, pp. 37–70

Hartung, Fritz, *Hardenberg und die preußische Verwaltung in Ansbach-Bayreuth von 1792 bis 1806* (Tübingen, 1908)

'Studien zur Geschichte der preußischen Verwaltung. Erster Teil. Vom 16. Jahrhundert bis zum Zusammenbruch des alten Staates im Jahre 1806', *Abhandlungen der Preußischen Akademie der Wissenschaften Jg. 1941 Phil.-hist. Klasse* (Berlin, 1942), no. 17

Deutsche Verfassungsgeschichte vom 15. Jahrhundert bis zur Gegenwart (Stuttgart, 1957)

Harvey, A. D., 'European Attitudes to Britain during the French Revolutionary and Napoleonic Era', *History*, 63 (1978), 356–65

Hase, Alexander von, 'Friedrich von Gentz "Von dem politischen Zustande von Europa vor und nach der Französischen Revolution" (1801). Analyse und Interpretation' (PhD dissertation, University of Erlangen, 1968)

'Friedrich Gentz: Vom Übergang nach Wien bis zu den "Fragmenten des Gleichgewichts" (1802–1806)', *HZ*, 211 (1970), 589–615

'Das konservative Europa in Bedrängnis: zur Krise des Gleichgewichtspublizisten Friedrich von Gentz (1805–1809), *Saeculum*, 29 (1978), 385–405

'Der Absolutismus an den Grenzen seiner selbst', *Archiv für Kulturgeschichte*, 73, 2 (1991), 351–77

Hausherr, Hans, *Verwaltungseinheit und Ressorttrennung vom Ende des 17. bis zum Beginn des 19. Jahrhunderts* (Berlin/East, 1953)

'Die Lücke in den Denkwürdigkeiten des Staatskanzlers Fürsten Hardenberg', in *Archivar und Historiker. Studien zur Archiv- und Geschichtswissenschaft zum 65. Geburtstag von Heinrich Otto Meissner* (Berlin, 1956), pp. 497–510

'Hardenberg und der Friede von Basel', *HZ*, 184 (1957), 292–335

'Stein und Hardenberg', *HZ*, 190 (1960), 267–89

'Bildungsreise und erste Heirat des Freiherrn Karl August von Hardenberg', *Ein Leben aus der Freien Mitte. Festschrift für Prof. Dr. Ulrich Noack* (Göttingen, 1961), pp. 37–56

Hardenberg, Eine politische Biographie. Vol. I. *1750–1800* edited by Karl Erich Born, Kölner Historische Abhandlungen 8 (2nd edn, Cologne and Graz, 1965)

Hardenberg, Eine politische Biographie. Vol. III. *Die Stunde Hardenbergs* (2nd edn, Cologne and Graz, 1965)

Heffter, Heinrich, 'Vom Primat der Aussenpolitik', *HZ*, 171 (1951), 1–20

Heidrich, Kurt, *Preussen im Kampfe gegen die französische Revolution bis zur zweiten Teilung Polens* (Stuttgart and Berlin, 1908)

Heigel, Karl Theodor, *Deutsche Geschichte vom Tode Friedrichs des Großen zur Auflösung des alten Reiches. Zweiter Band. Vom Feldzug in der Champagne bis zur Auflösung des alten Reiches (1792–1806)* (Stuttgart and Berlin, 1911)

Hellmuth, Eckhart (ed.), *The transformation of political culture: England and Germany in the late eighteenth century* (Oxford, 1990)

'Towards a comparative study of political culture. The cases of late eighteenth-century England and Germany', in Hellmuth (ed.), *The transformation of political culture*, pp. 1–36

Naturrechts-philosophie und bürokratischer Werthorizont. Studien zur preußischen Geistes und Sozialgeschichte des 18. Jahrhunderts, Veröffentlichungen des Max-Planck-Instituts für Geschichte 78 (Göttingen, 1985)

Hellwig, Leo, *Schulenburg-Kehnert unter Friedrich Wilhelm III (1798–1806)* (Berlin, 1936)

Henshall, Nicholas, *The myth of absolutism. Change and continuity in early modern European monarchy* (London and New York, 1992)

Herrmann, Alfred, 'Friedrich Wilhelm III und sein Anteil an der Heeresreform bis 1813', *Historische Vierteljahresschrift*, 11 (1908), 484–516

Herzig, Arno, *Unterschichtenprotest in Deutschland, 1790–1870* (Göttingen, 1988)

'Der Einfluß der französischen Revolution auf den Unterschichtenprotest in Deutschland während der 1790er Jahre', in Berding (ed.), *Soziale Unruhen in Deutschland*, pp. 202–18

Herzig, Arno and Sachs, Rainer, *Der Breslauer Gesellenaufstand von 1793. Die Aufzeichnungen des Schneidermeisters Johann Gottlieb Klose. Darstellung und Dokumentation*, Göttinger Beiträge zur Wirtschafts- und Sozialgeschichte, 12 (Göttingen, 1987)

Herzig, Arno, Stephan, Inge and Winter, Hans G. (eds.), *Sie und nicht Wir. Die Französische Revolution und ihre Wirkung auf Norddeutschland und das Reich. Bd.1 Norddeutschland.* Vol. II: *Das Reich* (Hamburg, 1989)

Heymann, Ernst, *Napoleon und die grossen Mächte 1806* (Berlin und Leipzig, 1910)

Hildebrand, Klaus, 'Geschichte oder "Gesellschaftsgeschichte"? Die Notwendigkeit einer politischen Geschichtsschreibung von den internationalen Beziehungen', *HZ*, 223 (1976), 328–57

'Staatskunst oder Systemzwang? Die "Deutsche Frage" als Problem der Weltpolitik', *HZ*, 228 (1979)

Hillgruber, Andreas, 'Methodologie und Theorie der Geschichte der internationalen Beziehungen', *GWU*, 27 (1976), 193–210

'Politische Geschichte in moderner Sicht', in Andreas Hillgruber, *Die Zerstörung Europas. Beiträge zur Weltkriegsepoche 1914 bis 1945* (Frankfurt/Main and Berlin, 1988), pp. 13–31

'Die Diskussion über den "Primat der Aussenpolitik" und die Geschichte der internationalen Beziehungen in der westdeutschen Geschichtswissenschaft seit 1945', in Hillgruber, *Die Zerstörung Europas*, pp. 32–50

Hinrichs, C., *Preußen als historisches Problem* edited by Gerhard Oestreich (Berlin, 1964)

Hintze, Otto, 'Stein und der preußische Staat. Eine Besprechung von Max Lehmann's Stein-Biographie I–II', *HZ*, 94 (1905), 412–46

Die Hohenzollern und ihr Werk. Fünfhundert Jahre vaterländischer Geschichte (Berlin, 1915)

'Die Entstehung der modernen Staatsministerien', in Oestreich (ed.), *Staat und Verfassung*, pp. 275–320

'Machtpolitik und Regierungsverfassung', in Otto Hintze (ed.), *Staat und Verfassung: Gesammelte Abhandlungen zur allgemeinen Verfassungsgeschichte*, edited by Gerhard Oestreich, introduced by Fritz Hartung (Göttingen, 1962), pp. 424–56

'Das monarchische Prinzip und die konstitutionelle Verfassung', in Oestreich (ed.), *Staat und Verfassung*, pp. 359–89

'Staatenbildung und Verfassungsentwicklung. Eine historisch-politische Studie', in Oestreich (ed.), *Staat und Verfassung*, pp. 34–51

'Staatsverfassung und Heeresverfassung', in Oestreich (ed.), *Staat und Verfassung*, pp. 52–83

'Weltgeschichtliche Bedingungen der Repräsentativverfassung', in Oestreich (ed.), *Staat und Verfassung*, pp. 140–85

'Liberalismus, Demokratie und auswärtige Politik', in Otto Hintze, *Soziologie und Geschichte. Gesammelte Abhandlungen zur Soziologie, Politik und Theorie der Geschichte*, edited and introduced by Gerhard Oestreich (Göttingen, 1964), pp. 200–4

'Preußische Reformbestrebungen vor 1806', in Oestreich (ed.), *Regierung und Verwaltung*, pp. 504–29

'Das preußische Staatsministerium im 19. Jahrhundert', in Otto Hintze, *Regierung und Verwaltung. Gesammelte Abhandlungen zur Staats-, Rechts-, und Sozialgeschichte*, edited and introduced by Gerhard Oestreich (Göttingen, 1967), pp. 530–619

Hölzle, Erwin, *Das Alte Recht und die Revolution. Eine politische Geschichte Württembergs in der Revolutionszeit 1789–1806* (Munich and Berlin, 1931)

Hoffmann, Karl, 'Innen- und Außenpolitik', *Deutsche Rundschau*, 189 (1921), 277–88

Hofmeister-Hunger, Andrea, *Pressepolitik und Staatsreform: die Institutionalisierung staatlicher Öffentlichkeitsarbeit bei Karl August von Hardenberg (1792–1822)*, Veröffentlichungen des Max-Planck Instituts für Geschichte (Göttingen, 1994)

Holzapfel, Kurt, 'Intervention oder Koexistenz. Preussens Stellung zu Frankreich 1789–1792', *ZfG*, 25, 7 (1977), 787–802

'La Prusse avant la paix de Bâle. Le torpillage du traités de subsides de la Haye par "le parti prussien de paix" (1794–1795)', *Annales Historiques de la Révolution Française*, 56 (1984), 229–39

Hubatsch, Walther, *Die Hohenzollern in der deutschen Geschichte* (Frankfurt, 1961)

Stein-Studien. Die preußischen Reformen des Reichsfreiherrn Karl vom Stein zwischen Revolution und Restauration (Cologne and Berlin, 1975)

Der Freiherr vom Stein und England (Köln, 1977)

Die Stein-Hardenbergschen Reformen, Erträge der Forschung 65 (Darmstadt, 1977)

Grundlinien preußischer Geschichte: Königtum und Staatsgestaltung, 1701–1871 (Darmstadt, 1983)

'Verwaltungsentwicklung von 1713–1803', in K. G. A. Jeserich, Hans Pohl and Georg-Christoph von Unruh, (eds.), *Deutsche Verwaltungsgeschichte.* Vol. I: *Vom Spätmittelalter bis zum Ende des Reiches* (Stuttgart, 1983), pp. 893–941

'Stein and Constitutional reform in nineteenth-century Germany: pre-conditions, plans and results', *Studies in Medieval and Modern German History* (Oxford, 1985), pp. 93–108

Huber, Ernst Rudolf, *Deutsche Verfassungsgeschichte*, vol. I: *Reform und Restauration 1789 bis 1830* (Stuttgart, 1957)

Hüffer, Hermann, *A. L. Mencken, der Großvater des Fürsten Bismarck, und die Kabinetsregierung in Preußen. Vortrag zum Antritt des Rektorates der Rheinischen Friedrich Wilhelms Universität am 18. Oktober 1890* (Bonn 1890)

Europa im Zeitalter der französischen Revolution. Vol. II: *Der Rastatter Kongreß und die zweite Koalition* (Bonn, 1890)

Die Kabinettsregierung in Preussen und Johann Wilhelm Lombard – Ein Beitrag zur Geschichte des preussischen Staates vornehmlich in den Jahren 1797 bis 1810 (Leipzig, 1891)

'Haugwitz nach der Schlacht bei Austerlitz', *Deutsche Zeitschrift für Geschichtswissenschaft* 6, 1 (1891), 102–4

'Die Beamten des älteren preussischen Kabinets von 1713–1808', *FBPG*, 5 (1892), 157–90

'Der Feldzug der Engländer und Russen in Holland im Herbst 1799 und die Stellung Preussens', *Historische Vierteljahresschrift*, 5 (1902), 161–95; 347–86

'Nachträgliche Bemerkungen zum Feldzuge der Engländer und Russen in Holland', *Historische Vierteljahrsschrift*, 5 (1902)

Hüttenberger, Peter and Molitor, Hansgeorg (eds.), *Franzosen und Deutsche am Rhein. 1789–1918–1945* (Essen, 1989)

Ingram, Edward, 'Lord Mulgrave's proposals for the reconstruction of Europe in 1804', *HJ*, 19 (1976), 511–20

Jany, Curt, *Geschichte der königlich-preussischen Armee bis zum Jahre 1807.* Vol. III: *1763–1807* (Berlin, 1929)

Jeserich, K. G. A. , Pohl, Hans and Unruh, Georg-Christoph von (eds.), *Deutsche Verwaltungsgeschichte.* Vol. I: *Vom Spätmittelalter bis zum Ende des Reiches* (Stuttgart, 1983)

Deutsche Verwaltungsgeschichte. Vol. II: *Vom Reichsdeputationshauptschluss bis zur Auflösung des Deutschen Bundes* (Stuttgart, 1983)

Johnston, Otto W., 'British espionage and Prussian politics in the age of Napoleon', *Intelligence and National Security*, 2 (1987), 232–44

Jones, A., 'Where "Governing is the use of words"', *HJ*, 19 (1976), 253–4

Julliard, Jacques, 'Political history in the 1980s. Reflections on its present and future', *Journal of Interdisciplinary History*, 12, 1 (1981), 29–44

Kallenberg, Fritz, 'Die Fürstentümer Hohenzollern im Zeitalter der Französischen Revolution und Napoleons', *Zeitschrift für die Geschichte des Oberrheins*, 111 (1963), 357–473

Kehr, Eckhart, 'Zur Genesis der preußischen Bürokratie und des Rechtsstaats', in *Der Primat der Innenpolitik. Gesammelte Aufsätze zur preußisch-deutschen Sozialgeschichte im 19. und 20. Jahrhundert*, edited by Hans-Ulrich Wehler (Berlin, 1975), pp. 31–52

Kell, Eva, 'Die Frankfurter Union (1803–1806). Eine Fürstenassoziation zur "verfassungsmäßigen Selbsterhaltung" der kleineren weltlichen Adelsherrschaften', *ZfHF*, 18 (1991), 71–97

Kieseritzky, Ernst, 'Die Sendung von Haugwitz nach Wien. November und Dezember 1805', (PhD dissertation, University of Göttingen, 1895)

Kircheisen, F. M., 'Pourquoi la guerre éclata en 1806 entre la France et la Prusse?', *Revue d'histoire diplomatique*, 43 (1929), 237–50

Kissinger, Henry A., 'Domestic structure and foreign policy', *Daedalus*, 95 (1966), 503–29

Klatt, Tessa, *Königin Luise von Preussen in der Zeit der Napoleonischen Kriege* (Berlin, 1937)

Klein, Ernst, 'Funktion und Bedeutung des Preußischen Staatsministeriums', *Jahrbuch für die Geschichte Mittel und Ostdeutschlands*, 9, 10 (1961), 195–261
'Johann Heinrich Gottlob Justi und die preussische Staatswirtschaft', *VSWG*, 8 (1961), 145–202

Klinkenborg, Melle, 'Die Stellung des Hauses Finckenstein am preußischen Hofe im 17. und 18. Jahrhundert', *Hohenzollern Jahrbuch*, 17 (1913), 156–72
'Materialen zur Geschichte des Geheimen Staatsministers Karl Wilhelm Finck von Finckenstein', *FBPG*, 28 (1915), 563–74
'Die Stellung des kgl. Kabinetts in der preuß. Behördenorganisation', *Hohenzollern Jahrbuch*, 19 (1915), 47–51

Klueting, Harm, *Die Lehre von der Macht der Staaten. Das außenpolitische Machtproblem in der 'politischen Wissenschaft' und in der praktischen Politik im achtzehnten Jahrhundert*, Historische Forschungen 29 (Berlin, 1986)

Knemeyer, Franz-Ludwig, 'Beginn der Reorganisation der Verwaltung in Deutschland', in K.G.A. Jeserich, Hans Pohl and Georg-Christoph von Unruh (eds.), *Deutsche Verwaltungsgeschichte*. Vol. II: *Vom Reichsdeputationhauptschluss bis zur Auflösung des Deutschen Bundes* (Stuttgart, 1983), pp. 120–54

Koch, Ursula, 'Französische Revolution und preußische Tagespublizistik', in Büsch and Neugebauer-Wölk (eds.), *Preußen und die revolutionäre Herausforderung seit 1789*, pp. 213–66

Kocka, Jürgen, 'Hitler sollte nicht durch Stalin un Pol Pot verdrängt werden', in *Historikerstreit*, pp. 132–42

Körholz, Franz, *Die Säkularisation und Organisation in den preußischen Entschädigungsländern Essen, Elten und Werden 1802–1806*, Münstersche Beiträge zur Geschichtsforschung NF 14 (Münster, 1907)

Kohnke, Meta, 'Das preußische Kabinettsministerium. Ein Beitrag zur Geschichte des Staatsapparates im Spätfeudalismus' (unpublished DPhil dissertation, University of Berlin/East, 1967)

'Das preußische Kabinettsministerium. Ein Beitrag zur Geschichte des Staats-apparates im Spätfeudalismus', *Jahrbuch für die Geschichte des Feudalismus*, 2 (1978), 313–56

'Bauernunruhen in der Altmark im Sommer 1794', *Jahrbuch für Regional-geschichte*, 16 (1989), 94–109

Kohnke, Meta (ed.), *Carl Wilhelm Cosmar. Geschichte des Königlich-preußischen Geheimen Staats- und Kabinetsarchivs bis 1806*, Veröffentlichungen aus dem Archiven Preußischer Kulturbesitz 32 (Cologne, Vienna and Weimar, 1993)

Koppen, Wilhelm, *Deutsche gegen Deutschland. Geschichte des Rheinbundes* (Hamburg, 1936)

Koselleck, Reinhart, *Preußen zwischen Reform und Revolution. Allgemeines Land-recht, Verwaltung, und soziale Bewegung von 1791–1848* (Stuttgart, 1975)

Koser, Reinhold, 'Die Gründung des Auswärtigen Amtes durch König Friedrich Wilhelm I im Jahre 1728', *FBPG*, 2 (1889), 161–97

'Die preußische Politik von 1786 bis 1806', *Deutsche Monatsschrift*, 6 (1907), 453–80; 612–37

Kossok, Manfred and Kross, Editha (eds.), *1789– Weltwirkung einer Grossen Revolution*, 2 vols. (Berlin, 1989)

Kraehe, Enno, *Metternich's German policy*. Vol. I: *The contest with Napoleon, 1799–1814* (Princeton, N.J., 1963)

Krauel, Richard, *Prinz Heinrich von Preussen als Politiker*, Quellen und Unter-suchungen zur Geschichte des Hauses Hohenzollern 4 (Berlin, 1902)

'Prinz Heinrich von Preussen in Rheinsberg', *Hohenzollern Jahrbücher*, 6 (1902), 12–37

'Eine Denkschrift des Freiherrn von Stein aus dem Jahre 1806', *HZ*, 102 (1909), 556–66

'Stein während des preussisch-englischen Konflikts im Jahre 1806', *PJ*, 137 (1909), 429–57

'Die Haltung Preussens in Fragen des Seekriegsrechts von 1783–1799', *FBPG*, 24 (1911), 183–226

'Die Beteiligung Preußens an der zweiten Bewaffneten Neutralität vom Dezember 1801', *FBPG*, 27 (1914), 189–245

'Preußen und England vor 100 Jahren', *Deutsche Revue* 31 (1906), 348–61

Kraus, Hans-Christof, 'Zum Verhältnis von politischer Ideen- und Sozialgeschichte. Bemerkungen zu Robert M. Berdahl: "The politics of the Prussian Nobility"', *Der Staat*, 30/2 (1991), 269–78

Krieger, Bogdan, 'Königin Luise und der Geheime Kabinetsrat Lombard', *Deutsche Revue*, 26 (1901), 200–11; 333–43

Krienen, Dag (review of Alexander Demandt (ed.), *Deutschlands Grenzen in der Geschichte*), *Der Staat*, 30/2 (1991), 304–7

Krill, Hans-Heinz, *Die Rankerenaissance. Max Lenz und Erich Marcks. Ein Beitrag zum historisch-politischen Denken in Deutschland 1880–1935* (Berlin, 1962)

Krockow, Christian Graf von, *Die Entscheidung. Eine Untersuchung über Ernst Jünger, Carl Schmitt, Martin Heidegger* (Frankfurt/Main, 1990)

Kroener, Bernhard R., 'Aufklärung und Revolution. Die preußische Armee am Vorabend der Katastrophe von 1806', Militärgeschichtliches Forschungsamt (ed.), *Die französische Revolution und der Beginn des*

Zweiten Weltkrieges aus deutscher und französischer Sicht (Herford and Bonn, 1989)

Krüdener, Jürgen von, *Die Rolle des Hofes im Absolutismus*, Forschungen zur Sozial- und Wirtschaftsgeschichte 19 (Stuttgart, 1973)

Krüger-Löwenstein, Uta, *Rußland, Frankreich und das Reich, 1801–1803. Zur Vorgeschichte der 3. Koalition* (Wiesbaden, 1972)

Krumeich, Gerd, *Aufrüstung und Innenpolitik in Frankreich vor dem Ersten Weltkrieg. Die Einführung der dreijährigen Dienstpflicht 1913–1914* (Wiesbaden, 1980)

Kunisch, Johannes, *Staatsverfassung und Mächtepolitik. Zur Genese von Staatenkonflikten im Zeitalter des Absolutismus* (Berlin, 1979)

Kutz, M., 'Die Deutsch-Britischen Handelsbeziehungen von 1790 bis zur Gründung des Zollvereins', *VSWG*, 56 (1969), 178–214

Lacoste, Yves, *Geographie und politisches Handeln. Perspektiven einer neuen Geopolitik* with a foreword by Mechtild Rössler (Berlin, 1990)

Laubert, Manfred, *Die preußische Polenpolitik von 1772 bis 1914* (Cracow, 1944)

Lawrence, Jon and Taylor, Miles, 'The poverty of protest: Gareth Stedman Jones and the politics of language – a reply', *Social History*, 18 (1993), 1–16

Ledermann, Richard, *Der Anschluß Bayerns an Frankreich im Jahre 1805*, Forschungen zur Geschichte Bayerns, 9 (Berlin, 1901), pp. 165–252

Lehmann, Max, 'Hardenberg's Memoiren', *HZ*, 39 (1878), 77–100

Scharnhorst. Vol. I: *Bis zum Tilsiter Frieden* (Leipzig, 1887)

'Ein Regierungsprogramm Friedrich Wilhelms III', *HZ*, 61 (1889), 441–60

'Der Ursprung des preussischen Kabinets', *HZ*, 63 (1889), 263–71

'Wöllner und die auswärtige Politik Friedrich Wilhelm II', *HZ* 62 (1889), 285–6

*Freiherr vom Stein.*Vol. I: *Vor der Reform, 1757–1807* (Leipzig, 1902)

'Das alte Preußen', *HZ*, 90 (1903), 385–421

Lenz, Max, 'Napoleon I und Preußen', *Cosmopolis: Internationale Revue*, 9 (1898), 580–95; 859–74

Levinger, Mathew, 'Hardenberg, Wittgenstein and the constitutional question in Prussia, 1815–1822', *German History*, 8 (1990), 257–77

'Imagining a nation: the constitutional question in Prussia, 1806–1815' (unpublished DPhil dissertation, University of Chicago, 1992)

Lübbe, Hermann, 'Zur Theorie der Entscheidung', *Collegium philosophicum. Studien Joachim Ritter zum 60. Geburtstag* (Stuttgart/Basel, 1965), pp. 118–40

'Dezisionismus in der Moral-Theorie Kants', in Hans Barion, Ernst-Wolfgang Böckenförde, Ernst Forsthoff and Werner Weber (eds.), *Epirrhosis. Festgabe für Carl Schmitt* (Berlin, 1968), pp. 567–78

Theorie und Entscheidung. Studien zum Primat der praktischen Vernunft (Freiburg, 1971)

'Dezisionismus- eine kompromittierte politische Theorie', *Praxis Philosophie. Praktische Philosophie. Geschichtstheorie* (Stuttgart, 1978), pp. 61–77

Lüdtke, Wilhelm, 'Preussen und Frankreich vom Bastillesturm bis Reichenbach', *FBPG*, 42 (1929), 230–62

'Friedrich Wilhelm II und die revolutionäre Propaganda (1789–1791)', *FBPG*, 44 (1932), 70–92

Luvaas, Jay, 'Napoleon's use of intelligence: the Jena campaign of 1805 [*sic*]', in *Intelligence and National Security*, 3, 3 (1988), 40–54

Luxenberg, Bruno, *Deutsche Brotpolitik* (Leipzig, 1941)

Mackesy, Piers, *The war in the Mediterranean, 1803–1810* (London, 1957)

War without victory. The downfall of Pitt, 1799–1802 (Oxford, 1984)

Mackinder, H. J., 'The geographical pivot of history', *The Geographical Journal*, 23, 4 (1904), 421–44

Mahan, Alfred Thayer, *The influence of sea power upon the French Revolution and empire, 1793–1812*, 2 vols. (London, 1893)

Mann, Golo, *Secretary of Europe. The life of Friedrich Gentz, enemy of Napoleon* (New Haven, 1946)

Marcks, Erich, *Deutschland und England in den grossen Europäischen Krisen seit der Reformation* (Stuttgart, 1900)

Die Einheitlichkeit der Englischen Auslandspolitik von 1500 bis zur Gegenwart (Stuttgart, 1910)

Englands Machtpolitik (Stuttgart, 1940)

Maschke, Günter, 'Zweideutigkeit der "Entscheidung" – Thomas Hobbes und Juan Donoso Cortes im Werk Carl Schmitts', in Helmut Quaritsch (ed.), *Complexio Oppositorum. Über Carl Schmitt. Vorträge und Diskussionsbeiträge des 28. Sonderseminars 1986 der Hochschule für Verwaltungswissenschaften Speyer* (Berlin, 1988), pp. 192–221

Masson, Frederic, 'Berlin il y a cent ans', *RHD*, 5 (1891), 28

Materna, Ingo and Ribbe, Wolfgang (eds.), *Brandenburgische Geschichte* (Berlin, 1995)

Mayerhoffer von Vedropolje, Eberhard, *1805, Der Krieg der dritten Koalition* (Vienna, 1905)

Mayfield, David and Thorne, Susan, 'Social history and its discontents. Gareth Stedman Jones and the politics of language', *Social History*, 17 (1992), 165–88

Meier, Ernst von, *Die Reform der Verwaltungsorganisation unter Stein und Hardenberg* (Leipzig, 1881)

Französische Einflüsse auf die Staats und Rechtsentwicklung Preussens im XIX Jahrhundert. Vol. II: *Preussen und die französische Revolution* (Leipzig, 1908)

Meinecke, Friedrich, *Das Leben des Generalfeldmarschalls Hermann von Boyen* (Stuttgart, 1896–9)

Die Idee der Staatsräson in der neueren Geschichte (Munich and Berlin, 1923)

Zur Geschichte der Geschichtsschreibung, edited and introduced by Eberhard Kessel (Munich, 1968)

Das Zeitalter der deutschen Erhebung, 1795–1815 (Bielefeld, 1913), translated as Friedrich Meinecke, *The age of German liberation, 1795–1815* (Berkeley, 1977)

Meissner, H. O., 'Zur neueren Geschichte des preußischen Cabinetts', *FBPG*, 36 (1924), 39–66

'Die monarchische Regierungsform in Brandenburg-Preussen', *Festschrift für Fritz Hartung* (Berlin, 1958), pp. 219–45

Melton, Edgar, 'The decline of Prussian *Gutsherrschaft* and the rise of the Junker as rural patron, 1750–1806', *German History*, 12 (1994), 334–50

Melville, Ralph and Reden-Dohna, Armgard von (eds.), *Der Adel an der Schwelle des bürgerlichen Zeitalters, 1780–1860* (Stuttgart, 1988)

Messerschmidt, Manfred, 'Nachwirkungen Friedrichs II. in Preußen-Deutschland', in Bernhard R. Kroener (ed.), *Europa im Zeitalter Friedrichs des Großen. Wirtschaft. Gesellschaft. Kriege* (Munich, 1989), pp. 269–88

Mettam, Roger, *Power and faction in Louis XIV's France* (Oxford, 1988)

Meusel, Friedrich, 'Die Aufhebung der Akzisefreiheit des Adels in Preußen (1799)', *FBPG*, 21 (1908), 559–63

Meyer, Christian, *Preussens innere Politik in Ansbach und Bayreuth in den Jahren 1792–1806* (Berlin, 1904)

Preußen und Frankreich, von 1795–1800, Hohenzollersche Forschungen, 7 (Munich, 1905), pp. 68–92

Michels, Robert, *Zur Soziologie des Parteiwesens in der modernen Demokratie. Untersuchungen uber die oligarchischen Tendenzen des Gruppenlebens*, edited by Werner Conze (Stuttgart, 1970)

Mittenzwei, Ingrid, *Preußen nach dem Siebenjährigen Krieg* (Berlin/GDR, 1979)

Möckl, Karl (ed.), *Hof und Hofgesellschaft in den deutschen Staaten im 19. und beginnenden 20. Jahrhundert*, Büdinger Forschungen zur Sozialgeschichte 18 (Boppard, 1990)

'Hof und Hofgesellschaft in den deutschen Staaten im 19. und beginnenden 20. Jahrhundert. Einleitende Bemerkungen', in Möckl (ed.), *Hof und Hofgesellschaft in den deutschen Staaten*, pp. 7–15

Möller, Detlev, 'Zur Politik der Hansestädte im Jahre 1806', *Zeitschrift des Vereins für Hamburgische Geschichte*. Vol. 41: *Festschrift für Heinrich Reinicke* (Hamburg, 1951), 330–51

Möller, Horst, 'Der Primat der Aussenpolitik: Preussen und die Französische Revolution', in Jürgen Voss (ed.), *Deutschland und die Französische Revolution* (Munich, 1983), pp. 65–81

'Preußische Aufklärungsgesellschaften und Revolutionserfahrung', in Büsch and Neugebauer-Wölk (eds.), *Preußen und die revolutionäre Herausforderung seit 1789*, pp. 103–17

Mohnhaupt, Heinz, 'Verfassung I: Konstitution, Status, Lex Fundamentalis', in Otto Brunner, Werner Conze and Reinhart Koselleck (eds.), *Geschichtliche Grundbegriffe*. Historisches Lexikon zur politisch-sozialen Sprache in Deutschland 6 (Stuttgart, 1990), pp. 832–62

Mommsen, Hans, *Der Nationalsozialismus und die deutsche Gesellschaft. Ausgewählte Aufsätze* (Hamburg, 1991)

Moran, Daniel, 'Clausewitz and the Revolution', *CEH*, 22, 2 (1989), 184–99

Moritz, Erhard, *Preussen und der Kosciusko-Aufstand 1794. Zur preussischen Polenpolitik in der Zeit der Französischen Revolution*, Schriftenreihe des Instituts für Allgemeine Geschichte an der Humboldt Universität Berlin 11 (East Berlin, 1968)

Müller, Hans-Heinrich, 'Der agrarische Fortschritt und die Bauern in Brandenburg vor den Reformen von 1807', *ZfG*, 12 (1964), 629–48

Müller, Harald, 'Forschungen zur deutschen Geschichte 1789–1848', *Zeitschrift für Geschichtswissenschaft*, Sonderband 1980, Historische Forschungen in der DDR, 1970–1980, Analysen und Berichte (Berlin, 1980), pp. 122–42

Müller, Heinrich, *Der letzte Kampf der Reichsritterschaft um ihre Selbstständigkeit 1789–1815* (Berlin, 1910)

Müller, Wilhelm, 'Zur Geschichte des Herzogs Karl Wilhelm Ferdinand in den Jahren 1792 und 1806', *Braunschweigisches Jahrbuch*, 38 (1957), 95–115

Müller-Weil, Ulrike, *Absolutismus und Außenpolitik in Preußen. Ein Beitrag zur Strukturgeschichte des preußischen Absolutismus*, Frankfurter Historische Abhandlungen 34 (Stuttgart, 1992)

Münchow-Pohl, Bernd von, *Zwischen Reform und Krieg. Untersuchungen zur Bewußtseinslage in Preußen 1809–1812*, Veröffentlichungen des Max-Planck-Instituts für Geschichte 87 (Göttingen, 1987)

Müsebeck, Ernst, 'Fragmentarische Aufzeichnungen Altensteins über die auswärtige Politik Preussens vom 28/29 Dezember 1805', *FBPG*, 28 (1915), 139–73

'Zur Geschichte der Reformbestrebungen vor dem Zusammenbruche des alten Preussens 1806', *FBPG*, 30 (1917), 115–46

Muhlack, Ulrich, 'Leopold von Ranke', in *Deutsche Geschichtswissenschaft um 1900* (Stuttgart and Wiesbaden, 1988), pp. 11–36

Narocnickij, Aleksej L., 'Russland und die napoleonische Hegemoniepolitik: Widerstand und Anpassung', in Aretin and Ritter (eds.), *Historismus und Moderne Geschichtswissenschaft*, pp. 163–83

Naudé, Albert, 'Der preußische Staatsschatz unter König Friedrich Wilhelm II und seine Erschöpfung', *FBPG*, 5 (1892), pp. 203–56

Naudé, Wilhelm, 'Die brandenburgisch-preußische Getreidehandelspolitik von 1713–1806', in [Schmoller's] *Jahrbuch für Gesetzgebung, Verwaltung und Volkswirtschaft im deutschen Reiche* 29 (1905), 161–90

Naujoks, Eberhard, *Die Französische Revolution und Europa 1789–1799* (Stuttgart, Berlin, Cologne, Mainz, 1969)

'Die Persönlichkeit Friedrichs des Grossen und die Struktur des preußischen Staates', *Historische Mitteilungen*, 2, 1 (1989), 17–37

Neue Deutsche Biographie, edited by the Historische Kommission der Bayerischen Akademie der Wissenschaften (Berlin, 1953–)

Neugebauer, Wolfgang, 'Zur neueren Deutung der preußischen Verwaltung im 17. und 18. Jahrhundert in vergleichender Sicht', in Otto Büsch and Wolfgang Neugebauer (eds.), *Moderne preussische Geschichte, 1648–1947. Eine Anthologie*, II (Berlin, 1981), pp. 541–97

Politischer Wandel im Osten. Ost- und Westpreußen von den alten Ständen zum Konstitutionalismus, Quellen und Studien zur Geschichte des östlichen Europa 36 (Stuttgart, 1992)

Neugebauer-Wölk, Monika, 'Preußen und die Revolutionen in Lüttich. Zur Politik des Christian Wilhelm von Dohm, 1789/90', in Büsch and Neugebauer-Wölk (eds.), *Preußen und die revolutionäre Herausforderung seit 1789*, pp. 59–76

Niedhart, Gottfried, 'Aufgeklärter Absolutismus oder Rationalisierung der Herrschaft', *ZfHF*, 6 (1979), 199–211

Nipperdey, Thomas, *Deutsche Geschichte 1800–1866. Bürgerwelt und starker Staat* (Munich, 1983)

Noack, Friedrich, *Hardenberg und das geheime Kabinett Friedrich Wilhelms III vom*

Potsdamer Vertrag bis zur Schlacht von Jena, Giessener Studien auf dem Gebiet der Geschichte 2 (Giessen, 1881)

Nolte, Paul, *Staatsbildung als Gesellschaftsreform: Politische Reformen in Preußen und den süddeutschen Staaten 1800–1820* (Frankfurt, 1990)

Novotny, Alexander, 'Über den Primat der äußeren Politik. Bemerkungen zu einem Gedankengang Leopold von Rankes', in *Österreich und Europa. Festgabe für Hugo Hantsch zum 70. Geburtstag* (Graz, Vienna, Cologne, 1965), pp. 311–23

O'Boyle, Lenore, 'Some recent studies of nineteenth-century European bureaucracy: problems of analysis', *CEH*, 19, 1 (1986), 386–408

O'Brien, Conor Cruise, *The great melody: a thematic biography and commented anthology of Edmund Burke* (London, 1992)

Oer, Rudolfine Freiin von, *Der Friede von Pressburg. Ein Beitrag zur Diplomatiegeschichte des napoleonischen Zeitalters* (Münster, 1965)

Die Säkularisation 1803 (Göttingen, 1970)

Oestreich, Gerhard, *Der brandenburgisch-preußische Geheime Rat von Regierungsantritt des großen Kurfürsten bis zu der Neuordnung im Jahre 1651. Eine Behördengeschichtliche Studie*, ed. F. Hartung, Berliner Studien zur neueren Geschichte (Würzburg/Aumühle, 1937)

'Bureaucracy, aristocracy, and autocracy' [review of Hans Rosenberg's *Bureaucracy, aristocracy, and autocracy*], *VSWG*, 52, (1965), 276–81

'Reichsverfassung und europäisches Staatensystem 1648–1789', in Oestreich (ed.), *Geist und Gestalt des frühmodernen Staates* (Berlin, 1969), pp. 233–52

Olden, Hans Peter, 'Napoleon und Talleyrand. Die französische Politik während des Feldzugs von 1805 in Deutschland' (PhD dissertation, University of Tübingen, 1928)

Oncken, Hermann, 'Über die Zusammenhänge zwischen aüßerer und innerer Politik', *Vorträge der Gehe Stiftung zu Dresden* (Dresden/Leipzig, 1918)

Oncken, Wilhelm, *Österreich und Preußen im Befreiungskriege. Urkundliche Aufschlüsse über die politische Geschichte des Jahres 1813*, 2 vols. (Berlin, 1876–9)

Das Zeitalter der Revolution, des Kaiserreiches und der Befreiungskriege, 2 vols. (Berlin, 1886)

Oppeln-Bronikowski, Friedrich von, *Abenteurer am preußischen Hofe 1700–1800* (Berlin, 1927)

Oppliger, Ernst, *Neuenburg, die Schweiz und Preussen 1798–1806* (Zurich and Leipzig, 1915)

Paret, Peter, *Yorck and the era of Prussian Reform, 1807–1815* (Princeton, 1966)

Parry, Geraint, 'Enlightened government and its critics in eighteenth-century Germany', *HJ*, 6 (1963), 178–92

Parry, Jonathan P., 'The state of Victorian political history', *HJ*, 26, 2 (1983), 469–84

'High and low politics in modern Britain', *HJ*, 29, 3 (1986), 753–70

Paulig, F. R., *Friedrich Wilhelm III., König von Preussen (1770–1840). Sein Privatleben und seine Regierung im Lichte neuer Foschungen* (Frankfurt/Oder, 1905)

Perthes, C.T., *Politische Zustände und Personen in Deutschland zur Zeit der französischen Herrschaft*, 2 vols. (Gotha, 1862)

Petzold, Horst, *Die Verhandlungen der 1798 von König Friedrich Wilhelm III. eingesetzten Finanzkommission*, (PhD dissertation, University of Göttingen, 1911)

Phillips, Walter Alison and Reade, Arthur H., *Neutrality: its history, economics and law*. Vol. II: *The Napoleonic period* (Columbia, 1936, repr. New York, 1976)

Poseck, E., *Louis Ferdinand. Prinz von Preussen. Eine Biographie* (Berlin, 1938, 1943 edition)

Preradovich, Nikolaus von, *Die Führungsschichten in Oesterreich und Preußen (1804–1918)* (Wiesbaden, 1955)

Press, Volker, 'Warum gab es keine deutsche Revolution? Deutschland und das revolutionäre Frankreich, 1789–1815', in Dieter Langewiesche (ed.), *Revolution und Krieg. Zur Dynamik historischen Wandels seit dem 18. Jahrhundert* (Paderborn, 1989), pp. 67–85

Quaritsch, Helmut, *Positionen und Begriffe Carl Schmitts* (Berlin, 1989)

Raack, R.C., *The fall of Stein*, Harvard Historical Monographs 58 (Cambridge, Mass., 1965)

Radtke, Wolfgang, *Die preußische Seehandlung zwischen Staat und Wirtschaft in der Frühphase der Industrialisierung*, Einzelveröffentlichungen der Historischen Kommission zu Berlin 30 (Berlin, 1981)

Ragsdale, Hugh, *Détente in the Napoleonic Era: Bonaparte and the Russians* (Lawrence, Kansas, 1980)

'Russia, Prussia and Europe in the policy of Paul I', *Jahrbücher für Geschichte Osteuropas*, 31 (1983), 81–118

Ragsdale, Hugh (ed.), *Paul I: a reassessment of his life and reign* (Pittsburgh, 1979)

Ranke, Leopold von, 'Das politische Gespräch', in Leopold von Ranke, *Das politische Gespräch und andere Schriftchen zur Wissenschaftslehre* edited by Erich Rothacker (Halle and Saale, 1925), pp. 10–36

'Die grossen Mächte', in Leopold von Ranke, *Völker und Staaten in der neueren Geschichte*, edited by L. von Muralt (Zurich, 1945), pp. 44–88

'A dialogue on politics', in Theodor von Laue (ed.), *Leopold von Ranke, the formative years* (Princeton, N.J., 1950)

Raumer, Kurt von, *Deutschland um 1800: Krise und Neugestaltung, 1789–1815*, Handbuch der deutschen Geschichte, Vol. III edited by Leo Just (Konstanz, 1961); vol. IV

'Politiker des Maßes? Talleyrands Strassburger Friedensplan, 17 Oktober 1805', *HZ*, 193 (1961), 286–368

'Prefecture Française – Montgelas und die Beurteilung der napoleonischen Rheinbundpolitik. Ein Bericht des württembergischen Gesandten Graf Taube, München 5 Juli 1806', in *Spiegel der Geschichte, Festgabe für Max Braubach zum 10 April 1964* (Munich, 1964), pp. 635–61

Real, Willy, *Von Potsdam nach Basel. Studien zur Geschichte der Beziehungen Preussens zu den europäischen Mächten vom Regierungsantritt Friedrich Wilhelm II. bis zum Abschluss des Friedens von Basel 1786–1795* (Stuttgart and Basle, 1958)

'Der Friede von Basel', *Baseler Zeitschrift für Geschichte und Altertumskunde*, 50 (1950), 27–112; 51 (1951), 115–228

'Die preussischen Staatsfinanzen und die Anbahnung des Sonderfriedens von Basel 1795', *FBPG*, N.F. 1 (1991), 53–100

Rein, Adolf, 'Über die Bedeutung der überseeischen Ausdehnung für das europäische Staaten-System. Ein Beitrag zur Bildungsgeschichte des Welt-Staatensystems', *HZ*, 137 (1928), 28–90

Reinhard, Wolfgang, *Freunde und Kreaturen. 'Verflechtung' als Konzept zur Erforschung historischer Führungsgruppen. Römische Oligarchie um 1600*, Schriften der Philosophischen Fachbereiche der Universität Augsburg 14 (Munich, 1979)

Ritter, Gerhard, *Die Dämonie der Macht: Betrachungen über Geschichte und Wesen des Machtproblems im politischen Denken der Neuzeit* (Munich, 1948)

Stein. Eine politische Biographie (Stuttgart, 1931, 3rd edn 1958)

Staatskunst und Kriegshandwerk. Das Problem des 'Militarismus' in Deutschland. Erster Band: Die altpreussische Tradition (1740–1890) (Munich, 1954), translated as *The sword and the sceptre. The problem of militarism in Germany.* Vol. I: *The Prussian tradition, 1740–1840* (London, 1972)

Roach, Elmo E., 'Anglo-Russian Relations from Austerlitz to Tilsit', *IHR*, 5 (1983), 181–200

Röhl, John, 'Introduction', in John Röhl and Nicolaus Sombart (eds.), *Kaiser Wilhelm II. New interpretations* (Cambridge, 1982)

Kaiser, Hof und Staat. Wilhelm II und die deutsche Politik (Munich, 1987)

Der Ort Kaiser Wilhelms II in der deutschen Geschichte (Munich, 1991)

Roider, Karl A., *Baron Thugut and Austria's response to the French Revolution* (Princeton, 1987)

'The Habsburg foreign ministry and political reform', *CEH*, 22 (1989), 160–82

Rosenberg, Hans, *Bureaucracy, aristocracy, and autocracy. The Prussian experience 1660–1815* (Cambridge, Mass., 1958)

'Die Überwindung der monarchischen Autokratie (Preußen)', in K. O. von Aretin (ed.), *Der Aufgeklärte Absolutismus* (Cologne, 1967), pp. 182–204

Roß, Günther, 'Das Leben des Freiherrn von Altenstein bis zum Jahre 1807', *FBPG*, 53 (1941), 91–128

Ross, Steven T., *European diplomatic history, 1789–1815. France against Europe* (New York, 1969)

Rössler, Hellmuth, *Oesterreichs Kampf um Deutschlands Befreiung. Die deutsche Politik der nationalen Führer Österreichs 1805–1815*, 2 vols. (Hamburg, 1940)

Rothfels, Hans, *Gesellschaftsform und auswärtige Politik* (Laupheim, 1951)

'Sinn und Grenzen des Primats der Außenpolitik', in Hans Rothfels, *Zeitgeschichtliche Betrachtungen. Vorträge und Aufsätze* (Göttingen, 1959), pp. 161–75

Rotthaus, Karl, 'Staatsform und auswärtige Politik. Eine Rankestudie', *PJ*, 179 (1920), 1–35

Rumler, Marie, 'Die Bestrebungen zur Befreiung der Privatbauern in Preußen, 1797–1806', *FBPG*, 37 (1925), pp. 31–76

Rumpf, Helmut, *Carl Schmitt und Thomas Hobbes* (Berlin, 1972)

Ruppel-Kuhfuss, Edith, *Das Generaldirektorium unter der Regierung Friedrich Wilhelms II.* (Würzburg, 1937)

Sahlins, Peter, 'Natural frontiers revisited. France's boundaries since the seventeenth century', *AHR*, 95, 5 (1990), 1423–51

Santelmann, Theodor, 'Die Beziehungen zwischen Bayern und Preußen 1799–1805', (unpublished DPhil dissertation, University of Munich, 1906)

Saring, Hans, 'Karl Friedrich von Beyme', *Jahrbuch für brandenburgische Landesgeschichte*, 7 (1956), 35–46

Satz, Siegmund, 'Die Politik der deutschen Staaten vom Herbst 1805 bis zum Herbst 1806 im Lichte der gleichzeitigen deutschen Publizistik' (DPhil dissertation, University of Berlin, 1908)

Schaeder, Hildegard, *Die Dritte Koalition und die heilige Allianz* (Königsberg and Berlin, 1934)

Scharf, Claus, *Katharina II, Deutschland, und die Deutschen*, Veröffentlichungen des Instituts für Europäische Geschichte Mainz 153 (Mainz, 1995)

Scheel, Heinrich, 'Probleme der deutsch-französischen Beziehungen 1789–1830', *ZfG*, 18/2 (1970), 163–71

'Die Stein-Hardenbergschen Reformen-der Beginn einer Revolution von oben', *Deutsche Historiker-Gesellschaft. Wissenschaftliche Mitteilungen*, 3 (1970), 51–4

Scheibert, Peter, "Quelques changements dans le code maritime". Zur Nachgeschichte der "Bewaffneten Neutralität", 1801–1805', in Peter Classen and Peter Scheibert (eds.), *Festschrift Percy Ernst Schramm zu seinem Siebzigsten Geburtstag von Schülern und Freunden zugeeignet*, vol. II (Wiesbaden, 1964), pp. 145–53

Scherer, Stephen, 'Alexander I, the Prussian royal couple, and European politics: 1801–1807', *The Michigan Academician*, 13/1 (1980), 37–44

Scheuner, Ulrich, *Das europäische Gleichgewicht und die britische Seeherrschaft* (Hamburg, 1943)

Schissler, Hanna, *Preußische Agrargesellschaft im Wandel. Wirtschaftliche, gesellschaftliche und politische Transformationsprozesse von 1764 bis 1847* Kritische Studien zur Geschichtswissenschaft 33 (Göttingen, 1978)

'The social and economic power of the Prussian Junkers', in Ralph Gibson and Martin Blinkhorn (eds.), *Landownership and power in modern Europe* (London, 1991), pp. 99–110

Schmidt, Adolf, *Preussens Deutsche Politik. 1785.1806.1849.1866.* (Leipzig 3rd edn, 1867)

Schmidt, Hans, 'Napoleon in der deutschen Geschichtsschreibung', *Francia*, 14 (1980), 530–60

Schmidt, H. D., 'The idea and slogan of perfidious Albion', *Journal of the History of Ideas*, 14 (1953), 604–16

Schmidt, Walther, 'Geschichte des niedersächsischen Kreises vom Jahre 1673 bis zum Zusammenbruch der Kreisverfassung', *Niedersächsisches Jahrbuch für Landesgeschichte*, 7 (1930), 1–134

Schmidt-Bückeburg, Rudolf, *Das Militärkabinett der preußischen Könige und deutschen Kaiser. Seine geschichtliche Entwicklung und staatsrechtliche Stellung, 1787–1918* (Berlin, 1933)

Schmitt, Carl, *Politische Theologie. Vier Kapitel zur Lehre von der Souveränität* (Munich and Leipzig, 1922)

Politische Romantik (2nd edn, Berlin, 1925)

Die geistesgeschichtliche Lage des heutigen Parlamentarismus (Berlin, 1926)

Der Begriff des Politischen (Hamburg, 1933, 1st edn, 1927)

Verfassungslehre (Berlin, 1928, reprinted 1983)

Der Leviathan in der Staatslehre des Thomas Hobbes (Hamburg, 1938)

Gespräch über die Macht und der Zugang zum Machthaber (Pfullingen, 1954)

'Der Zugang zum Machthaber. Ein zentrales verfassungsrechtliches Problem', in Carl Schmitt, *Verfassungsrechtliche Aufsätze aus den Jahren 1924–1954* (Berlin, 1958), pp. 430–9

Land und Meer. Eine weltgeschichtliche Betrachtung (Cologne, 1981)

Der Nomos der Erde im Völkerrecht des Jus Publicum Europaneum (Berlin, 1988)

Schmoller, Gustav, *Preußische Verfassungs-, Verwaltungs- und Finanzgeschichte* (Berlin, 1921)

Schneider, Hans, 'Die Entstehung des preußischen Staatsrats 1806–1817', *Zeitschrift für die gesammte Staatswissenschaft*, 102 (1942), 480–529

Der preussische Staatsrat (Munich, 1952)

Schnitter, Helmut, 'Revolution und Heer. Reformbestrebungen und Revolutionseinflüsse im preußischen Heer vor 1806. Lernfähigkeit und Lernbereitschaft einer feudal-absolutistischen Armee im Umfeld der Französischen Revolution 1789/1795', in Timmermann (ed.), *Die Französische Revolution und Europa*, pp. 689–701

Schnur, Roman, 'Land und Meer – Napoleon gegen England. Ein Kapitel der Geschichte internationaler Politik', in Roman Schnur, *Revolution und Weltbürgerkrieg. Studien zur Ouverture nach 1789* (Berlin, 1983), pp. 33–58

Schöllgen, Gregor, 'Sicherheit durch Expansion? Die aussenpolitischen Lageanalysen der Hohenzollern im 17. und 18. Jahrhundert im Lichte des Kontinuitätsproblem in der preußischen und deutschen Geschichte', *Historisches Jahrbuch*, 104 (1984), 22–45

Flucht in den Krieg? Die Aussenpolitik des kaiserlichen Deutschland (Darmstadt, 1991)

Die Macht in der Mitte Europas. Stationen deutscher Außenpolitik von Friedrich dem Großen bis zur Gegenwart (Munich, 1992)

Schroeder, Paul, 'The collapse of the Second Coalition', *JMH*, 59 (June 1987), 244–90

'Old wine in new bottles: recent contributions to British foreign policy and European international politics, 1789–1848', *Journal of British Studies*, 26 (1987), 1–25

The transformation of European politics, 1763–1848, Oxford History of Modern Europe (Oxford, 1994)

Schück, C. E., 'Friedrich Wilhelm III. und seine Räte für die innere Gestetzgebung Preußens, 1797–1807', *Abhandlungen der Schlesischen Gesellschaft für vaterländische Cultur*, Phil. Hist. Abt. 45 (1867), 44–70

Schulin, Ernst, *Handelsstaat England. Das politische Interesse der Nation am Aussenhandel vom 16. bis ins frühe 18. Jahrhundert* (Wiesbaden, 1969)

Schultz, H.-D., 'Deutschlands "natürliche Grenzen"', in Alexander Demandt (ed.), *Deutschlands Grenzen in der Geschichte* (Munich, 1990), pp. 33–88

Schultz, Helga, 'Gesellschaftlichen Strukturen und geistig-politisches Klima in Berlin 1789–1799', in Timmermann (ed.), *Die französische Revolution und Europa*, pp. 381–92

Schulz, Axel, *Die Gegenzeichnung. Eine verfassungsgeschichtliche Untersuchung*, Schriften zum öffentlichen Recht 339 (Berlin, 1978)

Schulze, Friedrich, 'Die Beurteilung Friedrich Wilhelms III. in der Geschichtsschreibung des 19. Jahrhunderts', *Studium Lipiense, Ehrengabe für Karl Lamprecht* (Berlin, 1909), pp. 339–43

Schulze, Winfried, *Landesdefension und Staatsbildung. Studien zum Kriegswesen des innerösterreichischen Territorialstaates (1564–1619)* (Vienna, Cologne and Graz, 1973)

Reich und Türkengefahr im späten 16. Jahrhundert. Studien zu den politischen und gesellschaftlichen Auswirkungen einer äußeren Bedrohung (Munich, 1978)

Schwennicke, Andreas, *Die Entstehung des Allgemeinen Landrechts von 1794*, IUS Commune. Veröffentlichungen des Max-Planck-Instituts für Europäische Rechtsgeschichte Frankfurt am Main Sonderhefte Studien zur Europäischen Rechtsgeschichte 61 (Frankfurt, 1993)

Schwertfeger, Bernhard, 'Der Kampf gegen die Französische Revolution und gegen Napoleon', in Fr. von Cochenhausen (ed.), *Die Verteidigung Mitteleuropas*, (Jena, n.d.), pp. 165–266

Scott, H. M., 'Aping the great powers: Frederick the Great and the defence of Prussia's international position, 1763–1786', *German History* 12 (1994), 286–307

The European nobilities in the seventeenth and eighteenth centuries, vol. II (London, 1994)

'Paul W. Schroeder's International System: the view from Vienna', *International History Review*, 16, 4 (1994), 661–880

'Introduction: Prussia from Rossbach to Jena', *German History*, 12 (1994), 279–85

Scott, H. M. (ed.), 'Special issue: Prussia from Rossbach to Jena', *German History*, 12 (1994)

Scott, H. M. and McKay, Derek, *The rise of the great powers, 1648–1815* (London and New York, 1983)

Seeber, Gustav, 'Preußen seit 1789 in der Geschichtsschreibung der DDR', in Seeber and Noack (eds.), *Preußen in der deutschen Geschichte nach 1789*, pp. 11–48

Seeber, Gustav and Noack, Karl-Heinz (eds.), *Preußen in der deutschen Geschichte nach 1789*, Akademie der Wissenschaften der DDR, Zentralinstitut für Geschichte (Berlin/East, 1983)

Seeley, J. R., *Life and times of Stein, or Germany and Prussia in the Napoleonic age*, 3 vols. (reprinted New York, 1968)

Seidel, Paul, 'Parade am Berliner Schlosse vor Kaiser Alexander I und König Friedrich Wilhelm III am 25 Oktober 1805', *Hohenzollern Jahrbuch*, 16 (1912)

Sellin, Volker, 'Politik', in Otto Brunner, Werner Conze and Reinhart Kozelleck (eds.), *Geschichtliche Grundbegriffe*, Historisches Lexikon zur politisch-sozialen Sprache in Deutschland 4 (Stuttgart, 1978), pp. 789–874

Sheehan, James J., 'The primacy of domestic politics: Eckart Kehr's essays on modern German history', *CEH*, 1, 2 (1968), 166–74

German history, 1770–1866, Oxford History of Modern Europe (Oxford, 1989)

Sherwig, J. H., *Guineas and gunpowder. British foreign aid in the wars with France* (Cambridge, Mass., 1969)

Shop, Arthur Lloyd, 'The Primacy of Domestic Politics: Eckhart Kehr and the Intellectual development of Charles A. Beard', *History and Theory*, 13/2 (1974)

Showalter, Dennis E., 'Hubertusberg (*sic*) to Auerstädt: the Prussian army in decline', *German History*, 12 (1994), 308–33

Sieburg, Heinz-Otto, 'Die französische Revolution im Spiegel der Presse und politischen Publizistik Deutschlands (1789–1801)', *Historische Mitteilungen*, 2 (1989), 39–60

Sieburg, Heinz-Otto (ed.), *Napoleon und Europa* (Cologne and Berlin, 1971)

Sieske, Günther, *Preussen im Urteil Hannovers, 1795–1806. Ein Beitrag zur Geschichte der politischen Publizistik in Niedersachsen*, Veröffentlichungen der Historischen Kommission für Niedersachsen 25, Niedersachsen und Preussen, vol. 2 (Hildesheim, 1959)

Simmel, Georg, *Soziologie. Untersuchungen über die Formen der Vergesellschaftung* (Leipzig, 1908)

Simms, Brendan, 'Fra *Land* e *Meer*. La Gran Bretagna, la Prussia e il problemo del decisionismo (1804–1806)', *Ricerche di Storia Politica*, 6 (1991), 5–34

'Anglo-Prussian relations, 1804–1806: the Napoleonic threat' (unpublished PhD dissertation, University of Cambridge, 1992)

'The road to Jena: Prussian high politics, 1804–1806', *German History*, 12 (1994), 374–94

'"An odd question enough". Charles James Fox, the crown and British policy during the Hanoverian crisis of 1806', *HJ*, 38, 3 (1995), 567–96

Simon, Walter, 'Prince Hardenberg', *Review of Politics*, 18 (1956), 88–99

Skalweit, August, *Die Getreidehandelspolitik und Kriegsmagazinverwaltung Preußens, 1756–1806*, Acta Borussica, Denkmäler der preußischen Staatsverwaltung im 18. Jahrhundert (Berlin, 1931)

Sombart, Nicolaus, *Die deutschen Männer und ihre Feinde. Carl Schmitt – ein deutsches Schicksal zwischen Männerbund und Matriarchatsmythos* (Munich and Vienna, 1991)

Sösemann, Bernd (ed.), *Gemeingeist und Bürgersinn. Die preußischen Reformen*, FBPG, NF 2 (Berlin, 1993)

Spranger, Eduard, 'Altensteins Denkschrift von 1807 und ihre Beziehungen zur Philosophie', *FBPG*, 18 (1905), 471–517

Srbik, Heinrich Ritter von, 'Das Österreichische Kaisertum und das Ende des Heiligen Römischen Reiches, 1804–1806', *Archiv für Politik und Geschichte*, 2 and 3 (1927), 133–71; 301–35

Deutsche Einheit Idee und Wirklichkeit vom heiligen Reich bis Königsgrätz. 4 vols. (Munich, 1935–42)

Stamm-Kuhlmann, Thomas, 'War Friedrich Wilhelm III. von Preußen ein Bürgerkönig?', *ZFHF*, 16 (1989), 441–60

'Preußens Reaktion auf die Französische Revolution', in *1789. Aspekte des Zeitalters der Reaktion. Eine Ring-Vorlesung der Christian-Albrechts Universität zu Kiel* (1990), pp. 181–9

'Der Hof König Friedrich Wilhelms III. von Preußen, 1797–1840', in Möckl (ed.), *Hof und Hofgesellschaft in den deutschen Staaten*, pp. 275–319

König in Preußens großer Zeit. Friedrich Wilhelm III, der Melancholiker auf dem Thron (Berlin, 1992)

'Die Rolle von Staat und Monarchie bei der Modernisierung von oben. Ein Literaturbericht mit ergänzenden Betrachtungen zur Person König Friedrich Wilhelms III.', in Bernd Sösemann (ed.), *Gemeingeist und Bürgersinn. Die preußischen Reformen*, FBPG, NF 2, (Berlin, 1993)

'Tätiges Leben und Melancholie im preußischen Königshaus: durch Charaktertypologie zum Epochenverständnis', in Hedwig Röckelein (ed.), *Biographie als Geschichte* (Tübingen, 1993), pp. 280–94

Steffens, Wilhelm, 'Rheingrenze und territoriale Entschädigungsfrage in der preussischen Politik der Jahre 1795–98. Zugleich ein Beitrag zur Steinforschung. Mit drei unveröffentlichten Denkschriften des Freiherrn von Stein', *Westfälische Forschungen*, 6 (1953), 149–81

Stern, Selma, *Karl Wilhelm Ferdinand, Herzog zu Braunschweig und Lüneburg*, Veröffentlichungen der historischen Kommission für Hannover, Schaumburg-Lippe und Bremen (Hildesheim and Leipzig, 1921)

Stollberg-Rillinger, Barbara, *Der Staat als Maschine. Zur politischen Metaphorik des absoluten Fürstenstaates* (Berlin, 1986)

Stribrny, Wolfgang, *Die Russlandspolitik Friedrichs des Großen (1764–1786)* (Würzburg, 1966)

Stürmer, Michael, *Die Grenzen der Macht. Begegnungen der Deutschen mit der Geschichte* (Berlin, 1992)

Süßheim, Karl, *Preussens Politik in Ansbach-Bayreuth 1791–1806*, Historische Studien 33 (Berlin, 1902)

Sweet, Paul, *Friedrich von Gentz: defender of the old order* (Madison, Wisc., 1941)

Sybel, Heinrich von, *Geschichte der Revolutionszeit von 1789 bis 1800*, vols. I and IX (Stuttgart, 1898)

Szabo, F. A. J., 'Prince Kaunitz and the balance of power', *IHR*, 1, 3 (1979), 401–8

'Prince Kaunitz and the primacy of domestic policy. A response', *IHR*, 2 (1980), 625–35

Szymanski, Hans, *Brandenburg-Preussen zur See, 1605–1815. Ein Beitrag zur Frühgeschichte der deutschen Marine* (Leipzig, n.d.)

Tabournel, Raymond, 'Les derniers volontés du Prince Henri de Prusse', *Revue des études historiques*, 69 (1903), 156–61

'La Reine Louise et le prince Henri de Prusse', *Revue des Etudes Historiques*, 71 (1905), 46–59

'Le prince Henri de Prusse et le Directoire 1795–1802', *Revue des Etudes Historiques*, 74 (1908), 5–41

Tarrasch, Fritz, *Der Übergang des Fürstentums Ansbach an Bayern* (Munich and Berlin, 1912)

Thielen, Peter Gerrit, 'Karl August von Hardenberg, 1750–1822', in *Männer der deutschen Verwaltung. 23 biographische Essays* (Cologne, 1963), pp. 23–34

Karl August von Hardenberg, 1750–1822. Eine Biographie (Cologne and Berlin, 1967)

Thimme, Friedrich, 'Die Okkupation des Kurfürstenthums Hannover durch die

Preussen im Jahre 1806' (DPhil dissertation, University of Göttingen, 1893)

Timmermann, Heiner (ed.), *Die französische Revolution und Europa, 1789–1799*, Dokumente und Schriften der Europäischen Akademie Otzenhausen 60 (Saarbrücken, 1989)

Treitschke, Heinrich von, *Deutsche Geschichte im neunzehnten Jahrhundert*. Vol. I: *Bis zum zweiten Pariser Frieden* (Leipzig, 1879)
    'Zur Geschichte der sächsischen Politik im Jahre 1806', *HZ*, 42 (1879), 566–8
    Historische und politische Aufsätze, 3 vols. (Leipzig, 1886)

Treue, Wilhelm, 'Preußens Wirtschaft vom Dreißigjährigen Krieg bis zum Nationalsozialismus', in Büsch (ed.), *Handbuch der preußischen Geschichte*, II, pp. 449–604

Trummel, W., 'Der Norddeutsche Neutralitätsverband, 1795–1801', *Beiträge für die Geschichte Niedersachsens und Westfalens*, 41 (Hildesheim, 1913)

Tschirch, Otto, *Geschichte der öffentlichen Meinung in Preußen im Friedensjahrzehnt vom Baseler Frieden bis zum Zusammenbruch des Staates (1795–1806)*, 2 vols. (Weimar, 1933/4)
    'Die Flugschrift: "Deutschland in seiner tiefen Erniedrigung" und ihr Verfasser', *HZ*, 165 (1942), 47–71

Tümpel, Ludwig, *Die Entstehung des brandenburgisch-preußischen Einheitsstaates im Zeitalter des Absolutismus 1609–1806*, Untersuchungen zur deutschen Staats- und Rechtsgeschichte 124 (Breslau, 1915)

Ullrich, Karl, 'Die deutsche Politik König Gustavus IV von Schweden in den Jahren 1799–1806' (PhD dissertation, University of Erlangen, 1914)

Ulmann, Heinrich, 'Preußen, die bewaffnete Meeresneutralität und die Besitznahme Hannovers im Jahre 1801', *Deutsche Zeitschrift für Geschichtswissenschaft*, 2 (1897/8), 254–68
    Russisch-preussische Politik unter Alexander I und Friedrich Wilhelm III, bis 1806 (Leipzig, 1899)

Usinger, Rudolf, 'Napoleon und der nordische Bund', *PJ*, 14 (1864), 577–616
    Napoleon, der rheinische und der nordische Bund (Berlin, 1865)

Vehse, Eduard, *Preussische Hofgeschichten*, vol. IV, re-edited by Heinrich Conrad (Munich, 1913)

Vetter, Klaus, 'Die Stände im absolutistischen Preußen. Ein Beitrag zum Absolutismus-Diskussion', *ZfG*, 24 (1976), pp. 1290–306
    Kurmärkischer Adel und preußische Reformen ((Weimar, 1979)
    'Der brandenburgische Adel und der Beginn der bürgerlichen Umwälzung in Deutschland', in Armgard von Reden-Dohna and Ralph Melville (eds.), *Der Adel an der Schwelle des bürgerlichen Zeitalters, 1780–1860* (Stuttgart, 1988), pp. 285–303

Vierhaus, Rudolf, 'Heinrich von Kleist und die Krise des Preussischen Staates um 1800', in Rudolf Vierhaus, *Deutschland im 18. Jahrhundert: Politische Verfassung, Soziales Gefüge, Geistige Bewegungen* (Göttingen, 1987), pp. 216–34
    'Die Revolution als Gegenstand der geistigen Auseinandersetzung in Deutschland, 1789–1830', in Roger Dufraisse and Elizabeth Müller-Luckner (eds.), *Revolution und Gegenrevolution, 1789–1830*, pp. 251–62

'"Sie und nicht wir." Deutsche Urteile über den Ausbruch der französischen Revolution', in Vierhaus, *Deutschland im 18. Jahrhundert*, pp. 202–15

Vogel, Barbara, *Allgemeine Gewerbefreiheit. Die Reformpolitik des preußischen Staatskanzlers Hardenberg (1810–20)*, Kritische Studien zur Geschichtswissenschaft 57 (Göttingen, 1983)

'Verwaltung und Verfassung als Gegenstand staatlicher Reformstrategie', in Bernd Sösemann (ed.), *Gemeingeist und Bürgersinn. Die preußischen Reformen*, FBPG, NF 2, pp. 25–40

Vogler, Günter and Egert, Ilonka, 'Stimmen zur Französischen Revolution in Preussen, 1789–1795. Argumente und Motive für das Pro und Contra', in Timmermann (ed.), *Die französische Revolution und Europa*, pp. 343–69

Voss, Jürgen (ed.), *Deutschland und die Französische Revolution* (Munich, 1983)

Wagner, Fritz, *England und das europäsche Gleichgewicht 1500–1914* (Munich, 1947)

Wahl, Adalbert, *Geschichte des europäischen Staatensystems im Zeitalter der französischen Revolution und der Freiheitskriege, 1789–1815* (Berlin, 1912)

Wallthor, Alfred Hartlieb von, 'Die Eingliederung Westfalens in den preußischen Staat', in Baumgart (ed.), *Expansion und Integration*, pp. 227–54

Walther, Rudolf, 'Man braucht mehr Platz', *Die Zeit*, 21.7.1995

Wangermann, Ernst, 'Preußen und die revolutionären Bewegungen in Ungarn und den österreichischen Niederlanden zur Zeit der Französischen Revolution', in Büsch and Neugebauer-Wölk (eds.), *Preußen und die revolutionäre Herausforderung seit 1789*, pp. 77–85

Ward, A. W. and Gooch, G. P., *The Cambridge history of British foreign policy, 1783–1919*. Vol. I: *1783–1815* (Cambridge, 1922)

Weber, Max, *From Max Weber: essays in sociology*, edited by H. H. Gerth and C. Wright Mills (New York, 1970)

Wehler, Hans-Ulrich, 'Moderne Politikgeschichte oder "Große Politik der Kabinette"', *GG*, 1 (1975), 344–69

'Geschichtswissenschaft heute', in Jürgen Habermas (ed.), *Stichworte zur 'Geistigen Situation der Zeit'*. Vol. II: *Politik und Kultur* (Frankfurt/Main, 1979), pp. 709–53; translation in Hans-Ulrich Wehler, 'Historiography in Germany today', in Jürgen Habermas (ed.), *Observations on the 'spiritual situation of the age'. Contemporary perspectives* (Cambridge, Mass., 1984), pp. 221–59

Deutsche Gesellschaftsgeschichte. Vol. I: *Vom Feudalismus des Alten Reiches bis zur Defensiven Modernisierung der Reformära 1700–1815* (Munich, 1987)

Aus der Geschichte lernen? (Munich, 1988)

Entsorgung der deutschen Vergangenheit? Ein polemischer Essay zum 'Historikerstreit' (Munich, 1988)

Weis, Eberhard, *Montgelas, 1759–1799. Zwischen Revolution und Reform* (Munich, 1971)

'Die außenpolitischen Reaktionen der deutschen Staaten auf die französische Hegemoniepolitik: zwischen Anpassung und Widerstand', in Aretin and Ritter (eds.), *Historismus und moderne Geschichtswissenschaft*, pp. 185–200

'Bayern und Frankreich in der Zeit des Konsulats und des Ersten Empire (1799–1815)', *HZ*, 237 (1983), 559–95

Deutschland und Frankreich um 1800. Aufklärung – Revolution – Reform, edited Walter Demel and Bernd Roeck (Munich, 1990)

'Preußen-Frankreich-Amerika. Revolution und Reformen', in Büsch and Neugebauer-Wölk (eds.), *Preußen und die revolutionäre Herausforderung seit 1789*, pp. 3–20

Werner, Karl Ferdinand (ed.), *Hof, Kultur und Politik im 19. Jahrhundert*, Pariser Historische Studien 21 (Bonn, 1985)

White, Charles Edward, *The enlightened soldier: Scharnhorst and the 'Militärische Gesellschaft in Berlin, 1801–1805'* (New York and London, 1989)

Wiedemann, Fritz, *Die Aussenpolitik Bremens im Zeitalter der Französischen Revolution 1794–1803* (Bremen, 1960)

Wienfort, Monika, *Monarchie in der bürgerlichen Gesellschaft. Deutschland und England von 1640 bis 1848*, Beiträge zur europäischen Gesellschaftsgeschichte 4 (Göttingen, 1993)

Wierichs, Marion, *Napoleon und das 'Dritte Deutschland'. Die Entstehung der Großherzogtümer Baden, Berg und Hessen* (Frankfurt, 1978)

Wilhelmy, Petra, *Der Berliner Salon im 19 Jh. (1780–1914)*, Veröffentlichung der historischen Kommission zu Berlin Bd. 73 (Berlin and New York, 1989)

Wilson, Peter, *War, state and society in Württemberg, 1677–1793* (Cambridge, 1995)

Windelband, Wolfgang, *Die auswärtige Politik der Grossmächte in der Neuzeit 1494–1919* (2nd edn, Stuttgart, 1925)

Gestalten und Probleme der Außenpolitik. Reden und Aufsätze zu vier Jahrhunderten (Berlin, Essen and Leipzig, 1937)

Winkler, Heinrich August, 'Gesellschaftsform und Außenpolitik. Eine Theorie Lorenz von Steins in zeitgeschichtlicher Perspektive', *HZ*, 214, 2 (1972), 335–62

Wittichen, Friedrich Carl, 'Zur Geschichte der öffentlichen Meinung in Preussen vor 1806', *FBPG*, 23 (1910), 35–70

Preussen und die Revolutionen in Belgien und Lüttich 1789–1790 (Göttingen, 1905)

Wittichen, Paul, 'Friedrich v. Gentz und die englische Politik 1800–1814', *PJ*, 110 (1902), 463–501

'Das preussische Kabinett und Friedrich von Gentz. Eine Denkschrift aus dem Jahre 1800', *HZ*, 89 (1902), 239–73

'Zu Gentz's Denkschrift über das preussische Kabinett', *HZ*, 91 (1903), 58–64

'Friedrich Gentz und Preußen vor der Reform', *FBPG*, 18 (1905), 203–27

'Zur inneren Geschichte Preussens während der Französischen Revolution. Gentz und Humboldt', *FBPG*, 19 (1906), 320–51

Witzleben, Alexander von, *Staatsfinanznot und sozialer Wandel. Eine finanz-soziologische Analyse der preußischen Reformzeit zu Beginn des 19. Jahrhunderts*, Studien zum modernen Geschichte 32 (Stuttgart and Wiesbaden, 1985)

Wohlfeil, Rainer, *Vom stehenden Heer des Absolutismus zur Allgemeinen Wehrpflicht (1789–1814)*, Handbuch zur deutschen Militärgeschichte 1648–1939 2 (Frankfurt/Main, 1964)

Wohlwill, Adolf, 'Frankreich und Norddeutschland von 1795–1800', *HZ*, 51 (1883), 385–433

'Zur Geschichte der diplomatischen Beziehungen zwischen Preussen und Frankreich (1800–1807)', *HZ* 62, 1 (1889), 1–41

Woolf, Stuart, *Napoleon's integration of Europe* (London and New York, 1991)

Wunder, Bernd, 'Zur Geschichte der deutschen Beamtenschaft, 1945–1985', *GG* 17/2 (1991), 256–77

'Rolle und Struktur staatlicher Bürokratie in Frankreich und Deutschland', in Berding, François and Ulmann (eds.), *Deutschland und Frankreich im Zeitalter der Französischen Revolution*, pp. 139–76

Zawadzki, W.H., 'The views of Prince Adam Czartoryski on reconstructing Europe (1801–1830)' (DPhil dissertation, University of Oxford, 1973)

A man of honour. Adam Czartoryski as a statesman of Russia and Poland, 1795–1831 (Oxford, 1993)

Zernack, Klaus, *Preußen – Deutschland – Polen. Aufsätze zur Geschichte der deutsch-polnischen Beziehungen*, edited by Wolfram Fischer and M. G. Müller (Berlin, 1991)

'Polen in der Geschichte Preußens', in Busch (ed.), *Handbuch der preußischen Geschichte*, pp. 377–448

'Preußen-Frankreich-Polen. Revolution und Teilung', in Büsch and Neugebauer-Wölk (eds.), *Preußen und die revolutionäre Herausforderung seit 1789*, pp. 21–40

Ziebura, Gilbert, 'Die Rolle der Sozialwissenschaften in der westdeutschen Historiographie der internationalen Beziehungen', *GG*, 16 (1990), 76–103

Ziekursch, Johannes, 'Die preussischen Landesreservebataillone 1805/06 – eine Reform vor der Reform?', *HZ*, 103 (1909), 85–94

Hundert Jahre schlesischer Agrargeschichte. Vom Hubertusburger Frieden bis zum Abschluss der Bauernbefreiung, Darstellungen und Quellen zur schlesischen Geschichte 20 (Breslau, 1915)

Zierke, Fritz, *Die deutsche Politik Hardenbergs in der ersten Periode seines Staatsmännischen Wirkens 1770–1807. Ein Beitrag zum Bilde des preussischen Staatskanzlers und zur Geschichte des preussisch-deutschen Problems im Zeitalter der Französischen Revolution* (Gelnhausen, 1932)

Zwehl, Hans Karl von, *Der Kampf um Bayern 1805. I. Der Abschluss der bayerisch-französischen Allianz* (Munich, 1937).

Index

adjutants, 63–4
adversarial politics, 305, 329, 337
  effect on Prussian decision-making, 314
Alexander I, Emperor of Russia
  (1770–1825), 104, 212, 254, 261
  meeting with Frederick William, 198
Allgemeines Landrecht, 306
  as *Ersatzverfassung*, 60–2
Alopeus, Count Magnus von, Russian
  ambassador to Berlin (1770–1840),
  183, 257
  and Rumbold affair, 160
  dispute with Haugwitz, 265
Altenstein, Karl von, Prussian bureaucrat
  (1770–1840), 65, 147, 325
  on primacy of foreign policy and
  domestic reform, 316
  memorandum of 1805, 274
Alvensleben, Philip Karl von, Prussian
  foreign minister (1745–1802), 55,
  146
  biographical details, 49
  'northerner' in annexation debate, 78,
  80
  opposition to war of intervention against
  France, 92
  opposition to Second Coalition, 96
  supports French alliance, 98, 151
  fears geopolitical exposure of Prussia,
  104
  and peasant unrest, 119
  opposition to reform, 126
  on the organisation of the executive, 132
  sidelined by Haugwitz, 133, 138–40
  death, 133
  on importance of foreign policy, 137
Amiens, treaty of (1802), 70
Ansbach-Bayreuth, 71, 278, 282
  French invasion of, 191,
antechamber of power, 16–18, 46–55,
  136, 137, 305, 323, 345, 330, 338,
  340

Armed Neutrality (1800–1), 64, 69, 76,
  83–4, 103–4, 110
Austerlitz, battle of (1805), 191, 222,
  224–5
  effect on Prussian high politics, 285–6
Austria, 67–9, 72, 78–9, 91, 96, 98–9,
  204, 212, 214–15, 217, 228, 230
  Austro-Prussian dualism, 105–8
  Prussian fears of separate peace, 211

Basle, Treaty of (1795), 67–8
Bavaria, 113, 277
  and collapse of Prussian power, 187
Beyme, Karl Friedrich, Prussian cabinet
  councillor (1765–1838), 18, 21, 51,
  144, 219
  biographical details, 48,
  on need for reform, 122
  opposes abolition of military exemptions
  for middle class, 125
  on the organisation of the executive,
  132–3
  on French offer of Hanover, 178–9
  and French infringements at Ansbach-
  Bayreuth, 196
  and treaty of Paris, 233
  on geopolitical exposure of Prussia, 234
  on closure of the ports, 249
  sidelined by secret policy, 256
  resigned to Napoleonic dominance,
  273–4
  on reform of the executive, 322–3
Britain, 83–5, 88, 230–1, 284, 294, 328
  and Prussia, 208–11, 225–9
  commercial tensions with, 108–11
  trade with, 125
  attempts to exploit Rumbold affair, 163,
  166
  attempts to force Prussia into alliance,
  170–6
  and subsidy negotiations with Prussia,
  197